SELECT DOCUMENTS ON ASIAN AFFAIRS

EAST ASIA

CHINA   KOREA   JAPAN

1947-50

SELECT DOCUMENTS ON ASIAN AFFAIRS

GENERAL EDITOR — S. L. POPLAI

EAST ASIA
CHINA   KOREA   JAPAN
1947-50

EDITED BY

VIDYA PRAKASH DUTT

ISSUED UNDER THE AUSPICES OF THE
INDIAN COUNCIL OF WORLD AFFAIRS

OXFORD UNIVERSITY PRESS

1958

Oxford University Press, Amen House, London E.C.4

GLASGOW   NEW YORK   TORONTO   MELBOURNE   WELLINGTON
BOMBAY   CALCUTTA   MADRAS   KARACHI   KUALA LUMPUR
CAPE TOWN   IBADAN   NAIROBI   ACCRA

Vidya Prakash DUTT

PRINTED IN INDIA BY PYARELAL SAH AT THE TIMES OF INDIA
PRESS, BOMBAY, AND PUBLISHED BY JOHN BROWN, OXFORD
UNIVERSITY PRESS, APOLLO BUNDER, BOMBAY I

GENERAL CONTENTS

JAPAN

EDITOR'S NOTE

THE documents received from Chinese sources do not necessarily observe uniformity in transliterating proper names. The following variations should be noted :

Mao Tze-tung and Mao Tse-tung ; Chen Chiyu and Chen Chi-yiu ; Wang Sao-au and Wang Shao-ao ; Li Chin-shen and Li Chi Shen ; Huang Yen-Pei and Huang Yen Pei ; Li Chang-ta and Li Chang Ta ; Liu Shao-chi and Liu Shao Chi; Ma Hsu-lun and Ma Hsu Lun; Peng Tze-min and Peng Tse Min ; Shen Chun-ju and Shen Chun Ju ; Tan Ping-shan and Tang Ping Shan ; Tsai Ting-kai and Tsai Ting Kai ; Kuo Mo-jo and Kuo Mo Jo ; Chang Po-chun and Chang Po Chun ; Fu Tso-yi and Fu Tso Yi.

CORRIGENDA

Please read :

Kim Kiu-sic on p. 375, l.18; 24 July 1948 on p. 613, l.26; 10 March 1948 on p. 466 (doc. 21); Kim Il Sung on p. 328, l.8, and pp. 333, 406, 447-9.

PREFACE

In 1949 the Research Board of the Indian Council of World Affairs decided to prepare a series of volumes entitled *Select Documents on Asian Affairs*. The volumes in the series would contain texts of policy speeches by national leaders and authoritative texts of laws, treaties and international agreements and other published papers, each volume covering a period of two to three years for one or more of the various countries or regions in Asia. The documents would be selected with a view to indicating the main lines of development in the political life of each country and its international relations.

This Volume is the second in the series, and is concerned with developments in East Asia (China, Korea and Japan) between August 1947 and January 1950.

The documents in this volume have been edited by Shri Vidya Prakash Dutt, who was Research Associate in the Council from February 1950 to May 1956. They are grouped according to the countries and relate to (i) political and economic developments and (ii) external relations. In the Chinese section they refer to the period of Kuomintang rule and to the establishment of the People's Republic. In the section on Japan, they refer mostly to the time of the occupation and in that on Korea to the period before the disastrous war which broke out there in June 1950. They include important statements of policy, laws, and communications, showing the major developments in these three countries. A short introduction seeks to give a connected account as a background to each section.

Like other publications of the Indian Council of World Affairs, this volume is the result of close and continuous co-operation between members of the Council's staff and scholars and experts in India and abroad to whom the Council is sincerely grateful for their ungrudging and valuable help.

The preparation of the volumes in the series has been made possible by special donations from the following institutions which supplement the Council's own resources : the Asian Relations Organization; the Institute of Pacific Relations; the University of Delhi; the University of Aligarh.

The Council gratefully acknowledges the generous assistance given by these institutions.

1 *January* 1958

S. L. POPLAI
Secretary General

CHINA

CHINA

PART ONE

POLITICAL, CONSTITUTIONAL
AND ECONOMIC DEVELOPMENTS

INTRODUCTION

THE SITUATION in China immediately after the Second World War, though not bleak and gloomy, gave serious cause for anxiety and concern. Economic prospects were not dismal but there was grave doubt about the prospects of peace and stability. From 1927 onwards a furious civil war, temporarily suspended in 1939 but which flared up intermittently till the end of World War II, had raged in China between the Communists and the Kuomintang. A continuation of the civil war, which was consuming all the national resources and blocking progress and development, would only spell ruin and chaos. Attempts were therefore made, mainly through the mediating efforts of the United States, to bring the Communists, the Kuomintang and other parties together to achieve national unity and peace. The increasing hostility between the Kuomintang and the Communists was seriously hampering the war effort and, alarmed at the deteriorating situation, the United States Ambassador in China, Patrick J. Hurley, had taken active measures of mediation between the Communists and the Nationalist Government. But the negotiations stalled over the question of adequate representation for the Communists in the Government to end the one-party Kuomintang rule and the reorganization of the Communist army. Mutual suspicions and the desire of the Nationalist Government to extend its rule over the areas under Communist control reduced the chances of a peaceful solution.

Later, in July 1945, the Kuomintang Government appointed a committee of seven persons, including members of the Kuomintang and of the Democratic League and political Independents, to negotiate with the Communists. The negotiations continued through September 1945 and on 11 October it was officially announced that an agreement had been reached to convene a Political Consultative Conference to discuss measures for the establishment of a constitutional government. However, there was no agreement on the basic question of political control in the liberated areas dominated by the Communists.

3

On 27 November, President Truman appointed General Marshall as his special representative in China to help bring the peace negotiations to a successful conclusion. The Political Consultative Conference, composed of representatives of the Kuomintang, the Chinese Communist Party, the Democratic League and the Youth Party, and of non-party delegates, met in Chungking from 10 to 31 January 1946. Prior to the convening of the Conference, a Committee of Three, with a representative each of the Communist Party and the National Government and General Marshall as Chairman, was set up to discuss the question of the cessation of hostilities and related matters. The Committee reached an agreement on 10 January providing for a cease-fire and the disposition of the Government troops, particularly in Manchuria, and for machinery for supervising the cessation of hostilities. The Political Consultative Conference was also able to reach agreement on Government and military reorganization. It was agreed to convene a National Assembly for the purpose of adopting a Constitution and giving a legal government to the country. Pending the convocation of the National Assembly, it was agreed that Generalissimo Chiang Kai-shek would set up a State Council, consisting of representatives from both the Kuomintang and the non-Kuomintang parties and individuals, which would be the supreme organ of the Government in charge of national affairs. The PCC resolutions also provided for the equality and legality of all political parties and the maintenance of the *status quo* in Communist 'liberated areas' until a settlement by the National Government after its reorganization.

A Military Subcommittee, composed of representatives of the Communists and the Kuomintang and with General Marshall as adviser, reached agreement on the reorganization of the armed forces, providing for a National Army of 60 divisions with 10 divisions from the Communist armies and the rest from Nationalist armies.

Although the PCC had taken progressive steps towards the bringing about of unification and peace in China, its decisions aroused opposition within the Kuomintang. There were powerful vested interests, both military and political, which were trying to sabotage unity efforts and which wanted to force a military decision under the illusion that the Communist areas would be conquered within a short time. They resorted to inspired mob actions and their efforts were directed towards substantial revisions in the peace accords. The situation was further complicated by the struggle for Manchuria which was all the time going on between the Communist and Government troops. Both sides were unwilling to commit themselves over reorganization and redistribution of troops. The military situation gradually worsened with the spread of hostilities to various points in

4

China proper. Each side took the stand that the other was provoking the fighting and could not be trusted to go through with an agreement. The peace negotiations had come to a stalemate, although protracted efforts both by General Marshall and Chinese third-party groups to break the deadlock continued to be made. In the meantime the Government's offensive against the Communist 'liberated areas' continued. Chiang Kai-shek wanted basic agreements to be worked out before he would order a cease-fire. He also desired the convening of the National Assembly before he would undertake the reorganization of the Government. The Communists, on the other hand, wanted the immediate reorganization of the Government and a cease-fire forthwith. They said that negotiations could not be fruitful as long as military hostilities continued.

The National Assembly met on 15 November with a limited representation from non-Kuomintang groups. The Communist Party and the Democratic League denounced the National Assembly and held that the Kuomintang had destroyed the PCC resolutions. The main question before the Assembly was the type of constitution that should be adopted by it. The Right-wing clique was working for the adoption of a constitution closely resembling that of 5 May 1936. However, the new Constitution adopted on 25 December 1946 was ostensibly a democratic document but the crucial point was the degree and manner of its enforcement.

On 6 January 1947 President Truman recalled General Marshall, bringing to an end a long and fruitless period of negotiations and discussions lasting for over a year. In his final statement General Marshall said that the almost overwhelming suspicion with which the Kuomintang and the Communists regarded each other had poisoned the atmosphere, and he blamed the dominant group of Kuomintang reactionaries and the extremist elements in the Communists for the failure of negotiations. He denounced the dominating influence of the military in the Kuomintang and was convinced that a campaign of force had been in progress and that the negotiations were used as a cover for this campaign.

Although prospects of a negotiated settlement had become very remote, some efforts were made to resume negotiations without any positive result. The Ministry of Information published a statement, on behalf of the National Government, which while outlining the course of negotiations contained fresh proposals for the resumption of political talks. The Communist Party rejected the proposals as not providing an adequate basis for peace negotiations and insisted that the Constitution must be annulled and the forces of the two parties must go back to the positions occupied by them prior to 13 January 1946 before any peace talks could take place. The Nationalist reaction was that no useful purpose would be served by any more attempts at negotiation and that the Government would go ahead with its own programme of national reconstruction and political democratization and would welcome the co-operation of other parties and groups. The question of reorganization of the National Government so as to end the period of political tutelage and bring about the participation of other groups was engaging the attention of the Government. The Communists and the Democratic League had already declared their dissociation from the projected reorganization, which was thus reduced to a question of giving a few positions to a couple of minor parties, the Youth Party and the Social Democrats.

On 1 March 1947 Chiang Kai-shek announced the reorganization of the Legislative Yuan and the Control Yuan. Fifty new members were appointed to the Legislative Yuan, of whom 17 were Kuomintang, 13 Youth Party, 12 Social Democrats, and 8 non-partisans. Twenty-five new members were added to the Control Yuan, of whom 9 belonged to the Kuomintang, 6 to the Youth Party, 7 to the Social Democrats, and 11 were non-partisans. Forty-four new members were named to the People's Political Council, of whom 11 were from the Kuomintang, 3 from the Youth Party, 11 Social Democrats and 11 non-partisans. These third-party members, however, did not command much following in the country and the problem of the civil war remained as acute as ever.

The Executive Yuan and the State Council were reorganized on 17 April 1947 and General Chang Chun became the President of the Executive Yuan or the Prime Minister. In a statement on 18 April he hailed the reorganization as another step towards the ending of political tutelage. The Government claimed that the period of political tutelage was over. It announced its political programme, which included familiar promises of economic reform and guarantees of civil liberties. It was doubtful, however, in view of past experience, how far this reorganization would change the actual situation by the genuine pursuit of progressive policies. The Kuomintang Party machine was dominated by the reactionary CC clique.[1]

Meanwhile, there was a growing deterioration in the general situation in all parts of China. The economic and financial situation continued its downward course during 1947. Prices continued to rise and the currency continued to fall. The civil war was not only a heavy drain on the national economy, it was impoverishing large masses of people. A rising anti-civil-war sentiment could be noticed among various sections of the people, and in academic and business circles. In May and June there were widespread student demonstrations

[1] The CC clique was the extreme Right-wing faction of the Kuomintang and was dominated by the two brothers Chen Li-fu and Chen Kuo-fu.

resulting in much violence and bloodshed. The students demanded the ending of the civil war, effective action to improve economic conditions, and relief for themselves. The rise in the price of rice led to minor rice riots at a number of places. The People's Political Council reflected popular uneasiness by passing in its last session, almost as a swan song, a resolution inviting the Communists for talks to end the civil war. However, it also asked for a continuation of the punitive action against the Communists. The Communists rejected the invitation as insincere.

Such a situation called for drastic reforms on the part of the National Government. The Standing Committee of the Central Executive Committee of the Kuomintang held an extraordinary session on 30 June and passed resolutions calling for continuation and expansion of the war against the Communists, integration of the San Min Chu I Youth Corps into the Kuomintang and preparations for elections in the coming autumn. These measures were manifestly inadequate to meet the critical situation. The State Council ordered general national mobilization on 4 July and it showed some awareness of the demands of the situation by promising reforms in its resolutions on mobilization. Generalissimo Chiang Kai-shek also showed a similar awareness when he said in his radio broadcast on 7 July, the tenth anniversary of the Sino-Japanese War : 'Unless drastic reforms are introduced, China may not be able to exist in the family of nations. Therefore, political, education, economic and social reforms, which should be made, shall not be delayed until the conclusion of the suppression campaign, but will be initiated right away.'

In view of the serious military and economic situation in China President Truman sent General Albert C. Wedemeyer as his special envoy in July 1947 on a fact-finding mission. General Wedemeyer presented his report to President Truman on 19 September. His report recommended in general that the United States provide military and economic aid to China under a programme of assistance over a period of at least five years.

The national mobilization resolution adopted by the State Council on 4 July declared the Communists to be in open rebellion which must be suppressed by the effective utilization of all the resources of the country. Thus the chapter of Kuomintang-Communist negotiations for a peaceful political solution of their differences came to an end and the civil war flared up in all its intensity. On 18 July the Government proclaimed measures for the implementation of the order for general mobilization. The Government also promised 'carefully-drafted' plans concerning the 'acceleration of economic reconstruction', the 'reform of local governments', the 'improvement of food and conscription administration', the 'mitigation of people's sufferings' and the 'protection of their basic rights'.

On 9 September the Central Executive Committee of the Kuomintang held its fourth plenary session at a time when the military and political situation was rapidly deteriorating. The meeting was called ostensibly to integrate the San Min Chu I Youth Corps with the Kuomintang but it had obviously to take note of the critical situation. The Generalissimo bitterly criticized his party members for their ineptness and failure to institute reforms. However, after this brilliant performance, the Generalissimo put his foot down on a specific plan of reform and the final manifesto published by the Executive Committee was a platitudinous document which contained nothing new or concrete to inspire hopes of firm action to implement the oft-repeated promises of radical reforms. Some sort of integration of the Youth Corps with the Kuomintang was effected in order to resolve the growing friction between the two organizations. The CC clique emerged stronger because it controlled the Youth Corps.

On the military front the Government's position was very insecure and unsatisfactory. Manchuria had practically slipped out of the hands of the Government. There had been large-scale infiltration in North China. In Manchuria, North China and Central China the Government troops were on the defensive while the Communists were having a free time conducting their hit-and-run raids. The alarming thing from the Kuomintang point of view was the sagging morale of the Nationalist troops and the increasing loss of the will to fight. Corruption and graft were on the increase and the general mood of apathy and cynicism was highly dangerous for the Kuomintang Government. The Government had yet to take effective action to stop the political and economic rot in the country. In fact, the Kuomintang members were preoccupied with the autumn elections.

Elections were held in late 1947. The people did not evince much interest in them. They were carefully stage-managed and resulted in strengthening the control of the CC clique. The National Assembly held its first meeting on 29 March 1948 to elect a President and a Vice-President. There was ill-concealed dissatisfaction with and criticism of the Government and of Chiang Kai-shek himself. Chiang Kai-shek admitted that the Government had lost seven of its best divisions in Manchuria and that it had made serious military mistakes. He promised to annihilate the Communists within six months. A large number of the Assembly members were in an angry mood and were highly critical of the Government. Dramatically the Generalissimo declined to accept the office of President, which immediately brought a clamour from all the groups that he should change his mind in this regard. Thus he enhanced his personal prestige and authority. However, the general dissatisfaction had not died down and despite direct pressure from Chiang Kai-shek, the Assembly refused to elect as Vice-President his nominee, Dr Sun Fo. Instead, it elected General Li Tsung-jen, a war-lord of Kwangsi, who had the support of the liberal members keen on instituting reforms in the administration. Li's election was generally regarded as a protest against the Government's handling of the situation under Chiang's leadership. After some wrangling and manœuvring, Dr Wong Wen-hao, an eminent geologist without any political following, was named Prime Minister. The new Cabinet consisted of individuals personally loyal to Chiang Kai-shek, who maintained his supreme position in the country.

Meanwhile, the deteriorating military situation was having its repercussions on the economic front. There were violent fluctuations in market prices in Shanghai and Nanking which were due in large measure to the deterioration of the military situation in Central China. The National Government seemed to be relying mainly on the proposed United States aid to help it out of the desperate situation. On 28 January 1948, the then Premier, General Chang Chun (Dr Wong's predecessor), proclaimed a ten-point programme of self-help expressing the Government's determination to undertake sweeping reforms in administrative, economic and military fields. The programme included land reforms, control and adjustment of Government expenditure, and a more stable monetary system. It was aimed at facilitating the current negotiations between Nanking and Washington for immediate American aid to China. On 2 April 1948 the American Congress passed the China Aid Act of 1948 which provided for 338 million dollars for economic aid and 125 million dollars for special grants to be administered through the ECA, and became a part of the Foreign Assistance Act of 1948. On 3 July the Sino-American Bilateral Agreement was formally signed in Nanking, including the basic document similar to the agreement between the US and the European Recovery Programme countries.

The growing discontent and disillusionment in China found another outlet in the form of student demonstrations in Peiping (later renamed Peking), Shanghai, Nanking and elsewhere in June and July against American policy in Japan. The anti-American sentiment had been gathering force in the country for some time and the American Embassy in Nanking reported that there was 'a common conviction . . . that the Generalissimo is, in fact, leading the country to ruin and chaos, and that he could not do so if it were not for the support which the American Government has given him.'[1] There

[1] *US Relations with China*, p. 906.

was also increasing apprehension over American efforts to strengthen Japan. Among the educated circles particularly the feeling was that America was building up Japan at the expense of China. The student riots were a culmination of this widespread fear of American-resurrected Japan becoming again a menace to China. The violence and strength of the anti-American demonstrations constrained the American Ambassador, Dr Stuart, to appeal to the public to take a more rational and balanced view of American policies. As a result of Government measures and Dr Stuart's appeal, the demonstrations subsided.

Public confidence in the Nanking Government was falling rapidly. Manchuria had practically been lost, North China was fast becoming a liability, Central China was being subjected to increasing Communist pressure, and even South China was not entirely free from guerilla activities. Economic conditions were growing intolerable. As a result of the alarming rise in rice prices, rice riots were reported in many parts of the country. In the spring of 1948, the Government introduced rationing of foodstuffs in Shanghai, Nanking, Tientsin, Peiping and Canton. Later, the American economic appropriations were utilized to import large quantities of food, cotton, fertilizer, petroleum and other essentials. The United•States aid was saving the economy from complete collapse. But the Government budget was even more unbalanced than that of the previous year and inflation continued unabated. On 11 June 1948 Dr Wong Wen-hao, the new Prime Minister, outlined at a special session of the Legislative Yuan his plan for improving conditions. Among his proposals were : reduction of the Government's civilian budget, erection of bases in South China, additional and regularized taxes levied on those most able to pay so that the burden would not fall entirely upon the countryside, and proper use of American aid. However, the catastrophic spiralling of commodity prices in Shanghai and other leading cities during the last two weeks of June pointed to the extreme gravity of the economic crisis confronting the country. The fall of Kaifung into Communist hands and the astounding depreciation of the Chinese national currency were the major causes for the price upheavals.

On 19 August 1948 the Nanking Government announced drastic currency reform measures. It decided to abolish the old Fapi and to issue a new currency called the Gold Yuan which was pegged at GY $4 to US $1. The conversion of old notes was fixed at CNC $3,000,000 to GY $1. The public and the banks were asked to turn in their gold and foreign currency for the new bills. The payment of salaries and wages on the cost of living indices was discontinued. Drastic measures to control prices, wages and salaries were to be taken after the conversion of the old currency.

The currency reform measures were successful for a few weeks, but the Government failed to take effective action to curtail expenditure or to increase revenue, and new currency continued to be issued in the previous volume to cover budgetary deficits. On the one hand, the Government was incurring loss of revenue through loss of territory, and, on the other hand, the Government's military expenditure was mounting. Prices in August 1948 were more than 3 million times their pre-war level. In 1948 there was a sharp increase in the velocity of currency circulation which sent prices to astronomical figures. The collapse of the Gold Yuan caused the Chinese middle class to lose considerable sums in hard-currency savings. It gave a fatal blow to their waning allegiance to the Kuomintang Government.

The Communists so far had not created any central authority to rule over their 'liberated areas'. They had organized local and provincial governments, including one for North China, for their own areas, but they had not yet formed a central government. Their territories were held together by a common military strategy and their organizational network. However, the Communists had all along made known their desire to hold a conference, in co-operation with liberal and Left-wing elements but excluding the conservative Kuomintang members, to elect a central government and adopt a constitution for China. They took a preliminary step in this direction when they called for a People's Political Consultative Conference in their May Day slogans. The call was directed towards anti-Nanking elements of China, chief among whom were those who had taken refuge in Hong Kong, like the Democratic League, the Revolutionary Committee of the Kuomintang, and other anti-Chiang groups and individuals. These latter had been suppressed by Chiang Kai-shek and they were looking more and more towards the Communists for co-operation and collaboration. The Communist appeal, therefore, found in them a very receptive audience. A number of them went to Communist territories to hold negotiations and in November 1948 there was a meeting at Harbin, attended by the leaders, where it was decided to convene a Preparatory Committee of the new People's Political Consultative Conference in 1949.

In the military field, the Communists had already changed their tactics. Instead of raiding cities and destroying communications, they issued a new directive which enjoined upon their armies to protect the new cities which came under their rule and not to damage them in any way. The tactics were changed in view of rapid Communist victories in Manchuria and North China. The emphasis now was on keeping the production equipment of cities intact because the Communists expected to be complete masters of them. The Communist soldiers were exhorted to display and maintain an iron sense of discipline and scrupulous dealings with the city population in order to win its confidence.

With the failure of the Nanking economic reforms, the Kuomintang headed fast towards disaster and defeat. During September and October 1948 the Nationalist armies in North China and Manchuria suffered decisive defeat. The Communists moved swiftly on the Manchurian front and by early November, with the fall of Mukden, had won the struggle for Manchuria. The Nationalists had lost 300,000 men, including the best of the American-trained divisions. The Communists next struck in North China and in the beginning of January 1949 captured Hsuchow, the railway hub of north central China. Tientsin fell on 15 January and Peiping on 31 January. Whereas in the beginning of 1948, the Nationalists had almost a three-to-one numerical superiority, the Communists now enjoyed superiority in numbers and at least equality in armaments. Chiang Kai-shek's soldiers were fast losing the will to fight and were deserting in increasing numbers. The end of the Kuomintang was in sight. President Chiang Kai-shek made desperate efforts to get more American aid as well as American military experts and made a direct appeal to President Truman for this purpose. The American Administration, however, did not think that more aid would make any substantial difference to the situation and therefore politely refused to step up aid beyond what had already been allocated under the China Act of 1948.

As the situation deteriorated, there was a rising demand, even among the Kuomintang members, for peace negotiations with the Communists. Even the Generalissimo had to take note of this feeling. The virtual collapse of military capacity, the failure of the monetary reforms, and the almost universal desire for peace compelled Chiang Kai-shek to express in his New Year's message of 1949 his willingness to enter into peace negotiations with the Communists. However, the tone of his message showed that his real desire was to continue the fighting. There developed a struggle in the leadership between the advocates of peace and those who wanted a fight to the finish. The Communists had already declared that they would not negotiate with the existing leadership but the peace group hoped to modify the Communist stand by removing Chiang Kai-shek from the helm. The advocates of peace finally had their way. On 8 January 1949 the Chinese Foreign Minister requested the American, British, Soviet and French Governments to act as intermediaries in the initiation of negotiations to bring about peace. The request was turned down by all the four Governments. On 21 January Chiang Kai-shek announced his decision to retire and left Nanking for Fenghua, transferring his duties and powers to Vice-President Li Tsung-jen, leader of the peace group, who immediately announced his intention to initiate peace talks with the Communists.

Acting President Li's task was by no means an easy one. On the one hand, the Communists, with complete victory in sight, were in no mood to dilute their victory by concessions to the defeated Kuomintang and had announced, on 14 January, their conditions for negotiations, which included punishment of 'war criminals', abolition of the Nanking Government, reorganization of the Kuomintang armies, agrarian reforms, and the calling of a Political Consultative Conference without 'reactionaries'. On the other hand, Chiang's retirement was more apparent than real. He still swayed the party organization, commanded the allegiance of most of the military commanders, and controlled the purse-strings. And he was at heart opposed to the peace talks and hoped that they would fail, providing him with an opportunity to stage a return.

Li hoped that by negotiating with the Communists, he might be able to salvage something out of the Kuomintang wreck. He hoped to rally round him moderate and liberal elements in the country which would give him bargaining points with the Communists and, even if the talks broke down, would strengthen the resistance under his leadership against the Communists. However, Li's attempts were unlikely to succeed because he did not control the armies and the treasury and he could not make any commitments on behalf of the Generalissimo. He was unable to have his way with Chiang and failed to attract the middle groups.

An unofficial Shanghai peace delegation had proceeded to Peking to discuss peace arrangements with the Communist leaders. Li Tsung-jen stated on 23 January 1949 that he was prepared to negotiate on the basis of Mao's eight peace terms. Negotiations between the Kuomintang and the Communists began formally in Peking on 2 April. On 15 April the Nanking delegation was handed the Communist draft Domestic Peace Agreement which substantially incorporated the eight demands of 14 January, and it was given until 20 April to accept or reject them. The Communists stated in their draft agreement that they would remove from the 'war criminal' list those Kuomintang leaders who would co-operate with them, and would include some Kuomintang leaders in the new Political Consultative Conference and Coalition Government. Li regarded these terms as amounting to virtual surrender and rejected them. At midnight on 20 April the Communist forces crossed the Yangtze River. On 23 April the Acting President, the Prime Minister, and the remaining officials left Nanking for Shanghai *en route* to Canton. The Communist forces captured Nanking on 24 April, Hankow on 16-17 May, Shanghai on 25 May and Tsingtao on 2 June. Before the end of the year the Kuomintang Government was expelled from the Chinese mainland and took refuge in Formosa.

In view of the imminent collapse of the Kuomintang, the Communists had already set about organizing a new government. All through 1948 there had been consultations between them and anti-Kuomintang groups and individuals. In June 1949 a preparatory committee of 134 delegates was established to complete the preliminaries for a new Political Consultative Conference. The new People's Political Consultative Conference held its first plenary session on 21 September 1949. The Conference was attended by 664 members, including 510 delegates from 45 representative units, among them being 14 democratic parties and groups, 9 regions, 6 army units, and 16 'people's organizations', representing workers, peasants, youth, women, students, industrialists, national minorities, overseas Chinese, religious circles, and scientific, cultural and educational workers. Besides, there were 77 specially invited persons and 77 alternates from the representative units. The Communist Party, the Revolutionary Committee of the Kuomintang and the Democratic League each received 16 seats. However, the Communists had a larger representation through army units, youth groups and people's organizations.

The CPPCC adopted a Common Programme, to which all parties and groups in the United Front in China undertook to subscribe, drafted an organic law for itself, established the Central People's Government of China, formulated the organic law of the new Government, and elected a Central People's Government Council, the highest organ of the State, which was given the task of organizing and supervising the administrative, judicial and military functions of the Government. Mao Tse-tung was named the Chairman of the Council and Chou En-lai the Prime Minister. On 1 October Mao Tse-tung formally proclaimed the inauguration of the People's Republic of China. Thus a new China arose on the ashes of the old one.

CHINA

PART I

POLITICAL, CONSTITUTIONAL AND ECONOMIC DEVELOPMENTS

THE NATIONALIST GOVERNMENT AND THE KUOMINTANG

Section Five
The Communists

Section Six
People's Republic of China

PART ONE

I CONSTITUTIONAL DEVELOPMENTS

I   1 *January* 1947

THE CONSTITUTION OF THE REPUBLIC OF CHINA

(*Adopted by the National Assembly on 25 December 1946 and promulgated by the National Government on 1 January 1947, it came into effect on 25 December 1947.*)

Preamble

The National Assembly of the Republic of China, by virtue of the mandate received from the whole body of citizens, and acting in accordance with the teachings of Dr Sun Yat-sen, Founder of the Republic of China, and in order to consolidate the authority of the State, safeguard the rights of the people, ensure social tranquillity and promote the welfare of the people, hereby adopts this Constitution and causes it to be promulgated for faithful and permanent observance by all in the country.

Ch. I.   General Provisions

Article 1.   The Republic of China, founded on the basis of the San Min Chu I (Three People's Principles), shall be a democratic republic of the people to be governed by the people and for the people.

Article 2.   The sovereignty of the Republic of China shall reside in the whole body of citizens.

Article 3.   Persons possessing Chinese nationality shall be citizens of the Republic of China.

Article 4.   The territory of the Republic of China, as represented by her existing geographical areas, shall not be altered except by resolution of the National Assembly.

Article 5.   All component racial groups in the Republic of China shall enjoy equal rights.

Article 6.   The National Flag of the Republic of China shall have a red background with a blue sky and a white sun in the upper left corner.

Ch. II.   Rights and Obligations of the People

Article 7.   All citizens of the Republic of China, irrespective of sex, religion, race, class or party affiliation, shall be equal before the law.

Article 8.   The people shall be guaranteed freedom of person. Except in case of apprehension *flagrante delicto* as otherwise provided for by law, no person shall be arrested or detained except by a judicial or a police organ in accordance with procedure prescribed by law. No person shall be tried or punished except by a law court in accordance with procedure prescribed by law. Any arrest, detention, trial or punishment not in accordance with procedure prescribed by law may be contested.

When a person is arrested or detained on suspicion of having committed a crime, the organ making the arrest or detention shall in writing inform the said person and his designated relative or friend of the reason for his arrest or detention, and shall within twenty-four hours, turn him over to a competent court for trial. The said person, or any other individual, may petition the competent court that a writ be served within twenty-four hours on the organ making the arrest for the surrender of the said person for trial.

The court may not reject the petition mentioned in the preceding paragraph, nor may it order the organ concerned to make an investigation and report first. The organ concerned may not refuse or delay to execute the writ of the court for the surrender of the said person for trial.

When a person is arrested or detained illegally, he, or any other person, may petition the court for an investigation. The court may not reject such a petition, and shall within twenty-four hours, pursue the investigation with the organ concerned, and proceed with the matter in accordance with law.

Article 9. Except those in active military service, no person shall be subject to trial by a military court.

Article 10. The people shall have freedom of domicile and of changing their domicile.

Article 11. The people shall have freedom of speech, academic instruction, writing and publication.

Article 12. The people shall have freedom of secret correspondence.

Article 13. The people shall have freedom of religious belief.

Article 14. The people shall have freedom of assembly and freedom to form associations.

Article 15. The people's right to life, right to work and right to property shall be inviolate.

Article 16. The people shall have the right to present petitions, file complaints or institute legal proceedings.

Article 17. The people shall have the rights of election, recall, initiative and referendum.

Article 18. The people shall have the right to take civil service examinations and to hold public offices.

Article 19. The people shall have the obligation to pay taxes in accordance with law.

Article 20. The people shall have the obligation to perform military service in accordance with law.

Article 21. The people shall have the right as well as the obligation to receive public education.

Article 22. All other freedoms and rights of the people that do not jeopardize the social order or general welfare shall be guaranteed under the Constitution.

Article 23. All the freedoms and rights enumerated in the preceding Articles may not be restricted by law, except for reasons of preventing infringement upon the freedoms of other persons, averting an imminent crisis, maintaining social order or advancing general welfare.

Article 24. Any public functionary who, in violation of law, infringes upon the freedoms or rights of any persons shall, in addition to being subject to disciplinary measures in accordance with law, be held accountable under the criminal and civil laws. The injured person may, in accordance with law, ask the State for indemnity.

Ch. III.   The National Assembly

Article 25. The National Assembly shall, in accordance with the provisions of the Constitution, exercise political powers on behalf of the whole body of citizens.

Article 26. The National Assembly shall be organized with the following components :

(1)   One delegate to be elected by every hsien, municipality or area of an equivalent status. In case its population exceeds 500,000, one additional delegate shall be elected for each additional 500,000. Areas of an equivalent status with the hsien or the municipality shall be prescribed by law.

(2)   Delegates of Mongolia shall be elected four for each league and one for each special banner.

(3)   The number of delegates to be elected by Tibet shall be prescribed by law.

(4)   The number of delegates to be elected by various racial groups in the border regions shall be prescribed by law.

(5)   The number of delegates to be elected by Chinese nationals residing abroad shall be prescribed by law.

(6)   The number of delegates to be elected by occupational groups shall be prescribed by law.

(7)   The number of delegates to be elected by women's organizations shall be prescribed by law.

21

Article 27. The functions and powers of the National Assembly shall be as follows :

(1) Election of the President and the Vice-President.

(2) Recall of the President or the Vice-President.

(3) Amendment of the Constitution.

(4) Referendum on amendments to the Constitution proposed by the Legislative Yuan.

With respect to the exercise of the powers of initiative and referendum, in addition to the authority stipulated in the above-mentioned (3) and (4), the National Assembly shall formulate measures pertaining thereto and enforce them, after the said two powers shall have been exercised in one-half of the hsien and municipalities of the whole country.

Article 28. Delegates to the National Assembly shall be elected every six years.

The term of office of the delegates to each National Assembly shall terminate on the day of convocation of the next National Assembly.

Incumbent government officials may not be elected delegates to the National Assembly in electoral areas where they hold office.

Article 29. The National Assembly shall be summoned by the President to meet ninety days prior to the date of expiration of each presidential term.

Article 30. The National Assembly may, in any of the following circumstances, convene an extraordinary session :

(1) When, in accordance with the provisions of Article 49 of the Constitution, a new President and a new Vice-President are to be elected.

(2) When, in accordance with a resolution of the Control Yuan, an impeachment of the President or the Vice-President is to be instituted.

(3) When, in accordance with a resolution of the Legislative Yuan, an amendment to the Constitution is to be proposed.

(4) When a meeting is requested by over two-fifths of the delegates to the National Assembly.

When an extraordinary session is to be called in accordance with the above-mentioned (1) and (2), the President of the Legislative Yuan shall issue the notice of convocation ; when it is to be called in accordance with the above-mentioned (3) and (4), it shall be convened by the President of the Republic.

Article 31. The National Assembly shall meet at the seat of the Central Government.

Article 32. No delegate to the National Assembly shall be held responsible outside the Assembly for opinions expressed or for votes cast in the Assembly.

Article 33. While the Assembly is in session, no delegate to the National Assembly shall, except in case of apprehension *flagrante delicto*, be arrested or detained without the permission of the National Assembly.

Article 34. The organization of the National Assembly, the election and the recall of delegates to the National Assembly, and the procedure whereby the National Assembly is to carry out its functions shall be prescribed by law.

Ch. IV. The President

Article 35. The President shall be the Head of the State and shall represent the Republic of China in foreign relations.

Article 36. The President shall command the nation's land, sea and air forces.

Article 37. The President shall, in accordance with law, promulgate laws and issue mandates with the counter-signature of the President of the Executive Yuan, or with counter-signatures of both the President of the Executive Yuan and of the heads of Ministries or Commissions concerned.

Article 38. The President shall, in accordance with the provisions of the Constitution, exercise the powers of concluding treaties, declaring war, and making peace.

Article 39. The President may, in accordance with law, declare martial law with the approval or confirmation of the Legislative Yuan. When the Legislative Yuan deems it necessary, it may, by resolution, request the President to terminate martial law.

Article 40. The President shall, in accordance with law, exercise the powers of granting general amnesty, pardons, remission of sentences and restitution of civil rights.

Article 41. The President shall, in accordance with law, appoint and remove civil and military officers.

Article 42. The President may, in accordance with law, confer honours and award decorations.

Article 43. In case of a natural calamity, an epidemic or a national financial or economic crisis that calls for emergency measures, the President, during the Legislative Yuan's recess, may, by resolution of the Executive Yuan Council and in accordance with the Emergency Decrees Act, issue an emergency decree proclaiming such measures as are necessary to cope with the situation. Such decree shall, within one month after issuance, be presented to the Legislative Yuan for confirmation ; in case the Legislative Yuan withholds confirmation, the said decree shall immediately become null and void.

Article 44. In case of any dispute between the various Yuan, unless there are relevant stipulations in the Constitution, the President may call a meeting of the Presidents of the Yuan concerned for consultation with a view to reaching an agreement.

Article 45. Any citizen of the Republic of China having attained the age of forty years shall be eligible to the office of President or of Vice-President.

Article 46. The election of the President and the Vice-President shall be prescribed by law.

Article 47. The term of office of the President and of the Vice-President shall be six years. They may be elected for a second term.

Article 48. The President shall, at the time of his inauguration, take the following oath :

'I do solemnly and sincerely swear before the people of the whole country that I shall observe the Constitution, faithfully perform my duties and strive to promote the people's welfare and defend the country. Under no circumstances shall I betray the people's trust. Should I break my oath, I shall submit myself to severe punishment by the State.'

Article 49. In the event of the President's office becoming vacant, the Vice-President shall succeed to the Presidency until the expiration of the original presidential term. In case the Presidency and the Vice-Presidency should both become vacant, the President of the Executive Yuan shall exercise the functions of the President and, in accordance with the provisions of Article 30 of the Constitution, convene an extraordinary session of the National Assembly to elect a new President and a new Vice-President, and the latter shall hold office until the completion of the term left unfinished by the preceding President.

In case the President should, due to any cause, become incapacitated, the Vice-President shall exercise the functions of his office. In case both the President and the Vice-President should become incapacitated, the President of the Executive Yuan shall exercise the functions of the President.

Article 50. The President shall vacate his office on the day his term expires. If by that time the succeeding President has not yet been elected, or if the President-elect and the Vice-President-elect have not yet assumed office, the President of the Executive Yuan shall exercise the functions of the President.

Article 51. The period during which the President of the Executive Yuan may exercise the functions of the President shall not exceed three months.

Article 52. The President shall not, without having been recalled or having vacated his office, be liable to criminal prosecution unless he is charged with having committed acts of rebellion or treason.

Ch. V. Administration

Article 53. The Executive Yuan shall be the highest administrative organ of the State.

Article 54. The Executive Yuan shall have a President, a Vice-President, a number of heads of Ministries and Commissions and a number of Ministers of State without Portfolio.

Article 55. The President of the Executive Yuan shall be nominated and appointed by the President of the Republic with the consent of the Legislative Yuan.

If the President of the Executive Yuan should resign or otherwise vacate his office during the recess of the Legislative Yuan, the Vice-President of the Yuan shall exercise his functions, but the President of the Republic shall, within forty days, request a meeting of the Legislative Yuan to confirm his nominee.

Pending such confirmation by the Legislative Yuan, the Vice-President of the Executive Yuan shall exercise the functions of the President of the Yuan.

Article 56. The Vice-President of the Executive Yuan, the heads of the various Ministries and Commissions and the Ministers of State without Portfolio shall be appointed by the President of the Republic upon the recommendation of the President of the Executive Yuan.

Article 57. The Executive Yuan shall be responsible to the Legislative Yuan in accordance with the following provisions:

(1) The Executive Yuan has the obligation to present to the Legislative Yuan its administrative policies and its administrative reports. Members of the Legislative Yuan have, during sessions of the Legislative Yuan, the right to interpellate the President and the heads of the Ministries and Commissions of the Executive Yuan.

(2) If the Legislative Yuan does not concur in any important policy of the Executive Yuan, it may, by resolution, ask the Executive Yuan to alter such a policy. With respect to such resolution, the Executive Yuan may, with the approval of the President of the Republic, request the Legislative Yuan to reconsider it. If, after reconsideration, two-thirds of the attending Members of the Legislative Yuan uphold the original resolution, the President of the Executive Yuan shall either abide by the same or resign.

(3) If the Executive Yuan deems a statutory, budgetary or treaty Bill passed by the Legislative Yuan difficult to carry out, it may, with the approval of the President of the Republic, request, within ten days after the delivery of the said resolution to the Executive Yuan, that the Legislative Yuan reconsider the same. If,

after reconsideration, two-thirds of the attending Members of the Legislative Yuan uphold the original resolution, the President of the Executive Yuan shall either abide by the same or resign.

Article 58. The Executive Yuan shall have an Executive Yuan Council to be composed of its President, Vice-President, heads of the various Ministries and Commissions and Ministers of State without Portfolio, with the President of the Yuan as Chairman.

Prior to submission to the Legislative Yuan of any statutory or budgetary Bill or any Bill concerning martial law, general amnesty, declaration of war, conclusion of peace, treaties or other important affairs, or concerning matters of common concern to the various Ministries and Commissions, the President and heads of the various Ministries and Commissions of the Executive Yuan shall present the said Bill to the Executive Yuan Council for discussion and decision.

Article 59. The Executive Yuan shall, three months before the beginning of every fiscal year, present to the Legislative Yuan the Budget for the following fiscal year.

Article 60. The Executive Yuan shall, within four months after the end of every fiscal year, present the Budget statement to the Control Yuan.

Article 61. The organization of the Executive Yuan shall be prescribed by law.

Ch. VI. *Legislation*

Article 62. The Legislative Yuan shall be the highest legislative organ of the State to be composed of popularly elected Members to exercise the legislative power on behalf of the people.

Article 63. The Legislative Yuan shall have the power to decide upon any statutory or budgetary Bill or any Bill concerning martial law, general amnesty, declaration of war, conclusion of peace, treaties and other important affairs of the State.

Article 64. Members of the Legislative Yuan shall be elected in accordance with the following provisions :

(1) Those elected by provinces and by municipalities under the direct jurisdiction of the Executive Yuan shall be five for each province or municipality with a population of less than 3,000,000. In case of a population exceeding 3,000,000, one additional Member shall be elected for each additional 1,000,000 persons.

(2) Those elected by Mongolian leagues and banners.

(3) Those elected by Tibet.

(4) Those elected by various racial groups in the border regions.

(5) Those elected by Chinese nationals residing abroad.

(6) Those elected by occupational groups.

The election of Members of the Legislative Yuan and the number of those to be elected in accordance with the above-mentioned (2) to (6) shall be prescribed by law.

The number of women to be elected in the above-mentioned categories shall be prescribed by law.

Article 65. Members of the Legislative Yuan shall serve a term of three years, and shall be eligible for re-election. The election of Members of the Legislative Yuan shall be completed not later than three months prior to the expiration of each term of office.

Article 66. The Legislative Yuan shall have a President and a Vice-President to be elected by and from among its Members.

Article 67. The Legislative Yuan may organize various committees.

Such committees may invite Government officials and private individuals concerned to be present at their meetings for consultation.

Article 68. The Legislative Yuan shall hold two sessions every year, to be convened by itself. The first session shall last from February to the end of May, and the second session from September to the end of December. When necessary, a session may be extended.

Article 69. In any of the following circumstances, the Legislative Yuan may hold an extraordinary session :

(1) At the request of the President of the Republic,

(2) Upon the petition of more than one-fourth of its Members.

Article 70. The Legislative Yuan shall not make proposals to increase expenditures listed in the Budget presented by the Executive Yuan.

Article 71. At meetings of the Legislative Yuan, the Presidents of the various Yuan and the heads of the various Ministries and Commissions concerned may be in attendance to present their opinions.

Article 72. Statutory Bills passed by the Legislative Yuan shall be sent to the President of the Republic and to the Executive Yuan. The President shall, within ten days after their receipt, promulgate them. However, the President may proceed with them in accordance with provisions of Article 57 of the Constitution.

Article 73. No Member of the Legislative Yuan shall be held responsible outside the Yuan for any utterances made or votes cast in the Yuan.

Article 74. No Member of the Legislative Yuan may, except in case of apprehension *flagrante delicto*, be arrested or detained without permission of the Legislative Yuan.

Article 75. No Member of the Legislative Yuan may concurrently hold a Government post.

Article 76. The organization of the Legislative Yuan shall be prescribed by law.

Ch. VII. Judiciary

Article 77. The Judicial Yuan shall be the highest judicial organ of the State and shall have jurisdiction over civil, criminal and administrative cases and over cases concerning disciplinary punishment of public functionaries.

Article 78. The Judicial Yuan shall have the power to interpret the Constitution and also the power to unify the interpretation of laws and decrees.

Article 79. The Judicial Yuan shall have a President and a Vice-President, who shall be nominated and appointed by the President of the Republic with the consent of the Control Yuan.

The Judicial Yuan shall have a number of Grand Justices to attend to matters stipulated in Article 78 of the Constitution, who shall be nominated and appointed by the President of the Republic with the consent of the Control Yuan.

Article 80. Judges shall be above party affiliations and shall, in accordance with law, hold trials independently and free of any interference.

Article 81. Judges shall hold office for life. No judge may be removed from office unless he has been found guilty of criminal offences or subjected to disciplinary punishment, or declared legally incompetent. No judge may, except in accordance with law, be suspended, transferred or have his salary reduced.

Article 82. The organization of the Judicial Yuan and of the law courts of various grades shall be prescribed by law.

Ch. VIII. Examination

Article 83. The Examination Yuan shall be the highest examination organ of the State and shall attend to matters such as examination, appointment, registration and ranking, checking of records, salary scales, promotion and transfer, safeguarding of tenures, commendation, compensation, retirement, and pension.

Article 84. The Examination Yuan shall have a President and a Vice-President and a number of members who shall be nominated and appointed by the President of the Republic with the consent of the Control Yuan.

Article 85. In the selection of public functionaries, a system of competitive examination shall be enforced, quotas of candidates shall be prescribed severally according to provinces and areas, and examinations shall be held by regions. No person may be appointed to a public office unless he has qualified through examination.

Article 86. The following qualifications shall be determined through examinations to be held by the Examination Yuan in accordance with law :

(1) Qualifications for appointment as public functionaries.

(2) Qualifications for practice in specialized professions and as technicians.

Article 87. The Examination Yuan may, with respect to matters under its charge, present statutory Bills to the Legislative Yuan.

Article 88. Members of the Examination Yuan shall be above party affiliations and shall, in accordance with law, independently carry out their functions.

Article 89. The organization of the Examination Yuan shall be prescribed by law.

Ch. IX. Control

Article 90. The Control Yuan shall be the highest organ of control of the State and shall exercise the powers of consent, impeachment, censure and auditing.

Article 91. The Control Yuan shall be composed of members to be elected by provincial and municipal councils, the local councils of Mongolia and Tibet, and Chinese nationals residing abroad. Their numbers shall be determined in accordance with the following provisions :

(1) Five members from every province.

(2) Two members from every municipality under the direct jurisdiction of the Executive Yuan.

(3) Eight members from Mongolian leagues and banners.

(4) Eight members from Tibet.

(5) Eight members from Chinese nationals residing abroad.

Article 92. The Control Yuan shall have a President and a Vice-President, to be elected by and from among its members.

Article 93. Members of the Control Yuan shall serve a term of six years and shall be eligible for re-election.

Article 94. When the Control Yuan exercises the power of the Constitution, it shall do so by resolution of a majority of the attending members.

Article 95. The Control Yuan, in the exercise of its powers, may send for orders issued by the Executive Yuan and its Ministries and Commissions and for other relevant documents for perusal.

Article 96. The Control Yuan, taking into account the functions of the Executive Yuan and its various Ministries and Commissions, may accordingly set up a number of committees to investigate their

measures with the view to ascertaining whether they have
violated any law or have been derelict in the performance of
their duties.

Article 97.   The Control Yuan may, on the basis of the investigations and resolutions of its committees, propose corrective measures
and forward them to the Executive Yuan and its appropriate Ministries and Commissions with request that improvements be effected.

When the Control Yuan deems a public functionary in the Central
or a local Government derelict in the performance of duty or when it
deems there has been violation of law, it may institute an indictment
or an impeachment. If it is a criminal offence the case shall be turned
over to a law court.

Article 98.   Any impeachment by the Control Yuan of a public
functionary in the Central or a local Government shall be instituted
upon the proposal of more than one member of the Control Yuan
and the endorsement, after due consideration, of more than nine
other members.

Article 99.   In instituting impeachments of personnel of the
Judicial Yuan or of the Examination Yuan for dereliction in the
performance of duty or for violation of law, the provisions of Articles
95, 97 and 98 of the Constitution shall be applicable.

Article 100.   Any impeachment of the President or the Vice-
President of the Republic by the Control Yuan shall be instituted
upon the proposal of more than one-fourth, and the endorsement,
after due consideration, of the majority of the members of the
Control Yuan, and the same shall be presented to the National
Assembly.

Article 101.   No member of the Control Yuan shall be held
responsible outside the Yuan for opinions expressed or for votes
cast in the Yuan.

Article 102.   No member of the Control Yuan may, except in
case of apprehension *flagrante delicto*, be arrested or detained without
the permission of the Control Yuan.

Article 103.   No member of the Control Yuan may concurrently
hold a public office or engage in professional practices.

Article 104.   In the Control Yuan, there shall be an Auditor-
General, who shall be nominated and appointed by the President
of the Republic with the consent of the Legislative Yuan.

Article 105.   The Auditor-General shall, within three months
after the presentation of the Budget statement by the Executive
Yuan, complete the auditing thereof in accordance with law, and
submit an auditing report to the Legislative Yuan.

Article 106.   The organization of the Control Yuan shall be
prescribed by law.

Ch. X.   *Powers of the Central and Local Governments*

Article 107.   The following matters shall be legislated upon and executed by the Central Government :

(1)   Foreign affairs.

(2)   National defence and military affairs concerning national defence.

(3)   Nationality law, and criminal, civil and commercial laws.

(4)   Judicial organization.

(5)   Aviation, national highways, State-owned railways, navigation, postal and telegraph services.

(6)   Central Government finance and national revenues.

(7)   Demarcation of national, provincial and hsien revenues.

(8)   State-operated economic enterprises.

(9)   Currency system and State banks.

(10)   Weights and measures.

(11)   Foreign trade policies.

(12)   Financial and economic matters affecting foreigners or foreign countries.

(13)   Other matters of the Central Government as stipulated in the Constitution.

Article 108.   The following matters shall be legislated upon and executed by the Central Government, which may delegate their execution to the provincial and hsien governments :

(1)   General rules governing provincial and hsien self-government.

(2)   Division of administrative areas.

(3)   Forestry, industry and mining, and commerce.

(4)   Educational system.

(5)   Banking and stocks and commodities.

(6)   Navigation and deep sea fishing enterprises.

(7)   Public utilities.

(8)   Co-operative enterprises.

(9)   Water and land communication and transportation affecting two or more provinces.

(10)   Water conservancy, waterways and agricultural and pastoral enterprises affecting two or more provinces.

(11)   Registration and ranking, appointment, supervision and protection of officials in the Central and local Governments.

(12)   Land legislation.

(13)   Labour legislation and other social legislation.

(14)   Eminent domain.

(15)   Census-taking and compilation of statistics.

(16)   Immigration and land reclamation.

(17)   Police system.

(18)   Public health.

(19)   Ordinary relief, compensation, and unemployment relief.

(20)   Preservation of ancient books, articles and monuments of cultural value.

With respect to the above-mentioned matters, the provinces may enact separate laws and rules, provided these do not contravene national laws.

Article 109.   The following matters shall be legislated upon and executed by the provinces, which may delegate their execution to the hsien :

(1)   Provincial education, public health, industries and communications.

(2)   Management and disposal of provincial property.

(3)   Administration of municipalities under provincial jurisdiction.

(4)   Province-operated enterprises.

(5)   Provincial co-operative enterprises.

(6)   Provincial agricultural, forestry, water conservancy, fishery and animal husbandry and public works.

(7)   Provincial finance and revenue.

(8)   Provincial debts.

(9)   Provincial banks.

(10)   Enforcement of provincial police administration.

(11)   Provincial charitable and public welfare enterprises.

(12)   Other matters delegated to the provinces in accordance with national legislation.

Except as otherwise provided for by law, any of the above-mentioned matters which concern two or more provinces may be undertaken jointly by the provinces concerned.

When any province, in undertaking matters in (1) of this Article experiences financial difficulties, it may, by resolution of the Legislative Yuan, receive a subsidy from the National Treasury.

Article 110.   The following matters shall be legislated upon and executed by the hsien :

(1)   Hsien education, public health, industries and communications.

(2)   Management and disposal of hsien property.

(3)   Hsien-operated enterprises.

(4)   Hsien co-operative enterprises.

(5)   Hsien agriculture and forestry, water conservancy, fishery and animal husbandry, and public works.

(6)   Hsien finance and revenue.

(7)   Hsien debts.

(8)   Hsien banks.

(9)   Administration of hsien police and defence.

(10)   Hsien charitable and public welfare enterprises.

32

(11) Other matters delegated in accordance with national legislation and the Provincial Self-Government Law.

Any of the above-mentioned matters covering more than two hsien may, except as otherwise provided for by law, be undertaken jointly by the hsien concerned.

Article 111. Should there occur any matter not enumerated in Articles 107, 108, 109 and 110, the same shall fall within the jurisdiction of the Central Government if it is national in nature, of the province if it is provincial in nature, and of the hsien if it is hsien in nature. Any dispute over jurisdiction shall be settled by the Legislative Yuan.

Ch. XI.   Local Government

SECTION 1.   THE PROVINCE

Article 112. A province may convene a Provincial Assembly to enact, in accordance with the General Principles of Provincial and Hsien Self-Government, a Provincial Self-Government Law, provided the same does not contravene the Constitution.

The organization of the Provincial Assembly and the election of the representatives shall be prescribed by law.

Article 113. The Provincial Self-Government Law shall, *inter alia*, provide for the following :

(1)   In each of the provinces, there shall be a Provincial Council. Members of the Provincial Council shall be elected by the people of the province.

(2)   In each of the provinces there shall be a provincial government with a provincial Governor, to be elected by the people of the province.

(3)   Relationship between the province and the hsien.

The legislative power of the province shall be exercised by the Provincial Council.

Article 114. The Provincial Self-Government Law, after enactment, shall be immediately submitted to the Judicial Yuan, which if it deems any part thereof unconstitutional, shall declare null and void such Article or Articles as contravene the Constitution.

Article 115. In the enforcement of the Provincial Self-Government Law, should a serious obstacle arise on account of any of its Articles, the Judicial Yuan shall first summon the parties concerned to present their views. Then the Presidents of the Executive Yuan, Judicial Yuan, Examination Yuan and Control Yuan shall form themselves into a committee, with the President of the Judicial Yuan as Chairman, to propose formulas for a solution.

Article 116. Provincial laws and regulations that are in contravention of national laws shall be null and void.

Article 117. In case of any doubt as to whether or not a provincial law or regulation contravenes a national law, an interpretation thereon shall be made by the Judicial Yuan.

Article 118. The self-government of municipalities under the direct jurisdiction of the Executive Yuan shall be prescribed by law.

Article 119. The local self-government system of the Mongolian leagues and banners shall be prescribed by law.

Article 120. The self-government system of Tibet shall be safeguarded.

SECTION 2. THE HSIEN

Article 121. The hsien shall enforce hsien self-government.

Article 122. The hsien may convene a hsien assembly and enact, in accordance with the General Principles of Provincial and Hsien Self-Government, a Hsien Self-Government Law, provided the same does not contravene the Constitution or the Provincial Self-Government Law.

Article 123. The people of the hsien shall, in accordance with law, exercise the rights of initiative and referendum in matters pertaining to hsien self-government, as well as the rights of election and recall of the magistrate and other hsien self-government officers.

Article 124. In each hsien, there shall be a hsien council. Members of the hsien council shall be elected by the people of the hsien.

The legislative power of the hsien shall be exercised by the hsien council.

Article 125. Hsien laws and regulations that are in contravention of national laws or provincial laws and regulations shall be null and void.

Article 126. In each hsien, there shall be a hsien government with a hsien magistrate, to be elected by the people of the hsien.

Article 127. The hsien magistrate shall attend to the enforcement of hsien self-government and to the execution of matters delegated by the Central and provincial Governments.

Article 128. The provisions governing the hsien shall apply *mutatis mutandis* to the municipality.

Ch. XII.   *Suffrage, Recall, Initiative and Referendum*

Article 129. The elections stipulated in the Constitution, except as otherwise provided for by the Constitution, shall be by universal, equal, and direct suffrage and by secret ballot.

Article 130. Any citizen of the Republic of China having attained the age of twenty years shall have the right of suffrage in accordance with law. Except as otherwise provided for by law and by the Constitution, any citizen having attained the age of twenty-three years shall have the right to be elected to office in accordance with law.

Article 131. All candidates in the elections prescribed in the Constitution shall openly campaign for election.

Article 132. Intimidation and material inducements shall be strictly forbidden in elections. Election disputes shall be settled by the courts.

Article 133. After being elected, a person may, in accordance with law, be recalled by his constituency.

Article 134. In the elections, the minimum number of women to be elected shall be decided upon, and measures pertaining thereto shall be prescribed by law.

Article 135. Regarding the number and election of representatives for interior areas where a different mode of living obtains, necessary measures shall be prescribed by law.

Article 136. The exercise of the rights of initiative and referendum shall be prescribed by law.

Ch. XIII. *Fundamental National Policies*

SECTION I. NATIONAL DEFENCE
Article 137. The national defence of the Republic of China shall have as its object the safeguarding of national security and the preservation of world peace.

The organization of national defence shall be prescribed by law.

Article 138. The land, sea and air forces of the whole country shall be above personal, regional or party affiliations, and shall be loyal to the State and protect the people.

Article 139. No political party or faction or private individual may make use of armed force as an instrument in the struggle for political power.

Article 140. No person in active military service may concurrently hold a civil office.

SECTION 2. FOREIGN POLICY
Article 141. In its external relations, the Republic of China shall, in keeping with a spirit of independence and on the basis of the principles of equality and reciprocity, cultivate good neighbourliness with other nations, respect treaties and the United Nations Charter, protect the rights and interests of Chinese nationals residing abroad, promote international co-operation, and advance the cause of right among nations and of world peace.

35

SECTION 3. NATIONAL ECONOMY

Article 142. National economy shall be based on the Principle of the People's Livelihood and seek to effect equalization of land ownership and control over private capital in order to attain fair distribution and sufficiency in national economy.

Article 143. All land within the territory of the Republic of China shall belong to the whole body of citizens. Private ownership of land, acquired by the people in accordance with law, shall be protected and restricted by law. Land owned by private individuals shall be liable to taxation, or Government purchase, according to its value.

Mineral deposits and natural power which may be economically utilized for the public benefit shall belong to the State and shall in no way be affected by the people's acquisition of the right of ownership over the land in question.

If the value of any piece of land shall have increased not through the exertion of labour or the employment of capital, the State shall levy thereon an increment tax, the proceeds of which shall be used for public welfare.

In the distribution of land and adjustment of title deeds the State shall, as a matter of principle, assist tiller-owners and persons who make use of the land themselves, and shall also regulate the size of land appropriate for cultivation and other purposes.

Article 144. Public utilities and other enterprises of a monopolistic nature shall, as a matter of principle, be under public operation. They may, if permitted by law, be operated by the people.

Article 145. With respect to private wealth and privately operated enterprises, the State shall restrict them by law if they are deemed prejudicial to a balanced development of the national economy.

Co-operative enterprises shall receive the encouragement and assistance of the State.

Private productive enterprises and foreign trade shall receive the encouragement, guidance and protection of the State.

Article 146. The State shall, by the use of scientific technique, undertake water conservancy projects, increase the productivity of land, improve agricultural conditions, plan the utilization of land, and develop agricultural resources in order to hasten the industrialization of agriculture.

Article 147. The Central Government, in order to attain a balanced economic development of provinces, shall give appropriate aid to economically poor provinces.

The provinces, in order to attain a balanced economic development of the hsien, shall give appropriate aid to economically poor hsien.

Article 148. Within the territory of the Republic of China, goods of all kinds shall be permitted to move freely from place to place.

Article 149. Financial institutions shall, in accordance with law, be subject to State control.

Article 150. The State shall establish throughout the country special financial institutions to aid the unemployed.

Article 151. With respect to Chinese nationals residing abroad, the State shall foster and protect the development of their economic enterprises.

SECTION 4.   SOCIAL SECURITY

Article 152. The State shall give adequate opportunity of employment to people who are capable of work.

Article 153. The State, in order to improve the livelihood of labourers and farmers and to improve their productive skill, shall enact laws and carry out policies for their protection.

Women and children engaged in labour shall, according to their age and physical condition, be accorded special protection.

Article 154. Capital and labour shall, in accordance with the principle of harmony and co-operation, promote productive enterprises. Mediation and arbitration of disputes between capital and labour shall be prescribed by law.

Article 155. The State, in order to promote social welfare, shall put into operation a Social Insurance System. To the aged, the infirm and the disabled among the people who are unable to earn a living, and to victims of natural calamities, the State shall give appropriate assistance and relief.

Article 156. The State, in order to consolidate the foundation of national existence and development, shall protect motherhood and carry out the policy of promoting the welfare of women and children.

Article 157. The State, in order to improve national health, shall extend throughout the country public health and medical services and the State Medicine System.

SECTION 5.   EDUCATION AND CULTURE

Article 158. The nation's educational and cultural services shall have as their aim the development among the citizens of national characteristics, a democratic spirit, traditional morality, good physique, scientific knowledge and the ability to earn a living.

Article 159. All citizens shall have an equal opportunity to receive education.

Article 160. All children of school age, to wit, those from six to twelve years, shall receive free primary education. Those from poor families shall be supplied with textbooks at the expense of the government.

All citizens above school age who have not received primary education shall receive such education free of charge, and shall likewise be supplied with textbooks at the expense of the government.

Article 161. Governments of various grades shall create scholarships to assist students of good scholastic standing and of exemplary conduct who lack the means to continue their school education.

Article 162. All public and private educational and cultural institutions in the country shall, in accordance with law, be subject to State supervision.

Article 163. The State shall pay due attention to the balanced development of education in different regions and shall promote social education in order to raise the cultural standard of the citizens in general. The National Treasury shall give cash grants to border regions and economically poor areas to help them meet their educational and cultural expenses. The Central Government may itself undertake the more important educational and cultural enterprises in such regions or give them financial assistance.

Article 164. Expenditure for educational programmes, scientific studies and cultural services shall be, in respect of the Central Government, not less than 15 per cent of the total national Budget ; in respect of the provinces, not less than 25 per cent of the total provincial Budget : and in respect of the municipality or hsien, not less than 35 per cent of the total municipal or hsien Budget. Educational and cultural foundations established in accordance with law shall, together with their property, be protected.

Article 165. The State shall safeguard the livelihood of those who work in the fields of education, sciences and arts, and shall, in accordance with the development of the national economy, increase their remuneration from time to time.

Article 166. The State shall encourage scientific discoveries and inventions and shall protect monuments and articles of historical, cultural or artistic value.

Article 167. The State shall give encouragement or subsidies to the following enterprises or individuals :

(1) Private educational enterprises in the country which have a good record.

(2) Chinese educational enterprises abroad which have a good record.

(3) Persons who have made discoveries or inventions in the fields of learning and technology.

(4) Persons who have rendered long and meritorious service to the cause of education.

Article 168. The State shall accord legal protection to the status of racial groups in the border regions, and shall give them special assistance in their local self-government undertakings.

Article 169. The State shall positively undertake and foster the development of education, cultural services, communications, water conservancy, public health and other economic and social enterprises for the benefit of racial groups in the border regions. With respect to the utilization of land, the State shall, after taking into account local climatic conditions and the nature of the soil, and in the light of the living habits of the local people, adopt measures to protect the land and to assist in its development.

Ch. XIV.   Enforcement and Amendment of the Constitution

Article 170. The term 'Law' as used in the Constitution, denotes any legislative Bill that shall have been passed by the Legislative Yuan and promulgated by the President.

Article 171. Laws that are in contravention of the Constitution shall be null and void.

In case of any doubt as to whether or not a law is in contravention of the Constitution, interpretation thereof shall be made by the Judicial Yuan.

Article 172. Ordinances that are in contravention of the Constitution or laws shall be null and void.

Article 173. Interpretation of the Constitution shall be done by the Judicial Yuan.

Article 174. Amendments to the Constitution shall be made in accordance with one of the following procedures :

(1) Upon the proposal of one-fifth of the total number of the delegates to the National Assembly and by a resolution of three-fourths of the delegates present at a meeting having a quorum of two-thirds of the entire Assembly, an amendment may be made.

(2) Upon the proposal of one-fourth of the members of the Legislative Yuan and by a resolution of three-fourths of the members present at a meeting having a quorum of three-fourths of the members of the Yuan, an amendment may be drawn up and submitted to the National Assembly for referendum. Such a proposed amendment to the Constitution shall be publicly announced six months prior to the opening of the National Assembly.

Article 175. Matters provided for in this Constitution which require separate enforcement measures shall be prescribed by law.

The preparatory procedure for the enforcement of this Constitution shall be decided upon by the Constitution-making National Assembly.

Text supplied by Chinese Embassy, New Delhi, 1948. Arts. 174-5, re-edited from Ch'ien Tuan-sheng, *The Government and Politics of China* (Harvard University Press, Cambridge, Mass., 1950), Appendix D.

2   18 *April* 1948

PROVISIONAL AMENDMENT TO THE CONSTITUTION PASSED BY THE NATIONAL ASSEMBLY GIVING THE PRESIDENT ADDITIONAL EMERGENCY POWERS

In accordance with the procedure stipulated in Paragraph 1 of Article 174, the following temporary provisions to be effective during the period of national crisis are hereby enacted :

The President during the period of national crisis may, by resolution of the Executive Yuan, take emergency measures to avert imminent danger to the security of the State or of the people, or to cope with any serious financial or economic crisis, without being subject to restrictions stipulated in Article 39 or Article 43 of the Constitution.

The emergency measures mentioned in the preceding paragraph may be modified or abrogated by the Legislative Yuan in accordance with Paragraph 2 of Article 57 of the Constitution.

The period of national crisis may be declared terminated by the President on his own initiative or at the request of the Legislative Yuan.

The President shall call an extraordinary session of the First National Assembly not later than 25 December 1950, to discuss all proposals pertaining to amendments to the Constitution. If at that time the period of national crisis has not yet been declared terminated in accordance with the foregoing provision, the extraordinary session of the National Assembly shall decide whether or not the temporary provisions are to remain in force or are to be abrogated.

China Magazine, May 1948, p. 23.

3   17 *April* 1947

THE POLITICAL PROGRAMME OF THE NATIONAL GOVERNMENT OF CHINA

The National Government of the Chinese Republic, with a view to establishing constitutional government and promoting democracy, has since the Political Consultative Conference (January 1946) decided to reorganize the Government and to invite individuals from political parties and groups other than the Kuomintang, as well as Independents, to participate. More than one year's persistent efforts have just resulted in a jointly formulated and agreed upon procedure for immediate completion of the Government reorganization. Besides, a political programme for the National Government after the re-organization, evolving from comprehensive and careful deliberations by all parties concerned, has just been approved, respectively, by the standing committees of the Young China Party, the Democratic Socialist Party and the Chinese Kuomintang ; it has also been agreed upon by the Independents who took part in the discussions. The embodiments of the political programme, which will be adhered to jointly by the reorganized National Government, are as follows :

(1) The programme of peaceful national reconstruction shall be the guiding principle of administration for the reorganized National Government, while all participating parties and Independents shall be jointly responsible for completing the interim procedure for inauguration of constitutional government.

(2) Co-operation among the various parties and groups shall be based upon the principles of 'political democratization' and 'nationa-lization of armed forces' under this common principle; no efforts will be spared towards political progress and national stability.

(3) In order to promote world peace and uphold the United Nations Charter, China should pursue a foreign policy of equality and good neighbourliness, without discrimination, towards all friendly nations.

(4) Settlement by political means shall remain the basic principle for solution of the Chinese Communist problem. If only the Chinese Communists show willingness for peace and the railway system can be completely restored, the Government will seek national peace and unity through political channels.

(5) The responsible Executive Yuan system shall be enforced as an experiment, in accordance with the spirit of the provisions of the Constitution. The Executive Yuan should abide by any decisions of the State Council and assume full responsibility for their execution, thus conforming to the principle of 'authority and responsibility'. Equal respect should be accorded to the functions and powers of the Legislative Yuan. In presenting a Bill to the Legislative Yuan, the Executive Yuan authorities shall be present to offer explana-tions, thereby ensuring co-ordination between the executive and legislative authority.

(6) Pending the inauguration of constitutional government any nomination to the presidency of the Executive Yuan shall be made by the President (of the Republic) with the previous concurrence of the various parties.

(7) Provincial administrations shall be governed by principles making a clear distinction between the military and civil authorities and allowing expediencies as local conditions warrant. In matters of

personnel and legislation, a thoroughgoing check-up will be made and reform instituted in order to enable the provincial Governments to attain the highest degree of efficiency possible.

(8) All laws promulgated and all institutions established to meet the needs of political tutelage shall, after reorganization of the National Government, be rescinded and abolished.

(9) Thorough adjustments shall be made in the tax system and financial set-up, the procedure of levying taxes shall be simplified, and the categories of land tax and additional levies shall be reduced, in order to alleviate the burdens of the people.

(10) Strict guarantee shall be accorded to the people's freedom of person, freedom of speech, freedom of publication and freedom of assembly. Any illegal arrest or interference shall be strictly forbidden. Where restrictions are deemed essential for the maintenance of social order or to avert a crisis, laws governing such restrictions shall be approved by the State Council.

(11) Foreign loans henceforth to be contracted shall be earmarked for purposes of stabilizing and improving the people's livelihood and of production and reconstruction.

(12) As far as possible, there should be participation of political parties and Independents in the political councils or provisional councils of the provinces, municipalities and hsien. Local governments in the various provinces should also include representatives of various parties and Independents, based on the principle of 'selection of the able and efficient'.

US Relations with China, pp. 740-41.

4   18 *April* 1947

STATEMENT BY GENERALISSIMO CHIANG KAI-SHEK
ANNOUNCING THE REORGANIZATION OF
THE STATE COUNCIL

The reorganization of the State Council which takes effect on 18 April is another step in the transition from Kuomintang tutelage to constitutional government in China. It gives representation, on the nation's highest policy-making body, to two minority parties and to the Independents.

The composition of the State Council under this reorganization is as follows :

Presidents of Yuan	..	..	..	..	5
Kuomintang	..	..	..	..	12

Social Democrats   4
Young China Party   4
Independents   4

At present the Presidents of all the five Yuan are Kuomintang members so that the total of Kuomintang seats is 17. But the assumption of any of these posts by members of other parties or by Independents would automatically reduce the Kuomintang representation.

The originally planned membership of the State Council consists of 40, with the Kuomintang numbering 20. In the present one, 29 seats have been occupied. If the remaining 11 should be filled, the Kuomintang membership will be 17 out of 40, or less than half.

In the case of the Social Democratic Party and the Young China Party, individuals will be selected by the groups themselves.   In the case of the Independents, selections will be made after talks with the individuals concerned.

The broadening of political representation on the State Council follows the election of minority party members to the Legislative and Control Yuan and thus establishes multi-party government. The next step is the forthcoming reorganization of the Executive Yuan under a new Premier with Cabinet Ministers assigned to minority parties and Independents, as well as the Kuomintang.

The effect of the reorganization of the Chinese Government is as follows : The control of the Government, hitherto exclusively under the Kuomintang, is broadened to control by the Kuomintang, Social Democratic Party, the Young China Party and Independents. The State Council will direct national affairs during the transitional period, carry out mandates of the last National Assembly and prepare for the inauguration of a constitutional government on 25 December 1947.

Chinese post-war political history has been divided into two phases. The first came with the attempt, with American mediation, to persuade the Communists to join the Government and merge their army into a national army. The second phase began with the National Assembly. Participation by the Social Democrats, the Young China Party and Independents in that body and in preparation of the Constitution meant that they supported the Government's effort to bring about constitutional government.

The world is not static. China's need for peace and reconstruction becomes more urgent every day. China must push vigorously ahead in order to achieve unity by the quickest means possible. Progress toward democracy and constitutionalism cannot wait indefinitely for the Communists.

If the Chinese Communist Party abandons its policy of seizing power by force and co-operates to achieve the unity of the nation, it still has the opportunity to join the Government and participate in the work of national reconstruction. For the sake of China's suffering people, it is to be hoped that the Communists will change their present attitude of open rebellion.

China Newsweek, No. 235, 24 April 1947.

II POLITICAL DEVELOPMENTS

5   10 *January* 1947

SPEECH BY CHOU EN-LAI ON THE POLITICAL SITUATION

This day last year saw the signing of the cease-fire order, and the opening of the Political Consultative Conference. Great were the changes in the situation, and rapid was the growth of the awakening of the people during the past year. Today a year ago, the people throughout the whole country were cheering for peace and cease-fire, but before long, the nation was again plunged into the abyss of civil strife. All of us have realized that, unless the rule by militarists is put to an end, China can never have peace. The people of the whole nation were celebrating the success of the Political Consultative Conference in January and February last year; but before long, the PCC agreements were completely overthrown by the reactionaries in the Kuomintang. All of us have realized that unless the system of individual dictatorship is removed, the democratic PCC line can never be realized. The people of the whole nation were welcoming President Truman's statement on China and General Marshall's mediation efforts in China a year ago, but before long the true nature of the China policy of the American imperialists was exposed, and the high-treason diplomacy of Chiang Kai-shek's régime was also fully unmasked. Since then, from tens of thousands of students to the broad masses of residents in big cities, people all over China have been shouting these slogans : 'US Army quit China', 'Oppose American intervention in China's internal affairs', 'Oppose Quisling style diplomacy', 'Oppose the Sino-American trade treaty', and the like.

In the changes during the past year, not only the KMT reactionaries have started anew the civil war and scrapped the PCC

agreements, but also the American witness who affixed his signature
on the cease-fire agreement has never again mentioned the January
cease-fire order. And the delegates of the Youth Party, the Social
Democrats, and a great part of the so-called social leaders who took
part in the PCC also participated in the illegal Kuomintang-con-
trolled 'National Assembly' which completely destroyed the PCC
line, whereby they formulated a dictatorial constitution which runs
diametrically counter to the PCC principles, thus deepening the
split of the nation. Only the Chinese Communists, genuine democratic parties and groups, genuine civic leaders and the broad masses
of the people have never for a moment ceased to uphold the January
cease-fire agreement, to fight for the PCC line, and to fight for the
realization of the demands that US troops withdraw from China,
and the United States stop interfering with China's domestic politics.
In looking back over the struggles during the past year, we can't
help but think of the martyrs of the 8 April incident who clamoured
for a cessation of hostilities, and for the implementation of the PCC
resolutions, and also of Messrs Wen, Li and Tao. The spirit with
which they fought bitterly against the reactionary bloc which had
tried to destroy the cease-fire agreement and the PCC resolutions
has been a constant source of inspiration to us.

Exactly one year after, and on the eve of his departure from
China, General Marshall issued a statement summarizing his mediation efforts during the past year. In the light of this statement of
his, I will now briefly touch upon a few important points.

General Marshall admitted that there is a reactionary group in
the Kuomintang which constitutes a dominant one in the Kuomintang Government, and which includes military and political leaders.
They oppose a coalition Government, have no confidence in internal
co-operation, but believe in the settlement of problems by armed
force. They have no sincerity in carrying out the PCC resolutions.
All these remarks are true. But what is to be regretted is that he
did not point out that Chiang Kai-shek is the highest leader of this
reactionary group. Chiang Kai-shek said a coalition Government
is tantamount to overthrowing the Government; inter-party conference is a spoils system conference. After the establishment of the
executive headquarters in Peiping last year, Chiang Kai-shek and
his group opposed the sending of field teams to Manchuria. After
the signing of the cease-fire agreement in Manchuria on 27 March,
Chiang Kai-shek ordered Tu Yu-Ming to launch a big offensive
there. The failure in the truce negotiations in June was caused
by Chiang Kai-shek's insistence on the withdrawal of Communist
troops from northern Kiangsu, Jehol and two other liberated areas
—an act which is a breach of the PCC resolutions. Immediately after

45

that, he conducted a large-scale fighting in China proper, and up
to now, he continues to act against the PCC agreements in massing
280 brigades (formerly divisions), 90 per cent of his total military
strength, to attack the Communist-held liberated areas. Up to the
end of last year, his armies invaded 174,000 square kilometres and
took 165 cities in the liberated areas. What are they if these are not
armed attacks ?

The PCC resolutions were completely violated by members of the
one-party 'National Assembly' and the decision of the Constitution
was made by Chiang Kai-shek. Therefore, the man who scrapped
the cease-fire pact and the PCC resolutions was none other than
Chiang Kai-shek himself.

Chiang Kai-shek's reactionary bloc wished by this means to maintain its feudal control. Even General Marshall admits that this
further weakens Chiang's Government. As to the disruptions of
economic and communication systems, they are attributable to the
civil war waged by Chiang Kai-shek. The yearly military expenses
constitute 80 per cent of the total State expenditures of Chiang's
Government. Added to these is the exploitation of the people by
bureaucratic capital. How can economic ruin be averted ?

General Marshall thinks that with the same bad Government and
still under the leadership of Chiang Kai-shek, but with the participation of a few Kuomintang liberals and minority parties such as the
Social Democratic Party and the Youth Party, a good Government
can ultimately be formed. Will it not be too cheap ? Without the
participation of the Communists in a coalition Government, the
dictatorial system instituted by Chiang Kai-shek cannot be
abolished, nor can a liberal Government be formed.

General Marshall understands full well that the Chiang Assembly
convened last year is a violation of PCC resolutions and procedures,
but he purposely says that the Constitution passed by it is a democratic constitution and its main parts are in full agreement with the
principles laid down by PCC. Even Communist demands are incorporated in it. This is a big bluff. The main parts of the Constitution
passed by Chiang's Assembly are in direct contravention to the PCC
principles. PCC favours the safeguarding of the liberties of the people,
but Chiang's Constitution restricts them. PCC is in support of the
granting of the right of self-government to racial minorities, but in
Chiang's Constitution, such a right is non-existent. PCC wants to
make the province the highest unit for regional autonomy, and let
it draft its own constitution so that there will be an equal division of
power, but Chiang's Constitution is pervaded with the idea of central-
ization of power, and the stipulation about the drafting of the
provincial constitution is cancelled. PCC desires the Cabinet system

to be instituted in the coalition Government, but Chiang's Constitution is all for the President system as contained in the 5 May draft Constitution. General Marshall relies on the enforcement of Chiang's Constitution and the reorganization of the Government for prolonging Chiang's dictatorship, but in this he is mistaken. The consequences will be that Chiang's Government will be further discredited and isolated and it will completely fail to gain the support of the people.

That being the case, will the Communists' opposition to Chiang's Constitution and the participation in the government under the present circumstances, and their demands of a return to the military positions of 13 January, the abolition of Chiang's Constitution and the convocation of an inter-party conference, be considered as a sign of unwillingness to make a fair compromise, as the Communists have been so accused by General Marshall? Quite the contrary. These are the most fair compromises and the lowest limit of the Communist demands for peace and democracy. Even General Marshall admitted that during last January and February the Communists were willing to reach a compromise. But, since last February, the Kuomintang reactionary group has repeatedly violated the PCC resolutions and the cease-fire pact. Up to now the Communists have tried to reach a compromise on the basis of the cease-fire pact signed last January and through the PCC line. These are really what General Marshall praised as a liberal and forward-looking charter.

If we make a comparison, Chiang Kai-shek is violating the cease-fire pact and deviating from the PCC line, whereas the Communists are observing the cease-fire pact and following the PCC line. Is Chiang Kai-shek trying to annihilate the Communists in the liberated areas or are the Communists trying to overthrow the Government? Is it fair if Chiang can refuse to accept the two Communist demands while the Communists must accept Chiang's Constitution and the positions of the two troops, not in accordance with the cease-fire pact?

No Chinese people will believe that the residents of the liberated areas are in the depth of their suffering. This is not an actual fact and is a blasphemy against the Communists. The Communists have worked for the welfare of the people for the last six years and have built up their reputation by their close attachment to the people. If the Communists agree to the occupation of the liberated areas by Chiang's troops and permit Chiang to force the residents to recognize the Constitution and to acknowledge his dictatorship, it will be a complete disregard of the people's suffering and the interest of the country. Besides, it will not lead to real peace.

There are many naïve persons who are too eager to have peace and who are too easily deceived by the apparent peace and do not

47

want to struggle for the minimum safeguards for peace. Chiang Kai-shek has perceived their weaknesses. When it was advantageous for Chiang to launch an attack, he would not hesitate to attack. But when he was defeated and required time to regroup his troops, for instance (he was in such a pass last January and February), he would favour the halting of the war and conducted the so-called peace talks. Let me ask how a fair compromise could be reached. Never. A fair compromise must be built on a basis which is beneficial to the people. That basis is the cease-fire pact signed last January by General Marshall and Chang Chun, Chiang's representative, and the PCC resolutions passed by Chiang Kai-shek. In General Marshall's report, he mentioned the PCC resolutions, but not the cease-fire pact. That was not just a slip of his memory. It was his intention to absolve himself of the responsibility of appending his signature to a pact and try to find a way out for the three-man military subcommittee and the Peiping executive headquarters. This further proves that the US Government has been helping Chiang to extend the civil war. It also explains why General Marshall hated very much the propaganda activities carried out by the Communists. Yes, the Communists had since last March repeatedly pointed out the error of the US policy in China, particularly the garrison of the United States forces in this country, their interference in the domestic affairs, and the invasion of the liberated areas. The Anping incident alluded to by General Marshall was one of the thirty-odd incidents.

The Chinese Communists have unremittedly exposed and lodged protests against American aid to Chiang Kai-shek's Government troops in the form of transportation, lend-lease materials, surplus property, warships and airplanes, military advisers and technical training, and the colonial policy of the American imperialists. [Here the broadcast was badly garbled.] Instead, the Chinese Communists were blamed for their being unable to accept the American mediation, something we must repudiate. General Marshall thought that the above-mentioned kinds of propaganda tend to arouse a bitter hatred of Americans, and are therefore of a vicious nature. The truth is that what aroused people is not abstract propaganda, but living facts. If facts such as those listed above continue to remain, then in the eyes of an independent and freedom-loving people they are vicious.

General Marshall has now returned to the United States to take up the post of Secretary of State. I hope that he will, taking the stand of the late President Roosevelt's China policy and for the sake of the traditional friendship between, and the interests of, the two Chinese and American peoples, review again the US-China policy during the past year. I hope that the United States will not repeat past mistakes but stop helping Chiang Kai-shek's Government in waging the civil war, evacuate American troops from China, and not intervene again in China's internal affairs, but will readjust relations between China and the United States. In so doing, it will be greatly helpful to the efforts of the Chinese people in their striving for peace, democracy, independence and freedom, and will also be beneficial to far faster pace and international co-operation.

We cannot forget this memorable day of the first anniversary of the issuance of the cease-fire order and the meeting of the PCC. We Chinese Communists pledge ourselves to continue to fight, and we believe that democratic people and our fellow countrymen throughout the country will fight for the complete realization of the PCC agreements and the PCC line. We will not cease our efforts until the aims are realized.

United States Relations with China (Department of State Publication 3575, August 1949), pp. 706-10.

6   20 *January* 1947

STATEMENT BY THE MINISTRY OF INFORMATION, CHINESE NATIONAL GOVERNMENT, ON THE COURSE OF NEGOTIATIONS WITH THE COMMUNISTS

With a view to establishing constitutional rule and completing national reconstruction, the Government has been consistently seeking for peace and unification. As far back as the beginning of the war of resistance, in order to pool together the nation's efforts, the Government called the People's Political Council, consisting of representatives of all political parties and Independents.

From start to finish, the Government has regarded the Communist problem as a political problem. The Kuomintang at its tenth CEC plenary session in 1942 and eleventh plenary session the following year persistently advocated an early solution through political means.

After May 1944 the Government has been negotiating with the Communist Party without let-up in the hope that a peaceful settlement could be reached.

When the Committee for Promotion of Constitutional Rule met on 1 March 1945, President Chiang Kai-shek, being convinced that the Communist problem, if left unsolved, would constitute a serious obstacle in the way of national unification and reconstruction, reiterated his determination of finding a peaceful solution without delay. He also proposed three steps leading towards constitutional government.

After victory, President Chiang Kai-shek invited the Communist leader, Mr Mao Tse-Tung, to Chungking for discussions. These discussions resulted in the Double Tenth Agreement with the announcement that negotiations would be continued on the basis of mutual trust and concessions so that satisfactory results will be achieved.

Since the Political Consultative Conference last January, agreements have been reached between the Government and Communists on military and communications problems with the help of United States special envoy General George C. Marshall. These agreements raised hope throughout the world that the Communist problem in China would be solved through political means.

The Government and Kuomintang, especially in the resolution of the party's second plenary session, repeatedly pledged support to the PCC resolutions and expressed their willingness to implement them in co-operation with the other political parties and Independents. The failure of realization of the PCC resolutions is due to the following factors :

One. According to the Sino-Soviet treaty, the National Government should take over the administration in the nine northeast provinces. When the Soviet troops began withdrawing, Communist troops obstructed in various ways the take-over work of the national army. In the middle of March last year the Communists occupied various places already taken over by the Government forces in Liaopel and attacked Szepingkai, Harbin and Tsitsihar. In order to fulfil its treaty obligations and assert its right to recover sovereignty over the northeast, the Government on 27 March reached an agreement with the Communists for sending truce field teams to the northeast. Unfortunately nothing was achieved, despite the efforts of the field teams under the Executive Headquarters; thus the northeast remains in chaotic conditions. The National Assembly scheduled by PCC to convene on 5 May had to be postponed.

Two. Since the Government returned to Nanking in May 1946, conflicts in the northeast were further intensified and communications in North China continued to be disrupted. The Government, jointly with the Communists, issued a cease-fire order for 15 days during which it hoped to put a full stop to the hostilities in the northeast, to restore communication lines throughout the country and to implement the army reorganization plan. On all these three points, the Government and the Communist Party had almost reached agreement. But though the deadline of the truce period was postponed three times, the Communists intensified their attacks during the interval, capturing Tehchow, Taian and attacking Tatung, Tsinan and the outer rim of Tsingtao. Again nothing was achieved.

Three. Before the National Assembly was convoked, in view of the confused domestic conditions and the countrywide demand for peace and especially the sincerity and earnest desire of the various political parties and Independents for the early termination of hostilities, the Government on 16 October proposed to the Communists an eight-point peace programme, in the hope that another cease-fire order would be issued and the National Assembly be called as scheduled to enact a Constitution. But despite the strenuous mediatory efforts of the minority parties, and despite the Government's intention to make concessions, the Communists stood adamant in their opposition to the compromise suggestion and demanded further postponement of the National Assembly. A deadlock was thus reached.

After the adjournment of the National Assembly, the Government, with the date set for the enforcement of the Constitution, made further efforts for the resumption of the peace talks. Through Dr J. Leighton Stuart, United States Ambassador, the Government informed the Communist Party of its willingness to send a representative to Yenan to resume the peace negotiations. But the Communists still insisted on the restoration of the troop dispositions extant on 13 January last year, and on the annulment of the Constitution adopted by the National Assembly, as the *sine qua non* conditions. But the fact is that great changes have occurred in the troop dispositions during the past year since 13 January. It is practically impossible to revert to the original positions. Moreover the withdrawal of Government troops from recovered areas would surely endanger the people's lives and property in those areas—a thing most incompatible with the Government's obligation to restore order, and protect the people and to prevent the recurrence of Communist terrorism.

If the Communists are really sincere to achieve peace, they should implement the army reorganization plan and other programmes reached in the Committee of Three. If so, there should be no need for any dispute over the temporary dispositions of the troops.

As regards the annulment of the Constitution, the National Assembly consisted of district, occupational and racial representatives and delegates from various political parties, in accordance with PCC resolution. The Assembly, therefore, was by no means a KMT-dominated Assembly. Moreover, the Constitution adopted by the Assembly embodies the very principles laid down by the Communist Party and the other parties represented in the Political Consultative Conference, and in the draft constitution reviewing committee. Therefore there should not be any reason for the Communists to object to the Constitution.

The above-stated fact clearly indicates that in order to achieve peace and unity, the Government has made the greatest possible concessions to appeal to the reasonable consideration of the Communists. Since political democratization and nationalization of troops were common objectives of the PCC there seems to be no reason why the Communists should cling to their prejudices and suspicions.

Now the war has been over for more than a year, peace and unity must be achieved without delay. It is fervently hoped that the Communists will appreciate the Government's earnest efforts to seek a political settlement and agree to resume negotiations. The Government is still ready to meet the Communists with tolerance and sincerity.

The Government therefore proposes the following four points for the resumption of the peace talks and Government reorganization. The four points are :

(1)   The Government is willing to send a representative to Yenan, or to invite Communist delegates to come to Nanking to resume the peace talks, or to call a round-table conference to be attended by representatives of the various parties and Independents.

(2)   The Government and the Communists will immediately order their troops to cease hostilities, and remain at their present positions and negotiate effective measures to ensure cessation of hostilities.

(3)   The Government is prepared to resume negotiations with the Communists for the enforcement of the army reorganization plan and the restoration of communications agreements in accordance with the principles laid down by the Committee of Three.

(4)   Before the full operation of the Constitution, the Government is willing to work out a just and equitable plan for solving the much controverted problem of regional administration.

United States Relations with China, pp. 697-9.

7   29 *January* 1947

STATEMENT BY LU TING-YI, CHIEF OF THE DEPARTMENT OF INFORMATION, CENTRAL COMMITTEE, CHINESE COMMUNIST PARTY, IN REPLY TO THE STATEMENT OF THE NATIONALIST GOVERNMENT

The entire content of the statement by the Kuomintang Ministry of Information is rejection of the two conditions raised by the

Chinese Communist Party for restoring peace negotiations—it is rejection of nullification of Chiang Kai-shek's false Constitution and of restoration of military positions of 13 January 1946. Moreover, it raises four points of a so-called peace proposal.

These four points have already been transmitted by Chiang Kai-shek to the Chinese Communist Party. It is clear that the so-called peace negotiations are a complete fraud and the so-called four points are employed to reject prerequisites for real peace negotiations. Inasmuch as these prerequisites are rejected, what kind of sincerity or peace negotiations remains to be spoken of ?

Nullifying Chiang Kai-shek's fake Constitution and restoring the military position of 13 January last year—these objectives must and can be attained. If Chiang can utilize every means of fraud and force to transfer 90 per cent of his military strength to attack liberated areas, why then cannot he transfer these armies back to the position of 13 January in pursuance of the needs of peace ? Already more than 300,000 war prisoners have been captured from Chiang's invading armies by people's liberation armies. From army and division commanders down to rank and file soldiers everyone expresses his unwillingness to fight a civil war and everyone yearns to make peace and return to the original positions. Why then must Chiang Kai-shek plunge them into civil war to become cannon fodder ? As for so-called 'during the past year changes in positions of both sides have been extremely great' and therefore restoration of military positions of 13 January last year is impracticable—is this not the clearest deception ? Another reason for the statement of the Kuomintang Ministry of Information rejecting restoration of military positions of 13 January last year is 'as soon as the Government withdraws from territories already recovered, people in those areas would have nothing to rely on for their lives and properties'. This is utter fabrication. Chiang Kai-shek's armies have occupied over 160 liberated area cities, 179,000 square kilometres of liberated area territory, where dwell over 20,000,000 people of liberated areas—equal to half the population of France. Before invasion and occupation by Chiang Kai-shek's troops peasants in these areas had already carried out 'land to tillers', democratic governments had already been established, traitors and Japanese collaborators had already been punished, people of all ranks and classes were living and working in peace and happiness. There were no scourges, no economic crises. After Chiang's troops invaded and occupied these places, the peasant's land was confiscated, Fascist secret police terrorized the populace, traitors, collaborators and local tyrants came back and were made officials by Chiang Kai-shek's Government. Chiang Kai-shek's officials and armies burned, murdered, raped, carried out exorbitant taxation, and conscription of soldiers and grain and corruption pervaded everywhere. Over 20,000,000 people again suffer from the boundless misery of Chiang Kai-shek's dictatorship.

Chiang Kai-shek in truth exhausts his energies in protecting traitors, secret police agents, evil gentry and corrupt officials. Where does he have even one minute in which to protect the lives and properties of the people ? Precisely for the sake of protecting the lives and properties of the people, Chiang Kai-shek's armies should be withdrawn from all of the invaded and occupied territories.

As for the so-called truce at present positions, Chiang Kai-shek's 'peace proposal', everyone should remember that truce at present positions has taken place three times since the truce order of last 13 January. The January truce order was the first time, the 27 March cease-fire order for Manchuria was the second time and the truce and peace negotiations of last January the third time. In each case the Chinese Communist Party made positive concessions, but the result of these concessions was that Chiang Kai-shek three times in succession broke the agreements. You don't mean to say that the Chinese people are all a bunch of blockheads, and, after all this, must we still give Chiang Kai-shek a fourth truce at present positions so that he can break it for the fourth time? So that he can entirely wipe out all liberated areas ? Who can guarantee that he will not do this ? The present so-called 'truce at present positions' of the Kuomintang is truce at 'present positions' after Chiang Kai-shek has completely torn up the truce order and PCC resolutions and launched unprecedented large-scale civil war.

This is in order to have the Chinese people recognize the results obtained by his use of military force in faithless betrayal of all agreements and trusts, and thus to encourage war-lords to carry out the idle dream of unity through force, and to encourage the reactionaries recklessly to tear up all agreements and wage large-scale civil war. Chiang Kai-shek repeatedly says he believes in 'political settlement' but his real activity is 'military settlement'. If the Chinese people were to agree to this, what hope for peace would there be ? If the Chinese Communist Party were to agree to this, what could they say to the people ? The Chinese Communist Party for the sake of the people's happiness absolutely cannot recognize the results achieved with military force thus in defiance of law. Therefore, the Chinese Communist Party absolutely cannot agree to the so-called 'truce at present positions'. The 90 per cent of Chiang Kai-shek's armies which have been illegally transferred must one and all return to their original positions. Otherwise there is absolutely no guarantee of peace.

With regard to the third and fourth points of Chiang Kai-shek's 'peace formula'—reorganization of armies, restoration of communications, local governments, et cetera—they have been raised and talked over innumerable times in the past, but either no results were reached or, if results were reached, they were torn up by Chiang Kai-shek. Before Chiang Kai-shek nullifies the false Constitution and restores positions of 13 January, these questions cannot be discussed at all. Hence the first point of Chiang Kai-shek's 'peace formula' alleging that the 'Government is willing to send a representative to Yenan for talks or even hold a round-table conference', et cetera, is not necessary before the two conditions of the Chinese Communist Party are carried out. The raising of such points by Chiang Kai-shek is but empty stalling to deceive people.

Chiang Kai-shek's fake Constitution must be nullified and can be nullified. This is the third fake Constitution since the country was called the Chinese Republic. Since the two fake Constitutions of Yuan Shih-kai and Tsao Kun were nullified why then cannot Chiang Kai-shek's fake Constitution be nullified, since Chiang Kai-shek has treacherously betrayed and violated PCC decisions by unilaterally calling the 'National Assembly' and passing the fake Constitution? The people have every reason to order him to nullify his fake Constitution.

The Kuomintang Ministry of Information states that the 'Chinese Communist Party has no reason whatsoever to oppose' this Chiang Kai-shek fake Constitution. It can, however, be asked, what reason has Chiang Kai-shek for manufacturing such a Constitution? Did the Chinese people not have reason for nullifying the fake Constitution of Yuan Shih-kai and Tsao Kun? Since Chiang Kai-shek has manufactured such a fake Constitution, not nullifying it would be tantamount to recognizing Fascist dictatorship, violating of laws and breaking of discipline by war-lords; where then can there be talk of political democracy and nationalization of armies? Hence the fake Constitution must be nullified.

The overwhelming bulk of public opinion at home as well as abroad heaped imprecations in concert on the 'National Assembly' called by Chiang Kai-shek. The Chinese Communist Party and democrats of all quarters long ago advised Chiang Kai-shek not to convene a one-party illegal National Assembly. But Chiang Kai-shek persisted in ignoring this. When Chiang Kai-shek's National Assembly opened we again advised him to dissolve it but he again refused to listen. Such unbridled lawlessness of Chiang Kai-shek will definitely not be permitted by the Chinese people. The Chinese people and real democrats will absolutely not recognize the validity of such an illegal National Assembly of division.

With regard to representatives of Chiang Kai-shek's 'National Assembly' most of them were appointed hand-picked and produced through bribed elections. Part of them were provisionally 'supplemented' by Chiang Kai-shek and his cronies. Among them are traitors. This National Assembly is worse than the rump assembly of Tsao Kun. Where are the 'representatives of all nationalities, all provinces and municipalities and all professions'? When was Chiang Kai-shek's fake Constitution ever finally examined by the Political Consultative Conference? Which of the main questions of principles, such as people's rights, autonomy of national minorities, relations between legislature and executive, distribution of powers between central and local governments in this fake Constitution, accords with PCC principles? The refusal of Chiang Kai-shek to nullify the malodorous Fascist fake Constitution is really a 'stubborn clinging to opinion', calamity to the entire country, betrayal of the people, betrayal of the nation and determination to be reactionary to the last!

Nullification of the false Constitution and restoration of the military positions of 13 January last year are minimum prerequisites for the restoration of peace negotiations. The reasons these are minimum prerequisites are: Chiang Kai-shek has already completely torn up his four promises, the truce order, the plan for reorganization of armies, the Manchurian cease-fire agreement, and the PCC decisions. He has assassinated Professors Li Kung-po, Wen I-to and other democratic figures. He has convoked an illegal 'National Assembly', concluded the Sino-American commercial treaty of national betrayal, launched large-scale civil war throughout the country, invaded and occupied so much of the liberated areas. After perpetrating all these lawless deeds Chiang Kai-shek still wants to negotiate for peace—of course, this cannot be done without first carrying out a few prerequisites. Otherwise, who can believe he has even a shred of sincerity? If we speak according to law, all bellicose elements of the Kuomintang should be punished as war criminals, all Kuomintang reactionaries and secret police agents who broke PCC decisions should be punished as Fascists, the Kuomintang Government officials who signed the Sino-American commercial treaty should be punished as traitors. Furthermore, they should have to compensate to people of liberated areas and of all China for colossal damages suffered from Chiang Kai-shek's launching of civil war. We have not raised all these just and equitable demands, however, but have only demanded nullification of the false Constitution and restoration of the military positions of 13 January last year. What is this if not the most extreme clemency toward Chiang Kai-shek?

To what degree of lawlessness has Chiang Kai-shek reached within the past year ? If we do not ask him to carry out our two minimum points, if we 'cease fire at present positions', forget all his past crimes and give him time to rest and regroup his troops, consolidate invaded areas, replenish his armies, 'reorganize government' and get $500,000,000 or more loans and military aid from the United States Government, then when he has strength to launch a large-scale offensive again, Chiang Kai-shek will certainly be more lawless. What happened last year is a good example.

Therefore, if we still want independence, peace and democracy, we must ask Chiang Kai-shek to nullify his fake Constitution and restore the positions of 13 January last year. We will never rest till this goal is attained. All deceptions will be in vain. Now that Chiang Kai-shek has rejected these two points and has brought forward his deceptive 'peace proposals' in conflict he will have to bear responsibility for all consequences.

United States Relations with China, pp. 699-702.

8   29 *January* 1947

FURTHER STATEMENT ON NEGOTIATIONS BY THE
NATIONALIST MINISTRY OF INFORMATION

It has been more than three months since the Government issued a cease-fire order on 8 November 1946. The Communists did not comply with this order, but instead have taken advantage of the opportunity and launched a general offensive on all fronts from the northeast to the eastern section of the Lunghai railway. The Communist offensive has been further intensified recently. For the cause of peace and the interest of the country and the people, the Government made one concession after another in the hope that a political solution could be found. It is indeed regrettable that the Communists refused both the Government proposal of sending a representative to Yenan for the resumption of negotiations and the four-point peace proposal of the Government.

Following the adoption, in the National Assembly, of a democratic constitution embodying the principles agreed upon by all parties in the PCC of last January, and having started discussions and preparations for the governmental reorganization plan by inviting all parties and groups to take part in the State Council, the Legislative Yuan, the Executive Yuan, and the Control Yuan, with a view to broadening the basis of the Government, the Government on 24 January requested Dr J. Leighton Stuart, United States Ambassador, to convey to the Communists the following four points :

First, the Government is willing to send a representative to Yenan or to invite Communist delegates to come to Nanking to resume the peace talks, or to call a round-table conference to be attended by representatives of the various parties and Independents.

Secondly, the Government and the Communists will immediately order their troops to cease hostilities and remain at their present positions and negotiate effective measures to ensure cessation of hostilities.

Thirdly, the Government is prepared to resume negotiations with the Communists for the enforcement of the army reorganization plan and the restoration of communications agreements in accordance with the principles laid down by the Committee of Three.

Fourthly, in the regions where hostilities are now taking place, the Government is ready to negotiate with the Communists for a fair and reasonable solution.

Now, the Communists have formally refused all peace negotiations and insisted upon the Government's acceptance of their dictates, namely the restoration of the military positions of 13 January 1946 and the abolition of the Constitution. This is equivalent to putting both the National Government and the National Assembly under the yoke of the Communist Party and subjecting them to the orders of the Communists. What would the Chinese Republic be like and what would be left of the rights of the people ?

During the one-year period after the PCC and the Committee of Three, the Government has spared no effort in inviting the Communist and the minority parties to join the Government.

All such endeavours in achieving an understanding with the Communists have been in vain. Since the Communists have taken such an obdurate stand, the only course at present is for the Government to carry out its fixed policy of 'political democratization'.

We hope that all party leaders as well as Independents will participate in the Government in accordance with their consistent patriotic attitude in order to expedite the preparations and scheduled realization of constitutional rule. We also hope that all parties will co-operate as one man in the gigantic task of national reconstruction, restoration of a balanced economy and improvement of the people's livelihood.

United States Relations with China, pp. 703-4.

9   7 *July* 1947

BROADCAST BY GENERALISSIMO CHIANG KAI-SHEK ON THE TENTH ANNIVERSARY OF THE SINO-JAPANESE WAR

My Fellow Countrymen,

On this, the tenth anniversary of the Double Seventh, I feel called upon to earnestly inform you of the following major happenings since the conclusion of the war : the change of our national situation, the crisis confronting our nation as a whole, the factors that will determine our destiny.

It was primarily to defend her domain, recover the northeast and preserve her sovereign and territorial integrity that China fought the Japanese aggressor. She will never attain her war aim so long as her sovereignty and territorial administration in the northeast remain unrestored, nor will the death of millions of Chinese soldiers and civilians be vindicated. The responsibility, therefore, falls equally on the shoulders of the survivors.

In the northeast, as everybody knows, there were no Chinese Communist rebels prior to the Japanese capitulation. In the one and a half years, however, since National troops entered that part of the country to take over sovereignty there, Communist rebels at different times launched five offensives against National troops. They besieged and attacked areas already taken over by the Government, carved up the territory, and slaughtered the populace.

Lately, the Communists' reply to the peace proposal from the People's Political Council was first, a barrage of vituperatives through their propaganda machine, and then a series of fanatical thrusts outside the Great Wall. The latest Communist offensive in the northeastern provinces, because of its unprecedented magnitude, is especially significant. Since early May, the Communists, in powerful thrusts, have thrown more than 300,000 men against various strategic bases. Finally, they focussed their attacks on one single locality, Szepingkai, employing a force that outnumbered the defenders ten to one. The battle raged for 18 days and nights.

Thanks to the fighting stamina of our forces, developed during the war against Japan, the invading Communists were given a decimating blow. Their plot to encircle Changchun and Kirin and seize Shenyang (Mukden) was crushed, and the tide of war turned in our favour.

Under no circumstances, however, will the Communist rebels abandon their consistent, insidious design of ruining their own fatherland. It cannot be conceded that the Szepingkai victory may have fundamentally removed the crisis facing the northeast. Everyone knows well just how the Chinese Communist rebels entered the northeast and how the various rebellious units there were organized.

The Chinese Communists patently are heirs to imperialistic Japan and the 'Manchoukuo' puppets, and they are now in the process of carrying out the pernicious plot to disintegrate China which was left unfinished by their Japanese predecessors. That plot would not permit restoration of northeast sovereignty to the Chinese nation, nor would it allow the Chinese nation to enjoy territorial and administrative integrity.

Worse still, the Chinese Communists have even made a cat's paw of remnant Japanese troops to ravage our territory and people at their command. In perversion, malignancy and treachery, the Chinese Communists indeed are worse than any bandit, traitor or puppet in Chinese history.

Fellow countrymen, we must realize that, in thus engaging in armed rebellion, the Communists aim to disintegrate all of China and our whole nation. They seek the total elimination of our national spirit and hereditary virtues, the eternal enslavement of our race, and the complete deprivation of the basic human attributes of independence and freedom.

Should the Communists, indulging in such bestial acts of destroying human instincts and suppressing human ethical concepts, be allowed to continue to exist, the Chinese nation would in the near future suffer the disaster of national extinction with indiscriminate, wholesale massacre, collective banishment and eternal slavery for all the composite racial groups.

The aim of our National Revolution is to build a new, independent, free China—of the people, governed for the people and by the people —on the basis of the Three People's Principles. To build such a nation requires, first of all, national unity and peace. Without national unity, however, there can be no national peace. Nor can there be democracy and liberty. National unity is all the more important for the people's welfare. Therefore, if national unity cannot be achieved, the ideal of national reconstruction will remain illusory and the Principles of Nationalism, Democracy and People's Livelihood can never be realized. The people naturally cannot enjoy normal life when their land is being devastated, their economy monopolized, their production destroyed and their communications disrupted by the Communists.

You may still remember my earnest appeal to the Communist Party after VJ Day: 'With the devastating war barely ended, there should not be any civil strife.' No responsible government or patriotic individual would let the country and the people fall into another war when they are still suffering from the ravages of a large-scale war.

We have never attempted to castigate communism as a theory or ideal. We continued to hope that the Communists might follow the course of democracy, as the Communists in Great Britain and the United States have done for so many years, by appealing to the electorate for support of their platform. We have been consistent for the past ten years, and even more so in the last year and a half, in our attitude towards the Communists. We have practised extreme tolerance and we have made substantial compromises and concessions, in the hope that the Communists would refrain from disrupting national unity, carrying on military regional domination, and undermining the foundation of the nation, and that they would contribute their share in national reconstruction. The Government was willing to give full consideration to their opinions. But no peace talk, no mediation, has succeeded in dissuading the Communists from staging a rebellion. We had no way of appealing to their conscience to give up their destructive policy in the interest of the nation and the people.

The activities of the Communist rebels in the past year or so were centred in the destruction of communication lines, industrial and mining plants and the already depleted farms. Every attempt of the Government to appeal for peace and every issuance of a cease-fire order only brought further expansion and attacks of the Communist rebels, which added more difficulties to the National armies and increased the sufferings and sacrifices of the people, thus creating unparalleled difficulties in our post-war social revival. Now all fellow countrymen can rest assured that the Communists, whose rebellious character does not seem to change for the better, have no faith in repentance, and apparently are determined to rebel to the last. Their ambition and intrigues will not be halted until the country is ruined and the world as a whole menaced. If we do not discern the treacherous plots of the Communists, and if we are not determined to quell their rebellion, not only will the people's livelihood be impoverished, but the whole country will be disintegrated.

It was the predetermined policy of the Chinese Communists to rebel against the Government after the conclusion of the war. After VJ Day, they openly launched the so-called 'join-the-army movement', 'social struggles', and 'people's liquidation', in the rebel areas. They looted what food and clothing they could find in order to conserve their rebellious strength. Not even the old men and women or the children are spared from their terrorism and wantonness. Youngsters in rebel areas must either follow their dictates or perish, and burial alive or torture are meted out if the slightest opposition is shown. If a man escapes from rebel control, his whole family is executed. Thousands upon thousands of our compatriots in rebel areas have become sacrifices to the Communists, who have opposed the Government and menaced the people.

In provinces away from the front, especially in large cities of Central and South China, there are still many who do not realize the gravity of our national crisis and the vicious and sinister terrorism of the Communists. They are deluding themselves into false security. They must realize that if it had not been for the struggles of our soldiers to quell the Communist rebellion, they could not maintain their normal living and would be placed in the same tragic conditions as people in North and Northeastern China. Therefore, if we weaken the strength of the National army, we shall deprive the people of their right to exist. Because the people remote from the front are not aware of the realities of the situation, the Communists instigate their reactionary elements everywhere to disseminate anti-civil war and anti-conscription of food and soldiers slogans in an attempt to confuse right and wrong, to drug people's minds, to bewilder the masses and finally weaken the national foundation. This has been done to prevent us from mustering our manpower and resources for suppressing the Communist rebellion and hastening reconstruction.

We can say that our people are being poisoned by Communist propaganda. It is evident that the Communists, in order to implement their plot to betray the country and the people, are trying to blindfold us and deaden our conscience. The aim of the Communists is to confuse the people so they will ignore their national consciousness and the disaster which confronts them and lose their faith in self-improvement and independence, thus falling spiritual captives to the Communists.

The existing confused situation is what the Communists hoped to create. An old saying goes, 'A bird nesting on a falling bough is unaware of imminent disaster.' As a matter of fact, if the nest eventually falls, none of the eggs will remain unbroken. Fellow countrymen, procrastination now will bring death in the near future. It will be too late for regret if we fall into the same pit as our compatriots in the rebel areas. Our country and the destiny of all our people face such a serious crisis that I cannot delay calling upon you to be on the alert.

Fellow countrymen, there are two ways before us and we must immediately choose between them. The first is to vacillate before the ravages and devastation of the Communists, and our whole people will perish. The other is to face the facts realistically, put down the rebellious elements and salvage our nation as well as ourselves. Shall we choose to quell the Communist rebellion with concerted efforts, so as to protect our sovereignty, hasten national unity and attain the goal of freedom and democracy ? Or, shall we procrastinate before Communist vandalism and see our villages pillaged, our kinsmen humiliated, our children compelled to become instruments of betrayal, and eventually our national life ruined ? We must remember how our compatriots are passing their days in North and Northeastern China.

The people in the northeast underwent more than a decade of Japanese subjugation and enslavement. But since the war ended, Communist terrorism, suppression, looting, and massacring have superseded imperial Japan's despotic rule. During the war, the people of North China sustained the greatest losses and underwent the severest tribulations. After the war, instead of having a breathing spell, they were again overrun, this time by the Communists, and thrown into another dark abyss. In their recent offensives the Communists made the 'people's militia' spearhead the attacks. Wherever the Communists hit, they looted and took prisoners, not sparing even dogs and poultry. Their wantonness surpassed even that of the Japanese. Whenever the Communists occupy a place, tens of thousands of the inhabitants, at great risk, move into the Government-controlled areas to find shelter, leaving their homes and property behind them. Their lamentations are the most tragic human utterances. How can those of us remote from the front who have the same ancestral origin remain indifferent to their lot? The aim of the Communist rebels is to exterminate the country and enslave us all. We must suppress the Communist rebels, otherwise we shall undergo the same sufferings in the near future.

With our rehabilitation work yet to be completed, I am fully aware that our people in the recovered areas are leading a hard life. At any rate, they obviously are far better off than their brethren in rebel areas where personal freedom, physical or spiritual, is absolutely forbidden. No whisperings are allowed even between father and son, husband and wife.

Therefore, not only does our suppression of the Communist rebels help to save our compatriots in the rebel areas, but it also helps to save ourselves. If we let the Communist rebellion spread unchecked, we would be inviting ruin. The ambition of the Communists is obvious, and it is our responsibility to quell them.

We suffered cruelly and sacrificed the lives of millions of soldiers and civilians during our war against the Japanese invaders. If we let the Communist rebels attain their goal of destroying the Government and erasing the history of our war of resistance, thus completing the unfinished task of the Japanese to exterminate China, how can the losses we suffered during the war be redeemed ?

Suppression of the Communist rebellion, therefore, is aimed at preserving the highest interests of the State and the basic rights of existence, democracy, and liberty of the people. Our struggle against the Communist rebels is as sacred as was our resistance against the Japanese aggressor.

The call to crush the Communist rebels is a continuation of the unfinished task of national reconstruction after our war against Japan. This is necessary, as I have told you, if we are to preserve the fruits of victory. Such a struggle is inevitable if we are to secure national independence and liberty. This being the case, the National troops who have fought and died for the cause should be respected by the people the same as those who fought and died in the Sino-Japanese war. Our 450,000,000 people must not shirk the responsibility of supplying sufficient food and munitions to the National troops at the front. In this task of saving the nation and protecting the people, all persons in areas at the front and in the rear should share their joys and sorrows and decide to live and die together.

Fellow countrymen, the Communist rebels' ambition has been completely exposed in the recent battles in the northeast. The national crisis has become more and more serious. Our people should not harbour the illusion that they may avoid participating in the struggle through some lucky occurrence or temporary peace. We must concentrate on our strength and redouble our efforts in suppressing the Communists and in reconstructing the nation, so as to eliminate the seeds of misfortune for our future generations. We must achieve national general mobilization with the same spirit as we did during the war of resistance, and we must multiply our efforts in eliminating the deficiencies we had during the war of resistance. We must not hesitate to contribute all our manpower, material strength and lives, if necessary, to the war of suppressing rebellion in a common effort to save our country and people. Only in this way can we preserve the fruits of our victory over Japan, achieve national independence and liberty and retain the hope of again securing social peace and order.

Fellow countrymen, the National Government has issued an order for the enforcement of national general mobilization. The purpose of the order is to awaken the people of the whole country to unify their purpose and to concentrate their efforts for the struggle. We must call on all patriotic Chinese to rise for the salvation of their country and themselves.

All the measures taken by the Government will be in accordance with law. The Government has implicit faith in the people's patriotic conscience and will let the people themselves serve the country spontaneously on the basis of the principle of nationalism. Every compatriot must love the country and the people, observe national laws, and perform his duty. He must make every effort to contribute his part in the suppression of the Communist rebellion and the promotion of national reconstruction.

The nation's social leaders should guide the people in promoting the cause in every possible way. Our youths in particular, upon whom our national existence depends, must discern right from wrong and fair from foul and promote nationalism to safeguard national existence. Unless the youths of China are willing to be Communist instruments and are indifferent about national extinction, they must recognize that they are descendants of Huang Ti and nationals of the Republic of China. If they wish the nation to achieve independence and existence, so that they may have freedom of thought without oppression by the Communists, they must be determined to face the national crisis. Those who go to schools should devote themselves to study, and those who are engaged in agriculture, industry and business must devote themselves to production, so as to increase national strength. Everybody must play his part and do his duty in an effort to stabilize social peace and order in the rear.

Our people must know that the nation-wide Communist rebellion is co-ordinated and linked up with the Communists' well-planned destruction of social order. Ever since the beginning of our resistance against the Japanese, the Communist Party has consistently disparaged the war efforts of the Government with vituperative propaganda in an effort to undermine the Government. This was done to arouse discord between the Government and the people, to weaken our strength in the war, to relegate the international position of the nation, to erase the history of our war of resistance, to minimize the people's faith in winning the war and to deaden the people's patriotism.

The Communists not only spread rumours and instigate riots in schools, among the people, in factories and in financial markets, but they also openly declare that such riotous and destructive actions are 'the second front' as distinguished from 'the first front', military operations. These two fronts are interdependent, so that military operations can disturb the community in the rear and riots in the rear can affect the troops at the front. This is malicious intrigue, and I must call it to your attention so that you may take timely precautions.

I can assure you that the Government's enforcement of national general mobilization will be in accordance with law. All military and administrative organs will respect the basic rights of the people. But anyone who disregards the national crisis and the principle of nationalism, and who is willing to take part in the work of 'the second front', disturbing social order and jeopardizing public safety under Communist direction, will be punished by the Government according to law, which is responsible for the maintenance of national existence and the people's welfare.

At this time, when the war of suppression against the Communist rebels is developing and National troops are fighting at the front, all our patriotic countrymen must struggle with one object in view—unified strength, definite aim and positive efforts—so as to solidify our military strength and achieve early suppression of the rebellious forces.

The Government's policy regarding the present situation can be seen in the resolution of the State Council. The national general mobilization has been promulgated not only for the suppression of the Communist rebellion, but also for national reform and reconstruction. Therefore, I wish to point out the following two matters :

First, we must work for national reconstruction. To carry the reconstruction work to completion, we must concentrate today on the suppression of the Communist rebellion by marshalling our spiritual and physical strength, thereby realizing internal unity. We must at the same time intensify our efforts to increase agricultural and industrial production so as to frustrate the Communist intrigue to undermine the national economy by throwing obstacles in the way of reconstruction.

The progress made in the promotion of and the preparation for the inauguration of constitutional democracy will not be impeded by the suppression campaign. The Communists renounced constitutional democracy by boycotting the National Assembly and obstructing the progress of national reconstruction, although they have proclaimed that they are dedicated to democracy. From this, we can see that the Communists are fundamentally opposed to the enforcement of constitutionalism in China and to the accomplishment of national reconstruction. If the Constitution is enforced in China, the Communists will have to relinquish their military forces, and they will be deprived of their chief reliance, rebellion.

If China adopts political democracy, the people will become masters of their own destiny, and dictatorship of the proletarian, advocated by the Communists, can never be realized. Following the institution of constitutional democracy, the Government will embark on the necessary work of economic reconstruction, and the Communists will be unable to create social disturbances and capitalize on them to establish a Soviet régime.

It is on this basis that I want to emphasize to my fellow countrymen, and especially to those who are actually striving for the realization of freedom in China and the democratization of our Government, that to attain constitutional democracy we must first eliminate the Communist rebels whose principles run counter to constitutional democracy and peaceful reconstruction. To save China from terror and chaos, we are duty bound to expedite the preparations for enforcement of the constitution, to carry out completely the Principle of People's Livelihood and safeguard the people's basic rights. This being our consistent policy, we shall never slacken our efforts towards its realization.

Second, we must exert our utmost to effect administrative reforms. We have committed ourselves to a dual political programme: to quell the Communist rebellion and introduce governmental reforms. Admittedly many defects exist in our administration. Weaknesses can also be found in our way of life. Immediately after the conclusion of the eight-year war, the Communist rebellion began, thus, we have been given no time to put our house in order. Our material resources, already drained by the war, are practically exhausted. The defects and weaknesses in the Government and in our way of life, which first made their appearance in the war, have now become more apparent. The sufferings of the people have immeasurably increased. Unless drastic reforms are introduced, China may not be able to exist in the family of nations. Therefore, political, educational, economic and social reforms, which should be made, shall not be delayed until the conclusion of the suppression campaign, but shall be initiated right away.

We should seek to increase our national strength, mitigate the people's sufferings, and concentrate our will power to effect a thoroughgoing reform, so as to overcome all difficulties confronting us. Constructive criticism and suggestions from the people on our political and economic policies and especially ways to alleviate the people's afflictions will be sincerely received by the Government, and measures for improvement will be instituted. It is also expected that people will report, with substantial evidence, mistakes made by governments of all levels, so that reforms may be made.

It was for the purpose of concentrating our efforts to effect an overall reform and remove all obstacles in the way of national reconstruction that national general mobilization was ordered. It is therefore positive rather than negative in nature ; it is nation-wide rather than local in scope. It is obligatory not only for the people, but for governments of all levels to seek improvement.

Dedicated to national revolution, I have struggled for the existence of the country and the people, the realization of the Three People's

Principles, unity in the nation and the inauguration of constitutional democracy. I have never been mindful of personal gains or losses, glories or eclipses. All I can offer you is my sincerity to save the country and the people. I cannot betray our founding father and our martyrs. I cannot betray the cause of national revolution, for which I have fought so long. I cannot betray the soldiers and the civilians who died in the War of Resistance. I must preserve to the best of my ability the achievements of the eight-year war. I must lead the nation to crush the enemies who are obstructing the realization of our principles, destroying national unity and interfering with our efforts for peaceful reconstruction. I shall not waver till the final aim is achieved.

My fellow countrymen, on this solemn occasion, I call for a re-dedication to the unfinished task of national reconstruction and a revival of the same spirit and energy manifested when we fought against the aggressors. At the conclusion of the war I said that the task of national reconstruction would be ten times more difficult than the military victory. In view of the accumulated effects of internal troubles and external aggressions over the last hundred years and the infirm basis on which this Republic was founded, we cannot make a new, independent, powerful and prosperous China in a day. But we can count on our long history, large population and the moral strength of our people. I am sure with these assets we shall be able to destroy the force that is hampering our reconstruction.

If only the entire population will rise up against the Communist rebels as they did against the Japanese, if only they will use the same determination and perseverance to deal with the Communist insurgents as they did in the War of Resistance, then the suppression of the Communist rebellion can be effected within a short period of time. Once this great difficulty is overcome, and the final obstacle removed, China will enter upon a glorious stage. We should not be distracted by Communist propaganda or dismayed by present difficulties, but should retain our self-confidence.

I hope we shall always remember our unflinching faith in ultimate victory during the War of Resistance and our strong determination to carry the work of national reconstruction to completion. By quelling the Communist rebellion and overcoming the last obstacle, we can expect to accomplish the important task of national reconstruction, and vindicate the sacrifice of soldiers and civilians who died in the War of Resistance and in the suppression campaign.

United States Relations with China, pp. 749-56.

10   13 *September* 1947

MANIFESTO OF THE FOURTH PLENARY
SESSION OF THE SIXTH KUOMINTANG
CENTRAL EXECUTIVE COMMITTEE

Ever since Dr Sun Yat-sen led us in our national revolution, our party has undertaken one historical mission after another for the nation. At every such juncture, our party, after re-examining the past, came forth with a new front of solidarity to carry its mission to a successful conclusion.

Toward the end of the Manchu dynasty, under the leadership of Dr Sun, the Hsin Chung Hui (China Regeneration Society) was reorganized into the Tung Men Hui (Revolutionary League). This subsequently led to the birth of the Republic of China. Then in the third year of the Chinese Republic (1914), the Kuomintang became the Chung Hua Ke Ming Tang (the Chinese Revolutionary Party). This brought about the downfall of the Yuan Shih-kai monarchy and the re-establishment of the Chinese Republic. In the thirteenth year of the Chinese Republic, the Chung Kuo Kuomintang (Chinese Nationalist Party) came into being as the result of another reorganization. This was soon followed by the Northern Expedition which ended with the elimination of the warlords and the unification of the country. In the twenty-seventh year of the Chinese Republic (1938), important resolutions reached at the extraordinary party congress and the formation of the San Min Chu I Youth Corps, laid the foundation for victory after eight long years of war against Japanese aggression. Now in this post-World War II period, history is again calling upon our party to take up the responsibility of quelling a domestic revolt and carrying on war-delayed reconstruction. Whereupon, our party has reached the momentous decision of combining the party and the San Min Chu I Youth Corps.

This step is taken, in the light of Dr Sun's own experience in party reorganization, to rally all party members, and unify our system of command, both for the sake of greater strength. In this way we shall be consolidating the foundation for our revolution, reinforcing our party's leadership in ideology, and enhancing the party's revolutionary spirit. With our forces thus marshalled, we can proceed to tackle the important and difficult tasks at hand, until we attain success in the second phase of our revolution.

The overthrow of the Manchu dynasty, the founding of the Chinese Republic, the eradication of the warlords, the abolition of unequal treaties, the victorious conclusion of the War of Resistance, all these epochal events of the past fifty years have borne witness to our party's important achievements in the cause of the principle of nationalism and that of people's rights. The establishment of representative assemblies at various levels in recent years, the promulgation of a constitution last December, and the forthcoming termination of the period of political tutelage, have given further evidence of our party's determination to persist in its efforts for the realization of democracy. The present military campaign to suppress the Communist rebellion and the general mobilization are for the purpose of unifying China and preserving her sovereignty and territorial integrity. On their outcome will depend China's chance of continued existence as an independent nation and the world's chance of a lasting peace.

As to the consummation of the principle of people's livelihood, it has been a principal aim of our party all these years. The pressing need of the moment is to relieve the people of their sufferings. In pre-war years, our accomplishments in reconstruction projects with a direct bearing on the people's livelihood were meagre, but even this little has been destroyed as a result of the war and post-war spoliation by the Communist rebels. Therefore, no more time must be lost in beginning anew those economic reconstruction projects that directly concern the people's livelihood. In this, as in other types of reconstruction, we should first exert our own utmost. Our party wishes to set this as a goal in our present endeavours.

We are aware of the difficulties now besetting our efforts, but at the same time we should be equally aware of the fact that our revolutionary strength is really greater than it has been during any previous period in our struggle. Previously with comparatively weak revolutionary strength at our disposal, we managed to overcome such difficulties as arose in various stages of our endeavours. Henceforth, so long as we respect ourselves but not to the extent of egoism, look within ourselves without becoming discouraged, and have confidence in ourselves without feeling self-satisfied, as before, we shall be able to attain our goals.

We must realize that unless we can continue to gather strength, ours cannot be called a revolutionary party. Those of us who cannot endure injustices and slights, and those who cannot stand trials and tribulations, are not qualified as members of a revolutionary party.

Our wish is that through unity and struggle, we can create a new life for the party, which will in turn generate a new revolutionary force to effect comprehensive political and economic reforms.

Bearing in mind the 2,000-year-old Chinese proverb, 'One handling public affairs need not say too much but should try his best under the circumstances,' we are henceforth willing to let deeds speak for themselves and actions bear witness to our determination.

We must not hesitate to make sacrifices if this is necessary to safeguard our national existence, nor should we hesitate to struggle for the realization of constitutional democracy ; nor should we fear to exert our efforts to improve the people's living conditions.

Our nation is now entering a period of constitutional government. To protect the Chinese Republic and safeguard our nation is a sacred duty, which neither our party as a whole, nor individual party members, can justifiably shirk. We wish to offer this as a common creed of guidance. We are particularly desirous that all our fellow countrymen, out of our common conceptions of a nation-State, and national consciousness, will, as one man, unite to work for the creation of a new China dedicated to the fulfilment of the Three People's Principles.

United States Relations with China, pp. 826-8.

II   28 *October* 1947

ANNOUNCEMENT BY THE CHINESE NATIONAL GOVERNMENT DECLARING THE CHINA DEMOCRATIC LEAGUE ILLEGAL

The Chinese people have known for a long time that the Democratic League has linked with the Communists and joined the rebellion. According to reports made by various local authorities who are responsible for the preservation of peace and order, the following examples are outstanding: Lo Ping-chi, a League member, has instigated mutiny among the troops in Manchuria ; a responsible League member for the northwest was responsible for the rebellion of Kung Chung-chou ; the student strikes in May and the recent labour strikes in Shanghai were incited by the League. Since the promulgation of the General Mobilization Order by the Government for the suppression of the Communist rebellion, the Hongkong and Malaya branches of the League have publicly opposed the order and indicated clearly that the League action and the action of the Communists are one and the same. Recently, Li Ying-fen, an important League member, mustered bandits in Szechuan in order to rise in rebellion and to co-operate with the Communist bandits of Li Hsien-nien. Other plots and underground work carried on by the League of which we have concrete proof are too numerous to mention. In view of the seriousness of the Communist rebellion and the rampant activities carried on by the League, the Government can no longer tolerate an organization which opposes the National Constitution and aims at the overthrow of the Government. For the preservation of peace and order in the rear this Ministry has to take adequate steps to check the activities of the League. The Democratic League is hereby pronounced illegal and local authorities responsible for the preservation of peace and order shall halt the illegal activities of the League and effect punishment according to the measures for the treatment of Communists stated in the General Mobilization Order.

United States Relations with China, pp. 839-40.

12   6 *November* 1947

ANNOUNCEMENT BY THE CHAIRMAN OF THE DEMOCRATIC LEAGUE DISSOLVING THE LEAGUE

The China Democratic League has consistently maintained its firm stand for democracy, peace and unity. Unfortunately, the war has become more and more intensified. In the face of this calamity, we, the Leaguers, could only grieve at being unable to do anything effective to serve the country. Recently, the Government ordered the outlawing of the League, prohibiting it from engaging in any activities. We, the Leaguers, could no longer be active. So we unanimously elected Huang Yen-Pei, member of the Standing Committee, as our representative, and dispatched him to the capital from Shanghai to negotiate with the Government concerning the problems relating to the dissolution of the League. The following are the measures proposed by the Government :

(1)   The Government has already outlawed the League and hopes that the League will dissolve itself voluntarily, so that the responsible officials of the League can be relieved of their responsibilities.

(2)   Concerning houses and other properties : (*a*) The properties belonging to the Communist Party, now in the League's custody, should be turned over to the Government ; (*b*) the houses belonging to the League can be retained for the time being ; (*c*) the houses appropriated by the Government for use of the League should be returned to the Government, and if they cannot be vacated immediately, they can be used temporarily ; (*d*) the private residences of League members will not be disturbed and (*e*) the houses located at Rue Chu Pao San, originally rented by the Communist Party, now in the League's custody, should likewise be handed over to the Government. If the houses are now used for school purposes and

cannot be vacated, arrangements for the use of the houses by the school should be worked out.

Mr Huang Yen-Pei gave the following answers to the above proposals :

(1)   Since the League has been outlawed by the Government, its only course is to notify all the Leaguers to cease all party activities, and, following the issue of the notification, the Leaguers themselves will be held personally responsible for their own activities and utterances.

(2)   The various points with respect to houses will be duly observed. However, one further point needs clarification, namely, while it is not known that the League originally had properties of its own, if there should prove to be any such properties, they should be disposed of by the League itself. Furthermore, the League submits the following two requests :

(3)   That the League members in various places be exempted from registering with the Government and enjoy all civil liberties to which they are legally entitled.

(4)   That League members in various places who are considered by the Government as having violated the law, and those who are already under arrest, should be treated by the Government in accordance with the law, and that the Measures for Dealing with the Communists in the Rear should not be applied to League members arrested under alleged but unproven Communist affiliations.

As to whether or not points (2), (3) and (4) can be carried out, we now await your reply. As for the various documents published in the Press, critical of the League, they are quite contrary to facts. However, we do not intend to argue or offer refutations now.

The following is the reply made by the Government :

(1)   If the League would obey the order announced by the spokesman of the Ministry of the Interior and formally declare its voluntary dissolution as well as cessation of all activities, then all League members everywhere could be exempted from registering with the Government and would be assured freedom within the law. However, if hereafter some still engage in illegal activities under false pretexts, they will be prosecuted by the security agencies in various places according to law.

(2)   If, after proper investigations by the judicial authorities, League members under arrest for alleged offences are found not to be Communist nor working for Communists, then the Measures for Dealing with the Communists in the Rear will not be applied to them.

Furthermore, all the points relating to houses and other properties will be carried out.

While publishing the foregoing record of the negotiations, we at the same time hereby notify all League members to stop all political activities as from this date. All personnel of the League's General Headquarters will resign *en bloc* as from this date and the General Headquarters will also dissolve as from this date.

CHANG LAN,
Chairman of the China Democratic League

United States Relations with China, pp. 834-6.

III KUOMINTANG ECONOMIC MEASURES

13*   19 *August* 1948

PRESIDENTIAL MANDATE ON FINANCIAL AND ECONOMIC EMERGENCY MEASURES.

Acting under the temporary provisions of the Constitution of the Republic of China, and in accordance with the decision of the Executive Yuan, this mandate on financial and economic emergency measures is hereby proclaimed. The principal objects are as follows:

I. As from this date, 'gold yuan' (dollar) to be adopted as the basic unit of currency, Gold Yuan notes to be issued and backed by 100 per cent reserve, and all *fapi*[1] and Northeast Circulation Notes outstanding to be redeemed within a stipulated period.

II. Gold, silver, silver currency and foreign currency notes held by the people to be bought over by the Government within a stipulated period, after which none whatsoever to be permitted to hold them.

III. Foreign exchange assets held abroad by nationals of this country to be registered within a stipulated period and placed under Government control, violations being liable to punishment.

IV. Finances to be reorganized and economic control strengthened, so as to stabilize prices and balance the national Budget and international payments.

With the foregoing objects in view, the following regulations are hereby promulgated together with this mandate, each being considered as a part thereof, namely, (1) Regulations governing the issuance of gold yuan notes, (2) Regulations governing the surrender of gold, silver and foreign currencies held by the people,

---

* Source for documents 13-17 is given at the end of document 17.
[1] Legal tender.

(3) Regulations governing the registration and control of foreign exchange assets held abroad by nationals of the Republic of China, and (4) Regulations governing the reorganization of finance and strengthening of economic control. Further, the Executive Yuan is hereby delegated with authority to issue such rules and/or supplementary measures in connexion with the various regulations as it may deem necessary for the enforcement of this mandate.

By Order of the President

14   19 *August* 1948

REGULATIONS GOVERNING THE ISSUANCE
OF GOLD YUAN NOTES

Article 1. As from date of promulgation of these Regulations, the basic unit of currency of the Republic of China shall be the gold yuan (dollar). Each yuan shall have a legal content of 0·22217 grams of fine gold. Gold yuan notes shall be issued by the Central Bank of China to be circulated at face value.

Article 2. The subsidiary units of the gold yuan shall be *chiao* (10 cents) and *fen* (cent), with 10 *fen* making 1 *chiao* and 10 *chiao* making 1 yuan.

Article 3. Gold yuan notes shall be of 5 denominations ; namely, 1 yuan, 5 yuan, 10 yuan, 50 yuan and 100 yuan.

Article 4. Gold yuan subsidiary coins shall be of 5 denominations ; namely, 1 *fen*, 5 *fen*, 1 *chiao*, 2 *chiao* and 5 *chiao*. These coins shall be made separately of copper, nickel and silver, as the case may be ; and the Central Bank of China may issue gold yuan subsidiary notes for circulation simultaneously.

Article 5. As from date of promulgation of these regulations, the issuance of *fapi* and Northeast Circulation Notes shall be discontinued. *Fapi* notes previously issued shall be converted at the rate of three million dollars to 1 gold yuan, and Northeast Circulation Notes at 300,000 dollars to 1 gold yuan. They shall be exchanged for gold yuan notes without limitation in amount before 20 November 1948. During the period of conversion, their temporary circulation shall be permitted at the aforesaid rates of conversion. Measures for dealing with Taiwan and Sinkiang currencies shall be adopted by the Executive Yuan separately.

Article 6. As from date of promulgation of these Regulations, all public and private accounting shall be kept on the basis of gold yuan. In all matters in which registration is required by law and the amount of value has to be specified, alteration in registration must be effected within six months following the promulgation of these Regulations.

Article 7. As from date of promulgation of these Regulations, all public and private rights and obligations in terms of *fapi* and/or Northeast Circulation Notes shall be computed and settled at the conversion rates stipulated in Article 5 of these Regulations. Measures for dealing with outstanding *fapi* bonds issued by the Government shall be adopted by the Executive Yuan separately. With the exception of the 36th Year US Gold Loan which shall be repaid according to its original regulations, the 27th Year Gold Loan, 29th Year Reconstruction Gold Loan, 31st Year Allied Victory US Gold Loan and 36th Year Short-Term Treasury Notes shall be converted at official exchange rates to a new gold yuan loan to be issued by the Government.

Article 8. Gold yuan notes issue shall be backed by 100 per cent reserve. The aforementioned note issue reserve shall be composed of : a minimum of 40 per cent gold, silver and foreign exchange, and the remainder in bonds and securities and Government owned properties designated by the Government.

Article 9. The total issue of gold yuan notes shall be limited to two billion yuan.

Article 10. For the inspection and custody of reserve of gold yuan note issue, a Gold Yuan Note Issue Reserve Supervisory Commission shall be established, the regulations governing its organization to be adopted by the Executive Yuan.

Article 11. Gold yuan notes must be countersigned by the Governor and the General Manager of the Issue Department of the Central Bank of China before they are put into circulation.

Article 12. The Central Bank of China must, at the end of each month, report the monthly total of gold yuan note issue to the Ministry of Finance and the Gold Yuan Note Issue Reserve Supervisory Commission.

Article 13. The Gold Yuan Note Issue Reserve Supervisory Commission must, at the end of each month, conduct an examination of the amount of gold yuan notes issued by the Central Bank of China and the conditions of their reserve. It shall prepare an inspection report, publish it officially, and submit same to the Executive Yuan, sending duplicate copies to the Ministry of Finance and the Central Bank of China.

Article 14. If and when the aforesaid Commission finds the reserve of the gold yuan note issue to be insufficient or the reserve in gold, silver and foreign exchange to be below the percentage stipulated in Section 2 of Article 8 above, it shall immediately notify the Central Bank of China to suspend note issue and to withdraw the amount of notes in excess of reserve, and at the same time report separately to the Executive Yuan and the Ministry of Finance.

Article 15. Upon receipt of the above-mentioned notification, the Central Bank of China must either immediately withdraw the excess amount of gold yuan notes issued or make up the deficit in issue reserve. Without the consent of the said Commission after further examination, the Central Bank may not increase the note issue.

Article 16. Counterfeiting, alteration or deliberate damaging of gold yuan notes is punishable according to the provisions of the Regulations Governing Punishment of Damage to the National Currency.

Article 17. These Regulations shall come into force on the date of promulgation.

15   19 *August* 1948

REGULATIONS GOVERNING THE SURRENDER OF GOLD, SILVER AND FOREIGN CURRENCIES HELD BY THE PEOPLE

Article 1. 'People' used in these regulations includes natural persons, juristic persons and other corporate bodies within the territories of the Republic of China.

Article 2. As from date of promulgation of these Regulations, the circulation, transaction or holding of gold, silver, silver currency and foreign currency notes is prohibited within the territories of the Republic of China.

Article 3. People holding gold, silver, silver currency and/or foreign currency notes must convert them to gold yuan notes at the Central Bank of China or any of its appointed banks, before 30 September 1948, according to the following provisions :

(1) In the case of gold, each *shih liang* (31·25 grams) of required fineness to be exchanged for 200 gold yuan notes ;

(2) In the case of silver, each *shih liang* of required fineness to be exchanged for three gold yuan notes ;

(3) In the case of silver dollar coins, each dollar to be exchanged for two gold yuan notes ; and

(4) In the case of United States currency notes, each dollar to be exchanged for four gold yuan notes ; notes in other foreign currencies to be exchanged at the exchange rates of the Central Bank of China.

Article 4. Holders of gold, silver, silver currency and foreign currency notes, aside from exchanging them for gold yuan notes under the provisions of the preceding Article, may according to their wish dispose of them in one of the following two ways :

(1) For purchase of the 36th Year US Gold Loan Bonds ; United States currency notes may be used in their original forms for buying the said bonds ; gold, silver, silver currency and/or other foreign currency notes may be similarly used by conversion at the rates stipulated in the preceding Article.

(2) For deposit with the Central Bank of China ; foreign currency notes may be deposited in their original currencies ; and gold, silver and silver dollars may be deposited after conversion to United States currency at the rates stipulated in the preceding Article. The deposits referred to in the preceding paragraph may be used for the payment of imports covered by import licences or for other purposes approved by the Ministry of Finance.

Article 5. Gold, gold sand and silver produced by domestic mines shall be bought over by the Central Bank of China or its appointed banks at prices to be fixed by them from time to time, and shall not be subject to the restrictions laid down in Article 3 above.

Article 6. Gold and/or silver required as raw materials by medical and industrial establishments or for other legitimate uses may be bought upon application to and approval by the Ministry of Finance.

Article 7. People holding gold and/or silver ornamental articles shall be permitted to continue such holding and to transfer them, but the gold and/or silver contents of such articles may not be bought or sold at prices exceeding the conversion rates stipulated in Article 3 of these Regulations.

Article 8. People may not manufacture gold ingots and bars into gold ornamental articles.

Article 9. No gold, silver, silver dollars and foreign currencies may be carried out of the country. But a person who carries out gold ornaments not exceeding a total of two *shih liang* and/or silver ornaments not exceeding a total of 20 *shih liang*, or a person who carries for travelling expenses foreign currency notes equivalent in total to not over United States $100 and covered by a certificate issued by the bank selling such foreign currency notes, is excepted from the above restriction.

Article 10. Persons who carry gold, silver, silver currency, gold or silver ornaments or foreign currency notes into the country must declare them before the Customs authorities. With the exception that a person is permitted to bring in and to hold gold ornaments not exceeding a total of 20 *shih liang*, any amount in excess thereof must be surrendered to the Central Bank of China or its appointed banks and be converted to gold yuan notes according to the stipulations of Article 3 above. Aside from the amount of gold and silver ornaments permitted to be brought in under the preceding paragraph, travellers in transit or tourists who bring in gold, silver and/or foreign currency but must later take the same out of the country, shall at the time of entrance to the country declare such belongings before the Customs authorities and hand them over to the Central Bank of China or its appointed banks for custody, but they may claim the same back at the time of their departure from the country. But those who fail to apply and claim back such holdings within six months following their entrance to the country shall be required to convert them to gold yuan notes according to the stipulations of Article 3 above.

With the exception of the Central Bank of China, no Chinese or foreign bank, unless duly appointed by the Central Bank of China, may buy, hold or take custody of gold, silver, silver currency or foreign currency notes.

Article 12. In case of violations of the stipulations of Articles 3 and 4 of these Regulations involving failure to effect the required conversion or deposit within the prescribed period, or violations of any stipulations contained in Articles 8, 9, 10 and 11 of these Regulations, the gold, silver, silver currency and/or foreign currency notes concerned shall all be confiscated.

Article 13. In case of violations of the stipulations of Article 7 of these Regulations, or violations of the stipulations of Article 11 involving unauthorized purchase of gold, silver, silver currency or foreign currency notes, the objects concerned shall be liable to confiscation ; and, in addition, where violations of Article 7 involve transaction in gold ornaments at prices exceeding the prescribed conversion rates, or where violations of Article 11 involve unauthorized purchase of gold or foreign currency notes, such violations shall also be subject to punishment according to the Regulations Governing Punishment of Transactions in Gold and Foreign Currencies.

Article 14. In case of violations of the stipulations of Articles 4 and 5 of these Regulations involving failure to effect the required conversion or deposit within the prescribed period, or violations of Articles 7 to 11 if the violations are discovered and objects concerned are confiscated as a result of information furnished to the authorities in charge, 40 per cent of the confiscated value shall be given as reward to the informant.

Article 15. These Regulations shall come into force on the date of promulgation.

REGULATIONS GOVERNING THE REGISTRATION AND CONTROL OF FOREIGN EXCHANGE ASSETS HELD ABROAD BY NATIONALS OF THE REPUBLIC OF CHINA

Article 1. By virtue of the stipulations of Article 3, Section 9, of the National General Mobilization Law, foreign exchange assets are hereby designated as one of the resources subject to national general mobilization ; and in accordance with the stipulations of Article 7, Section 1 of the same law, the use, removal and transfer of such assets are hereby placed under control.

Article 2. For the purpose of realizing the above-mentioned object, registration shall be required of foreign exchange assets held abroad by nationals of the Republic of China.

Article 3. 'Nationals of the Republic of China' used in these Regulations includes natural persons, juristic persons and other corporate bodies.

Article 4. 'Foreign exchange assets' used in these Regulations refers to current and fixed deposits abroad, foreign currencies, gold ingots and bars held abroad, and all rights and benefits arising from payments derived or derivable abroad, including foreign currency securities of any foreign Government or the Chinese Government, stocks and shares, bonds and Treasury notes, land title deeds, insurance policies, annuities, forward payments collectable, advance payments in buying and selling, margin deposits in security transactions as well as all negotiable instruments.

Article 5. With the exception of those nationals whose normal livelihood is verified to be established abroad and who are considered as Overseas Chinese, all nationals of the Republic of China, shall, before 31 December 1948, file declaration and registration according to prescribed forms with the Central Bank of China or its appointed banks with respect to the foreign exchange assets they hold abroad as of 21 August 1948. Where any foreign exchange asset is acquired after 21 August 1948, the declaration and registration of the same must be effected within two months following its acquisition.

Article 6. Nationals of the Republic of China who presently reside abroad and who are subject to the restrictions of the preceding Article may file the registration of their foreign exchange assets in accordance with the stipulations of the preceding Article with the local or nearby office of the Chinese embassy, legation, consulate or special commissioner of the Wai-chiaopu.[1] Nationals referred to in the preceding paragraph who hold foreign exchange assets of a

[1] Ministry of Foreign Affairs.

value not exceeding US $3,000, or its equivalent in other foreign currencies, are exempted from registration.

Article 7. Foreign exchange assets required to be registered under these Regulations include assets which are held in trust for any national of the Republic of China by any agent, trustee, broker, or any juristic person or other corporate body registered abroad. Foreign exchange assets referred to in the preceding paragraph, regardless of whether they are held jointly with a foreign national or foreign juristic person or other corporate body and whether they are under independent or joint control, must be declared and registered with respect to the portion held by the Chinese national concerned.

Article 8. As from date of promulgation of these Regulations, no national of the Republic of China shall be allowed to transfer his foreign exchange assets to any natural person, juristic person or other corporate body whatsoever at home or abroad with the intention of evading the registration.

Article 9. With respect to foreign exchange assets required to be registered under these Regulations, all bank deposits and foreign currencies, as well as benefits derived from assets or the sale thereof, must be transferred in their original currencies to, and deposited in, the Central Bank of China or any of its appointed banks, with the exception of the prescribed amount which the holder may be permitted to keep by approval of the Ministry of Finance according to the following provisions :

(1) Living and medical expenses for a national and his family residing abroad ;

(2) Educational expenses for a national or his children during the period of study abroad ; and

(3) Expenses for travelling abroad and return trip to China for a national or his family.

The nationals referred to in the preceding paragraphs are limited to those who are already abroad previous to the promulgation of these Regulations. The amount allowed to be kept shall be fixed separately.

Article 10. Foreign exchange deposits transferred to and deposited in the Central Bank of China or its appointed banks may be utilized according to the following provisions :

(1) For legitimate purposes approved by the Ministry of Finance ;

(2) For payment of imports covered by import licenses ; and

(3) For conversion to gold yuan notes, purchase of the 36th Year US Gold Bonds or Gold Yuan Bonds to be issued by the Government.

Article 11.   Nationals of the Republic of China who violate any stipulation of Articles 5 to 8 of these Regulations shall, in accordance with the stipulations of Article 5 of the Provincial Regulations Governing Punishment of Infringement of the National General Mobilization Law, be liable to imprisonment under seven years and may also be subject to fines. In case of above-mentioned violations of the stipulations of these Regulations, the foreign exchange assets held abroad shall, following the imposition of punishment, be confiscated by the Government after consultations with the foreign Government concerned.

Article 12.   Where violations of Articles 3 to 8 of these Regulations are discovered and punishment and confiscation are enforced as a result of information furnished to the authorities in charge, 40 per cent of the value shall be given as reward to the informant.

Article 13.   In each of the municipalities of Nanking, Shanghai, Tientsin, Canton and Hankow (and other localities to be designated by the Executive Yuan), a commission on direction or declaration and registration of foreign exchange assets of nationals of the Republic of China shall be established immediately following the promulgation of these Regulations.   The commission shall consist of the Mayor, Chairman of the Municipal Council, a representative of the Ministry of Finance, a representative of the Central Bank of China, and 3 to 5 other members to be appointed by the Mayor from among the members of the Municipal Council and other local bodies organized according to law. The Mayor and Chairman of the Municipal Council shall be conveners of the commission, the administrative staff of which shall be furnished by the Ministry of Finance, Central Bank of China and the local municipal government. The functions of the aforesaid commission shall be as follows :

(1)   To acquaint the local community with the contents of these Regulations ;

(2)   To direct and assist the applicants in the matter of registration ;

(3)   To be responsible for ascertaining the rich people and merchants in the local community and advising them in the observance of these Regulations ; and

(4)   To receive secret information regarding evasion of declaration of foreign exchange assets and to refer such cases to the authorities in charge.

Article 14.   In localities abroad designated by the Executive Yuan, the Chinese embassy, legation and/or local consulate shall be responsible for organizing a commission similar to the commission described in the preceding Article, the detailed rules to be adopted by the Executive Yuan.

Article 15. These Regulations shall come into force on the date of promulgation.

17   19 *August* 1948

REGULATIONS GOVERNING FINANCIAL
REFORM AND ECONOMIC CONTROL

Article 1. These Regulations are adopted with a view to balancing the national Budget, adjusting international payments, and strengthening measures for the stabilization of prices and wages as well as the control of banking and financial operations.

Article 2. Revenues from various taxes are to be vigorously increased. Where tax rates are lower than their respective pre-war standards, they are to be adjusted accordingly, and rates on luxuries are to be raised.

Where existing laws require revision in connexion with the aforesaid development of tax revenues, the Ministry of Finance shall immediately submit recommendations to the Executive Yuan for transmission to the Legislative Yuan.

Article 3. Where charges made by state-operated public utilities and communications enterprises are lower than their respective pre-war standards, they may be adjusted accordingly so as to make the enterprises self-supporting. Subsidies provided by the National Treasury shall be limited to areas that are subject to destruction by military activities.

Article 4. All state-operated enterprises must as far as possible economize expenses and remove superfluous personnel. Those having surplus profits shall be ordered by the respective Ministries and Commissions in charge to remit all such profits to the National Treasury.

Article 5. The sale of 'surplus supplies' as well as supplies and properties taken over from the enemy and puppets shall be accelerated as far as possible in order to augment Treasury receipts.

Article 6. Personnel in all civil and military organizations as well as the number of soldiers are to be strictly checked; no false report to be condoned.

Article 7. The budget of national receipts and expenditures for the second half-year of the 37th Year shall, following the issuance of gold yuan notes, be compiled anew in terms of gold yuan in accordance with this mandate on emergency measures. Where actual conditions require revision of estimates, the Executive Yuan shall request the Legislative Yuan for re-examination.

Article 8. Government organs and people requiring foreign exchange for legitimate purposes may buy foreign exchange upon approval of the Government. Existing regulations governing control of foreign exchange by the Central Bank of China are to be revised according to the relevant stipulations of this mandate.

Article 9. Control of imports and exports shall be adjusted according to the following provisions :

(1) Beginning with the 7th quarter,[1] the import quota shall be cut down by at least one-fourth on the basis of the average set for the 5th and 6th quarters.[2]

(2) In case of quota goods referred to in the preceding Paragraph and of certain other categories of goods to be designated, people may apply for permission to pay the value of such imports out of their foreign currency deposits in the Central Bank of China.

(3) All foreign exchange realized by exporters from exports shall be sold to the Central Bank of China at the exchange rates fixed between gold yuan and foreign currencies.

(4) In case of supplies that may be exported, their production shall be encouraged and restrictions may be imposed on their domestic consumption.

Article 10. Overseas Chinese remittances shall be sold to the Central Bank of China at the exchange rates fixed between gold yuan and foreign currencies, and Government banks are to extend to them all facilities.

Article 11. The foreign exchange rates to be used in connection with Articles 8, 9 and 10 above shall be fixed in the following manner :

(1) One United States dollar to 4 gold yuan.

(2) Rates for other foreign currencies to be fixed from time to time by the Central Bank of China in relation to the exchange rate between the United States dollar and the gold yuan.

Article 12. In case of supplies that must be imported from abroad, strict economy in their consumption is to be exercised according to the following provisions :

(1) In Shanghai and other cities designated by the Executive Yuan, licences for all kinds of motor cars shall be reduced by one-quarter to one-third within two months following the promulgation of these Regulations, and strict restrictions shall be enforced with respect to the quantity of gasoline consumed by such cars.

(2) As from 15 September 1948, the sale of articles whose importation is prohibited shall be banned in designated cities, and violations shall be dealt with as smuggling, detailed rules to be adopted by the

[1] August-October 1948.
[2] February-July 1948.

Ministry of Industry and Trade together with the Ministry of Finance.

Article 13. In all cities throughout the country, prices of all commodities and services shall be charged on the levels prevailing in each particular city on 19 August 1948, when converted in gold yuan at the prescribed rates. Local authorities shall see to it that this limitation is strictly enforced.

Article 14. After the conversion of prices of all commodities and services in terms of gold yuan according to the stipulations of the preceding Article, the Regulations Governing Punishment of Violations of Price Restrictions must be strictly enforced. No increase in price shall be permitted unless approved by the authorities in charge for special reasons.

Article 15. All public utilities and communications enterprises shall collect charges in terms of gold yuan ; aside from adjustments that may be made by state-operated enterprises according to the provisions of Article 3 above and those made by private enterprises in keeping with the same Article as well as with actual costs, all of which adjustments being subject to approval of the authorities in charge, no increase may be sanctioned hereafter unless for special reasons.

Article 16. In Shanghai and other cities designated by the Executive Yuan, inspection of godowns and registration of incoming and outgoing cargoes shall be enforced. Violations of the Regulations Governing Prohibition of Hoarding and Profiteering in Articles of Daily Necessity during the Emergency Period shall be punished strictly according to law.

Article 17. As from date of promulgation of these Regulations, newspapers, news service dispatches and other printed matter shall not publish the black-market prices of gold, silver or foreign currencies or of any kinds of articles of daily necessity. Violations shall be punishable according to the stipulations of Article 10 of the Temporary Regulations Governing Punishment of Infringement of National General Mobilization.

Article 18. As from date of enforcement of the gold yuan unit, all arrangements regarding payment of salaries and wages on the basis of the cost-of-living index shall be discontinued.

Article 19. The salaries of civil and military officials shall be paid in gold yuan notes according to the following standard. The basic amount shall be 40 dollars to be paid in full in gold yuan notes. Twenty per cent of the sum in excess of 40 dollars up to 300 dollars shall be paid in gold yuan notes, and ten per cent shall be paid in gold yuan notes for any amount above 300 dollars. The pay and food rations of the enlisted men shall be paid in gold yuan notes according to the pre-war basic amount without discount.

Article 20. Civil and Army personnel and soldiers in the Nanking-Shanghai area shall be paid according to the standard prescribed in the preceding Article. In other areas where the original cost-of-living index numbers are higher or lower than those in the Nanking-Shanghai area, a certain percentage of increase or decrease in pay according to the aforesaid standard shall be fixed by the Executive Yuan, based on the difference between the respective index numbers in such areas and those in the Nanking-Shanghai area for the month of July 1948.

Article 21. The pay for employees and labourers in state-operated enterprises shall be made in gold yuan according to the stipulations of Articles 18, 19 and 20 above. Excepting that employees of such enterprises may be allowed an additional pay not exceeding 30 per cent of the pay which civil employees of corresponding ranks or grades receive, any portion of pay which such an employee actually receives in excess of the maximum limit must be abolished.

Article 22. The salaries and wages for employees and labourers in private enterprises shall all be converted and paid in gold yuan, but the pay for half a month shall not exceed the equivalent amounts which such persons were entitled to receive in terms of *fapi* according to the original arrangements of the enterprises concerned during the first half-month of August 1948.

Article 23. During the period of enforcement of these Regulations, closure of factories, strikes and go-slow strikes are prohibited. Violations shall be liable to punishment according to the stipulations of Section (4) of Article 5 of the Provisional Regulations Governing Punishment of Infringement of National General Mobilization Law.

Article 24. Government banks and other financial institutions shall absolutely stop the extension of loans of a commercial nature and shall be charged with the duty of examining the utilization of funds and the results thereof in connexion with loans which they may be authorized to extend. Appropriate measures to this end shall be adopted by the authorities in charge and be strictly enforced.

Article 25. Commercial banks and native banks shall strictly observe the Banking Law and all regulations of financial control in the operation of their business activities. They shall not engage in any form of operations involving dealings in commodities. Violations shall be subject to cancellation of their business licences and shall also be dealt with as hoarding and profiteering.

Article 26. Credit co-operative societies, besides accepting deposits from their members and employing such deposits and the societies' capital funds for extension of credits to their members, are prohibited from engaging in other business activities of banking institutions. Violations shall be punished according to Regulations Governing Illegitimate Banking Establishments, aside from being ordered to be disorganized.

Article 27. With exception of banking institutions, no company or shop whatsoever may receive deposits or extend loans. Violations shall be punished according to Regulations Governing Illegitimate Banking Establishments, aside from being ordered to be disorganized.

Article 28. The Ministry of Finance shall inspect the business activities of Chinese banks maintaining branch offices abroad, and shall order the abolition within a prescribed period of those branch offices whose record is found unsatisfactory.

Article 29. Any banking institution shall have its business licence revoked if found to have committed one of the following offences :

(1) If the clearance of its bills has been stopped by the clearing house ;

(2) If it violates economic control regulations ; or

(3) If its capital is too small and its business cannot be developed in the proper way.

Article 30. The Ministry of Finance shall, by reference to the provisions of the pre-war Banking Law with regard to the minimum capital of banks, revise the requirements concerning the minimum amounts of capital of banks, native banks and trust companies in the various areas and upon approval of its recommendations by the Executive Yuan, shall order the banks concerned to increase their capital up to the required minimum amounts within two months. The increase of capital shall consist of not less than 50 per cent in cash. Any bank unable to effect the required increase in capital within the prescribed period shall be ordered to suspend business and be liquidated within a fixed period.

Article 31. The stock exchange in Shanghai and Tientsin shall suspend business temporarily and may not reopen unless approved by the Executive Yuan.

Article 32. Market interest rates shall be lowered and domestic remittance charge shall be adjusted by areas, so as to enliven financial activities and protect production enterprise. Effective measures to these ends shall be taken by the Ministry of Finance and the Central Bank of China.

Article 33. These Regulations shall come into force on the date of promulgation.

China Information Bulletin, Vol. I, No. 16, New York, 1 September 1948.

IV THE CIVIL WAR

18   18 *July* 1947

THE OUTLINE FOR THE IMPLEMENTATION OF
MOBILIZATION TO SUPPRESS REBELLION AND
COMPLETE CONSTITUTIONAL GOVERNMENT
ADOPTED BY THE STATE COUNCIL

Article 1. This outline has been formulated in accordance with the stipulation of the programme for the enforcement of national general mobilization to suppress the Communist rebellion, remove obstacles to democracy and realize constitutional government as scheduled, which was adopted by the State Council, and the provisions of the National General Mobilization Act (promulgated by the National Government on 29 March 1942, and put into effect on 5 May 1942).

Article 2. Enforcement of constitutional government and conducting of elections in connexion therewith shall all be expedited as stipulated.

Article 3. Manpower necessary for military, labour and other services required to suppress the rebellion shall be fully mobilized. Any action to evade or obstruct such services shall be punished in accordance with law.

Article 4. All materials required to suppress the rebellion, including foodstuffs, clothing, medicine, oil, coal, iron and steel, transportation and communication equipment, and other supplies needed by the military, shall be immediately mobilized. Any action to evade or obstruct requisitioning of such supplies, hoard them or profiteer from them shall be punished in accordance with law.

Article 5. Close co-operation shall be maintained between management and labour in all enterprises. All disputes shall be mediated or arbitrated in accordance with law. Sabotage, the in-outs or any other actions hampering production or disturbing social order shall be punished in accordance with law.

Article 6. In order to stabilize the people's livelihood, the Government may institute restrictions or controls over market prices of daily necessities, salaries and wages, the flow of materials, use of capital and other financial activities.

Article 7. The Government shall, in accordance with law, take punitive measures against assemblies where speeches or other actions incite the people to rebellion.

Article 8. In areas recovered from rebels, authorities concerned shall consolidate security measures and maintain social order. When necessary, loans may be extended, taxes in the areas suspended and social relief and medical aid carried out.

Article 9. Refugees from rebel-held areas shall be given adequate relief, assistance and accommodation by authorities concerned.

Article 10. Authorities concerned shall direct needs. In case of a shortage in capital, Government banks may grant loans in order to increase supplies. If necessary, the Government may exercise control over finished products.

Article 11. In areas free from the Communist rebels, local administration shall be revamped and social peace and order safeguarded. To improve the people's livelihood, priority shall be given to urgent projects of production, transportation, irrigation and water conservancy.

Article 12. Equitable taxation shall be increased and unnecessary expenditure curtailed in order to finance the suppression of the rebellion.

Article 13. Measures shall be formulated to enforce thrift and increase efficiency, for observance by both the Government and the people.

Article 14. Basic rights of the people shall be fully respected and adequately safeguarded. Any impingement thereupon shall be strictly prohibited, unless necessitated by laws and decrees required for the implementation of mobilization and the suppression of the rebellion.

Article 15. Where there is need for separate detailed measures for the implementation of the outline, such measures shall be drawn up by the Ministers and commissions of the Executive Yuan concerned, and, after their approval by the Yuan, promulgated by mandates for enforcement.

Article 16. Violation of Articles 3 to 7 of the outline or any action that would be outlawed and restrained in accordance with the stipulations of these Articles shall be punished in accordance with the provisional penal regulations for obstructors of the National General Mobilization Act (promulgated by the National Government on 29 June 1942, and put into force on 1 August 1942).

Public functionaries who, in the exercise of authority delegated to them under the outline, break the law or neglect their duties shall be punished in accordance with law.

Article 17. In addition to the stipulations of the outline, the Executive Yuan may, in accordance with the provisions of the National General Mobilization Act, at any time issue mandates to expedite the suppression of the rebellion.

Article 19. The outline shall be promulgated for enforcement after approval by the State Council.

US Relations with China, pp. 756-8.

19   22 December 1947

EMERGENCY REGULATIONS GOVERNING PUNISHMENT FOR CRIMES ENDANGERING THE CHINESE REPUBLIC DURING THE PERIOD OF BANDIT-SUPPRESSION

Article 1. These Regulations shall be applied during the period of bandit-suppression.

Article 2. Offenders against Item 1 of Article 100 or Item 1 of Article 101 of the Criminal Code shall be sentenced to death, or life imprisonment. Offenders against the same through plotting with any foreign country or its appointed agents shall be sentenced to death. Those who make ready or secretly plot to commit the crime of either of the two above-mentioned items of the Code shall be sentenced to prison terms of over ten years. Offenders against the same who self-surrender shall get a reduction of punishment or grant of pardon.

Article 3. Those who participate in any organization or meeting which aims at committing the crime of the preceding Article shall be sentenced to prison terms of below five years. Those who commit the same but self-surrender shall get a reduction of punishment or grant of pardon.

Article 4. Those who self-surrender and get a grant of pardon in accordance with the regulation of the preceding two Articles may be sent to a reformatory to receive reformatory instruction. The length of the period of reformatory instruction shall be below three years and over one year. In case of necessity the period may be, through consideration, prolonged to a length within the legally set range.

Article 5. Those who commit any one of the following crimes shall be sentenced to death, or life imprisonment, or prison terms of over ten years :

(1) Handing troops over to the bandit or leaving troops to the command and training of the bandit.

(2) Bringing troops to surrender to the bandit.

(3) Handing over to the bandit or destroying and rendering useless any strategic point, naval base, structure of military field, naval

vessel, bridge, aeroplane, railroad, military vehicle, military equipment, ammunition, military baggage, ration or other military supply,
telegraphic material, or any material for communication or transportation.

(4)   Agitating military men to neglect duty or to violate army
discipline or to escape and rebel.

(5)   Smuggling or handing over to the bandit any secret document,
map, chart, information or article concerning any strategic point,
naval base, military camp, naval vessel, aeroplane or other structure
of the military field.

(6)   Recruiting soldiers or labourers or raising funds for the bandit.

(7)   Serving as spy of the bandit.

(8)   Supplying the bandit with, selling to the bandit, or buying
in or transporting for the bandit any article for use of the army, or
manufacturing for the bandit any military equipment, ammunition,
or raw material for the making of any such.

(9)   Supplying the bandit with, selling to the bandit, or buying
in or transporting for the bandit any military bedding, uniform,
ration, or other material that may be used to manufacture beddings
or uniforms, or may serve as substitute of ration.

(10)   Act intending to hinder bandit-suppression, to break the
peace, or to upset the currency.

Those who made an abortive attempt but whose preparation or
secret plot possesses the same intention as that of the preceding
item shall be sentenced to prison terms of over seven years. Those
who commit the crime of the preceding item but self-surrender shall
get a reduction of punishment or grant of pardon.

Article 6.   Those who use literature, pictures or speeches to
propagandize for the bandit shall be sentenced to prison terms of
over three years and below seven years.

Article 7.   Offenders against Item 1 of Article 2, or Item 1 of
Article 3, or Sub-Item 3 under Item 1 of Article 4 of Regulations
Governing the Punishment of Robbers and Bandits shall be sentenced to death, life imprisonment, or prison terms of over ten
years.

Article 8.   With the exception of military men who shall be
court-martialled, other offenders against these Regulations shall be
tried before a special criminal court.

The organization of the special criminal court mentioned in the
preceding item shall be jointly regulated by the Executive Yuan
and the Judicial Yuan.

Article 9.   The trial of those who should be punished in accordance with what is regulated in the Outline of the Mobilization for
Bandit-Suppression and the Completion of the Application of

Constitutionalism shall follow the regulation of the preceding Article.

Article 10. The trial mentioned in the preceding Article may permit advocates to appear in court and to defend.

Article 11. The area of enforcement of these Regulations shall be determined by the National Government of the Republic of China and shall be proclaimed in the form of an order.

Article 12. These Regulations shall be enforced from the date of their promulgation.

Hsin Sheng Pao, Taiwan, 23 December 1947.

20   4 *April* 1948

SPEECH BY GENERALISSIMO CHIANG KAI-SHEK TO THE KUOMINTANG CENTRAL EXECUTIVE COMMITTEE ON THE ELECTION OF THE PRESIDENT OF THE CHINESE REPUBLIC

The convocation of the National Assembly is a great event in the history of China. On the current situation as well as on the course of political development in decades to come it is bound to exercise a most profound and decisive influence. Problems confronting the National Assembly are many. In tackling any one of them, especially that of the presidency and vice-presidency, we must have all seriousness of mind and a sense of grave responsibility to the nation and posterity. We must carefully study our revolutionary history, analyse the prevailing circumstances, understand the people's psychology and visualize the future of the country. Above all, we must uphold our late leader Dr Sun's lofty ideal 'everything for the people', and make our choice with far-sight and circumspection. I, therefore, propose to explain to you with all sincerity the conclusions I have drawn on these questions after careful deliberation.

Before I present to you my views on the question of the presidency and vice-presidency, I wish to make clear three points : First, the ultimate aim of our Party is to save and reconstruct the country. Aside from the paramount interest of the state, the Party has no interest of its own. We have no partisan or personal considerations. Secondly, the only ambition our comrades should have is how to serve the country and the people. We can best render our service only when we perform our duty wholeheartedly, each in his respective post. Thirdly, our late leader Dr Sun, when leading the revolutionary movement, always took cognizance of the past and gave practical and realistic consideration to existing circumstances. The above three points are what we have to bear in mind when we take decisions on momentous issues. Hence I wish to remind you of a bitter lesson of history and draw a parallel between it and the present situation.

At the beginning of the Republic Dr Sun Yat-sen was the president of the Provisional Government. Hardly had three months elapsed when the majority of party comrades advocated Dr Sun's withdrawal from the Government in order to make the peace negotiations between the North and South a speedy success. They were mistaken in regarding the provisional constitution, the parliament and the cabinet as constitutional democracy itself. They did not realize that Peiping still was the citadel of reactionary influence with the northern war-lords actually in control of everything. In other words, the foundation of the Republic was extremely feeble. At that juncture, our Party, in order to safeguard this foundation, should not have relinquished the presidency. But to Dr Sun's pleadings our comrades turned a deaf ear. So he failed. And his failure was also that of the Revolution of 1911. The result was the tragic history of the last thirty-odd years and the enormous sufferings of the people. The situation today is, however, fundamentally different from that of 1911. On account of the contributions we made during the Northern Expedition and the War of Resistance the foundation of the Republic has been greatly strengthened. The idea of democracy has become a popular sentiment. In these circumstances, our Party does not need to keep the post and honour of the presidency. On the contrary, we should develop Dr Sun's ideal 'everything for the people' to the fullest extent. In other words, we can entrust to persons outside the party the grave responsibility of making the Constitution a living thing. Only in this manner, I believe, shall we rally the support of the people in our common and gigantic tasks of suppressing the rebellion and national reconstruction.

After careful deliberation I consider that the qualifications for the first president should be as follows : First of all, he must be a person who comprehends the essentials of the Constitution. He must have the ability and will to uphold the Constitution, observe it and carry it into practice. To choose the man capable of obeying and enforcing the law is the surest guarantee of the success of constitutional democracy. In the second place, he must be a person inspired by the ideal of democracy and imbued with a democratic spirit. I believe that a true democrat is always a true patriot. I believe that he will, in accordance with the Constitution, carry out the Three People's Principles and build up China as a country by the people, of the people, and for the people. In the third place he must be a person

93

loyal to the basic policy of suppressing the rebellion and national reconstruction. It takes a true democrat to fully comprehend the incompatibility between a dictatorship and a constitutional government. In the fourth place, he must be one who has a profound understanding of our history, culture and national traditions. It is evident that the Communists are determined to undermine the very existence of our country. They are all equally determined to destroy our history, culture and national traditions. Finally, he must be one who follows world trends and has a rich knowledge of contemporary civilization. He will lead China towards the ideal of universal brotherhood, make China an independent and self-respecting country and guide her to take her rightful place in the family of nations. I sincerely hope that my views will be shared by all of you, especially those who are holding responsible positions. Let a person outside our Party with such qualifications be nominated as candidate to the presidency. Let all of us support him and help him to be elected. As for myself, being the leader of the Party, I may be the logical candidate for nomination by the Party to the presidency. I believe, however, that since you have been with me for so many years, you must understand that I do not care for high honour and important post. My only concern has always been how to give my best to serve my people. I am ever ready to assist the president in carrying out the democratic principles embodied in the Constitution. I shall contribute what I have and what I am as a soldier to defend the country.

As long as the nation remains disunited, I am determined not to run for the presidency.

This does not mean that I shall shirk the responsibility towards our revolutionary cause and our beloved country. Aside from the presidency and vice-presidency, I shall not fail to answer the call of the new Government. I have been with my people and army throughout these twenty years of great trial and tribulation. Patriotic soldiers and citizens have supported me in uniting and defending the country. They have given their very best. They have sustained great sacrifices. I have the moral obligation to do my utmost so as not to disappoint them and to forfeit the confidence they have placed in me. I shall contribute whatever I can to co-operate with the people, the army and my party comrades towards our common goal. For the good of the country and the good of the people, I am convinced that I should not run for the presidency. This is not mere modesty. It is my sincere conviction. The only hope I cherish is : how to lay a sound and solid foundation for China's constitutional government.

In a word, I propose that our Party will nominate an outstanding non-partisan to be candidate to the presidency.

Comrades, I hope you will appreciate my sincerity, trust my judgement, endorse my opinion and make a decision !

United States Relations with China, pp. 847–9.

21   1 *January* 1949

NEW YEAR MESSAGE OF GENERALISSIMO CHIANG KAI-SHEK

My Fellow Countrymen :

On this thirty-eighth anniversary of the founding of the Republic of China and the first anniversary after the introduction of constitutional government, I observe with great regret that our national reconstruction efforts have come to a state of suspension and the Three People's Principles still remain to be achieved.

Since the end of the war against Japan, the main object of the Government has been to lay down a firm foundation for peace and reconstruction so as to alleviate the suffering of the people. The task which the Government considered as of great importance was to recover the Northeast, thereby preserving China's national sovereignty and territorial integrity. But, unfortunately, we have not been able to do this.

On the other hand, Tsinan was lost to the Communists and Chinchow, Changchun, and Mukden fell into their hands in succession. The Mukden tragedy of 1931 has repeated itself. Commercial and industrial cities as well as cultural centres in North and East China are now being menaced by the Communists.

During this national crisis I cannot but blame myself for my inadequate leadership. I am sorry that I have not lived up to the high expectation of the people.

The military situation has entered upon an exceedingly perilous stage. The fate of the nation and the historical and cultural continuity of our people will soon be decided. The issue of this struggle will determine whether the Chinese people will continue to live as free men and women or as slaves, and whether they will live at all or perish.

Everyone is concerned over the policy which the Government has pursued in dealing with the situation. We are convinced that all patriotic citizens will not tolerate the Communist method of 'liquidation' and 'struggle' and that they are not willing to abandon their liberty and to remain inactive at this critical moment.

But we are also fully aware that military operations have increased the people's burden and that they hope for an early conclusion of the war. Shouldering the responsibility of the conduct of national affairs, I have carefully studied the situation and considered the wishes of the people.

The Father of our Republic once said : 'The aim of national reconstruction of the Republic of China is peace.' Being a strong believer in the Three People's Principles and abiding by Dr Sun Yat-sen's bequeathed teachings, I did not have any intention to fight the Communists at the end of the war.

Immediately after VJ Day, the Government declared its principles for peace and reconstruction. Later it went one step further by seeking to solve the Communist question by means of political consultation.

In the subsequent one and a half years, the Communists disregarded every agreement and obstructed every peace effort that was made. As a result, these agreements and the programmes which were agreed upon were not implemented.

In the end, the Communists started an all-out rebellion, thereby endangering the very existence of the nation. Unwillingly, the Government was forced to order a general mobilization and to proceed with the anti-Communist campaign. I am sure that these historical facts are still vivid in your minds.

Communism has already had a history of twenty-five years in China. In this period I have never for a moment given up the hope that the Communists would place the national interests above that of their own, would follow the regular courses as befitting a political party, and would join hands with the Government in finding ways to work for peace and national existence.

Such was the purpose of the political consultation which took place shortly after the war, and such remains the objective of the Communist-Suppression Campaign. The key to the problem of peace or war and to the happiness or suffering of the people is not in the hands of the Government, nor can the problem be solved by popular appeal for peace to the Government alone. The problem can be decided only by the Communists. So the sincerity of the Communists for peace must be ascertained before the problem can be solved.

If the Communists are sincerely desirous of peace, and clearly give such indication, the Government will be only too glad to discuss with them the means to end the war.

If a negotiated peace is not detrimental to the national independence and sovereignty, but will contribute to the welfare of the people ; if the Constitution is not violated and constitutionalism preserved, the democratic form of government maintained, the entity of the armed forces safeguarded ; and if the people's free mode of living and their minimum living standard are protected, then I shall be satisfied.

In my devotion to the cause of the National Revolution, I have known nothing except loyalty to the nation, service to the people and the realization of the Three People's Principles, thereby fulfilling my sacred duties as a Revolutionist. If peace can be secured, I am not at all concerned about my own position. In this I will follow only the consensus of the people.

If, on the other hand, the Communists are not sincerely desirous of peace and will insist on continuing their armed rebellion, the Government, with no other alternative, will fight them to the finish. As the political nerve centre of the country, the Nanking-Shanghai area will be held at all costs, and the Government is determined to throw in all available forces for a decisive victory. I firmly believe that the Government will win out in the end, and it also will mark the turning point of the war.

The people of the nation should realize that only by carrying on this war of self-defence can a real peace be secured ; and only by making sacrifices can a glorious victory be won. It has been almost forty years since I joined the National Revolution. In every major and prolonged battle, I have suffered many setbacks and have been subjected to vicious propaganda. No matter how serious was the reverse, I never lost confidence in the final victory. And as a rule, victory was obtained in the end.

National spirit, justice, and righteousness, such as they are generally recognized, must constitute our mainstay in this fight. The brutal force of the Communists can wrest from us the Northwest, but it can never subdue our national spirit.

The Communists can penetrate into our heartland, but they can never soil our national character. Righteousness is the strength for victory, and right will always triumph over might. We of this generation have seen the greatest cataclysm in our history ; we have on our shoulders an unprecedented mission.

We can, we must, endure temporary afflictions and sacrifices and struggle for the existence of the nation, the continuity of our history and culture, our free way of living, and the prosperity of our offspring.

My countrymen, at this time of national crisis, I feel all the more keenly the weightiness of my responsibilities and the difficulties in fulfilling my mission. It is my hope that all patriotic countrymen will advise me and join hands in the fight for the sanctity of the Constitution, the maintenance of China's territorial and sovereign integrity, the freedoms of the people, and the continuance of our culture.

Dr Sun said: 'Final victory belongs to the one who struggles until victory.' I hope that all of us will bear this motto in mind.

United States Relations with China, pp. 920-2.

22   22 *January* 1949

STATEMENT BY FIFTY-FIVE REPRESENTATIVES OF DEMOCRATIC PARTIES AND GROUPS SUPPORTING THE EIGHT PEACE CONDITIONS OF THE COMMUNISTS

We have now successively arrived in the Liberated Areas. We recollect the call to the entire country by the Central Committee of the Communist Party of China last May, first proposing the convoking of a new Political Consultative Conference including all democratic parties and groups, people's organizations and democratic figures to speed up the overthrow of the traitorous, dictatorial rule of Nanking and realize a people's democratic coalition government. We unanimously held the definite view that this advocacy for settlement of national affairs was precisely in accord with the demands of the masses of people of the entire country. Therefore, we were the first to cable our support and then came one after another to the Liberated Areas. We wish, united under the leadership of the Communist Party of China, to exert our humble efforts in the course of the people's liberation war, to work together for the swift success of the Chinese people's democratic revolution, and the early realization of an independent, free, peaceful and happy new China.

Our first impression on arriving in the Liberated Areas has filled us with joy. The Liberated Areas are full of the atmosphere of democracy and freedom, and a vibrant, forward-moving spirit. Production and construction are taking great strides forward. Social order is excellent. All strata, workers, peasants, businessmen and intelligentsia, are able to stand at their own stations, exerting their efforts in work and supporting the front. Members of the Communist Party, especially, set the example through their own deeds. They display an extraordinary spirit of heroic self-sacrifice, acting as the vanguard of the people, fearing no hardship.

The hard-fighting, meritorious People's Liberation Army launches successive offensives with stupendous power. During the past three months they wiped out over one million of Chiang Kai-shek's troops, liberated all Manchuria, and nearly all of North and Central China. The military offensive now points to south of the Yangtze River.

Beyond doubt, China will obtain full liberation in the year 1949.

Under these circumstances, the reactionary KMT Nanking bloc under the wing of American imperialism is really just about to crumble into dust. Since their military struggles have proved hopeless, they are changing their tricks and attempting to carry out political plots to drag out their existence. As far back as when the troops of Chiang Kai-shek began to collapse on the Northern front, American imperialism had launched its conspiratorial activities, employing an enormous, double-edged scheme of disrupting the Chinese revolution. On the one hand, they scheme to foment an opposition within the revolutionary camp, hoping to block or slow down the revolutionary advance. On the other hand, they incite the reactionary Nanking bloc to launch a peace offensive so as to win time for the remnant of the counter-revolutionary forces to make a final desperate struggle south of the Yangtze or in border provinces. We should be on guard against this.

Today, we must clearly declare our belief : We hold that the revolution must be carried through to the very end. There is no possibility for compromise or conciliation between the revolution and the counter-revolution. We should bear well in mind the bitter lessons of the repeated defeats since the 1911 Revolution. The Chinese people's revolution is today directed against imperialism, feudalism and bureaucratic capitalism. They are the greatest enemies obstructing the realization of independence, democracy, freedom and happiness for China. If they are not thoroughly swept away, no genuine peace in fact as well as in name can be realized.

Therefore, we must relentlessly smash the hypocritical peace offensive instigated by Chiang Kai-shek and American imperialism. Even more, we must raise our vigilance within our people's democratic camp, set our ranks in order, march in step, strengthen our solidarity to prevent the infiltration of counter-revolutionary forces. The people's democratic dictatorship should embrace representatives of the broadest strata of the people, but cannot include the germs of counter-revolution. It should bring full freedom to the greatest majority of the people, but cannot give a handful of reactionaries freedom to oppose the people. Therefore, we firmly believe that persons throughout the entire country who are really striving for democratic revolution should exert their efforts together so that there is no room for an opposition foothold within the people's democratic camp or for the existence of a so-called middle road.

At this time, when the reactionary rule is tottering on the brink of collapse, the peace offensive is assuming more variegated forms. The New Year's Day broadcast of China's number one war criminal, Chiang Kai-shek, made public the first howls for peace. But this was simply a fraud. Putting aside his glaring historic crimes of bringing calamity upon the country and the people, Chiang Kai-shek shamelessly raised such conditions as: 'If only peace negotiations do not harm the integrity of national independence and enable the people to recuperate and prosper, if only we do not have to destroy the sacred Constitution and disrupt the democratic constitutional régime, if only the body politic of the Chinese People's Republic is preserved, the legitimacy of traditional institutions of the Chinese People's Republic is not discontinued, if only there are real guarantees for the army and the people to maintain their free way of life and the minimum living standards of the present, then I personally have no other desire.'

With these conditions, the régime of the Chiang Kai-shek dynasty headed by the Four Families would rule in unbroken line for generations. What 'other desire' could he have, indeed?

For this reason, he emphasized at the end that he would 'grapple to the end' with the Communist Party of China and appealed for 'the armies and people together, the whole country together, to struggle in unison'. This is Chiang Kai-shek's ultimate aim.

Today is the final test for we people of China. We believe that our Chinese people weighted down by calamitous sufferings will surely not be cheated again by the reactionary plots of Chiang Kai-shek and America. But in the character of a few people exists the weakness of holding harmony as the highest virtue and indulgence as magnanimity and benevolence. Over an essence of slovenly submission they throw the cloak of heavenly compassion. This is the final psychological ground on which the enemy conducts a peace offensive. This is also the enemy's greatest hidden aid. In order to destroy the remnants of the enemy, we should uproot this final hidden aid.

The achievements gained by the people's democratic revolution under the leadership of the Communist Party of China were not lightly won. If anyone today slovenly gives in by indulging the enemy so that the great revolutionary cause collapses on the threshold of victory, he becomes a criminal against the Chinese revolution and against the Chinese nation.

But we are very happy and elated at having read the recent statement on the current situation issued by Mao Tze-tung, Chairman of the Central Committee, Communist Party of China. To carry the revolution through to the very end and shatter the peace offensive, he keenly, firmly, comprehensively and sternly exposed the plots of the Chiang Kai-shek-American bloc and raised eight conditions[1] for genuine people's democratic peace :

(1) Punish war criminals.

(2) Abrogate the bogus constitution.

(3) Abolish the bogus 'legitimacy of traditional institutions'.

(4) Remould all reactionary armies in accordance with democratic principles.

(5) Confiscate bureaucratic capital.

(6) Reform the agrarian system.

(7) Abrogate treaties of national betrayal.

(8) Convoke a Political Consultative Conference without the participation of reactionary elements, establish a democratic coalition government, take over all power from the Nanking KMT reactionary Government and all its levels of government.

These eight conditions are a relentless counter-blow at the shameless demands raised by Chiang Kai-shek. We thoroughly support these eight conditions. Beyond all doubt, the common will of the people of the whole country is reflected here. We hope that the people of all China and all comrades-in-arms in the democratic united front will unite together, and adopt the necessary action to carry out firmly this common will of the people so that these eight peace conditions can be realized in their entirety.

Today is the era in which we people straighten our backs and reshape history. We must create a free way of life in which the people are the masters, and create the highest possible standard of living. This does not mean to 'maintain the minimum living standards of the present' as Chiang Kai-shek demanded of us. Chiang Kai-shek wants us to be the slaves of the Four Families and American imperialism from first to last, but we want to be the real masters of a people's democratic republic. In order to achieve this, all of the eight conditions raised by Mr Mao Tze-tung are indispensable.

[1] The Communist Party put the following eight conditions on 14 January 1949 as a basis for peace talks with the Kuomintang :

(1) Strict punishment of war criminals.

(2) Abolition of the constitution.

(3) Abolition of the Kuomintang legal system.

(4) Reorganization of Nationalist troops according to democratic principles.

(5) Confiscation of 'bureaucratic' capital.

(6) Reformation of the land system.

(7) Abolition of 'treasonous treaties'.

(8) Convocation of a Political Consultative Conference with non-participation of 'reactionary elements', establishment of a democratic coalition government, taking over all authority of the 'Kuomintang reactionary Government' and all its strata.

Let us repeat these conditions in another form :

War criminals must be tried and punished ; the bogus constitution and bogus legitimacy of traditional institutions must be abolished ; all reactionary armies must be remoulded in accordance with democratic principles ; bureaucratic capital must be confiscated ; the agrarian system must be reformed ; treaties of national betrayal must be annulled ; all power of the reactionary Nanking Government and all its levels of government must be taken over ; and the new Political Consultative Conference soon to be convoked and the democratic coalition government soon to be established must refuse participation by reactionary elements.

To sum up : the people's revolution must be carried to the very end. The day on which the revolution is carried to the very end is the day of the advent of genuine peace and complete liberation. The strength of the liberated peoples is matchless. Look at our friend and neighbour, the Soviet Union : after only 32 years of construction, it has become the strongest fortress of peace in the whole world. We people of China are double the people of the Soviet Union in number, and have in addition favourable geographic conditions. We dare to believe that after we have smashed the reactionary government we can in a shorter time construct a peaceful, democratic, free new China, a people's democratic republic.

A bright perspective lies before us. We should exert our efforts in unison.

LI CHI-SHEN, SHEN CHUN-JU, MA HSU-LUN, KUO MO-JO, TAN PING-SHAN, PENG TZE-MIN, CHANG PO-CHUN, LI SHI-CHIU, TSAI TING-KAI, CHOU CHIEN-JEN, FU TING-YI, CHANG NAI-CHI, LI TEH-CHUAN, HU YU-CHIN, SHA CHIEN-LI, MAO TUN, CHU HSUEH-FAN, CHEN CHIYU, HUANG CHEN-SHENG, CHU YUN-SHAN, TENG CHU-MIN, CHIEN PO-TSAN, WANG SHAO-AO, WU HAN, HSU KUANG-PING, CHU TU-NAN, CHIU CHE, HAN CHAO-NGO, FENG YU-FANG, HSU PAO-CHU, TIEN HAN, HUNG SHEN, HOU WAI-LU, SHEN TZE-CHIU, HUAN HSIANG, YANG KANG, TSAO MENG-CHUN, LIU CHING-YANG, CHANG MAN-YUN, SHIH FU-LIANG, SUN CHI-MENG, YEN HSIN-MIN, LI MIN-HSIN, MEI KUNG-PIN, SHEN CHIH-YUAN, CHOU YING, AN OA, WU MAO-SUN, HO CHU, LIN YI-YUAN, LAI YA-LI, KUNG TEH-CHIH, YUAN CHEN, SHEN CHIANG, WANG YUN-JU.

China Digest, Vol. V, No. 8, 8 February 1949, pp. 9-11.

23

27 January 1949

ACTING PRESIDENT LI'S TELEGRAM TO MAO TZE-TUNG
ACCEPTING EIGHT PEACE CONDITIONS AND URGING
SPEEDY PEACE TALKS

Dear Mr Jun-chih,

Since the break of the Political Consultative Conference for over three years the civil war has been carried on in succession to the eight years of War of Resistance. The constitution of the nation has been greatly injured and the sufferings brought to the people have been numerous. To stop war and to seek for peace have become the unanimous cry of the entire nation today. Therefore, ever since the first day I led the administration, I have made my decision to spend, with the greatest sincerity, the greatest effort toward the promotion as well as realization of peace. The statement which I issued on the 22nd and the letters which I sent to Messrs Jen-ch'ao, Heng-shan, Po-chun and Tung-sun have repeatedly expressed what has been my original wish. I lament over the nation's being shattered to such an extreme and the people's being made to suffer to such a depth today. Wives and children are separated from their husbands and parents. People who cry for food and clothing are found everywhere. All these are brought forth by war.

Once in the past the Kuomintang and the Chinese Communist Party worked together towards the Chinese revolution under the guidance of Dr Sun Yat-sen. It is unfortunate that due to a divergence in political opinion they finally started this fight among brothers, thus leading both the people and nation into catastrophe. Touching the present while recollecting the past, would not one feel pain in the heart ? If we do think that the purpose of revolution is to increase the benefit of the people and nation and the motive of revolution is founded on the will of the majority of the people, there is no reason why the Kuomintang and the Chinese Communist Party should, under the present situation, continue to resort to force of arms, to kill each other and to aggravate the sufferings of the people and nation, regardless of how different the opinions and political views of the two parties may be. In other words, there is no other path to take except to follow the will of the people of the entire nation, to stop the war and to seek for peace through political settlement. Otherwise, our sins will never be redeemed.

You repeatedly stated in the past that you are willing to seek for peaceful settlement. Now you can see that the Government side has expressed its sincere wish for peace through both words and action. All that was demanded in the past by the people of various circles of the nation, such as the release of political prisoners, freedom of speech and the guarantee for other freedoms of the people, has been put into practice step by step. Facts are here to prove ; nobody can say it is otherwise. It is therefore hoped that you will summon your comrades and together with them speedily enable the realization of peace talk, and that you will, on this very day, appoint and send delegates over to discuss and decide on a place for peace talk as well as to start the peace talk. If the war could be stopped a day earlier, thousands and thousands of human lives would be saved and thousands and thousands would not be made widows and orphans. If we could only sympathize with the age for its grief and be sincere with each other, everything would reach settlement. The Government side has already acknowledged the eight conditions which your side suggested as the basis for peace talk. If such talks were proceeded with, all problems would be solved through discussion. However, if one side demanded the opposite side to first fulfil certain conditions before the discussion of the two sides even started, how could it be called a peace talk ? If the love and hatred, the right and wrong of the past were still over-emphasized, how could there be any end to revenge after revenge ? In that case I am afraid that both you and I would be sinners of the race for ages to come. Moreover, the broadcast of your side says that the Government's initiation of peace is the secret plot of the Government and a certain country. This point of view is evidently based upon certain prejudice. Since the War of Resistance the foreign policy which I stand for has been to make friends of the good and to be friendly with neighbours. There is no differentiation of high and low. We should closely co-operate with any country which is helpful to peace and the reconstruction of our nation. Henceforth the same principle will be followed in order to safeguard the peace of East Asia and independence of our nation. You who are wise should approve it. As a whole, the affairs of today do not pertain to the honour or disgrace of a single party or a single person. They are rather what the pulse of the nation and the life and death of the people are attached to. I personally have not the slightest prejudice or intention of loss or gain. To speedily eliminate the ravages of the soldiery and to bring forth peace and happiness, thus releasing responsibility from my shoulder and fulfilling my original wish, are what I incessantly pray for.

I write specially to present you all these. I shall be obliged if you will give me a reply.   Yours sincerely,

                                                                LI TSUNG-JEN

Hsin Chiang Jih Pao, Tihua, 28 January 1949.

24

15 *April* 1949

THE DOMESTIC PEACE AGREEMENT PROPOSED BY THE DELEGATION OF THE COMMUNIST PARTY OF CHINA TO THE KUOMINTANG DELEGATION

In the 35th year of the Republic of China, the Nanking Government, with the help of the United States Government, violated the will of the people, and destroyed the Truce Agreement and the Political Consultative Conference resolutions and launched civil war on a nationwide scale against the Chinese people and the Chinese People's Liberation Army under the name of opposing the Communist Party of China. This war has, up till the present, lasted two years and nine and a half months. Because of this, the people throughout the country suffered colossal calamities. The nation's financial and material resources suffered tremendous losses and national sovereignty also suffered new losses. The people of the whole country have always expressed their dissatisfaction with the Nanking national Government for its violation of the standpoint of Dr Sun Yat-sen's revolutionary Three People's Principles, (its) violation of Dr Sun Yat-sen's correct policies of uniting with the Soviet Union and the Communist Party of China and supporting peasants and workers and the violation of Dr Sun Yat-sen's Revolution Will made just before his death. The people of the country particularly expressed their opposition to the launching of the present civil war on an unprecedented scale by the Nanking national Government and the erroneous political, military, financial, economic, cultural and diplomatic policies and measures adopted by it because of this civil war. The people throughout the country have completely lost trust in the Nanking national Government. And the troops of the Nanking national Government have already been defeated by the People's Liberation Army led by the Communist Party of China and commanded by the Chinese People's Revolutionary Military Committee during the present civil war. Based on the above-mentioned situation, the Nanking national Government proposed to the Communist Party of China, on 1 January of the 38th year of the Republic of China, to conduct negotiations to cease civil war and to return to a state of peace.

On 14 January, the Communist Party of China made a statement, agreeing to the above-mentioned proposal of the Nanking national Government. It also proposed eight terms : punishment of war criminals ; abolition of the bogus constitution ; abolition of the bogus legitimacy of traditional institutions ; reorganization of all reactionary troops according to democratic principles ; confiscation of bureaucratic capital ; carrying out of agrarian reform ; abrogation of treaties of national betrayal; convocation of a new Political Consultative Conference without the participation of reactionary elements, establishment of a democratic coalition government and taking over of all powers of the Nanking KMT reactionary Government and all its subordinate governments of various levels as the basis for peace negotiations by both parties. These eight basic terms were agreed to by the Nanking national Government. The Communist Party of China and the Nanking national Government, therefore, sent their delegations and empowered them with full powers to conduct negotiations and sign an agreement. The delegates of both parties met in Peiping and, first of all, affirm that the Nanking national Government should bear full responsibility for the present civil war and all its erroneous policies and agree to conclude this agreement.

Article 1

CLAUSE 1. To distinguish between right and wrong and clarify responsibility, both the delegation of the Communist Party of China and the delegation of the Nanking Government (later referred to in brief as both parties in this document) affirm that the war criminals in the Nanking national Government who should be responsible for launching and executing the present civil war should be punished in principle, but they may be dealt with individually in accordance with the following conditions :

(*a*) All war criminals, no matter who they are, provided they differentiate between right and wrong, repent completely, are really earnest and sincere and show it with deeds, thus favouring the progress of the cause of the People's Liberation, favouring the peaceful solution of the domestic question, are permitted to cancel their criminal name of war criminals and will be treated clemently.

(*b*) All war criminals, no matter who they are, who are incorrigible in their crimes, who hinder the advancement of the cause of the People's Liberation, who are inimical to the using of the peace method to settle the domestic question or even incite rebellion, should be severely punished. Those among them who lead troops in rebellion should be put down by the Chinese People's Revolutionary Military Committee responsible to carry this out.

CLAUSE 2. Both parties affirm that the action of the Nanking national Government in pronouncing General Okamura, Japanese war criminal invading China, as not guilty and releasing him on 26 January of the 38th year of the Republic of China and in allowing two hundred and sixty other Japanese war criminals to return to Japan on 31 January of the same year are wrong. These Japanese war criminals should be promptly dealt with anew as soon as the Democratic Coalition Government of China, namely, the New Central Government representing the people throughout China, is established.

Article 2

CLAUSE 3. Both parties affirm that the 'Constitution of the Republic of China' passed by the 'National Assembly' convoked in November of the 35th year of the Republic of China by the Nanking national Government should be abolished.

CLAUSE 4. After the abolition of the 'Constitution of the Republic of China', the fundamental law to be observed by the state and people of China should be handled in accordance with the resolutions of the New Political Consultative Conference and the Democratic Coalition Government.

Article 3

CLAUSE 5. Both parties affirm that all the Nanking national Government's legitimacy of traditional institutions should be abolished.

CLAUSE 6. In places reached and taken over by the People's Liberation Army and after the establishment of the Democratic Coalition Government, the People's Democratic Institutions should be established whilst all reactionary decrees should be cancelled.

Article 4

CLAUSE 7. Both parties affirm that all armed forces of the Nanking national Government (all the army, navy, air force, gendarmes, communication police, local troops and all military institutions, schools, factories and rear service organizations etc.) should be reorganized into the People's Liberation Army in accordance with democratic principles. After the signing of the domestic peace agreement, a reorganization committee of a nationwide character should be immediately established and be responsible for this reorganization work. The reorganization committee is to consist of seven to nine members, four to five of which are to be appointed by the People's Revolutionary Military Committee, three to four appointed by the Nanking national Government with one of the members appointed by the People's Revolutionary Committee as director and one of the members appointed by the Nanking national Government as assistant director. In places reached and taken over by the People's Liberation Army, branch committees of a regional character of the reorganization committee should be set up when necessary. The proportion of the members of both parties in the branch committee and the appointment of directors and assistant directors will be similar to that of the national reorganization committee. A reorganization committee should be separately set up for the reorganization of the navy and air force. All matters relating to the People's Liberation Army's moving into and taking over in the areas at present administered by the Nanking national Government will be stipulated in the orders issued by the Chinese People's Revolutionary Military Committee. When the People's Liberation Army marches in, the armed forces belonging to the Nanking national Government must not resist.

CLAUSE 8. Both parties agree that the reorganization plans in each region are to be carried out in two stages :

(1) The first stage is one of assembling and regrouping.

(a) All the armed forces belonging to the Nanking national Government (army, navy, air force, gendarmes, communication police and local troops etc.) should be assembled and regrouped. The principles of regrouping : the reorganization committee should, in accordance with the actual local conditions, order these armed forces in the areas reached and taken over by the People's Liberation Army to move, area by area over different periods, to the designated places for assembling and regrouping in their original designation, formation and number.

(b) All the armed forces belonging to the Nanking national Government should, before the arrival and taking over by the People's Liberation Army, be responsible for maintaining local order and preventing the occurrence of any sabotage acts in the big and small cities, important communication lines, rivers, ports and rural areas quartered by them.

(c) In the above-mentioned areas, when the People's Liberation Army arrives and takes over, armed forces of the Nanking national Government should, in accordance with the orders of the reorganization committee and its branch committees, conduct peaceful handing over and move to the designated places. While moving to, and after arriving at, the designated places, armed forces of the Nanking national Government should strictly observe discipline and must not undermine local order.

(d) When armed forces of the Nanking national Government leave the places in which they are originally stationed in compliance with the orders of the reorganization committee and its branch committees, local police or peace preservation troops stationed in these places must not be withdrawn, but should undertake the maintenance of local order and security and obey the command and orders of the People's Liberation Army.

(e) During the period of movement and assembling, the grain and fodder outfits and other military supplies of all armed forces of the Nanking national Government are to be entirely solved by the reorganization committee, its branch committee and the local governments.

(f) With regard to all military institutions (ranging from the Ministry of National Defence to the headquarters of the combined service forces and the institutions, schools, factories and storehouses etc. belonging to them), all military installations (naval ports, forts and air bases etc.) and all military materials of the Nanking national Government, the reorganization committee and its branch committees are to order them, according to the actual situation of the various areas, to hand over area by area at different periods to the People's Liberation Army and its military control committees in various places for taking over.

(2) The second stage is the stage of reorganization area by area.

(a) After the army units of the Nanking national Government (infantry, cavalry, special army units, gendarmes, communication police and local troops) have moved to designated places and have been assembled and regrouped area by area over different periods, the reorganization committee should work out plans for reorganization area by area at specified periods according to the actual conditions in the various areas. The principle of reorganization should be to reorganize the above-mentioned army units which have been assembled and regrouped into regular forces of the People's Liberation Army according to the democratic system and regular troop formation of the People's Liberation Army. The reorganization committee and its branch committee are responsible for dealing with soldiers who have been ascertained to be old or disabled and should really be discharged and who personally wish to retire, and officers who personally wish to retire or take up other occupations, and accord them facilities to return home and to settle down so that everyone has an occupation and will not be without a living, thus giving rise to misconduct.

(b) After the navy and air force of the Nanking national Government have moved to the designated places and have been assembled and regrouped area by area over different periods, they will be reorganized according to their original designation, formation and number by the navy and air force reorganization committee in accordance with the democratic system of the People's Liberation Army.

(c) After all armed forces of the Nanking national Government have been reorganized into the People's Liberation Army, they should without fail strictly observe the three great disciplines and eight points for attention of the People's Liberation Army and loyally carry out the military and political systems of the People's Liberation Army.

(*d*) After reorganization, retired officers and men should respect the various local People's Governments and observe the laws and decrees of the People's Governments. The People's Governments and people of various localities should look after these retired officers and men and not treat them with discrimination.

CLAUSE 9. After the signing of the domestic peace agreement, all armed forces of the Nanking national Government must neither conscript nor recruit soldiers or personnel. They must undertake the responsibility of protecting all their arms, ammunition and all equipment, all military institutions, installations and all military materials. They must not engage in any acts of sabotage, concealment, transfer or sale of these objects.

CLAUSE 10. If, after the signing of the domestic peace agreement, there are any armed forces of the Nanking national Government who resist the carrying out of the reorganization plan, the Nanking national Government should assist the People's Liberation Army to enforce its execution, in order to ensure its thorough implementation.

Article 5

CLAUSE 11. Both parties agree that the enterprises and property of bureaucratic capital (including banks, factories, mines, vessels, companies and shops) acquired or usurped through political prerogatives and plutocratic influence during the rule of the Nanking national Government should be confiscated and become state-owned.

CLAUSE 12. In areas not yet reached and taken over by the People's Liberation Army, the Nanking national Government should be responsible for the supervision of the bureaucratic capitalist enterprises and property mentioned in Clause 11 and the flight, concealment, damage, transfer and secret sale of the above-mentioned are not permitted. Those that have been removed should be frozen on the spot and further removal and flight abroad or damage is prohibited. Enterprises and property of bureaucratic capital abroad should be declared state-owned.

CLAUSE 13. In areas reached and taken over by the People's Liberation Army, the enterprises and property of bureaucratic capital mentioned in Clause 11 should be confiscated by the local military control committee or institutions appointed by the Democratic Coalition Government. If private shares are in them, they should be sorted out. After they have been certified to be private shares and not secretly transferred bureaucratic capital, they should be recognized, and their owners are free to remain shareholders or withdraw their shares.

CLAUSE 14. Enterprises of bureaucratic capital of the period prior to the rule of the Nanking national Government and during the rule of the Nanking national Government, which are not big nor harmful to national economy and people's livelihood are not to be confiscated. However, the enterprises and property of certain persons, as for example the enterprises and property of reactionaries who have committed heinous crimes and have been prosecuted by the people and proved to be the case should still be confiscated.

CLAUSE 15.   In cities where the People's Liberation Army is not yet in control, municipal and county governments under the Nanking national Government should be responsible for protecting the local people's democratic forces and their activities, and must not suppress nor undermine them.

Article 6

CLAUSE 16.   Both parties affirm that the feudal land ownership system in rural areas of all China should be reformed systematically. After the arrival of the People's Liberation Army, reduction of rents and interest should in general be carried out first and land distribution later.

CLAUSE 17.   In areas not yet reached and taken over by the People's Liberation Army, the local government subordinate to the Nanking national Government should be responsible for protecting the organizations and activities of the peasant masses, and must not suppress or undermine them.

Article 7

CLAUSE 18.   Both parties agree that all diplomatic treaties and agreements concluded during the rule of the Nanking national Government, and other public and secret diplomatic documents and files should be handed over by the Nanking national Government to the Democratic Coalition Government and be examined by the Democratic Coalition Government. Among them, all which are detrimental to the Chinese people and country, especially those having the nature of selling out national rights, should be abrogated, revised or re-concluded according to their different cases.

Article 8

CLAUSE 19.   Both parties agree that after the signing of the domestic peace agreement and before the formation of the Democratic Coalition Government, the Nanking national Government and its machinery of yuans, departments and commissions should temporarily perform their functions. But they must consult with the Chinese People's Revolutionary Military Committee in their dealings and help the People's Liberation Army in the take-over and hand-over of affairs in various areas. After the formation of the Democratic

Coalition Government, the Nanking national Government will immediately hand over to the Democratic Coalition Government and proclaim its own termination.

CLAUSE 20. When the Nanking national Government and its various levels of local governments and all their subordinate machinery are being handed over, attention must be paid by the People's Liberation Army, People's Governments of various localities and the Democratic Coalition Government of China to absorb all patriotic and useful persons from their working personnel, give them democratic education and give them employment in suitable posts so that they will not become displaced.

CLAUSE 21. Before the arrival of and taking over by the People's Liberation Army, the Nanking national Government and its subordinate local governments of provinces, cities and counties should undertake to maintain order and security in their areas, take care of and protect all government organizations and state-owned enterprises (including banks, factories, mines, railways, postal and telegraph offices, aircraft, vessels, companies, warehouses and all communication facilities) and the movable and immovable property belonging to the state. No destruction, loss, removal, concealment or sale is allowed. Libraries, archives, curios, valuables, gold, silver foreign currencies and all properties and assets which have been removed or concealed should be frozen immediately, pending taking over. As for those which have been sent abroad or are originally abroad, the Nanking national Government should be responsible for bringing them back or keeping them for handing over.

CLAUSE 22. In areas reached or taken over by the People's Liberation Army, all the powers and property and wealth of the state in the area should be immediately taken over through the Military Control Committee of the areas and the local People's Government or institutions commissioned by the Coalition Government.

CLAUSE 23. After the delegation of the Nanking national Government has signed the domestic peace agreement and the agreement has been implemented by the Nanking national Government, the delegation of the Communist Party of China is willing to be responsible for proposing to the preparatory committee of the New Political Consultative Conference that the Nanking national Government may send a number of patriotic elements as representatives to the New Political Consultative Conference ; after obtaining the approval of the preparatory committee of the New Political Consultative Conference, the representatives of the Nanking national Government may attend the New Political Consultative Conference.

CLAUSE 24. After the Nanking national Government has sent its representatives to the New Political Consultative Conference, the

Communist Party of China is willing to be responsible for proposing to the New Political Consultative Conference that the Democratic Coalition Government should include a number of patriotic elements from the Nanking national Government in the interest of co-operation.

The delegations of both parties hereby state : We hereby take the responsibility of signing this agreement for the sake of the liberation of the Chinese people and the independence and liberty of the Chinese nation, and for the sake of the early conclusion of the war and restoration of peace, to facilitate the commencement of the great work of production and reconstruction on a nation-wide scale, and to enable the country and the people stably to attain prosperity, strength and happiness. It is hoped that the people of the entire country will unite together to struggle for the complete realization of this agreement. This agreement will immediately come into force after it is signed.

China Digest, Vol. VI, No. 2, 3 May 1949, pp. 19-22.

V THE COMMUNISTS

25   4 *January* 1947

MEMORANDUM BY LU TING-YI, CHIEF OF THE DE-PARTMENT OF INFORMATION OF THE CHINESE COMMUNIST PARTY, ON THE 'EXPLANATION OF SEVERAL BASIC QUESTIONS CONCERNING THE POST-WAR INTERNATIONAL SITUATION'

It is now the new year—1947. We wish to make an all-sided examination of the whole international situation in order to dispel certain misconceptions in this realm.

During the past year and more and right up to the present time, owing to the complicated changes in the situation and to demagogic propaganda intentionally spread about widely by the Chinese and foreign reactionaries, there are still some people in the camp of democracy in China whose understanding of several basic questions concerning the post-war political situation is not in accord, or not wholly in accord, with the real state of affairs. These people include some Communists, some Left-wing critics, some middle of the road critics. The purpose of this article is to offer a general explanation of these several basic questions.

I. Mao Tze-tung's Prediction

Sixteen months have elapsed since the victory in the anti-Fascist war. These sixteen months have been a period of extremely complicated changes in the international political situation. The course of changing affairs has taken many twists and turns—one sort of conditions prevailed at the London Foreign Ministers' Conference in September a year before last, there was a change at the time of the Moscow Foreign Ministers' Conference in December of the same year, in February and March of last year another change took place, and from September of last year yet another change occurred. After the many changes of the past sixteen months we have ample surety in saying : The development of the international situation is entirely in accord with the prediction of Comrade Mao Tze-tung.

In 'On Coalition Government', a political report of Comrade Mao Tze-tung to the 7th National Convention of the Chinese Communist Party, in April 1945, he made the following prediction of a new world situation following World War II :

'This new situation differs greatly from that of the first world war and the so-called 'peaceful' period which followed. At that time there was not a Soviet Union like the present one, nor was there such a degree of consciousness as now expressed by the people of Great Britain, America, China, France, and other anti-Fascist Allies, and naturally there could not be such a present world unity headed by three Great Powers or five Great Powers. Now we are living in an entirely new situation. There now exist in the world peoples and their organized forces who have been awakened and united, and are in the course of becoming more so. This determines the objective to which the wheels of world history are moving, and the path which should be followed to attain it.

'The defeat of the Fascist aggressor countries and the emergence of a general peace situation do not mean that there will be no more struggle. The widely spread remnant forces of Fascism will certainly continue to make trouble. The anti-democratic forces remaining in the camp of the anti-Fascist war against aggression will continue to oppress the people. Therefore after the realization of international peace, the struggle between the anti-Fascist masses of the people and the remnant forces of the Fascists, and between democracy and anti-democracy will continue to occupy a major part of the world. A most widespread people's victory can only be the outcome of a long period of energetic forces to overcome the remnant Fascist forces and the anti-democratic forces. To attain this is certainly not very quick or very easy, but it will nevertheless certainly come. The victory of the anti-Fascist war—the just World War II—has opened the road to victory for the people's struggle in the post-war period, and it is only after such a victory that a stable and lasting peace can be guaranteed. This is the bright future lying before the people of the world.'

I hope all readers will carefully read these words of Comrade Mao Tze-tung several times. This will be helpful to a comprehension of the basic questions concerning the present international situation.

II. Two Basic Points

These words of Comrade Mao Tze-tung bring out two basic points :

(1) Victory in the anti-Fascist war has opened the way to progress for democratic forces in all nations. The extent of progress of these democratic forces will be incomparably greater than after the first world war. The attack by the anti-democratic forces on the peoples of all nations must of necessity come. But the democratic forces will in the necessity of things be able to overcome the anti-democratic forces, will secure their own victory and win a firm and lasting international peace. These are the two necessities: (1) that the anti-democratic forces will of necessity attack and (2) that the democratic forces will of necessity be victorious.

Thus, all erroneous pessimistic contentions are swept clean away. These pessimistic contentions are : alleging that the extent of the progress of the democratic forces after World War II is smaller than that after World War I ; allegations about the 'super colossal' reactionary strength of American imperialism and Chiang Kai-shek and about how they will oppress the people of China and the whole world till they will be unable to draw breath ; allegation that World War III is inevitable or will soon arrive ; that a firm and lasting peace cannot be attained, etc. All these points of view are obviously erroneous. The reason for committing those errors have been misled by the temporary and outside appearance of might of international and internal reactionary forces or been blinded by reactionary propaganda thereby under-estimating the strength of the people.

(2) The struggle between the forces of democracy and anti-democracy will cover a greater part of the world. That is to say, in the world there is a Socialist Soviet Union in which there have long been no anti-democratic forces and therefore there is no internal struggle between democracy and anti-democracy. Other places in the world besides the Soviet Union—that is the whole of the capitalist world—are filled with struggle between democracy and anti-democracy. Thus, following World War II, the actual dominant political contradiction in the world between democratic and anti-democratic forces is within the capitalist world and not between the capitalist world and the Soviet Union and also not between the

Soviet Union and the United States. Speaking more concretely, the present dominant contradictions in the world are contradictions between the American people and the American reactionaries, the Anglo-American contradictions and the Sino-American contradictions.

Thus, the propaganda of the reactionaries in China and abroad is thoroughly confuted so that no good-hearted people will be misled by such propaganda. Such demagogic propaganda is : that the actual dominant political contradiction in the present world is between capitalist and socialist countries, that the Soviet-American contradictions are dominant and the Anglo-American and Sino-American contradictions are secondary ; the socialist and capitalist countries cannot peacefully co-operate, the Soviet-American war is inevitable, etc.

We will elucidate below : 1. Who are anti-democratic forces ? What is their present and will be their future ? 2. Who are demo-cratic forces ? What is their present and will be their future ?

III. World Reactionaries, Their Smokescreen and Their Real Activities

After World War II, the American imperialists took the place of Fascist Germany, Italy and Japan, becoming a fortress of the world reactionary forces. So-called reactionary forces are precisely the American imperialists with addition of reactionaries in various countries (China's Chiang Kai-shek, Great Britain's Churchill, France's De Gaulle, etc.) and other Fascist remnants (Spain's Franco Government, Japan's Yoshida Cabinet, Germany's von Papen and Schacht, etc.). The reactionaries of all countries and the Fascist remnants have now all become traitors directly or indirectly supported and protected by the American imperialists selling out the people of all countries.

The American war-time industrial production has more than doubled in comparison with pre-war figures. During the war, American monopoly capital underwent tremendous development. At the same time, a batch of war-lords arose in America. After the conclusion of the war, this batch of monopoly capitalists and mili-tarists, this bloc of an extremely small handful of fanatical aggressors, advocated a policy of imperialist aggression to expand markets, wrest away markets, colonies and semi-colonies of other capitalist countries, primarily oppressing the great colonial imperialist count-ries England and France and oppressing China, while at the same time exercising a sole domination over Japan and Latin America. The American imperialists are carrying out this aggression under slogans of 'open door policy and equal opportunity', etc. to be in an overwhelming position to drive others away and monopolize the market. In addition to all this, the American imperialists are undertaking large-scale military preparations against all capitalist countries, colonies, and semi-colonial countries, under all sorts of pretexts. Their military bases are spread over many countries, outside the Soviet Union. The American imperialists have through 'peaceful' means occupied many 'Pearl Harbours' in various countries, saying on the other hand that this is to 'prevent another Pearl Harbour'.

In February and March of 1946, the world reactionaries schemed to incite a war against the Soviet Union. This was characterized by the reactionary speech of Churchill. This speech has aroused great vigilance in the people, as it should. But Churchill's agitation has met with the opposition of the people of the whole world. The attempt of the reactionaries has suffered a bitter defeat.

The 'anti-Soviet war' propaganda launched by Churchill was regarded as a treasure and inherited by the American imperialists. Why do the American imperialists love this kind of propaganda? Their purpose is not to launch an anti-Soviet war at present, but to use it as a smokescreen in order to carry out their large-scale aggressive actions abroad and oppression of the American people at home.

What is the meaning of the 'anti-Sovietism'? Hitler's 'anti-Sovietism' meant enslaving the German people and invading the whole of Europe. Fascist Japan's 'anti-Sovietism' meant oppressing the Japanese people and aggressing against countries on both sides of the Pacific. The American reactionaries' 'anti-Sovietism' at present only means enslaving the American people and world domination.

But the anti-Soviet slogan of the American reactionaries at present differs from that of the former Fascist Germany and Japan. Germany is close to the Soviet Union. In addition to other conditions, Fascist Germany was able to attack the latter. Japan is also near the Soviet Union. Owing to the fact that its strength was weaker than Fascist Germany, Fascist Japan could only attack China and the Pacific and was defeated before it had time to invade the Soviet Union. The United States is far away from the Soviet Union with a large area lying between. In this neutral area, there are capitalist countries, colonial and semi-colonial countries of three continents, Europe, Asia, and Africa. In addition to other conditions, it is very difficult for the United States to attack the Soviet Union : therefore the actual meaning of the 'anti-Soviet' slogan of America in the post-war period is only to oppress the American people and invade through 'peaceful' means all countries besides the Soviet Union.

Certainly there is a contradiction between the American monopoly capital and war-lords on the one side and the Socialist Soviet Union on the other. It is a contradiction between the new and old worlds, one of the world's basic contradictions. The social and political system of the Soviet Union is much stronger than American capitalism. The Soviet Union is the defender of world peace. Ambition and graft of the American and world reactionaries are impossible of realization as long as the Soviet Union exists; therefore the American and world reactionaries hate the Soviet Union, and they certainly will persist in an anti-Soviet struggle. But anti-Soviet propaganda is one thing and anti-Soviet war is another. We cannot say that the American imperialists do not want to attack the Soviet Union ; but the American imperialists cannot attack the Soviet Union before they have succeeded in suppressing and putting under their control the American people and all capitalist, colonial and semi-colonial countries. To oppress and put under their control these countries is impossible. Therefore, the contradiction between the United States and Soviet Union, though it is one of the basic contradictions, is not an imminent one, not a dominant one in the present political situation. This has been proved by the development of events during the past 16 months. The actual policy of the American imperialists is to attack through 'peaceful' means the American people and oppress all capitalist, colonial and semi-colonial countries. However, the American imperialists will keep under cover these activities in which they are actually engaged. The American imperialists have no way to attack the Soviet Union, yet they are talking loudly about the anti-Soviet war. Obviously the slogan is only a smokescreen.

Why do the American imperialists use this smokescreen ? Why should we expose this smokescreen ? The purpose of the American imperialists in smokescreening their activities is to divert the attention of the American people, the broad masses of all capitalist countries besides America and all colonial and semi-colonial countries so that they will be off guard against attacks by the American imperialists. With the unpreparedness of the American people and the other countries, the American imperialists can more easily fascistize their own country and turn other countries into American colonies and dependencies. If we fail to expose this smokescreen of American imperialism or fail to pay due attention to this important work, we shall more or less be lured into the trap of the American imperialists or be a mouthpiece speaking for the American imperialists, the common enemy. Therefore, we should not be fooled by the smokescreen of the reactionaries and lose our own judgement, bewildered by such demagogic propaganda as : 'The dominant contradiction in the present world is between capitalist and socialist countries', 'World War III is inevitable', etc. The only road to follow and the only duty for each and everyone in the democratic camp to fulfil is to expose the reactionaries' smokescreen and to call the people in America, in all capitalist, colonial and semi-colonial countries to fight for their own existence and to resist the attacks and aggressions of the American imperialists, their real enemies.

IV. *World Democratic Strength*

Standing against the world reactionaries—the imperialists of America and their running dogs in various countries—is world democratic might.

Besides the Soviet Union, which is the main pillar, the world democratic forces are made up of three sections : the broad masses of the American people, the broad masses of the people of all capitalist countries besides America, and the broad masses of the people of all colonial and semi-colonial countries. In terms of class make-up, they include everyone from workers and farmers right up to patriotic elements and advocates of peace among the bourgeoisie.

The American people made heroic contributions during the anti-Fascist war. The object of their self-sacrificing struggle was the winning of world peace and democracy and a happy life for themselves. After the conclusion of the war, however, the American people were faced with the following situation : After the defeat of foreign reactionaries loomed domestic reactionaries. They were precisely those monopoly capitalists who fattened on speculation and ill-gotten riches during the war. In the field of domestic policy this batch of monopoly capitalists and their reactionary spokesmen in the government raise prices of goods to press down living standards of the people, crack down on strikes in order to cancel people's liberties, encourage anti-Sovietism to divert the attention of the American people so that they will be off guard against attacks by the monopoly capitalists. In the field of foreign policy, the American reactionaries do not call themselves 'isolationists', but rather 'internationalists'. But these 'internationalists', however, are international aggressionists and not democratic international co-operationists. These reactionary elements have their men in both American Democratic and Republican Parties. The world aggression of these reactionaries has seriously spoiled the reputation of America, ruined international friendship and is brewing a danger of war.

This is why the American people, including enlightened members of the American bourgeoisie represented by Wallace, will certainly rise for a determined struggle with the reactionaries.

Capitalist countries outside of America, principally England and France, suffered great wounds from war and compared to America they are second or third class countries. They are objects of aggression by American imperialism. The law of uneven development of capitalism forces them resolutely to resist American oppression.

These capitalist countries are now struggling for economic recovery from the wounds of war and are at the same time in the following situation : On the one hand is the democratic movement of the people of their own country, and the demand for independence and autonomy on the part of colonies and semi-colonial countries and on the other is the savage aggression of the American imperialism. The line being taken by reactionaries like Churchill and de Gaulle within these countries is to rely on America to oppose the democratic movement of the people of their own country and the independence movement of the peoples of colonies and semi-colonies. The price paid for this reactionary line is that it inevitably leads these countries sinking to the position of American dependencies. The people in these capitalist countries have another line : winning democratic and social reform for their own country and getting colonial and semi-colonial people's independence and autonomy and co-operation with the Soviet Union, in order to resist the aggression of American imperialism and maintain national independence. Beyond all shadow of doubt, the people's line will be victorious. This line will obtain the endorsement of all classes of people including enlightened members of the bourgeoisie. On the other hand, the line of the reactionaries must certainly fail, because it will meet with the opposition of the whole nation.

Take the most important among those capitalist countries—Great Britain, for instance. In the post-war period, she is exerting her efforts to effect economic recovery. Her exports are gradually rising and this is something about which the American imperialist elements are not happy. American imperialism schemes to break the sterling bloc by exploiting the need of England for loans and in the name of so-called 'defence against the Soviet Union's attacks' wants England to enter into a military alliance with her. These are all serious preparatory steps for swallowing up England. England's far-flung dependencies and colonies—Canada, South (Africa), Australia, the Atlantic Islands, the Middle East, Palestine and Arabia, Egypt and the Mediterranean and finally India, Burma and elsewhere —are all scenes of American imperialistic attacks on England under the American imperialist policy of world domination. In certain places, these clashes have already become or are brewing up armed struggles. In the future, the possibility exists of America's inciting aggressive wars against other capitalist countries (first of all Great Britain).

The Attlee-Bevin Cabinet which continues the Conservative Party's foreign policy in Great Britain has done many evil deeds in concert with American imperialism and on many questions has expressed a mutual sympathy and understanding or a common action with American imperialism. The policy of American imperialism, however, cannot but force the English people gradually into consciousness. The gradual increase of votes in the British Lower House against Bevin's foreign policy is a proof of this. In the circumstances of the daily growing consciousness of the British people, it will be very difficult for Great Britain to continue her present foreign policy and the time for her to change her foreign policy is already not distant.

Thus it is with England and it will be even more so with France. In the circumstances of the daily growing consciousness of the French people, France certainly will not follow the road of American imperialists.

The American imperialistic policy of aggression on all capitalist countries must of necessity arouse the opposition of these countries. After the Second World War, there are no grounds . . . for the so-called 'capitalist encirclements of the Soviet Union'. Just the contrary, because of the peaceful democratic international policies and policies of peaceful competition and friendly commerce with all countries on the part of the Soviet Union and because England, France and other countries must resist the American aggression, escape the blows of the economic crisis and furthermore restore their economies, these countries must co-operate and trade with the Soviet Union. So-called capitalist encirclement therefore does not exist.

The American policy with regard to all colonial and semi-colonial nations is to transform them into American colonies or dependencies. The American imperialistic policy towards China is a typical example. There is no difference in nature between the policy of American imperialism towards China and the policy of Japanese Fascists towards China, although there are differences in form. The venomous treachery of means employed by American imperialism however surpasses that of Japanese imperialism. After the defeat of Japanese imperialism, America supports Chiang Kai-shek and other reactionaries in oppressing the Chinese people. In Japan, it supports Yoshida and other reactionaries in oppressing the Japanese people, and helps them to revive the policy of aggression towards China. At the present time the reactionaries of both China and Japan are occupying the same position as running dogs of America, and the peoples of both China and Japan are in the same position bearing the oppression of American imperialism. The self-defence war now being waged by the Chinese people against Chiang Kai-shek and the American imperialists is, in its nature, a war for the motherland. It is an all-national war obtaining the full support of the entire nation. This kind of war for the motherland has been taking place in Indo-China, India, Iran, Greece etc. These wars are fought against American imperialism and its running dogs in various countries. They are directly or indirectly against American imperialism and for winning world peace and democracy.

The contradiction between American imperialism and the democratic forces in the capitalist world is not being slackened, but instead is growing and developing.

When the American economic crisis arrives, and the American imperialists, because of this, tighten up their attacks, these contradictions will become sharp. Such a period is not far off because the American economic crisis will arrive this year or next.

V.   United Front on World Scale

The world anti-democratic forces are the American imperialists and reactionaries in various countries. Since the world anti-democratic forces are in unison attacking the American people, the people of various capitalist countries, colonies and semi-colonial countries must also act in unison to form a world-wide united front against American imperialism and reactionaries in all countries. This world-wide united front, this colossal army comprising well over one billion people is precisely the world democratic might.

This world-wide united front cannot possibly be of any other character than that of a united front hunting for world peace and democracy and the independence of all nations against American imperialism and its running dogs in various countries. This united front will undoubtedly have the sympathy and moral support of the socialist Soviet Union.

This united front on a world scale will characterize a new page in world history : that is the history of the world from the end of the Second World War down to today when the stable and lasting peace of the world is ensured. The Chinese movement for independence, peace and democracy is an important part of this chapter of world history.

Within each capitalist country, colony and semi-colonial country, there will be an extremely broad united front as in China against the American imperialists and the reactionaries within each country.

The immediate cardinal task before the peoples and democratic forces of all countries is a struggle for the realization of this world-wide united front and a united front within each country.

VI.   Relative Strength of Forces

Facts in more than one year following the victory in the anti-Fascist war prove that the rate of world progress is very fast, and some events have developed faster than we had expected. The scope of development of democratic forces in all countries of the world is far greater than that after World War I.

The progress of people in the capitalist world during the past year and more is manifested in : (1) Firm establishment of new democratic regimes in various countries of eastern and southern Europe; (2) Progress by leaps and bounds of the peoples of England and France; (3) The flourishing development of the struggles of the peoples of colonies and semi-colonial countries with China at their head for independence and autonomy; (4) The rapid Leftward trend of the peoples of Germany, Italy and Japan; (5) The high tide of the American strike movement and the occurrence of the Wallace incident (the Wallace incident expresses a split among the American bourgeoisie, just as the British Labour Party's opposition in England expressed a split among the British bourgeoisie) ; (6) A broad development of democratic forces in all countries of South America.

The scope and speed of the progress of people and the development of democratic forces in the capitalist world is really startling.

The international position of the most progressive country in the world—the socialist Soviet Union—has risen greatly. At present she is devoting all her strength to the peaceful constructive work of a new Five Year Plan. The completion of her first year's industrial production plan one month ahead of its schedule shows that it is entirely possible to complete and over-fulfil this new plan for construction. The struggle of the Soviet Union in the realm of small nations achieved great victories in the recent Foreign Ministers' conferences and the United Nations Assembly. A plot of American and British reactionaries to isolate the Soviet Union following Churchill's reactionary utterances of March last year has been smashed. Victories of the Soviet Union in economic construction and in foreign policy will greatly influence the history of world development, and will be beneficial to peoples of all countries.

The world reactionary forces are outwardly strong, but hollow inside. Moreover, they are becoming daily more isolated. American imperialism reaches the highest peak of capitalist development, but precisely because of this, it is weaker than capitalism in any earlier period. The higher they climb, the harder they fall—the American economic crisis which will arrive this year or next cannot but be turbulent in its nature. The reactionary foreign and domestic policies of the American imperialists will necessarily lead, and have led, to the opposition of the broadest masses of people both within and without the country. This will daily result in the masses turning against them and their allies deserting them. All running dogs of the American imperialists in various countries, as for example, China's Chiang Kai-shek, cannot but become traitors, and in their countries meet with the opposition of the entire nation. Therefore they cannot but rapidly isolate themselves, turned against by the masses and deserted by their allies. It is thus with China's Chiang Kai-shek and with reactionaries of all countries. The reactionary forces will collapse in the long run. They really appear very ferocious for a time, and can even frighten the feeble-minded people out of their will, so that they express pessimism and disappointment, lose their self-confidence, and even give in and surrender to reactionaries. But the broad masses of people and all men of strong will cannot be frightened away. The people in the course of their own practical experience will recognize not only the reactionary nature of the reactionaries, but also their feebleness. They will recognize that attacks of the reactionaries on the people can be smashed.

To sum up : world progress, the successes of the Soviet Union, and the American crisis are three factors of decisive significance in the history of the future development of the world.

VII.   Road to Victory

The present time is still a period when world reaction can be cocky, baring its fangs and extending its talons. This is primarily because the struggles of the peoples in the various countries have not entered a higher stage and at the same time this is also because the American economic crisis has not yet arrived. But even in this kind of period, the reactionary forces have already revealed that they are hollow within and outwardly strong. When the struggles of the peoples of all countries reach a higher development and the American economic crisis has broken out, that will be the time when the grand arrogance of the reactionaries will collapse. This is already not far distant. Before the arrival of this time, the people of each country will meet with difficulties, and in individual countries and regions, may even meet with very serious difficulties. Difficulties of this kind, however, can and must be conquered. The present task is for everyone to exert all efforts and to overcome these difficulties.

Following the development of the three factors—world progress, Soviet successes and the American crisis—the democratic forces will become even stronger and the relative strength of the democratic and anti-democratic forces will become more beneficial to the people. But it is not to be imagined that the reactionary forces will voluntarily abdicate to the democratic forces. Therefore before we have attained what comrade Mao Tse-tung calls the 'broadest victory of the people' and the 'ensurance of stable and enduring peace', there is still a long and tortuous struggle ahead. The Chinese Communists and the Chinese people will fear no difficulties. They will fight on till the complete victory of the democratic cause and the winning of the peace and independence of their nation. We have the strongest confidence in this brilliant future, but the world bourgeoisie on the other hand have completely lost confidence in their future. The terrorism whipped up by the anti-democratic forces in various countries after the war against the forces of the people, their terror at the strength of the Soviet Union, their fanatical oppression of the peoples, their horror of the truth, their complete reliance on lies for a living—these all are manifestations of their complete loss of confidence. It is certainly not accidental that all newspapers of the Chinese bourgeoisie express an unprecedented pessimism and disappointment with regard to their future.

In general, everything has changed after the Second World War, and is still continuing to change. How strong the people have become—how conscious, how organized, determined, and full of confidence ! How maniacally savage the reactionaries have become —outwardly strong yet inwardly feeble, turned against by the masses and deserted by their allies, devoid of all confidence in their future ! It may be forecast categorically that the face of China and the world will be vastly different after three to five more years. All comrades of our party and all people of China must resolutely fight for a new China and a new world.

United States Relations with China, pp. 710-19.

26   25 *December* 1947

MAO TZE-TUNG'S REPORT ON 'THE PRESENT
SITUATION AND OUR TASKS' TO THE CENTRAL
COMMITTEE OF THE COMMUNIST PARTY

[*Note.*—This is the fifth important document which Mao Tze-tung has published since 1937. The first was 'On Protracted War' (1938) being an analysis of the nature of China's war against Japan. The second 'On A New State' (1938) discusses the stalemate during the development of the war against Japan. The third, 'New Democracy' (1939) gives the broad outline for the future development of China ; the fourth 'On Coalition Government' (1945) explains the nature of China's prospective democratic coalition government.]

A. A Turning-Point in History

The revolutionary war of the Chinese people has now reached a turning-point. That is, the Chinese People's Liberation Army has repelled the attacks of the millions of reactionary troops of Chiang Kai-shek, running dog of America ; and has enabled itself to go over to the offensive. As far back as the first year of the war, from July 1946 to June 1947, the People's Liberation Army had repelled Chiang Kai-shek's offensives on several battle fronts, forcing him over to the defensive. And since the first quarter of the second year of war, between July and September 1947, the People's Liberation Army has gone over to the offensive on a nation-wide scale, and smashed Chiang Kai-shek's counter-revolutionary plans of continuing to head the war toward the Liberated Areas for the purpose of thorough destruction of the Liberated Areas. At present, the war is already not waged mainly in the Liberated Areas but in Kuomintang controlled areas : the main forces of the People's Liberation Army have already fought into Kuomintang controlled areas. The Chinese People's Liberation Army in this land of China has reversed the counter-revolutionary wheels of American imperialism and the Chiang Kai-shek gang of brigands on to the road to ruin ; they have pushed forward their own revolutionary wheels along the road to victory.

This is a turning-point in history. It is the turning-point from growth to extermination in the twenty years' counter-revolutionary rule of Chiang Kai-shek. It is the turning-point from growth to extermination in more than one hundred years' rule of imperialism in China.

This is a great event. This event is great in character because it occurs in a country having a population of 450,000,000, and once it has taken place, it will of necessity go toward nation-wide victory. This event is furthermore great in character because it occurs in the eastern part of the world in which is a population totalling more than one billion (half of mankind) suffering under the oppression of imperialism ; the passing over of the Chinese people's war of Liberation from the defensive to the offensive cannot but bring about jubilation and encouragement among these oppressed nations. At the same time, it is also a kind of aid to the oppressed peoples now struggling in the various countries of Europe and the Americas.

B. 'We must defeat Chiang Kai-shek'

From the very day on which Chiang Kai-shek launched the counter-revolutionary war, we said that we not only must, but moreover can, defeat Chiang Kai-shek. We must defeat Chiang Kai-shek, because the war launched by him is a counter-revolutionary war directed by American imperialism against the independence of the Chinese nation and the liberation of the Chinese people.

The tasks of the Chinese people, after the conclusion of World War II and the overthrow of Japanese imperialism, were to effect new democratic reforms politically, as well as economically and culturally, to realize the unity and independence of the nation and to change from an agricultural country into an industrial country. But precisely at this time, after the victorious conclusion of World War II, American imperialism and its running dogs in various countries have replaced German and Japanese imperialism and their running dogs, and organized a reactionary camp against the Soviet Union and the new democratic countries of Europe, against the workers' movement in the capitalist countries, against the national movement in the colonies ; and against the liberation of the Chinese people. At such a time the Chinese reactionary clique headed by Chiang Kai-shek acted as the running dog of American imperialism, exactly like the running dog of Japanese imperialism, Wang Ching-wei. They sold out China to America, unleashed war, opposed the Chinese people and obstructed the advance of the cause of the Chinese people's liberation. Hence, at such a time as this, had we displayed weakness and yielded, had we not dared resolutely to arise to fight the counter-revolutionary war with revolutionary war, China would have become a world of darkness, and the future of our nation would have been sacrificed. The Chinese Communist Party led the Chinese People's Liberation Army in resolution, waging a patriotic, just, revolutionary war against the offensive of Chiang Kai-shek. Basing its belief on the science of Marxism-Leninism, the Chinese Communist Party clearly estimated the international and domestic situation, and knew that all the attacks of domestic and foreign reactionaries not only must, but moreover could be defeated. At the time when the skies seemed to be dark, we pointed out that this was but a temporary phenomenon ; the tempest would soon be over, the light of dawn was just ahead.

At the time when Chiang Kai-shek's gang of brigands launched a nation-wide counter-revolutionary war in July 1946, they considered that only 3 to 6 months were required in which to defeat the People's Liberation Army. They considered that they had 2,000,000 regular army troops, more than 1,000,000 irregular troops and more than 1,000,000 personnel and troops of rear area military organizations—a total military strength of more than 4,000,000 men ; they had already utilized time to complete preparations for the offensive ; they again controlled the big cities ; they held a population of more than 300,000,000 ; they had taken over all the equipment of the 1,000,000 troops of the Japanese army invading China ;

they had obtained the huge military and financial aid of the United States Government. Furthermore, they considered that the Chinese People's Liberation Army had already fought itself weary in the course of the eight years of anti-Japanese war, and was far behind the KMT army in numbers and equipment ; the Chinese liberated areas still only had a population of a little over 100,000,000, the reactionary forces of feudalism in most of these areas had not yet been eradicated ; the land reform was still not universal and thorough ; the rear of the People's Liberation Army was not yet consolidated. On the basis of all these, the Chiang Kai-shek gang, heedless of the Chinese people's yearning for peace, once and for all tore up the Truce Agreement signed between the Communist and Kuomintang parties in January 1946, and the Resolutions of the Political Consultative Conference of various parties and groups, and launched an adventurous war. At that time, we said that our enemy's superiority in military strength was only a temporary phenomenon, a factor playing only a temporary role ; the aid of American imperialism was likewise a factor playing only a temporary role ; while the anti-popular nature of Chiang Kai-shek's war, and the support or opposition of the people are factors playing a constant role ; and in these respects, the People's Liberation Army held superiority. The war of the People's Liberation Army is of a patriotic, just, and revolutionary nature which must of necessity obtain the support of the people throughout the country. This is the political basis for victory over Chiang Kai-shek. The experience of eighteen months of war fully bears out our judgement.

C.   Principal Methods by which the People's Liberation Army defeats Chiang

Seventeen months of combat (July 1946 to November 1947—December not yet included) destroyed a total of 1,690,000 of Chiang Kai-shek's regular and irregular troops, of which 640,000 were killed or wounded and 1,050,000 were taken prisoner. Our troops were thus enabled to repel the offensives of Chiang Kai-shek, preserve the basic regions of the Liberated Areas and go over to the offensive. Militarily speaking, we were able to do this because we carried out a correct strategic line. Our military principles are :

  (1) First strike scattered and isolated enemies, and later strike concentrated, powerful enemies.

  (2) First take small and middle-sized towns and cities and the broad countryside, and later take big cities.

  (3) The annihilation of enemy manpower, and not the holding or taking of cities and places, is the major objective. The holding or taking of cities and places is the result of the annihilation of enemy

manpower, which often has to be repeated many times before they can be finally held or taken.

(4) In every battle to concentrate an absolutely superior force (double, triple, quadruple and sometimes even five or six times those of the enemy), to encircle the enemy on all sides, and strive for their annihilation with none escaping from the net. Under specific conditions, adopt the method of dealing the enemy smashing blows, that is, concentrating all forces to strike the enemy's centre and one or both of the enemy's flanks, aiming at the destruction of a part of the enemy and the routing of another part so that our troops can swiftly transfer forces to annihilate other enemy groups. Avoid battles of attrition in which the gains are insufficient to make up for the losses or in which the gains simply balance the losses. Thus we are in an inferior position taken as a whole (numerically speaking). But our absolute superiority in every section and in every specific campaign guarantees the victory of each campaign. As time goes by, we shall become superior, taken as a whole, until the enemy is totally destroyed.

(5) Fight no unprepared engagements, fight no engagement in which there is no assurance of victory. It is necessary to work hard for the preparation of every engagement ; and for assurance of victory based on the relative conditions between ourselves and the enemy.

(6) Promote and exemplify valour in combat, fear no sacrifice nor fatigue nor continuous actions (that is, to continue fighting several battles in a short period without rest).

(7) Strive hard to annihilate the enemy while in movement. At the same time, pay close attention to the tactics of attacking positions to wrest strongpoints and cities from the enemy.

(8) With regard to the question of storming cities, resolutely wrest all enemy strongpoints and cities which are weakly defended. At favourable opportunities wrest from the enemy all strongpoints and cities which are defended to a medium degree and where circumstances permit. Wait until conditions mature and then wrest all enemy strongpoints and cities which are powerfully defended.

(9) Replenish ourselves by the capture of all enemy arms and most of his personnel. The source of men and materials for our army is mainly at the front.

(10) Be skilled at utilizing the intervals between two campaigns for rest, regrouping and the training of troops. The period of rest and regrouping should not in general be too long. As far as possible do not let the enemy have breathing space.

All the above are the principal methods by which the People's Liberation Army defeats Chiang Kai-shek. These methods were forged by the People's Liberation Army in the course of prolonged warfare with domestic and foreign enemies, and are entirely suitable to our present conditions. The Chiang Kai-shek gang of brigands and the military personnel of American imperialism in China are well aware of these military methods of ours. Chiang Kai-shek has many times called together his generals and field grade officers for training, issuing to them for study our military books and documents obtained in battle, and attempting to seek counter-measures. The American military personnel suggest this and that strategy and tactics to Chiang Kai-shek, for destroying the People's Liberation Army, directly train troops for Chiang Kai-shek, and supply him with military equipment. But none of these efforts can save the Chiang Kai-shek gang of brigands from defeat. This is because our strategy and tactics are founded on the basis of a people's war, and no anti-popular army can utilize our strategy and tactics. The establishment of strong and powerful revolutionary political work of the People's Liberation Army based on a people's war and on the objectives of the solidarity between the Army and the people, the solidarity of commanders and fighters, and the disintegration of the army—this is a vital factor for victory over the enemy.

When we dodged the mortal blows of the superior enemy, trans-ferring our military forces to seek the destruction of the enemy in movement and abandoning many, many cities on our own initiative, our enemy was jubilant. They considered that this was their victory and our defeat. They went dizzy over the so-called successes of a moment. On the second day of Kalgan's occupation Chiang Kai-shek ordered the convening of his reactionary National Assembly, as if his reactionary rule would henceforth be as secure as the Tai Moun-tain. [Editor's note : Taishan, one of China's five famous mountains.] The American imperialists were also cutting joyous capers, as if their wild schemes of converting China into an American colony could henceforth be carried out without hindrance. But, as time went by, Chiang Kai-shek and his American masters changed their tune. Now, this is the time when all domestic and foreign enemies are dominated by their pessimistic sentiments. They heave great sighs, loudly crying their crisis, and not even a trace of joy is to be seen.

In the course of eighteen months, most of Chiang Kai-shek's high-ranking frontline commanders have been dismissed or replaced because of their military defeats. Among them are Chengchow's Liu Chih, Hsuchow's Hsueh Yueh, North Kiangsu's Wu Chi-wei, South Shantung's Tang En-po, North Honan's Wang Chung-lien, Mukden's Tu Yu-ming and Hsiung Shih-hui, Peiping's Sun Lien-chung and others. Chiang Kai-shek's Chief of the General Staff, Chen Cheng,

empowered with the direction of overall operations, was also deprived
of this power of command, and demoted to commander on a single
battle front—Manchuria. But during the period in which Chiang
Kai-shek himself replaced Chen Cheng as overall commander, there
developed the situation in which Chiang's armies passed over from
the offensive to the defensive and the People's Liberation Army
passed over from the defensive to the offensive. Chiang Kai-shek's
reactionary clique and their American masters should now be aware
of their own mistakes. They regarded all the efforts of the Chinese
Communist Party for a long period after the Japanese surrender,
in striving for peace and opposing civil war, and representing the
yearnings of the Chinese people, as expressions of cowardice and
feebleness. They over-estimated their own strength, under-estimated
revolutionary strength, adventurously unleashed war ; and thereby
fell into the trap they themselves had laid. The strategic calculations
of the enemy have thoroughly miscarried.

D.   Satisfy demands of poor Peasants and unite middle Peasants

At present, the rear areas of the People's Liberation Army are
much more consolidated than they were eighteen months ago. That
is the outcome of our Party's firmly siding with the peasants in
reforming the agrarian system. During the anti-Japanese war, for
the sake of establishing an anti-Japanese united front with the
Kuomintang and uniting all people who at the time were still capable
of resisting Japan, our party on its own initiative changed from the
policy before the anti-Japanese war of confiscating landlords' lands
and distributing them to the peasants, to that of reducing rents and
interest—this was entirely necessary.

After the Japanese surrender, the peasants urgently demanded
land and we therefore made a timely decision to change the agrarian
policy of reducing rents and interest to one of confiscating the lands
of the landlord class and distributing them to the peasants. The
directive issued by our Party's Central Committee on 4 May 1946
expressed this change. In September 1947, our party convened a
national agrarian conference, worked out the basic programme on
Chinese agrarian law, and immediately carried it out universally
throughout the various areas. This step not only affirmed the line
of last year's 4 May directive, but also made clear-cut rectifications
of certain unthoroughness (the landlords obtaining more land and
properties of rich peasants being left untouched in principle). The
Basic Programme on Chinese Agrarian Law stipulates that under the
principle of eliminating the agrarian system of feudal and semi-feudal
exploitation and carrying out the agrarian system of land to the
tillers, the land shall be equally distributed according to population.

This is the most thorough method for eliminating the feudal system, and is entirely in conformity with the demands of the broad masses of Chinese peasants. For the sake of resolutely and thoroughly carrying out agrarian reform, not only peasant unions of the broadest mass character, and their elected committees, comprising farm labourers, poor peasants and middle peasants, must be organized in the villages, but also, and first of all, poor peasants leagues, and their elected committees, comprising the masses of poor peasants and farm labourers, must be organized in the villages. These shall be the legal organs for carrying out agrarian reform, and the poor peasants league should become the backbone leading all rural struggles. Our line is to rely on poor peasants and solidly unite with middle peasants to destroy the feudal and semi-feudal exploitation system of the landlord class and old-type rich peasants. The land and properties which should be distributed to landlords and rich peasants shall not exceed those distributed to the peasant masses. But neither should the ultra-Left, erroneous policy carried out between 1931 and 1934, the so-called 'distribute no land to landlords, and poor land to the rich peasants' be repeated. Although the proportion of land-lords and rich peasants in the village population may be greater or smaller in various places, generally speaking they make up only approximately 8 per cent (reckoned in families), but the land they hold, generally speaking, makes up 70 to 80 per cent of all land. Therefore, the object which our agrarian reform opposes is a very small number of people, whereas the number of people (families) in the villages who can and should participate in the agrarian reform united front make up as much as over 90 per cent.

Two basic principles must be noted here : firstly it is necessary to satisfy the demands of the poor peasants and farm labourers—this is the most basic task of agrarian reform. Secondly it is necessary to resolutely unite the middle peasants and not to injure the basic principles, and the tasks of our agrarian reform will surely be triumphantly completed. In accordance with the principle of equal distribution, the surplus land and a portion of the properties of old-type rich peasants should be taken for distribution because China's rich peasants in general have a heavy feudal and semi-feudal exploiting nature—most rich peasants at the same time collect land rents and engage in usury, and their conditions of hiring labour are semi-feudal. Also because the land they hold is very great in quantity and very good in quality, the demands of the poor peasants and farm labourers cannot be satisfied if equal distribution is not carried out. But, in accordance with the stipulations of the Basic Programme on Chinese Agrarian Law, there should in general be differentiation between the treatment of rich peasants and landlords.

In the course of agrarian reform, the middle peasants express
their approval of equal distribution of land because equal distribution does not harm the middle peasants. In the equal distribution,
the land of a portion of the middle peasants remains unchanged, the
land of another portion increases. Only a portion of well-to-do middle
peasants have a small quantity of surplus land, and they are willing
to hand it over for equal distribution—this is because after equal
distribution their land tax burden is lighter. Nevertheless, in the
carrying out of equal distribution in the various areas, it is still
necessary to heed the opinions of the middle peasants ; if they do
not agree, concessions should be made to them. In the confiscation
or distribution of the land and properties of the feudal classes,
attention should be paid to the needs of certain middle peasants.
In the demarcation of class composition, care must be taken not to
assign those who are really middle peasants erroneously to the rich
peasant category. Active elements among the middle peasants must
be absorbed into peasant union committees and the government and
their work. With regard to the burden of land taxation and support
of the war, just and equitable principles should be adopted. All these
are the concrete policies that must be adopted by our Party in
carrying out this strategic task of solidly uniting the middle peasants.

The entire Party must understand that the thorough reform of the
agrarian system is the basic task of the present stage of the Chinese
revolution. If we can universally and thoroughly solve the agrarian
question, we shall have obtained the most basic condition required
for conquering all enemies.

E.   Reorganize and purify the Party Ranks

For the sake of resolutely and thoroughly carrying out agrarian
reform and consolidating the rear areas of the People's Liberation
Army, it is necessary to reorganize and purify the ranks of the party.
The movement for the reformation of ideology and style of work
within our Party during the period of the anti-Japanese war in
general attained success. This success lay, in the main, with the fact
that our Party's leading organs as well as many cadres have gone a
step further in their grasp of such a basic orientation as the integration of the universal truth of Marxism-Leninism with the concrete
practice of the Chinese revolution. In this respect, our party has
taken a great stride forward in comparison with the several historical
periods prior to the anti-Japanese war. However, the question of
impure composition and working style of the Party's local organizations, and especially of the Party's primary rural organizations,
was solved. During the eleven years from 1937 to 1947, our Party
organization developed from several tens of thousands of Party

members to 2,700,000 Party members—this is a huge leap forward.
It has made our Party an unprecedentedly powerful Party. It
provided us with the possibilities of defeating Japanese imperialism
and repelling the offensives of Chiang Kai-shek, and leading the
liberated areas of more than 100,000,000 population and a People's
Liberation Army 2,000,000 strong. But along with this also came
defects. That is, many landlord, rich peasant, and lumpen-proletarian
elements took this opportunity to slip into our Party. They domi-
nate many party, government and mass organizations in the rural
areas; took them over, bully and oppress the people, and distort the
Party's policies, causing these organizations to become alienated
from the masses of the people, preventing agrarian reform from being
thorough. Such serious conditions place before us the task of reorganizing and purifying the ranks of the Party. If this task is not solved,
we cannot make progress in the rural areas. The Party's national
agrarian conference thoroughly discussed this question, and
stipulated appropriate steps and methods. These steps and methods
are now being resolutely carried out in the various areas along with
the equal distribution of land. Among them, the first in importance
is the unfolding of criticism and self-criticism within the Party,
thoroughly to expose erroneous thinking and serious phenomena
deviating from the Party's line in the organization of various areas.
All party comrades must realize that the solution of this question of
impurities within the Party, reorganizing and purifying the ranks of
the Party, enabling the Party to completely stand on the same
direction with the broadest labouring masses and lead them forward,
is a decisive link in solving the agrarian questions and supporting
the prolonged war.

F. Economic Structure of New China

(1) State Economy ; (2) Agricultural Economy Developing from
individual towards Collective.

Confiscate the land of the feudal classes and put it under the
ownership of the peasants ; confiscate the monopoly capital headed
by Chiang Kai-shek, T. V. Soong, H. H. Kung, and Chen Li-fu and
put it under the ownership of the New Democratic State ; protect
national industry and commerce. These are the three great economic
platforms of the New Democratic Revolution. The four families—
Chiang, Soong, Kung and Chen—during their twenty years in power
have amassed enormous capital worth 10 to 20 billion American
dollars, and monopolized the economic pulse of the entire country. This
monopoly capital, merged with state power, becomes state monopoly
capitalism. This monopoly capitalism intimately merged with foreign
imperialism and the domestic landlord class and old-type rich

peasants, becomes compradore-feudal, state-monopoly capitalism. This is the economic foundation of Chiang Kai-shek's reactionary régime. This state-monopoly capitalism not only oppresses workers and peasants, but also oppresses the petty-bourgeoisie and injures the middle bourgeoisie. This state-monopoly capitalism reached its highest peak during the anti-Japanese war and after the Japanese surrender ; it prepared full material conditions for the new democratic revolution. This capital is popularly called bureaucratic capital in China. This bourgeoisie is called bureaucratic bourgeoisie, that is, China's big-bourgeoisie. Apart from doing away with the special privileges of imperialism in China the object of the new democratic revolution within the country is to eliminate the exploitation and oppression of the landlord class and the bureaucratic bourgeoisie (big-bourgeoisie), transform compradore-feudal relations of production, and liberate all the fettered productive forces. The petty-bourgeoisie and middle bourgeoisie oppressed and injured by these classes and their state power, although they too are bourgeoisie, may, however, participate in the New Democratic Revolution or maintain neutrality. They have no connexions or comparatively fewer connexions with imperialism ; they are the real national bourgeoisie. Wherever the state power of new democracy extends, these classes must be firmly and unhesitantly protected. Among the upper petty-bourgeoisie and middle bourgeoisie in the areas ruled by Chiang Kai-shek, there is a portion with reactionary political tendencies, small in number, the Rightest elements of these classes. They disseminate illusions for American imperialism and Chiang Kai-shek's reactionary bloc and oppose the people's democratic revolution. As long as their reactionary tendencies can still influence the masses, we should carry on a work of exposure among the masses who receive their influence, strike at their political influence among the masses to liberate the masses from their influence. But political blows are one thing, and economic extermination is another. If we confuse these two things, we shall commit errors. The objects which the New Democratic Revolution is to eliminate are only feudalism and monopoly capitalism, only the landlord class and the bureaucratic bourgeoisie (big-bourgeoisie), not capitalism in general and not the petty-bourgeoisie and the middle bourgeoisie. Owing to the backwardness of China's economy, it will still be necessary to permit the existence for a long period of the capitalist economy represented by the broad petty-bourgeoisie and the middle bourgeoisie, even after the nation-wide victory of the revolution. Furthermore in accordance with the division of labour in national economy, the development of a section among them beneficial to the national economy will still be necessary ; they will still be an indispensable part of the entire national economy. The petty-bourgeoisie mentioned here refers to the small-scale industrial and commercial capitalists who hire workers and shop employees. But besides this, there are the broad independent, small, industrial and commercial business men who do not hire workers or shop employees. With regard to these small industrial and commercial business men, it goes without saying that they should be firmly protected. After the nation-wide victory of the revolution, owing to the fact that the new democratic state will have in its hands the enormous state capital which controls the economic pulse of the entire country, taken over from the bureaucratic bourgeoisie, and will also have in its hands the agricultural economy emancipated from the feudal system, although for quite a long time it will basically still be scattered and individual, nevertheless it can be guided step by step to develop in the direction of cooperation in the future. The existence and development of small and middle capitalist elements are, under these conditions, not at all dangerous. The same applies to the new rich peasant economy which will necessarily come into being in the rural areas after the agrarian revolution.

The adoption of ultra-Left, erroneous policies toward petty-bourgeoisie and middle bourgeoisie economic elements as our party did in the period from 1931 to 1934—'excessively high working conditions, excessively high income tax rates; infringing on industrial and commercial elements in agrarian reform; not taking as our own objectives the development of production, the flourishing of economy, nor taking into account both public and private interests and benefits to both labour and capital, but taking as our objectives short-sighted, unilateral so-called welfare of the toilers'—absolutely must not be permitted to recur. If this kind of mistake is repeated, it will necessarily injure the interests of the labouring masses and of the New Democratic State. There is a provision in the Basic Programme on Agrarian Law: 'The property and legal operation of industrial and commercial business men should be protected from infringement.' The industrial and commercial business men mentioned here refer to all independent, small industrial and commercial business men, and all small and middle capitalist elements.

To sum up, the economic structure of new China is, (1) state economy—this is the leading element; (2) agricultural economy developing step by step from an individual towards a collective one; (3) the economy of independent small industrial and commercial business men, and the economy of small and middle private capital —these are the entire national economy of new democracy. The guiding principle of the national economy of new democracy, for its part, must closely pursue the general objective of developing production, a flourishing economy, taking into account both public and private interests and benefits to both labour and capital. All principles, policies and methods which deviate from these general objectives are erroneous.

G.   United Front Enlarged

The People's Liberation Army issued a manifesto in October 1947, in which it was stated : 'Unite the workers, peasants, soldiers, students and commercial elements, all oppressed classes, all people's organizations, all democratic parties and groups, all national minorities, overseas Chinese everywhere and other patriotic elements—unite to organize a national united front to strike down the dictatorial government of Chiang Kai-shek and establish a democratic coalition government.' This is the most basic political platform of the People's Liberation Army as well as of the Chinese Communist Party. Regarded on the surface, our revolutionary national united front in this period appears to have shrunk in comparison with that during the anti-Japanese war. But in reality, it is only in the present period, it is only after Chiang Kai-shek sold out the national interests to American imperialism and launched an anti-popular nation-wide internal war, and it is only after the crimes of American imperialism and Chiang Kai-shek's reactionary ruling bloc had been completely exposed before the Chinese people that our national united front really enlarged. During the anti-Japanese war, Chiang Kai-shek and the Kuomintang had not completely lost prestige among the Chinese people, they still had many deceptive functions. It is different now. All their deceptions have been laid bare by their own deeds. They have no masses whatsoever, and they are already completely isolated. Contrary to the Kuomintang, the Chinese Communist Party has not only obtained the confidence of the broadest masses of the people in the Liberated Areas, but has also obtained the support of the broad masses of the people in the Kuomintang controlled areas and in the Kuomintang controlled big cities. If in 1946 there was still a section of people among the intelligentsia of the upper petty-bourgeoisie and middle bourgeoisie under Chiang Kai-shek's rule who still cherished ideas of a so-called 'third road', these ideas have now become bankrupt.

Owing to our Party's adoption of a thorough agrarian policy, our Party has been enabled to obtain the loyal support of masses of peasants much broader than during the anti-Japanese war. Owing to the aggression of American imperialism, the oppression of Chiang Kai-shek, and our Party's correct line of resolutely protecting the interests of the masses, our party has obtained the sympathy of the broad masses of the working class, peasant classes, petty-bourgeoisie and middle bourgeoisie in the areas under Chiang Kai-shek's rule. These masses unceasingly raise high the struggle against American imperialism and Chiang Kai-shek's reactionary government because they suffer from hunger, because they are politically oppressed and because Chiang Kai-shek's anti-popular civil war has snatched away all of the people's roads to life ; their basic slogans are anti-hunger, anti-oppression, anti-civil war and anti-American intervention in China's domestic affairs. Before the anti-Japanese war, during the anti-Japanese war and even for a period after the Japanese surrender, such an extent was never reached. Therefore, we say that our new democratic revolutionary united front is now broader and also more consolidated than at any period in agrarian policy and urban policy, and is moreover closely connected with such a general political situation as the victories of the People's Liberation Army, Chiang Kai-shek's going over from the offensive to the defensive, the People's Liberation Army's going over from the defensive to the offensive and the entering of the Chinese revolution into a new period of upsurge. The people have now seen that the extinction of Chiang Kai-shek's rule is already inevitable, and they therefore place their hopes on the Chinese Communist Party and the People's Liberation Army— this is a very natural reason.

Without the broadest united front, comprising the overwhelming majority of the entire national population, the victory of the Chinese New Democratic Revolution is impossible. But this is not all, this united front must also be under the firm leadership of the Chinese Communist Party. Without the firm leadership of the Chinese Communist Party, no revolutionary united front can be victorious. In 1927 when the war of the Northern Expedition reached its high tide, the capitulationists in our Party's leading organs voluntarily abandoned leadership of the masses of peasants, petty-bourgeoisie and middle bourgeoisie, and especially abandoned leadership over the armed forces, causing the revolution of the time to meet with defeat. During the anti-Japanese war, our Party opposed a kind of thought analogous to this capitulationist thought, that is, yielding to the Kuomintang's anti-popular policies, trusting the Kuomintang more than the masses, not daring to give free rein to the setting of the struggle in motion, not daring to enlarge Liberated Areas and the People's Armies in Japanese occupied areas, presenting the leadership of the anti-Japanese war to the Kuomintang. Our Party carried on a resolute struggle against this kind of feeble, incompetent, decadent thinking which violated the principles of Marxism-Leninism ; and resolutely carried out the political line of 'developing progressive forces, winning over middle-of-the-road forces, and isolating diehard forces',

and resolutely enlarged the Liberated Areas and the People's Liberation Army. This not only guaranteed that our Party could conquer
Japanese imperialism during the period of Japanese aggression;
but also that guaranteed our Party could with no losses turn over
smoothly to the pathway of opposing Chiang Kai-shek's counter-
revolutionary war with a people's revolutionary war when Chiang
Kai-shek waged a counter-revolutionary war after the Japanese
surrender; and within a short period of time win great victories.
All Party comrades must bear these historic lessons well in mind.

H. The Light of Dawn is just before Us

In 1946 when the Chiang Kai-shek reactionary bloc launched a
nation-wide, anti-popular internal war, they dared to be adventurous
not only because they relied on their own superior military strength,
but also principally because they relied on American imperialism
which they believed to be extraordinarily powerful and matchless
throughout the world, holding the atomic bomb in its hands. They
believed that on the one hand American imperialism could succour
them with a steady stream of military and financial necessities;
and on the other hand they wildly imagined the so-called 'necessity of
war between the United States and the Soviet Union' and the so-called
'necessary outbreak of a World War III'. Such reliance on American
imperialism is a common characteristic of reactionary forces in
various countries throughout the world following the conclusion
of World War II. This fact reflects the seriousness of the blow dealt
to world capitalism by World War II, the feebleness of the reactionary forces in the various countries and their psychological
panic and loss of confidence; it reflects the powerful might of the
revolutionary forces of the whole world which causes the reactionaries
of various countries to feel that there is no way out except to rely
on the aid of American imperialism. But in reality, is American
imperialism after World War II as powerful as Chiang Kai-shek and
the reactionaries of the various countries imagine? Can it really pour
a steady stream from America to succour Chiang Kai-shek and the
reactionaries of the various countries? Not in the least. The economic
strength of American imperialism which grew during World War II
has met with an unstable and daily shrinking domestic and international market. Further shrinking of this market will lead to the
outbreak of economic crisis.

American war prosperity is merely a momentary phenomenon.
Its strength is only superficial and temporary. Crisis, like a volcano,
is daily menacing American imperialism; American imperialism is
sitting right on this volcano. This situation forced American imperialist elements to establish a plan for enslaving the world, to plunge

like wild beasts into Europe, Asia and other places, muster the reactionary forces of various countries—these dregs spat out by the people—to organize the imperialist anti-democratic front against all democratic forces headed by the Soviet Union and prepare war, scheming at some remote time in the future to unleash World War III and defeat the democratic forces. This is a wild plan. The democratic forces of the whole world must, and entirely can, defeat this plan. The strength of the world anti-imperialist camp exceeds that of the imperialist camp. The superiority is with us, not with the enemy. The anti-imperialist camp headed by the Soviet Union has already been formed.

With no crisis, on the rise and cherished by the broad masses of the people of the whole world, the strength of the Socialist Soviet Union now already exceeds that of imperialist America, seriously menaced by crisis, on the decline and opposed by the broad masses of the people of the whole world. The various new democratic countries of Europe are consolidating themselves internally and uniting with one another. The anti-imperialist forces of the people of various European capitalist countries headed by France and Italy are growing. Within the United States exist people's democratic forces daily growing stronger. The peoples of Latin America are not at all slaves subservient to America. A mighty national liberation movement has arisen throughout all Asia. All forces of the anti-imperialist camp are uniting and developing forward. The Communist Parties of nine European countries have organized an information bureau and published a summons to battle, calling on the people of the whole world to arise in opposition to imperialist plans for enslavement. This summons to battle has inspired the oppressed peoples of the whole world, pointed out to them their direction of struggle, and consolidated their confidence in victory. In the face of this summons to battle, the reactionaries of the whole world are in confusion and consternation. All anti-imperialist forces of the various Eastern countries should also unite to oppose the oppression of imperialism and the reactionaries within each country, taking as the objective of their struggle the liberation of the more than a billion oppressed people of the east. We should hold our destinies in our own hands. We should clear away all weak and incompetent thinking within our ranks. All viewpoints which over-estimate the strength of the enemy and under-estimate the strength of the people are erroneous. Together with the democratic forces of the whole world, we need only exert our efforts, and we can surely defeat the imperialist's plans for enslavement, block a third world war so that it cannot take place, overthrow the oppression of all reactionaries and win victory of eternal peace for mankind. We are clearly aware of the fact that there will still be all kinds of obstructions and difficulties in our path of advance; we should prepare to cope with the greatest degree of resistance and struggle on the part of all foreign and domestic enemies. Only if we are able to grasp the science of Marxism-Leninism, have faith in the masses, stand closely together with the masses and lead them forward, are we entirely capable of surmounting any obstacle and conquering any difficulty and our strength is matchless. This is the historic era in which the capitalism and imperialism of the whole world are moving towards their doom, in which the socialism and democracy of the whole world are moving towards victory. The light of dawn is just before us. We should put forth our efforts.

China Digest, Vol. III, No. 4, 13 January 1948, pp. 3-5, 14-18.

27   1 *May* 1948

MAY DAY SLOGANS OF THE COMMUNIST PARTY URGING EARLY CONVOCATION OF A PEOPLE'S REPRESENTATIVE ASSEMBLY

(1) May Day this year is the day of the march to nation-wide victory of the Chinese people. Salute to all commanders and fighters of the Chinese People's Liberation Army, liberators of the Chinese people ! Hail to the great victories of the People's Liberation Army on all fronts !

(2) May Day this year is the day of the march toward doom of the mortal enemy of the Chinese people.

(3) May Day this year is the day of the unprecedented maturing of the consciousness of the labouring people and all oppressed people of China. Hail to the solidarity of the working class of all liberated areas and of the entire country ! Hail to the victory and advance of the agrarian reform work of the peasants of all liberated areas and the entire country ! Hail to the advance of the movement for freedom of the youth and intelligentsia of the entire country !

(4) Labouring people of the entire country, unite ; ally with the intelligentsia, liberal bourgeoisie, all democratic parties and groups, social luminaries and other patriotic elements ; consolidate and expand the united front against imperialist, feudal and bureaucratic capitalist forces ; fight together to destroy KMT reactionaries and build a new China.

(5) All democratic parties and groups, people's organizations and social luminaries, speedily convene a political consultative

conference, discuss and carry out the convoking of a people's representative assembly to establish a democratic coalition government !

(6) Everything for victory at the front! Workers and employees of the liberated areas: furnish the front with more and better arms, ammunition and other war materials ! Working personnel in the rear line of the liberated areas: improve the organization of work in support of the front line !

(7) Salute to the workers and employees of the liberated areas exerting their efforts for the production of munitions ! Salute to the workers and employees of the liberated areas exerting their efforts for the restoration of industry, mining and communications ! Salute to the engineers and technicians of the liberated areas exerting their efforts for the improvement of technique ! Salute to all liberated areas' personnel exerting their efforts in rear service and institution work ! Salute to the labour heroes, meritorious servants of the people, and model workers of all branches of industry and service in all liberated areas !

(8) Workers, employees and economic personnel of the liberated areas, consistently and unswervingly support the labour movement and industrial policy of developing production, making the economy prosperous, taking into account both public and private interests and benefiting both labour and capital !

(9) Workers and employees of the liberated areas, strive to increase output, raise the quality and reduce the cost of industrial goods ! Furnish the markets with more and better necessities for the people's livelihood !

(10) Workers and employees of the liberated areas, promote a new attitude to labour, cherish your implement, save raw materials, abide by labour discipline, oppose all sluggish, wasteful and harmful conduct ; study technique and raise production !

(11) Workers and employees of the liberated areas, strengthen solidarity within the working class, strengthen the solidarity of workers and technicians, establish the master-workman-apprentice relationship of 'respect the master-workman and cherish the apprentice' !

(12) Workers and employees of private-operated enterprises in the liberated areas, establish with the capitalists a reasonable relationship of benefits to both labour and capital, and strive for the development of the national economy in common !

(13) Trade unions of the liberated areas, work together with the democratic government to guarantee a proper standard of living for workers and employees, establish workers' welfare undertakings and overcome the problems in the lives of working people !

(14) Workers and employees of the liberated areas and those of the areas controlled by Chiang Kai-shek, unite ; establish a united organization of the workers of the entire country ; fight for the liberation of the working class of the entire country !

(15) Salute to the workers and employees heroically fighting for survival and freedom in the areas controlled by Chiang Kai-shek ! Welcome the workers and employees from areas controlled by Chiang Kai-shek to come to the liberated areas and participate in industrial construction !

(16) Workers and employees in areas controlled by Chiang Kai-shek, support the liberation army with action, do not manufacture or transport munitions for the KMT reactionaries ! When the liberation army occupies a city, maintain civic order on your own initiative, protect public and private enterprises, do not permit destruction by Chiang Kai-shek's troops !

(17) Workers and employees in areas controlled by Chiang Kai-shek, ally with oppressed national industrialists and commercial elements, strike down the rule of bureaucratic capitalists, oppose the aggression of American imperialism !

(18) The working class and the whole people of the entire country, unite ; oppose the intervention of American imperialists in China's domestic affairs and their encroachment on China's sovereignty ; oppose the American imperialists fostering the revival of the forces of Japanese aggression !

(19) The working class of China and the working class of all countries, unite ; oppose American imperialist oppression of the national liberation movements, democratic movements, and trade union movements of Asia, Europe and the Americas !

(20) Salute to the working class of all countries of the world aiding the liberation war of the Chinese people and the Chinese trade union movement !

Salute to the working class of all countries refusing to transport and unload materials to aid Chiang Kai-shek, from American and other imperialists ! Salute to the working class and peoples of all countries resisting American imperialist aggression !

(21) Long live the unity of the labouring people and all oppressed people of China !

(22) Long live the victory of the Chinese People's Liberation War !

(23) Long live the liberation of the Chinese Nation !

China Digest, Vol. IV, No. 1, 18 May 1948, pp. 9-11.

JOINT STATEMENT OF THE DEMOCRATIC PARTY AND
OTHER NON-COMMUNIST LEADERS SUPPORTING THE
COMMUNIST CALL FOR A PEOPLE'S REPRESENTATIVE
ASSEMBLY (EXTRACTS)

[Two telegrams—one to all countrymen and one to Communist
Chairman Mao Tze-tung—were jointly sent on 5 May by various
democratic parties and individuals in response to the May Day
Slogans of the Communist Party. Signatories included Marshal Li
Chai-sum, Mme Liao Chung-kai (both of the Kuomintang Revolu-
tionary Committee), Shen Chun-ju, Chang Po-chun (both of the
Chinese Democratic League), Ma Hsu-lun, Wang Sao-au (both of
the Chinese Democracy Promotion Society), Peng Tse-min (the
Chinese Farmers and Workers' Democratic Party), Chen Chi-yiu
(the Chi Kung Tong Party), Li Chang-ta (the Chinese People's
National Salvation Group), General Tsai Ting-kai (Kuomintang
Democratic Promotion Association), Tan Ping-shan (San Min Chu I
Comrades Society), Kuo Mo-jo (non-partisan) and others. The
following are extracts from the messages—*Editor*.]

TO ALL NEWSPAPERS AND ORGANIZATIONS IN AND OUTSIDE THE
COUNTRY AND TO ALL FELLOW COUNTRYMEN

The betrayal of national sovereign rights by the Nanking reactionary régime is unprecedented in history. Its collusion with
the American imperialists in recent years induced surrender of
political, economic, military and other national interests. It hazarded
the multiparty Political Consultative Council and broke up the five
agreements arrived thereat, and therefore prolonged the civil war
which is causing great slaughter. Our nation is now none other than
a dependent of the United States of America, and our fellow countrymen are threatened with the danger of being victimized by a third
world war.

When thinking over this sad state of affairs, we read the fifth item
of the May Day Slogans promulgated by the Chinese Communist
Party, which says, 'All democratic parties and groups, people's
organizations and social luminaries, speedily convene a political
consultative conference, discuss and carry out the convoking of a
people's representative assembly to establish a democratic coalition
government !' This stands for the people's demands in the present
situation, and coincides with our intentions. This is important to
the future of our nation, and we have communicated our approval
to the Communists. We here urge that all people of the country

should promptly concentrate on this matter and discuss methods, in order to uproot reaction and realize democracy.

TO MR MAO TZE-TUNG, CHAIRMAN OF THE CHINESE COMMUNIST PARTY, AND ALL FELLOW COUNTRYMEN IN THE LIBERATED AREAS

The people are not deceived by the democratic camouflage of the Nanking reactionary régime. The march of the Liberation Army and the uprisings of armed people everywhere are heralding the people's victory. We have just read the fifth item of your May Day Slogans. We herein express our response and support to your call, and hope by its realization to meet our national renaissance.

China Digest, Vol. IV, No. 1, 18 May 1948, p. 11.

29   10 *June* 1948

DIRECTIVE OF THE NORTH-EAST BUREAU OF THE
CENTRAL COMMITTEE OF THE COMMUNIST PARTY ON
'HOW TO ADMINISTER NEWLY OCCUPIED CITIES'

(1) A short-term military administration is to be carried out in newly occupied cities. During the initial period after a city is taken, the military administration must be shouldered by the highest commanding organ of the forces storming the city. For this purpose, a military administrative committee including responsible members of the local party organization and government should take up full responsibility for protecting the newly occupied city. The duration of the military administration which is dependent on military conditions and conditions in the city shall be decided by a yet higher military commanding organ. When the city has on the whole returned to peace and order, military administration is to be declared ended, and all the authority administering the city is to be handed over to the municipal government, while a definite number of troops is to be assigned as the city's garrison force.

(2) The administrative military organ during the initial period, and the municipality and the city party committee that take over later, have full power to deal with all cases and criminals violating the urban policy and law. But they must maintain close contact with upper leading organs, the North-east Administrative Council and the North-east Bureau of the Chinese Communist Party's Central Committee, from which instructions must be obtained before settling all important matters, and reports made after their settlement.

(3) Troops storming a city and troops entering a city must observe the following regulations :

(*a*) Education on the party's urban policy and industrial and commercial policy must be widely carried out among military, government and rear service personnel and fighters. The forces assigned to storm a city should be educated before the fighting on taking great care of a city and on discipline upon entering a city to protect industry and commerce. A check must be made to see whether such education is widespread and deep.

(*b*) The force assigned to storm a city has only the duty of protecting industry and commerce in the city ; it has no power to confiscate and deal with them. A city-storming force has no right to confiscate or deal with Chiang Kai-shek's government-operated enterprises, banks, commercial stores, municipal organs, hospitals, schools, storehouses and private enterprises and commercial shops. It must send out necessary troops to protect them and prevent any unauthorized person from arbitrarily entering these premises and moving away machinery, materials and equipment during or after the fighting.

(*c*) Enemy personnel who may be taken prisoner by the city-storming force are limited to enemy armed forces and resisting personnel who bear arms ; criminals whom they may arrest are limited to enemy military spies, elements subverting economic and social order, and obvious important war criminals. No law-abiding enemy functionaries, personnel of economic and educational organs and policemen should be taken prisoner or arrested. They must be given duties and remain at their original posts under the orders of definite organs and personnel, to watch over their original organs, factories, storehouses, materials and documents. They must also continue to carry on necessary work, awaiting inventory and turning over. They must not slow down work, damage or sabotage.

(*d*) Materials that can be dealt with by a force assigned to storm a city are limited to ammunition, weapons and other war materials and supplies on the battlefields. But individual units have no right to handle military supplies of this category ; they must properly take care of them and send an inventory to the highest headquarters and political department of the city storming forces, who should report to general army headquarters for unified dealing. Rear service personnel can only follow the army and do supply work for their unit ; they are to be absolutely prohibited from over-stepping their own duties. Thus, all captured materials will be handed over to the responsible authorities (this is one of the three great disciplines of the People's Liberation Army) and make possible suitable and equitable distribution.

(*e*) After the fighting is over all troops of the city-storming force with the exception of a definite number of troops necessary to maintain order in the city should withdraw outside the city. Before withdrawal they should clearly hand over the factories, storehouses, banks and municipal organs they have watched. No troops are allowed to billet in factories, hospitals, schools and churches.

(*f*) Mete out reward and punishment. Those with merit in observing the industrial and commercial policy and urban policy should be rewarded. Those who violate these policies must be thoroughly taken to task, and dealt with according to the severity of their case, in accordance with law.

China Digest, Vol. IV, No. 5, 13 July 1948, pp. 6-7.

30   19 *August* 1948

THE ORGANIC OUTLINE OF THE NORTH CHINA PEOPLE'S GOVERNMENT, ADOPTED BY THE NORTH CHINA PROVISIONAL PEOPLE'S REPRESENTATIVE ASSEMBLY

In order to meet the needs arising from the recent developments in North China and the demands of the people, the North China Provisional Representative Assembly decides to establish the North China People's Government by amalgamation of the two border governments of Shansi-Chahar-Hopei and Shansi-Hopei-Shantung-Honan, and adopts the following organic outline of the North China People's Government.

Article 1. The North China People's Government shall be organized in accordance with the following organic outline.

Article 2. The North China People's Government shall have a Chairman, three Vice-Chairmen, and thirty-nine State Councillors. They shall compose the State Council.

Article 3. The State Councillors of the North China People's Government shall be elected by the present sessions of the North China Provisional People's Representative Assembly and its subsequent sessions. The Chairman and Vice-Chairmen of the State Council shall be elected by the State Councillors from among themselves.

Article 4. The North China People's Government shall exercise the governing powers in North China. It shall have power to promulgate laws and issue orders ; it shall formulate provisions and regulations in accordance with the administrative policy and other resolutions adopted by the North China Provisional People's Representative Assembly.

Article 5. The North China People's Government shall have the power to administer the following affairs decided by the State Council of the Government :

(*a*) Matters stipulated in Article 4.

(*b*) To execute resolutions adopted by the North China Provisional Representative Assembly and North China People's Representative Assembly.

(*c*) To organize man and material power to support the war.

(*d*) To elect the North China People's Representative Assembly and various levels of people's representative bodies.

(*e*) The demarcation of administrative districts, and organic provisions for various levels of people's government.

(*f*) Appointment and removal of heads of ministries, departments, commissions, general manager of the North China Bank and officials above the rank of Administrative Bureau Chief.

(*g*) Preliminary and final budget estimates of the whole area.

(*h*) Matters relating to production, reconstruction, finance, land, census, cultural activities, public security, judicial policy and programme of the whole area.

(*i*) Matters relating to the organization of the people's armed forces of the whole area.

(*j*) Other essential matters.

Article 6. The promulgation of resolutions adopted by the State Council shall be signed by the Chairman and Vice-Chairmen.

Article 7. The Chairman of the North China People's Government shall have the following powers :

(*a*) To summon the State Council of the North China People's Government to meet and to preside over it as Chairman.

(*b*) To direct, supervise and examine the execution of decisions of the North China Provisional People's Representative Assembly, and the State Council of the North China People's Government, by various levels of people's administrative organs.

(*c*) To administer routine and emergency matters of the North China People's Government, but matters affecting the State Council of the North China People's Government shall be presented for confirmation.

(*d*) - To represent the North China People's Government in outside relations.

Article 8. The Vice-Chairmen of the North China People's Government shall assist the Chairman in the execution of his duties stipulated in the above Article. In case the Chairman is unable to discharge his duties, the Vice-Chairmen shall act in his place.

Article 9.   The North China People's Government shall establish the following ministries, departments, court, bank and secretariat to which shall be entrusted the various duties under the supervision of the Chairman.

(1)   Ministry of Interior.
(2)   Ministry of Education.
(3)   Ministry of Finance.
(4)   Ministry of Industry and Commerce.
(5)   Ministry of Agriculture.
(6)   Ministry of Public Enterprises.
(7)   Ministry of Communications.
(8)   Ministry of Health.
(9)   Ministry of Public Security.
(10) Ministry of Justice.
(11) North China Financial and Economic Commission.
(12) North China Conservancy Commission.
(13) North China People's Court.
(14) North China People's Supervisory Department.
(15) Bank of North China.
(16) The Secretariat.

The above administrative organs may be enlarged, abolished or merged as it deems necessary for the performance of their functions.

Article 10.   The ministries shall each have a Minister; the commissions shall each have a Director; the People's Supervisory Department, a President; the North China People's Court, a President; the Bank of North China, a General Manager; the Secretariat, a Secretary-General.

As a principle, posts for ministers, presidents, directors, and general manager, shall be held concurrently by State Councillors of the North China People's Government. But the aforementioned posts may be filled by non-state councillors upon appointment by the North China People's Government at the instance of its Chairman. The various ministries, commissions, court, department, bank and secretariat may establish deputy posts to assist performance of their functions.

Article 11.   The North China Supervisory Department shall be the highest supervisory organ under which a People's Supervisory Council shall be established. It shall consist of the President of the Supervisory Department, and five to nine members appointed by the State Council of the North China People's Government. The People's Supervisory Council shall investigate, impeach and sentence public employees of all ranks in administrative and judicial organs, and public enterprises guilty of breaches of law, negligence of duty, act of embezzlement and wasting, and other offences detrimental

149

to the interests of the Government and the people. The People's Supervisory Council may receive petitions from the people against public employees guilty of the above offences.

The People's Supervisory Council, in the exercise of its power, may investigate public offices, and organs concerned. The offices and organs under investigation shall be obliged to accept investigation and provide necessary information.

Any decision of the People's Supervisory Council which involves verdicts requiring trial by court may be sent to the Court ; any decision which requires action from administrative and public organs may be referred to the offices concerned.

Article 12. The North China People's Court shall be the highest tribunal in North China area. But verdicts for important cases shall be reviewed by the Ministry of Justice. Cases involving death sentences shall be approved by the President of the Court and the execution shall be carried out by decree.

Article 13. All public announcements and directives which involve policy, programme, and important planning, shall be issued in the name of the Chairman and Vice-Chairmen.

Matters concerning specific duties or of a technical nature, may be announced under the signature of the Minister, President, Director or General Manager concerned.

Article 14. The regulations governing the organization of the various ministries, councils, departments, bank, and the secretariat shall be drawn by the North China People's Government.

Article 15. In order to carry out resolutions adopted by the North China Provisional People's Representative Assembly, the North China People's Representative Assembly, and the State Council of the North China People's Government, and to administer matters affecting the administration of various organs, the North China People's Government shall establish an Administrative Affairs Council. This Council shall consist of a chairman, vice-chairmen, ministers, presidents, directors, general manager of the Bank of North China, and the Secretary-General. The Chairman shall have the power of making the final decision.

Article 16. The power to amend and alter the present organic outline shall be exercised by the North China People's Representative Assembly.

Article 17. The present law shall come into force on the day of its adoption by the North China Provisional People's Representative Assembly.

China Digest, Vol. V, No. 3, 30 November 1948, pp. 8-9.

31   25 *April* 1949

EIGHT-POINT PROCLAMATION FOR THE PEOPLE'S LIBERATION ARMY

The KMT reactionaries have rejected the peace terms and insisted on pursuing their criminal war against the nation and the people. The people of the entire country are hoping that the People's Liberation Army will quickly exterminate the KMT reactionaries. We have ordered the People's Liberation Army to advance boldly, to wipe out all KMT reactionary troops daring to offer resistance, arrest all incorrigible war criminals, liberate the people of the entire country, safeguard the independence and integrity of the territory and sovereignty of China, and realize the true peace and democratic unity for which the people of the entire country crave.

We profoundly hope that people of all walks of life will render help to the People's Liberation Army wherever they advance. We hereby issue an eight-point proclamation which we shall observe jointly with the whole people.

(1) The lives and property of all people will be protected. It is hoped that all people, regardless of class, faith or profession, will maintain order and adopt a co-operative attitude towards the People's Liberation Army, while the People's Liberation Army will adopt a co-operative attitude towards people of all walks of life. If there are counter-revolutionary elements or other disruptive elements who take advantage of the situation to create disturbances, and to loot or destroy, they will be punished without fail.

(2) National industry, commerce, agriculture and pasturage will be protected. All privately operated factories, stores, banks, warehouses, vessels, wharves, farms, pastures etc. will be protected against any encroachment. It is hoped that workers and employees of all trades will continue production and that all business will operate as usual.

(3) Bureaucratic capital will be confiscated. All factories, stores, banks, warehouses, vessels, wharves, railroads, postal, telegraph, telephone, electric light, water utilities and agricultural and livestock farms etc. operated by the reactionary KMT Government and big bureaucratic elements will be taken over by the People's Government. If the above-mentioned involve private shares of national industrialists, business men or farmers, the ownership rights of the persons concerned will be recognized after investigation has established their claims. All personnel working in enterprises of bureaucratic capital before taking over by the People's Government must remain at their posts as usual. They must furthermore be responsible

for the protection of materials, machines, charts, accounts, files, etc., pending inventory and taking over. Those who have performed meritorious actions in protecting the above-mentioned will be rewarded. Those who sabotage and disrupt will be punished. Those willing to continue to serve after the People's Government has taken over will be employed in accordance with their capabilities so that they will not become displaced.

(4) All public and private schools, hospitals, cultural and educational institutions, athletic fields and all other public welfare enterprises will be protected. It is hoped that all personnel working in these institutions will remain at their posts as usual. The People's Liberation Army will protect them against any encroachment.

(5) Apart from incorrigible war criminals and counter-revolutionary elements with heinous crimes, the People's Liberation Army and People's Government will not capture, arrest or submit to indignities high and low ranking officials under the KMT central, provincial, municipal, county government of different levels; delegates of the National Assembly; members of the Legislative and Control Yuans; People's Political Council members; police personnel and heads of *Pao Chia* organizations in districts, townlets and villages unless they carry out armed resistance or engage in sabotage. The above-mentioned persons are enjoined to stay at their posts, obey the order of the People's Liberation Army and the People's Government, and take the responsibility for safeguarding the property and archives of the various institutions pending taking over and disposal. The People's Government will employ, according to their individual cases, those persons with any ability, provided they do not engage in counter-revolutionary activities and their personal record is not seriously besmeared. Punishment will without fail be meted out to those who take the opportunity to sabotage, steal, engage in graft, embezzle public funds, abscond with public property and archives or who refuse to hand over to the proper authorities.

(6) In order to ensure peace and security in urban and rural areas and to maintain public order, all stray soldiers should report to the People's Liberation Army or People's Government in that area. Those who voluntarily report and also hand over all their arms will have no action taken against them. Those who refuse to report or conceal their arms will be arrested and examined. Persons who harbour stray soldiers and fail to report them to the proper authorities will also receive due punishment.

(7) The feudal land ownership system in the rural areas is irrational, but it must be eliminated only after preparation and stage by stage. Generally speaking, reduction of rent and interest should be carried out first, and land distribution later. Moreover, the land

problem can only be really solved after the People's Liberation Army has arrived and work has been carried on for a comparatively long time. The masses of peasants should organize themselves, assist the People's Liberation Army to carry out all kinds of preliminary reform work, and at the same time exert their efforts to cultivate the land, maintain the present agricultural level and then to raise it step by step in order to improve the livelihood of the peasants and to supply the urban markets with grain for the population. Land and houses in the cities cannot be dealt with similarly to those in the rural areas.

(8)   The security of the lives and property of all foreign nationals will be protected. It is hoped that all foreign nationals will do their work as usual and preserve order. All foreign nationals must observe the laws and decrees of the People's Liberation Army and the People's Government. They must not engage in espionage activities or acts against the cause of the independence of the Chinese nation and of the people's liberation. They must not harbour Chinese war criminals, counter-revolutionary elements and other criminals. Otherwise, they will be dealt with according to the laws of the People's Liberation Army and the People's Government.

The discipline of the People's Liberation Army is strict. The People's Liberation Army practices fair trading, and is not allowed to take even so much as a needle or a piece of thread from the people.

It is hoped that all people will live and work in peace and security and will not be needlessly alarmed by listening to rumours.

(Signed)

MAO TZE-TUNG,
*Chairman of the Chinese People's
Revolutionary Military Committee*

CHU TEH,
*Commander-in-Chief of the Chinese
People's Liberation Army*

25 April 1949

China Digest, Vol. VI, No. 2, 3 May 1949, pp. 9 and 18.

VI   PEOPLE'S REPUBLIC OF CHINA

32   15 *June* 1949

MAO TZE-TUNG'S SPEECH AT THE PREPARATORY MEETING OF THE NEW POLITICAL CONSULTATIVE CONFERENCE AT PEKING

Fellow delegates,

The preparatory meeting of our New Political Consultative Conference opens today. The task of this meeting is to accomplish all preparatory work necessary for the swift convening of the New Political Consultative Conference through which a democratic coalition Government will be formed so as to lead the people throughout the country to clean up the remnant forces of the KMT reactionaries with all speed and to unify all China for carrying out, systematically and step by step, the political, economic, cultural and national defence reconstructions on a nation-wide scale. People throughout the country hope that we shall do this and we should do it.

The convening of the New Political Consultative Conference was proposed to the country by the Communist Party of China on 1 May 1948. Democratic parties and groups, people's organizations, and democratic personages of all circles throughout the country, national minorities in the country and overseas Chinese abroad promptly responded. The Communist Party of China, other democratic parties and groups, people's organizations and democratic personages of all circles throughout the country, national minorities in the country and overseas Chinese abroad all deem that the rule of imperialism, feudalism, bureaucratic capitalism and the KMT reactionary clique must be overthrown, a Political Consultative Conference embracing the representatives of democratic parties and groups, people's organizations, democratic personages of all circles, national minorities in the country and overseas Chinese abroad must be convened to announce the establishment of the People's Democratic Republic of China and elect a democratic coalition Government representing this Republic. Only thus can our great motherland free herself from her semi-colonial and semi-feudal fate and travel along the road of independence, freedom, peace, unity, strength and prosperity. This is the common political basis. It is the common political basis for the unified struggle of the Communist Party of China, other democratic parties and groups, people's organizations, democratic personages of all circles, national minorities in the country and overseas Chinese abroad. It is also the common political basis for the unified struggle of people throughout the country. This political basis is so firm that no divergent opinion has been raised by any conscientious democratic party or group, people's organization or democratic personage. They all hold that only such a course is the correct direction for solving all of China's problems.

People throughout the country supported the People's Liberation Army and won the war. This great people's liberation war has lasted three whole years since it began in July 1946. This war was launched by the KMT reactionaries with the help of foreign imperialism. The KMT reactionaries treacherously tore up the January 1946 Truce Agreement and the resolutions of the Political Consultative Conference and launched this civil war against the people. But within only three years they have been defeated by the heroic People's Liberation Army. Not long ago, the People's Liberation Army advanced bravely and crossed the Yangtze River after the peace plot of the KMT reactionaries was exposed. Nanking, capital of the KMT reactionaries, has been taken. Shanghai, Hangchow, Nanchang, Wuhan and Sian have also been liberated. The various field armies of the People's Liberation Army are advancing in the southern and north-western provinces in a great march never witnessed in the history of China. In three years, the People's Liberation Army has wiped out 5,590,000 reactionary KMT troops. Up to the present, KMT remnant forces including regular and irregular troops and military organizations and schools in the rear number only about one and a half million men. The clearing of these enemy remnants will still take some time, but it will not be long before they are cleaned up.

This is the victory of the people throughout the country and is also the victory of the peoples of the world. All except for the imperialists and reactionaries of various countries are jubilant over this great victory of the Chinese people. The struggle of the Chinese people against their enemies and the struggle of the peoples of the world against their enemies bear the same meaning. Together the people of China and peoples of the world witnessed the following fact : the imperialists directed the reactionaries in China to oppose the Chinese people brutally with counter-revolutionary war, the Chinese people victoriously struck down the reactionaries with revolutionary war.

At this point, I think it is necessary to call your attention to the fact that the imperialists and their running dogs, the Chinese reactionaries, will not take their defeat in this land of China lying down. They will still work in collusion with each other and use all possible means to oppose the Chinese people. They will, for example, send their lackeys to penetrate into China to carry out work of disintegration and disruption. This is inevitable and they will certainly not forget this work. They will, for instance, egg on the Chinese reactionaries, or may in addition even come out with their own forces, to blockade the seaports of China. They will do this if it is still possible for them to do so. Furthermore, if they choose to be adventurous, they may even send part of their armed forces to encroach on China's frontiers, a possibility which cannot be ruled out. We must fully take all this into account. Decidedly we must not, because of our victories, relax our vigilance towards the wild retaliatory plots of imperialist elements and their running dogs. Whoever relaxes his vigilance will be politically disarmed and thus lose his initiative. Under these circumstances, people throughout the country must unite, and smash firmly, thoroughly, cleanly and completely all the anti-popular conspiratorial schemes of the imperialists and their lackeys, the reactionaries in China. China must be independent, China must be liberated, the affairs of China must be decided on and dealt with by the Chinese people themselves and not an inkling of intervention by any imperialist country should be allowed.

The revolution of China is a revolution by the masses of the people of the entire nation. Except for the imperialists, feudalists, bureaucratic bourgeoisie, KMT reactionaries and their henchmen, everybody is our friend. We have a broad and consolidated revolutionary united front which is so broad that it includes the working class, peasant class, petty-bourgeoisie and national bourgeoisie, and which is so consolidated that it has the powerful will and inexhaustible capacity to vanquish all enemies and conquer all difficulties. We are now in an era in which the imperialist system is heading towards complete collapse. The imperialists are bogged down in an inescapable crisis, and no matter how they still want to continue to oppose the Chinese people, the Chinese people have the means to win final victory.

At the same time, we wish to declare to the whole world : we only oppose the imperialist system and its conspiratorial scheme against the Chinese people. We are willing to negotiate for the establishment of diplomatic relations with any foreign government on the basis of principles of equality, mutual benefits and mutual respecting of territorial sovereignty, provided it is willing to sever relations with the Chinese reactionaries and cease to help or work in collusion with them, and provided it adopts a real, and not hypocritical, attitude of amity towards the China of the people. The Chinese people is willing to carry out friendly co-operation with peoples of all countries in the world in restoring and developing international trading relations so as to favour the development of production and bringing about of a flourishing economy.

Fellow delegates, all conditions for convening the New Political Consultative Conference to form the democratic coalition Government have matured. The people throughout the country look forward eagerly to the convening of the conference and setting up of the Government. I believe that the work which we have begun can satisfy this hope and moreover it will not be long before this hope is satisfied.

Once the democratic coalition Government of China is formed, its major work will be : first, to clean up the remnants of the reactionary clique and suppress their disruptive activities ; secondly, to use all means and exert our utmost efforts in rehabilitating and developing the economic work of the people while at the same time rehabilitating and developing the people's cultural and educational work.

Once the destiny of China is in the hands of the people, the Chinese people will see a China rising like the sun from the East and shining with its brilliant rays and see her swiftly clearing away the dirt left behind by the reactionary Government, heal the scars of war and build up a new, strong and prosperous People's Democratic Republic of China which will be true to its name.

Long live the People's Democratic Republic of China !

Long live the Democratic Coalition Government !

Long live the great unity of people throughout the country !

China Digest, Vol. VI, No. 6, 28 June 1949, pp. 3-4.

33   29 *September* 1949

COMMON PROGRAMME OF THE CHINESE PEOPLE'S
POLITICAL CONSULTATIVE CONFERENCE (CPPCC)

Preamble

The great victories of the Chinese people's war of liberation and people's revolution have ended the era of the rule of imperialism, feudalism and bureaucratic capitalism in China. From the status of the oppressed, the Chinese people has become the master of a new society and a new state, and replaced the feudal, comprador, fascist, dictatorial Kuomintang reactionary rule with the republic of the people's democratic dictatorship. The Chinese people's dictatorship is the state power of the People's Democratic United Front of the Chinese working class, peasantry, petty-bourgeoisie, national bourgeoisie and patriotic democratic elements based on the alliance of workers and peasants and led by the working class. The Chinese People's Political Consultative Conference composed of the representatives of the Communist Party of China, all democratic parties and groups, people's organizations, all areas, People's Liberation Army, all national minorities, overseas Chinese and patriotic democratic elements is the form of organization of the Chinese people's democratic united front. The Chinese People's PCC, representing the will of the people throughout the country, proclaims the establishment of the People's Republic of China and organizes the people's own central government. The Chinese People's PCC unanimously agrees that the new democracy, namely the people's democracy, shall be the political foundation for national construction of the People's Republic of China. The Chinese People's PCC has also worked out the following Common Programme which should be observed in common by all units participating in the Chinese People's PCC, all levels of the people's government and people throughout the country.

I. General Principles

Article 1. The People's Republic of China is a state of New Democracy, that is, people's democracy. This republic carries out the people's democratic dictatorship led by the working class, based on the alliance of workers and peasants, and rallying all democratic classes and all nationalities in China. This republic opposes imperialism, feudalism and bureaucratic capitalism and strives for the independence, democracy, peace, unification, prosperity and strength of China.

Article 2. The Central People's Government of the People's Republic of China must undertake to wage the people's war of liberation to the very end, to liberate all the territory of China and accomplish the cause of unifying China.

Article 3. The People's Republic of China must abolish all prerogatives of imperialist countries in China, confiscate bureaucratic capital for ownership by the people's state ; systematically transform the feudal and semi-feudal land ownership system into the system of peasant land ownership ; protect the public property of the state and the property of co-operatives, protect the economic interests and private property of workers, peasants, petty bourgeoisie and national bourgeoisie ; develop the people's economy of New Democracy and steadily transform the country from an agricultural into an industrial country.

Article 4. The right of the people of the People's Republic of China to elect and be elected is prescribed by law.

Article 5. The people of the People's Republic of China shall have freedom of thought, speech, publication, assembly, association, correspondence, person, domicile, movement from one place to another, religious belief and the freedom of holding processions and demonstrations.

Article 6. The People's Republic of China abolishes the feudal system which holds women in bondage. Women shall enjoy equal rights with men in political, economic, cultural and educational and social life. Freedom of marriage for men and women shall be enforced.

Article 7. The People's Republic of China must suppress all counter-revolutionary activities, severely punish all Kuomintang counter-revolutionary war criminals and other obdurate, arch counter-revolutionary elements who collude with imperialism, commit treason to the Motherland and oppose the cause of people's democracy. Reactionary elements, feudal landlords, bureaucratic capitalists in general, must, according to law, also be deprived of their political rights within a necessary period after they have been disarmed and their special power abolished, but they shall at the same time be given a means of living and compelled to reform themselves through labour to become new men. If they continue their counter-revolutionary activities they shall be severely punished.

Article 8. It is the duty of every national of the People's Republic of China to defend the Motherland, to observe the laws, to maintain labour discipline, to protect public property, to perform public service and military service and pay taxes.

Article 9. All nationalities in the People's Republic of China have equal rights and duties.

Article 10. The armed forces of the People's Republic of China, that is, the People's Liberation Army, the people's public security forces and people's police, are armed forces belonging to the people. Their tasks are to defend the independence, integrity of territory and sovereignty of China and the revolutionary fruits and all legitimate rights and interests of the Chinese people. The Central People's Government of the People's Republic of China shall endeavour to consolidate and strengthen the people's armed forces to enable them to accomplish their tasks effectively.

Article 11. The People's Republic of China unites with all peace and freedom loving countries and peoples throughout the world, first of all the Soviet Union, all people's democracies and all oppressed nations, and stands in the camp for international peace and democracy to oppose jointly imperialist aggression and defend lasting world peace.

II. Organs of State Power

Article 12. The state power of the People's Republic of China belongs to the people. All levels of the people's congress and all levels of the people's government are the organs for exercising state power by the people. All levels of the people's congress shall be elected through universal suffrage by the people. All levels of the people's congress shall elect the respective levels of the people's government. The various levels of the people's government shall be the organs for exercising state power at their respective levels when their respective people's congresses are not in session. The All-China People's Congress is the supreme organ of state power. The Central People's Government shall be the supreme organ for exercising state power when the All-China People's Congress is not in session.

Article 13. The Chinese People's PCC is the form of organization of the people's democratic united front. It shall be composed of the representatives of the working class, the peasantry, revolutionary servicemen, intellectuals, the petty bourgeoisie, the national bourgeoisie, national minorities, overseas Chinese, and patriotic democratic elements.

Pending the convocation of the All-China People's Congress, to be elected through universal suffrage, the plenary session of the Chinese People's PCC shall exercise the functions and powers of the All-China People's Congress, enact the statute of the Central People's Government of the People's Republic of China, elect the Central People's Government Council of the People's Republic of China and vest it with the authority of exercising state power.

After the convocation of the All-China People's Congress elected through universal suffrage, the Chinese People's PCC shall submit proposals on fundamental policies relating to the construction work of the country, and other important measures, to the All-China People's Congress or to the Central People's Government.

Article 14. Military control shall be enforced in all places newly liberated by the People's Liberation Army, and the Kuomintang reactionary organs of state power shall be abolished. The Central People's Government or military and political organs at the fronts shall appoint personnel to organize military control Commissions and local people's governments to lead the people in establishing revolutionary order and suppressing counter-revolutionary activities and, when conditions permit, to convene conferences of the representatives of all circles.

Pending the convocation of the local people's congresses elected through universal suffrage, the local conferences of representatives of all circles shall gradually assume the functions of the local people's congresses.

The duration of military control shall be determined by the Central People's Government in accordance with the military and political conditions of the given locality.

In all places where military operations have ended, agrarian reform has been thoroughly carried out and people of all circles have been fully organized, elections through universal suffrage shall be held immediately to convene local people's congresses.

Article 15. All levels of organs of state power shall put into practice democratic centralism. Its main principles are : the people's congress is responsible and accountable to the people. The people's government council is responsible and accountable to the people's congress. Within the people's congress and the people's government council, the minority shall abide by the decisions of the majority. The appointment of the people's governments of various levels shall be confirmed by the people's government of the higher level. The people's government of the lower level shall obey the people's government of the higher level and all local people's governments throughout the country shall obey the Central People's Government.

Article 16. The jurisdiction of the Central People's Government and the local people's governments shall be defined in accordance with the nature of the various kinds of affairs and shall be prescribed by decrees of the Central People's Government Council so as to benefit both national unification and conform to the needs of local circumstances.

Article 17. All laws, decrees and judicial systems of the Kuomintang reactionary government oppressing the people are abolished and laws and decrees protecting the people shall be enacted and the people's judicial system shall be established.

Article 18. All state organs must enforce a revolutionary working style of honesty, simplicity and service to the people, must severely punish graft, forbid extravagance and oppose the bureaucratic working style of estrangement from the masses of the people.

Article 19. People's supervisory organs shall be set up in the people's governments at county and municipal level and above, to supervise the execution of duties by the various levels of state organs and public functionaries, and indict organs and functionaries who violate the law or are derelict in the performance of their duties. Individuals or people's organizations have the right to indict before the people's supervisory organs or judicial organs any state organ or any public functionary violating the law or derelict in performing their duties.

III. *Military System*

Article 20. The People's Republic of China shall build up a unified army, that is the People's Liberation Army and the people's public security forces, which shall be under the command of the People's Revolutionary Military Council of the Central People's

Government and which shall institute a unified command, unified system, unified formation and unified discipline.

Article 21. The People's Liberation Army and the people's public security forces shall, in accordance with the principle of unity between the officers and rank and file and unity between the army and the people, set up a political system of work and educate the commanders and fighters of these in a revolutionary and patriotic spirit.

Article 22. The People's Republic of China shall strengthen the modernized land force and establish an air force and a navy to consolidate national defence.

Article 23. The People's Republic of China shall enforce the system of people's militia to maintain local order, lay the foundation for national mobilization and prepare for the enforcement of an obligatory military service system at the appropriate moment.

Article 24. The armed forces of the People's Republic of China shall, during peace time, systematically take part in agricultural and industrial production to assist in national construction work provided this does not hinder military tasks.

Article 25. Dependents of revolutionary martyrs and revolutionary servicemen who suffer from privation shall receive preferential treatment from the state and from society. The People's Government shall appropriately provide the means of livelihood and resettlement for disabled servicemen and retired servicemen who have participated in the revolutionary war.

IV. Economic Policy

Article 26. The basic principle for economic construction of the People's Republic of China is to attain the goal of developing production and of creating a prosperous economy through the policies of taking into account both public and private interests, benefits to both labour and capital, mutual aid between city and countryside and interflow of goods at home and between China and countries abroad. The state shall co-ordinate and regulate state-owned economy, co-operative economy, individual economy of peasants and handicraftsmen, private capitalist economy and state capitalist economy in spheres of operation, supply of raw materials, markets, labour conditions, technical equipment, policies of public finance and trade etc., so that all components of the social economy can play their part and effect division of work and co-operate under the leadership of the state-owned economy to promote the development of the entire social economy.

Article 27. The agrarian reform is the essential condition for the development of the productive power and the industrialization of the country. In all areas where the agrarian reform has been carried out, the right of ownership over the land obtained by peasants shall be protected.

In areas where the agrarian reform has not yet been carried out, the peasant masses must be set in motion to organize peasant organizations and to realize the slogan 'land to the tiller' through such measures as the elimination of local bandits and despots, the reduction of rents and interest and the distribution of land.

Article 28.   State-owned economy is of a socialist nature. All enterprises vital to the economic life of the country and to the people's livelihood shall come under unified operation of the state. All state-owned resources and enterprises are the common property of all the people. They are the main material basis of the People's Republic for the development of production and the creation of a prosperous economy and are the leading forces of the entire social economy.

Article 29.   Co-operative economy is of a semi-socialist nature and is an important component of the entire people's economy. The People's Government shall foster its development and accord it preferential treatment.

Article 30.   The People's Government shall encourage the active operation of all private economic enterprises beneficial to national welfare and people's livelihood and shall foster their long term development.

Article 31.   The economy based on co-operation between state and private capital is of a state-capitalist nature. Whenever necessary and possible, private capital shall be encouraged to develop along the direction of state-capitalism, for example, towards joint operations with state-owned enterprises or in joint operations with the State or operation of state-owned enterprises and exploitation of state-owned enterprises and exploitation of the state-owned resources through the form of concessions.

Article 32.   The system of workers taking part in the administration of production shall, at present, be put into practice in state-owned enterprises, that is, factory administrative committees shall be set up under the leadership of the factory director. In privately operated enterprises, collective contracts should be signed by the employer and the trade union, representing the workers and employees in order to carry out the principle of benefits to both labour and capital. At present, an eight to ten-hour day shall in general be enforced in publicly and privately operated enterprises, but this may be dealt with at discretion under special circumstances. The People's Government shall fix the minimum wage according to the conditions in various places and trades. Labour insurance shall be gradually instituted. The special interests of juvenile and women workers shall be protected. Inspection of industries and mines shall be carried out to improve safety devices and sanitary facilities of the industries and mines.

Article 33. The Central People's Government shall as early as possible draw up a general plan for rehabilitating and developing the main branches of public and private economy of the entire country, determine the division of work and co-operation between the central and local governments in economic construction, and carry out unified co-ordination of the mutual relations between the economic departments of the central and local governments. Under the unified leadership of the Central People's Government, the various economic departments of the central and local governments should give full play to their creativeness and initiative.

Article 34. Agriculture, Forestry, Fishery and Stock-raising : In all areas where the agrarian reform has been thoroughly carried out, the People's Government shall take as its central task the organization of peasants and all labour power which can be employed in agriculture to develop agricultural production and by occupations, and shall guide the peasants step by step to organize various forms of mutual aid labour, and production co-operation according to the principle of free choice and mutual benefit. In newly-liberated areas, every step of the agrarian reform should be linked up with reviving and developing agricultural production. The People's Government should, in accordance with the plan of the state and needs of the people's livelihood, restore the output of grain, industrial raw materials and export goods to the pre-war production level and surpass this within the shortest possible time. Attention should be paid to building and repairing irrigation works, taking preventive measures against floods and drought, restoring and developing live-stock-raising, increasing the use of fertilizers, improving farm tools and seeds, taking preventive measures against pests and plant diseases, relieving the victims of natural calamities and systematically carrying out irrigation for land reclamation.

Forests shall be protected and afforestation shall be developed according to plan.

Fishing grounds along the seacoast shall be protected and the aquatic-products industry shall be developed.

Livestock-raising shall be protected and developed and preventive measures taken against plague.

Article 35. Industry : To lay down the foundation for the industrialization of the country, work shall be centred on the planned, systematic rehabilitation and development of heavy industry such as mining, steel and iron industries, and light industry, the machine building industry, the electrical and the main chemical industries. At the same time, the production of the textile industry and other industries beneficial to the national welfare and people's livelihood shall be restored and increased so as to meet with the daily consumption needs of the people.

Article 36. Communications : Railways and highways must be swiftly restored and transport facilities increased; rivers must be dredged and water-way transportation expanded; postal and telegraphic services must be improved and developed; various communication facilities must be built up and civil aviation inaugurated step by step according to plan.

Article 37. Commerce : All legitimate public and private trading shall be protected. Control of foreign trade shall be enforced and the policy of protecting trade shall be adopted. Domestic free trade shall be adopted under a unified economic plan of the state, but commercial speculations disturbing the market are strictly prohibited. The state-owned trading organs shall undertake to adjust supply and demand, stabilize commodity prices and foster the people's co-operatives. The People's Government shall adopt necessary measures to encourage the people to deposit their savings, to facilitate overseas remittance, and channelise the idle capital in society and the commercial capital not beneficial to the national welfare and the people's livelihood into industry and other productive undertakings.

Article 38. Co-operatives : The broad masses of the working people shall be encouraged and assisted to develop co-operatives according to the principle of voluntariness. Supply and marketing co-operatives, consumers co-operatives, credit co-operatives, producers co-operatives and transport co-operatives shall be organized in towns and villages and consumers co-operatives shall first be organized in factories, institutions and schools.

Article 39. Finance : Financial enterprises shall be strictly controlled by the state. The right of issuing currency belongs to the state. The circulation of foreign currencies within the country is forbidden. Buying and selling of foreign exchange, foreign currencies, gold and silver shall be handled by the state banks. Private financial enterprises operating within the law shall be subjected to state supervision and direction. Severe punishment shall be meted out to all who engage in financial speculation and undermining of the financial enterprises of the state.

Article 40. Public Finance : The system of budget and final account shall be instituted. The financial spheres of the central and local governments shall be defined. Retrenchment and economy shall be enforced. The balancing of the Budget shall be gradually attained and capital accumulated for the country's production.

The taxation policy of the state shall be based on the principle of ensuring supplies for the revolutionary war and taking into account the rehabilitation and development of production and the needs of national construction. The taxation system shall be simplified and just distribution of the burden effected.

V. *Cultural and Educational Policy*

Article 41. The culture and education of the People's Republic of China are new democratic, that is, national, scientific and popular. The main tasks of the cultural and educational work of the People's Government shall be the raising of the cultural level of the people, training of personnel for national construction work, liquidating of feudal, compradore, Fascist ideology and developing of the ideology of serving the people.

Article 42. Love for the fatherland and the people, love of labour, love of science and the care for public property shall be promoted as the public spirit of all nationals of the People's Republic of China.

Article 43. Efforts shall be made to develop the natural sciences to place them at the service of industrial, agricultural and national defence construction. Scientific discoveries and inventions shall be encouraged and rewarded and scientific knowledge shall be popularized.

Article 44. The application of a scientific historical viewpoint to the study and interpretation of history, economics, politics, culture and international affairs shall be promoted. Outstanding works of social science shall be encouraged and rewarded.

Article 45. Literature and the arts shall be promoted to serve the people, to awaken the political consciousness of the people, and to encourage the labour enthusiasm of the people. Outstanding works of literature and the arts shall be encouraged and rewarded. The people's drama and cinema shall be developed.

Article 46. The method of education of the People's Republic of China is the unity of theory and practice. The People's Government shall reform the old educational system, subject-matter and teaching methods systematically, according to plan.

Article 47. In order to meet the widespread needs of revolutionary work and national construction work, universal education shall be carried out, middle and higher education shall be strengthened, technical education shall be stressed, the education of workers during their spare time and education of cadres who are at their posts shall be strengthened, and revolutionary political education shall be accorded to young intellectuals and old-style intellectuals in a planned and systematic manner.

Article 48. National sports shall be promoted. Public health and medical work shall be extended and attention shall be paid to safeguarding the health of mothers, infants and children.

Article 49. Freedom of reporting true news shall be safeguarded. The utilization of the Press to slander, to undermine the interests of the state and the people and to provoke world war is prohibited. The people's broadcasting work and the people's publication work shall be developed and attention paid to publishing popular books and newspapers beneficial to the people.

VI. Policy Towards Nationalities

Article 50. All nationalities within the boundary of the People's Republic of China are equal. Unity and mutual help shall be effected among them to oppose imperialism and the public enemies within these nationalities so that the People's Republic of China will become a big family of fraternity and co-operation of all nationalities. 'Great Power nationalism' and chauvinism shall be opposed and acts of discrimination, oppression and splitting the unity of the various nationalities shall be prohibited.

Article 51. Regional autonomy shall be carried out in areas where national minorities are congregated, and autonomous organs of the various nationalities shall be set up according to their respective population and the size of the region. The various nationalities shall have an appropriate number of representatives in the local organs of state power in places where various nationalities live together and in the autonomous areas of national minorities.

Article 52. The nationalities within the boundary of the People's Republic of China have the right to join the People's Liberation Army and organize local people's public security forces in accordance with the unified military system of the state.

Article 53. All national minorities have the freedom of developing their dialects and languages, preserving or reforming their customs, habits and religious beliefs. The People's Government shall help the masses of the people of all national minorities to develop their political, economic, cultural and educational construction work.

VII. Foreign Policy

Article 54. The principles of the foreign policy of the People's Republic of China are the safeguarding of the independence, freedom and integrity of territory and sovereignty of the country, supporting of lasting international peace and friendly co-operation between the peoples of all countries, and opposition to the imperialist policy of aggression and war.

Article 55. The Central People's Government of the People's Republic of China shall examine the treaties and agreements concluded between the Kuomintang and foreign governments, and recognize, or abrogate, revise or renew them according to their respective contents.

Article 56. The Central People's Government of the People's Republic of China may negotiate and establish diplomatic relations on the basis of equality, mutual benefit and mutual respect for territory and sovereignty with foreign governments which sever relations with the Kuomintang reactionaries and adopt a friendly attitude towards the People's Republic of China.

Article 57. The People's Republic of China may restore and develop trading and commercial relations with foreign governments and people on the basis of equality and mutual benefit.

Article 58. The Central People's Government of the People's Republic of China shall do its utmost to protect the legitimate rights and interests of Chinese residing abroad.

Article 59. The People's Government of the People's Republic of China shall protect law-abiding nationals in China.

Article 60. The People's Republic of China shall accord the right of asylum to foreign nationals who seek refuge in China because they are oppressed by their own governments for supporting the people's interests and taking part in the struggle for peace and democracy.

The Common Programme and other Documents,
(Reprinted from *Labour Monthly*, December, 1949).

34   30 *September* 1949

DECLARATION BY THE CHINESE PEOPLE'S
POLITICAL CONSULTATIVE CONFERENCE

Fellow countrymen of the whole country,

The first plenary session of the Chinese People's PCC has victoriously accomplished its task.

This conference is composed of the delegates of all the political parties and groups, people's organizations, People's Liberation Army, various areas, various nationalities, overseas Chinese and patriotic democratic elements throughout the country. The conference represents the will of the people throughout the country and demonstrates their unprecedentedly great unity.

This great unity was achieved through protracted heroic struggle by the Chinese people and the People's Liberation Army under the leadership of the Chinese Communist Party after defeating the reactionary Kuomintang Government of Chiang Kai-shek which is aided by American imperialism. For a century and more, the advanced elements of the Chinese people, among whom were outstanding elements like the great revolutionary Sun Yat-sen who led the 1911 Revolution, had led the broad masses of the people to wage ceaseless and unswerving struggle to overthrow the oppression of imperialism and the Chinese reactionary government, and they have now attained their goal. As we are holding the conference, the Chinese people has defeated its enemy, changed the features of China and founded the People's Republic of China. We, four hundred and seventy-five million Chinese people, have now stood up and the future of our nation is boundlessly bright.

Under the leadership of the people's leader Chairman Mao Tzetung, our conference has, with one will and in accordance with the principles of New Democracy, drawn up the Statute of the Chinese People's PCC, the Statute of the Central People's Government of the People's Republic of China and the Common Programme of the Chinese People's PCC, decided that the capital of the People's Republic of China be located at Peking, chosen a red flag with five stars as the national flag of this republic, adopted the 'March of the Volunteers' as the present national anthem, adopted the calendar similar to that of most countries in the world, and elected the National Committee of the Chinese People's PCC and the Central People's Government Council of the People's Republic of China. From now on, a new era has opened in the history of China.

Fellow countrymen throughout the country, the founding of the People's Republic of China has been proclaimed and the Chinese people has its own Central Government. This Government will carry out people's democratic dictatorship within the boundary of China in accordance with the Common Programme. This Government will command the People's Liberation Army to wage the revolutionary war to the very end, exterminate the remnant enemy troops, liberate all territory of the country and fulfil the great cause of unifying China. This Government will lead the people throughout the country to surmount all difficulties, carry out large-scale economic and cultural construction, sweep away poverty and ignorance left behind by the old China, gradually improve the material life of the people and raise their cultural life. This Government will protect the people's interests and suppress all conspiratorial activities of counter-revolutionary elements. This Government will strengthen the people's army, navy and air force, consolidate national defence, protect the integrity of territory and sovereignty of China and oppose all aggression of imperialist countries. This Government will unite with all peace and freedom-loving countries, nations and people, first of all the Soviet Union and the new democratic countries, as allies to oppose jointly the imperialist plots for provoking war and strive for world lasting peace.

Fellow countrymen throughout the country, we should be further organized. We should organize the overwhelming majority of the people in China in the political, military, economic, cultural and other organizations, overcome the loose, disorganized state of the old China, and support the People's Government and the People's Liberation Army with the great collective power of the people's masses to build up the independent, democratic, peaceful, unified, prosperous and strong new China.

Eternal Glory to the people's heroes who fell in the people's liberation war and the people's revolution !

Long live the great unity of the Chinese people !

Long live the People's Republic of China !

Long live the Central People's Government !

New China News Agency—*Daily News Release*, 1 October 1949, (Nos. 153-82) p. 2.

35   *27 September* 1949

ORGANIC LAW OF THE CHINESE PEOPLE'S POLITICAL CONSULTATIVE CONFERENCE

I. *General Provisions*

Article 1. The Chinese People's Political Consultative Conference (referred to in this text as Chinese People's PCC) is the organization of the democratic united front of the entire Chinese people. Its aim is to unite all democratic classes and all nationalities throughout China through the unity of all democratic parties and groups and people's organizations, to exert joint efforts in carrying out New Democracy, opposing imperialism, feudalism and bureaucratic capitalism, overthrowing the reactionary rule of the Kuomintang, eliminating overt and covert remnant counter-revolutionary forces, healing the wounds of war, rehabilitating and developing the people's economic, cultural and educational work, consolidating national defence, and uniting with nations and countries in the world which treat us on a footing of equality, to establish and consolidate the independent, democratic, peaceful, unified, prosperous and strong People's Republic of China of people's democratic dictatorship, led by the working class and based on the alliance of workers and peasants.

II.   Participating Units and Delegates

Article 2.   Democratic parties and groups and people's organizations which agree to Article I of this Organic Law may take part in the Chinese People's PCC after being approved by the National Committee of the Chinese People's PCC through consultation. Individuals may, upon invitation agreed on through consultation by the National Committee of the Chinese People's PCC, also take part in the plenary sessions of the Chinese People's PCC and are eligible for election to its National Committee.

Article 3.   The units, the number of delegates and nominees taking part in each session of the Chinese People's PCC shall be decided through consultation by the National Committee of the previous session of the Chinese People's PCC. The units, number of delegates and nominees taking part in the first plenary session of the Chinese People's PCC shall be determined by the Preparatory Committee of the Chinese People's PCC through consultation.

Article 4.   All participating units and delegates have the obligation to abide by and execute all resolutions passed by the plenary session of the Chinese People's PCC and by its National Committee.

In the event of participating democratic parties and groups and people's organizations disagreeing with resolutions passed by the plenary session or by the National Committee, they have to abide faithfully by the said resolutions in accordance with the democratic principle of the minority submitting to the majority, and must not violate them, but they may reserve their divergent opinions for discussion at the next session. If they fundamentally disagree with important resolutions, they are at liberty to withdraw from the Chinese People's PCC upon application.

Article 5.   If units or delegates to the Chinese People's PCC or members of its National Committee seriously violate the Organic Law and the Common Programme or important resolutions of the Chinese People's PCC, they shall in accordance with the gravity of the offence be warned, or be asked to recall their delegates, or have their membership to the committee disqualified, or be cancelled as a representative unit. In the event of disagreement, appeal may be made to the next plenary session.

III.   Plenary Session

Article 6.   The plenary session of the Chinese People's PCC shall be summoned triannually by the National Committee. The National Committee may, when necessary, convene the session earlier or postpone its convening.

The first plenary session of the Chinese People's PCC shall however be summoned by the Preparatory Committee of the Chinese People's PCC.

Article 7. The plenary session of the Chinese People's PCC has the following powers and functions :

(1) Enacting or amending the Organic Law of the Chinese People's PCC.

(2) Drawing up or amending the programme of New Democracy, that is, the Common Programme of the Chinese People's PCC, to be observed in common by all democratic parties and groups and people's organizations participating in the Chinese People's PCC.

(3) Exercising the functions and powers of the All-China People's Congress prior to its convocation through universal suffrage.

(*a*) Enacting or amending the Organic Law of the Central People's Government of the People's Republic of China.

(*b*) Electing the Central People's Government Council and vesting it with the power of exercising state authority.

(*c*) Handing over resolutions to the Central People's Government of the People's Republic of China concerning fundamental policies or important measures relating to the cause of democratic revolution of the people throughout the country or national construction work.

(4) Submitting proposals on fundamental policies and important measures relating to national construction work to the All-China People's Congress and the Central People's Government after the convocation of the All-China People's Congress through universal suffrage.

(5) Electing the National Committee of the Chinese People's PCC.

Article 8. More than half of the total number of delegates are required to form the quorum of the plenary session of the Chinese People's PCC. There must be the concurrence of more than half of the delegates present at the session before a resolution may be passed.

Article 9. The plenary session of the Chinese People's PCC shall have a presidium elected by the plenary session, and the number of the members of the presidium shall be prescribed by each plenary session extemporaneously.

Article 10. The plenary session of the Chinese People's PCC shall have a secretary-general elected by the plenary session and a number of assistant secretaries-general appointed by the presidium. A secretariat shall be set up under the secretary-general and his assistants.

Article 11. The plenary session of the Chinese People's PCC may organize various committees. The organization-regulations pertaining to them shall be separately stipulated.

Article 12.   The rules of procedure of the plenary session of the Chinese People's PCC shall be drawn up by the presidium.

IV.   National Committee

Article 13.   A national committee shall be set up after the closing of the plenary session of the Chinese People's PCC and shall have the following functions and powers :

(1) Ensuring the implementation of the resolutions of the plenary session and of the National Committee of the Chinese People's PCC.

(2) Consulting on and submitting proposals to the Central People's Government of the People's Republic of China.

(3) Assisting the Government in mobilizing the people to participate in the work of people's democratic revolution and national construction.

(4) Consulting on and submitting the joint list of candidates of all participating units of the Chinese People's PCC for the election of deputies to the All-China People's Congress.

(5) Consulting on and determining the units, number of delegates and nominees of the next plenary session of the Chinese People's PCC and to summon it.

(6) Directing the work of the local democratic united front.

(7) Consulting on and dealing with affairs concerning the internal co-operation of the Chinese People's PCC.

Article 14.   The members and alternates of the National Committee of the Chinese People's PCC shall be elected by the plenary session of the Chinese People's PCC ; the number of the members and alternates shall be determined by each plenary session extemporaneously.

The National Committee of the Chinese People's PCC shall meet semi-annually and the meeting shall be called by the Standing Committee of the National Committee. The Standing Committee may, when necessary, call the meeting earlier or postpone it.

Article 15.   A certain number of Standing Committee members, a chairman and a certain number of vice-chairmen shall be elected by and from among the members of the National Committee of the Chinese People's PCC to form the Standing Committee to take charge of the affairs of the National Committee.

Article 16.   The National Committee of the Chinese People's PCC shall have a secretary-general elected by the National Committee, and a certain number of assistant secretaries-general appointed by the Standing Committee of the National Committee. A secretariat shall be set up under the secretary-general and his assistants.

173

Article 17. Regulations for the work of the National Committee of the Chinese People's PCC shall be drawn up by the Standing Committee of the National Committee.

V. *Local Committees*

Article 18. Local committees of the Chinese People's PCC may, in accordance with the resolutions of the National Committee of the Chinese People's PCC, be set up in major cities, important areas and provincial capitals as organs for consultation and ensuring the implementation of resolutions by the democratic parties and groups and people's organizations in these places.

Article 19. The organization-rules of the local committees of the Chinese People's PCC shall be drawn up or ratified by the National Committee of the Chinese People's PCC.

VI. *By-Laws*

Article 20. The Organic Law shall be put into effect after being adopted by the plenary session of the Chinese People's PCC.

New China News Agency—*Daily News Release,* 1 October, 1949 (Nos. 153-82), pp. 62-4.

36   29 *September* 1949

ORGANIC LAW OF THE CENTRAL PEOPLE'S GOVERNMENT

I. *General Principles*

Article 1. The People's Republic of China is a state of the people's democratic dictatorship, led by the working class, based on alliance of workers and peasants, and uniting all democratic classes and the various nationalities within the country.

Article 2. The Government of the People's Republic of China is a government of the people's congress system based on the principle of democratic centralism.

Article 3. Prior to the convocation of the All-China People's Congress by universal franchise, the plenary session of the Chinese People's Political Consultative Conference shall perform the functions and exercise the power of the All-China People's Congress, enact the Organic Law of the Central People's Government of the People's Republic of China, elect the Central People's Government Council of the People's Republic of China and vest it with the authority to exercise state power.

Article 4. The Central People's Government Council represents the People's Republic of China in international relations and assumes the leadership of the state apparatus at home.

Article 5. The Central People's Government Council shall set up the Government Administration Council as the highest executive body for state administration ; the People's Revolutionary Military Council as the supreme military command of the state ; and the Supreme People's Court and the People's Procurator-General's Office as the highest judicial and supervisory bodies of the country.

II. *The Central People's Government Council*

Article 6. The Central People's Government Council shall consist of the Chairman and six Vice-Chairmen of the Central People's Government and of fifty-six Council Members elected by the plenary session of the Chinese People's Political Consultative Conference. It shall have a Secretary-General elected by and from the Central People's Government Council.

Article 7. The Central People's Government Council shall exercise the following authority, in accordance with the Common Programme enacted by the plenary session of the Chinese People's Political Consultative Conference :

(1) Enacting and interpreting the laws of the state, promulgating decrees and supervising their execution.

(2) Determining the administrative policies of the state.

(3) Annulling or revising any decisions and orders of the Government Administration Council, which do not conform to the laws and decrees of the state.

(4) Ratifying, abrogating or revising treaties and agreements concluded by the People's Republic of China with foreign countries.

(5) Dealing with questions of war and peace.

(6) Approving or revising the state budget and financial statement.

(7) Promulgating acts of general amnesty and pardon.

(8) Instituting and awarding orders, medals, and titles of honour of the state.

(9) Appointing or removing of government personnel as follows :

(*a*) Appointment or removal of the Premier and Vice-Premiers and Members of the Government Administration Council ; Secretary-General and Assistant Secretaries-General of the Government Administration Council ; Chairmen, Vice-Chairmen, and Members of the various Committees and Commissions ; Ministers and Vice-Ministers of the various Ministries ; President and Vice-Presidents of the Academy of Sciences ; Directors and Deputy Directors of the various Administrations ; and Manager and Assistant Managers of the Bank.

175

(*b*) Appointment or removal or confirmation of the appointment or removal, on the recommendation of the Government Administration Council, of chairmen, vice-chairmen and chief administrative personnel of people's governments in various major administrative areas, provinces and municipalities.

(*c*) Appointment or removal of ambassadors, ministers and plenipotentiary representatives to foreign states.

(*d*) Appointment or removal of the Chairman, Vice-Chairmen and Members of the People's Revolutionary Military Council; of the Commander-in-Chief, Deputy Commander-in-Chief, Chief of Staff, Deputy Chief of Staff, Director and Assistant Director of the General Political Department of the People's Liberation Army.

(*e*) Appointment or removal of the President and Vice-Presidents and Committee Members of the Supreme People's Court, the Procurator-General, Deputy Procurator-General and Committee Members of the People's Procurator-General's Office.

(10) Preparing for and convening the All-China People's Congress.

Article 8. The Chairman of the Central People's Government shall preside over the meetings of the Central People's Government Council and shall direct its work.

Article 9. The Vice-Chairmen and Secretary-General of the Central People's Government shall assist the Chairman in the discharge of his duties.

Article 10. Sessions of the Central People's Government Council shall be convened by the Chairman once every two months. The Chairman may convene the session earlier or postpone it when conditions demand it or upon the request of more than one-third of the Members of the Central People's Government Council or upon the request of the Government Administration Council. More than one-half of the Council Members constitute a quorum and the adoption of any resolution demands the concurrence of over one-half of the Members present at the session.

Article 11. The Central People's Government Council shall have a Secretariat and may set up other subordinate working bodies when necessary.

Article 12. The Central People's Government Council shall enact its own organizational regulations.

III. *The Government Administration Council*

Article 13. The Government Administration Council shall consist of a Premier, a number of Vice-Premiers, a Secretary-General and a number of Council Members appointed by the Central People's Government Council.

Members of the Government Administration Council may concurrently hold posts as Chairmen of the various Committees or Commissions or as Ministers of the various Ministries.

Article 14. The Government Administration Council shall be responsible and accountable to the Central People's Government Council. When the Central People's Government Council adjourns, the Government Administration Council shall be responsible and accountable to the Chairman of the Central People's Government.

Article 15. The Government Administration Council shall exercise the following authority on the basis and in application of the Common Programme of the Chinese People's Political Consultative Conference, and of the laws and decrees of the state and of the administrative policies stipulated by the Central People's Government Council :

(1) Issuing decisions and orders and verifying their execution.

(2) Annulling or revising the decisions and orders of the Committees, Ministries, Commissions, Academy, Administrations, and Bank and governments of all levels, which do not conform to the laws and decrees of the state and of the decisions and orders of the Government Administration Council.

(3) Submitting Bills to the Central People's Government Council.

(4) Co-ordinating, unifying and directing the interrelations, the internal organizations and the general work of the Committees, Ministries, Commissions, Academy, Administrations and Bank and other subordinate bodies.

(5) Directing the work of local people's governments throughout the country.

(6) Appointing or removing, or confirming the appointment or removal of the chief administrative personnel of country and municipal level and above, not included in Article 7, Section 9(*b*).

Article 16. The Premier of the Government Administration Council shall direct the Council's affairs. The Vice-Premiers and the Secretary-General of the Government Administration Council shall assist the Premier in the discharge of his duties.

Article 17. Once a week the Government Administration Council shall hold meetings convened by the Premier. The Premier may convene the meeting earlier or postpone it when conditions demand it, or upon the request of over one-third of the Council Members. Over one half of the Members of the Government Administration Council constitute a quorum and the adoption of a resolution demands the concurrence of over one half of the Members present at the meeting.

The decisions and orders of the Government Administration Council shall come into force when signed by the Premier or signed by the Premier and countersigned by the heads of the Committees, Ministries, Commissions, Academy, Administrations, or Bank concerned.

Article 18. The Government Administration Council shall set up Committees of Political and Legal Affairs, of Financial and Economic Affairs, of Cultural and Educational Affairs, of People's Control, and shall set up the following Ministries, Commissions, Academy, Administrations, and Bank, which shall direct their respective departments of state administration :

Ministry of the Interior, Ministry of Foreign Affairs, Information Administration, Ministry of Public Security, Ministry of Finance, People's Bank, Ministry of Trade, Customs Administration, Ministry of Heavy Industry, Ministry of Fuel Industry, Ministry of Textile Industry, Ministry of Food Industry, Ministry of Light Industry, (industries not included in the four mentioned above), Ministry of Railways, Ministry of Posts and Telecommunications, Ministry of Communications, Ministry of Agriculture, Ministry of Forestry and Land Reclamation, Ministry of Water Conservancy, Ministry of Labour, Ministry of Cultural Affairs, Ministry of Education, Academy of Sciences, Press Administration, Publications Administration, Ministry of Public Health, Ministry of Justice, Commission of Legislative Affairs, Commission of the Nationalities' Affairs, Commission of Overseas Chinese Affairs.

The Committee of Political and Legal Affairs shall direct the work of the Ministry of the Interior, the Ministry of Public Security, the Ministry of Justice, the Commission of Legislative Affairs, and the Commission of the Nationalities' Affairs.

The Committee of Financial and Economic Affairs shall direct the work of the Ministries of Finance, of Trade, of Heavy Industry, of Fuel Industry, of Textile Industry, of Food Industry, of Light Industry, of Railways, of Posts and Telecommunications, of Communications, of Agriculture, of Forestry and Land Reclamation, of Water Conservancy, of Labour, and of the People's Bank, and of the Customs Administration.

The Committee of Cultural and Educational Affairs shall direct the work of the Ministry of Cultural Affairs, the Ministry of Education, the Ministry of Public Health, the Academy of Sciences, the Press Administration, and the Publications Administration.

In order to carry out their work, the responsible Committees may issue decisions and orders to the Ministries, the Commissions, the Academy, the Administrations and the Bank under their direction and to other subordinate bodies and may verify their execution.

178

The Committee of People's Control shall be responsible for the supervision over the execution of duties by government institutions, and public functionaries.

Article 19.   The Ministries, Commissions, Academy, Administrations and the Bank may announce decisions and issue orders within their jurisdiction and may verify their execution.

Article 20.   The Government Administration Council shall have a Secretariat to deal with the routine work and to take charge of the files, archives and seals of the Government Administration Council, etc.

Article 21.   The organizational regulations of the Government Administration Council, the Committees, Ministries, Commissions, the Academy, the Administrations, the Bank and the Secretariat shall be enacted or ratified by the Central People's Government Council.

Article 22.   The Central People's Government Council may, when necessary, decide on the increase or reduction of the number or on the merging of the Committees, Ministries, Commissions, the Academy, Administrations, the Bank and the Secretariat.

IV.   *The People's Revolutionary Military Council*

Article 23.   The People's Liberation Army and other people's armed forces throughout the country shall come under the unified control and command of the People's Revolutionary Military Council.

Article 24.   The People's Revolutionary Military Council shall have a Chairman, a number of Vice-Chairmen, and a number of Council Members.

Article 25.   The organization of the People's Revolutionary Military Council and the system of its administration and command shall be determined by the Central People's Government Council.

V.   *The Supreme People's Court and the People's Procurator-General's Office*

Article 26.   The Supreme People's Court is the highest judicial body of the country, and is charged with the direction and supervision of the judicial work of all levels of judicial bodies of the country.

Article 27.   The Supreme People's Court shall have a President and a number of Vice-Presidents and a number of Committee Members.

Article 28.   The People's Procurator-General's Office shall have the supreme supervisory power to ensure the strict observance of the law by all government institutions and public functionaries as well as by nationals of the country.

Article 29. The People's Procurator-General's Office shall have a Procurator-General, a number of Deputy Procurators-General and a number of Committee Members.

Article 30. The organizational regulations of the Supreme People's Court and of the People's Procurator-General's Office shall be enacted by the Central People's Government Council.

VI. Right of Amendment and Interpretation of this Organic Law

Article 31. The right of amendment of the Organic Law of the Central People's Government belongs to the plenary session of the Chinese People's Political Consultative Conference ; while the latter is not in session, it belongs to the Central People's Government Council. The right of interpretation of this Organic Law belongs to the Central People's Government Council.

The Common Programme and Other Documents, pp. 29-40.

37   1 *October* 1949

PROCLAMATION OF THE CENTRAL
PEOPLE'S GOVERNMENT

The people throughout China have been plunged into bitter suffering and tribulations since the Chiang Kai-shek Kuomintang reactionary government betrayed the fatherland, conspired with imperialists and launched the counter-revolutionary war. However, our People's Liberation Army, supported by the people throughout the country, fighting heroically and selflessly to defend the territorial sovereignty of the fatherland, to protect the people's lives and property, to relieve the people of their sufferings and to struggle for their rights, has eliminated the reactionary troops and overthrown the reactionary rule of the National Government.

Now, the war of the people's liberation has been fundamentally won and the majority of the people throughout the country have been liberated.

On this foundation, the first session of the Chinese People's Political Consultative Conference, composed of the delegates of all democratic parties and groups, people's organizations, the People's Liberation Army, various regions, various nationalities, overseas Chinese and patriotic democratic elements of the whole country, has been convened. Representing the will of the people throughout the country, this session of the Chinese People's Political Consultative Conference has enacted the Organic Law of the Central People's Government of the People's Republic of China, elected Mao Tze-tung as Chairman of the Central People's Government, and Chu Teh, Liu Shao Chi, Soong Ching Ling, Li Chi Shen, Chang Lan and Kao Kang as Vice-Chairmen of the Central People's Government and Chen Yi, Ho Lung, Li Li San, Lin Po Chu, Yeh Chien Ying, Ho Hsiang Ning, Lin Piao, Peng Teh Huai, Liu Po Cheng, Wu Yu Chang, Hsu Hsiang Chien, Peng Chen, Po Yi Po, Nieh Jung Chen, Chou En Lai, Tung Pi Wu, Saifudin, Jao Shu Shih, Tan Kah Kee, Lo Jung Huan, Teng Tsu Hui, Ulanfu, Hsu Teh Li, Tsai Chang, Liu Ke Ping, Ma Yin Chu, Chen Yun, Kang Sheng, Lin Feng, Ma Hsu Lun, Kuo Mo Jo, Chang Yun Yi, Teng Hsiao Ping, Kao Chung Min, Shen Chun Ju, Shen Yen Ping, Chen Shu Tung, Seeto Meitong, Li Hsi Chiu, Huang Yen Pei, Tsai Ting Kai, Hsi Chung Hsun, Peng Tse Min, Chang Chih Chung, Fu Tso Yi, Li Chu Chen, Li Chang Ta, Chang Po Chun, Cheng Chien, Chang Hsi Jo, Chen Ming Shu, Tan Ping Shan, Chang Nan Hsien, Liu Ya Tsu, Chang Tung Sun, and Lung Yun as Council Members to form the Central People's Government Council, proclaimed the founding of the People's Republic of China, and decided that Peking shall be the capital of the People's Republic of China.

The Central People's Government Council of the People's Republic of China took over office today in this capital and unanimously made the following decisions :

Proclamation of the formation of the Central People's Government of the People's Republic of China.

Adoption of the Common Programme of the Chinese People's Political Consultative Conference as the policy of the Government.

Election of Lin Po Chu from among the Council Members as Secretary-General of the Central People's Government Council.

Appointment of Chou En-lai as Premier of the State Administration Council and concurrently as Minister of the Ministry of Foreign Affairs, Mao Tze-tung as Chairman of the People's Revolutionary Military Council of the Central People's Government, Chu Teh as Commander-in-Chief of the People's Liberation Army, Shen Chun Ju as Chief Justice of the Supreme People's Court, and Lo Jung Huan as Procurator-General of the People's Procurator-General's Office and entrusting them with the task of early formation of the various organs of the Government to carry out the work of the Government.

At the same time, the Central People's Government Council decided to declare to the Governments of all other countries that this Government is the sole legal government representing all the people of the People's Republic of China. This Government is willing to establish diplomatic relations with any foreign Government which is willing to observe the principles of equality, mutual benefit and mutual respect of territorial integrity and sovereignty.

(Signed) MAO TZE-TUNG,
Chairman of the Central
People's Government of the
1 October 1949   *People's Republic of China*

Daily News Release, No. 154, New China News Agency, 3 October 1949.

CHINA

PART TWO

EXTERNAL RELATIONS

INTRODUCTION

CHINA'S EXTERNAL RELATIONS during this period have revolved round the United States and the Soviet Union, particularly the former. The United States took active interest in China since the end of World War II and has had intimate relations with her. During the war, with a view to expediting the effective execution of the war against Japan, the United States was interested in the ending of the civil conflict between the Kuomintang and the Communists and the restoration of national unity. The popular Chinese sentiments and the American policy led to unity talks in early 1944 but, unfortunately, the talks did not make much headway. The chief advocate of the military necessity of unity between the Kuomintang and the Communists, General Joseph W. Stilwell, who was Chiang Kai-shek's Chief of Staff, was recalled at the latter's instance, and American policy shifted to support of the Kuomintang, though still interested in internal peace and unity. The new policy was one of refusing Chiang Kai-shek an unlimited commitment but giving him considerable military and economic aid.

When Japan surrendered in August 1945, the bulk of the Kuomintang armies was in the interior with headquarters in Chungking, while Communist forces were operating in Manchuria and North China. Both were anxious to get control of the Japanese-occupied areas but the Kuomintang was at an obvious disadvantage. In this situation the United States came to the aid of Chungking, by flying three Nationalist armies to key positions in East and North China for the purpose of accepting the Japanese surrender, and by landing over 50,000 marines in North China.

America was beginning to recognize the pivotal position of China in East Asia and its importance for American-Soviet relations, since the Soviet Union was also deeply interested in a friendly and peaceful China. Historically, American interest had been confined to trade, investments, and missionary activity but the war had broadened America's interest in and recognition of the importance of China. In February 1945 at the Yalta Conference the American President and the British Prime Minister had given many concessions to the Soviet Union in order to obtain the latter's early participation in the war against Japan. The United States also encouraged

183

China in concluding a'treaty with the Soviet Union in order to normalize diplomatic relations in East Asia. The Chinese-Soviet Treaty of Friendship and Alliance of August 1945 conceded special rights to the Soviet Union in Manchuria, Port Arthur and Dairen in return for the latter's support to the Nationalist Government and recognition of Chinese sovereignty over Manchuria and Sinkiang. These arrangements were, of course, made at a time when there was every hope of continued Allied co-operation in peace time and the 'cold war' had not raised its ugly head. With the rupture of the wartime alliance and the increasing estrangement of the Soviet Union and the United States, these agreements came in for much criticism and many held them responsible for the downfall of the Kuomintang.

It was becoming increasingly obvious that the Kuomintang was unable to destroy the Communists by military action. In the attempt to recover all China the Nationalist armies had suffered several defeats. The American Administration realized that it was not possible for Generalissimo Chiang Kai-shek to secure a complete victory in the civil war and was, therefore, interested in achieving unity through peaceful means. The then American Ambassador, Patrick J. Hurley, was instrumental in bringing the two contending parties together for negotiations in August 1945. The talks were, however, stalled over the questions of the reorganization of the National Government and the Communist armies. Events in China brought to the surface differences in the United States over policy towards China. While one view was to give unlimited aid to Chiang Kai-shek, the majority feeling, particularly in the Administration, was for going slow in view of the acute economic and other problems facing China and the danger of Chiang Kai-shek over-extending his forces. Ambassador Hurley was an advocate of large-scale aid to the Generalissimo but as he found himself in a minority, he resigned in November 1945. On 27 November President Truman appointed General Marshall as his special representative in China to help bring the peace negotiations to a successful conclusion. The President also declared that the United States had no intention of undertaking military intervention in order to influence the course of the Chinese civil strife.

In spite of General Marshall's patient efforts and protracted negotiation, his mission failed to achieve its objective. The deep-seated bitterness and suspicion between the two chief contending parties, the various violations of the truce from both sides and the desire of the extreme right wing of the Kuomintang to force a military win led to the failure of General Marshall's efforts. On 6 January 1947 President Truman recalled General Marshall, thus bringing to an end a long and fruitless period of negotiations and discussions, begun in January 1946. In his final statement on 7 January, before leaving China, he said that the almost overwhelming suspicion with which the Kuomintang and the Communists regarded each other had poisoned the atmosphere and he blamed the dominant group of Kuomintang reactionaries and the extreme elements in the Communists for the failure of negotiations. He denounced the dominating influence of the military in the Kuomintang Government and was convinced that a campaign of force had been in progress and that the negotiations were used as a cover for this campaign. His conclusion was that liberal elements in the Government and in the minority parties should assume the leadership under Chiang in order to attain unity through good government. In spite of American warnings, the extreme right wing did not think that in the event of their precipitating a military conflict, the United States would stop aid to them. They also hoped for increasing American-Soviet tension which would compel the USA to identify itself with them.

The failure of the Marshall Mission heightened the controversy in America over the China policy. There was an increasing demand, led by the Republicans, for a shift in the American policy and large-scale aid to the Kuomintang. The Administration, however, was not inclined towards this course. It was aware of the internal weaknesses of the Kuomintang Government and was highly doubtful of its ability to make effective use of American aid. It was also deterred by the feelings of Chinese middle groups and intellectuals whose war-weariness and suffering had already made them receptive to the Communist propaganda that America was using China as a pawn in the East-West struggle. However, the US Government had not washed its hands of the Nationalist Government. Although it had not lifted the embargo on arms purchases by the Nationalist Government, it continued to give aid to it in various forms. Since the war American aid had taken such forms as lend-lease, the transfer of surplus property and naval vessels. American military advisers were still in China. The economy was being bolstered by UNRRA supplies, which were financed mainly by America, and by the loan and credit agreements and the Surplus Property Agreement of August 1946. Out of a total UNRRA expenditure of $658,400,000 in China during 1945-7, the American share constituted $474,000,000. The US Government continued its efforts to persuade the Chinese Government to undertake far-reaching reforms but met with little success. In April 1947 the US Ambassador noted that the extreme right wing was still dominant in the Kuomintang.

The deteriorating military and economic situation forced the Chinese Government to renew efforts to obtain American financial and economic assistance. On 8 May 1947 the Nationalist Government put in a request for a loan of $1,000,000,000. General Marshall was unwilling to accede to this request. He felt that the effectiveness of the reorganization of the Chinese Government had still to be tested and that the Chinese economy was still bedevilled by inflation. He, however, indicated that he was considering the most effective ways of helping China which could be justified to Congress.

The deteriorating situation in China served to increase the growing division of opinion in America over the Administration's China policy. The Chinese Government also stepped up its propaganda in the United States through what is known as the 'China Lobby'. It blamed the Yalta Conference as the root of all troubles of the Kuomintang Government. The American Government's policy of partial withdrawal and limited help was being increasingly criticized as inept and ineffective. Although the Administration still stuck to its stand, it was under pressure to take some action in the direction of aid to China. In the spring and summer of 1947 the American marines in North China, borrowing from the Soviet practice, 'abandoned' considerable quantities of munitions which were 'secured' by Nationalist Government forces. On 27 June the Secretary of State ordered the removal of the embargo on arms purchases in the USA by the Nationalists. Finally on 9 July 1947 President Truman instructed General Robert C. Wedemeyer, who had been Commander of American Forces in China during 1944-6 and had cordial relations with Generalissimo Chiang Kai-shek and the Chinese military command, to go to China on a fact-finding mission. Among the instructions—which were kept secret at that time—were that he should impress upon the Chinese Government the need to take speedy and effective action on reforms in the administration and economy in order to facilitate American aid and that such aid would be subject to the supervision of American representatives.

In China it was generally assumed that General Wedemeyer was coming to China to announce a new programme of American aid. The official circles, therefore, were pleased with the decision. On 12 July the Chinese Foreign Minister welcomed General Wedemeyer as 'an old friend of China' and anticipated stronger American support. The Chinese middle groups were apprehensive at the prospect of more American aid to the Government, while the Communists denounced the mission for planning to prop up Chiang Kai-shek's 'moribund régime'. General Wedemeyer arrived in Nanking on 23 July 1947 and visited the chief cities for a month, talking to both officials and non-officials. On 16 August the Government gave him a memorandum claiming considerable progress in political, economic, educational and social reforms since the war. The memorandum was intended to impress the General with the achievements of the Kuomintang régime and thus provide justification for large-scale American aid. Adhering strictly to his instructions, General Wedemeyer had made no commitment for American aid to China and already Kuomintang circles were displaying impatience at the unwillingness of the General to make any promises.

General Wedemeyer was requested by Chiang Kai-shek to address a joint meeting of the Ministers of the Nationalist Government and the State Council on 22 August 1947. The Generalissimo asked Wedemeyer to speak frankly and freely. General Wedemeyer took the Generalissimo at his word and made a scathing criticism of the corruption, inefficiency and incompetence of the administration and appealed for thorough-going reforms and inspiring leadership. The General's plain speaking aroused bitter resentment in Kuomintang circles. They had hoped for considerable American assistance, but they had, instead, to hear some unpleasant home-truths, with no promise of aid. His speech elicited a sharp reply from the Chinese Prime Minister, General Chang Chun, who said on 2 September that General Wedemeyer did not know many things and that he paid more attention to people outside the Government than to those inside. He claimed that the Government was already carrying out many of the reforms advocated by the General.

General Wedemeyer returned to Washington on 19 September and submitted his report to the President. After making a survey of the general scene in China, and pointing out the weaknesses, shortcomings and limitations of the Nationalist régime, he recommended a programme of long-term financial, military and advisory aid, spread over a period of five years, to the Chinese Government under constant and close American supervision and direction. He also recommended that Manchuria be placed under five-Power guardianship, or, alternatively, United Nations trusteeship. The Wedemeyer recommendations in effect asked that the United States put the Chinese Government under US tutelage and direct its civil war effort. The American Government, however, was not prepared to adopt such a course. It could not take over the Chinese Government and administer its economic and military affairs and was, therefore, opposed to undertaking a commitment of indefinite duration, scope and cost. It had also to take account of the heavy burden of foreign aid which the United States was assuming elsewhere, particularly in Europe, which, in American strategy, came first because of its industry and well-developed democratic institutions. The US Government did not want to take the risk of over-committing its strength. General Wedemeyer's report was not published at that time in view of its highly controversial recommendations, especially in regard to Manchuria. The report was published later in the White Paper on China in August 1949.

The disappointment over the fruitlessness of General Wedemeyer's visit caused much resentment in China. It happened to coincide with the misgivings that the Chinese were increasingly feeling over America's policy towards Japan, which the Chinese felt America was building up at the cost of China. The bitterness and frustration resulting from these happenings led to suggestions in Nanking that China should now try to get closer to the Soviet Union. An indication of this trend was given by the Chinese Prime Minister when on 9 September 1947 he told the Kuomintang Central Executive Committee that China had a similar policy towards Japan as the USSR and that China was opposed to America's policy of strengthening Japan. In these circumstances, he said, China would have to strengthen its relations with the Soviet Union. It was, however, generally felt that Nanking was not seriously contemplating such a course and that it was intended rather as a pressure tactic to extract more aid from the United States.

The apprehensions over American policy in Japan came at a time when there had already been a slow growth of anti-American sentiment in the country. The Chinese Leftists and Communists had been denouncing Chiang Kai-shek's Government as subservient to the United States. They had been accusing the United States of financing the civil war in China and had maintained that but for American aid Chiang Kai-shek could not have been able to resist the popular demand for peace, unity and reforms. These attacks fell on the receptive ears of the war-weary intellectual and middle class circles. The gathering storm of anti-American sentiment burst out in June and July 1948 in student demonstrations against American policy in Japan. There were demonstrations and riots in Peiping, Shanghai, Nanking and elsewhere. The anti-American demonstrations were assuming alarming proportions and Ambassador Stuart was constrained to issue a public statement appealing to his relationship with Chinese academic groups and counselling sanity. Finally the Government cracked down on the movement, which gradually died down.

The Wedemeyer mission had further split American opinion over China policy. The fundamental issues were whether or how to give the Nationalist Government further aid and how much importance should be attached to reforms. On account of increasing American-Soviet tension these questions were more and more being examined within the 'cold war' context. The Republicans were taking the lead in demanding all-out aid for Chiang's Government. They accused the Democratic Administration of 'neglecting' China and betraying it to communism. The continued deterioration in the Chinese Government's position only served to make the demand for aid more insistent. Generalissimo Chiang Kai-shek had told a visiting group of members of the Military Affairs Committee of the House of Representatives on 11 October 1947 that if the Chinese Government were finally defeated, it would not be because of Russia or the Chinese Communists but because the United States had failed to give assistance at a time of desperate need. The Chinese Communists, in his view, were thorough-going satellites of Moscow, and were constantly in receipt of supplies from the USSR. Similar views were expressed by the supporters of the Chinese Government in the United States. The American Administration was being subjected to heavy pressure. Faced with the task of piloting the European Recovery Programme through a predominantly Republican Congress, it had to take cognizance of this mounting demand and, therefore, set to work on a programme of aid to China. On 18 February 1948 its proposals were laid before Congress along with a special message from President Truman. The President recommended that Congress authorize $570,000,000 for China to provide assistance until 30 June 1949. After protracted debates Congress passed on 2 April 1948 what came to be known as the China Aid Act, sanctioning $400,000,000 for a twelve-month period. Of this amount $275,000,000 was earmarked for economic aid and $125,000,000 for military aid.

The China Aid Act stipulated that an agreement should be negotiated with China which should resemble those concluded with countries receiving ECA aid. Such a Sino-American agreement was concluded on 3 July 1948. By its terms the Chinese Government undertook to make the best possible use of its economic assets and the aid given by the United States, to promote the development of agriculture and industry on a sound basis, to take all necessary measures for bringing about financial stability, and to reduce barriers to increased foreign trade. The organization of aid to China was entrusted to the ECA which set up a China Programme Division and sent a mission to China. The China Aid Act also authorized a specified amount of expenditure on rural reconstruction. In order to facilitate this task an agreement was signed on 5 August 1948 setting up a Sino-American Rural Reconstruction Commission.

The $125 million earmarked for military aid was used to finance purchases by the Chinese Government of arms, ammunition, and equipment for its army, air force, and navy. The American Government had also taken steps to implement General Wedemeyer's recommendation that military advisory help to China should be expanded and extended. In October 1947 the State Department had agreed to the participation of the Army Advisory Group in the instruction of Chinese troops in Formosa. In the spring and summer of 1948 such authorization was also given for army training establishments at Nanking, Hankow, Canton and Chengtu. In November 1947 Major-General David Barr, Head of the Army Advisory Group, was permitted to give confidential advice to the Chinese High Command. However, this advice generally went unheeded and, therefore, resulted in no substantial improvement.

The aid programme was intended to give a breathing spell to the Kuomintang Government which was, however, declining too rapidly for that. Already in February 1948 Ambassador Stuart had reported to Washington that the Chinese Government might soon lack the minimum of popular support necessary for its survival. Chiang's group, he wrote, hoped to sustain itself with whatever aid it could get, believing that in the final analysis it would be saved by a Soviet-American war. The decisive defeats which the Kuomintang suffered in 1948 again faced the United States with basic policy decisions. In his instructions of 12 and 13 August 1948 to the American Ambassador in Nanking, the Secretary of State, General Marshall, made it plain that while the Administration did not support any move for a coalition with the Chinese Communists, the United States wanted to retain a free hand to cope with the state of flux and confusion into which China was apparently entering. He favoured a policy of 'wait and see'. Actuated by the fear of Communist domination of China, Ambassador Stuart suggested to the State Department towards the end of October 1948 increased assistance to the Nanking Government. The suggestion was unacceptable to General Marshall who in his reply cited the Ambassador's own despatches to the effect that the Chinese Government was incapable of saving itself and could not be saved by anything short of armed intervention on a scale which America was unable and unwilling to undertake.

This view was endorsed by senior American military officers in China. The American Ambassador reported to Washington on 6 November 1948 : 'We gathered together senior military personnel, JUSMAG and Service Attachés, who, after discussing the military situation, were unanimous that short of actual employment of United States troops no amount of military assistance could save the present situation in view of its advanced stage of deterioration. Agreeing that employment of United States troops was impossible, it was the conclusion of the group that there was no military step China or the United States could take in sufficient time to retrieve the military situation.' Major-General David Barr expressed his opinion in a report of 16 November to the Department of the Army that 'no battle has been lost since my arrival due to lack of ammunition or equipment. Their military débâcles in my opinion can all be attributed to the world's worst leadership and many other morale-destroying factors that led to a complete loss of the will to fight.'

In view of the débâcle that faced the Nationalist Government, renewed efforts were made by it to get more aid as well as a firm declaration of support from the United States. The Nationalist Government tried through its chief UN delegate, Dr T. F. Tsiang, to persuade General Marshall, who had come to Paris to attend the UN General Assembly, to get the US Administration to send a top military adviser to direct the operations of the Chinese forces. General Marshall, however, was not willing to accede to this request. Generalissimo Chiang Kai-shek followed this up by making a personal appeal to President Truman, who received the Generalissimo's letter on 9 November 1948. The Generalissimo put all the responsibility for the disastrous situation in China on the non-observance by the Soviet Union of the Sino-Soviet Treaty of Friendship. He asked for aid and support in China's fight for freedom. President Truman gave a polite refusal on 13 November and indicated that no aid beyond that sanctioned by the China Aid Act would be forthcoming.

Thus thwarted in their attempt to get the United States more heavily committed in the Chinese civil war and faced with a desperate situation, the Nationalists made a bid to secure Big Four mediation in order to save something from the disaster that loomed. On 8 January 1949 the Chinese Foreign Minister addressed identical notes to the American, British, French, and Soviet Governments soliciting their good offices in the initiation of negotiations with the Chinese Communist Party with a view to obtaining a restoration of peace. The replies of all the four Powers were unfavourable. The United States Government in its reply of 12 January recounted its past experience when General Marshall conducted the peace negotiations and declared that it did not believe any useful purpose would be served by its attempting to act as an intermediary in the prevailing situation. The Soviet Government in its reply of 17 January rejected the Chinese plea on the ground that it would militate against the Soviet policy of non-interference in the internal affairs of other countries, and suggested, instead, direct negotiations between the Nanking Government and the Chinese Communists.

Meanwhile, events in China were taking their remorseless course. Towards the close of 1949 the Chinese Communists had driven the Kuomintang from the Chinese mainland to Formosa. Towards the end of September 1949 they had called the Chinese People's Political Consultative Conference which adopted the Common Programme and proclaimed the new régime. The Common Programme laid down the principles and objectives of the foreign policy of New China. The objectives were to be 'the safeguarding of the independence, freedom, and integrity ... of the country, supporting of ... international peace and friendly cooperation between the peoples of all countries and opposition to the imperialist policy of aggression and war'. The new Government was empowered to establish diplomatic relations on the basis of 'equality, mutual benefit and mutual respect for territory and sovereignty'.

The Communists, however, left it in no doubt that in international politics New China was a part of the Communist bloc. The Chinese People's PCC declared: 'This Government will unite with all peace and freedom-loving countries, nations and people, first of all the Soviet Union and the new democratic countries, as allies to oppose jointly the imperialist plots for provoking war and strive for world lasting peace.' This was followed up by a speech by Liu Shao-chi, one of the Chinese Communist Party's chief theoreticians and a Vice-Chairman of the new Government, on 8 October 1949 at the occasion of the inaugural conference of the Sino-Soviet Friendship Association, where he enlarged upon China's need for alliance with the Soviet Union and the benefits accruing to China from this alliance.

On 1 October 1949 the Central People's Government invited foreign Powers to recognize the new régime. The Soviet Union was the first to accord its recognition, on 2 October. Soviet recognition was followed by recognition by the Eastern European countries. India extended recognition to the People's Government on 30 December. Pakistan and Ceylon followed suit. The new régime was recognized by various countries of Asia and Europe, but the United States and France were the two big countries who were not prepared to accord recognition to it. The United States Government, mindful of the uncompromising opposition of the US Congress, was unwilling to consider the recognition of the Chinese Communist Government. It also led the opposition to the admission of China to the United Nations. The Central People's Government made repeated efforts to oust the Kuomintang and secure its own membership of the UN. The Chinese Foreign Minister, Chou En-lai, sent cables to the UN General Assembly in November 1949 and

January 1950 repudiating the Kuomintang delegates and demanding admittance for delegates appointed by the new régime. A number of countries, including India, strongly favoured giving New China a seat in the United Nations but the United States' determined opposition was successful in keeping New China out.

PART II

EXTERNAL RELATIONS

THE NATIONALIST GOVERNMENT

Section One
Relations with the United States   Page

THE PEOPLE'S REPUBLIC

Section Two
Relations with the Soviet Union

Section Three
The United Nations

PART TWO

I RELATIONS WITH THE UNITED STATES

38   7 *January* 1947

STATEMENT BY GENERAL MARSHALL, SPECIAL REPRESENTATIVE OF PRESIDENT TRUMAN, ON THE FAILURE OF HIS PEACE MISSION TO CHINA

The President has recently given a summary of the developments in China during the past year and the position of the American Government toward China. Circumstances now dictate that I should supplement this with impressions gained at first hand.

In this intricate and confused situation, I shall merely endeavour here to touch on some of the more important considerations—as they appeared to me—during my connexion with the negotiations to bring about peace in China and a stable democratic form of government.

In the first place, the greatest obstacle to peace has been the complete, almost overwhelming suspicion with which the Chinese Communist Party and the Kuomintang regard each other.

On the one hand, the leaders of the Government are strongly opposed to a communistic form of government. On the other, the Communists frankly state that they are Marxists and intend to work toward establishing a communistic form of government in China, though first advancing through the medium of a democratic form of government of the American or British type.

The leaders of the Government are convinced in their minds that the Communist-expressed desire to participate in a government of the type endorsed by the Political Consultative Conference last January had for its purpose only a destructive intention. The Communists felt, I believe, that the Government was insincere in its apparent acceptance of the PCC resolutions for the formation of the new government and intended by coercion of military force and the action of secret police to obliterate the Communist Party. Combined with this mutual deep distrust was the conspicuous error by both parties of ignoring the effect of the fears and suspicions of the other party in estimating the reason for proposals or opposition regarding the settlement of various matters under negotiation. They each sought only to take counsel of their own fears. They both, therefore, to that extent took a rather lopsided view of each situation and were susceptible to every evil suggestion or possibility. This complication was exaggerated to an explosive degree by the confused reports of fighting on the distant and tremendous fronts of hostile military contact. Patrol clashes were deliberately magnified into large offensive actions. The distortion of the facts was utilized by both sides to heap condemnation on the other. It was only through the reports of American officers in the field teams from Executive Headquarters that I could get even a partial idea of what was actually happening and the incidents were too numerous and the distances too great for the American personnel to cover all of the ground. I must comment here on the superb courage of the officers of our Army and Marines in struggling against almost insurmountable and maddening obstacles to bring some measure of peace to China.

I think the most important factors involved in the recent breakdown of negotiations are these : On the side of the National Government, which is in effect the Kuomintang, there is a dominant group of reactionaries who have been opposed, in my opinion, to almost every effort I have made to influence the formation of a genuine coalition government. This has usually been under the cover of political or party action, but since the Party was the Government, this action, though subtle or indirect, has been devastating in its effect. They were quite frank in publicly stating their belief that co-operation by the Chinese Communist Party in the Government was inconceivable and that only a policy of force could definitely settle the issue. This group includes military as well as political leaders.

On the side of the Chinese Communist Party there are, I believe, liberals as well as radicals, though this view is vigorously opposed by many who believe that the Chinese Communist Party discipline is too rigidly enforced to admit of such differences of viewpoint. Nevertheless, it has appeared to me that there is a definite liberal group among the Communists, especially of young men who have turned to the Communists in disgust at the corruption evident in the local governments—men who would put the interest of the Chinese people above ruthless measures to establish a Communist ideology in the immediate future. The dyed-in-the-wool Communists do not hesitate at the most drastic measures to gain their end as, for instance, the destruction of communications in order to wreck the economy of China and produce a situation that would facilitate the overthrow or collapse of the Government, without any regard to the immediate suffering of the people involved. They completely distrust the leaders of the Kuomintang and appear convinced that every Government proposal is designed to crush the Chinese Communist Party. I must say that the quite evidently inspired mob actions of last February and March, some within a few blocks of where I was then engaged in completing negotiations, gave the Communists good excuse for such suspicions.

However, a very harmful and immensely provocative phase of the Chinese Communist Party procedure has been in the character of its propaganda. I wish to state to the American people that in the deliberate misrepresentation and abuse of the action, policies and purposes of our Government this propaganda has been without regard for the truth, without any regard whatsoever for the facts, and has given plain evidence of a determined purpose to mislead the Chinese people and the world and to arouse a bitter hatred of Americans. It has been difficult to remain silent in the midst of such public abuse and wholesale disregard of facts, but a denial would merely lead to the necessity of daily denials ; an intolerable course of action for an American official. In the interest of fairness I must state that the Nationalist Government publicity agency has made numerous misrepresentations, though not of the vicious nature of the Communist propaganda. Incidentally, the Communist statements regarding the Anping incident which resulted in the death of three Marines and the wounding of twelve others were almost pure fabrication, deliberately representing a carefully arranged ambuscade of a Marine convoy with supplies for the maintenance of Executive Headquarters and some UNRRA supplies, as a defence against a Marine assault. The investigation of this incident was a tortuous procedure of delays and manœuvres to disguise the true and privately admitted facts of the case.

Sincere efforts to achieve settlement have been frustrated time and again by extremist elements of both sides. The agreements reached by the Political Consultative Conference a year ago were a liberal and forward-looking charter which then offered China a basis for peace and reconstruction. However, irreconcilable groups within the Kuomintang, interested in the preservation of their own feudal control of China, evidently had no real intention of implementing them. Though I speak as a soldier, I must here also deplore the dominating influence of the military. Their dominance accentuates the weakness of civil government in China. At the same time, in pondering the situation in China, one must have clearly in mind not the workings of small Communist groups or committees to which we are accustomed in America, but rather of millions of people and an army of more than a million men.

I have never been in a position to be certain of the development of attitudes in the innermost Chinese Communist circles. Most certainly, the course which the Chinese Communist Party has pursued in recent months indicated an unwillingness to make a fair compromise. It has been impossible even to get them to sit down at a conference table with Government representatives to discuss given issues. Now the Communists have broken off negotiations by their last offer which demanded the dissolution of the National Assembly and a return to the military positions of 13 January which the Government could not be expected to accept.

Between this dominant reactionary group in the Government and the irreconcilable Communists who, I must state, did not so appear last February, lies the problem of how peace and well-being are to be brought to the long-suffering and presently inarticulate mass of the people of China. The reactionaries in the Government have evidently counted on substantial American support regardless of their actions. The Communists by their unwillingness to compromise in the national interest are evidently counting on an economic collapse to bring about the fall of the Government, accelerated by extensive guerrilla action against the long lines of rail communications—regardless of the cost in suffering to the Chinese people.

The salvation of the situation, as I see it, would be the assumption of leadership by the liberals in the Government and in the minority parties, a splendid group of men, but who as yet lack the political power to exercise a controlling influence. Successful action on their part under the leadership of Generalissimo Chiang Kai-shek would, I believe, lead to unity through good government.

In fact, the National Assembly has adopted a democratic Constitution which in all major respects is in accordance with the principles laid down by the all-party Political Consultative Conference of last January. It is unfortunate that the Communists did not see fit to participate in the Assembly since the Constitution that has been adopted seems to include every major point that they wanted.

Soon the Government in China will undergo major reorganization pending the coming into force of the Constitution following elections to be completed before Christmas Day 1947. Now that the form for a democratic China has been laid down by the newly adopted Constitution, practical measures will be the test. It remains to be seen to what extent the Government will give substance to the form by a genuine welcome of all groups actively to share in the responsibility of government.

The first step will be the reorganization of the State Council and the executive branch of Government to carry on administration pending the enforcement of the Constitution. The manner in which this is done and the amount of representation accorded to liberals and to non-Kuomintang members will be significant. It is also to be hoped that during this interim period the door will remain open for Communists or other groups to participate if they see fit to assume their share of responsibility for the future of China.

It has been stated officially and categorically that the period of political tutelage under the Kuomintang is at an end. If the termination of one-party rule is to be a reality, the Kuomintang should cease to receive financial support from the Government.

I have spoken very frankly because in no other way can I hope to bring the people of the United States to even a partial understanding of this complex problem. I have expressed all these views privately in the course of negotiations ; they are well known, I think, to most of the individuals concerned. I express them now publicly, as it is my duty, to present my estimate of the situation and its possibilities to the American people who have a deep interest in the development of conditions in the Far East promising an enduring peace in the Pacific.

United States Relations with China, pp. 686-9.

39   24 *August* 1947

LT-GENERAL WEDEMEYER'S STATEMENT ON THE CONCLUSION OF HIS MISSION IN CHINA

As promised in the initial Press release, the inquiry into economic, political, military and social conditions has been undertaken without commitment or prejudgement.

All members of the mission have striven for objectivity and impartiality. To that end we have travelled widely to escape influences peculiar to any one area, visiting Mukden and Fusan, Manchuria ; Peiping, Tientsin, Tsingtao and Tsinan in North China ; Nanking, Shanghai and Hankow in Central China ; Canton in South China, and also Taiwan (Formosa).

Successful efforts were made to reach all classes and categories of people as measured by economic position, intellectual attainment and divergent political viewpoints. Foreign business men and officials were interviewed. We have seen officials of national and local governments, members of various political organizations, many of whom were frankly critical of the Government and some of whom were far Left in their views.

We have received approximately 2,000 letters, a small proportion of which were anonymous. These letters contained suggestions which we were able to follow up advantageously.

The last week of our stay in China was devoted chiefly to analysing an enormous mass of data and in relating political, economic and other items together to reach sound judgements and conclusions.

Varied as were the views, there is one point on which all the hearts and minds of China unite : Throughout strife-torn China there is a passionate longing for peace, an early, lasting peace. I wish the means of attaining it were as easily discernible.

After VJ Day the Chinese people rightfully expected to enjoy the fruits of hard-earned victory. They endured hardships and dangers and suffered untold privations in their efforts to expel the ruthless invader.

In China today I find apathy and lethargy in many quarters. Instead of seeking solutions of problems presented, considerable time and effort are spent in blaming outside influences and seeking outside assistance.

It is discouraging to note the abject defeatism of many Chinese, who are normally competent and patriotic, and who instead should be full of hope and determination.

Weakened and disrupted by long years of war and revolution, China still possesses most of the physical resources needed for her own rehabilitation. Recovery awaits inspirational leadership and moral and spiritual resurgence wh:ch can only come from within China.

While I am fully aware of the interests and problems of particular individuals or groups within the country, I am profoundly concerned over the welfare of the Chinese people as a whole. It is my conviction that if the Chinese Communists are truly patriotic and interested primarily in the well-being of their country, they will halt the voluntary employment of force in efforts to impose ideologies. If they are sincere in a desire to help the Chinese people, they can better do so by peaceful means, in lieu of the violence and destruction which have marked these tragic months.

Equally important, the existing Central Government can win and retain the undivided, enthusiastic support of the bulk of the Chinese people by removing incompetent and/or corrupt people who now occupy many positions of responsibility in the Government, not only national but more so in provincial and municipal structures.

There are honourable officials who show high efficiency and devotion to duty, who strive to live within ridiculous salaries and such private means as they possess, just as there are conscientious business men who live up to a high code of commercial ethics. But no one will misunderstand my emphasis upon the large number whose conduct is notoriously marked by greed, incompetence or both.

To regain and maintain the confidence of the people, the Central Government will have to effect immediately drastic, far-reaching political and economic reforms. Promises will no longer suffice. Performance is absolutely necessary. It should be accepted that military force in itself will not eliminate Communism.

On taking leave, all members of the mission join in expressing sincere gratitude for the assistance uniformly given by the Generalissimo and all patriotic Chinese with whom we had contact. All Americans hope and pray that China will achieve the unity, prosperity and happiness which her people so richly deserve and of which they have been unjustly deprived for so many years.

United States Relations with China, pp. 763-4.

40   19 *September* 1947

LT-GENERAL WEDEMEYER'S REPORT TO PRESIDENT TRUMAN

Memorandum for the President

My dear Mr President : In compliance with your directive to me of 9 July 1947, the attached 'Report on China-Korea' is respectfully submitted.

In consonance with your instructions, advisers from State, Treasury, War and Navy Departments accompanied me on a two months fact-finding mission in the Far East. The principal cities and some rural areas in China and Korea were visited. Successful efforts were made to reach all categories of people as measured by economic position, intellectual attainment and divergent political viewpoints. Conferences were held with public officials and with private citizens in all walks of life. Approximately 1,200 memoranda from individuals and groups were received and considered.

The report includes pertinent data in appendices which may be of interest and assistance to appropriate Government departments and agencies. The report presents against a global background my estimates of the situations, current and projected, in both China and Korea, and recommends what I deem to be sound courses of action for achievement of United States objectives in the Far East.

Respectfully yours,

A. C. WEDEMEYER
Lieutenant-General, US Army

REPORT TO THE PRESIDENT

CHINA

Part I—General Statement

China's history is replete with examples of encroachment, arbitrary action, special privilege, exploitation, and usurpation of territory on the part of foreign Powers. Continued foreign infiltration, penetration or efforts to obtain spheres of influence in China, including Manchuria and Taiwan (Formosa), could be interpreted only as a direct infringement and violation of China's sovereignty and a contravention of the principles of the Charter of the United Nations. It is mandatory that the United States and those other nations subscribing to the principles of the Charter of the United Nations should combine their efforts to ensure the unimpeded march of all peoples toward goals that recognize the dignity of man and his civil rights and, further, definitely provide the opportunity to express freely how and by whom they will be governed.

Those goals and the lofty aims of freedom-loving peoples are jeopardized today by forces as sinister as those that operated in Europe and Asia during the ten years leading to World War II. The pattern is familiar—employment of subversive agents; infiltration tactics; incitement of disorder and chaos to disrupt normal economy and thereby to undermine popular confidence in government and leaders; seizure of authority without reference to the will of the people—all the techniques skilfully designed and ruthlessly implemented in order to create favourable conditions for the imposition of totalitarian ideologies. This pattern is present in the Far East, particularly in the areas contiguous to Siberia.

If the United Nations is to have real effect in establishing economic stability and in maintaining world peace, these developments merit high priority on the United Nations' agenda for study and action. Events of the past two years demonstrate the futility of appeasement based on the hope that the strongly consolidated forces of the Soviet Union will adopt either a conciliatory or a co-operative attitude, except as tactical expedients. Soviet practice in the countries already occupied or dominated completes the mosaic of aggressive expansion through ruthless secret police methods and through an increasing political and economic enslavement of peoples. Soviet literature, confirmed repeatedly by Communist leaders, reveals a definite plan for expansion far exceeding that of Nazism in its ambitious scope and dangerous implications. Therefore in attempting a solution to the problem presented in the Far East, as well as in other troubled areas of the world, every possible opportunity must be used to seize the initiative in order to create and maintain bulwarks of freedom.

Notwithstanding all the corruption and incompetence that one notes in China, it is a certainty that the bulk of the people are not disposed to a Communist political and economic structure. Some have become affiliated with Communism in indignant protest against oppressive police measures, corrupt practices and maladministration of National Government officials. Some have lost all hope for China under existing leadership and turn to the Communists in despair. Some accept a new leadership by mere inertia.

Indirectly, the United States facilitated the Soviet programme in the Far East by agreeing at the Yalta Conference to Russian re-entry into Manchuria, and later by withholding aid from the National Government. There were justifiable reasons for these policies. In the one case we were concentrating maximum Allied strength against the Japanese in order to accelerate crushing defeat and thus save Allied lives. In the other, we were withholding unqualified support from a government within which corruption and incompetence were so prevalent that it was losing the support of its own people. Further, the United States had not yet realized that the Soviet Union would fail to co-operate in the accomplishment of world-wide plans for post-war rehabilitation. Our own participation in those plans has already afforded assistance to other nations and peoples, friends and former foes alike, to a degree unparalleled in humanitarian history.

Gradually it has become apparent that the World War II objectives for which we and others made tremendous sacrifices are not being fully attained, and that there remains in the world a force presenting even greater dangers to world peace than did the Nazi militarists and the Japanese jingoists. Consequently the United States made the decision in the spring of 1947 to assist Greece and Turkey with a view to protecting their sovereignties, which were threatened by the direct or inspired activities of the Soviet Union. Charges of unilateral action and circumvention of the United Nations were made by members of that organization. In the light of its purposes and principles such criticisms seemed plausible. The United States promptly declared its intention of referring the matter to the United Nations when that organization would be ready to assume responsibility.

It follows that the United Nations should be informed of contemplated action with regard to China. If the recommendations of this report are approved, the United States should suggest to China that she inform the United Nations officially of her request to the United States for material assistance and advisory aid in order to facilitate

China's post-war rehabilitation and economic recovery. This will demonstrate that the United Nations is not being circumvented, and that the United States is not infringing upon China's sovereignty, but contrarywise is co-operating constructively in the interest of peace and stability in the Far East, concomitantly in the world.

The situation in Manchuria has deteriorated to such a degree that prompt action is necessary to prevent that area from becoming a Soviet satellite. The Chinese Communists may soon gain military control of Manchuria and announce the establishment of a government. Outer Mongolia, already a Soviet satellite, may then recognize Manchuria and conclude a 'mutual support agreement' with a *de facto* Manchurian government of the Chinese Communists. In that event, the Soviet Union might accomplish a mutual support agreement with Communist-dominated Manchuria, because of her current similar agreement with Outer Mongolia. This would create a difficult situation for China, the United States and the United Nations. Ultimately it could lead to a Communist-dominated China.

The United Nations might take immediate action to bring about cessation of hostilities in Manchuria as a prelude to the establishment of a Guardianship or Trusteeship. The Guardianship might consist of China, Soviet Russia, the United States, Great Britain and France. This should be attempted promptly and could be initiated only by China. Should one of the nations refuse to participate in Manchurian Guardianship, China might then request the General Assembly of the United Nations to establish a Trusteeship, under the provisions of the Charter.

Initially China might interpret Guardianship or Trusteeship as an infringement upon her sovereignty. But the urgency of the matter should encourage a realistic view of the situation. If these steps are not taken by China, Manchuria may be drawn into the Soviet orbit, despite United States aid, and lost, perhaps permanently, to China.

The economic deterioration and the incompetence and corruption in the political and military organizations in China should be considered against an all-inclusive background lest there be disproportionate emphasis upon defects. Comity requires that cognizance be taken of the following :

Unlike other Powers since VJ Day, China has never been free to devote full attention to internal problems that were greatly confounded by eight years of war. The current civil war has imposed an overwhelming financial and economic burden at a time when resources and energies have been dissipated and when, in any event, they would have been strained to the utmost to meet the problems of recovery.

The National Government has consistently, since 1927, opposed Communism. Today the same political leader and same civil and military officials are determined to prevent their country from becoming a Communist-dominated state or a Soviet satellite.

Although the Japanese offered increasingly favourable surrender terms during the course of the war, China elected to remain steadfast with her Allies. If China had accepted surrender terms, approximately a million Japanese would have been released for employment against American forces in the Pacific.

I was assured by the Generalissimo that China would support to the limit of her ability an American programme for the stabilization of the Far East. He stated categorically that, regardless of moral encouragement or material aid received from the United States, he is determined to oppose Communism and to create a democratic form of government in consonance with Dr Sun Yat-sen's principles. He stated further that he plans to make sweeping reforms in the Government including the removal of incompetent and corrupt officials. He stated that some progress has been made along these lines but, with spiralling inflation, economic distress and civil war, it has been difficult to accomplish fully these objectives. He emphasized that, when the Communist problem is solved, he could drastically reduce the Army and concentrate upon political and economic reforms. I retain the conviction that the Generalissimo is sincere in his desire to attain these objectives. I am not certain that he has today sufficient determination to do so if this requires absolute overruling of the political and military cliques surrounding him. Yet, if realistic United States aid is to prove effective in stabilizing the situation in China and in coping with the dangerous expansion of communism, that determination must be established.

Adoption by the United States of a policy motivated solely toward stopping the expansion of Communism without regard to the continued existence of an unpopular repressive government would render any aid ineffective. Further, United States prestige in the Far East would suffer heavily, and wavering elements might turn away from the existing Government to communism.

In China (and Korea), the political, economic and psychological problems are inextricably mingled. All of them are complex and are becoming increasingly difficult of solution. Each has been studied assiduously in compliance with your directive. Each will be discussed in the course of this report. However, it is recognized that a continued global appraisal is mandatory in order to preclude disproportionate or untimely assistance to any specific area.

The following three postulates of United States foreign policy are pertinent to indicate the background of my investigations, analyses and report :

The United States will continue support of the United Nations in the attainment of its lofty aims, accepting the possible development that the Soviet Union or other nations may not actively participate.

Moral support will be given to nations and peoples that have established political and economic structures compatible with our own, or that give convincing evidence of their desire to do so.

Material aid may be given to those same nations and peoples in order to accelerate post-war rehabilitation and to develop economic stability, provided :

That such aid shall be used for the purposes intended.

That there is continuing evidence that they are taking effective steps to help themselves, or are firmly committed to do so.

That such aid shall not jeopardize American economy and shall conform to an integrated programme that involves other international commitments and contributes to the attainment of political, economic and psychological objectives of the United States.

Part II—China

Political

Although the Chinese people are unanimous in their desire for peace at almost any cost, there seems to be no possibility of its realization under existing circumstances. On one side is the Kuomintang, whose reactionary leadership, repression and corruption have caused a loss of popular faith in the Government. On the other side, bound ideologically to the Soviet Union, are the Chinese Communists, whose eventual aim is admittedly a Communist state in China. Some reports indicate that Communist measures of land reform have gained for them the support of the majority of peasants in areas under their control, while others indicate that their ruthless tactics of land distribution and terrorism have alienated the majority of such peasants. They have, however, successfully organized many rural areas against the National Government. Moderate groups are caught between Kuomintang misrule and repression and ruthless Communist totalitarianism. Minority parties lack dynamic leadership and sizeable following. Neither the moderates, many of whom are in the Kuomintang, nor the minority parties are able to make their influence felt because of National Government repression. Existing provincial opposition leading to possible separatist movements would probably crystallize only if collapse of the Government were imminent.

Soviet actions, contrary to the letter and spirit of the Sino-Soviet Treaty of 1945 and its related documents, have strengthened the Chinese Communist position in Manchuria, with political, economic and military repercussions on the National Government's position both in Manchuria and in China proper, and have made more difficult peace and stability in China. The present trend points toward a gradual disintegration of the National Government's control, with the ultimate possibility of a Communist-dominated China.

Steps taken by the Chinese Government toward governmental reorganization in mid-April 1947 aroused hopes of improvement in the political situation. However, the reorganization resulted in little change. Reactionary influences continue to mould important policies even though the Generalissimo remains the principal determinative force in the Government. Since the April reorganization, the most significant change has been the appointment of General Chen Cheng to head the civil and military administration in Manchuria. Projected steps include elections in the Fall for the formation of a constitutional government, but, under present conditions, they are not expected to result in a government more representative than the present régime.

Economic

Under the impact of civil strife and inflation, the Chinese economy is disintegrating. The most probable outcome of present trends would be, not sudden collapse, but a continued and creeping paralysis and consequent decline in the authority and power of the National Government. The past ten years of war have caused serious deterioration of transportation and communication facilities, mines, utilities and industries. Notwithstanding some commendable efforts and large amounts of economic aid, their overall capabilities are scarcely half those of the pre-war period. With disruption of transportation facilities and the loss of much of North China and Manchuria, important resources of those rich areas are no longer available for the rehabilitation and support of China's economy.

Inflation in China has been diffused slowly through an enormous population without causing the immediate dislocation which would have occurred in a highly industrialized economy. The rural people, 80 per cent of the total Chinese population of 450 million, barter foodstuffs for local handicraft products without suffering a drastic cut in living standards. Thus, local economies exist in many parts of China, largely insulated from the disruption of urban industry. Some local economies are under the control of Communists, and some are loosely under the control of provincial authorities.

14   209

The principal cause of the hyperinflation is the long-continued deficit in the national Budget. Present revenue collections, plus the profits of nationalized enterprises, cover only one-third of governmental expenditures, which are approximately 70 per cent military, and an increasing proportion of the Budget is financed by the issuance of new currency. In the first six months of 1947 note-issue was tripled but rice prices increased sevenfold. Thus prices and governmental expenditures spiral upwards, with price increases occurring faster than new currency can be printed. With further price increases, budget revisions will undoubtedly be necessary. The most urgent economic need of Nationalist China is a reduction of the military budget.

China's external official assets amount to $327 million (US) on 30 July 1947. Privately-held foreign exchange assets are at least $600 million and may total $1500 million, but no serious attempt has been made to mobilize these private resources for rehabilitation purposes. Private Chinese assets located in China include probably $200 million in gold, and about $75 million in US currency notes. Although China has not exhausted her foreign official assets, and probably will not do so at the present rates of imports and exports until early 1949, the continuing deficit in her external balance of payments is a serious problem.

Disparity between the prices of export goods in China and in world markets at unrealistic official exchange rates has greatly penalized exports, as have disproportionate increases in wages and other costs. Despite rigorous trade and exchange controls, imports have greatly exceeded exports, and there consistently has been a heavy adverse trade balance.

China's food harvests this year are expected to be significantly larger than last year's fairly good returns. This moderately encouraging situation with regard to crops is among the few favourabe factors which can be found in China's current economic situation.

Under inflationary conditions, long-term investment is unattractive for both Chinese and foreign capital. Private Chinese funds tend to go into short-term advances, hoarding of commodities, and capital flight. The entire psychology is speculative and inflationary, preventing ordinary business planning and handicapping industrial recovery.

Foreign business enterprises in China are adversely affected by the inefficient and corrupt administration of exchange and import controls, discriminatory application of tax laws, the increasing role of government trading agencies and the trend towards state ownership of industries. The Chinese Government has taken some steps toward improvement but generally has been apathetic in its efforts.

Between 1944 and 1947, the anti-inflationary measure on which the Chinese Government placed most reliance was the public sale of gold borrowed from the United States. The intention was to absorb paper currency, and thus reduce the effective demand for goods. Under the circumstance of continued large deficits, however, the only effect of the gold sales programme was to retard slightly the price inflation and dissipate dollar assets.

A programme to stabilize the economic situation was undertaken in February 1947. The measures included a wage freeze, a system of limited rationing to essential workers in a few cities, and the sale of government bonds. The effect of this programme has been slight, and the wage freeze has been abandoned. In August 1947, the unrealistic official rate of exchange was replaced, for proceeds of exports and remittances, by a free market in foreign exchange. This step is expected to stimulate exports, but it is too early to determine whether it will be effective.

The issuance of a new silver currency has been proposed as a future measure to combat inflation. If the Government continued to finance budgetary deficits by unbacked note issue, the silver would probably go into hoards and the price inflation would continue. The effect would be no more than that of the gold sales in 1944-7, namely, a slight and temporary retardation of the inflationary spiral. The proposal could be carried out, moreover, only through a loan from the United States of at least $200 million in silver.

In the construction field, China has prepared expansive plans for reconstruction of communications, mines and industries. Some progress has been made in implementing them, notably in the partial rehabilitation of certain railroads and in the textile industry. Constructive results have been handicapped by a lack of funds, equipment and experienced management, supervisory and technical personnel.

On 1 August 1947, the State Council approved a 'Plan for Economic Reform'. This appears to be an omnibus of plans covering all phases of Chinese economic reconstruction but its effectiveness cannot yet be determined.

Social – Cultural

Public education has been one of the chief victims of war and social and economic disruption. Schoolhouses, textbooks and other equipment have been destroyed and the cost of replacing any considerable portion cannot now be met. Teachers, like other public servants, have seen the purchasing power of a month's salary shrink to the market value of a few days' rice ration. This applies to the entire educational system, from primary schools, which provide a medium to combat the nation's grievous illiteracy, to universities, from which must come the nation's professional men, technicians and administrators. The universities have suffered in an additional and no less serious respect—traditional academic freedom. Students participating in protest demonstrations have been severely and at times brutally punished by National Government agents without pretence of trial or public evidence of the sedition charged. Faculty members have often been dismissed or refused employment with no evidence of professional unfitness, patently because they were politically objectionable to Government officials. Somewhat similarly, periodicals have been closed down 'for reasons of military security' without stated charges, and permitted to reopen only after new managements have been imposed. Resumption of educational and other public welfare activities on anything like the desired scale can be accomplished only by restraint of officialdom's abuses, and when the nation's economy is stabilized sufficiently to defray the cost of such vital activities.

Military

The overall military position of the National Government has deteriorated in the past several months and the current military situation favours the Communist forces. The Generalissimo has never wavered in his contention that he is fighting for national independence against the forces of an armed rebellion nor has he been completely convinced that the Communist problem can be resolved except by force of arms. Although the Nationalist Army has a preponderance of force, the tactical initiative rests with the Communists. Their hit-and-run tactics, adapted to their mission of destruction at points or in areas of their own selection, give them a decided advantage over the Nationalists, who must defend many critical areas including connecting lines of communication. Obviously large numbers of Nationalist troops involved in such defensive roles are immobilized whereas Communist tactics permit almost complete freedom of action. The Nationalists' position is precarious in Manchuria, where they occupy only a slender finger of territory. Their control is strongly disputed in Shantung and Hopei Provinces where the Communists make frequent dislocating attacks against isolated garrisons.

In order to improve materially the current military situation, the Nationalist forces must first stabilize the fronts and then regain the initiative. Further, since the government is supporting the civil war with approximately seventy per cent of its national budget, it is evident that steps taken to alleviate the situation must point toward an improvement in the effectiveness of the armed forces with a concomitant programme of social, political and economic reforms, including a decrease in the size of the military establishment. Whereas some rather ineffective steps have been taken to reorganize and revitalize the command structure, and more sweeping reforms are projected, the effectiveness of the Nationalist Army requires a sound programme of equipment and improved logistical support. The present industrial potential of China is inadequate to support military forces effectively. Chinese forces under present conditions cannot cope successfully with internal strife or fulfil China's obligations as a member of the family of nations. Hence outside aid, in the form of munitions (most urgently ammunition) and technical assistance, is essential before any plan of operations can be undertaken with a reasonable prospect of success. Military advice is now available to the Nationalists on a General Staff level through American military advisory groups. The Generalissimo expressed to me repeatedly a strong desire to have this advice and supervision extended in scope to include field forces, training centres and particularly logistical agencies.

Extension of military aid by the United States to the National Government might possibly be followed by similar aid from the Soviet Union to the Chinese Communists, either openly or covertly—the latter course seems more likely. An arena of conflicting ideologies might be created as in 1935 in Spain. There is always the possibility that such developments in this area, as in Europe and in the Middle East, might precipitate a third world war.

Part IV—Conclusions

The peaceful aims of freedom loving peoples in the world are jeopardized today by developments as portentous as those leading to World War II.

The Soviet Union and her satellites give no evidence of a conciliatory or co-operative attitude in these developments. The United States is compelled, therefore, to initiate realistic lines of action in order to create and maintain bulwarks of freedom, and to protect United States strategic interests.

The bulk of the Chinese are not disposed to communism and they are not concerned with ideologies. They desire food, shelter and the opportunity to live in peace.

China

The spreading internecine struggle within China threatens world peace. Repeated American efforts to mediate have proved unavailing. It is apparent that positive steps are required to end hostilities immediately. The most logical approach to this very complex and ominous situation would be to refer the matter to the United Nations.

A China dominated by Chinese Communists would be inimical to the interests of the United States, in view of their openly expressed hostility and active opposition to those principles which the United States regards as vital to the peace of the world.

The Communists have the tactical initiative in the overall military situation. The Nationalist position in Manchuria is precarious, and in Shantung and Hopei Provinces strongly disputed. Continued deterioration of the situation may result in the early establishment of a Soviet satellite government in Manchuria and ultimately in the evolution of a Communist-dominated China.

China is suffering increasingly from disintegration. Her requirements for rehabilitation are large. Her most urgent needs include governmental reorganization and reforms, reduction of the military budget and external assistance.

A programme of aid, if effectively employed, would bolster opposition to Communist expansion, and would contribute to gradual development of stability in China.

Due to excesses and oppressions by Government police agencies basic freedoms of the people are being jeopardized. Maladministration and corruption cause a loss of confidence in the Government. Until drastic political and economic reforms are undertaken United States aid cannot accomplish its purpose.

Even so, criticism of results achieved by the National Government in efforts for improvement should be tempered by a recognition of the handicaps imposed on China by eight years of war, the burden of her opposition to Communism, and her sacrifices for the Allied cause.

A United States programme of assistance could best be implemented under the supervision of American advisers in specified economic and military fields. Such a programme can be undertaken only if China requests advisory aid as well as material assistance.

Part V—Recommendations

It is recommended :

That the United States Government provide as early as practicable moral, advisory, and material support to China in order to contribute to the early establishment of peace in the world in consonance with the enunciated principles of the United Nations, and concomitantly to protect United States strategic interests against militant forces which now threaten them.

That United States policies and actions suggested in this report be thoroughly integrated by appropriate Government agencies with other international commitments. It is recognized that any foreign assistance extended must avoid jeopardizing the American economy.

China

That China be advised that the United States is favourably disposed to continue aid designed to protect China's territorial integrity and to facilitate her recovery, under agreements to be negotiated by representatives of the two Governments, with the following stipulations :

That China inform the United Nations promptly of her request to the United States for increased material and advisory assistance.

That China request the United Nations to take immediate action to bring about a cessation of hostilities in Manchuria and request that Manchuria be placed under a Five-Power Guardianship or, failing that, under a Trusteeship in accordance with the United Nations Charter.

That China make effective use of her own resources in a programme for economic reconstruction and initiate sound fiscal policies leading to reduction of budgetary deficits.

That China give continuing evidence that the urgently required political and military reforms are being implemented.

That China accept American advisers as responsible representatives of the United States Government in specified military and economic fields to assist China in utilizing United States aid in the manner for which it is intended.

United States Relations with China, pp. 764-74.

41   *2 September* 1947

KUOMINTANG PREMIER CHANG CHUN'S PRESS
INTERVIEW ON THE STATEMENT BY
LT-GENERAL WEDEMEYER

Premier Chang Chun in an exclusive interview with the United Press today declared there will be no change in either the domestic or foreign policy of the Chinese Government as a result of the Wedemeyer Mission and said: 'There were many things which Wedemeyer did not know.'

The Premier said while he met Lieutenant-General Albert C. Wedemeyer several times during the American envoy's visit to China, Wedemeyer did not hold any 'serious' discussions with him. 'General Wedemeyer paid more attention to people outside the Government than in it', Chang said.

The Prime Minister said that many of the reforms suggested in the Wedemeyer farewell statement 'were already being carried out before the General visited China. Perhaps General Wedemeyer thought he was not away from China for a long time and still knows China well,' Chang said.

'There were many people who wanted to see Wedemeyer and could not. And there were many things not known to the General.' Chang said Wedemeyer got lots of help from his advisers 'and the General perhaps thought these materials were quite enough'.

Criticized by People

The Premier said that he personally was good friends with Wedemeyer and recognized the good intentions of the General 'but as a representative of the President of the United States Wedemeyer's statement caused a lot of criticism among the Chinese people'.

The Prime Minister said he hopes that in time the critics will understand Wedemeyer's good intention 'and Wedemeyer will understand the persons who criticized his statement'.

Asked whether his assertion that there would be no change in Chinese domestic policy as the result of the Wedemeyer statement means that he did not agree with Wedemeyer's contention that 'drastic and far-reaching political and economic reforms' were necessary, Chang replied that such changes were already provided for in the form of the new constitution and forthcoming national election.

Question of Method

Chang said that such changes however must be made 'step by step' according to a schedule already decided upon by the Chinese Government. 'We are improving,' the Premier said. 'Minor affairs should not be mixed up with matters of policy. It is a question of method. Chinese policy is fixed and will not change either domestically or foreign.

'Our American friends say the Chinese Government is not efficient. We are studying ways and means and we know we have a lot to learn from the United States and Western countries. But changes in China involve many things—old customs, systems and procedures. This does not mean we are not trying to improve our present administration and there are many things we can do now. But many must wait.

'We know, for example, that the period of political tutelage is not good and we are trying to conclude it as soon as possible. But it is not feasible to end the tutelage period until the Constitution is put into operation. Many similar changes can only be done after the Constitution is operative.'

The Premier said that even since the government reorganization the National Government has heavier responsibility and much more work but nevertheless it is bending all effort to usher in the constitutional period.

Government Determined

'In spite of all obstacles, the Government is determined to finish this work this year,' Chang asserted.

He said a lot of people had expressed doubts about whether the Government really intended to hold the national elections this Fall and has suggested that they might be postponed because of the civil war. 'The policy is to hold the elections,' Chang declared. 'And the Government is not going to change that policy in spite of obstacles.'

The Premier touched on other matters which had been the subject of criticism from 'American friends' such as export and import regulations about which business men felt keenly and he said the Government was effecting improvements but foreign critics should not expect a change overnight.

Chang said the specific reactions of the Chinese Government to the Wedemeyer Mission were contained in a Note handed to Wedemeyer a few days prior to the General's departure which he said represented both his views and the views of the Chinese Government.

Chang received me in his spacious office at the Executive Yuan late in the afternoon. He was dressed in a grey civilian suit and spoke Chinese during the formal part of the interview and English during the informal chat. The interview lasted 45 minutes. Samson Shen of the Chinese Information Office acted as the interpreter.

United States Relations with China, pp. 815-16.

42   *28 August* 1947

COMMUNIST RADIO COMMENT ON
THE WEDEMEYER MISSION

North Shensi, 28 August : People here all laugh at Wedemeyer's 24 August departing statement. They say that he is playing another deceptive trick to cover up his imperialistic activities in China by 'criticizing' Chiang's Government, talking of 'peace'.

However, from Wedemeyer's statement one can clearly see these three points : (1) There is no way to cover up the corruption of Chiang Kai-shek's dictatorial rule. (2) There is no way to deny the demand of the Chinese people for ending Chiang's dictatorial rule and US aggression. (3) Even the imperialist Wedemeyer cannot distort the fact that the might of the people of liberated areas, especially that of the people's liberation army, is invincible. The statement shows that even a bloodthirsty butcher like Wedemeyer now sees that to support this evil Government of Chiang is difficult under the present circumstances when the peoples of the world including the US are so bitter against Fascists like Chiang. Although Wedemeyer has quit China and has unhappily accepted that 'military force in itself will not eliminate Communism', yet his promise to equip Chiang's troops and other plots are being put into practice. It is very possible that he will urge Washington for further aid to Chiang to prop up the Kuomintang Government from imminent collapse. Chiang Kai-shek will also exert all his effort for a final struggle and American imperialists will rush aid to Chiang.

People of the liberated areas have known these things too well and they will never be cheated by 'peace' uttered by a hypocrite like Wedemeyer. Real peace can only be attained when Chiang's corrupt rule is thoroughly smashed and American imperialistic force completely driven out of China.

United States Relations with China, pp. 816-17.

43   *6 September* 1947[1]

MEMORANDUM FROM THE NATIONALIST GOVERNMENT TO LT-GENERAL WEDEMEYER OUTLINING ITS ACHIEVEMENTS

On VJ Day the Chinese Government found itself confronted with the following problems :

(1) The question of the Chinese Communists who were maintaining a regular armed force of 310,000 men in addition to a larger number of their so-called 'militia'. The presence of a large number of yet unsurrendered and undisarmed Japanese and puppet government troops in Manchuria was offering opportunities to the Chinese Communists to acquire more and better equipment.

(2) An inflation, which had developed during the long years of war and was threatening the economic life of the nation.

(3) The complete standstill of over 90 per cent of China's railways and the acute shortage of inland shipping which made the work of

---

[1] The memorandum was handed to Lt-Gen. Albert C. Wedemeyer before his departure and transmitted to Secretary Marshall by Ambassador Stuart on 6 September 1947.

repatriation and of restoring order in areas formerly held by the Japanese or puppet forces extremely difficult and rendered it impossible for many pre-war industries to revive even though the plants were partially recovered.

(4) The need for the rehabilitation of rural economy after eight years of neglect and destruction during enemy occupation resulting in widespread shortage of farm labour, livestock and fertilizers and in consequent critical reduction of agricultural production. The total annual production of cotton, for example, was reduced to about 5,320,000 piculs or shih tan, ⅓ of the 1937 level, which was 16,180,000 piculs or shih tan.

(5) There were in China proper more than one million Japanese soldiers and approximately an equal number in Manchuria ; 600,000 puppet government troops scattered in various parts of China proper and another 330,000 of them in Manchuria ; and as a result of Soviet participation in the Far Eastern war, a large Soviet force estimated at 600,000 to 700,000 men deployed in different parts of Manchuria.

(6) And last, but by no means the least, the question of the fulfilment of commitments made by the Government, before and during the war, of the convocation of the National Assembly, the drafting and adoption of a national constitution, the return by the Kuomintang of the responsibility of government to the people, the termination of one-party rule, and the lifting of censorship. These were the most difficult problems that the Government had to deal with all at once on VJ Day. The weight of responsibility that so suddenly fell on the Government was far greater than the Government machine then existing could adequately cope with. Not only were the tasks themselves heavy and complicated but they were also in many cases new to the experience of the Government.

In the repatriation of Japanese soldiers and civilians and in the timely despatch of Chinese troops by air and by sea to many areas to take over from the enemy, the Chinese Government was substantially aided by the United States forces in China. Credit must also be given to UNRRA and CNRRA for their contribution toward the solution of many problems in connexion with the repatriation of displaced persons and such relief and rehabilitation work as could be undertaken immediately. Meanwhile, the Government itself was tackling all the problems it could in the circumstances. (1) It set about reorganizing the army and reducing the national budget. (2) An immediate attempt was made following VJ Day to restore communications systems, such as railways, highways, waterways, public utility services and conservancy works. (3) Mines and iron works (including a number of those the equipment of which had been largely removed by the Soviet Army from Manchuria or destroyed by the

Communists) were reopened and textile and other precarious industries were salvaged. (4) Efforts were made afresh to lay down the
foundations for local self-government, such as the reorganizing and
restaffing of municipal and hsien offices, the organization of the Pao-
Chia system in villages and towns, and the rehabilitation of schools
of various grades. (5) Wherever practicable, measures were also
taken to revitalize rural economy. In the case of cotton, the extension work carried out by the Government in the past one and one-
half years is now expected to result in a production of eleven million
piculs or shih tan this year, a 100 per cent increase over the production for the year of VJ Day. Each of these jobs involved considerable
administration, funds and personnel.

When one assesses the work of the Government in this period one
should bear in mind the fact that the social institutions in China were
not yet fully adapted to modern conditions, that a large portion of
her territory was under enemy occupation for many years, and that
the new economic foundations that had been prepared since 1927
were impaired by the enemy. The immensity and complexity of the
task of recovery that followed in the wake of victory must be taken
into account.

There can be no doubt that the Government would have achieved
greater results and China's politico-economic position would be
brighter if the greater part of the Government's constructive effort
had not been thwarted at each turn by the non-settlement of the
Communist issue and the continuance of the war-time legacy—
inflation.

The infiltration of the Chinese Communists into Manchuria during
and following the Soviet occupation constituted a new factor in the
Communist impasse after VJ Day. The armed opposition of the
Communists was the greatest single destructive force against all the
efforts of the Government in carrying out rehabilitation and in restoring law and order, particularly in areas formerly held by the Japanese.
When every possible effort was being made, for instance, to restore
the main communication lines, mobile Communist squads were
actively engaged in demolition work disrupting newly repaired railways, cutting telegraph and telephone lines, and causing havoc in the
countryside.

As a result of the inability on the part of the Chinese Government
to disarm and accept surrender from the large number of Japanese
and puppet government troops in Manchuria, the attitude of the
Communists towards the Government became increasingly challenging and uncompromising. After the meeting of the National Assembly
last November and December, the Communists openly denounced
the adopted Constitution. It was then clear that all hopes of a political

settlement had gone. For by that time the Communists had decided on the immediate launching of a large-scale military offensive. No one could feel more profoundly disappointed than the Government itself at such a turn of events, at a time when so much reconstruction work called for its undivided attention and immediate action.

While the Communist issue remained unsettled, the plan for army reorganization could not materialize owing to Communist obstruction thus hampering the reduction of the armed forces. As a result, a policy of retrenchment in national budget could not be put into effect, and inflation developed to such an extent as to threaten every fabric of our political and economic life. It led to the lowering of the efficiency of the Government administration and the undermining of the morale of the army. The bulk of the civil servants were not paid enough to meet anew the requirements of a bare subsistence. As a result, many Government employees were forced to seek concurrent work in order to maintain their living, while others turned to more lucrative jobs.

To this day there has been no substantial improvement in the treatment of these long-suffering civil servants. However, considering the straitened circumstances of the civil servants in general, it is astonishing to find that the great bulk of them are carrying on without failing in their duties. The loyalty of these people recalls to mind the stolid endurance of the Chinese masses who bore the brunt of the long war against Japanese aggression.

Whatever one may say of the National Government in China, one cannot possibly accuse it of not having steadily pursued the preparatory work for a democratic government as laid down by their leader, Dr Sun Yat-sen. It has always been the unanimous opinion of the leaders of the Kuomintang that unless it could lead the nation into a multi-party and representative government, it could not be said to be in any way carrying out the principles on which the party was founded. No one of any importance in the party has ever questioned the need to terminate the so-called 'period of political tutelage' as soon as the basic conditions stated by Dr Sun have been fulfilled. In this respect, the party as a whole, never once swerved from its aim.

When Sino-Japanese hostilities broke out in 1937, the momentous decision to resist the enemy was accompanied by a nationwide effort to preserve, as far as possible, the political and economic foundation that had been laid since 1927. Above all, the general opinion of the party was such that the interlude of war should not nullify the preparatory work for representative government that had already been undertaken.

In 1938, the People's Political Council was founded to provide a broader basis of representative opinion for the guidance of Government policy. Except for matters of military strategy and security, the Council served as a war-time organ of public opinion. Here, in the midst of a life-and-death struggle, the National Government decided to invite and accept open questions and criticism and thus to promote representative government. This invaluable tradition has happily continued to this day. Although the 200 members of the first People's Political Council were all elected by the Government from different professions and on the basis of geographical distribution, it was widely acknowledged to be a fairly representative body of the politically conscious sections of the country. Early in 1940, the second People's Political Council met with 240 members, of which 90 were for the first time elected by the various provisional provincial and municipal councils, both on a regional and a professional basis. When the third People's Political Council met in 1942, 164 out of the total 240 members were elected by the provincial and municipal councils. Today, the People's Political Council, in the last phase of its existence, has 362 members, of which 227 were re-elected by provincial and municipal councils.

In September 1938, two months after the first People's Political Council held its inaugural meeting, the National Government promulgated the regulations of the provisional provincial council. Today, such councils have been organized in nearly all the provinces. Here again, the percentage of elected councillors was increased after each meeting, so that in many provinces the members of such councils are now entirely elected representatives. The municipal and hsien councils have also been conducted along the same lines. Thus, while the war was being fought and its priority acknowledged, no effort was spared in preserving the continuity of the effort towards the building up of basic democratic institutions and practices.

Shortly after VJ Day, Press censorship was lifted in spite of the existence of a number of factors which might still have argued for its continuance. The National Assembly was convened and the draft constitution adopted in November 1946. The one-party rule had come to an end, although the Kuomintang was still by far the majority party in the Government. The Youth Party and the Demo-Socialist Party are now also represented in the Government.

No observer who is acquainted with Chinese events in the past can possibly fail to notice the existence today of a far greater body of public opinion than had ever existed before. This has come about since VJ Day as a result of the lifting of censorship, the convocation of the National Assembly, the presence of other parties in the Government, the emergence of a responsible Cabinet in the new Executive Yuan and, above all, the effect of the periodic open discussions at the People's Political Council. The defence by the Government of its own policy and administration has in turn a stimulating effect on the growth of public opinion. It brings the Government closer to the people.

Since the Kuomintang gained power it may have committed errors in regard to methods for the attainment of its political goal, but never has it for any period deviated from its general political direction. Exigencies of circumstances may at times have retarded the progress of its work, but in the twenty odd years of its government, it has never been known to recede from a step once it has been taken.

China's critics are prone to lose sight of the vastness of the country, the weaknesses of its traditional political, economic and social structures, and the complexity of the problems with which she is confronted. Their views and judgement are apt to be based too much on the situation of a given moment without due regard to the background.

It may be well for us to review briefly the period between 1927 and 1937, a period in which the strength of the Kuomintang was put for the first time to a real test, and in which the Government never had a continued peace for more than a few months. In 1926, when the Government was still in Canton, it launched upon a punitive expedition against the war lords. In 1927, when the National Government was established in Nanking there were still war lords to reckon with ; there was internal political opposition to overcome from the Communists as well as remnants of the old régime who were ever ready to lend a hand in any port against the Government ; there was no street in Chungking where one could not find public opium dens and such conditions prevailed in many other cities ; extraterritorial rights continued and the attitude of the major Powers, not excluding the United States, towards the new Government was one of critical scepticism. Since 18 September 1931, when the Japanese started their open aggression, the Government had to resist the enemy on the one hand and on the other to suppress the armed rebellion of the Communists in the south.

But in spite of all this, the Government during this hard-pressed period of ten years was able to launch upon a national constructive programme.

In 1937, it had completed almost 5,000 kilometres of railways, 100,000 kilometres of highways ; had built schools, parks, hospitals and civic centres in many cities, trebled the number of middle schools and doubled that of universities and colleges. The number of middle school and vocational school students totalled nearly 600,000 in 1936. It was estimated that illiteracy decreased by almost 20 per cent in those ten years. Modern ordnance works began in 1926 and, at the time of the Lukouchiao incident, China was already able to supply, from her own arsenals, practically all her infantry divisions with rifles, hand grenades, machine guns, trench mortars and various accessories. A national anti-narcotic movement was launched during this period. The number of drug addicts rapidly decreased and by the end of 1938 no public opium den was to be found in areas under the control of the National Government.

When the full-fledged war broke out in 1937, Japanese financial experts predicted that China's finances would collapse within a few months of the war. During the eight years of war China faced financial problems as enormous as they were complicated but as a result of certain vigorous measures taken before the war, such as the adoption of a managed currency, concentration of gold and silver reserves, the reform of the taxation and banking systems, the Chinese Government was able to pass through the early—in fact the most critical— part of the war without any serious financial crisis.

In short the period between the establishment of the National Government in Nanking in 1927 and the beginning of war with Japan in 1937 was one of severe trial for the Kuomintang. However, the Government concentrated its effort on the two-fold task of suppressing Communist rebellion and resisting the Japanese aggression and this gigantic undertaking received the single-minded support of the entire populace. Moreover, the relations between China and her neighbours were at that time not so complicated as they are. The Government was therefore able to turn this difficult decade into a constructive period. Commerce and industries developed while the people both in rural districts and cities were able to plan and look ahead. Industrial production reached in 1936 a level higher than in any previous year. A general feeling of prosperity and growth prevailed.

The complexity of the problems of today may be greater than those of the pre-war years, but the dangers and difficulties which beset the present Government are reminiscent of those that confronted the nation during the early years of war (1937-42), when China was forced to fight Japan single-handed. Whether the present Government, for which the Kuomintang is practically still responsible, will be able to overcome these fresh dangers and difficulties as it did in the war and pre-war periods remains to be seen.

It is, however, clear that there is no weakening of determination on the part of the present Government and the Kuomintang to face the new challenge. As to the lines of policy with which the Government will meet the challenge, several things are uppermost in the minds of its leaders. First, the Communists as an armed political party must be suppressed. No half measures should be considered. The Government fully realizes that the success or failure of this fight against the Communist peril will not only decide its own fate but also the life or death of China as a sovereign Power. In fact, the outcome of the struggle is bound up with the peace and security of the whole of the Far East. Second, the inflation menace must be brought under control; there should be no further delay in initiating some effective programme in this regard because this is the very root of many political, economic and social ills. Third, in the provinces which are free from Communist menace, economic rehabilitation work must be intensified as far as Government resources permit. This must be accompanied by necessary political reform in the local government. Last, the Government must pursue its political goal, the building up of a democratic constitutional government, without fear or hesitation. Whatever difficulties the present Communist rebellion and other political factors may cause to the accomplishment of this task, the Government must proceed to give effect to the Constitution adopted at the end of last year. No real form of democracy is built in a day and it is the consensus of opinion of the Government that the best way to achieve it is to start it as soon as you can.

United States Relations with China, pp. 817-22.

44   5 *June* 1948

US AMBASSADOR STUART'S STATEMENT
ON ANTI-AMERICAN STUDENT AGITATION

It is with real regret that I find myself compelled to take cognizance publicly of a growingly dangerous situation which affects not only the interests of the United States, but, I am firmly convinced, the vital interests of China as well. I am, of course, referring to the campaign against American policy in Japan. I know you will understand that my sorrow at having to do this is all the greater because most of my life has been spent in Chinese academic circles and because the primary object of my life work has been to assist them in some small measure in increasing the welfare and the mature responsibility of Chinese students to themselves and their country.

It is therefore difficult for me to have to admit that the core of anti-American agitation on the question of Japan is coming from the Chinese student groups. I do not pretend to know who initiated this agitation or for what purpose. I have received varying reports as to its origin and intent. Perhaps all reports are partially valid. What I do know is that it is seriously damaging the traditional cordiality between the United States and China and that if it continues it can have most unfortunate results. It is all the more regrettable that this movement should start at a time when the United States is embarking upon a large-scale and serious programme to assist China in its present tragic plight. At a time when the American people are being called upon to assist in the rehabilitation of war-torn areas throughout the world and, I should add, are only too glad to do so, they may well wonder when these efforts are greeted by unreasonable and irresponsible attacks on American policy.

I would be most reluctant to believe that university circles which initiate or follow the anti-American agitation really believe the arguments which they use against my country. We are charged with fostering the restoration of Japanese military and economic imperialism. These charges are demonstrably false. Immediately after the victorious conclusion of our war against Japan, the United States on behalf of the Allied Powers who destroyed Japanese power, proceeded to disband the Japanese Army, Navy, Air Force and General Staff. I defy anyone to produce a single shred of evidence that any part of Japanese military power is being restored or that there is any intention on the part of the United States other than to assure that it will never rise again. The basis of Japanese aggression was its overseas empire. It has now lost that empire and cannot regain it without military power. You may rest assured the American people and Government will make sure it does not do so.

As for Japanese economic and industrial power, the United States, again on behalf of the Allied Powers, proceeded to destroy or dismantle all Japanese war industries. We are now faced with a situation where we must restore enough of Japanese economic life to enable the Japanese people to become self-supporting. No one can expect the American taxpayer to continue indefinitely paying the Japanese bills. Japan must be allowed a chance for self-support or it will be a continuing liability not only to the United States but also to China. An indigent country can never become a peace-loving and democratically-minded people. If it be argued that industry can be converted to war-time purposes, I admit the truth of the allegation. In modern warfare, any production is susceptible of war uses. Food is a war product. Textiles are a war product. Any of the articles of consumption are necessary in modern warfare. It will be our responsibility to ensure that these products are used for peaceful purposes. This task will be made immeasurably easier if we co-operate thereon. It will be immeasurably more difficult if we squabble among ourselves.

If it be charged that the revival of Japanese economy will be a threat to Chinese economy, then I deny it. Certainly the demands of the peoples of the world for goods and services are far greater than anything all the countries in the world in the predictable future can hope to satisfy. On the contrary, the indefinite continuation of an indigent Japan will continue to lower the standards of living of the world. The world will be deprived of what Japan can produce. It will continue to be a drain on our already depleted resources. As a hungry and restless people, it will continue to be a threat to peace. Such a situation is made to order for Communism. If we are sincere in our profession, that Communism, in the general interest, must be stopped, then we must remove the causes which encourage Communism.

If those of you who agitate or who participate in the agitation against the United States on the question of Japan disagree with what I have said, then you must be prepared to face the consequences of your actions. If in your hearts you know that I am right, and still continue your agitation for other and secret purposes, then I say to you that it is time you examined your consciences. If by dishonest means you are attempting to accomplish some clandestine purpose, you are not only damaging the United States, you are also damaging your own country. You are also damaging your own standing and reputation as students and intellectuals of China whose best and most honest efforts are so desperately needed today by your country. You are the ones who are in the best position in China to know the truth. If you betray it you also betray yourselves. If you are not true to yourselves then most assuredly you cannot be true to anyone or anything else.

I hardly need protest my affection for Chinese student groups. If my life has not proven that, then it has been a total failure. I trust then that you will take the harsh words I have felt compelled to speak in the spirit in which they are intended. My greatest wish is the peace and welfare of all peoples of the world. Unless China and the United States can approach each other with mutual trust and confidence, that peace and welfare are endangered. I have confidence that the students of China will not knowingly lend themselves to evil purposes or betray the trust which has been placed in them by their country.

At the same time I want to assure you that I am fully aware of how much the Chinese people suffered at the hands of the Japanese and how heroically China resisted aggression. I was a prisoner of the Japanese myself and I know what it meant. I also know that the American people are aware of the tremendous Chinese sacrifices and are deeply grateful for that selfless contribution to the defeat

of our common enemy. But I would also say that despite the understandable bitterness of China toward Japan, the best guarantee
against a recurrence of the tragedy is wisdom, calmness and unity
of purpose. In the present distraught situation of the world, mis-
understanding among ourselves is the luxury we can least afford.

Your interests in Japan and those of my country are identical.
We do not want a Communist Japan, and our surest method of
preventing such a calamity is to enable the Japanese people to earn
their own living.

United States Relations with China, pp. 869-71.

45   18 *February* 1948

PRESIDENT TRUMAN'S MESSAGE TO THE UNITED
STATES CONGRESS RECOMMENDING A PROGRAMME
OF AID TO CHINA

To the Congress of the United States :

On several occasions I have stated that a primary objective of the
United States is to bring about, throughout the world, the conditions
of a just and lasting peace. This is a cause to which the American
people are deeply devoted.

Since VJ Day we have expended great efforts and large sums of
money on the relief and rehabilitation of war-torn countries, to aid
in restoring workable economic systems which are essential to the
maintenance of peace. A principle which has guided our efforts to
assist these war-torn countries has been that of helping their peoples
to help themselves. The Congress is now giving careful consideration to a most vital and far-reaching proposal to further this
purpose—the programme for aid to European recovery.

I now request the Congress to consider the type of further assistance which this country should provide to China.

A genuine friendship has existed between the American people
and the people of China over many years. This friendship has been
accompanied by a long record of commercial and cultural association and close co-operation between our two countries. Americans
have developed a deep respect for the Chinese people and sympathy
for the many trials and difficulties which they have endured.

The United States has long recognized the importance of a stable
Chinese nation to lasting peace in the Pacific and the entire world.
The vast size and population of China make her an important factor

in world affairs. China is a land which has a rich tradition and culture and a large and energetic population. It has always been our desire to see a strong, progressive China making a full contribution to the strength of the family of nations.

With this end in view, we have supported the National Government of China since it first came to power 20 years ago. China and the United States were allies in the war against Japan, and as an ally we supported China's valiant war efforts against the Japanese. Since the Japanese surrender we have provided a great deal of additional assistance. Military aid was given the Chinese Government, not only to help defeat the Japanese invaders but also to assist in reoccupying Japanese-held areas. The United States contributed the major share of the extensive aid received by China under the programme of the United Nations Relief and Rehabilitation Administration. We made available to the Chinese Government at minimum cost large quantities of surplus goods and equipment of value to China's economy. We are currently extending further aid to China under our foreign-relief programme.

Nevertheless, the Chinese Government and people are still labouring under the double and interrelated burden of civil war and a rapidly deteriorating economy. The strains placed upon the country by 8 years of war and the Japanese occupation and blockade have been increased by internal strife at the very time that reconstruction efforts should be under way. The wartime damage to transport and productive facilities has been greatly accentuated by the continued obstruction and destruction of vital communications by the Communist forces.

The civil warfare has further impeded recovery by forcing upon the Government heavy expenditures which greatly exceed revenues. Continual issuances of currency to meet these expenditures have produced drastic inflation, with its attendant disruption of normal commercial operations. Under these circumstances, China's foreign-exchange holdings have been so reduced that it will soon be impossible for China to meet the cost of essential imports. Without such imports, industrial activity would diminish and the rate of economic deterioration would be sharply increased.

The continued deterioration of the Chinese economy is a source of deep concern to the United States. Ever since the return of General Marshall from China, the problem of assistance to the Chinese has been under continuous study. We have hoped for conditions in China that would make possible the effective and constructive use of American assistance in reconstruction and rehabilitation. Conditions have not developed as we had hoped, and we can only do what is feasible under circumstances as they exist.

We can assist in retarding the current economic deterioration and thus give the Chinese Government a further opportunity to initiate the measures necessary to the establishment of more stable economic conditions. But it is, and has been, clear that only the Chinese Government itself can undertake the vital measures necessary to provide the framework within which efforts toward peace and true economic recovery may be effective.

In determining the character and dimensions of the programme which might be suited to this purpose, we have had to take into account a number of diverse and conflicting factors, including the other demands on our national resources at this time, the availability of specific commodities, the dimensions and complexities of the problems facing the Chinese Government, and the extent to which these problems could be promptly and effectively alleviated by foreign aid. United States assistance to China, like that provided to any other nation, must be adapted to its particular requirements and capacities.

In the light of these factors, I recommend that the Congress authorize a programme for aid to China in the amount of $570,000,000 to provide assistance until 30 June 1949.

The programme should make provision for the financing, through loans or grants, of essential imports into China in the amount of $510,000,000. This estimate is based upon prices as of 1 January 1948, since it is impossible at present to predict what effect current price changes may have on the programme. Revised dollar estimates can be presented in connexion with the request for appropriations if necessary. The essential imports include cereals, cotton, petroleum, fertilizer, tobacco, pharmaceuticals, coal, and repair parts for existing capital equipment. The quantities provided for under this programme are within the limits of available supplies. The financing of these essential commodity imports by the United States would permit the Chinese Government to devote its limited dollar resources to the most urgent of its other needs.

The programme should also provide $60,000,000 for a few selected reconstruction projects to be initiated prior to 30 June 1949. There is an urgent need for the restoration of essential transportation facilities, fuel and power operations, and export industries. This work could be undertaken in areas sheltered from military operations and could help in improving the supply and distribution of essential commodities.

As in the case of aid to European recovery, the conduct of this programme of aid should be made subject to an agreement between China and the United States setting forth the conditions and procedures for administering the aid. The agreement should include assurances that the Chinese Government will take such economic, financial, and other measures as are practicable, looking toward the ultimate goal of economic stability and recovery. The United States would, of course, reserve the right to terminate aid if it is determined that the assistance provided is not being handled in accordance with the agreement or that the policies of the Chinese Government are inconsistent with the objective of using the aid to help achieve a self-supporting economy.

Pending establishment of the agency which is to be set up for the administration of the European recovery programme, the assistance to China should be carried forward under the existing machinery now administering the foreign relief programmes. Legislation authorizing the Chinese programme should make possible transfer of the administration of the Chinese programme to the agency administering our aid to European recovery. The need for authority in the administering agency to make adjustments in the programme from time to time will be as great here as in the European recovery programme.

The proposed programme of aid to China represents what I believe to be the best course this Government can follow, in the light of all the circumstances. Nothing which this country provides by way of assistance can, even in a small measure, be a substitute for the necessary action that can be taken only by the Chinese Government. Yet this programme can accomplish the important purpose of giving the Chinese Government a respite from rapid economic deterioration, during which it can move to establish more stable economic conditions. Without this respite the ability of the Chinese Government to establish such conditions at all would be doubtful. The achievement of even this limited objective is of such importance as to justify the proposed programme of aid.

I recommend, therefore, that this programme be given prompt and favourable consideration by the Congress.

HARRY S. TRUMAN

United States Relations with China, pp. 981-3.

46   3 *April* 1948

THE CHINA AID ACT

Sec. 401. This title may be cited as the 'China Aid Act of 1948'.

Sec. 402. Recognizing the intimate economic and other relationships between the United States and China, and recognizing that disruption following in the wake of war is not contained by national frontiers, the Congress finds that the existing situation in China endangers the establishment of a lasting peace, the general welfare and national interest of the United States, and the attainment of the objectives of the United Nations. It is the sense of the Congress that the further evolution in China of principles of individual liberty, free institutions, and genuine independence rests largely upon the continuing development of a strong and democratic national government as the basis for the establishment of sound economic conditions and for stable international economic relationships. Mindful of the advantages which the United States has enjoyed through the existence of a large domestic market with no internal trade barriers, and believing that similar advantages can accrue to China, it is declared to be the policy of the people of the United States to encourage the Republic of China and its people to exert sustained common efforts which will speedily achieve the internal peace and economic stability in China which are essential for lasting peace and prosperity in the world. It is further declared to be the policy of the people of the United States to encourage the Republic of China in its efforts to maintain the genuine independence and the administrative integrity of China, and to sustain and strengthen principles of individual liberty and free institutions in China through a programme of assistance based on self-help and co-operation : *Provided*, That no assistance to China herein contemplated shall seriously impair the economic stability of the United States. It is further declared to be the policy of the United States that assistance provided by the United States under this title should at all times be dependent upon co-operation by the Republic of China and its people in furthering the programme: *Provided further*, That assistance furnished under this title shall not be construed as an express or implied assumption by the United States of any responsibility for policies, acts, or undertakings of the Republic of China or for conditions which may prevail in China at any time.

Sec. 403. Aid provided under this title shall be provided under the applicable provisions of the Economic Co-operation Act of 1948 which are consistent with the purposes of this title. It is not the purpose of this title that China, in order to receive aid hereunder, shall adhere to a joint programme for European recovery.

Sec. 404. (*a*) In order to carry out the purposes of this title, there is hereby authorized to be appropriated to the President for aid to China a sum not to exceed $338,000,000 to remain available for obligation for the period of one year following the date of enactment of this Act.

(*b*) There is also hereby authorized to be appropriated to the President a sum not to exceed $125,000,000 for additional aid to China through grants, on such terms as the President may determine and without regard to the provisions of the Economic Co-operation Act of 1948, to remain available for obligation for the period of one year following the date of enactment of this Act.

Sec. 405. An agreement shall be entered into between China and the United States containing those undertakings by China which the Secretary of State, after consultation with the Administrator for Economic Co-operation, may deem necessary to carry out the purposes of this title and to improve commercial relations with China.

Sec. 406. Notwithstanding the provisions of any other law, the Reconstruction Finance Corporation is authorized and directed, until such time as an appropriation is made pursuant to section 404, to make advances, not to exceed in the aggregate $50,000,000, to carry out the provisions of this title in such manner and in such amounts as the President shall determine. From appropriations authorized under section 404, there shall be repaid without interest to the Reconstruction Finance Corporation the advances made by it under the authority contained herein. No interest shall be charged on advances made by the Treasury to the Reconstruction Finance Corporation in implementation of this section.

Sec. 407. (*a*) The Secretary of State, after consultation with the Administrator, is hereby authorized to conclude an agreement with China establishing a Joint Commission on Rural Reconstruction in China, to be composed of two citizens of the United States appointed by the President of the United States and three citizens of China appointed by the President of China. Such Commission shall, subject to the direction and control of the Administrator, formulate and carry out a programme for reconstruction in rural areas of China, which shall include such research and training activities as may be necessary or appropriate for such reconstruction : *Provided*, That assistance furnished under this section shall not be construed as an express or implied assumption by the United States of any responsibility for making any further contributions to carry out the purposes of this section.

(*b*) In so far as practicable, an amount equal to not more than 10 per centum of the funds made available under sub-section (*a*) of section 404 shall be used to carry out the purposes of sub-section (*a*) of this section. Such amount may be in United States dollars, proceeds in Chinese currency from the sale of commodities made available to China with funds authorized under sub-section (*a*) of section 404, or both.

United States Relations with China, pp. 991-3.

ECONOMIC AID AGREEMENT BETWEEN THE UNITED
STATES OF AMERICA AND THE REPUBLIC OF CHINA

The Government of the Republic of China and the Government
of the United States of America :

Considering that it is the policy of the Government of the United
States of America to extend economic assistance to the people and
the Government of China in accordance with the provisions of the
China Aid Act of 1948 ; and

Considering that it is the policy of the Government of China to
undertake a vigorous programme of self-help in order to create more
stable economic conditions in China, and to improve commercial
relations with other countries ;

Have agreed as follows :

Article 1. The Government of the United States of America
undertakes to assist China, by making available to the Government
of China or to any person, agency or organization designated by
the latter Government such assistance as may be requested by it
and approved by the Government of the United States of America.
The Government of the United States of America will furnish this
assistance under the provisions, and subject to all of the terms,
limitations and conditions, of the China Aid Act of 1948 (other than
Section 404(*b*) thereof), acts amendatory and supplementary thereto
and appropriation acts thereunder, and will make available to the
Government of China only such commodities, services and other
assistance as are authorized to be made available by such acts. The
Government of the United States of America may suspend or
terminate any time the assistance under this Article.

Article 2. (1) In order to achieve the maximum improvement
of economic conditions through the employment of assistance
received from the Government of the United States of America, the
Government of China undertakes :

(*a*) to adopt or maintain the measures necessary to ensure efficient
and practical use of economic resources available to it, including

(i) such measures as may be necessary to ensure that the commodities and services obtained with assistance furnished under this
Agreement are used for purposes consistent with this Agreement ;

(ii) to the extent practicable, measures to locate, identify and
put into appropriate use in furtherance of its efforts to improve
economic conditions, in China, assets, and earnings therefrom which
belong to nationals of China and which are situated within the United
States of America, its territories or possessions. Nothing in this

clause imposes any obligation on the Government of the United States of America to assist in carrying out such measures or on the Government of China to dispose of such assets ;

(*b*) to promote the development of industrial and agricultural production on a sound economic basis ;

(*c*) to initiate and maintain financial, monetary, budgetary and administrative measures necessary for the creation of more stable currency conditions and for the promotion of production and marketing of goods for domestic consumption and export ; and

(*d*) to co-operate with other countries in facilitating and stimulating an increasing interchange of goods and services with other countries and in reducing public and private barriers to trade with other countries.

(2) The Government of China will take the measures which it deems appropriate to prevent, on the part of private or public commercial enterprises, business practices or business arrangements affecting international trade which have the effect of interfering with the purposes and policies of this Agreement.

Article 3. (1) The Government of China undertakes to make all practicable efforts to improve commercial relations with other countries, including measures to improve the conditions affecting the carrying on of foreign trade by private enterprises in China.

(2) The Government of China, in carrying out the provisions of paragraph (1) of this Article, will, among other measures, administer such import and exchange controls as are, or may be, made necessary by the exigencies of China's international balance of payments and the foreign exchange resources available to the Government of China, in a uniform, fair and equitable manner.

(3) The Government of the United States of America and the Government of China will consult, upon the request of either, regarding any matter relating to the application of the provisions of this Article.

Article 4. (1) All commodities provided by the Government of the United States of America pursuant to this Agreement shall be processed and distributed by commercial enterprises or by private or Chinese Government agencies, and in accordance with terms and conditions, agreed upon from time to time between the Government of the United States of America and the Government of China.

(2) The Government of China, in consultation with representatives of the United States of America, will take all appropriate steps designed to achieve fair and equitable distribution within the areas under its control of commodities provided by the Government of the United States of America pursuant to this Agreement and of

similar commodities imported into China with other funds or produced locally. To the extent that circumstances and supply availabilities permit, a distribution and price control system shall be
inaugurated or maintained in urban centres of China with the intent
of ensuring that all classes of the population shall receive a fair share
of imported or indigenously produced essential civilian supplies.
In permitting expendable commodities made available under this
Agreement to be utilized in support of the Chinese efforts to improve
consumption and price controls, it is understood that the Government of the United States of America takes no responsibility for the
success of these urban programmes.

(3) The prices at which supplies furnished by the United States
of America pursuant to this Agreement will be sold in China shall
be agreed upon between the Government of the United States of
America and the Government of China.

Article 5. (1) The provisions of this Article shall apply only
with respect to assistance which may be furnished by the Government of the United States of America on a grant basis pursuant to
this Agreement.

(2) The Government of China agrees to establish a special
account in the Central Bank of China in the name of the Government of China (hereinafter called the special account) and to make
deposits in Chinese currency to this account as follows :

(a) The unencumbered balance at the close of business on the
day of the signature of this Agreement in that special account in
the Central Bank of China in the name of the Government of China
established pursuant to the Agreement between the Government of
China and the Government of the United States of America made on
27 October 1947, and any further sums which may from time to
time be required by such Agreement to be deposited in that special
account. It is understood that sub-section (e) of section 114 of the
Foreign Assistance Act of 1948 constitutes the approval and determination of the Government of the United States of America with
respect to the disposition of such balance referred to in that
Agreement.

(b) The unencumbered balances of the deposits made by the
Government of China pursuant to the exchange of notes between the
two Governments dated 30 April 1948.

(c) Amounts commensurate with the indicated dollar cost to the
Government of the United States of America of commodities, services
and technical information (including any costs of processing, storing,
transporting, repairing or other services incident thereto) made
available to China on a grant basis pursuant to this Agreement less,
however, the amount of deposits made pursuant to the exchange of

notes referred to in sub-paragraph (b). The Government of the United States of America shall from time to time notify the Government of China of the indicated dollar cost of any such commodities, services and technical information and the Government of China will deposit in the special account at such times as may be specified by the Government of the United States of America a commensurate amount of Chinese currency computed at a rate of exchange to be agreed upon between the Government of the United States of America and the Government of China. The Government of China will upon the request of the Government of the United States of America make advance deposits in the special account which shall be credited against subsequent notifications pursuant to this paragraph.

(3)   The Government of the United States of America will from time to time notify the Government of China of its requirements for administrative expenditures in Chinese currency within China incident to operations under the China Aid Act of 1948 and the Government of China will thereupon make such sums available out of any balances in the special account in the manner requested by the Government of the United States of America in the notification.

(4)   The Government of China will further make such sums of Chinese currency available out of any balances in the special account as may be required to cover : (a) Expenditures required to carry out the purposes of the Joint Commission on Rural Reconstruction in China as provided for by Section 407 of the China Aid Act of 1948 ; and (b) Costs (including port, storage, handling and similar charges) of transportation from any point of entry in China to the consignee's designated point of delivery in China of such relief supplies and packages as are referred to in Article 7.

(5)   The Government of China shall dispose of any remaining balance in the special account only for such purposes as may be agreed from time to time with the Government of the United States of America including in particular :

(a)   Sterilization as a measure of monetary and financial stabilization ;

(b)   Expenditures incident to the stimulation of productive activity and the development of new sources of wealth including materials which may be required in the United States of America because of deficiencies or potential deficiencies in the resources of the United States of America ;

(c)   Expenditures upon projects or programmes the external costs of which are being covered in whole or in part by assistance rendered by the Government of the United States of America or by loans from the International Bank for Reconstruction and Development; or (*d*) Expenditures upon uncompleted relief or work relief projects undertaken pursuant to the Agreement between the Governments of the United States of America and of China of 27 October 1947.

(6) The Government of China will maintain the value in terms of United States dollar equivalent of such amount of the special account as is :

(*a*) Indicated by the Government of the United States of America as necessary for administrative expenditures referred to in paragraph (3) of this Article ;

(*b*) Required for the purposes of paragraph (4) of this Article ; and

(*c*) Agreed between the two Governments to be necessary to defray the expenses in Chinese currency associated with reconstruction projects or programmes the external costs of which are met in whole or in part by assistance rendered by the Government of the United States of America pursuant to the Agreement. The Government of China will carry out this provision by depositing such additional amounts of Chinese currency as the Government of the United States of America may from time to time determine after consultation with the Government of China.

(7) Any unencumbered balance remaining in the special account on 3 April 1949 shall be disposed of within China for such purposes as may hereafter be agreed between the Governments of the United States of America and of China, it being understood that the agreement of the United States of America shall be subject to approval by Act or joint resolution of the Congress of the United States of America.

Article 6. (1) The Government of China will facilitate the transfer to the United States of America for stockpiling or other purposes of materials originating in China which are required by the United States of America as a result of deficiencies or potential deficiencies in its own resources upon such reasonable terms of sale, exchange, barter or otherwise and in such quantities and for such period of time as may be agreed to between the Governments of the United States of America and of China after due regard for the reasonable requirements of China for domestic use and commercial export of such materials. The Government of China will take such specific measures as may be necessary to carry out the provisions of this paragraph. The Government of China will, when so requested by the Government of the United States of America, enter into negotiations for detailed arrangements necessary to carry out the provisions of this paragraph.

(2) The Government of China will, when so requested by the Government of the United States of America, negotiate such arrangements as are appropriate to carry out the provisions of

paragraph (9) of sub-section 115(*b*) of the Foreign Assistance Act of 1948 which relates to the development and transfer of materials required by the United States of America.

(3) The Government of China, when so requested by the Government of the United States of America, will co-operate, wherever appropriate, to further the objectives of paragraphs (1) and (2) of this Article in respect of materials originating outside of China.

Article 7. The Government of China will, when so requested by the Government of the United States of America, enter into negotiations for agreements (including the provision of duty-free treatment under appropriate safeguards) to facilitate the entry into China of supplies of relief goods donated to or purchased by United States voluntary non-profit relief agencies and of relief packages originating in the United States of America and consigned to individuals residing in China.

Article 8. (1) The two Governments will, upon the request of either of them, consult regarding any matter relating to the application of this Agreement or to operations or arrangements carried out pursuant to this Agreement.

(2) The Government of China will communicate to the Government of the United States of America in a form and at intervals to be indicated by the latter after consultation with the Government of China :

(*a*) Detailed information regarding projects, programmes and measures proposed or adopted by the Government of China to carry out the provisions of this Agreement ;

(*b*) Full statements of operations under this Agreement, including a statement of the use of funds, commodities and services received thereunder, such statements to be made in each calendar quarter ;

(*c*) Information regarding its economy and any other relevant information which the Government of the United States of America may need to determine the nature and scope of operations, and to evaluate the effectiveness of assistance furnished or contemplated under this Agreement.

(3) The Government of China will assist the Government of the United States of America to obtain information relating to the materials originating in China referred to in Article 6 which is necessary to the formulation and execution of the arrangements provided for in that Article.

Article 9. (1) The Government of China will keep the people of China fully informed of the progress achieved by the Government of China in implementing the undertakings contained in this Agreement designed to achieve more stable economic conditions in China, and it will provide continuously information to the people of China regarding the nature and extent of assistance furnished pursuant to this Agreement. It will make such information available to the media of public information and will take practicable steps to ensure that appropriate facilities are provided for the dissemination of such information.

(2) The Government of the United States of America will encourage the dissemination of such information and will make it available to the media of public information.

(3) The Government of China will make public in China in each calendar quarter full statements of operations under this Agreement, including information as to the use of funds, commodities and services received.

Article 10. (1) The Government of China agree to receive a Special Mission for Economic Co-operation which will discharge the responsibilities of the Government of the United States of America in China under this Agreement.

(2) The Government of China will, upon appropriate notification from the Ambassador of the United States of America in China, consider the Special Mission and its personnel as part of the Embassy of the United States of America in China for the purposes of enjoying the privileges and immunities accorded to that Embassy and its personnel of comparable rank. The Government of China will further accord appropriate courtesies to the members and staff of the Joint Committee on Foreign Economic Co-operation of the Congress of the United States of America and will grant them the facilities and assistance necessary to the effective performance of their responsibilities.

(3) The Government of China will extend full co-operation to the Special Mission and to the members and staff of the Joint Committee. Such co-operation shall include the provision of all information and facilities necessary to the observation and review of the carrying out of this Agreement, including the use of assistance furnished under it.

Article 11. (1) The Governments of the United States of America and of China agree to submit to the decision of the International Court of Justice any claim espoused by either Government on behalf of one of its nationals against the other Government for compensation for damage arising as a consequence of governmental measures (other than measures concerning enemy property or interests) taken after 3 April 1948 by the other Government and affecting property or interests of such national including contracts with or concessions granted by duly authorized authorities of such other Government. It is understood that the undertaking of each Government in respect of claims espoused by the other Government pursuant to this paragraph is made in the case of each Government under the authority of and is limited by the terms and conditions of such effective recognition as it has heretofore given to the compulsory jurisdiction of the International Court of Justice under Article 36 of the Statute of the Court. The provisions of this paragraph shall be in all respects without prejudice to other rights of access, if any, of either Government to the International Court of Justice or to the espousal and presentation of claims based upon alleged violations by either Government of rights and duties arising under treaties, agreements or principles of international law.

(2) The Governments of the United States of America and of China further agree that such claims may be referred in lieu of the Court to any arbitral tribunal mutually agreed upon.

(3) It is further understood that neither Government will espouse a claim pursuant to this Article unless the national concerned has exhausted the remedies available to him in the administrative and judicial tribunals of the country in which the claim exists.

Article 12. (1) This Agreement shall become effective on this day's date. It shall remain in force until 30 June 1950, and, unless at least six months before 30 June 1950 either Government shall have given the other notice in writing of intention to terminate the Agreement on that date, it shall remain in force thereafter until the expiration of six months from the date on which such notice shall have been given. Article 5 shall remain in effect until all the sums in the currency of China required to be disposed of in accordance with its own terms have been disposed of as provided in such Article.

(2) This Agreement may be amended at any time by agreement between the two Governments.

(3) The Annex to this Agreement forms an integral part thereof.

(4) This Agreement shall be registered with the Secretary-General of the United Nations.

Annex

(1) It is understood that the requirements of paragraph 1(*a*) of Article 2, relating to the adoption of measures for the efficient use of resources would include, with respect to commodities furnished under the Agreement, effective measures for safeguarding such commodities and for preventing their diversion to illegal or irregular markets or channels of trade.

(2) It is understood that the Government of China will not be requested, under paragraph 2(*b*) of Article 8 to furnish detailed information about minor projects or confidential commercial or technical information the disclosure of which would injure legitimate commercial interests.

(3) It is understood that the Government of the United States of America in making the notifications referred to in paragraph 2 of Article 10 would bear in mind the desirability of restricting, so far as practicable, the number of officials for whom full diplomatic privileges would be requested. It is also understood that the detailed application of Article 10 would, when necessary, be the subject of inter-governmental discussion.

United States Relations with China, 1949, pp. 994-1001.

48   5 *August* 1948

EXCHANGE OF NOTES BETWEEN THE UNITED STATES GOVERNMENT AND THE REPUBLIC OF CHINA, PROVIDING FOR THE ESTABLISHMENT OF A SINO-AMERICAN JOINT COMMISSION ON RURAL RECONSTRUCTION

(I) *Note from the American Ambassador to the Chinese Minister for Foreign Affairs :*

Excellency : I have the honour to refer to Section 407 of the China Aid Act of 1948 enacted by the Government of the United States of America (hereinafter referred to as the Act), which provides among other things, for the conclusion of an agreement between China and the United States of America establishing a Joint Commission on Rural Reconstruction in China. In pursuance of the general principles laid down in the Act, and in particular Section 407 thereof, I have the honour to bring forward the following proposals regarding the organization of the Joint Commission and related matters :

(1) There shall be established a Joint Commission on Rural Reconstruction in China (hereinafter referred to as the Commission) to be composed of two citizens of the United States of America appointed by the President of the United States of America and three citizens of the Republic of China to be appointed by the President of China. The Commission shall elect one of the Chinese members as chairman.

(2) The functions and authority of the Commission shall, subject to the provisions of the above-mentioned Section of the Act, be as follows : (*a*) to formulate and carry out through appropriate Chinese Government agencies and international or private agencies in China a co-ordinated programme for reconstruction in rural areas of China (hereinafter referred to as the programme) ; (*b*) to conclude arrange-

ments with the agencies referred to in the preceding paragraph
establishing a basis for their co-operation ; (c) to recommend to the
Governments of the United States of America and of China within
the limits prescribed by the Act the allocation of funds and other
assistance to the programme, and to recommend to the Government
of China the allocation of such other funds and assistance as are
deemed essential to the success of the programme ; (d) to establish
standards of performance for implementation of the programme, including the qualifications, type and number of personnel to be used
by co-operating agencies in the programme, and to maintain a constant
supervision of all phases of the programme with authority to recommend changes in or stoppage of any phase of the programme; (e) to
appoint such executive officers and administrative staff as the Commission deems necessary to carry out the programme, it being understood that the chief executive officer shall be a citizen of China.
Salaries, expenses of travel, and other expenses incident to the
administrative functions of the Commission itself shall be paid from
funds made available under Section 407(B) of the Act.

(3) In its programme the Commission may include the following
types of activity to be carried out in agreement with the agencies
referred to in paragraph 2(a) : (a) A co-ordinated extension-type
programme in agriculture, home demonstration, health and education
for initiation in a selected group or Hsien in several provinces to
include a limited number of subsidiary projects suited to conditions
in the areas where the programme is developed, in such fields as agricultural production, marketing, credit, irrigation, home and community industries, nutrition, sanitation, and education of a nature
which will facilitate the promotion of all projects being undertaken ;
(b) Consultation with the Chinese Government concerning ways and
means of progressively carrying out land reform measures ; (c) Subsidiary projects in research, training and manufacturing to be carried
out in suitable locations to provide information, personnel and
materials required by the programme; (d) projects to put into effect
over a wider area than provided for in the co-ordinated extension-
type programme specified in (a), any of the above lines of activity
which can be developed soundly on a larger scale, of which examples
might be the multiplication and distribution of improved seeds, the
control of rinderpest of cattle, the construction of irrigation and
drainage facilities and the introduction of health and sanitation
measures ; (e) related measures in line with the general objectives of
this programme; (f) the distribution of the assistance in this programme
on the principle of giving due attention to strengthening rural
improvement in areas where selected projects can be progressively
developed and where their development will contribute most

effectively to the achievement of purposes for which this programme is undertaken but that the principle of distributing aid will not be controlled by proportionate or geographical consideration *per se*.

(4) In respect of any decision of the Commission, the approval of the Government of China shall be obtained prior to its execution if the Commission or its chairman, with the concurrence of the Chinese members, deems it necessary.

(5) The Commission shall publish in China and transmit to the Government of the United States of America and the Government of China, in such form and at such times as may be requested by either of the two Governments, full statements of operations, including a statement on the use of funds, supplies and services received, and will transmit to the two Governments any other matter pertinent to operations as requested by either of the two Governments. The Government of China will keep the people of China fully informed of the intended purpose and scope of the programme and of the progress achieved by the Commission in implementing the programme, including the nature and extent of the assistance furnished by the Government of the United States of America.

(6) The Government of China will, upon appropriate notification of the Ambassador of the United States of America in China, consider the United States members and personnel of the Commission as part of the Embassy of the United States of America in China for the purpose of enjoying the privileges and immunities accorded to that Embassy and its personnel of comparable rank. It is understood that the Ambassador of the United States of America in China in making the notification will bear in mind the desirability of restricting so far as practicable the number of officials for whom full diplomatic privileges and immunities would be requested. It is also understood that the detailed application of this paragraph would, when necessary, be a subject of inter-governmental discussion.

(7) All supplies imported into China for use in the programme shall be free of customs duties, conservancy dues, and other charges imposed by the Government of China on similar supplies which are imported through regular commercial channels.

(8) The Government of the United States of America and the Government of China will consult with respect to problems incident to the interpretation, implementation and possible amendment of the terms of the agreement embodied in this exchange of Notes whenever either of the two Governments considers such action appropriate.

(9) The Government of the United States of America reserves the right at any time to terminate or suspend its assistance or any part thereof provided under this exchange of Notes. Assistance furnished by the Government of the United States of America under Section 407 of the Act and pursuant to this exchange of Notes shall not be construed as an express or implied assumption by the Government of the United States of America of any responsibility for making any further contributions to carry out the purpose of Section 407 of the Act or of this exchange of Notes.

(10) This note and Your Excellency's reply accepting the above proposals on behalf of the Government of China will constitute an agreement between the two Governments in the sense of Section 407 of the Act. Subject to the provisions of paragraph 8 and 9, this exchange of Notes will remain in force until 30 June 1949 or, upon the request of either Government transmitted to the other Government at least two months before 30 June 1949, until the date of termination of the Economic Aid Agreement between the two Governments concluded on 3 July 1948.

I avail myself [etc.]   J. LEIGHTON STUART

(II) *Note from the Chinese Minister for Foreign Affairs to the American Ambassador :*

Excellency : I have the honour to acknowledge receipt of your Note of today's date which reads as follows :

[Here follows the text of the preceding note.]

On behalf of the Government of China I have the honour to accept the proposals contained in the Note quoted above.

In recognition of the importance of the programme as one of the essential means of achieving the objectives in seeking which the Governments of China and of the United States of America unite under the Economic Aid Agreement between the two Governments concluded on 3 July 1948, the Government of China undertakes to afford to the execution of the programme the full weight of its support and to direct co-operating agencies of the Government of China including the local officials concerned to give such assistance and facilities as are essential to the success of their undertakings under the programme.

I avail myself of this opportunity to renew to your Excellency the assurances of my highest consideration.

WANG SHIH-CHIEH

United States Relations with China, 1949, pp. 1004-6.

49   9 *November* 1948

GENERALISSIMO CHIANG KAI-SHEK'S LETTER TO
PRESIDENT TRUMAN APPEALING FOR MORE AID

I have the honour to acknowledge receipt of Your Excellency's
reply dated 16 October 1948, for which I am deeply grateful.

The Communist forces in Central China are now within striking
distance of Shanghai and Nanking. If we fail to stem the tide,
China may be lost to the cause of democracy. I am therefore compelled to send to Your Excellency again a direct and urgent appeal.

The general deterioration of the military situation in China may
be attributed to a number of factors. But the most fundamental is
the non-observance by the Soviet Government of the Sino-Soviet
Treaty of Friendship and Alliance, which, as Your Excellency will
doubtless recall, the Chinese Government signed as a result of the
well-intentioned advice from the United States Government. I need
hardly point out that, but for persistent Soviet aid, the Chinese
Communists would not have been able to occupy Manchuria and
develop into such a menace.

As a co-defender of democracy against the onrush and infiltration
of communism throughout the world, I appeal to you for speedy
and increased military assistance and for a firm statement of
American policy in support of the cause for which my Government
is fighting. Such a statement would serve to bolster up the morale
of the armed forces and the civilian population and would strengthen
the Government's position in the momentous battle now unfolding
in North and Central China.

My Government would be most happy to receive from you as
soon as possible a high-ranking military officer who will work out
in consultation with my Government a concrete scheme of military
assistance, including the participation of American military advisers
in the direction of operations.

As the situation demands your Excellency's full sympathy and
quick decision, I shall appreciate an early reply.

CHIANG KAI-SHEK

United States Relations with China, pp. 888-9.

50   12 *November* 1948

PRESIDENT TRUMAN'S LETTER TO GENERALISSIMO
CHIANG KAI-SHEK REPLYING
TO THE APPEAL FOR AID

My dear President Chiang: This is in acknowledgement of your letter delivered to the White House on 9 November through the good offices of your Ambassador, Dr V. K. Wellington Koo.

As I stated in my letter of 16 October 1948, everything possible is being done to expedite the procurement and shipment to China of the weapons and ammunition being obtained in this country under the China Aid Programme. I am again emphasizing to the appropriate officials the urgency of your needs and the necessity of prompt action. In this connexion, I have just been informed that one shipment of arms and ammunition sailed from Guam on 4 November and another from Japan on 7 November *en route* to China. I have also been informed that a further shipment of ammunition sailed from the West Coast of the United States on 9 November and is scheduled to reach China about 24 November.

A message of 9 November from the Secretary of State to Ambassador Stuart, containing Secretary Marshall's reply to a request from the Chinese Foreign Minister for military aid and the visit of a high-ranking United States officer to China, apparently crossed Your Excellency's message in transmission. The Secretary authorized Ambassador Stuart to inform the Foreign Minister that the United States National Military Establishment was making every effort to expedite shipments of military material purchased in this country under the China Aid Act. He also authorized Ambassador Stuart to point out the inherent difficulties involved in an attempt on the part of a newly appointed foreign official to advise the Chinese Government regarding its courses of action in the present dilemma, even if such an official would be completely conversant with all the numerous complexities of the situation, and to point out the even greater difficulties for a foreign official not familiar with China.

However, Major-General Barr, Director of the Joint United States Military Advisory Group in China, is conversant with the current situation and his advice has always been available to you.

Your attention may have been called to my public statement on 11 March 1948, in which I stated that the United States maintained friendly relations with the Chinese Government and was trying to assist the recognized Government of China to maintain peace. I also stated that I did not desire Communists in the Chinese Government.

Secretary Marshall stated publicly on 10 March 1948 that the Communists were now in open rebellion against the Chinese Government and that the inclusion of the Communists in the Government was a matter for the Chinese Government to decide, not for the United States Government to dictate. I believe that these statements and the action of my Government in extending assistance to the Chinese Government under the China Aid Act of 1948 have made the position of the United States Government clear.

You will understand the desire of the United States Government to support the cause of peace and democracy throughout the world. It is this desire that has led this Government to extend assistance to many countries in their efforts to promote sound economies and stable conditions without which the peoples of the world cannot expect to have peace and the principles of democracy cannot grow. It was with that hope that the United States Government has extended assistance in various forms to the Chinese Government. I am most sympathetic with the difficulties confronting the Chinese Government and people at this time and wish to assure Your Excellency that my Government will continue to exert every effort to expedite the implementation of the programme of aid for China which has been authorized by the Congress with my approval.

Very sincerely yours,
HARRY S. TRUMAN

United States Relations with China, pp. 889-90.

51   8 *January* 1949

CHINESE FOREIGN MINISTER'S APPEAL TO THE UNITED STATES GOVERNMENT FOR MEDIATION IN THE CIVIL WAR

Aide-Mémoire

The Chinese people, true to their peaceful traditions, have always devoted themselves to the pursuit of international as well as domestic peace. In their long history, it was only when they were in the face of the danger of aggression that they took up arms in self-defence. For this reason, the people rose to resist the Japanese invaders, and later, through their close co-operation with their allies, World War II was carried to a successful conclusion. On the eve of victory, China took an active part in organizing and founding the United Nations in the hope that a foundation for world peace might thus be laid and international disputes settled by pacific means. For, it has long been through the maintenance of peace that the continuity and development of human civilization can be ensured.

Following the surrender of Japan, the National Government immediately took steps to initiate and carry on peace negotiations with the Chinese Communist Party. Through the good offices personally offered by General Marshall the Political Consultative Council was set up and a number of meetings took place. Unfortunately, the failure to reach a mutually satisfactory settlement led to a renewal of hostilities. Although these efforts proved abortive at the time, the Government and the people have never since abandoned the hope that hostilities may still be brought to an end.

However, in the wake of the long, gruelling struggle against Japan, this renewed conflict has inflicted untold suffering upon the masses and prevented the Government from carrying out the plans of reconstruction which it had prepared during the war with Japan. The ravages of war followed by rapid deterioration of the economic life of the nation make it imperative that peace be restored as soon as possible.

As nations today are unavoidably interdependent and international peace and stability depends largely upon the degree to which international co-operation can be achieved, it would be difficult for any nation to confine the effect of its own unsettled conditions to itself. The Chinese Government is, therefore, most anxious that her internal situation would not in any way become an impediment to the progress of world peace.

In consideration of the above facts, the President of the Republic of China, in his New Year message on 1 January, announced without hesitation his determination for the restoration of peace in the country. The decision thus proclaimed by the President has since received the general support of the people, who have through numerous messages and public statements echoed their prompt support for a peaceful settlement of the questions at issue between the Government and the Communists.

The United States Government has on many occasions in the past demonstrated its friendly concern over the state of affairs in China and has co-operated with the Chinese Government for the promotion of international peace. The Chinese Government wishes hereby to assure the United States Government of its sincere desire for a peaceful settlement with the Chinese Communist Party and particularly to avail itself of this opportunity to ascertain the views of the United States Government on this subject. The Chinese Government will welcome any suggestion by the United States Government which may lead to an early restoration of peace in China. The Chinese Government further signifies its readiness, through the possible intermediary of the United States Government, to initiate negotiations with the Chinese Communist Party with a view to attaining the end stated above.

Similar notes are being communicated to the French, the Soviet and the British Governments. An early reply from the United States Government will be greatly appreciated.

United States Relations with China, pp. 922-3.

52   12 *January* 1949

UNITED STATES REPLY TO THE CHINESE GOVERNMENT'S REQUEST FOR MEDIATION

The United States Government has received and has given careful consideration to the *aide-mémoire* delivered by the Chinese Minister for Foreign Affairs to the United States Ambassador at Nanking on 8 January 1949.

It is noted in the *aide-mémoire* that the Chinese Government is most anxious that the internal situation in China should not in any way become an impediment to the progress of world peace. It is also noted that the Chinese Government took steps immediately following the Japanese surrender to initiate and carry on peace negotiations with the Chinese Communist Party.

It will be recalled that these negotiations in September and October 1945 resulted in agreement for the convening of a Political Consultative Conference, to be composed of representatives of all political parties as well as non-party Chinese leaders, for the purpose of forming a constitutional government in which all Chinese parties and groups would be represented. It will also be recalled that subsequent to these negotiations clashes between the armed forces of the Chinese Government and of the Chinese Communist Party became increasingly widespread. It was at this juncture in December 1945 that the United States Government, motivated by the same anxiety as that expressed in the Chinese Government's *aide-mémoire* under acknowledgement with respect to the danger to world peace from the internal situation in China and desirous of doing everything within its power to assist in bringing peace to China, offered its good offices in the hope that a peaceful settlement of their differences could be achieved by the Chinese themselves along the lines of the agreement reached in September and October. In furtherance of that Chinese agreement and with the consent of the Chinese Government and the Chinese Communist Party, General Marshall shortly after his arrival in China on 21 December exerted his good offices in assisting the Chinese Government and the Chinese Communist Party to reach an agreement for a cessation of hostilities with the hope that discussions by the Chinese of their differences could be conducted in an atmosphere of peace.

Following the convening of the Political Consultative Conference and its approval of resolutions providing for the settlement of political differences and the establishment of a constitutional government to include all parties and groups in China, General Marshall again exerted his good offices in connexion with the agreement reached for the reorganization of all Chinese armed forces and their amalgamation into a national army responsible to a civilian government.

The negotiations between the Chinese Government and the Chinese Communist Party subsequently broke down and the various agreements were not implemented. The United States Government, therefore, after having made every effort to assist the Chinese in bringing peace to China through implementation of the fundamental political agreements arising out of the Chinese Government's negotiations with the Chinese Communist Party immediately after the Japanese surrender, considered that it had no alternative to withdrawal from its position as an intermediary.

In the light of the foregoing, it is not believed that any useful purpose would be served by the United States Government's attempting, in accordance with the Chinese Government's suggestion, to act as an intermediary in the present situation.

United States Relations with China, pp. 290-1.

53   *February* 1949*

ECONOMIC AID TO CHINA UNDER
THE CHINA AID ACT OF 1948

Part I—Introduction

At the time the China Aid Act was passed, China was in the grip of the longest sustained inflation in modern history. Her external resources had dwindled from approximately a billion dollars on VJ Day to less than one-quarter of that sum at the beginning of 1948. Foreign trade was at a low ebb. Continuation of deficit financing to support the civil war against the Communists kept the fires of inflation burning ; the currency inflation in turn caused production and other constructive business activity to stagnate and contributed greatly to a popular loss of confidence in the National Government.

*Excerpts from document published by the Economic Co-operation Administration, Washington, in February 1949.

While the military strength of the Communists was increasing, Nationalist strength was being sapped by military defeats, sinking morale among the troops, and a crumbling economic front in the rear of the Government's armies.

Character of the 1948 Economic Aid Programme for China

The China Aid Programme was not originally conceived as something that could by itself turn back or even arrest these trends. It was described as an effort to 'assist in retarding the current economic deterioration and thus give the Chinese Government further opportunity to initiate the measures necessary to the establishment of more stable economic conditions'.

The programme of economic aid was organized and carried on against a background of continuing civil war and progressive contraction of the area and resources under the control of the National Government. It has been directed toward bringing economic assistance as directly as possible to areas and people who have needed the type of assistance which could be supplied by the use of US dollars.

Food has been provided through a controlled ration system to nearly 13,000,000 inhabitants of seven major Chinese cities. Cotton financed under the programme has kept the mills operating in China's largest industry, providing cloth for direct consumption, for barter to encourage the bringing of indigenous food into the cities, and for export to earn foreign exchange that can be used to pay for more imports. Petroleum has kept in operation basic utilities, transport facilities and industries, and also provided goods for which the farmers in the countryside are prepared to exchange their produce. Fertilizer imports have been planned for use in the production of spring crops in 1949. A Joint Commission on Rural Reconstruction has been established, and has formulated principles and a programme for attacking some of the root causes of poverty and unrest among China's vast rural population. An industrial programme of replacement of machinery and reconstruction projects has been initiated with the participation of private American engineering firms; although actual procurement and construction had to be suspended for the most part due to uncertainties connected with the civil war, much useful engineering survey work has been done. A 'counterpart' fund in local currency, established by agreement with the Chinese Government and managed jointly by Chinese and Americans, has been used to maintain many hospitals, welfare programmes, and dike-building projects.

In spite of the growing chaos around them, these activities, by and large, have been managed with care and have been carried out successfully within their own limited terms of reference. In the case of the commodity programme particularly, the supplies provided have been an important and at times crucial factor in keeping unrest to a minimum in the main cities of the coastal areas controlled by the Nationalist Government. In this narrow but significant sense, therefore, the efforts of ECA in China have been constructive and useful. Supplies financed by the USA have been and are being effectively distributed to the people intended to receive them.

Economic Aid in a Setting of General Deterioration

But the atmosphere surrounding these efforts has been one of continuing discouragement and defeat for those who had hoped the Chinese National Government, after a decade of upheaval and in face of all difficulties, could and would do the things that needed to be done if it were to provide an adequate counter-force to the Communists in China. The incapacity of the Government to put into effect the reforms which it had in January announced its intention of initiating ; the inability of the Nationalist commanders to lead and inspire an effective military effort against the growing Communist threat ; a series of ill-conceived economic and financial measures which made the situation behind the lines even worse than it needed to be ; the widening breach between the people and their Government—all these were factors so demoralizing in their effect that it became only a matter of time until the Government would reach the brink of disaster.

Chinese economic problems cannot be separated from problems which are ordinarily termed political and military. The inflation itself, dramatic as it has been, is only a symptom of broader and deeper problems. The prodigious increase in the issue of currency has been a devastating economic fact, but the reason for it is to be sought in the military fact that more than two-thirds of all currency issued has been used directly to support the Government's military efforts. Sudden increases in the velocity of circulation can be related directly to sudden drops in public confidence due to military defeats.

On 19 August 1948, the Chinese Government published a series of apparently sweeping financial reforms, in an attempt to arrest the runaway inflation of the Chinese National Currency (CN), and draw in for public use the large private holdings of foreign exchange. The drastic and dramatic reforms, including the introduction of a new Gold Yuan (GY) currency, seemed to hold the inflation in suspense for more than a month. But they did nothing to increase revenues or to reduce expenditures ; thus they failed to attack the basic cause of the inflation, which is the gross unbalance of the Government's budget. Internal contradictions in the new regulations soon appeared. A new commodity tax was not put into effect because it would have meant breaking the price ceilings set forth in the same regulations. Although the Government reported collection of more than US $150 million worth of foreign exchange, it had to pay out in return so large an amount of the new Gold Yuan currency, without any compensating increase in supplies or production, that the new currency rapidly depreciated further both in real value and in the esteem of the Chinese people.

With these economic influences at work, the resumption of the inflationary spiral and a breakdown of the attempt to maintain 19 August ceiling prices was inevitable. Attempts to enforce arbitrary price ceilings in Shanghai, and to a less extent in other cities, brought about an almost complete stagnation of economic activity. The more strictly the regulations were enforced, the less food came into the cities, and the worse the situation became. Finally, in November, the regulations became so ineffective and disruptive of economic activity that they were officially revoked in the face of a downward slide of the Gold Yuan which has continued thereafter.

Internal financial deterioration and the maintenance of artificial exchange rates have held down official receipts by the Chinese Government from exports and inward remittances. Although China has had to draw down also some $100 million from her contracted dollar assets, official holdings of foreign exchange may have exceeded slightly, at the end of 1948, the balance existing when the China Aid Act was passed. This has been due in part to the existence of the China Aid Programme itself, which has paid for most of China's basic commodity imports since June 1948. But it has been due also to two factors unfavourable to China: first, the fact that imports outside the ECA programme were held to a level so low as to impair seriously production and trade; and second, the fact that private exchange holdings were called in under the 19 August regulations in such a way as to heighten the inflation and at the same time to wipe out extensively middle class savings. Thus the balancing for a time of China's official international payments accounts was achieved at a prohibitive internal cost.

China's drawings upon restricted foreign exchange resources were largely for current requirements, not for importations of capital equipment. The Government even sold valuable productive properties in order to meet current outlays.

A further debilitating effect of the civil war was to be found in the phenomenon of 'disinvestment' within China, which contrasted with the process of expanding investment in the ECA-aided countries of Europe. In a setting of spiralling inflation and universal uncertainty as to the future, private capital was almost wholly directed into non-productive channels of financial speculation and hoarding of goods for sale at higher prices ; banks demonstrated an increasing reluctance to extend long-term credit for industrial investment. As a result, not only did China's productive plant fail to expand, but existing productive facilities deteriorated. The lack of repairs and rehabilitation of productive capacity has lowered output.

These facts, taken together, point to a steady decline in the overall productive capacity of the Chinese economy during 1948.

The relationship between military defeat and economic deterioration has been further demonstrated in the case of coal and food supplies.

Coal production in China during 1948 was at about the same level as 1947. Supplies reaching consuming areas, however, were sharply reduced, particularly during the latter half of the year, as mining centres were cut off or fell into Communist hands. An especially serious loss toward the end of the year, was that of the output from the Kailan Mines north of Tientsin, which were supplying more than half of the coal produced in the whole of Nationalist China.

The output of foodstuffs in 1948 reached a post-war peak at a level roughly equal to that of pre-war years. In spite of this recovery in the agricultural regions, China's urban centres were able to meet their food requirements only with the continuing assistance afforded by substantial shipments from abroad. Factors contributing to this situation were Communist occupation of producing areas in Manchuria and much of north China and the consequent disruption of distribution patterns ; and, in accessible areas—particularly during the autumn months—an increasing unwillingness on the part of farmers to market their crops in view of rigid price controls and continuing currency depreciation.

Similar trends could be noted in every other sector of the economy. Mill output of cotton textiles held up during the first half of the year at 1947 levels and then began to drop sharply. Operable rail mileage in Nationalist hands was reduced by 2,500 kilometres despite the rehabilitation of lines in the south. Shipping capacity was maintained but the pressure of military needs reduced the amount available for commercial requirements. Costly air traffic increased under the necessity of supplying cities besieged by Communist armies. During the last few months of the year, important cities in north and central China were virtually cut off from major supply sources and economic activity became thoroughly demoralized. ECA imports, in the latter part of the year, played an increasingly large role in supplying urban areas with essential foods and raw materials.

Preliminary Review of the ECA China Aid Programme

Within a few weeks after the Economic Co-operation Administration came into being, economic aid to China was an operating reality.

Initial funds from the Reconstruction Finance Corporation were advanced to ECA, a 'Programme No. 1' for using these funds was approved by the Administrator, and the first procurement authorization was issued. An exchange of notes between the Secretary of State and the Chinese Ambassador in Washington set up interim arrangements for providing assistance pending conclusion of a formal bilateral agreement. Mr Roger D. Lapham was appointed Chief of the ECA Mission to China, arriving at his post in Shanghai the first week of June. The Chinese Government created a Council for US Aid, a cabinet level committee to deal with the ECA Programme. To 'backstop' the Mission, a China Programme Division was created in the ECA Headquarters office. And on 3 July, three months after the Foreign Assistance Act was approved, the formal Economic Aid Agreement between China and the United States was signed by the Chinese Foreign Minister and the US Ambassador to China.

The ECA Mission to China was faced with the problem of getting itself organized quickly for the job ahead. To speed up the process, it took over and adapted to the new purpose the China Relief Mission which had been responsible in China for the US Foreign Relief Programme under Public Law 84 (Eightieth Congress). ECA also inherited some continuing functions of a relief character, including the distribution of PL 84 supplies which had not reached end-users by the time that law expired, on 30 June 1948. ECA likewise continued support to a number of special projects started by the China Relief Mission and financed from a local currency 'Special Account'.

Operating under a strict limitation on dollar administrative expenses, the Mission has made a maximum use of alien staff, paid in local currency. ECA has arranged for a part of the work of supervising and controlling portions of the programme to be done by private firms and voluntary relief agencies.

The programme itself has consisted of three parts : the provision of a limited number of basic commodities (food, fuel, cotton, fertilizer and coal) ; the initiation of an industrial replacement and reconstruction programme; the formation and support of a Joint Commission on Rural Reconstruction in China. In addition, ECA has participated in the management and use of a Special Account, or 'counterpart' fund, in Chinese currency provided by the Chinese Government. Of the total $275 million appropriation for the ECA China Programme, $203·8 million was earmarked for commodities, $67·5 million for the industrial programme, $2·5 million for dollar expenditures on the rural reconstruction programme, and $1·2 million for administration.

The commodity programme called for average ECA imports into China of supplies costing roughly $20 million a month. As of 31

December $194 million of the commodity funds had been authorized for procurement, and about $112 million worth of these supplies had arrived in China. The commodity programme was, therefore, well up to schedule. But obligations against the industrial programme had been limited to allotments of money for 'preproject' engineering survey work. Towards the end of the year, some of the projects were about ready to start actual procurement and construction work ; but in December, it was necessary to suspend allocations for such work pending clarification of the political and military situation in China. Similarly, the Rural Reconstruction Commission was only emerging from the planning stage at the end of 1948, and had tapped only a small part of the $2·5 million set aside for its US dollar expenses.

In all phases of the programme, as much emphasis as practicable has been placed on the use of commercial channels of supply and distribution. The food programme is the sole exception as regards supply ; rice from Southeast Asia and wheat and flour from the USA have been bought and shipped by the Commodity Credit Corporation, an agency of the US Department of Agriculture. The major portion of the petroleum products, most of which originate in the Persian Gulf, have been procured and shipped by private oil companies. American cotton has been shipped by American firms and received in China by American cotton importers. Fertilizer, coming from a variety of sources under allocations by the International Emergency Food Committee, has likewise been supplied through private commercial channels.

After each commodity shipment arrives in China, the ECA Mission keeps track of its receipt, processing, distribution, and end-use. Food is distributed through the first general civilian rationing system ever developed in China's urban areas, with the Chinese Government and ECA each providing a part of the total ration requirements. Cotton becomes yarn, yarn becomes cloth, and the end-products are used for export, for barter and for domestic sale —all under the watchful observation of a Joint Management Board in which ECA participates. Petroleum products are distributed by the importing companies, who themselves assist in end-use control and reporting, and provide detailed sales records for each product to the ECA Mission. As of 31 December 1948, fertilizer had not been distributed since it was for use in 1949 spring production ; a part, it was planned, would be handled in direct exchange with farmers for rice, a part sold through commercial channels and a part used by the Rural Reconstruction Commission. The small amount of coal imported before the end of the year went directly to utilities and other users under the supervision of the ECA China Mission. Medical supplies imported by ECA's predecessor in China, the US China Relief Mission, are distributed by a special group set up by agreement between the Ministry of Health and voluntary agencies. Pesticides, also inherited from the China Relief Mission, have been distributed largely through commercial channels, the remainder being earmarked for agricultural demonstration purposes.

The industrial programme started with an intensive investigation of proposed replacement and reconstruction projects conducted by a special Reconstruction Survey Group. This group faced a double problem—an extensive need for replacement and reconstruction equipment, and a serious lack of the engineering and management skills needed in China to make certain that such equipment would be effectively absorbed into the economy. The group prepared tentative recommendations for allocation among approved projects from the $67·5 million set aside for this purpose. The projects thus recommended were largely limited to the field of basic industry and transportation—the largest provisional allotments proposed being for power plants, coal mines, the rehabilitation of railroads, and the manufacture of fertilizer. The Survey Group also developed procedures for making maximum use of private American engineering firms as 'project engineers' to help individual projects in drawing up plans, procuring the right equipment, and making sure that equipment is correctly installed and effectively operated. To manage the whole scheme, ECA and the Chinese Government agreed to retain a high-grade American firm of management engineers.

The uncertainties in the China situation had in December caused the suspension of all but survey work under this programme, leaving open the possibility of selected projects being carried forward as circumstances permit. The technique adopted for administering this programme may prove to be of significance in relation to future programmes involving industrial projects in under-developed countries.

The Joint Commission on Rural Reconstruction in China was established in accordance with Section 407 of the China Aid Act to 'formulate and carry out a programme for reconstruction in rural areas of China'. Initiated on 5 August by an exchange of notes between the Chinese and US Governments, the Joint Commission consisted of three Chinese and two American members, appointed in September by the Presidents of China and of the United States.

Intensive planning and survey work were undertaken by the Commission after the members had agreed on the general statement of objectives and principles. In general, the Commission has been moving in the direction of : assisting people in rural areas to improve their living conditions, increase food production, and develop local self-government ; strengthening and improving the operations of

Government agencies concerned with rural problems; stimulating local movements and private agencies in efforts on behalf of the rural people ; and affording to progressive elements in the population real opportunities to participate in the programme. The Joint Commission operates under the supervision of the Administrator, who has delegated his authority in this field to the Chief of the ECA Mission to China. The American members and staff of the Commission are ECA staff members engaged in full-time work with the Commission.

A special concern of the ECA in connexion with the China Programme has been the development of sources of strategic materials required by the USA. Although China is a major producer of three such materials—tin, tungsten, and antimony—the limitations upon funds for stockpiling purposes have made it impracticable to pick up antimony and tungsten which are available for purchase in China. Extensive investigations on the development and supply of tin concentrates and tin metal, however, had resulted before the end of December 1948 in a tentative arrangement for tin purchasing as part of a general scheme for rationalizing the supply of metal and the development of processing facilities in Yunnan Province.

The special local currency account, or counterpart fund, provided for in the Economic Aid Agreement with China, differed from corresponding accounts in Europe, two of its features being unique. The first is an arrangement for deposits of local currency, which leaves the timing of deposits in the discretion of the US Government ; this discretion is used to relate deposits to actual needs for the local currency, without large surpluses which would rapidly shrink in value. The second unique feature is a 'maintenance of value' clause which provides that for certain important uses the Chinese Government would protect appropriations made from the special account against currency depreciation, by expressing the appropriation in terms of some more stable unit, such as US dollars or a basic commodity like rice or cotton yarn.

Since it was clear from the outset that the sterilization of the entire special account would not by itself be an important influence toward control of the inflation, the Chinese Government and the ECA, after consultation with the National Advisory Council in Washington, followed a policy of making expenditures from the account for important public purposes which might not otherwise be provided for, if such expenditures were of demonstrated urgency. The main categories of expenditures have been for administrative costs, the expenses of delivering relief packages and supplies in China, local currency costs of projects sponsored by the Joint Commission on Rural Reconstruction, expenditures on special projects in the field of water conservancy, health and welfare, and the internal costs to date of the replacement and reconstruction programme, in cases where money could not be raised from other sources. It was estimated, according to the plans envisaged during 1948, that the total of these expenditures would amount to less than half of the total potential account.

By the end of December 1948, notifications of US grant aid had been given to the Chinese Government to the amount of $94,470,926. According to preliminary and tentative estimates, pending final determination upon a formula for computing exchange rates, Gold Yuan equivalent to approximately $9,543,000 had been requested for deposits, and the equivalent of approximately $5,839,000 had been spent.

Part II—Economic Aid Programme for China to 31 December 1948:
Scope and Rationale

The President, in his message of 18 February 1948 to Congress on aid to China recommended authorization of an economic aid programme in the amount of $570 million to provide assistance over a fifteen-month period extending to 30 June 1949. Of this amount, $510 million was estimated as required for financing essential commodity imports into China, 'which would permit the Chinese Government to devote its limited dollar resources to the most urgent of its other needs', and $60 million was recommended for 'a few selected reconstruction projects to be initiated prior to 30 June 1949'. 'Essential imports' cited included cereals, cotton, petroleum, fertilizer, tobacco, pharmaceuticals, coal and repair parts for existing capital equipment. Reduced to a twelve-month basis, the programme of economic assistance proposed by the President would have called for approximately $403 million for commodity shipments to China and an additional $60 million for aid to selected reconstruction projects.

The China Aid Act of 1948 authorized for expenditure during the ensuing twelve-month period (3 April 1948 to 2 April 1949) $338 million for economic assistance to China, of which $275 million has been appropriated, and an additional $125 million for aid to China through grants 'on such terms as the President may determine and without regard to the provisions of the Economic Co-operation Act of 1948'.

The programme of economic aid to China administered by the ECA during 1948 has been limited to expenditures within the $275 million appropriated by the Congress.

In Section 407 of the China Aid Act of 1948 (Public Law 472, Title IV), the Congress authorized for 'a programme for reconstruction in rural areas in China' an amount 'equal to not more than 10 per cent' of the funds made available for economic assistance under the Act, which amount could be 'in United States dollars, proceeds in Chinese currency from the sale of commodities made available . . . or both'. Thus a third category of assistance was specified. The China Aid Act did not further stipulate the relative magnitude of expenditures to be incurred in behalf of the three general types of limited assistance contemplated, namely: a commodities programme, an industrial reconstruction programme, and a rural reconstruction programme.

Related to these three types of aid within China and available for helping to carry them out was a special local currency or 'counterpart' fund, established by the Chinese Government pursuant to the terms of an 'Economic Co-operation Agreement between the United States of America and the Republic of China'.

In administering economic aid to China, as approved by Congress, the ECA has faced the obligation to ensure as efficient use as possible, under prevailing conditions, of the $275 million appropriation provided by Congress, recognizing that the assistance thus furnished would, to be fully effective, have to be supplementary to, and not a substitute for, vigorous efforts on the part of the Chinese Government and people.

With limited resources and under prevailing conditions in China, it has not been possible for the ECA to undertake a comprehensive approach to China's broad problems of budgetary and financial stabilization and economic recovery. It has been necessary, instead, to concentrate upon a few restricted activities designed to furnish some assistance at critical points in the Chinese economy; to maximize in the aid programme, where possible, the use of private trade channels as one means of sustaining a degree of normal economic activity; and to devise effective end-use controls designed to ensure efficient utilization of all the economic aid provided.

Initiation of the Programme

On 30 April 1948 Notes were exchanged between the Secretary of State and the Chinese Ambassador in Washington, setting up interim arrangements for the initiation of the China Aid Programme, pending the negotiation of a bilateral economic aid agreement. These Notes (a) confirmed the Chinese Government's adherence to the purposes and policies set forth in Section 2 of the China Aid Act of 1948; (b) specified that prior to the conclusion of an agreement under Section 405 of the China Aid Act and until 3 July 1948, the extension of aid to China, as authorized by Section 404(a) of the Act, would be provisionally governed, subject to agreed modifications, by the Agreement negotiated in connexion with the United States Foreign Relief Programme, dated 27 October 1947; and (c) recorded an understanding relating to the establishment of a special mission for economic co-operation to China, together with an assurance that the Chinese Government would extend the fullest co-operation to representatives of the United States Government concerned with operations in implementation of the China Aid Act.

Bilateral Agreement

Section 405 of the China Aid Act provided that an agreement should be 'entered into between China and the United States containing these undertakings by China which the Secretary of State, after consultation with the Administrator for Economic Co-operation, may deem necessary to carry out the purposes of this title and to improve commercial relations with China'. Consequently, negotiations were begun in early June between the United States Embassy in Nanking and the Chinese Ministry of Foreign Affairs regarding the terms of a bilateral economic co-operation agreement between the two countries. These negotiations were concluded satisfactorily and the Agreement was signed on 3 July 1948 by Ambassador J. Leighton Stuart and the Chinese Minister of Foreign Affairs, Wang Shih-chieh. (For the full text of the Agreement see Document 47 above.)

In general, the Agreement with China followed the pattern of the bilateral agreements being negotiated simultaneously between the United States and those European countries which participated in the Organization for European Economic Co-operation. The language of certain articles was made almost identical for those undertakings specified by Title I of the Foreign Assistance Act which applied in principle to the Chinese as well as to the European situation. Because of certain basically different aspects of the Chinese situation, however, some standard articles were modified considerably in the China Agreement, or unique provisions were added. In view of conditions prevailing in China, the scope of joint control, particularly with respect to prices and allocations, was broader under the terms of the China Agreement than under the European bilateral agreements. One unique article in the China Agreement, that calling for improvement of commercial relations, was required specifically by Section 405 of the China Aid Act.

The Agreement with China set forth a number of undertakings by the Chinese and/or the US Government relating to the following :

provision of aid to the Chinese Government in accordance with the terms of the China Aid Act of 1948 (other than Section 404(*b*) thereof) ; measures for improvement of general economic conditions including effective use of aid goods, appropriate use of private Chinese assets in the USA, development of industrial and agricultural production, creation of more stable currency conditions, co-operation with other countries to increase international trade, and prevention of commercial arrangements which interfere with the purposes of the Agreement ;

improvement of commercial relations with other countries, with particular reference to the conditions affecting foreign trade by private enterprises in China ;

fair and equitable distribution of aid goods, and of similar goods produced locally or imported with other funds, and the methods of determining terms, conditions and prices for distribution of aid goods ;

deposits of Chinese currency in value commensurate with the value of US aid provided on a grant basis, and the principles governing disposal of such deposits ;

facilitating the acquisition by the USA from China of materials in short supply in the USA ;

negotiation of duty-free treatment for imports into China of relief goods by private agencies or individuals ;

joint consultation, and provision of information by the Chinese Government, regarding matters relevant to the Agreement ;

publicity within China regarding provision of aid under the agreement ;

establishment in China of, and treatment to be accorded to, a US Special Mission for Economic Co-operation ;

settlement, by reference to an agreed upon international tribunal, of claims espoused by either Government on behalf of its nationals against the other Government for compensation for damage arising as a consequence of governmental measures taken after 3 April 1948 ;

entry into force, amendment and duration of the Agreement.

Advisory Bodies

Two advisory bodies have on request furnished helpful counsel and guidance on broad questions relating to the planning and conduct of the ECA China Aid Programme : The National Advisory Council on International Monetary and Financial Problems, established by Congress, and the Public Advisory Committee for the China Programme, appointed by the Administrator under authority granted in Public Law 472, Section 107 (*b*).

Members of the National Advisory Committee for the China Programme have been: Isaiah Bowman, President-Emeritus of Johns Hopkins University and a member since 1940 of the Permanent International Commission for China and the United States ; Arthur B. Foye, senior partner of the international public accountant firm of Haskins and Sells and, since 1945, president of the Far East-America Council of Commerce and Industry ; Paul V. McNutt, former ambassador and United States high commissioner to the Philippines, and president and chairman of the Board of United Service to China ; Elizabeth Luce Moore, former chairman of the USO Council, one of the founders in 1940 of United China Relief, and a trustee of Wellesley College, of the China Institute in America, and of the United Board for Christian Colleges in China ; and Walter S. Robertson, former minister-counsellor for economic affairs at the United States Embassy in Chungking, and a principal assistant to General George C. Marshall during his special mission to China in 1945-6.

ECA Mission to China

Authority for the establishment of a special ECA Mission to China is contained in Public Law 472, Sections 109 and 403.

The organization of the China Mission began with the appointment of Roger D. Lapham, former mayor of San Francisco, as Chief of the Mission. The appointment was made on 5 May 1948, and Mr Lapham arrived in China on 7 June, accompanied by initial members of a Reconstruction Survey Group. Staffing of the Mission has been kept at a minimum consistent with the efficient performance of ECA economic aid functions in China. As on 31 December 1948, 89 Americans and 355 non-Americans were on duty with the Mission.

Clearances between ECA Headquarters and the China Mission are conducted through a China Programme Division in Washington. This is a staff office of 20 persons which facilitates the integration, without needless duplication, of China operations within the general framework of ECA financing and supply operations.

Relations with the Chinese Government

To provide for an orderly conduct of relations between the Chinese Government and the ECA China Mission, the Government appointed a Council for United States Aid (CUSA), with the Prime Minister as Chairman, which includes in its membership the Ministers of Foreign Affairs, Finance, and Communications, the Governor of the Central Bank, the Chairman of the National Resources Commission, the Mayor of Shanghai and the Chairman of the Chinese Technical Mission to the United States.

The Economic Co-operation Agreement between the United States and the Chinese Governments, signed at Nanking on 3 July 1948 by the United States Ambassador and the Chinese Minister for Foreign Affairs, provided the framework of understanding and agreements on the basis of which ECA operations in China have been conducted. The text of the Agreement appears in the final section of this paper.

Take-over from US China Relief Mission

The first organizational problem faced by the Chief of the ECA Mission to China was the need to make provision for the orderly transition from the work of the US China Relief Mission, which had been responsible for the $45,000,000 interim relief programme in China, previously provided under Public Law 84, to the new programme under ECA direction. Arrangements were made for the temporary transfer of considerable numbers of the personnel in the China Relief Mission, in order to ensure the orderly liquidation of that Mission's responsibilities under the supervision of ECA, and at the same time to utilize, for the benefit of the ECA programme, the experience of personnel already available in China, who had been working with a programme similar in certain respects to the China Aid Programme.

Take-over responsibilities included principally the receipt and distribution of residual China Relief Mission supplies, responsibility for residual proceeds from the sale of such supplies, and the carrying on or liquidation of various local currency projects agreed to by the China Relief Mission.

Approximately 25,000 tons of CRM rice and flour valued at about $3·8 million were on hand on 30 June 1948, which were taken over and distributed under the supervision of the ECA Mission through the rationing system. Approximately $5·2 million worth of medical supplies and $670,000 worth of pesticides were on order in the United States, to be delivered during the early months of the ECA programme. The general policy governing distribution of medical supplies has been to distribute them for the greater part free of charge and in large part in outlying areas where it has not been feasible to ship ECA bulk supplies. About a third of the pesticides has been reserved for the use of the Rural Reconstruction Commission, the remainder being sold through normal commercial channels or distributed free by the Ministry of Agriculture through agricultural demonstration centres.

There was virtually no cash balance in the CRM local currency account at the time of the ECA takeover. However, commitments had been entered into for over 260 projects predicated on anticipated proceeds from the sale of undistributed rice and flour. The ECA, accordingly, assumed responsibility for the orderly completion or liquidation of these projects. In July and August, the equivalent of US $197,600 was disbursed from the local currency Special Account for these purposes, about 55 per cent for public works, 43 per cent for medical purposes, and 2 per cent for miscellaneous projects. After August, considerable weeding out was done in order to reduce the number of projects to a number which would permit adequate supervision and these have been included in the overall ECA-CUSA programme for the Special Account.

Organization

Headquarters of the ECA Mission to China were established in Shanghai, and regional offices in Nanking, Peiping, Tientsin, Tsingtao, Canton and Taipeh (or Taiwan or Formosa).

The approved pattern of the Mission as of 31 December 1948 is reflected in the accompanying organizational chart. The principal functions of each organizational unit within the Mission are set forth in the Appendix.

Assistance has been given to the Mission by ECA Headquarters in the recruitment of American personnel and the co-ordination of personnel procedures, fiscal activities, and administrative management in accordance with Headquarters procedures and in compliance with foreign service requirements of the State Department.

Administrative Expenses

The ECA China Programme has operated under a limitation, for administrative expenses incurred in US dollars, of $1·2 million —less than one-half of one per cent of the amount appropriated for the current China programme. This necessitated rigid economies in the planning of staff requirements, and a maximum use of other agencies and means in order to develop an effective field organization. The $1·2 million ceiling did not apply to administrative costs provided from counterpart local currency funds in China, from which source approximately three-fifths of the administrative costs of the Mission are being met.

Administrative expenses, with the benefit of special arrangements referred to below, were held, up to the end of December 1948, within an amount provisionally estimated at approximately $560,000. However, a large percentage of these expenses were incurred during the last quarter of the calendar year 1948. This was attributable chiefly to two factors (a) the fact that the ECA China Mission was not fully staffed, and operations in China were not in full swing, until the October-December quarter; and (b) the necessity of incurring increased expenses (notably for extensive transfers of supplies and personnel, including the removal of some dependents) as a result of unsettled and uncertain conditions in north and central China. A third factor contributing to higher costs was beginning to appear at the end of the year, namely, the necessity, with the excessive rate of depreciation of Chinese currency, of meeting certain administrative expenses out of US dollars instead of local currency.

Payment for expenses incurred on behalf of American members of the Mission, including travel for members and dependents, is governed by US Foreign Service regulations which are mandatory with respect to ECA employees.

Military developments in China have made necessary budgetary provisions for the voluntary removal of certain dependents and household effects from threatened areas. As of 31 December 1948 some dependents and women employees with children were being evacuated, and some members of the Mission had been reassigned in accordance with changing programme plans.

The use of consulting engineers or engineering firms on a contract basis, in connexion with the development of surveys and plans for reconstruction projects in the industrial field, has made it possible to have competent engineering surveys and to prepare for supervising this part of the programme without incurring direct administrative expenditures in excess of the ceiling on administrative costs.

A similar saving has been effected in the case of the rural reconstruction programme. As indicated above, the Congressional appropriation for this programme, to be supervised by a Joint Commission on Rural Reconstruction, was 'an amount equal to not more than 10 per centum' of the appropriation for economic aid to China, which amount could be in US dollars, proceeds in Chinese currency from the sale of commodities made available to China, or both. From the ceiling of $27·5 million thus established for the rural reconstruction programme, $2·5 million was tentatively earmarked for availability in US dollars, to be used principally for salaries, dollar administrative requirements and essential procurement of agricultural supplies and educational media. The Joint Commission's allotments for both programme and administration represent a programme cost and are thus not chargeable to the limitation on administrative funds for the China Mission.

To avoid needless administrative duplication and expense, administrative arrangements were entered into between the State Department and the China Programme of ECA, in which the State Department agreed to provide communication facilities and to assume disbursing functions with respect to US dollars and to perform such minor services, in return for which ECA would reimburse the State Department, either through direct payment or through the provision of agreed services as needed by American or alien personnel.

Economies in time and space facilities were effected by the takeover of office and warehouse space and equipment previously utilized by the China Relief Mission operating under P.L. 84. Effective co-ordination with the Chinese Government Council for US Aid (CUSA) was facilitated by a provision for CUSA offices in the same location as those of the ECA China Mission.

The civil war, with its attendant disruption of rail services, has made necessary an almost exclusive use of air travel on the part of the members of the Mission in China, including chartered flights when necessary. Telegraph work-loads in excess of available capacities through diplomatic or military channels have necessitated a considerable use of commercial telegraph facilities for unclassified operational messages.

Through the economies and special arrangements outlined above, direct administrative expenses charged against the ECA programme in China were, as of 31 December 1948, within an administrative budget based upon the $1·2 million limitation for the one-year period of the authorizing legislation. And it was expected that administrative expenses incurred in the course of operations through 2 April 1949, would, despite the rising costs referred to above, be kept within this limitation.

Commodities Programme

The commodities programme has had as its aim the provision of a continued flow to China of certain key commodities essential to the maintenance of minimum economic activity and subsistence in the urban centres of China. As indicated above, resources available for ECA commodity imports into China were not of a sufficient order of magnitude to reduce substantially the great unbalance in the Chinese national budget or to solve the nation's balance of payments problem by providing all essential imports which could not be financed by the Chinese themselves. It was essential, therefore, to concentrate upon the commodities which were of most strategic importance in helping to bolster China's internal economy. Commodities procured under the ECA programme have included food, cotton, petroleum, fertilizer, and coal. In addition, as mentioned above, some residual medical supplies and pesticides were taken over by the ECA, from the earlier US Foreign Relief Programme, for distribution. The scope and character of each of these commodity programmes are discussed below.

Procurement and Shipment

Following consultation with the National Advisory Council, ECA decided to finance commodities for China entirely on a basis of grants, not loans. The reason for this action lay in the state of the Chinese Government's external finances, as described in an earlier section of this paper.

Commodity procurement has been conducted by two methods, through private trade channels for cotton, fertilizer, petroleum and coal, and through the US Department of Agriculture for rice, wheat and flour.

Cotton has been purchased through ECA financing by the Chinese Textile Industries, Inc., a quasi-governmental corporation, from US cotton brokers submitting bids through agents in Shanghai. Fertilizer has been purchased by the Central Trust of China from suppliers presenting bids, overall quantities purchased being governed by the size of International Emergency Food Committee allocations to China. Petroleum products have been purchased from suppliers on the basis of recommendations submitted by a joint Chinese-American sub-committee of CUSA, these recommendations being based on the pre-war supply pattern ; although this method of selecting suppliers has to some extent reduced the scope of price competition, prices paid for petroleum have been carefully scrutinized in the light of Section 202 of Public Law 793.

Procurement of wheat and flour has been from United States surpluses, purchases being made by the Commodity Credit Corporation of the US Department of Agriculture from private suppliers on the basis of competitive bidding. These purchases have been against US Department of Commerce allocations, determining the total quantity of US wheat exportable to China. Rice has also been procured by the Commodity Credit Corporation, pursuant to Section 121, Public Law 472, chiefly in Siam and Burma, purchases being made against IEFC allocations.

Up to 31 December 1948, more than 99% of the ECA-financed cargo tonnage originating in the United States and delivered to China had been shipped in US flag vessels; this was far in excess of the overall requirement for ECA (in section 111(a) of Public Law 472) 'that at least 50% of the gross tonnage of commodities, procured within the United States out of funds made available under this title and transported abroad on ocean vessels, is so transported on United States-flag vessels to the extent such vessels are available at market rates'.

Procurement and Pricing of Commodities in China

Aid in providing essential commodities has been regarded by the ECA as a supplement to, and not a substitute for, production and supply efforts by the Chinese Government. This has been especially true with regard to the food programme, in connexion with which the ECA China Mission has undertaken to secure as effective performance as possible by the Government in providing from indigenous sources a substantial share of the food supplies required for the cities receiving ECA food shipments. In order to minimize the degree of subsidy to private consumers at the expense of government income, the China Mission has undertaken, with varying results, to exert its influence in favour of the selling of rationed food at, or near to, actual market prices ; the same is true with respect to cotton goods and petroleum products. Similar influence has been exerted, as far as practicable, with regard to prices for coal, rates for electric power, or levels at which any enterprise, directly or indirectly assisted by ECA, sells its products.

End-Use Control

Measures essential to effective end-use control have been carefully developed for each of the commodity programmes, in order to assure that supplies provided through ECA would go to the recipients for which they were intended, to furnish maximum assistance to people and institutions within China, to support efforts of the Government to increase production and stabilize economic conditions, and generally to secure the best results attainable through the expenditure of ECA dollars.

Food has been distributed through a controlled rationing system in major cities of China, and a detailed record has been kept of individual recipients of this aid ; ECA representatives attend as observers the meetings of City Food Committees, and ECA investigators inspect and report on all phases of operations under the rationing programme. The cotton aid programme is directed in China by a Joint Management Board whose decisions require CUSA and ECA concurrence ; a system has been established for following cotton through conversion into yarn, the conversion of yarn into cloth, and the subsequent domestic use or export of the resulting textiles. Petroleum has been distributed primarily by major oil companies which themselves help to make sure that ECA-financed oil goes only to the uses for which it is allocated ; a joint CUSA-ECA Petroleum Committee estimates requirements and supervises distribution. Control arrangements are being developed to insure that fertilizer will be distributed in a way that will achieve maximum effect in increasing food production.

Further details with respect to end-use controls are contained in the description below of the several commodity programmes, and in the Appendix.

270

Food

The interior of China—including countryside, towns and cities—has normally been relatively self-sufficient in foodstuffs, but the larger coastal cities have in recent decades become increasingly dependent, for part of their food supply, on imports from abroad. As previously indicated, the problem of food supplies for these cities became acute in the spring of 1948 due to the disruption of communications and trade by the civil war, spiralling inflation, and increasing strains upon the Government's foreign exchange resources.

Inception of Food Rationing in Post-war China

Food rationing in post-war China was first developed in the programme of the United States China Relief Mission. Under this programme the US Government provided—for the five major coastal cities of Shanghai, Nanking, Canton, Peiping and Tientsin—approximately 200,000 tons of rice, wheat and flour, of which more than 150,000 tons was distributed before the end of June 1948. Contributions from the Chinese Government approximately matched this tonnage, with the result that between March and the close of June about 300,000 tons of food was sold at prices considerably lower than those prevailing on the open market to between 11 and 12 million inhabitants of these cities.

Each individual, under the rationing programme, was limited to a monthly purchase of 16·5 pounds of rice or flour, although no one was limited in the amount that might, if available, be purchased at inflated prices on the open market.

This programme was an innovation in China. Food rationing on a major scale had not previously been practised there as it has in most other countries of the world where shortages posed a problem of equitable distribution of available supply. Chinese officials considered the matter long and carefully before undertaking the responsibility for a programme which depended for its success upon the development and maintenance of relatively complicated administrative machinery. However, once started, the administration of the programme was carried out with a record of competence, precision and honesty that became a source of gratification to all parties concerned, including the Chinese officials responsible for the operation.

Seven-city Rationing Programme

Following the first arrival of ECA food supplies in China, it was decided that the rationing programme should be continued as the best means of applying US aid in an equitable manner, of retarding somewhat the rapid rate of price increase, and of providing an added source of revenue to the Government. Under the ECA programme, the number of cities participating in rationing was extended to include Swatow and Tsingtao. In the latter city, the US Navy maintained a base in an area which was surrounded by Communists and cut off from local sources of food supply.

The somewhat fluctuating population of the seven cities participating in the rationing programme ranged, in total, between 12·7 and 13 million during 1948.

Under arrangements agreed upon between the ECA China Mission and the Chinese Government Council for US Aid (CUSA), agreement was reached on the setting up, within the Chinese Government's Ministry of Food, of an Office of Emergency Food Procurement (OEFP), which was to handle indigenous purchasing for the rationing programme. The OEFP undertook initially to procure from indigenous sources approximately 60 per cent of the total food required for the operation of the rationing system, and ECA approximately 40 per cent.

Emergency Feeding Programmes

In addition to this rationing programme for seven cities, a limited emergency feeding programme for Mukden was developed while that city remained in Nationalist hands. Nearly one thousand tons of flour delivered under this emergency programme were cooked and fed directly to key groups of workers with appropriate publicity. The resultant increase in morale was notable until, with the Communist assault on Mukden, the programme had to be suspended. Some 400 tons of ECA flour in Chinchow awaiting airlift to Mukden were captured by the Communists during their rapid advance in that sector.

In order to cope with the heavy influx of refugees into Tsingtao from the war zones and to compensate for the reduced supplies of indigenous food coming into the city because of Communist occupation of surrounding territory, the ECA China Mission has also provided, in that city, continuing support for a special Refugee Feeding Project originally instituted under the CRM programme. This project, conducted outside the rationing programme in co-operation with municipal authorities, consists of open-air kitchens which prepare and serve daily portions of rice congee to an estimated 100,000 refugees. Damaged rice, sweepings and poorer grades of rice unsuitable for rationing, which are received in ECA shipments from south-east Asia, are set aside for this project in Shanghai, for trans-shipment to Tsingtao. The bulk of shipments have been made via vessels of the US Navy, which considers the project a necessary emergency measure effective in the maintenance of orderly conditions in Tsingtao. Requirements for the project are 1,300 tons per month.

August 19 Regulations and Indigenous Procurement

An element of subsidy was inherent in the seven-city rationing plan. But it was never intended that the prices of rationed cereals would be allowed to fall far below open market prices. At first, prices for rationed foods were adjusted monthly to a level approximately 5 per cent below prevailing open-market rates and held there throughout the ensuing month, regardless of price rises in the open market. Thus the Government was in a position to obtain much needed revenue from sales of rationed rice and flour, even though some slight subsidy accrued to the people, for the US supplies thus sold cost the Government nothing and all local currency returns from this sale constituted a net gain.

Under the Government's 19 August reform measures, however, ration prices, particularly in the central and north China cities, were set well below market prices, with the result that the dependence of the programme on governmental subsidies became heavy during the period until November when these measures were drastically revised. As the military, political and economic situation deteriorated, the Government deemed it expedient to use the rationing programmes to provide an outright subsidy to all the people in the urban coastal cities in an effort to mitigate public discontent. At this time, wages were lagging so far behind essential commodity prices that the city populations began to be unable to purchase minimum requirements of daily necessities. ECA officials reluctantly acquiesced in the selling of US-contributed food supplies along with indigenous supplies, at what to the Government were ruinously subsidized prices, but warned that the policy would prove exceedingly costly.

Since ECA funds for food procurement were limited, it appeared advisable at the outset to conserve them in large part to provide foodstuffs for the 1948-9 winter and spring months and thus assure rationing supplies at the time of the year when food is normally less plentiful. The Chinese Government agreed to find and deliver the foodstuffs needed for rationing during the last quarter of 1948, with the understanding that the ECA would undertake to supply a major portion of the ration during the first quarter of 1949 and to deliver additional food thereafter to the extent of availability of funds from the 1948 appropriation.

Difficulties developed in the implementation of this plan. The obtaining of indigenous supplies by the Chinese OEFP was slow and erratic ; its attempts to purchase domestic food supplies were inspired by lack of sufficient appropriations and by the disparity between official and black-market prices. There was a failure to act quickly to procure domestic supplies in quantity when the harvests were in. Anticipated purchases of rice in Burma did not materialize.

Some flour was collected at Shanghai for the ration in the cities of north China, but commandeering by the military of the ships selected for the transport of these supplies caused considerable delay in their movement. As indicated above, the unsuccessful economic regulations promulgated by the Government on 19 August 1948 resulted in the exclusion from China's major cities of normal free-market supplies of indigenous foods. The acute shortages, dramatized by all-night queues in front of food shops, were intensified by a partial breakdown of the rationing system during October. At the middle of October none of the cities except Canton and Tsingtao had even been able to start the October ration, and one city was still trying to fulfil the September ration commitment.

Throughout this period, the ECA China Mission pressed for the lifting of arbitrary food price ceilings in the cities, for a realistic pricing of rationed foods, and for more vigorous efforts by the OEFP to procure indigenous supplies.

Speed-up of ECA Deliveries

Steps were also taken to speed up ECA deliveries of wheat, previously scheduled for the first quarter of 1949, in order to move up to November and December the resumption of ECA's contribution to the ration system. Some success was achieved in the acceleration of ECA shipments to China—which proved to be of crucial importance in allaying unrest in major cities—and in the development of more realistic pricing for rationed food, but indigenous procurement efforts by the Chinese Government continued to lag.

Reported shipments as of 31 December 1948, under procurement programmes 1, 2 and 3 (for the second, third and fourth quarters of 1943) were valued at approximately $37,000,000 for the purchase of 129,000 tons of rice and 107,000 tons of wheat and flour. In addition, about 25,000 tons of rice and flour had been received as residue from the China Relief Mission and 9,000 tons of rice had been borrowed from Hongkong to relieve a threatened November food shortage in Shanghai. Of these amounts, approximately 120,000 tons of rice and 30,000 tons of wheat and flour had before the end of December been released for the rationing programmes. Additional Programme 3 stocks either *en route*, loading or waiting for shipment, at the end of 1948, totalled 27,000 tons of rice from Siam and Burma and 56,000 tons of wheat and flour from the United States.

Supervision of Rationing Programme

Although administered by Chinese Government officials, the ECA food programme in China has been carefully supervised by ECA representatives who have insisted upon the maintenance of high standards of performance and honesty. Mindful of the considerable pilfering and misuse of food supplies previously delivered under the UNRRA programme, ECA has paid utmost attention to the problem of end-use control. Strict supervision and careful checking have been applied to every phase of distribution in order to assure that all ECA-financed food supplies allocated to the rationing programme actually reach the end recipient. A detailed description of rationing and end-use control under the ECA food programme is contained in the Appendix.

The United States has delivered its contributions to the rationing programmes regularly and on time. ECA officials in China have manifested constant concern that the rationing programme should be conducted for the benefit of the people as a whole. These facts are well known to the millions of persons affected, and have done much to sustain their faith in the friendship of the American people.

Cotton

The first step in the cotton programme involved an easing of pressure upon China's strained foreign exchange resources by ECA financing of existing consignment contracts with early delivery dates; these contracts were between the China Textile Industries, Inc., and the agents in Shanghai of American cotton shippers. All of the cotton involved was programmed for supply from the United States. In the course of authorizing procurement of this cotton, provision was made for joint supervision, by the Government and the ECA China Mission, of processing and distribution of raw cotton after arrival in China.

The total cotton programme developed under the current China Aid Programme involved an expenditure of nearly $70 million. During October 1948, the first of this cotton reached the mills and the system of control and reporting of end-use was perfected. As of 31 December, cotton in the amount of 299,038 bales, costing approximately $52·7 million, had arrived in China and was being allocated and distributed to the mills ; 51,000 bales of yarn and 557,000 bolts of cloth (40 yards each) had been received back from the mills.

Under the ECA China aid programme, all cotton is procured through private trade channels. Cotton shipments to China are continuing under schedules designed to maintain production and employment while avoiding any undue advance stock-piling.

The Chinese textile industry with about 3,900,000 operable spindles is China's largest manufacturing industry and raw cotton is one of China's vital imports. Not only are the cloth and yarn produced of great significance to the Chinese economy, but a high level of employment among the textile workers is important to the maintenance of relative stability in industrial centres, particularly in Shanghai.

Raw Cotton Supply Problem

Before the war, cotton grown in China supplied the bulk of the fibre required to keep the textile mills in operation. Due to some reduction in cotton acreage and, more important, to the extensive disruption of internal transportation trade caused by the civil war (see accompanying map), indigenous cotton has gone largely into household use and China has had to depend on imports for more than a third of the cotton used in her mills. In the year 1947-48, mill consumption was about 1,950,000 bales ; imports of cotton were about 700,000 bales (as compared with a pre-war level of imports of 340,000 bales). Procurement was in considerable part from India, and limited quantities were purchased also from British East Africa, Burma and Egypt.

Provision of the necessary foreign exchange for cotton importation has been for China a problem of increasing proportions. The ECA programme, which financed 300,000 bales in 1948 and in January of 1949 was in process of financing an additional 100,000 bales, has been a major factor in the sustaining of production and employment in China's textile industry during the latter part of 1948.

Use and Control of ECA Cotton Imports

The plan developed for the use of ECA cotton imports called for the conversion of the cotton into yarn under arrangements involving processing or trading at a fixed ratio under which raw cotton is paid for by the processing and in most cases by conversion of the resulting yarn into cotton cloth. The Council for United States Aid (CUSA) and the ECA Mission to China agreed upon a division of the yarn and cloth produced from ECA cotton, with 50 per cent to be used for domestic consumption and the rest to be exported—the proceeds to be used for purchase of additional raw cotton. Exports under this programme had up to 31 December 1948 earned an equivalent of more than $4·5 million in foreign exchange, all sales being to countries of south-east Asia. Domestic distribution is largely by direct sale through commercial channels ; some of the textiles, however, have been used in barter schemes, as described below, designed to bring more food into the cities. More than 2,000 bales of yarn and cloth made from ECA cotton were bartered in Nanking, Shanghai and Nanchang for 33,000 piculs of rice at a time when no other grain was moving into these cities from producing areas.

The arrangements adopted followed careful planning and careful negotiation by the Mission with the Chinese Government. The conversion, storage and disposition of ECA-financed cotton shipments to China are under the control of a Joint Management Board, and full records of each stage of the process are kept for end-use control purposes. Details of the end-use control mechanism developed are presented in the Appendix.

Petroleum

Since production of crude oil in China is negligible, the country is almost wholly dependent upon imports of petroleum products required in the operation of utilities, transport facilities, and manufacture and for household use. The cutting off of coal from north China, as a result of the civil war, increased greatly during the year the relative importance of petroleum products for power and industrial units in which they could be substituted for coal.

Taken as a whole, petroleum imports were vital to the operation of China's limited transport facilities and industrial plant. Diesel and fuel oil were essential to the operation of power plants and other utilities. These types, as well as motor and aviation gasoline and lubricants, were essential to the operation of water, rail and air transport. The use of kerosene, normally in wide demand for household lighting and fuel in rural districts and towns lacking electric power, has been restricted by disruptions in transport, but there has been continuing demand in the more accessible areas.

Use of Normal Trade Channels

The petroleum programme involved, at first, negotiations on the part which each of the petroleum distributing concerns and the large end-users in China would play in the importation and distribution of the products. The problems involved were largely settled about the middle of 1948, and firm authorizations were thereupon prepared for issuance.

As a result, the importation and distribution of petroleum products under the ECA China Aid Programme have been entirely through normal trade channels and the bulk of the business is handled by the Standard Vacuum Oil Co., the Shell Company of China, Ltd., the California-Texas Oil Co., and the Chinese Petroleum Corporation (an agency of the Chinese Government). A number of small importers and distributors have also participated in the programme. The oil companies at first charged somewhat higher prices for petroleum products to China than to other destinations in order to recover thereby the foreign exchange component of internal distribution costs. Such price differentials were not satisfactory either to the Chinese Government or ECA : consequently ECA has indicated its willingness to finance only such petroleum shipments as are priced on a cost-and-freight basis and are within the US market price as provided in Section 202 of the Appropriation Act (Public Law 793).

As of 31 December 1948, the Central Bank of China had financed petroleum brought into China under the ECA China Aid Programme to a value of about $28 million, for which amount the Central Bank of China was to be reimbursed by ECA as rapidly as the requisite documentation is furnished ECA by the Central Bank of China.

In view of the Central Bank's straitened foreign exchange position, ECA Headquarters on 26 November 1948 authorized an advance of $15 million to the Central Bank to enable it, pending reimbursement by ECA, to continue financing the release and distribution of petroleum products in China. Shortly before the end of the year, the reimbursement procedure was abandoned, and arrangements were made to finance all future petroleum shipments (and releases from bonded tanks of products already in China) by letter of commitment to US banks. In connexion with the new procedure, the ECA Mission to China was given the responsibility of approving each shipment or release in advance, in order to avoid undue stock-piling of petroleum products in Chinese ports.

Administration of Petroleum Programme

Requirements programmes have been prepared on a quarterly basis by the CUSA-ECA Petroleum Committee, which includes both active members and observers from CUSA and ECA. Up to the end of 1948, prices within China were determined by the Oil Allocation Committee, with approval of the Executive Yuan ; the CUSA-ECA Petroleum Committee has sought Executive Yuan approval of a plan to authorize a CUSA-ECA, EIB (Export-Import Board) Price Adjustment Committee in Shanghai to make periodic reviews and price adjustments on its own initiative, in order to keep prices on a realistic basis and prevent the oil companies from sustaining losses because of currency fluctuations.

With ECA assistance, production has been continued at the Kaohsiang refinery in Taiwan to which, at the end of 1948, 225,000 barrels of crude oil were being provided monthly for conversion into motor gasoline, diesel and fuel oil and kerosene. The plan under which this assistance has been given was developed on the basis of recommendations by an independent firm of engineers engaged for the purpose by the Chinese Government upon the suggestion of ECA.

End-use control of the petroleum products imported into China has presented fewer administrative problems for the ECA than end-use control of other commodities. Distribution of ECA-financed petroleum products in China is generally of two types : distribution to large users (for example, fuel oil for the Shanghai Power Company) and distribution by individual companies to end-users (for example, retail distribution of gasoline through filling stations to car owners). Since the companies are the distribution agents, and the major distributors are two American companies and one British company, these firms themselves provide a considerable measure of end-use control and are able to do most of the end-use reporting required, subject to necessary spot-checking by the ECA Mission.

Fertilizer

Procurement of fertilizer has proceeded within the limitation of availabilities for China from existing world supplies, as reflected in allocations by the International Emergency Food Council. Although increased use of fertilizers offers promise of substantial increases in indigenous food production, its widespread application during the post-war period has been impeded by a lack of extensive previous experience in the use of chemical fertilizers in China, except in Formosa ; by a shortage of extension personnel and organization to train Chinese farmers in the effective application of modern fertilizers ; and by the difficulty of devising effective distribution and end-use control systems within China. Under plans being perfected at the end of 1948, it was expected that substantial distribution to end-users, particularly in Formosa and south China, would occur during the first quarter of 1949, and that a reasonable minimum of fertilizer could be made available in China for the spring planting.

ECA Procurement of Fertilizers

Under the current China Programme, ECA is financing the procurement of approximately 75,000 metric tons of chemical fertilizers, at a cost of approximately US $8·9 million ; this should be of material benefit in increasing rice production in some districts, particularly in sections of Formosa and south China. It was at first planned to spend US $13·8 million on fertilizers. Subsequently, arrangements were made whereby the Bank of China, the Central Bank and the Taiwan Provincial Government undertook to finance from their own resources the procurement of a portion of the nitrogenous fertilizers allocated to China by the International Emergency Food Committee ; ECA thereupon reduced its fertilizer commitment by $4·9 million. Under these arrangements China is in a position to acquire during 1948-49, through ECA and Government procurement, 116,000 metric tons of ammonium sulphate and ammonium phosphate. Having been used by Chinese farmers who have previously employed chemical fertilizers, these types are considered the most practical under prevailing agricultural practice.

Aid to Food Production in China

Fertilizers provided by ECA are primarily for use in increasing yields of lowland rice, which should mean a corresponding decrease in dependence upon importations of rice from abroad.

It has been found, through scientific experimentation and practice, that one unit of nitrogenous fertilizer can produce an average increase in yield of at least 2 units of clean rice or about 3 units of paddy rice, all by weight. Theoretically, therefore, one dollar's worth of fertilizer should produce three dollars worth of grain (in terms of each equivalent to the import cost of an equal amount of food). However, owing to high transportation and internal handling costs and the low price of rice at producing centres in China, a somewhat smaller gain is realized. Nevertheless, the use of chemical fertilizer is the most effective means known to augment food production in China.

The total annual domestic production of chemical fertilizers in China, at the 1948 rate, was only about 81,000 metric tons (36,000 ammonium sulphate, 35,000 superphosphate and 10,000 calcium cyanamide). A provisional allotment from ECA of $5·5 million to China's domestic fertilizer industry, aimed to increase substantially production capacity, had to be suspended at least temporarily, towards the end of the year, due to disturbed civil war conditions.

At the end of 1948, the first 10,000 tons of ECA fertilizer was scheduled to reach Shanghai in January 1949. This instalment, on the basis of an agreement with the Farmer's Bank, was to be distributed to farmers who, during November and December, had advanced rice for the food rationing programme. Plans were developed for the distribution, through commercial channels in south China and Taiwan and through the Joint Rural Reconstruction Commission, of additional shipments totalling about 61,000 tons.

Coal

China's principal coal-producing centres have been in north China and Manchuria. As indicated on the accompanying map*, military developments together with the cutting of vital transportation routes during 1948 interrupted the flow of coal from north China producing areas to consuming areas in central China.

Arrangements were made, therefore, for ECA procurement on an emergency basis of limited stocks from Japan through the Supreme Command, Allied Powers, Pacific (SCAP) organization. Before the end of 1948, coal in the amount of 15,000 tons had been obtained from Japan at a cost of about $280,000, and there was a prospect that further emergency procurement would be required.

* Not included here.—*Editor.*

Medical Supplies

About $5 million worth of medical supplies were procured for China under Public Law 84, the US Foreign Relief Programme. Most of these supplies arrived in China after the expiration of the China Relief Mission on 30 June 1948 ; they became, therefore, an ECA responsibility. As of December, nearly 90 per cent of the supplies programmed by the China Relief Mission had arrived in China.

The reception, storage and transportation phases of the medical supply programme have worked smoothly and losses from pilferage and improper handling have been negligible. Special medical ware-housing units established have operated with a high degree of efficiency. On the basis of careful allocation and distribution planning by the Council for US Aid, the ECA Mission to China, the Ministry of Health and the International Relief Committee, the distribution of these supplies was proceeding regularly at the end of 1948.

Distribution from Shanghai was being accelerated in view of the rapidly changing political and military situations ; additional ware-houses were being stocked in Canton and Taipeh (on the island of Taiwan), leaving in Shanghai only supplies required in that area. It was expected that final distribution of medical supplies to end-users would be completed by 31 May, 1949.

Pesticides

ECA also took over from the China Relief Mission responsibility for $537,000 worth of pesticides which reached China during 1948 ; most of these supplies arrived too late for distribution during the lifetime of the China Relief Mission.

Plans were developed and agreed upon between ECA and the Chinese Government in September, for allocations of 35 per cent of these pesticides to the Joint Rural Reconstruction Commission, 15 per cent to the Ministry of Agriculture and Forestry for free distribution at agricultural demonstration centres, and the remaining 50 per cent for sale through commercial channels. Sales during October and November were principally in south Kiangsu and north Chekian areas bordering the Shanghai district and were concluded in time to give needed protection to crops. When seasonal demand from farmers in these districts ceased, sales efforts were directed to south China where, with a long growing season, the need for insecticides continued during ensuing months. In Taiwan, where the use of agricultural insecticides is best known, the only channels through which farmers had been accustomed to obtain their supplies in the past had not, at the end of the year, been utilized in accordance with original plans due to lack of requisite co-operation in making supplies quickly available to consumers.

Special Barter Arrangements

A barter programme, of an emergency nature, was developed, initially on a small scale. Difficulties experienced by the Chinese in obtaining their quota of domestic food supplies for the rationing programme were such that CUSA and ECA undertook to exchange limited quantities of cloth and yarn (manufactured from aid cotton) for rice and other indigenous food grains.

About 200 tons of cloth were sent to Nanking, for example, to be used in exchange for rice, about 150 pounds of rice being obtained for each piece of grey cloth 40 yards long.

In villages near Shanghai a similar type of exchange was developed, and in Changsha, commercial centre of a large rice-producing area in northern Hunan, a beginning was made. Such exchanges up to the end of 1948, were experimental in character. The results attained indicated that considerable quantities of rice could be obtained in this manner, and it was planned that regular supplies of yarn and cloth to be used for this purpose would shortly be advanced to the Office of Emergency Food Procurement, with ECA observing OEFP operations and ensuring strict end-use accounting.

In north China ECA representatives were, at the end of November, negotiating with representatives from General Fu Tso-yi's headquarters and local grain dealers. A contract was under consideration calling for 120,000 pieces of cloth to be used in exchange for domestic wheat, flour, and coarse grains, the foodstuffs to be used in a selective rationing plan for workers in essential services. This plan was disrupted by military developments in the Peiping-Tientsin area.

Two principal purposes were served by such barters of cloth and yarn for food : (1) the obtaining of additional supplies of food for use in the rationing programmes and (2) the distribution of yarn and cloth in interior areas, in many cases direct to the farmers without passing through middlemen, thus reducing opportunities for cloth and yarn to fall into the hands of speculators.

Shipping

Mention has been made of the fact that more than 99 per cent of ECA-financed commodities shipped from the United States to China during 1948 were carried in US vessels.

Internal administrative rulings defining what types of transportation expenditures are eligible for reimbursing from ECA funds, written principally for application to Europe, are generally applied to China. However, due to emergency conditions in China the Administration has seen fit to depart from its general rules on special occasions. These departures involve the payment of partial freight in dollars to certain Chinese ships chartered to move rice from Siam and Burma. The rice, procured by US representatives using ECA funds, has been moved to China on an exacting schedule to meet ECA's feeding programme in principal Chinese cities. About $727,000 for freight thus provided before the end of December 1948 made possible the movement of 39 Chinese ships carrying about 155,000 metric tons of rice.

These movements of rice from south-east Asia to China have not taken place exclusively in Chinese ships ; funds are made available to US representatives to enable them to use American ships interested in the traffic. However, only one American ship was used for this purpose in 1948 ; the cost *via* this vessel was $7·50 per ton as compared with the current Chinese rate of $2·00 per ton from Siam. The Chinese rate towards the end of 1948 was $3·50 per ton from Burma as compared with an estimated $10·00 per ton in American vessels. It is considered doubtful whether the dollars provided to the Chinese cover the out-of-pocket expenses of the ships involved, which do receive some additional compensation in Chinese currency from counterpart funds.

The reason for close scheduling of shipping carrying food into China has been to import sufficient amounts to prevent starvation and riots, at the same time avoiding stockpiling of quantities that might be lost as a result of the war. In addition to scheduling rice shipments, considerable authority was delegated to the ECA Mission in China to divert US wheat and flour shipments, as well as shipments of other commodities, to meet changing situations. When the military situation in the vicinity of Tientsin deteriorated, several American ships about to discharge in ports serving that area were diverted to Tsingtao.

Industrial Reconstruction and Replacement Programme

A total of $70 million was originally programmed for industrial reconstruction and replacement projects in China. The legislative history of the China Aid Act indicated considerable Congressional interest in this significant aspect of proposed assistance to China. Extensive, painstaking preparations were made, including the sending to China of a special Reconstruction Survey Group, in order to ensure the most productive use of the funds made available for industrial reconstruction and replacement purposes.

Necessity for Suspension

However, due to developments in the civil war situation in China, it became necessary for the Administrator, on 21 December 1948, to announce that work on the reconstruction and replacement programme was, to a large extent, being suspended—exceptions being made in connexion with the completion of certain pre-project engineering studies which had already reached an advanced stage of development. Preparatory work on some of the projects, located in areas of Manchuria or north China involved in or threatened by military developments, had already in fact been suspended. The series of defeats sustained by the Nationalist forces in the fall and early winter of 1948, jeopardizing the Government's position not only at its remaining bases in north China but also in the Yangtze Valley, had resulted in chaotic conditions and major uncertainties throughout many of the regions in which reconstruction and replacement projects had been planned.

The suspension did not eliminate the possibility of renewed activity on selected projects in areas remaining accessible, in the event that such a partial resumption of the reconstruction and replacement programme should at any future time be deemed feasible and expedient. At the time of suspension, all of the projects were still in the pre-project engineering stage, no funds having as yet been actually committed for procurement.

The following paragraphs present a brief summary of the problems encountered in the field of industrial replacement and reconstruction, the planning and preparatory work undertaken, and the practical arrangements developed for the initiation and execution of replacement and reconstruction projects in China. A listing, with brief descriptions, of the projects for which 'provisional allotments' were made prior to the suspension of this part of the programme appears in the Appendix.

Planning and Preparatory Work

Initial planning had called for an expenditure of $60 million for reconstruction and $10 million for replacement work; as a result of the work of the Reconstruction Survey Group, however, much greater proportionate emphasis was placed upon replacements needed to increase the productivity of existing enterprises.

Initial members of the Survey Group reached China on 7 June 1948. The Group, consisting of 4 engineers, 2 economists, a lawyer and a businessman (Charles L. Stillman), who served as its head, operated as a part of the ECA Mission to China. After several months' review of conditions in China by the members of this Group, the ECA Mission developed, in agreement with the Chinese Government, a tentative programme designed to make a significant start towards the reconstruction or rehabilitation of certain railroads, electric power plants, fertilizer manufacturing units, and coal, tin and antimony mines—all in non-Communist China.

The programme finally recommended by the Survey Group and tentatively approved by the Administrator prior to the enforced suspension of this aspect of ECA assistance to China called for approximately $25 million worth of new reconstruction or development, $35 million to be spent for replacement assistance, and $7·5 million for engineering services and reserves, making a total of $67·5 million ; the remaining $2·5 million was earmarked for foreign exchange expenditures required in connexion with the rural reconstruction programme. Most of the projects planned were in the fields of basic industry and transportation—approximately $13·5 million being provisionally allotted for railway rehabilitation, $17·25 million for power plants, $11 million for coal mines and $5·5 million for fertilizer manufacture.

Following extensive consideration within ECA of the possibility of extending assistance to certain types of replacement and reconstruction projects on a loan basis, and after subsequent consultation with the National Advisory Council, it was tentatively determined that projects currently under consideration would be provided on an outright grant basis, leaving open the possibility of future reconsideration of loan proposals.

Problems of Industrial Reconstruction in China

The Chinese in taking back control of their country after eight long years faced many problems. The areas reoccupied had been swept over by Japanese armies, by Chinese armies, and by Chinese and American air forces. Communist raids and damage by armies of both sides in the civil war had continued in many regions. Nearly all existing industrial facilities were in deplorable condition due to a variety of causes dating back to the opening of the Sino-Japanese War in 1937. Railroads, partially restored during the UNRRA period, needed further assistance. Further problems were presented for foreign exchange shortages, internal economic and financial difficulties evidenced in extreme inflation, seriously inadequate transportation and a general disruption of Government and of industrial management, both public and private.

Elimination of much foreign participation in Chinese affairs, as a result of the war and the ending of extraterritoriality, inevitably left a gap in the nation's economic and industrial life. Particularly in the industrial areas, foreign participation in management and control of properties had been of significance in their development and effective operation. Following the war, foreign-flag shipping was excluded from Chinese river and coastal waters, resulting in higher transportation costs and less adequate services. The Chinese were unable to develop comparable services in a short time.

285

When Taiwan (the island of Formosa) was returned to *de facto* Chinese control after fifty years of Japanese occupation, US military forces removed nearly all Japanese from the island. The removal of those who had exercised management, control and possessed requisite technical knowledge meant that this relatively highly developed island had to be staffed at management and technical levels with Chinese personnel who lacked previous knowledge of the properties involved and who faced, in addition to normal maintenance problems, a large replacement problem resulting from bombing damage inflicted during the war by US air forces.

Considerable quantities of industrial materials and equipment had been made available to China through previous aid programmes, notably the UNRRA programme, and through Chinese Government procurement from the Pacific islands of United States surplus supplies after the war. China had not been able to absorb all of these supplies during the first three post-war years. The ECA faced, therefore, the problem not only of making sure that equipment under the ECA China aid programme was put to effective use, but of helping also to get into operation residual stockpiles of equipment already in China.

Most of China's industrial plant had been badly undermaintained throughout the long war years, and requisite training of personnel had been largely discontinued. Although China's industrial development was still in its early stages, the effective functioning of the nation's limited industrial plant was regarded as vital for the production of goods essential to the reducing of China's dependence upon external aid, and for an effective approach to the problem of inflation.

The essence of the problem facing ECA, then, was an extensive need for replacement and reconstruction equipment and a lack of the foreign assistance in engineering and management requisite to the effective absorption of such equipment into the Chinese economy. A solution to this problem required a unique approach. Engineering and management assistance would have to be furnished along with the equipment. The ECA, in approaching this problem, needed also to bear in mind objectives implicit in the legislative history of the ECA : to maximize the use of private trade channels, to encourage both internal production and international trade and to avoid impairment of the US economy.

Insufficiency of technical knowledge and experience in management had been a recurrent problem encountered in efforts to help Chinese industry. This made necessary a provision of technical and managerial help along with material assistance. The Survey Group developed a unique plan of action for the meeting of this need. It recommended that each industrial project applying for, and receiving a tentative allotment for, ECA assistance be required to engage the services of a private engineering firm to help in surveying and planning the work needing to be done and in the procurement and installation of requisite equipment. The Survey Group further recommended that the Chinese Government and ECA jointly engage a high-grade American engineering management firm to assist in supervising the entire scheme, in order to ensure that this part of the China Aid Programme would, as a whole, be conducted with the benefit of outstanding engineering talent and experience. These recommendations contemplated ECA payment for such engineering services under the 'technical assistance' provision in Section III (a) (3) of the Foreign Assistance Act of 1948. These recommendations, in which the Chinese Government concurred, were approved by the Administrator as a tentative basis on which further development of the programme might proceed.

In anticipating the types of firms best equipped to undertake, on behalf of provisionally approved projects, the requisite work of pre-project engineering analysis and subsequent assistance in procurement and installation, consideration was given both to engineering firms without previous experience in China and to concerns which had been active in developing production and trade in China. Some of the latter, with worldwide connexions, extensive local experience and competent resident managers and staffs of engineers, both Chinese and foreign, could, it was believed, make valuable contributions, under appropriate safeguards, to the success of the programme.

Practical Arrangements Developed

After consideration of all aspects of this complicated programme, the Chinese Government and the ECA Mission to China agreed to form a non-voting consultative Joint Committee composed of three representatives of the Chinese Government and two representatives of the ECA Mission to supervise the carrying out of the replacement and reconstruction projects. This arrangement was in accord with the principles of the Economic Aid Agreement between China and the United States which specifies that programmes are to be carried out by mutual agreement.

It was decided to engage the services of an outstanding American management engineering firm to assist the Joint Committee. This was a distinct change from methods hitherto employed for previous aid programmes by either government or by the United Nations for the UNRRA programme. Previous practice had involved efforts to co-ordinate the work of Chinese and non-Chinese staffs, without use in most cases of special engineering consultants or of normal business and trade channels for functions which might be performed efficiently and economically by private enterprise. The Joint Committee, representing both governments, decided to retain in a technical capacity the J. G. White Engineering Corporation of New York City. The principal function of this corporation, it was agreed, would be to furnish technical supervision, with a group of from six to ten US engineers, of the projects approved under the tentatively authorized $70 million ECA replacement and reconstruction programme in China. The staff was not itself to undertake any 'projects', but to assist the Joint Committee in selecting, recommending for approval, and supervising a wide range of industrial projects.

The procedure adopted may be outlined briefly as follows :

Private or public enterprises desiring assistance under the programme would present initial applications to the Joint Committee which would refer them to the J. G. White Corporation for analysis and recommendation ; projects provisionally approved by the Joint Committee were to be given 'provisional allotments'.

As soon as a 'provisional allotment' was made, the successful applicant was to select an engineering firm as its 'project engineer', this selection requiring ratification by the Joint Committee set up by the Chinese Government and the ECA China Mission.

The project engineer would draw up a bill of materials with detailed specifications, search world markets for necessary equipment and supplies which could be procured on the most expeditious and economical terms, and present a fully justified 'project' to the Joint Committee.

Upon approval of the project by the Joint Committee, the project engineer would arrange for the procurement and delivery of approved equipment and material, and assist the applicant in achieving prompt installation and use.

Financing was to be done by ECA by a letter of commitment to a US bank, in effect guaranteeing letters of credit (a) to suppliers of equipment or materials under approved projects, and (b) to the project engineer for his approved fee.

At each stage of this procedure, the J. G. White Engineering Corporation was to act as technical staff to the Joint Committee, the Committee taking action only after receiving the recommendations of its technical staff on such matters as : approval of the selection of project engineering firms, approval of fees and charges by these firms, approval of the detailed specifications and sources of procurement of equipment for the projects, and approval of prices of materials to be procured. Before any programme was approved, the applicant and the project engineer would be required to submit to the Joint Committee a sworn affidavit containing information with respect to their profit margins and their methods of seeking materials, including competitive bidding. Arrangements could be made for the technical staff of the Joint Committee to accept sealed bids on items where relationships between the project engineer and the supplier indicated that such protection would be desirable.

These procedures taken together represented a new pattern for publicly financed industrial projects in under-developed areas. As such, they provided a unique approach towards the solution of a large continuing problem, that of grafting branches of modern technology into the great trunks of agrarian economy in Asia and other under-developed parts of the world. An uninterrupted testing of this approach was unfortunately precluded by events in China.

Rural Reconstruction Programme

During the deliberations of the House Foreign Affairs Committee in February and March of 1948 on prospective aid to China, consideration was given to the fundamental and extensive needs of the Chinese economy in the field of rural reconstruction. Some new light had been thrown on this problem by a special agricultural mission sent to China by the President in 1946. Valuable experience in dealing with certain aspects of the problem had been gained through the Chinese Mass Education Movement headed by Dr James Y. C. Yen. Information from these and other sources was weighed by the Committee with the result that rural reconstruction was included in subsequent China aid legislation as a specific field in which programme funds might be spent.

Section 407 of the China Aid Act

Authorization for inclusion of a special rural reconstruction programme was provided in Section 407 of the China Aid Act of 1948— the full text of which appears in the Appendix. This section authorized the Secretary of State, after consultation with the Administrator, 'to conclude an agreement with China establishing a Joint Commission on Rural Reconstruction in China, to be composed of two citizens of the United States appointed by the President of the United States and three citizens of China appointed by the President of China'. Such Commission, it was provided, subject to the direction and control of the Administrator, was to formulate and carry out a programme for reconstruction in rural areas of China, including such research and training activities as might be necessary or appropriate for such reconstruction.

The Act authorized an expenditure, for this rural reconstruction programme, of an amount equal to not more than 10 per cent of the funds made available for economic aid to China under the China

Aid Act. This placed an upper limit of $27·5 million upon the funds which could be used for the rural reconstruction programme. It was stipulated that the amount could be made available in US dollars, proceeds in Chinese currency from the sale of ECA commodities, or both.

Establishment of Rural Reconstruction Commission

Following a period of negotiation, notes were exchanged on 5 August 1948 between the United States Ambassador to China and the Chinese Government Ministry of Foreign Affairs, providing an agreement for the establishment of a Rural Reconstruction Commission in accordance with the terms of the China Aid Act of 1948. The text of these notes is quoted in the section on Documents, below.

Following the conclusion of this agreement, appointments were made by the Chinese and the United States Governments to the Rural Reconstruction Commission, the Chinese members being Dr Chiang Monlin (former President of the Peking National University, former Minister of Education, and recently Executive Secretary of the Chinese Government Executive Yuan), Chairman ; Dr James Y. C. Yen (for 25 years the leader of China's internationally known Mass Education Movement) ; and Dr T. H. Shen (outstanding Chinese agriculturist). The United States members appointed by the President on 19 September 1948, were Dr John Earl Baker (former Director of the China International Famine Relief Commission and former adviser to the Chinese Government), and Dr Raymond T. Moyer (US Department of Agriculture authority on Chinese agriculture). On 1 October, the Commission held its first meeting.

Objectives and Principles

The problem of rural reconstruction in China is one of enormous magnitude and complexity. Intensive and lengthy discussion was required to reach general agreement among members of the Commission with respect to questions of aim, emphasis, organization and methods of work. On 18 October 1948 agreement was reached on a general statement of the objectives and principles of the Joint Commission on Rural Reconstruction. The text of this statement follows :

'I.   *Objectives*
(a)   To improve the living conditions of the rural people.
(b)   To increase the production of food and other important crops.
(c)   To develop the potential power of the people to reconstruct their own communities and the nation, thus to lay the foundation of a strong and democratic China.

(d) To help build up and strengthen appropriate services of government agencies—national, provincial and *hsien*—that are established to carry out measures pertaining to rural reconstruction.

(e) To help stimulate and revitalize enterprises of the Rural Reconstruction Movement and other private agencies doing rural reconstruction work.

(f) To offer liberals, educated youths and other constructive elements, opportunities to participate in a programme of service.

'II. *Principles*

(1) Relating to Programme

(a) The emergency nature of the present situation shall be given paramount consideration in deciding on the nature and location of programme and projects.

(b) First consideration shall be given to projects which will contribute most directly and immediately to the welfare of the rural people, with special emphasis to be given to the improvement of their economic conditions.

(c) A literacy programme, supplemented by audiovisual aids, shall be an essential part of this programme, as a means of furthering education, organizing the people, and developing and selecting rural leadership.

(d) New projects in rural reconstruction deserve encouragement, but unless they can show evidence of self-help and self-support for a reasonable length of time, financial aid shall not be considered.

(e) Projects which already have been proved successful, under rural conditions, and which are reasonably simple and inexpensive, shall be broadcast on a large scale.

(f) In general, preference shall be given to those agencies engaged in rural reconstruction having a sound foundation and experienced staff and organization.

(2) Relating to Procedure

(a) The programme formulated by the Commission shall be carried out in co-operation with existing agencies.

(b) A correlated approach shall be adopted wherever possible, since the various aspects of rural reconstruction are interrelated, the success of one depending on the success of the other.

(c) A direct extension-type of adult education shall be emphasized as the most effective and quickest means of promoting the understanding, acceptance and correct use of recommended practices.

(d) Local initiative shall be fostered and local resources, both human and material, shall be mobilized for the purposes of the programme.

(e)   Assistance to a project in any province shall be contingent upon the willingness of the provincial and local officials concerned to co-operate fully in efforts to carry it out, and to take other steps, themselves, that are essential to the attainment of results expected of the project.'

On 26 October 1948, 'A Memorandum of Understanding Between the Economic Co-operation Administration and the Joint Commission on Rural Reconstruction in China, Defining Their Respective Spheres of Administrative Responsibility' was signed by the Chairman of the Joint Rural Reconstruction Commission and the Acting Chief of the ECA Mission to China. This agreement established procedures for the presentation of budget estimates by the Joint Commission and the allocation of US dollar funds for material and technical assistance and of local currency from the counterpart funds for expenses incurred within China. And arrangements were agreed upon for the recruitment, administrative supervision and direction of Commission personnel.

Based on the objectives and principles quoted above, the Commission worked out the main outlines of a programme, which was divided into four parts with the following aims:

To increase in supplying areas the domestic production of agricultural commodities currently in serious short supply in China and supplied in part by the United States ECA programme, particularly foodstuffs;

To establish centres in which a broad integrated programme would be started under appropriate agencies of the Government, through projects related to local government administration, land reform, agriculture, rural public health and rural social education;

To carry out a large-scale effort in adult education as a means of developing the potential power of the people and raising their level of understanding, thus enabling them to participate more intelligently in solving their present problems; and

To assist significant projects in rural reconstruction established in numerous centres through local initiative and resources.

When Nanking became threatened by military action, it was decided to move the Commission's operational headquarters to Canton. At the same time, a decision was made to focus major attention first on the development of a programme in provinces south of the Yangtze River, and to concentrate upon projects susceptible of prompt development and usefulness, in such fields as irrigation, dyke repair, public health, and the control of serious animal diseases.

Surveys and Organization

To put this initial programme promptly into effect a trip was taken by members of the Commission to Szechwan and Hunan provinces to inspect existing efforts on behalf of the rural population and to consult with responsible persons concerning projects for which assistance had been requested. Steps also were taken to set up regional offices in Chungking (Szechwan), Changsha (Hunan), and Kwellin (Kwangsi), and a central office in Canton (Kwangtung), while retaining a regional office in Nanking. Tentative plans to carry out some phases of a rural programme from two offices in north China had to be suspended on account of troubled civil war conditions there. Headquarters of the Commission were moved to Canton on 5 December 1948.

To assist the Commission in carrying out its plans, competent persons were selected as heads for three of the four divisions of work, and, at the end of the year, able appointees were under consideration for the fourth division and to represent the Commission in three of the most important regional offices. A staff of Chinese and American specialists was being assembled to advise the Commission and help carry out its programme, although uncertainties in the general situation caused the Commission to proceed gradually in building up such a staff.

The impression gained by the Commission in visits to provinces in west and south China was that these provinces were at the time relatively free from acute tension then felt in the lower Yangtze area, and that local officials and private agencies were anxious to proceed with rural reconstruction measures along the general lines formulated by the Joint Commission. Steps were taken, therefore, to get into operation, in an initial programme, specific projects to which the Commission was prepared to allocate assistance.

Initial Projects

Projects for which detailed plans were being developed included the following :

A broad integrated programme in rural reconstruction in the third prefecture of Szechwan province, initiated by the Mass Education Movement and local leaders, assistance to include grants for the development of educational, agricultural and farm organization projects, and loans for irrigation and weaving projects.

The completion of 11 irrigation projects already under way in Szechwan province, which would provide for the irrigation of 191,000 mow (about 30,000 acres) of land by the end of April 1949.

The establishment of a system to multiply and distribute improved rice, corn and cotton varieties in Szechwan province.

The repair of dykes in the Tung T'ing Lake area of Hunan province, which would restore to production and protect from flooding land normally producing around two-thirds of the amount of rice annually imported into China before the war, to be completed by the end of April 1949.

An integrated programme of rural reconstruction in Hunan, for which definite plans were yet to be received and agreed upon.

The establishment in Hunan province, the 'rice bowl' of central China, of the beginnings of an improved system of rice production and marketing, including the multiplication and distribution of improved seed varieties and the establishment of more modern milling and warehousing centres.

Projects involving co-operation with various Ministries of the National Government were being considered in consultation with these Ministries after specific project plans were reasonably well developed. Steps were being taken to set up appropriate committees of specialists to advise the Commission and to assist in carrying out phases of the rural reconstruction programme; the first committee established was for work in the field of public health in rural areas, with a former Minister of Health as Chairman. In accordance with a request of the Rural Reconstruction Commission, a private public relations firm completed in November a special study of the facilities available for a widespread educational effort under the Commission's sponsorship.

Detailed plans for the irrigation projects in Szechwan, for the dyke repair project in Hunan, for certain parts of the programme sponsored by the Mass Education Movement in Szechwan, and for several other projects, were being reviewed in December with a view to early allocations of funds. The Commission also expected to make early announcement of projects to which it would initially allocate assistance in Kwangtung province, and trips were planned to Kwangsi, Fukien and Taiwan to study projects for which aid had been requested.

Specific plans for broader programmes with a major emphasis on education, it was anticipated, might not be completed before the end of February 1949. Tentative planning, conditional upon developments, called for an extension of some assistance to such integrated programmes during the spring of 1949. It was expected, however, under prevailing conditions, that available funds under the current programme would necessarily be allocated principally to projects of a short-range nature, emphasizing increases in agricultural production and improvements in rural health conditions.

Strategic Materials

Article VI, paragraph 1, of the Economic Co-operation Agreement between the United States and the Republic of China (the full text of which is quoted in the section on Documents, below) provided that the Chinese Government would facilitate the transfer to the United States, for stockpiling or other purposes, 'materials originating in China which are required by the United States of America as a result of deficiencies or potential deficiencies in its own resources upon such reasonable terms of sale, exchange, barter or otherwise and in such quantities and for such period of time as may be agreed to between the Governments of the United States of America and of China for domestic use and commercial export of such materials'. The Government of China agreed to undertake 'such specific measures as may be necessary to carry out the provisions of this paragraph' and 'when so requested by the Government of the United States of America, to enter into negotiations for detailed arrangements necessary to carry out the provisions of this paragraph'.

Article V, paragraph 4, of the same agreement, provided that expenditures in Chinese currency from the Special Account (described below) would be 'only for such purposes as may be agreed from time to time with the United States of America, including expenditures incident to the stimulation of production activity and the development of new sources of wealth including materials which may be required in the United States of America because of deficiencies or potential deficiencies in the resources of the United States of America'.

A preliminary investigation was conducted by members of the Reconstruction Survey Group, with a view to promoting increased production and export to the United States of strategic materials available in China and required by the United States, particular attention being given to tin, antimony and tungsten in south and south-west China. Such procurement, it was felt—to the extent that it could be developed—would, in addition to increasing the supplies of minerals needed by the United States, serve the double purpose in China of increasing local employment and augmenting the country's slender foreign exchange resources.

Production and Procurement Problems

It was found that foreign exchange policies and controls connected therewith since VJ Day, related to the Government's attempts to deal with the inflation, had exerted a depressing influence upon the production and export of these minerals, making it impossible for exporters, by and large, to obtain by negotiations through official channels fair and realistic prices for their goods. Only on rare occasions, when official exchange rates were for short periods realistic, were such exporters able to secure reasonable returns upon their produce. Initial negotiations looking towards the acquisition of these materials were aimed in part at securing the agreement of the Chinese Government to changes of policy designed to remove some of the obstacles to the flow of materials through legitimate channels of trade to the US, at prices fair to the producers.

Additional difficulties in procurement and export of such materials to the United States were attributable to shortage of productive equipment in China and to lack of transportation facilities from relatively inaccessible parts of China where such materials existed. Efforts towards helping to meet both these needs were clearly needed if production and procurement were to be developed on any appreciable scale.

Initial Arrangements

Following the aforementioned survey, the ECA China Mission before the end of 1948 began to work out arrangements with Chinese tin interests to make their product available for export to the United States. After receipt of pertinent information from ECA, the Reconstruction Finance Corporation in Washington offered to purchase from China considerable quantities of tin concentrates, to be refined in the US where efficient smelter operation could extract a maximum percentage of high-grade tin ; and to buy some tin metal in China for stockpile purposes. Preliminary negotiations were in progress at the end of the year to effect procurement arrangements, which were complicated by the necessity of effecting purchases through barter by the use of commodities or silver, instead of depreciated local currency.

Special Local Currency Account

Provision for the establishment of a special local currency account, or counterpart fund, was contained in Article V of the Economic Co-operation Agreement between the Governments of China and the United States.

Unique Provisions in the Bilateral Agreement

The article referred to provided for two unique features in connection with the special local currency account, or counterpart fund, in China. The first was a provision that deposits would be made in the account only when requested by the United States ; thus deposits could be requested at a rate sufficient to cover actual expenses that had to be met currently, without the accumulation of large balances which would rapidly depreciate in value as a result of the inflation. The second was a provision that the Chinese Government would 'maintain the value' of allotments made from the Special Account—for such important purposes as administrative costs, rural reconstruction and the internal expenses of industrial projects—by 'depositing such additional amounts of currency as the Government of the United States of America may from time to time determine after consultation with the Government of China'. The value of allotments to be thus maintained could be recorded in terms of such standard and relatively stable measures of value as quantities of cotton yarn, rice or American dollars.

Support for China Relief Mission Projects

Shortly after the establishment of the ECA Mission in China, discussions were initiated with the Chinese Government pertaining to the setting up and operation of the special local currency account. While these discussions were in progress, provisional arrangements were made for the use of counterpart funds made available by the Chinese Government in support of existing projects in the fields of medical services, relief and welfare, conservancy work, and agricultural improvement which had been previously supported from a local currency account created in connexion with the operation of the US China Relief Mission. These projects, which had theretofore been regarded as ending on 30 June 1948, were in some cases selected by action of the Chinese Government in consultation with the ECA for continuation after that date.

Preliminary Studies and Proposals

After careful study of special questions involved in setting up the special local currency account in China, and in the light of discussions with the Government, the ECA China Mission prepared in September 1948 a tentative proposed programme of local currency utilization which outlined in some detail projected uses for the counterpart funds in the fields of conservancy, public works, agriculture, medical and health activities and welfare.

Concurrently, analysis was undertaken of the financial and economic problems in China which needed to be considered in determining the manner in which the counterpart funds would be utilized. These problems included : the extensive deficit spending of the Government, concomitant with the continued prosecution of the civil war ; the inflationary effect of the enforcement of the Government's short-lived 19 August economic regulations ; the continuation of certain inflationary practices of the Government ; the progressive deterioration in economic production ; the disruption of transportation in disturbed areas ; and the loss of public confidence in the currency resulting in widespread hoarding of supplies and excessively rapid turnover of the currency.

Technical problems requiring study included determination of the exchange rates governing payments of local currency counterpart funds into the Special Account ; the timing of deposits ; and policies to be followed with regard to the disposition of Special Account funds.

Studies and proposals received from the Mission, in relation to these problems, were further analysed in Washington prior to consultations with the National Advisory Council.

Establishment of the Special Account

Following these consultations, authorization was given to the ECA China Mission to negotiate with the Chinese Government on questions relating to the establishment of the Special Account, deposits into such account, and purposes for which funds from the account might be utilized.

The Special Account was established in the Central Bank of China. It was agreed that, in order to avoid depreciation of cash balances in the account as a result of the inflation, deposits would be made only as called for by the ECA China Mission, in most cases a short time before withdrawal and expenditure.

Utilization of Counterpart Funds

It was further agreed that withdrawals could be made to cover all mandatory expenditures from the account, as called for in the Bilateral Agreement, including the Chinese currency portion of the following expenses : administrative costs of the ECA China Mission ; costs of delivering private relief gift packages in China ; and costs of the Joint Commission on Rural Reconstruction. It was estimated that expenditures of these types would amount to roughly 12 per cent of the total account.

From the outset, it was clear that 'sterilization' of local currency Special Account funds could not of itself be the key to controlling the Chinese inflation. The basic cause of the inflation was the magnitude of the Government's deficit financing, which in turn was due to the exigencies of the civil war and shaken public confidence in the currency, which led to excessively rapid rates of circulation of the note issue.

On the other hand, it was apparent that an easy money policy in the use of the Special Account would be inflationary, the effect of such a policy being similar to that of greatly increasing the Government's monthly budget deficit through excessive note issue.

The ECA China Mission, in the light of discussions of this problem with the National Advisory Council in Washington followed, therefore, a policy of agreeing only to expenditures from the account which could be regarded as of demonstrated urgency and which in many cases would have offsetting deflationary benefits. Broad categories of non-mandatory expenditures on which the ECA China Mission could agree with the Chinese Government as being appropriate uses for the Special Account included : emergency expenditures which, at the discretion of the Chief of the ECA China Mission, could be considered as consistent with the objectives of the China Aid Act—expenditures envisaged in this category being for such purposes as emergency procurement of indigenous food for the rationing programmes ; expenditures on certain carefully screened projects, chiefly in the fields of conservancy, health and welfare ; and expenditures, when necessary, to ensure prompt installation and proper utilization of capital equipment under the replacement and reconstruction programme. The total of these expenditures, it was expected, should amount to less than half of the potential local currency account.

Exchange Rates

A persistent problem with respect to the Special Account has been that of agreeing with the Chinese Government upon appropriate rates at which deposits would be made in terms of US currency—that is, rates reflecting commensurate value in Chinese currency, at given times, for US dollar aid provided. A rapid decline in the value of the new gold yuan and reluctance of the Chinese Government to negotiate formally on a basis other than official exchange rates led, pending a settlement of this question, to deposits being made as advances, without final agreement before the end of 1948 on commensurate value in terms of US dollars.

Deposits and Withdrawals

As of 31 December 1948, deposits into the Special Account totalled, in round numbers, 157,289,000 gold yuan, equivalent (on the basis of rough tentative estimates prior to agreement on applicable exchange rates) to US $9,543,000. Withdrawals on the same date totalled, in round numbers, 150,333,000 gold yuan, equivalent, according to similarly tentative estimates, to US $5,839,000—the equivalent of approximately $1,342,000 being for ECA administrative expenses in China, $2,498,000 for administrative expenses of the Chinese Council for United States Aid, $1,803,000 for special projects, $53,000 for engineering services, and $143,000 for expenses incurred by the Joint Commission on Rural Reconstruction.

Before the end of 1948, the local counterpart funds thus jointly managed by ECA and the Chinese Government had enabled many worthy institutions and projects to continue operations in spite of inflation and civil war.

United States Relations with China, pp. 1006-42.

54   21 *March* 1949

SUMMARY OF UNITED STATES GOVERNMENT'S ECONOMIC, FINANCIAL AND MILITARY AID AUTHORIZED FOR CHINA SINCE 1937

Since the commencement of hostilities between China and Japan in 1937 the United States Government has authorized aid to China in the form of grants and credits totalling approximately $3,523 million, of which $2,422 million has been in the form of grants and $1,101 million as credits. About 40 per cent of the total, or $1,515·7 million, was authorized prior to VJ Day to contribute towards the stabilization of China's war-time economy and to enable the Chinese Government to obtain military, agricultural and industrial goods essential to the conduct of the war with Japan.

United States Government grants and credits to China authorized since VJ Day have amounted to approximately $2,007·7 million, representing sixty per cent of the total, of which $1,596·7 million has been as grants and $411 million on credit terms. This aid was designed to assist the Chinese Government in the reoccupation of liberated areas and the repatriation of Japanese, to meet some of China's urgent relief and rehabilitation needs, and, in the case of the present ECA programme, to help retard the rate of economic deterioration in China and to encourage the adoption of effective self-help measures on the part of the Chinese Government. The Chinese Government has elected to use $125 million authorized by the China Aid Act of 1948 (included in the total of grants above) to purchase items of a military nature.

The totals of United States aid given above do not include sales to the Chinese Government of United States Government military and civilian-type surplus property which have been made since VJ Day, except where these sales were made on credit terms. In such cases, the amount of the credit involved has been included in the total of United States credits authorized. Surplus property with a total estimated procurement cost of over $1,078·1 million has been sold to China for an agreed realization to the United States of $232 million, of which $95·5 million is to be repaid on credit terms. There are no available estimates of the fair value of this surplus property at the time of its sale. Neither do the aid totals include certain ammunition transferred by the United States Marines in connexion with their withdrawal from north China.

United States aid to China reviewed herein does not reflect assistance through provision of advisory personnel in cultural, economic and military fields ; nor does it include United States contributions through certain United Nations' programmes in China—the International Children's Emergency Fund, the International Refugee Organization, the World Health Organization, and advisory social welfare services.

The various measures of United States Government aid authorized for China since 1937, together with the miscellaneous sales to China of United States Government surplus property, are summarized in the table on the next page and described briefly in the text that follows.

DESCRIPTION OF INDIVIDUAL CATEGORIES OF US AID

(Paragraph numbers correspond with numbers of items listed in table on next page).

(1) *Pre-VJ Day Export-Import Bank Credits :* Export-Import Bank credits extended prior to VJ Day were general commodity credits, used to purchase a considerable variety of American industrial and agricultural products and services. Repayment was arranged by contracts between United States and Chinese Government agencies for the sale of strategic minerals or wood oil. Of the $120 million total authorized, $117 million was disbursed and the balance, approximately $3 million, expired. Of the amount disbursed, $112·8 million had been repaid as of 31 December 1948. Credit authorizations were as follows :

				Million
Universal Trading Corporation	..	..	12/13/38	$25·0
Universal Trading Corporation	..	..	3/7/40	20·0
Central Bank of China	..	..	..	10/17/40	25·0
Central Bank of China	..	..	..	11/30/40	50·0
Total	..			$120·0

(2) On 1 April 1941, the Secretary of the Treasury entered into an agreement with the Government of China and the Central Bank of China to purchase Chinese Yuan up to an amount equivalent to US $50 million to further the monetary and financial co-operation of the two governments and the stabilization of the United States

UNITED STATES GOVERNMENT ECONOMIC, FINANCIAL AND MILITARY AID TO CHINA SINCE 1937

(In millions of US dollars)

	Grants	Credits	Sales of US Government Excess and Surplus Property		
			Procurement value	Realization by US	
				Initial	Ultimate (Sum of Credits & Initial Realization)
PRE-VJ DAY					
ECONOMIC					
1 Export-Import Bank Credits Authorized	….	120	….	….	….
2 Stabilization fund agreement, 1941	….	50	….	….	….
3 1942 Treasury Credit (PL 442)	….	500	….	….	….
Total economic aid	….	670	….	….	….
MILITARY					
4 Lend-lease	825·7	….	….	….	….
Total military aid	825·7	20	….	….	….
Total pre-VJ day aid	825·7	690	….	….	….
POST-VJ DAY					
ECONOMIC					
5 Lend-lease 'pipeline' credit	….	51·7	….	….	….
6 UNRRA–US Contribution	474·0	….	….	….	….
7 BOTRA–US Contribution	3·6	….	….	….	….
8 Export-Import Bank Credits Authorized	….	82·8	….	….	….
9 Civilian Surplus Property Transfers (Under 30 August 1946, bulk sale agreement)	….	55	900	120	175
10 OFLC dockyard facilities sales	….	4·1	n.a.	….	4·1
11 Maritime Commission ship sales	….	16·4	77·3	9·8	26·2
12 US Foreign Relief Programme	46·4	….	….	….	….
13 ECA Programme	275	….	….	….	….
Total economic aid	799·0	210·0	977·3	129·8	205·3

UNITED STATES GOVERNMENT ECONOMIC, FINANCIAL AND MILITARY AID TO CHINA SINCE 1937—
Continued.

(In millions of US dollars)

| | Grants | Credits | Sales of US Government Excess and Surplus Property | | |
| | | | Procurement value | Realization by US | |
				Initial	Ultimate
POST-VJ DAY—*Continued*					
MILITARY					
14 Lend-lease	513·7	181·0			
15 Military Aid under SACO	17·7	20			
16 Sale of excess stocks of US Army in West China			n.a.		(a) 20·0
17 Ammunition Abandoned and Transferred by US Marines in North China (over 6,500 tons)	(b)				
18 Transfer of US Navy Vessels (PL 512)	(c) 141·3				
19 Sales of surplus military equipment (total accepted by Chinese Government)			100·8	6·7	6·7
20 Grant Under China Aid Act of 1948	125				
Total military aid	797·7	201·0	100·8	6·7	26·7
Total post-VJ day aid	1,596·7	411·0	1,078·1	136·5	232·0
GRAND TOTAL	2,422·4	1,101·0	1,078·1	136·5	232·0

(a) Down payment covered under item 9. See textual explanation.
(b) No estimate of total value available.
(c) Vessels valued at procurement cost.

303

dollar—Chinese Yuan rate of exchange. This agreement did not provide for collateralization of such purchases, as did a previous stabilization agreement of 1937 which therefore cannot be considered as representing aid to the Chinese Government in the strict sense of the term. It was further agreed in connexion with the 1941 agreement that a Stabilization Board be established, to which the Chinese Government banks were to contribute $20 million. Purchases of Chinese Yuan under this agreement amounted to US $10 million and were repaid in April 1943.

(3) *1942 Treasury Credit* (PL 442): On 7 February 1942, Congress passed Public Law 442, authorizing the Secretary of the Treasury, with the approval of the President, to make available to China funds not to exceed $500 million and promptly made appropriations for this purpose. An agreement of 21 March 1942 between the United States and China established this amount as a credit in the name of the Chinese Government. Between the date of the agreement and VJ Day, the Chinese Government drew on this credit to the extent of $485 million, the balance having been drawn since VJ Day.

At the time of this congressional action, strategic bases of the United Nations were being lost to the Japanese offensive in the Pacific and southeast Asia, and effective land lines of communication with China were being severed. It was of vital importance to the United States Government that China, which had resisted Japanese aggression for 5 years, should be strengthened and encouraged to continue the war against Japan. Since opportunities for giving effective material aid to China, such as was being rendered to allies in more accessible areas through lend-lease, were not great, the $500 million credit was characterized by the Secretary of the Treasury and in House Report No. 1739 as 'the financial counterpart of lendleasing war materials'.

Funds provided under the agreement of 21 March 1942 were used mainly by the Chinese Government to purchase gold for sale in China as an anti-inflationary measure and to provide reserves for the redemption of Chinese Government savings and victory bonds denominated in United States dollars. A total of $220 million was withdrawn in gold, much of which was shipped to China, largely during 1945, to be sold internally in an effort to control inflation by reducing currency in circulation and keeping down the price of gold.

A total of $200 million was reserved out of the 1942 credit for the redemption of Chinese Government United States dollar security issues. A reserve of $100 million was established for payment of Chinese United States dollar savings certificates, and another $100 million was earmarked for the payment of Chinese United States dollar victory bonds. In 1946, this earmarking was abandoned, and the funds became available for imports and other foreign payments as measures were promulgated governing payment of foreign currency bonds held in China which provided that such bonds would be redeemed in Chinese currency. It was also provided, however, that registered bondholders outside China would be paid in foreign currency.

Of the balance of $80 million of the credit, $55 million was spent for purchase of bank notes in the United States, and $25 million was used to import textiles into China.

Final settlement of the terms of this credit has not yet been negotiated.

(4) *Pre-VJ Day Lend-Lease :* China was declared eligible for lend-lease aid on 6 May 1941. During that first year until the blocking of the Burma Road in April 1942, lend-lease aid was aimed especially at improving transport over the Burma Road, which, due to the Japanese blockade, was the only land route into China. Although amounts carried by this route were greatly increased, they were still small. Delivery by air cargo plane from Assam in India over the 18,000 foot hump of the Himalayas, begun in April 1942, was the only means of lend-lease supply until the completion in January 1945 of the Ledo Road from India across Burma. Lend-lease materials supplied prior to VJ Day were primarily military in character, but included considerable quantities of industrial and transportation equipment essential to the Chinese war effort. All but approximately $200 million of the $845·7 million in lend-lease aid extended prior to VJ Day is considered to have been on a grant basis. Terms of settlement of the $20 million balances are subject to negotiation.

The following table presents a break-down by major categories of Pre-VJ Day lend-lease aid :

Ordnance and Ordnance Stores	$153,333,189·94
Aircraft and Aeronautical Material ..	187,339,849·94
Tanks and Other Vehicles	94,177,927·72
Vessels and Other Watercraft	35,561,264·12
Miscellaneous Military Equipment.. ..	47,085,115·94
Facilities and Equipment	9,928,803·33
Agricultural, Industrial and Other Commodities	46,505,983·26
Testing and Reconditioning of Defence Articles	204,393·63
Services and Expenses	271,611,693·00
Total ..	$845,748,220·88

These figures are compiled from reports received by the Treasury Department from United States Government agencies as of 30 June 1948.

(5) *Lend-Lease 'Pipeline' Credit:* An agreement between the United States and China dated 14 June 1946 authorized the delivery on 3(c) credit terms of civilian-type equipment and supplies contracted for but undelivered on VJ Day under the war-time lend-lease programme. It was subsequently determined that a total of $51·7 million in equipment and supplies could be furnished under contracts covered by this agreement. The Chinese Government had been billed for 'pipeline' shipments totalling $50·3 million in value as of 30 November 1948.

(6) *UNRRA:* The UNRRA programme for China was estimated on 31 December 1947 to involve the procurement of goods valued at approximately $517·5 million, allocated as follows:

		(Millions)
Food	.. ..	133·2
Clothing	.. ..	113·4
Medical Supplies	.. ..	31·7
Agricultural Rehabilitation	.. .. ..	72·5
Industrial Rehabilitation	.. ..	166·7
	Total ..	517·5

The estimate of the total value of the goods procured under the UNRRA programme has since been revised upward to $526·8 million. This figure does not include shipping and insurance costs, which, in the case of China, are roughly estimated to have added an average of about 25 per cent. This brings the total estimated cost of the UNRRA China programme to $658·4 million. Since the United States contribution to all UNRRA funds was approximately 72 per cent, it may be said that the United States contribution to the China programme amounted to 72 per cent of $658·4 million, or $474·0 million.

(7) *BOTRA:* $5 million of UNRRA funds were allocated to the Board of Trustees for Rehabilitation Affairs (BOTRA), an international body established by the Chinese Government to control the use of UNRRA supplies and funds remaining after the conclusion of its China programme. Since the United States contribution to the entire UNRRA programme was approximately 72 per cent, it may be estimated that the United States contribution to the BOTRA fund was $3·6 million.

(8) *Post-VJ Day Export-Import Bank Credits :*

(*a*) Credits Authorized for China : Export-Import Bank credits have been authorized for China since VJ Day for specific rehabilitation purposes. Individual credits are as follows :

Borrower	To Finance	Date	Amount (Millions)
Yungli Chemical Industry	Machinery, equipment and services ..	21-3-45	$16·0
Central Bank of China.	Cotton	1-3-46	33·0
Republic of China ..	Cargo Vessels ..	20-2-46	4·2
Republic of China ..	,, ,, ..	..	....
Republic of China ..	Equipment, materials and engineering services	20-2-46 20-2-46	2·6 8·8
Republic of China ..	Railway Repair Materials	20-2-46	16·7
Republic of China ..	Coal mining equipment materials and supplies	13-3-46	1·5
Total ..			$82·8

Of the $82·8 million credit authorized since VJ Day, $65·4 million had been disbursed as of 31 December 1948. Thus a balance of $17·4 million remains undisbursed, including the $16 million credit to Yungli Chemical Industries, Ltd. Owing to the delay in concluding the detailed arrangements for disbursing the Yungli credit it was necessary for the Export-Import Bank to postpone the expiry date until 31 December 1950.

Of the total amount disbursed since VJ Day, 12·2 million had been repaid as of 31 December 1948, leaving 53·2 million outstanding.

(*b*) The $500 Million Earmark for China : In recognition of the magnitude of China's requirements for reconstruction and the possibilities for economic development under orderly conditions, the United States Government gave consideration after VJ Day to making available substantial funds for this purpose. In April 1946, following the recommendation of General Marshall and approval by the National Advisory Council, the Export-Import Bank authorized the earmarking until 30 June 1947 of $500 million of the Bank's funds for the possible extension of individual credits to the Chinese Government and private Chinese interests. It was contemplated that such credits would be confined to particular projects and would be subject to the usual criteria governing the Bank's lending operations. No implementing agreements were consummated between the Bank and the representatives of the Chinese Government.

During 1946 and the first half of 1947, the Chinese Government discussed numerous proposals for credits with the Export-Import Bank, for some of which General Marshall and the Department of State recommended favourable consideration. Most of the proposals were not adequately supported by economic and financial data and analysis, and many of them were overlapping and without any indication of priority. The principal reason, however, for the Bank's refusal to take favourable action on Chinese credit proposals was its inability to find reasonable assurances of repayment.

In accordance with the terms of its authorization, the earmarking of $500 million for China lapsed on 30 June 1947. However, on 27 June 1947 the Export-Import Bank announced that, the expiration of the earmarked funds notwithstanding, it was prepared to consider Chinese credit applications in accordance with its general policies. While the Chinese Government has subsequently applied for substantial credits, none have been extended by the Bank, primarily, again, because of inability to find reasonable assurances of repayment.

(9) *Civilian-type Surplus Property Sales (Under 30 August 1946 Bulk Sale Agreement)* : The sale to China of United States surplus fixed installations and movable property located in India and China and on seventeen Pacific islands was authorized or recognized under an agreement between the two governments dated 30 August 1946. The property sold under this agreement included every type of supply used by an expeditionary force except combat material, vessels, and aircraft, all of which were specifically excluded from the contract. The total procurement cost of the property involved, initially computed at approximately $824 million, is now estimated at $900 million. Vehicles of all types accounts for about one-third of the total, construction equipment about one-sixth, and air force supplies and equipment about one-eighth. The remainder was composed principally of communication equipment, tools, shop equipment, industrial machinery, electrical equipment, medical equipment, and chemicals. Approximately $873·4 million at procurement cost had been declared surplus under this agreement as of 30 September 1948.

Property originally valued at $240 million, included in the above total, had been sold under a number of miscellaneous sales contracts prior to the conclusion of the agreement but incorporated in whole or in part in the consideration set forth in the agreement. This property consisted chiefly of fixed installations and stocks of equipment in China and India and small ships from the Pacific area. The sales value of this property was agreed in the contract as $74 million. It had been turned over, for the most part, to the Chinese Government prior to 31 August 1946, and consisted of the following individual transactions:

(a)   The Calcutta stockpile, having a sales price of approximately $25,000,000. This group of property, which had been sold to China under an earlier agreement, was composed largely of trucks and spare parts together with other supplies related to the repair and maintenance of motor vehicles.

(b)   The small-ship programme, with the sales price of approximately $28,000,000. Ships included in this programme cover all varieties of small noncombat types.

(c)   Materials and supplies required for the support of air forces with a sales value of approximately $6,000,000. This package of equipment, originated as a part of the lend-lease programme, had already been assembled for subsequent delivery to the Chinese when hostilities terminated.

(d)   The Army's sale of property in west China, having a basic sales price of $25,000,000 (US) plus $5,160,000,000 (Chinese) of which the $5,000,000 down payment is incorporated in the consideration covering the bulk sale. This sale was occasioned by the withdrawal of the Army from west China in 1945, and included a broad assortment of expeditionary supplies.

(e)   Miscellaneous small sales with a sales value of approximately $10,000,000. These cover all types of property which had been purchased by the Chinese Government prior to the date of the bulk sale. Two major categories, which combined represent almost one-half the total, are railroad equipment purchased in France and an assortment of quartermaster supplies composed largely of mosquito-bars, blankets, and bath towels.

The agreement of 30 August 1946 provided for a total realization by the United States of $175 million, as follows: (1) $150 million offset against the United States' war-time indebtedness to China, (2) the equivalent in Chinese currency of US $20 million to be available over 20 years to the United States for research, cultural, and educational activities in China, and (3) the equivalent in Chinese currency of US $35 million to be available over 20 years for acquisition by the United States of property in China and for current governmental expenses. While these considerations total $205 million, the United States at the same time agreed to establish a

$30 million fund to be used by China to cover the cost of shipping and technical services arising out of the property transfer. Thus the United States' net realization under the agreement was $175 million.

(10) *OFLC Dockyard Facilities Sales :* On 15 May 1946 OFLC agreed to furnish the Chinese Government surplus supplies and equipment for dockyards at Shanghai and Tsingtao, with repayment to be made in thirty annual instalments. However the agreement provided that the United States might, at its opinion, request of China certain goods and services for United States Navy and other Government-owned vessels, with the cost of such goods and services considered as part of China's annual payments of interest and principal. Transfers of United States surplus under this agreement have now been completed. As of 31 October 1948, OFLC sales totalled $4·1 million at fair value.

(11) *Maritime Commission Ship Sales :* Since VJ Day the Maritime Commission has sold the Chinese Government 43 vessels with a total sales price of $26·2 million under the Merchant Ship Sales Act of 1946. Of this amount, $16·4 million was on Maritime Commission credit terms. The balance was paid in cash, obtained in part through an Export-Import Bank credit. (See item 8 above.) The total wartime procurement cost of the 43 vessels was $77·3 million.

The following sales are included in the total :

No.	Type			Sales Price
10	N–3	..	..	$4,300,000
10 8	} Liberty and } N–3	..	..	9,300,000
8 4	} C1–M–VI and } C1–S–AY1	..	..	10,000,000
3	VC2–A–P2 ..	..	..	2,600,000
	Total	..		$26,200,000

(12) *US Foreign Relief Programme :* Public Law 84, approved 31 May 1947, authorized the initial appropriations for the United States Foreign Relief Programme. China's allocation out of these appropriations amounted to approximately $28·4 million. A supplementary appropriation of $18 million for the China programme was authorized under Public Law 393, approved 23 December 1947.

Deliveries to China under the United States Foreign Relief Programme were made during the first half of 1948, as follows :

Cereals	..	..	..	..	..	$35,412,900
Seeds	..	..	..	..	..	88,400
Pesticides	..	..	..	..	..	609,900
Medical Supplies	..	..	..	..	..	5,185,300
Estimated shipping costs	..	..	..	..		5,084,500
				Total	..	$46,381,000

(13) *ECA Programme :* The current programme of economic aid for China was authorized on 3 April 1948, in the China Aid Act of 1948 (Title IV of the Foreign Assistance Act of 1948). This Act authorized to be appropriated $338,000,000 for economic assistance to China, to be available for obligation for a period of one year from the date of enactment. The Act further provided for creation of a Joint Commission on Rural Reconstruction in China. It was specified that in so far as practicable a maximum of ten per cent of the funds made available for economic assistance should be allotted to the Rural Reconstruction Programme, in the form of United States dollars, proceeds in Chinese currency from the sale of ECA commodities, or both.

The Appropriation Act passed on 28 June (PL 793) appropriated $275,000,000 for economic aid to China of which not more than $1,200,000 was to be obligated for administrative expenses.

The original ECA Programme for China consisted of the following four major categories of expenditures :

(a)	A commodity programme, through which ECA finances the importation of food, petroleum, cotton, fertilizer, and coal into China, and supervises the use within China of these commodities ..	$203,800,000
(b)	Participation with the Chinese Government in a Joint Commission on Rural Reconstruction	2,500,000
(c)	A programme of industrial replacement and re-construction, together with related engineering services	67,500,000
(d)	Administration in Washington, D.C., and China	1,200,000
	Total ..	$275,000,000

311

The following amounts had been authorized for procurement under the ECA commodity programme by 11 March 1949:

Rice	$44,580,000
Wheat/Flour	20,617,000
Petroleum	46,000,000
Cotton	69,790,000
Fertilizer	9,202,000
Coal	286,000
Total ..	$190,475,000

Dollar expenditures for the rural reconstruction programme to date have amounted to less than $50,000. The Commission's expenses have been met largely through withdrawals of Chinese currency from the 'counterpart fund' provided by the Chinese Government.

Procurement authorizations under the industrial reconstruction and replacement programme have been suspended due to the military situation in China, but pre-project engineering is continuing on a number of projects. A total of $1,550,500 had been authorized for expenditure as of 11 March 1949, mainly for engineering surveys.

(14) *Post-VJ Day Lend-Lease :* Lend-lease aid was furnished China after VJ Day to assist the Chinese Government in the re-occupation of liberated areas and in the disarmanent and evacuation of Japanese troops. Under the direction of General Wedemeyer, Chinese armies were moved by air to their new reoccupation assign-ments at a cost of approximately $300 million. Though the 'thirty-nine division' programme ceased as of VJ Day, transfers of army ground material and equipment were continued. Lend-lease transfers of aircraft and air equipment after VJ Day were effected in order to assist the Chinese in the creation of a modern air force. A military-aid agreement of 28 June 1946 provided for the continuation of military lend-lease on a reimbursable basis. This agreement autho-rized expenditures up to $25 million for the reoccupation of China between 30 June and 31 October 1946, and up to $15 million for training Chinese military, air force, and naval personnel between 30 June 1946, and 31 December 1947. Expenditures under these programmes are included in the total figure of lend-lease aid.

As of 30 June 1948 a grand total of $781·0 million in post-VJ Day lend-lease transfers had been reported to the Treasury Department by United States Government agencies. Of this amount, $50·3 million represented deliveries on 3(c) credit terms under the lend-lease 'pipeline' agreement (see item 5 above), and $36 million covered United States Navy vessels originally lend-leased to China but subsequently transferred under the terms of PL 512 (see item 18 below). Of the balance of $694·7 million, $181·0 million is considered subject to payment. Settlement of this amount is now under negotiation.

Listed below are the major categories of Post-VJ Day Lend-Lease supplies :

Ordnance and Ordnance Stores	$117,869,076·94
Aircraft and Aeronautical Material	43,683,604·63
Tanks and Other Vehicles	96,009,610·08
Vessels and Other Watercraft	49,940,642·57
Miscellaneous Military Equipment ..	99,762,611·71
Facilities and Equipment	36,198·74
Agricultural, Industrial and Other Commodities	37,918,928·21
Testing and Reconditioning of Defence Articles	2,338·88
Services and Expenses	335,817,910·56
Total ..	$781,040,922·32

(15) *Military Aid Under SACO :* Supplies valued at $17,666,929·70, consisting primarily of ordnance, were furnished China between 2 September 1945 and 2 March 1946 by the United States Navy under the Sino-American Co-operative Organization agreement. The supplies were made available in exchange for certain services provided by the Chinese Government.

(16) *Sale of Excess Stocks of United States Army in West China :* The sale of a broad assortment of military supplies in west China was made on the departure of United States forces from that area. This property was transferred for a sales price of $25 million (US) plus $5·16 billion (Chinese). Down payments of $5·16 billion (Chinese) and $5 million (US) were made in the form of offsets against the United States indebtedness to China. [The $5 million (US) down payment was incorporated in the realized return to the United States under the surplus property sales agreement of 30 . August 1946—see item 9 above.] It was agreed that $20 million (US) would be paid over a period of time by China. The terms of repayment are subject to negotiation.

(17) *Ammunition Abandoned and Transferred by US Marines in North China :* Between April and September 1947 the United States Marines abandoned or transferred at no cost to the Chinese Government over 6,500 tons of ammunition in connexion with their withdrawal from North China. Included was a wide variety

of small arms and artillery ammunition, grenades, mines, bombs, and miscellaneous explosives. No estimate of the total value of this material is available.

(18) *Transfer of United States Navy Vessels Under PL 512 :* PL 512 authorized the President to transfer 271 naval vessels to the Chinese Government on such terms as he might prescribe. On 8 December 1947, an agreement was signed between the United States Government and the Republic of China relative to the implementation of this Act. A total of 131 vessels with a procurement cost of $141·3 million had been transferred to the Chinese Navy under PL 512 as of 31 December 1948 on a grant basis. This figure includes approximately $36 million representing vessels originally lend-leased to China but subsequently transferred under PL 512.

(19) *Sales of Surplus Military Equipment :* The United States continued to make military equipment available to the Chinese Government following the termination of lend-lease through the transfer of surplus US equipment at a small fraction of its original procurement cost. As of 30 November 1948, China had accepted declared military surplus totalling $100·8 million in value at procurement cost, or $6·7 million at sales price. Of the total accepted, $99·8 million (procurement cost) had been shipped. The following is a listing, in summary form, of military surplus shipments :

		Procurement cost	Sales price
(1)	130 million rounds of 7·92 ammunition (sold by OFLC under contract dated 25 June 1947)	$ 6,564,992·58	$656,499·27
(2)	150 C-46 airplanes (sold by War Assets Administration under contract dated 22 Dec. 1947).	34,800,000·00	750,000·00
(3)	OFLC transfers, 1 Jan. 1948-30 Nov. 1948 :		
	Ammunition, Cal. ·30 to 155 Howitzer	21,419,116·91	554,534·33
	Air Force material and equipment, including 159 aircraft and 683 engines	34,895,332·52	4,365,929·29
	Ordnance, signal, and other military equipment (10,304 tons)	2,158,938·17	269,867·29
	Total ..	$99,838,380·18	(1) $6,596,830·18

(1) A portion of the total military surplus shipments was financed by the Chinese Government from the $125 million grants authorized under the China Aid Act of 1948 (see item 20 below).

(20) *$125 Million Grant Under the China Aid Act of 1948* : Section 404(*b*) of the China Aid Act of 1948 (Title IV of the Foreign Assistance Act of 1948) authorized to be appropriated to the President a sum not to exceed $125,000,000 for additional aid to China through grants, on such terms as the President might determine. The legislative history of the Act made it clear that Congress intended that these funds should be made available to the Chinese Government for such purposes as it might specify. The grants have been used by China to purchase items of a military nature. As of 11 March 1949 the Department of the Treasury had paid a total of $124,148,891·99 of the $125 million appropriated. Disbursements were made to the Chinese Government direct or to United States Government agencies requested by the Chinese Government to engage in procurement activities, as follows :

Recipient	Materials Procured	Amount
US Government Agencies :		
Department of the Army	Arms, ammunition, medical supplies, motor vehicles, spare parts, etc.	$64,437,061·68
Department of the Navy	Naval vessels, reconditioning of naval vessels, ammunition ..	6,892,020·00
Department of the Air Force	Miscellaneous air force equipment and aviation gasoline	7,750,000·00
Bureau of Federal Supply	Petroleum products, ordnance raw materials	13,765,522·12
Office of Foreign Liquidation Commissioner	Surplus aircraft, aircraft spares, ammunition, etc.	(1)2,690,910·88
Republic of China	Miscellaneous supplies and equipment, from commercial sources ..	28,613,377·31
	Total ..	$124,148,891·99

(1) In addition, OFLC has received by direct payment from the Chinese Government $1,045,693·8 of the $28,613,377·31 paid to the Chinese Government by the Treasury Department.

As of 31 December 1948, materials purchased for $60,958,791·38 under the $125 million grants had been shipped to China.

In accordance with the President's Directive of 2 June 1948, the Department of State examines the documentation submitted by the Chinese Government to determine that the request is not in excess of the total represented by the invoices or other supporting data, and authorizes the Treasury to make the appropriate payments to the Chinese Government. Under the President's Directive of 28 July 1948, the Chinese Government may arrange for the procurement or furnishing of supplies or services by any agency of the United States Government, subject to the approval of the Secretary of State as to the availability of funds. In such instances, the agency concerned is authorized to submit to the Department of State requests for reimbursement of appropriations or for advance payments. The Department has been able to certify fully documented requests for payment by the Treasury Department within a few days after receipt.

United States Relations with China, pp. 1042-53.

II   RELATIONS WITH SOVIET UNION

55   5 *October* 1949

LIU SHAO-CHI'S SPEECH AT THE INAUGURAL CONFERENCE OF THE SINO-SOVIET FRIENDSHIP ASSOCIATION

The history of the last thirty years has clearly proved that the peoples of the two great nations, China and the Soviet Union, love each other like brothers.

More than thirty years ago, the Tsarist Government pursued the policy of invading China which evoked the opposition of the Chinese people; such opposition was entirely justified. But, after the overthrow of the Tsarist Government and the victory of the October Revolution, the situation underwent a complete change. The people of the Soviet Union, under the leadership of the great Lenin and Stalin, carried out an unprecedentedly friendly policy towards the Chinese people, while the Chinese people also began to accept the friendship of the people and government of the Soviet Union with an unprecedentedly friendly attitude.

The success of the Great October Revolution gave all mankind and also the oppressed Chinese people great hopes, just as Comrade Stalin said: 'The October Revolution greatly promoted the liberation cause of the oppressed nations of the West and the East . . . building a bridge between the socialist West and the enslaved East.' It was only under the inspiration of the October Revolution that the advanced elements of China grasped the weapon of Marxism-Leninism after their long groping, and used this weapon earnestly to analyse and solve problems in China. The Communist Party of China consequently came into being in 1921 and the face of the Chinese Revolution was changed anew.

This historical development was understood by Dr Sun Yat-sen who had led the 1911 Revolution. Disappointed over the realities of old China and the old democracy of the Anglo-American type, he welcomed the October Revolution and the Communist Party of China, and, as a result of this the three policies of allying with Russia, allying with the Communist Party and assistance to the peasants and workers were formed in 1924. At that time, the government of the Soviet Union voluntarily abrogated all its prerogatives in China and all unequal treaties concluded with the old government of China during the Tsarist period, and rendered truly friendly help to Sun Yat-sen and the revolutionary government of that time. It was just because of this aid that the revolutionary Northern Expedition War was victoriously launched. In March 1925, Dr Sun Yat-sen in his will to his successors just before his death exhorted 'We must ally ourselves in a common struggle with those peoples of the world who treat us on a footing of equality, so that they may co-operate with us in our struggle.' This means that alliance must be made with the Soviet Union.

But after the death of Dr Sun Yat-sen, his will was entirely violated by his successors, the Chiang Kai-shek reactionary bloc. In 1927, when China's Great Revolution was on the way to winning brilliant victory through Kuomintang-Communist co-operation and the aid of the Soviet Union, Chiang Kai-shek sold out the Chinese Revolution, betrayed the Chinese people and Dr Sun Yat-sen, and switched over from uniting the Soviet Union and the Communist Party into opposing them and from helping the peasants and workers into riding roughshod over them, and furthermore launched ten years of brutal Civil War. The Chiang Kai-shek bloc became the running dog of imperialism and the representative of the interests of the feudal comprador class. The friendship and co-operation between the two great nations, China and the Soviet Union, were seriously obstructed and undermined.

In 1937, when the armed forces of Japanese imperialism invaded China and China's Anti-Japanese War broke out, the Soviet Union was the first to aid China's war of resistance with manpower and materials, disregarding the past crimes of the Kuomintang.

Despite the great destruction suffered by her, the Soviet Union quickly participated in the war against Japan after winning the war in Europe, annihilated the Japanese Kwantung Army and helped China to liberate the north-east. During the present People's Liberation War, the Soviet Union extended trading facilities to our northeast Liberated Area. The existence of the powerful Soviet Union and the growth of the people's democratic forces in the world especially pinned down a great part of the forces of imperialism, thus enabling the Chinese People's Liberation War to be won rapidly.

Now the Chinese People's Liberation War and the People's Great Revolution have won a basic victory and will soon win complete victory. The Chinese People's Political Consultative Conference has been convened. The formation of the Central People's Government of the People's Republic of China was proclaimed on 1 October of this year. The Soviet Union was the first to recognize and establish new diplomatic relations with the Chinese People's Government on the second day of the proclamation of the founding of the People's Republic of China.

These facts of the past thirty years demonstrate the steadfast friendship of the Soviet people and the Soviet Government towards the Chinese people.

In his letter to the Soviet Union just before his death, Dr Sun Yat-sen said : 'The day will soon dawn when the Soviet Union will welcome a strong and independent China as friend and ally and in the great war for freedom of the oppressed nations of the world, these two nations will march forward hand in hand to win victory.' This day cherished by Dr Sun Yat-sen has not only dawned, but has entirely become reality. Henceforth, Chinese history has entered an entirely new era. This has also enabled the friendship between the Chinese and Soviet peoples to enter into friendship and co-operation between these two peoples. Henceforth there will be boundless development and consolidation for the friendship and co-operation between these two peoples. The close co-operation of these two great nations will be matchless in the world and will play a decisive role in the direction of world development. The close co-operation of these two great nations is, therefore, one of the best interests of mankind and especially the best interest of the Chinese people. We therefore greatly prize this friendship and co-operation. We will not allow any impeding or undermining of this friendship and co-operation, because they run counter to the best interests of the great majority of the Chinese people.

China is an economically backward country with industrial production occupying only one-tenth of its total production. At present the Chinese economy has suffered great destruction and the prime task of the Chinese people today is to rehabilitate and develop speedily the people's economy so as to industrialize China. Without the friendly help of the Soviet people and Soviet Government these tasks would have been much more difficult. For instance, the rapid restoration of our railways was due to the help of the Soviet Union. And for instance, with the help of the Soviet Union, the rehabilitation of the iron and steel industry in Anshan, Shihchingshan etc. was able to proceed at a much faster speed. The sincere friendly help rendered by the Soviet Union to the Chinese people is therefore one of the favourable conditions for rehabilitating and developing Chinese economy. The Chinese people should particularly prize their friendship and co-operation with the Soviet people for this reason and also because the Soviet people has been nurtured by the teachings of the great Lenin and Stalin. Such a people is full of boundless sincere friendship of internationalism towards the Chinese people and peoples of the world. Their help to the Chinese people is unconditional and they ask for nothing in return. This help is the same as that of the Chinese Communists who serve the people unconditionally and ask for nothing in return. Such a friendly spirit of internationalism is incomprehensible to persons with the old bourgeois viewpoint. For instance, when we served the workers and peasants in factories and rural villages, persons looked at us curiously when they saw that we were unafraid of troubles, hardship and danger and did things for them without asking anything in return. This was because they had never seen such magnanimous and selfless persons who could serve the people unconditionally. The communists and people of the Soviet Union are just as magnanimous and selfless as the Chinese communists and can serve the Chinese people unconditionally. This is because communists throughout the world including those in China are a completely new type of people hitherto unknown in history. These people are endowed with a boundless sincere friendly spirit of internationalism and can serve the people in any part of the world unconditionally and indiscriminately. That was why comrade Mao Tze-tung said : We can only look for genuine friendly aid from the Soviet Union front.

For example, the Soviet Union has now sent more than two hundred specialists to serve in the northeast and other parts of China. When I asked them about the conditions for their services in China, these specialists said : Stalin had instructed them to impart all their knowledge and technique to the Chinese people. When the Chinese people had mastered the knowledge and could run their factories and enterprises without difficulty and no longer needed their services in China, they would return to the Soviet Union.

After arriving in China, they are assigned jobs by China. When they are assigned to various factories, enterprises and economic departments, they work under the responsible Chinese personnel. They only act as advisers, and their pay is the same as that of Chinese engineers of the same grade. They do not receive the very high pay demanded by American and British engineers. Never before in China have foreign engineers worked under such conditions as theirs. It is only Soviet specialists who voluntarily ask for such conditions.

Trade between the Soviet Union and China has now begun. The trading conditions proposed by the Soviet Union are entirely friendly and self-denying and could never be possible with the capitalist countries. These are some of the concrete manifestations of the spirit of internationalism of the Soviet people.

We specially prize this friendship and co-operation between the Chinese and Soviet peoples because the path traversed by the Soviet people is the path which we Chinese people will soon take. The experience of the Soviet people in national construction is worthy of careful study by the Chinese people. The Chinese revolution attained the victory of the day because we learnt from the Soviet Union in the past and took 'Russia as the teacher'. Henceforth, we are going to build up the country, and must likewise take 'Russia as the teacher' and study the experience in national construction of the Soviet people. The Soviet Union has now much scientific knowledge which is entirely new and unknown to the rest of the world. We can learn such scientific knowledge only from the Soviet Union. For example, in the fields of economics, banking, public finances, commerce, education, etc. the Soviet Union has an entirely new set of theories which other countries of the world do not have, not to mention her advanced political science and military science. Soviet culture is an entirely new culture. The pressing task before the Chinese people today is to absorb the new culture of the Soviet Union and to make it our orientation for building up the New China. Hence we are especially in need of the friendly aid and co-operation of the Soviet people.

Thirty-two years ago Russia was still a backward country. But such conditions have now changed, and she is no longer a backward nation but an advanced state. The Soviet Union has not only the most advanced political and military systems in the world, but her science and technology have caught up and outstripped those of the most advanced countries in the world. Only by correcting this viewpoint of a number of Chinese who believe that Russia is still backward can it be possible for Chinese people to learn from the Soviet Union, unhindered and on a large scale.

The industrialization of capitalist countries took over one hundred years while it took only twenty to thirty years in the Soviet Union. We can also industrialise China within twenty years because of the help to the Chinese people extended by the Soviet Union in the spirit of internationalism. Therefore, the close friendship and co-operation between the Chinese and the Soviet peoples are particularly worthy of being prized.

Since the friendship and co-operation between the Chinese and Soviet peoples have such a great significance, our enemies, the imperialists and reactionaries, are not unaware of it. They will consequently concentrate on the undermining of our friendship and co-operation. They are now using various means such as spreading rumours, creating dissension, inveigling and intriguing to undermine Sino-Soviet friendship and co-operation and attempt to create suspicion and dissension between the peoples of these two nations. We must be on our guard against this.

Representing the will of the Chinese people throughout the country, we have undertaken the preparatory work of the Sino-Soviet Friendship Association because of the above mentioned reasons. The purpose of this work is the strengthening, furthering and consolidating of the fraternal friendship and co-operation between the two great nations. We had decided to set up our general associations at the new people's capital Peking and will set up general branches, branches and sub-branches throughout the country. The general association has already finished its preparatory work and its inauguration has been announced today. Some of the general branches, branches and sub-branches have also been formed such as those in the northeast, while some are in the process of preparation and will soon be set up. The fact that the broad masses in various places have enthusiastically joined the Sino-Soviet Friendship Association proves that the Chinese people want most earnestly and urgently to co-operate closely with the Soviet people.

We are greatly honoured that the Soviet delegation of culture, arts and science workers led by Comrades Alexander A. Fadeyev and K. M. Simonov are attending today's inaugural conference. This symbolizes that our conference today is really the great unity of 'Sino-Soviet friendship'. The Soviet comrades headed by Comrade Alexander A. Fadeyev and Comrade K. M. Simonov have participated in the inaugural ceremony of the founding of our state on the 2nd and the 3rd. Today, you are also attending the inaugural conference of the Sino-Soviet Friendship Association. You are our very good international friends at the founding of our People's Republic. You have probably noticed the aspirations of our Chinese people. Sino-Soviet friendship is indivisible from the work of defending world peace and also from the construction work of our country. One of the great events during the founding of our state is the strengthening of Sino-Soviet friendship and the defence of world peace.

We wish good health to the Soviet delegation and other international representatives and success to the conference.

Long live the great Chinese people ! Long live the great Soviet people ! Long live the immortal friendship and co-operation between the peoples of the Soviet Union and China ! Long live Generalissimo Stalin, the great revolutionary teacher of the working people of the world !

Daily News Release, New China News Agency, No. 289, 8 October 1949.

III   RELATIONS WITH UNITED NATIONS

56   *18 November* 1949

CHOU EN-LAI'S CABLE TO THE SECRETARY-GENERAL OF THE UNITED NATIONS REPUDIATING THE DELEGATION OF THE KUOMINTANG GOVERNMENT

Mr Trygve Lie, Secretary-General of the United Nations Organization :

The Central People's Government of the People's Republic of China was formally formed on 1 October. On the day of its formation, Chairman Mao Tse Tung of the Central People's Government solemnly proclaimed to the world : The Central People's Government of the People's Republic of China is the sole legal government representing all the people of the People's Republic of China.

The Central People's Government of the People's Republic of China has now fundamentally liberated the territory and people of all China and also won the enthusiastic support of the people throughout the country while the Kuomintang reactionary government is now in exile and dispersed and its remnant forces will soon be eliminated ; this reactionary government has lost all *de jure* and *de facto* grounds for representing the Chinese people.

The so-called 'delegation of the Chinese national government' participating in the United Nations Organization and attending the present session of the United Nations General Assembly in the name of the Chinese people has therefore become the tool of a handful of exiled elements, and is absolutely unqualified to represent the Chinese people.

On behalf of the Central People's Government of the People's Republic of China, I formally demand that the United Nations Organization immediately deprive the 'delegation of the Chinese national government', in accordance with the principles and spirit of the United Nations Charter, of all rights to further represent the Chinese people in the United Nations, so as to conform to the wishes of the Chinese people.

CHOU EN-LAI,
*Foreign Minister of the Central
People's Government of the
People's Republic
of China*

UN Document A/1123, 21 November 1949.

57   19 *January* 1950

CHOU EN-LAI'S NOTE TO THE PRESIDENT OF THE GENERAL ASSEMBLY OF THE UNITED NATIONS INTIMATING APPOINTMENT OF THE CHIEF CHINESE DELEGATE TO THE UNITED NATIONS

On the 8th of January, 1950, I addressed to the United Nations a note demanding the United Nations and the Security Council to expel the illegitimate delegates of the Chinese Kuomintang reactionary remnant clique. Mr Trygve Lie has kindly replied acknowledging the receipt of this note of protest and stating that copies of it have been given to the member delegations to the Security Council.

I would like to inform you further, Messrs President and Secretary-General, that the Central People's Government of the People's Republic of China has appointed Chang Wen Tien, Chairman of the Delegation of the People's Republic of China, to attend the meetings and to participate in the work of the United Nations including the meetings and work of the Security Council.

Also may I request you, Messrs President and Secretary-General to answer the following two questions :

(1) When will the illegitimate delegates of the Chinese Kuomintang reactionary remnant clique be expelled from the United Nations and from the Security Council ? I consider the continued presence to this day of the illegitimate delegates of such a reactionary remnant clique in the United Nations and the Security Council as completely unjustified. They should be expelled immediately.

323

(2)   When can the legitimate Delegation of the People's Republic of China under the chairmanship of Chang Wen Tien attend the meetings and participate in the work of the United Nations and the Security Council ? I consider that this delegation should attend the meetings and participate in the work without delay.

An early reply will be appreciated.

[Peking, 19 Jan.—The Central People's Government of the People's Republic of China today appointed Chang Wen Tien as head of the delegation to attend and participate in the work of the United Nations and its Security Council.

He is a member of the Central Committee of the Communist Party of China and of its Political Bureau. He is also a member of the Standing Committee of the North-east Bureau of the Chinese Communist Party Central Committee and member of the North-east People's Government Council.

Chang Wen Tien is 50 years old and was born in Nanhwei county, Kiangsu Province. He joined the Communist Party of China in 1925 and has taken part in the work of the leading organ of the Central Committee of the Party since 1931. When the Central Committee of the Communist Party of China led the Chinese people's revolutionary army to make the famous 25,000 *li* Long March between the winter of 1934 and 1935, he was a member of the organization which directed the march. He was again elected member of the Central Committee at the 7th Congress of the Communist Party of China in 1945.]

Daily News Release, New China News Agency, No. 262, 20 January 1950.

KOREA

KOREA

INTRODUCTION

FROM 1906 to the end of the second world war, Korea remained under Japanese rule. The Cairo Declaration of 1 December 1943, issued by President Roosevelt, Sir Winston Churchill and Generalissimo Chiang Kai-shek, promised that 'in due course Korea shall become free and independent'. This promise was reaffirmed in the Potsdam Declaration which was also adhered to by the Soviet Union. The qualification 'in due course' was added, it seems, because it was felt that after a long period of rigorous subjection the Koreans might not be ready to assume immediately the responsibilities of self-government. On 22 September 1945, after the Japanese surrender, General MacArthur required the Japanese Government to issue directions to its forces in Korea north of the 38th parallel to surrender to the Soviet forces and to those south of the 38th parallel to surrender to the United States forces. Thus Korea came to be divided at the 38th parallel, though it was not intended to be a lasting division; it was described as a fortuitous line adopted because of the immediate needs of the moment.

At Moscow in December 1945, the United States, the Soviet Union and the United Kingdom decided that a provisional Korean democratic government should be set up for all Korea. To assist in the formation of this government a Joint Commission, consisting of the representatives of the US and Soviet Commands, was established. The government was to be set up 'in consultation with Korean democratic parties and social organizations'. The Joint Commission and the Provisional Government were to propose for consideration the terms of a five-year Four-Power trusteeship agreement.

The Joint Commission was set up in March 1946 but reached an impasse very soon. The proposal of international trusteeship was unacceptable to all but the extreme leftists in Korea. The Soviet Government took the position that only those groups should be consulted which had expressed a willingness to accept fully and freely the Moscow decisions. Since it meant eliminating all but the Communists and fellow-travellers, the United States refused to accept the Soviet stand and the Joint Commission was deadlocked.

One of the main causes for the political impasse was the different approaches of the American and Soviet Governments towards the problems of Korea. These reflected themselves in different, and often opposite, policies adopted by the two governments in their own zones of occupation. In the Soviet zone the Soviet authorities took quick and effective measures to reorganize the political and economic structure according to their wishes. The leftists were brought into the forefront and given the leadership of the Soviet zone. Various political parties were united in a single new People's Party and a Provisional People's Committee dominated by the Communists was established on 9 February 1946. This was followed by the formation of an all-Korean Cabinet, with Kim Sung as Premier. Steps were also taken to establish a North Korean army. A programme of agrarian reform and redistribution of land was put through, and industrial reorganization was undertaken. The administration was efficient and incorruptible. Strong action was taken against those Koreans who were considered traitors. Along with these popular measures, there was intolerance and suppression of opposition which resulted in a large exodus of dissatisfied elements to South Korea.

In South Korea, on the other hand, the United States pursued different objectives and different methods to achieve them. The Americans did not pick out a Korean group or groups through which to work from the beginning ; instead, they worked through the Japanese during the first months of occupation. In January 1946 a US Military Government régime took over authority and gradually gave administrative but not political responsibility to the Koreans. The United States chose to ally itself with conservative and feudal elements. An Advisory Council consisting of conservative Koreans was constituted in February 1946. It was replaced in November by an Interim Legislative Assembly, half of whose members were selected by a system of indirect elections, the other half being appointed by the Military Government. The election plans evoked much opposition and led to strikes and riots. The leftists complained that the Military Government was suppressing all but conservative activity in a reign of terror, and the US authorities countercharged that the Communists were instigating the agitation. The elections conducted in such an unhealthy atmosphere further strengthened the position of the conservatives. The division of political parties into two extreme sections plagued the politics of South Korea. The leftists wanted a full-blooded programme of land reform and were opposed to the Americans. The conservatives could maintain their influence and position only through their economic strength and the support of the police and the administration. The middle groups lacked both organization and following.

The growing hostility between the two zones, resulting in the practical severance of relations between the two, disrupted the economic unity of Korea. The economies of North and South Korea were in many ways complementary to each other. South Korea was a rice and grain producing area but was poor in essential minerals and industries. North Korea, on the other hand, had abundant mineral deposits and well-developed hydro-electric plants but was short of foodstuffs. The disruption of normal economic relations between the two zones caused much suffering and hardship to the people in the two areas.

In an exchange of notes in May 1947 General Marshall and Mr Molotov arrived at an agreement calling for the resumption of the meetings of the Joint Commission. It was decided that in order to facilitate consultations with a wide range of Korean groups and parties, they would be asked to pledge support to the decisions of the Moscow Conference, particularly to the Four-Power Trusteeship plan. However, the rightist organizations in Korea had no intention of doing so ; on the contrary, they renewed their opposition to the trusteeship proposal and even revived their Anti-Trusteeship Committee. Thus when the Joint Commission met, it was again faced with the same dilemma. The Soviet delegate insisted that only those parties and groups should be consulted and associated with the work of the Commission who had accepted the decisions of the Moscow Conference. The American authorities were not willing to accept this restriction because it would have meant the exclusion of practically all but the leftists. By mid-July 1947 the deadlock in the Commission was complete.

The Joint Commission had reached the end of its tether. It was now up to the higher authorities to unravel the knot. On 26 August 1947, US Acting Secretary of State Lovett made new proposals to Molotov for resolving the Korean tangle. He suggested the holding of separate elections in the two zones under UN supervision and the formation of a National Assembly from among the two provisional legislatures, which would in turn establish a provisional government. The four signatories to the Moscow agreement would then hold talks with the provisional government on the political future of Korea. The US note, therefore, proposed the holding of a Four-Power Conference in Washington to discuss these proposals. These proposals were rejected out of hand by the Soviet Union, and Molotov in his note of 4 September maintained that framing measures for the establishment of a Korean provisional government was the task of the Joint Commission and that the latter body could still perform that task. He intimated the refusal of the Soviet Union to participate in the proposed Four-Power Conference at Washington.

In view of the Soviet refusal it was pointless to go ahead with the conference. The United States then decided to submit the matter to the United Nations. On 23 September 1947, the United Nations General Assembly, despite Soviet opposition, decided to place the Korean question on its agenda. The Soviet Union opposed the consideration of the Korean question by the United Nations on the ground that, like other questions connected with the conclusion of peace treaties, it was exclusively a matter for discussion and decision between the Big Four, and was therefore outside the competence of the United Nations. As a counter-measure to the General Assembly decision, the Soviet delegation on the Joint Commission proposed the withdrawal of both Soviet and American troops by the beginning of 1948 leaving the Koreans to organize their own government. The Soviet Government reiterated this proposal in a note to the United States on 9 October. The United States in its reply of 18 October maintained that the question of the withdrawal of troops was an integral part of the problem of establishing an independent government for a unified Korea for whose achievement the United States had already submitted proposals in the General Assembly.

In a counter-move to the Soviet proposals for the withdrawal of foreign troops from Korea, the United States proposed in the General Assembly on 17 October 1947 that elections be held in the two zones of Korea. On the basis of these elections a National Assembly for all Korea should be constituted and a new government for the whole of Korea would be elected by the National Assembly. This government would assume full powers and enter into negotiations with the occupying Powers for the withdrawal of foreign troops. The US proposals provided for a UN Temporary Commission on Korea to supervise all these steps. The Soviet Union had first maintained that the question of Korea was outside the competence of the United Nations but when it failed to get the majority of the Assembly to accept this point of view, the Soviet delegate, Mr Gromyko, proposed that the Assembly should hear the views of the elected representatives of the Korean people before taking any decision on the question. The American view was that it was not possible to decide who the properly elected Korean representatives were.

The American resolution, with some amendments, was adopted by the Assembly by 43 votes to none, with 6 abstentions. The Soviet Union and its Eastern European allies did not participate in the voting. In fact, the Soviet Union gave notice during the discussion on the American resolution that if a Commission was appointed without prior consultation with the Korean representatives, the Soviet Union would not participate in the work of the Commission. The Temporary Commission set up by the General Assembly was to consist of Australia, Canada, China, El Salvador, France, India, the Philippines, Syria and the Ukraine. In accordance with Soviet policy, the Ukraine refused to serve on the Commission.

The Commission held its first meeting in Seoul on 12 January 1948. Some of the rightist leaders in South Korea, led by Dr Syngman Rhee, called for immediate elections in South Korea while the leftist leaders along with some rightist politicians were opposed to partial election and supported the proposal of withdrawal of all foreign troops from Korea. The Commission's attempts to contact the North Korean authorities proved fruitless. When the UN Secretary-General approached the Soviet authorities, he was reminded by Mr Gromyko that the Soviet Union had not recognized the Commission. The Commission was also refused permission to enter North Korea. In the circumstances it was obvious that the Commission's activities would be limited to South Korea. It was, therefore, decided by the Commission on 6 February 1948 to consult the UN Interim Committee, which had been established at the Second Session of the General Assembly and which had been denounced by the Soviet Union as an illegal body, on whether it was open to the Commission to implement the Assembly's resolution in South Korea only. The Interim Committee decided on 26 February that the Commission should go ahead with its programme in such parts of Korea as were accessible to it. Australia and Canada voted against this decision because they felt that it would tend to perpetuate the division of Korea.

The Interim Committee's resolution gave the green light for holding elections in South Korea only. This was exactly what Dr Rhee and his associates were demanding. It was vigorously opposed by the leftists, the moderates led by Dr Kim Kiu-sic, and some right-wing groups headed by Kim Koo. It was felt that separate elections and the establishment of a government in South Korea would invite a similar course in North Korea by the Soviets and thus the division of Korea would tend to become permanent.

The Commission was divided in its opinion, with Australia and Canada strongly opposed to holding separate elections and China strongly favouring such a course. The Commission decided by a small majority to implement the resolution of the Interim Committee.

The South Korean leaders who were opposed to holding separate elections started negotiations with the North Korean leaders for bringing about a unified Korea. The North Koreans responded by inviting the South Korean leaders to a political conference in Pyongyang for devising measures to establish an all-Korean coalition government. Both Kim Kiu-sic and Kim Koo accepted the invitation and went to Pyongyang to attend the conference which opened on 22 April 1948. The conference was attended by 545 delegates, including 240 from the south. It passed resolutions calling for the withdrawal of foreign troops and the establishment of a government for the whole of Korea. The leaders of the two zones held a further conference in

Pyongyang on 30 April after which they issued a public statement announcing their resolve not to recognize the results of elections in South Korea, and to unite to form a provisional government for the whole of Korea and hold free elections for an all-Korean Assembly.

Elections in South Korea were fixed for 10 May 1948. Violence and terrorism were often used during the election campaign, and there were frequent charges of intimidation. The elections resulted in the victory of the conservatives and Dr Syngman Rhee emerged as the leader of the majority of the members of the National Assembly. How far the elections were free and fair has been a matter of acrimonious controversy. The UN Temporary Commission was satisfied that a reasonable degree of free atmosphere existed during the elections and stated in its resolution of 25 June that the result was a 'valid expression of the free will of the electorate'. However, the Commission's observations were naturally limited to small areas and allegations of intimidation and other unfair practices were levelled not only by the leftists but also by moderates and rightists of various shades.

The National Assembly met on 31 May 1948, adopted a constitution for the Republic of Korea on 12 July, and elected Syngman Rhee as the first President of the Republic. Calling for the unification of Korea, Rhee issued the warning that the North Korean leaders would be treated as traitors if they continued to sell the country to a foreign Power. The Republic was formally inaugurated on 15 August 1948 and the American Military Government was terminated the same day. Government authority was transferred from the military command and its civilian agencies to the newly constituted Republic. On 24 August an agreement was signed between President Rhee and the American military commander, General Hodge, providing for the transfer of jurisdiction over the security forces, including the police and coast-guard, to the new Government. On 11 September the United States and the Korean Republic reached a financial and property agreement by which the latter received as a gift all ex-Japanese assets or receipts therefrom which had been in the possession of the military government. Additional credits to the South Korean Government were provided by the United States by an agreement of 10 December.

As had been feared, the moves in South Korea provoked similar measures in North Korea. The North Korea leaders denounced the elections in South Korea and announced that they would hold elections in August 1948 for a 'Supreme People's Assembly' in order to establish a single Korean Government. Elections to this Assembly were held on 25 August and followed the Soviet pattern of a single list of candidates. The North Koreans claimed that a large proportion

of the voting population in South Korea had secretly participated in the election. The People's Assembly proclaimed the Democratic People's Republic of Korea on 9 September 1948. It also
adopted a constitution and named Kim Sung, Prime Minister of
the People's Republic. On 10 September the Supreme People's
Assembly appealed to both the occupying Powers to withdraw
their troops from Korea. The Soviet Union replied on 19 September
that it would withdraw all its troops by 1 January 1948. It sent
a Note to the United States Government informing it of its decision
and calling upon it to do likewise. The United States announced on
21 September that it would reduce its troops in Korea but that
there would be no final withdrawal until the forthcoming Third
Session of the General Assembly had considered the Korean question.
In its reply of 28 September to the Soviet Note the American Government maintained that the withdrawal of troops was an integral
part of the entire Korean question which would be considered by
the General Assembly at its next meeting. On 8 October Kim
Sung addressed a request to Marshal Stalin for the establishment of
diplomatic relations between the Soviet Union and the North Korean
régime. Marshal Stalin indicated his willingness in his reply of
October 10. The relations between the two countries were further
cemented by the conclusion in Moscow on 17 March 1949 of an
Agreement on Economic and Cultural Co-operation between the
Soviet Union and the People's Democratic Republic of Korea.
Thus two separate régimes had come into being, each created in
the image of its occupying Power.

The Korean imbroglio once again came up for discussion before
the General Assembly in its third session in December 1948. The
first question that led to heated discussion was the bid by both the
North Korean Government and the South Korean Government to
secure recognition by the United Nations. The Czechoslovak delegation introduced a resolution with a view to getting a North Korean
representative to take part in the discussion on the Korean question
while China countered this with a resolution inviting a South Korean
representative to speak to the Political Committee. The Committee
rejected the Czechoslovak resolution by a vote of 34 to 6 and accepted that of China by 39 to 6. Regarding the general question of Korea,
a joint resolution was moved by Australia, China and the United
States providing for the recognition of the South Korean Government
and the setting up of a United Nations Commission in Korea to supervise the withdrawal of occupation forces and to lend its good offices
for the unification of Korea. The Soviet Union, on the other hand,
moved a resolution which called for the termination of the Temporary
Commission on Korea without providing for any successor to it.

333

On 8 December 1948 the Political Committee adopted the three-Power joint resolution and rejected the Soviet resolution. The General Assembly endorsed this decision on 12 December by 48 to 6 votes with one abstention. The resolution in its final form declared that the South Korean régime was established as a result of elections which were a valid expression of the free will of the electorate in such part of Korea as were accessible to the Temporary Commission, and that it was the only such government in Korea. It also provided for the establishment of a further commission on Korea which was entrusted with the task of observing the withdrawal of all occupation forces and bringing about the unification of Korea. After these decisions of the General Assembly, the United States accorded recognition to the Republic of Korea on 1 January 1949 and Great Britain, many other countries of Western Europe and some countries in Asia followed suit.

On 30 December the Soviet Union announced that it had completed withdrawal of its troops from Korea. However, the UN Commission was again denied access to North Korea, and the Commission in its resolution of 23 May 1949 declared that it had been unable to observe and verify the withdrawal of Soviet troops. The United States which had been progressively reducing its troops informed the Commission that it intended to withdraw all combat forces from Korea by the end of June 1949. The Commission observed the withdrawal of American troops, which was completed by 29 June 1949. The United States left behind a military advisory group to train the forces of the South Korean Republic.

All the efforts of the UN Commission to contact the North Korean authorities directly or indirectly, through appeals to the Soviet authorities, were unavailing. In these efforts it was not only the Communists who were uncooperative but the South Korean Government was also unhelpful. The South Korean Government denounced the North Korean régime as a puppet régime and wanted to bring the northern zone under its rule, an intention which was fully reciprocated, only the other way round, by the North Korean régime. Both sides were talking of 'liberating' the other and were anxious to use force to secure their aim. As the UN Commission remarked in its report to the Fourth Session of the General Assembly which met in October 1949, the spirit of compromise was non-existent in Korea. The General Assembly voted to prolong the life of the Commission for further attempts to bring about peaceful unification of Korea, but events inside the country were fast moving towards a crisis. Threats and counter-threats and a growing tension bedevilled the situation. The prospects of peaceful unification were becoming more and more dim.

KOREA

PART I

POLITICAL AND CONSTITUTIONAL DEVELOPMENTS

Section One
US and USSR Disagreement on a Political Solution

Section Two
UN General Assembly's Search for a Political Solution

Section Three
Korean Efforts for a United Korea

Section Four
Democratic Republic of Korea (South)

Section Five
People's Republic of Korea (North)

PART II

EXTERNAL RELATIONS

Section One
South Korea
Relations with the United States

Section Two
North Korea
Relations with the Soviet Union

PART ONE

I   US AND USSR DISAGREEMENT ON A POLITICAL SOLUTION

I   26 *August* 1947

UNITED STATES NOTE TO THE SOVIET UNION
PROPOSING FOUR-POWER CONFERENCE ON THE
MOSCOW AGREEMENT ON KOREA (LETTER FROM
R. A. LOVETT TO V. M. MOLOTOV)

For almost two years the Government of the United States has
devoted its utmost efforts to carrying out the terms of the Moscow
Agreement on Korea. The present stalemate in the Joint Commission negotiations and the failure of that Commission to accomplish
even the first task of its mission have made it abundantly clear to
all that bilateral negotiations on the subject of consultation with
Korean political parties and organizations will only serve to delay
the implementation of this agreement and defeat its announced
purpose of bringing about early independence for Korea. The United
States Government cannot in good conscience be a party to any such
delay in the fulfilment of its commitment to Korean independence
and proposes that the four Powers adhering to the Moscow Agreement meet to consider how that agreement may be speedily carried
out.

The United States Government therefore submits for the consideration of your government the enclosed outline of proposals
designed to achieve the aims of the Moscow Agreement on Korea.
The United States Government proposes that these suggestions
be considered at an early date by the Powers adhering to that
Agreement. It is therefore hoped that the Soviet Chargé d'Affaires
at Washington or an authorized deputy may be designated
to participate in four-Power conversations on this problem at
Washington beginning on 8 September 1947.

It is believed that the Joint Commission's report on the status of
its deliberations might be helpful in consideration of the United
States proposals during these four-Power conversations. The United
States proposals during these four-Power conversations. The United
States Delegation has accordingly been instructed to endeavour to
reach agreement with the Soviet Delegation on a joint report to be
submitted not later than 5 September 1947.

Copies of this letter are being transmitted to the Foreign Ministers of the United Kingdom and China together with invitations to participate in the four-Power conversations referred to above.

UNITED STATES PROPOSALS REGARDING KOREA

(1) In both the USSR and US zones of Korea there shall be held early elections to choose wholly representative provisional legislatures for each zone. Voting shall be by secret, multi-party ballot on a basis of universal suffrage and elections shall be held in accordance with the laws adopted by the present Korean legislatures in each zone.

(2) These provisional zonal legislatures shall choose representatives in numbers which reflect the proportion between the populations of the two zones, these representatives to constitute a national provisional legislature. This legislature shall meet at Seoul to establish a provisional government for a united Korea.

(3) The resulting Provisional Government of a united Korea shall meet in Korea with representatives of the four Powers adhering to the Moscow Agreement on Korea to discuss with them what aid and assistance is needed in order to place Korean independence on a firm economic and political foundation and on what terms this aid and assistance is to be given.

(4) During all the above stages the United Nations shall be invited to have observers present so that the world and the Korean people may be assured of the wholly representative and completely independent character of the actions taken.

(5) The Korean Provisional Government and the Powers concerned shall agree upon a date by which all occupation forces in Korea will be withdrawn.

(6) The provisional legislatures in each zone shall be encouraged to draft provisional constitutions which can later be used as a basis for the adoption by the national provisional legislature of a constitution for all of Korea.

(7) Until such time as a united, independent Korea is established, public and private Korean agencies in each zone shall be brought into contact with international agencies established by or under the United Nations and the presence of Korean observers at official international conferences shall be encouraged in appropriate cases.

Korea 1945 to 1948, US Department of State, Publication No. 3305, October 1948, pp. 43-4.

2   4 *September* 1947

SOVIET NOTE REPLYING TO THE UNITED STATES
PROPOSAL OF FOUR-POWER CONFERENCE ON KOREA
(LETTER FROM V. M. MOLOTOV TO GEORGE MARSHALL)

Acknowledging the receipt of Mr Lovett's letter of 26 August,
I deem it necessary to draw your attention to the fact that the
preliminary elaboration of measures for assisting the formation of a
Provisional Korean Democratic Government, in accordance with
the decision of the Moscow Conference of the Three Foreign Ministers
is in the charge of the Joint Commission composed of representatives of the Soviet Command in Northern Korea and the American
Command in Southern Korea. According to the Moscow decision,
the recommendations drawn up by the Joint Commission are to be
submitted for the consideration of the four Governments, including
the Governments of Great Britain and China, prior to final decisions being taken on them. Furthermore, the Governments of Great
Britain and China are to take part, jointly with the Governments of
the USSR and the USA, in the examination of measures proposed
by the USSR-US Joint Commission to help and assist (trusteeship)
in the political, economic and social progress of the Korean people, the
development of democratic self-government and the establishment
of the national independence of Korea, with a view to working out
an agreement concerning a four-Power trusteeship of Korea.

The task of the USSR-US Joint Commission, as is well known, is
to assist the formation of a single Provisional Democratic Government for all Korea.

The Joint Commission has indeed still done very little in this
respect, but this situation is chiefly the result of the position taken
by the American delegation on the question of consultation by the
Commission with Korean democratic parties and social organizations, as was noted in my last letter to you. If the American delegation had manifested a proper desire to assist the formation of a real
democratic government in Korea, the work of the Joint Commission
would have been more fruitful, the task laid upon it might have been
performed, and there would not have been that state of stagnation
in the work of the Joint Commission which is referred to in Mr
Lovett's letter as a stalemate.

As you know, the Soviet delegation, desirous of resolving the situation which has arisen in the Joint Commission, and anxious to expedite
the work of forming a Provisional Korean Democratic Government,
agreed to the proposal of the American delegation not to consult orally
with the Korean democratic parties and social organizations, and

on 26 August made a new proposal, namely, to set up a consultative body—a Provisional All-Korean People's Assembly—consisting of representatives of the democratic parties and social organizations of all Korea. This proposal should not, in our opinion, meet with objection on the part of the American delegation, since it would remove the difficulties which the Joint Commission has encountered.

It is necessary to add to the above that the effective realization of the measure outlined in the proposal of the Soviet delegation is possible only on the basis of the free and unhampered activity of democratic parties and organizations, representatives of which in Southern Korea are now being subjected to arrest and other repressive measures, which is incompatible with the principles of democracy and law, as well as with the obligations which the Governments of the USA and the USSR have taken upon themselves with regard to Korea.

In respect to the assertions contained in Mr Lovett's letter regarding the attitude of the Soviet delegation in the Joint Commission, the substance of which is that the Soviet delegation has allegedly not displayed adequate understanding for the American delegation's proposals, I see no necessity to dwell on these assertions since they are obviously without foundation.

I cannot, on the other hand, refrain from expressing regret at such actions unilaterally taken by you as the sending of an invitation to the Governments of Great Britain and China to take part in the discussion of this question and the fixing of a place and date for the conference.

Your proposal that the question of forming a Provisional Korean Democratic Government should be submitted to the Governments of the four countries is considered by the Soviet Government to be inexpedient, since the Joint Commission has not yet by far exhausted all its possibilities in respect to the working out of agreed recommendations, which is quite possible. The 'United States Proposals Regarding Korea' set forth in Mr Lovett's letter are likewise unacceptable. These proposals could not but result in further disuniting Korea, since they envisage the formation of separate provisional legislative assemblies in South and North Korea (in the Soviet and American zones), whereas the vital task is to secure as soon as possible the formation of a single, if provisional, organ of government—an All-Korean Provisional Democratic Government. The American proposals would not put an end to the present situation in Korea—the division of the country into two zones, to the termination of which all our efforts should be directed—but, on the contrary, would perpetuate this abnormal situation.

In view of the fact that the proposal to examine the question of Korea at a joint conference of representatives of the four Powers does not follow from the Moscow Decision of the Three Foreign Ministers on Korea, and bearing in mind the above considerations, the Soviet Government does not think it possible to accept the proposals made in Mr Lovett's letter.

I am sending copies of this letter to the Governments of Great Britain and China.

The Soviet Union and the Korean Question (Documents), Ministry of Foreign Affairs of the USSR, Moscow, 1948, pp. 36-8.

3   *26 September* 1947

STATEMENT OF CHIEF SOVIET DELEGATE TO THE US-USSR JOINT COMMISSION ON KOREA PRO- POSING THE WITHDRAWAL OF SOVIET AND AMERICAN TROOPS FROM KOREA

The Soviet delegation in the USSR-US Joint Commission has made repeated declarations insisting on the strict implementation of the Moscow Decision of the Three Foreign Ministers on Korea.

With the help of the great Allies, the Korean nation is to receive its democratic government and its independence. The principal document expressing the desire of the Allied states to render the Korean nation assistance in its revival as a state is the Moscow Decision of the Three Foreign Ministers on Korea. That decision sets forth the programme of the Allies concerning the restoration of Korea as a free and independent state.

It is well known that the majority of the Korean people, the Korean democratic parties and social organizations, have expressed their approval of this decision. It is also known that certain political parties and their reactionary leaders have come out, and are coming out, against the Moscow Decision. The reactionary leaders and their protectors are to blame for the fact that to this day no Provisional Democratic Government of Korea has been formed.

The Soviet delegation, which represents the Soviet Command in Korea, and which for the past year and a half has been following all the political events and the sentiments and aspirations of the Korean people, is in a position to affirm that from the very first days of their liberation from the yoke of Japanese imperialism the Korean people began to display immense interest in political life, and have been striving to acquire skill in administering their state independently.

Already in August 1945, when the Soviet Army came to Korea, the Korean people everywhere set up popular government bodies in the shape of People's Committees in the localities, and a Central People's Committee as the organ of a people's republic. These government bodies were made up of representatives of all sections of the Korean people.

The Soviet delegation is also in a position to affirm that in the two years of their activity the People's Committees in North Korea, acting as popular government bodies, have carried out a tremendous amount of work and have put into effect a number of democratic reforms supported and approved by the people. It should be noted, however, that great difficulties are encountered in the course of this work. These difficulties consist in the fact that the leading personnel lack the necessary experience in dealing with state problems. True enough, we know that people are not born with experience, that experience is acquired in the course of practical activity. That is why the five-year trusteeship term envisaged in the Moscow Decision of the Three Ministers is quite sufficient for national government personnel to grow up in Korea.

A different situation has developed in South Korea. The People's Committees are not recognized as popular government bodies by the American Military Command. The People's Committees in South Korea are permitted no part in the administration of political and economic life, and consequently it has been made difficult for leading government personnel to grow up from the ranks of the Korean people.

No democratic reforms have been carried out. The democratic parties and social organizations which support the Moscow Decision on Korea, their leaders, their members, and even persons sympathizing with these organizations, are subjected to harsh persecutions.

The reactionary leaders of certain political parties in southern Korea, who are opposed to democratic reforms and to Korea's development along democratic lines, have come out, and are coming out, against the Moscow Decision of the Three Foreign Ministers. The reason they give is that the Moscow Decision provides for trusteeship which, they allege, the Korean people cannot accept.

The Korean reactionary Press, and for that matter certain American newspapers too, have tried to spread among the Korean people the belief that trusteeship was instituted on the demand of the Soviet Union, that the Soviet Union, allegedly, is out to seize Korea and establish there a Soviet régime.

The Soviet delegation considers it necessary to deny the rumours emanating from reactionary circles to the effect that the Soviet Union intends to seize Korea and establish there a Soviet régime, to brand them as fabrications, as hostile to the Soviet Union. At the Conference of the Three Foreign Ministers in Moscow, as we all know, the question of Korea was discussed at the initiative of the American delegation. In the American draft it was suggested that a single administration should be set up in Korea, headed by the two commanders, who were to govern Korea until trusteeship was established. The American draft provided for setting up an administrative body of representatives of four states (the USA, China, the United Kingdom and the USSR), which was to act on behalf of the United Nations and the people of Korea. This administrative body was to exercise such executive, legislative and judicial power as might be necessary for effectively governing Korea until a Korean government was formed. Furthermore, the administrative body was to exercise its powers and functions through a High Commissioner. This method of governing Korea was to operate for five years. That term could be prolonged for another five years, which actually meant that Korea would be governed under a mandate for ten years. The American draft did not envisage the formation of a Korean government.

Naturally, the Soviet Union could not agree to those proposals of the American delegation—firstly, because Korea had not been a belligerent state and had not fought against the Allies, and, secondly, because a five-year term was ample for the re-establishment of Korea as a state, for setting up state institutions, and for training personnel capable of independently administering the state.

The Soviet delegation submitted its draft proposals to the Ministers. The Soviet proposals reckoned with the interests and aspirations of the Korean people and provided for the formation of a Provisional Korean Democratic Government which was to participate in working out measures for helping and assisting (trusteeship) in the political, economic and social progress of the Korean people, in the development of democratic self-government and the establishment of Korea's independence as a state.

The proposal of the Soviet delegation was adopted at the conference of Ministers with minor amendments. It will be clear to every Korean who compares the American proposals on Korea submitted to the Foreign Ministers with the decision which was adopted by the Three Ministers that the Moscow Decision is the more progressive one with regard to Korea, that it takes into consideration the interests of the Korean people. The Korean reactionaries are opposed to this decision because they do not want Korea to develop along democratic lines, they do not want the democratic reforms demanded by the Korean people.

We are certain that the Korean people will not be deceived or intimidated by the hue and cry and the slander. There are parties and leaders in Korea who are closely linked with the people, know their desires and aspirations, and are capable of deciding for themselves as to what is best for them : arbitrary rule, tyranny, disfranchisement, poverty and colonial dependence, or freedom, democratic rights and a free, democratic independent Korean state. The Korean nation is not to be bought with riches from overseas ; it has plenty of wealth in its own country, and once it is the master of that wealth it can in a brief space of time become one of the advanced nations of Asia.

The Soviet delegation, furthermore, cannot understand the attitude of the American delegation, which thinks that, inasmuch as there are Koreans who want no trusteeship, the latter may be dispensed with. The Soviet delegation is for trusteeship only because it has been provided for by the Moscow Decision, which was signed by our Ministers and must be implemented with all exactitude.

The Soviet delegation cannot understand why the American delegation, while taking a benevolent attitude towards the activities of a small handful of Korean reactionaries flaunting the slogan of fighting against trusteeship, shows no desire to implement the Moscow Decision on Korea which the American Government itself adopted. The Soviet delegation on its part has bent all efforts, in strict pursuance of the Moscow Decision, to accelerate the formation of a single Democratic Government for the whole of Korea. However, the attitude taken by the American delegation has so far prevented the formation of such a government.

The Soviet delegation believes that the idea that trusteeship can be dispensed with while American and Soviet troops are on Korean territory would be a fraud on the Korean people. Korea can be a free and independent state only when it has its own democratic government supported by the people, and when the American and Soviet troops are withdrawn from its territory.

The Soviet Union's attitude to small nations has always been, and is, one of respect ; it has always striven and will continue to strive for their independence and sovereignty. The Soviet delegation therefore holds that the Koreans may be given the opportunity to form a government by themselves, without the aid and participation of the Allies, on condition that the American and Soviet troops are withdrawn from Korea. The Soviet delegation declares that, if the American delegation agrees to the proposal that all foreign troops should be withdrawn in the beginning of 1948, the Soviet troops will be prepared to leave Korea simultaneously with the American troops.

The Soviet delegation has no other proposals to make. In the process of the work of the Joint Commission it has explained fully enough its view on the ways of re-establishing Korea as an independent democratic state.

The Soviet delegation is waiting for an answer and for proposals from the American delegation.

The Soviet Union and the Korean Question (Documents), Ministry of Foreign Affairs of the USSR, Moscow, 1948, pp. 42-6.

4   *9 October* 1947

LETTER FROM SOVIET FOREIGN MINISTER V. M. MOLOTOV TO US SECRETARY OF STATE GEORGE MARSHALL ON ESTABLISHING AN INDEPENDENT KOREAN GOVERNMENT

The position taken up by the delegation of the United States of America in the USSR-US Joint Commission in Seoul bears witness that the USA delegation is not desirous of continuing the work of the Joint Commission with the object of achieving, on the basis of strict observance of the Moscow Agreement on Korea, agreed decisions on matters connected with the formation of a Provisional Korean Democratic Government.

In contravention of the Moscow Agreement on Korea and the understanding reached between the Governments of the USSR and the USA in May 1947 regarding the conditions for the resumption of the work of the Joint Commission, the USA delegation insists that not only democratic parties and groups of northern and southern Korea which signed the declaration of support of the aims of the Moscow Agreement and which loyally adhere to the terms of this declaration shall take part in the formation of the Korean government, but also reactionary groups which, although they have signed the declaration, are combating the Moscow Agreement and continue to belong to the so-called 'Anti-Trusteeship Committee', which is contrary to the aforesaid understanding between the Governments of the USSR and the USA. Naturally, the Soviet delegation, which consistently upholds the principles of the Moscow Agreement, cannot agree to this.

The attitude of the USA delegation had made it impossible to form a Provisional Korean Democratic Government in conformity with the Moscow Agreement, thus hampering the re-establishment of Korea as a single democratic state.

In view of this situation, the Government of the USSR instructed the Soviet delegation to submit a new proposal to the Joint Commission in Seoul, viz., the Koreans shall be given the opportunity

to form a government themselves, without the assistance or participation of the United States of America or the Soviet Union, on
condition that the American and Soviet troops are withdrawn from
Korea. If the Government of the USA agrees with the proposal to
withdraw all foreign troops from Korea in the beginning of 1948,
the Soviet troops will be ready to leave Korea simultaneously with
the American troops.

Notwithstanding the fact that this proposal was made by the
Soviet delegation at a meeting of the Joint Commission as far back
as 26 September, the USA delegation has regrettably not given a
reply to it to this day, a situation which cannot but retard the settlement of the Korean question.

As regards the proposal made in Mr Lovett's letter of 17 September
that the Korean question should be examined in the General Assembly of the United Nations, the attitude of the Soviet Government,
as you know, has already been stated by the Soviet delegation at
the General Assembly.

I am sending copies of this letter to the Governments of Great
Britain and China.

The Soviet Union and the Korean Question, pp. 47-8.

5   18 *October* 1947

UNITED STATES NOTE REPLYING TO THE SOVIET
PROPOSALS FOR ESTABLISHING AN INDEPENDENT
KOREAN GOVERNMENT (LETTER FROM R. A. LOVETT
TO V. M. MOLOTOV)

In your letter of 9 October 1947, you state that the position taken
by the United States delegation in the Joint Soviet-American Commission at Seoul has delayed a decision on the Korean question and
you refer to the proposal made by the Soviet delegation in Seoul on
26 September 1947, for the immediate simultaneous withdrawal of
the United States-Soviet occupation forces to which you state no
reply has been received.

The Secretary of State announced on 17 September that the
problem of setting up an independent Government for a unified
Korea would be presented to the General Assembly of the United
Nations and on 23 September the General Assembly voted to place
this question on its agenda. In the opinion of the United States
Government the question of withdrawal of occupation forces from
Korea must be considered an integral part of the solution of that
problem.

The United States delegation to the General Assembly meeting in New York City has now had circulated to the various delegations for their consideration a proposed resolution which is designed to bring about the early establishment of an independent Korean Government representative of the will of the Korean people, and the consequent speedy withdrawal of all occupation forces. In submitting this proposal to the Secretary General, specific attention was called to the Soviet proposal for the simultaneous withdrawal of troops with the statement of the United States' hope that having both proposals before it the General Assembly would be able to recommend a solution of the problem. A copy of the United States proposals was delivered to the Soviet delegation in New York prior to its being communicated to the Secretary General of the United Nations for transmission to the other delegations.

In view of the continued inability of the Soviet and United States delegations in the Joint Commission to agree on how to proceed with their work and the refusal of the Soviet Government to participate in discussions on this problem with the other Governments adhering to the Moscow Agreement on Korea, the United States Government considers it is obligated to seek the assistance of the United Nations in order that, as the Secretary of State said on 17 September, 'the inability of two powers to reach agreement' should not further delay the early establishment of an independent, united Korea.

Copies of this letter have been furnished to the Governments of the United Kingdom and China.

Korea 1945 to 1948, Department of State Publication 3305, Washington D.C., 1948, pp. 50-1.

II   UN GENERAL ASSEMBLY'S SEARCH FOR A POLITICAL SOLUTION

6   17 *September* 1947

SPEECH BY US SECRETARY OF STATE GENERAL MARSHALL, INTRODUCING THE KOREAN PROBLEM IN THE UN GENERAL ASSEMBLY (EXCERPT)

I turn now to the question of the independence of Korea. At Cairo in December 1943, the United States, the United Kingdom, and China joined in declaring that in due course Korea should become free and independent. This multilateral pledge was reaffirmed in the

Potsdam Declaration of July 1945 and subscribed to by the Union of Soviet Socialist Republics when it entered the war against Japan. In Moscow in December of 1945, the Foreign Ministers of the USSR, the United Kingdom, and the United States concluded an agreement designed to bring about the independence of Korea. This agreement was later adhered to by the Government of China. It provided for the establishment of a Joint US-USSR Commission to meet in Korea and, through consultations with Korean democratic parties and social organizations, to decide on methods for establishing a provisional Korean government. The Joint Commission was then to consult with that provisional government on methods of giving aid and assistance to Korea, any agreement reached being submitted for approval to the four Powers adhering to the Moscow Agreement.

For about two years the United States Government has been trying to reach agreement with the Soviet Government, through the Joint Commission and otherwise, on methods of implementing the Moscow Agreement and thus bringing about the independence of Korea. The United States representatives have insisted that any settlement of the Korean problem must in no way infringe the fundamental democratic right of freedom of opinion. That is still the position of my Government. Today the independence of Korea is no further advanced than it was two years ago. Korea remains divided at the 38th parallel with Soviet forces in the industrial north and United States forces in the agricultural south. There is little or no exchange of goods or services between the two zones. Korea's economy is thus crippled.

The Korean people, not former enemies but a people liberated from 40 years of Japanese oppression, are still not free. This situation must not be allowed to continue indefinitely. In an effort to make progress the United States Government recently made certain proposals designed to achieve the purposes of the Moscow Agreement and requested the Powers adhering to that Agreement to join in discussion of these proposals. China and the United Kingdom agreed to this procedure. The Soviet Government did not. Furthermore, the United States and Soviet Delegations to the Joint Commission have not even been able to agree on a joint report on the status of their deliberations. It appears evident that further attempts to solve the Korean problem by means of bilateral negotiations will serve only to delay the establishment of an independent, united Korea.

It is therefore the intention of the United States Government to present the problem of Korean independence to this session of the General Assembly. Although we shall be prepared to submit suggestions as to how the early attainment of Korean independence

might be effected, we believe that this is a matter which now requires the impartial judgement of the other members. We do not
want to have the inability of two Powers to reach agreement delay
any further the urgent and rightful claims of the Korean people to
independence.

UN Official Records of the Second Session of the General Assembly, Plenary Meetings,
Vol. I, 16 September–13 November 1947, Lake Success, New York, pp. 21-2.

7   13 *November* 1947

SOVIET REPRESENTATIVE ANDREI GROMYKO'S SPEECH AT THE UN GENERAL ASSEMBLY ON THE KOREAN QUESTION

Taking into account the importance of the question of Korea,
the delegation of the Soviet Union considers it essential to outline
its position with regard to this question at the plenary meeting of
the General Assembly. It is essential to do so if only because the
resolution adopted by the First Committee, which is now submitted
to the General Assembly for confirmation, does not provide a solution for this question. Furthermore, this resolution which, as is
known, has been imposed by the United States of America only
serves to complicate the whole question, because the basis of this
resolution is not the interests of the Korean people, but the designs
of the United States which has undermined and continues to undermine an appropriate and equitable solution of the question of the
future of Korea. The delegation of the Union of Soviet Socialist
Republics expressed the attitude of the Government of the Soviet
Union with regard to the Korean question, and cast light upon all
the details of the various aspects of this important question in an
attempt to assist the other delegations in reaching their conclusions.

In this connexion, we based ourselves upon the circumstances
that the position of the Soviet Union with regard to Korea was
usually pictured in a distorted fashion and in an incorrect light,
and was often just simply distorted. This was done by the Government of the United States of America, by its official representatives
here in the United States of America and in southern Korea. Of
course, the detailed discussion of this question in the First Committee relieved the delegation of the Soviet Union of the need for
embarking upon the details of this question at the plenary meeting
of the General Assembly.

Therefore, I shall merely touch upon the most important questions which arise in connexion with the resolution submitted by the First Committee. I shall deal principally with the Soviet Union and United States proposals concerning the problem of Korea.

First of all, it is essential to point out that the Government of the Soviet Union applied every effort to reach a solution to the question of Korea which would be fully in accordance with the obligations which the Soviet Union, the United States and the United Kingdom had taken upon themselves, obligations to which China subsequently adhered, obligations which were set forth in the Moscow Agreement of 27 December 1945.

According to that Agreement, the Allied Powers were to ensure the restoration of Korea as an independent state, the establishment of an interim Korean democratic government and the establishment of conditions calculated to assist the country's development upon democratic bases. Moreover, the United States and the Soviet Union which, as is known, maintain troops upon Korean territory took special obligations upon themselves under that agreement which I have just mentioned.

With the help of a Joint Commission which was established in accordance with this Agreement, the United States and the Soviet Union obligated themselves to prepare recommendations which, after consideration by the Governments of the four Powers, were to govern the United States and the Union of Soviet Socialist Republics in adopting the final decisions for achieving the aim which I have indicated, the aim being the establishment of an independent democratic Korean Government.

The Agreement set forth the methods by which the Governments of the two Powers were to settle the questions before them. It was provided that the Joint Commission, in preparing its recommendations, was to consult with democratic political parties and social organizations of Korea. This is easy to understand since it is impossible not to take into account the opinion of the Korean people when decisions are taken which will determine their future.

Unfortunately, the work of the Joint Commission reached a deadlock almost from the inception of its mission because the United States refused to implement its obligations, in the first instance, with regard to the consultation which I have mentioned. Regardless of the obligations taken upon themselves by both Governments to consult with democratic parties and social organizations, the representatives of the United States in the Joint Commission insisted upon consultations with anti-democratic parties and organizations which, moreover, had fought against the Moscow Agreement, and the United States categorically objected to consultations with democratic parties and organizations of South Korea.

The United States objected to consultations with the All-Korean Confederation of Labour, the All-Korean Women's Association, the All-Korean Youth Alliance, the All-Korean Peasants Union—comprised of more than three million peasants—and many other organizations.

At the very beginning of the work of the Joint Commission, it became clear that the obligations which the United States had taken upon itself in accordance with the Moscow Agreement, in essence, were a manoeuvre, because the behaviour of the United States representatives in the Commission was diametrically opposed to what was provided for under that Agreement.

Through its representatives on the Joint Commission, and also through letters of the Minister of Foreign Affairs of the Union of Soviet Socialist Republics—V. M. Molotov—letters which were addressed to Secretary of State Marshall of the United States of America, the Government of the Soviet Union repeatedly insisted upon the need to implement the exact terms of the Moscow Agreement.

After an interruption in its work which lasted from May 1946 through April 1947, the Joint Commission again renewed its sessions. However, no appreciable results ensued because the position taken by the Government of the United States with regard to consultation was in contradiction to the Moscow Agreement on the establishment of an independent democratic Korean State. The United States would not budge from this position. Thus, the United States Government flagrantly violated its obligations and made impossible the implementation of the Moscow Agreement.

I consider it essential to make this clear again because the United States delegation to this General Assembly, following the example of the United States representative on the Joint Soviet-American Commission in Korea, is distorting the true state of things in an attempt to accuse the Soviet Union and condemn the Soviet Union because it has been impossible to settle the Korean question so far, although, as is well known, the United States delegation was unable to cite a single fact in order to confirm these declarations or its position as a whole. This causes small wonder since the very facts served to expose the true situation in Korea.

The delegation of the Soviet Union, as well as several other delegations, cited numerous such facts before the First Committee. These facts expose, as I have said, the true situation in Korea ; they expose the double game being played by the United States with regard to the Korean question. These facts serve to justify and confirm the position of the Soviet Union, which insisted upon the need of strictly implementing the obligations which the Allied Governments had taken upon themselves with regard to Korea.

I cannot but point to the fact that the State Department of the United States of America, as well as the United States representatives on the Joint Soviet-American Commission in Korea, released *communiqués* to the Press which systematically were divergent from the facts. The falsification of facts became their accustomed method, and this only served to cast new doubts upon the intentions of the leading circles of the United States with regard to settling the question of Korea in agreement with other states and in full accordance with the genuine interests of the Korean people through the establishment of an independent and democratic Korea.

In this respect, a kind of competition took place between the State Department and the Military Command of the United States of America in Southern Korea. All this tendentious propaganda and hubbub could not conceal the desire to bury or pigeonhole the entire Moscow Plan for the settlement of the Korean question and to replace it with some special United States plan which apparently pursued its own designs in Korea, if we base our considerations not upon the official statements made by the representatives of the United States of America, but if we base them upon the facts.

Everything having been done for the United States and the Soviet Union to act in full accordance with the obligations they had taken on themselves with regard to Korea, and having convinced itself that the Government of the United States, for some reason, did not wish to implement these obligations but merely lengthen and undermine the work of the Joint Soviet-American Commission, on 26 September of this year the Government of the Soviet Union, through its representatives on the Joint Commission, submitted its new proposals with regard to Korea.

The substance of these proposals, as is well known, is that all foreign troops on Korean territory were to be evacuated from Korea at the beginning of 1948. Thus, it was stipulated that the Korean people was to settle its internal affairs alone, without interference ; it was to organize elections to representative bodies ; it was to establish a national government of Korea ; it was to establish its own armed forces and to organize the whole internal political and economic life of the country upon a democratic basis, without any pressure or interference from outside.

It is not difficult to have it perfectly clear in one's mind that the Soviet Union proposals are fully in accordance with the interests of the Korean people, interests which cannot but correspond with our own interests for the maintenance of international peace and security. The Soviet Union proposals provide for a radical solution of the Korean question, removing all difficulties and complications which had arisen with regard to the implementation of the obligations which the Allied governments had taken upon themselves. These new proposals, by affording to the Korean people an opportunity to settle all its internal state affairs without interference, give and provide for the simplest solution of the Korean question.

To this it may be added that the Soviet Union proposals are in full accord with the national dignity and the national feeling of the Korean people. They meet its natural feeling of national dignity, and if one considers all that, the meaning of these proposals will become perfectly clear.

What is the reaction in Korea to these new Soviet Union proposals ? The Korean people, as we know fully well, met these Soviet Union proposals with full approval ; not only did the democratic leaders and the democratic parties and not only did the social organizations of Korea welcome these proposals ; more than that, these proposals were welcomed by many leaders of the rightist parties and organizations. This fact was published and reported repeatedly in the last few days, and in the American Press in particular. For instance, this fact was reported in *The New York Times* of 5 November of this year, in an article by Rosenthal.

Among the Korean people, only sworn enemies of the Koreans object to the evacuation of foreign troops. Those who object are hopeless reactionaries, upon whom the United States Military Command in Southern Korea leans, in its activities. These men know that they dare not meet their own people face to face, if and when the United States troops are withdrawn from Korea. They are prepared to trade and bargain with Korea, provided they get what they want on the barrel-head. They are prepared to sell and betray the interests of their people in order to please their foreign masters.

As regards the leading circles of the United States of America, it may be seen from the position of the United States delegation to the General Assembly that the new Soviet Union proposals completely mixed up the cards in the hand of these circles.

As is well known so far, an important role in American propaganda on Korea was played by assertions to the effect that the United States are interested in a most rapid evacuation of foreign troops from Korea. However, when the new Soviet Union proposals were submitted for the evacuation of all foreign troops from Korea, instead of supporting these proposals, the United States began to object to them strenuously. Thus, the United States showed the hypocrisy of its assertions about its desire to evacuate its troops from Korea as rapidly as possible.

When the Soviet Union proposals were discussed in the First Committee, the United States delegation, in substance, eschewed a discussion of the gist of these proposals and confined itself to several particular comments which were hardly connected in themselves. This bore witness to the fact that the United States delegation was afraid to consider these proposals, but was well aware that it was unable to give any kind of convincing proof against the proposals of the Soviet Union.

In the meantime, the United States delegation in the First Committee hammered one point. It requested and demanded a rapid vote upon its proposals which, as is well known, are substantially opposed to and different from the Soviet Union proposals. The proposals of the United States put everything upside down. The evacuation of foreign troops from Korean territory, according to these proposals, must not precede the election of representative organs and the establishment of a democratic government in Korea, but on the contrary, this evacuation is considered as a concluding measure in a chain of events proposed in the United States plan. As a matter of fact, no definite time limits whatever are established for the evacuation of foreign troops from Korea under the United States plan. The United States proposal contains a formula which does not obligate anybody to do anything, a formula to the effect that the armies are to be evacuated as rapidly as possible after elections have taken place and after a new government has been established. Is it not obvious what are the designs of the authors of this proposal ? Under the United States plan, the carrying out of elections to representative organs, including elections to the national assembly of Korea and the establishment of a national government, must take place while foreign troops are present in that country. Naturally, this cannot be evaluated otherwise than as an attempt to run the elections while foreign interference in the internal affairs of Korea is taking place, with a view to ensuring the election to the representative bodies and the inclusion in the Government of persons upon whom the United States military authorities have been leaning for a long time—in other words, sworn reactionaries who are concerned not so much with the fate of the Korean people as with their own profit and benefits for themselves and their foreign protectors.

This whole American plan is not one which would permit the Korean people freedom to express its will. At the same time, it serves the purpose of reactionary anti-democratic groups in Korea, because it is calculated to help them remain in power. As we see it, the designs in the United States plan are quite simple. Unfortunately, these plans and designs do not correspond with the interest of the

Korean people or with common interests for the establishment and maintenance of international co-operation, because the United States proposals, in their implementation, would amount not to the establishment of a democratic Korean Government, but the establishment of an anti-democratic government which would depend upon the United States, and would, in fact, become a colony of the United States.

This conclusion is patent and unavoidable, particularly if we take into account the whole character of the United States proposal, which, as is well known, is at the basis of the Resolution adopted by the First Committee. This conclusion will also become patent when we take into account the attitude of the Government of the United States towards the Soviet Union proposals for evacuation and consultation.

In order to shield and to screen the true gist of the United States proposal, the delegation of the United States submitted a proposal, which was also adopted by the First Committee, for the establishment of a so-called temporary commission of the United Nations, which, according to the plans of the champions of this proposal, is supposed to ensure control over Korea during the elections and during the establishment of the Korean national government. However, the establishment of this commission would not change the substance of the matter. More than that, the decision for the establishment of the commission makes this whole United States plan still more blatant and unacceptable to all those who want to see the establishment of a genuine democratic Korea rather than to play with words, behind which are concealed reactionary projects calculated to achieve the enslavement of the Korean people by United States monopolies. The establishment of such a commission is unacceptable because it contradicts the principle of national self-determination of the Korean people, and would simply transform this commission into a screen which would hide the one-sided actions of the United States in southern Korea, actions which, as I have already pointed out, are designed to transform Korea into a United States colony.

If we look at the actions of the United States rather than the words of the United States, if we look at the policy of the United States in southern Korea, that is, the policy of the United States Military Government in southern Korea, this conclusion becomes unavoidable. What I have said is further confirmed by the practices which the United States military authorities in southern Korea engaged in from the very beginning of the occupation.

When the question was being discussed in the First Committee, the Soviet Union delegation cited numerous facts which bore witness to the effect that the United States military authorities in southern Korea had engaged upon an anti-democratic campaign. The United States has placed its hope and faith in southern Korea upon narrow reactionary groups isolated from the Korean people, and the United States is furthering the activities of these groups which are directed against democratic parties and organizations. The United States, moreover, by its connivance, by its protection, furthers and promotes terroristic activities of semi-fascist organizations which have taken the road of open struggle against democratic forces of the country up to the point of the physical destruction of well-known leaders of Korean democratic parties and social organizations.

The Soviet Union delegation, in the First Committee, made numerous statements, and discussed numerous examples which confirmed the correctness of what I have just said. This policy of the United States military authorities in southern Korea has brought upon the United States military authorities the lawful indignation of the whole Korean people. This becomes clear if one reads the letter of the National Unified Democratic People's Front in northern Korea. This letter was written in the name of the various political organizations which are part of the Front. It was written two months ago, and it was sent to the Governments of the United States and the Soviet Union.

This letter reads as follows: 'What has been happening in southern Korea lately exceeds what had happened in the darkest days of reaction run rampant . . . '

The letter exposes the anti-democratic policy of the American military command. The delegation of the United States, for reasons which are clear, continues to be silent with regard to this remarkable document.

Almost daily, the world Press, including the American Press, publishes reports to the effect that reactionary and terroristic semi-fascist groups in southern Korea, acting with the connivance and support of the American authorities, are becoming more and more impudent. The discontent of the people—workers, peasants and educated people—grows day by day ; and small wonder, since in southern Korea no democratic reforms have been carried out, in contradistinction to what has happened in northern Korea.

The land, which for hundreds of years was the dream of the Korean peasant, still has not been distributed among those who are entitled to it—the peasants. The peasant in southern Korea still remains landless as distinguished from the peasant in northern Korea, where democratic reforms have taken place. Under these circumstances, could the Korean peasant be expected to support the prevailing order in southern Korea ? Of course he cannot.

Therefore, one should not wonder at the statement of the correspondent of *PM*, a newspaper, Mark Gayn. This correspondent visited Korea, and, on 3 November 1947, he wrote that 'the Russians have created a lot of friends for themselves. We have none.' We agree with this despatch of this correspondent.

I might adduce numerous facts to the effect that the status of Korean workers in southern Korea is no better than the status of the peasant. However, the whole world is well aware of that. The status of the workers is proved and evidenced by numerous strikes and protest demonstrations against the policies of the American authorities in southern Korea, and against the policies of the henchmen of the Americans—the Korean reactionaries.

If we take all that into account, can we wonder that numerous persons who have visited Korea harshly criticized the activities of the American military command there as soon as they got back from that land? Even Americans are indignant when they observe the situation which prevails in southern Korea. They indicate that the position not only has failed to improve but, on the contrary, it is becoming worse and worse; and that American authorities are completely indifferent to the fate of the Korean people.

That same correspondent of the newspaper *PM*, Mark Gayn, reports a conversation with regard to the status of the peasantry. He conversed with a certain American official on that subject. Of course, I am dealing with southern Korea. That official would have the correspondent believe that the Koreans apparently are accustomed to their system.

If we take all these facts into account, it becomes clear why the delegation of the United States has objected categorically to the consideration of the Korean question in the General Assembly in the presence of elected representatives of the Korean people. Apparently the United States delegation was afraid to hear the voice of the Korean people. The United States delegation presumably was afraid to hear the truth about the situation in southern Korea; and the delegation of the Soviet Union insisted upon hearing the truth from the representatives of the Korean people. The delegation of the Soviet Union insisted that the General Assembly cannot consider the substance of the Korean question without having heard the opinions of the representatives of the Korean people. As you well know, the representatives of the United States succeeded in stifling the voice of the Korean people in the General Assembly.

The resolution adopted by the First Committee was accepted in the absence of these representatives of the Korean people. This is a result of the ignoring of the interests of the Korean people. Such decisions are incompatible with the national dignity of the Korean people.

The significance of the United States proposal will become still clearer if we take into account not only the practice of the military authorities of the United States of America in southern Korea but also if we look at the statements of some official American statesmen about Korea, and the significance and importance of Korea to the United States of America.

In the course of the discussion in the First Committee, the Soviet Union delegation pointed to General Hodge's statement to the effect that the Americans have dug-in in Korea and that the Americans will remain there until they will have accomplished their mission. The Soviet Union delegation also pointed to the statement of the former Assistant Secretary of State, General Hilldring, who expressed fear that the evacuation of American troops from Korea would bring about serious reaction in the East. We have to pay due tribute to the tenor of these remarks. Such declarations shed light upon the plans of the United States, with regard to southern Korea in particular, because southern Korea is being fused into the economy of the United States more and more by the American authorities in Korea. Politically, southern Korea is being transformed into a centre of reaction in East Asia. Territorially, apparently, Korea is being considered as a base *sui generis* of the United States of America. It is not in vain that sections of the United States Press have already stressed the strategy of Korea. They made transparent and clear hints as to how and against whom such a base can be or should be utilized.

The eyes of these organs of the press are directed from Korea to the north, and to the northwest. These are the conditions under which we are asked to accept the United States plan for the settlement of the Korean question, a plan which is not at all designed to settle that question, but is merely calculated to create more complications and difficulties on the road towards the settlement of the question. It is clear that the responsibility for the situation is, in the first instance, borne by those who would impose such plans upon us. The Soviet Union will expose in the future, as it did before, all the designs of those who, under the banner of the United Nations, want to utilize Korea for interests which have nothing in common with the maintenance of international peace and security. The Soviet Union will attempt to reach a settlement on the question of the future of Korea which will correspond with the basic national interests of the Korean people, and which would at the same time, be fully in agreement and in accordance with our common interests in the cause of strengthening the peace and security of the nations of the world.

The Soviet Union, in the First Committee, has already pointed out that the substance of the Korean question cannot be considered in the General Assembly, and that the General Assembly cannot adopt decisions in the absence of the representatives of the Korean people.

Since the majority in the First Committee decided to consider this question in its substance, and to adopt a decision, the delegation of the Union of Soviet Socialist Republics declared that it did not consider it possible to take part in the voting on any proposal bearing upon the substance of the question, for reasons which I have already outlined. For these very same reasons, the Soviet Union delegation does not find it possible to participate in the vote on the resolution submitted by the Political Committee. It cannot, therefore, vote in this plenary meeting of the General Assembly.

Korea, 1945 to 1948, pp. 51-61.

8   14 *November* 1947

RESOLUTION OF THE UN GENERAL ASSEMBLY ESTABLISHING THE UNITED NATIONS TEMPORARY COMMISSION ON KOREA

A

Inasmuch as the Korean question which is before the General Assembly is primarily a matter for the Korean people itself and concerns its freedom and independence, and

Recognizing that this question cannot be correctly and fairly resolved without the participation of representatives of the indigenous population,

The General Assembly

(1) *Resolves* that elected representatives of the Korean people be invited to take part in the consideration of the question ;

(2) *Further resolves* that in order to facilitate and expedite such participation and to observe that the Korean representatives are in fact duly elected by the Korean people and not mere appointees by military authorities in Korea, there be forthwith established a United Nations Temporary Commission on Korea, to be present in Korea, with right to travel, observe and consult throughout Korea.

B

The General Assembly,

Recognizing the urgent and rightful claims to independence of the people of Korea ;

Believing that the national independence of Korea should be re-established and all occupying forces then withdrawn at the earliest practicable date ;

Recalling its previous conclusion that the freedom and independence of the Korean people cannot be correctly or fairly resolved without the participation of representatives of the Korean people, and its decision to establish a United Nations Temporary Commission on Korea (hereinafter called the 'Commission') for the purpose of facilitating and expediting such participation by elected representatives of the Korean people,

(1) *Decides* that the Commission shall consist of representatives of Australia, Canada, China, El Salvador, France, India, Philippines, Syria, Ukrainian Soviet Socialist Republic ;

(2) *Recommends* that the elections be held not later than 31 March 1948 on the basis of adult suffrage and by secret ballot to choose representatives with whom the Commission may consult regarding the prompt attainment of the freedom and independence of the Korean people and which representatives, constituting a National Assembly, may establish a National Government of Korea. The number of representatives from each voting area or zone should be proportionate to the population, and the elections should be under the observation of the Commission ;

(3) *Further recommends* that as soon as possible after the elections, the National Assembly should convene and form a National Government and notify the Commission of its formation ;

(4) *Further recommends* that immediately upon the establishment of a National Government, that Government should, in consultation with the Commission : (*a*) constitute its own national security forces and dissolve all military or semi-military formations not included therein ; (*b*) take over the functions of government from the military commands and civilian authorities of north and south Korea, and (*c*) arrange with the occupying Powers for the complete withdrawal from Korea of their armed forces as early as practicable and if possible within ninety days ;

(5) *Resolves* that the Commission shall facilitate and expedite the fulfilment of the foregoing programme for the attainment of the national independence of Korea and withdrawal of occupying forces, taking into account its observations and consultations in Korea. The Commission shall report, with its conclusions, to the General Assembly and may consult with the Interim Committee (if one be

established) with respect to the application of this resolution in the light of developments ;

(6) *Calls upon* the Member States concerned to afford every assistance and facility to the Commission in the fulfilment of its responsibilities ;

(7) *Calls upon* all Members of the United Nations to refrain from interfering in the affairs of the Korean people during the interim period preparatory to the establishment of Korean independence, except in pursuance of the decisions of the General Assembly ; and thereafter, to refrain completely from any and all acts derogatory to the independence and sovereignty of Korea.

UN Official Records of the Second Session of the General Assembly, Resolutions 16 September–29 November 1947, Document No. A/519, pp. 16–181.

9   6 *February* 1948

STATEMENT BY THE UNITED NATIONS TEMPORARY
COMMISSION ON KOREA ON NON-PARTICIPATION
OF THE SOVIET GOVERNMENT IN THE COMMISSION

The United Nations Temporary Commission on Korea has taken note of the following facts :

That the Commission was informed by the Secretary-General of the United Nations on 25 January 1948 that the attitude of the Government of the Ukrainian Soviet Socialist Republic in the matter of appointing a representative to the Temporary Commission on Korea remains the same as presented by the Ukrainian delegation at the second session of the General Assembly ;

That a cable was received by the Secretariat of the Commission from the United Nations headquarters on 23 January 1948 quoting the Permanent Representative of the Union of Soviet Socialist Republics to the United Nations, Mr Gromyko, as follows :

'In connexion with your letter of 18 January 1948 transmitting the text of a letter from the Acting Chairman of the Commission on Korea, in which he expresses desire to visit the Commander of Soviet troops in Northern Korea, we find it necessary to remind you of the negative attitude taken by the Soviet Government towards the establishment of the United Nations Temporary Commission on Korea as already stated by the Soviet delegation during the second session of the General Assembly of the United Nations' ;

That the Commission requested the Secretary-General of the United Nations, on 16 January 1948, to remind the Government of the Soviet Union of the Secretary-General's letter of 24 November 1947 drawing attention to paragraph 6 of the substantive part of the General Assembly resolution calling on Member States concerned to afford every assistance and facility to the Commission in the fulfilment of its responsibilities, and that no reply has been received from the Soviet Government either to the letter of 24 November 1947 or to the reminder ;

That, up to date, the Commission has received no reply to the letter addressed to General Korotkov expressing the desire of the Acting Chairman of the Commission to exchange the appropriate courtesies with the officers commanding the armed forces in North and South Korea, which letter was despatched to North Korea by train on 20 January 1948, while the train which left Pyongyang on 30 January 1948 did not carry any message from the Soviet authorities in North Korea ;

That efforts were made to deliver other communications from the United Nations Temporary Commission on Korea to North Korea, but that the Soviet officials would neither sign for nor accept the communications transmitted by the Commission.

UN Document A/AC. 18/23, 16 February 1948.

10–11   6 *February* 1948 & 11 *February* 1948

RESOLUTIONS OF THE TEMPORARY COMMISSION ON CONSULTATION WITH THE UN INTERIM COMMITTEE

I   *6 February 1948*

The United Nations Temporary Commission on Korea,

Having considered that the negative attitude of the Soviet Authorities with regard to the work of the Commission has made it clear that it will not be possible for the Commission to exercise for the time being the functions conferred upon it by the General Assembly under the resolutions of 14 November 1947 in the part of Korea occupied by the Armed Forces of the Union of Soviet Socialist Republics,

Having considered that the General Assembly, in resolution II of 14 November 1947, paragraph 5, authorized the Commission to consult with the Interim Committee with respect to the application of this resolution in the light of developments ;

Having considered the preliminary results of the work of its Sub-Committees and in particular the consultations held to date by Sub-Committee 2 ;

Resolves

(1) That the Commission shall consult with the Interim Committee with respect to the application of the resolutions of 14 November in the light of developments ;

(2) That the Chairman, accompanied by the Assistant Secretary-General shall represent the Commission during the consideration of this question by the Interim Committee ;

(3) That in the accomplishment of this mission the Chairman shall be guided by such directives as the Commission may formulate.

2   *11 February 1948*

The United Nations Temporary Commission on Korea,

Having resolved to consult with the Interim Committee of the General Assembly ;

Resolves that this consultation should take place on the following questions :

(1) Is it open to or incumbent upon the Commission, under the terms of the General Assembly resolutions of 14 November 1947, and in the light of developments in the situation with respect to Korea since that date, to implement the programme as outlined in resolution II in that part of Korea which is occupied by the armed forces of the United States of America ?

(2) If not,

(*a*) Should the Commission observe the election of Korean representatives to take part in the consideration of the Korean question, as outlined in resolution I of 14 November 1947, provided that it has determined that elections can be held in a free atmosphere ? and

(*b*) Should the Commission consider such other measures as may be possible and advisable with a view to the attainment of its objectives ?

UN Doc. A/AC. 18/6, 6 February 1948 ; *UN Doc.* A/AC. 18/27, 17 February 1948.

12   *26 February* 1948

RESOLUTION OF THE UN INTERIM COMMITTEE
ON THE GENERAL ASSEMBLY
RESOLUTION ON KOREA (EXTRACT)

The Interim Committee,

Bearing in mind the views expressed by the Chairman of the United Nations Temporary Commission on Korea ;

Deeming it necessary that the programme set forth in the General Assembly resolutions of 14 November 1947 be carried out and as a necessary step therein that the United Nations Temporary Commission on Korea proceed with the observance of elections in all Korea, and if that is impossible, in as much of Korea as is accessible to it ; and

Considering it important that the elections be held to choose representatives of the Korean people with whom the United Nations Temporary Commission on Korea may consult regarding the prompt attainment of freedom and independence of the Korean people, which representatives, constituting a National Assembly, may establish a National Government of Korea ;

Resolves

That in its view it is incumbent upon the United Nations Temporary Commission on Korea, under the terms of the General Assembly resolution of 14 November 1947, and in the light of developments in the situation with respect to Korea since that date, to implement the programme as outlined in Part B of the resolution in such parts of Korea as are accessible to the Commission.

Report of the Interim Committee of the General Assembly (5 January–5 August 1948), General Assembly Official Records : Third Session, Supplement No. 10 (A/578, A/583, A/605, A/606), Paris 1948, p. 21.

13   *28 April* 1948

RESOLUTION OF THE TEMPORARY COMMISSION
ON OBSERVING THE KOREAN ELECTIONS

In order to comply with the provisions of the resolution passed at its 22nd meeting, on 12 March,

Having satisfied itself as a result of its extensive field observations in various key districts of south Korea that there exists in south Korea in a reasonable degree a free atmosphere wherein the democratic rights of freedom of speech, press and assembly are recognized and respected,

The United Nations Temporary Commission on Korea *resolves :*

To confirm that it will observe the elections announced by the commanding General of the United States Forces in Korea to be held on 10 May 1948.

Korea 1945 to 1948, p. 72.

14   25 *June* 1948

RESOLUTION OF THE TEMPORARY COMMISSION ON FREE BALLOTING IN THE KOREAN ELECTIONS

The United Nations Temporary Commission on Korea,

Having observed, in accordance with the terms of the Resolution of 14 November 1947 adopted by the General Assembly of the United Nations, the elections which were held on 10 May 1948 in that part of Korea accessible to the Commission ;

Having previously declared that there existed in that part of Korea a reasonable degree of free atmosphere wherein the democratic rights of freedom of speech, press and assembly were recognized and respected (document A/AC. 19/68) ;

Having taken into account the reports of its observation groups that such a free atmosphere existed during the elections ;

Having satisfied itself that the electoral procedures which it recommended had on the whole been correctly applied ;

Resolves :

To record its opinion that the results of the ballot of 10 May 1948 are a valid expression of the free will of the electorate in those parts of Korea which were accessible to the Commission and in which the inhabitants constituted approximately two-thirds of the people of all Korea.

Korea 1945 to 1948, pp. 72-3.

15   12 *December* 1948

RESOLUTION OF THE UN GENERAL ASSEMBLY ON THE PROBLEM OF THE INDEPENDENCE OF KOREA

The General Assembly,

Having regard to its resolution No. 112(II) of 14 November 1947, concerning the problem of the independence of Korea ;

Having considered the report of the United Nations Temporary Commission on Korea (hereinafter referred to as the 'Temporary Commission'), and the report of the Interim Committee of the General Assembly regarding its consultation with the Temporary Commission ;

Mindful of the fact that, due to difficulties referred to in the report of the Temporary Commission, the objectives set forth in the resolution of 14 November 1947 have not been fully accomplished, and in particular that unification of Korea has not yet been achieved;

(1) *Approves* the conclusions of the reports of the Temporary Commission;

(2) *Declares* that there has been established a lawful government (the Government of the Republic of Korea), having effective control and jurisdiction over that part of Korea where the Temporary Commission was able to observe and consult and in which the great majority of the people of all Korea reside; that this Government is based on elections which were a valid expression of the free will of the electorate of that part of Korea and which were observed by the Temporary Commission; and that this is the only such Government in Korea:

(3) *Recommends* that the occupying Powers should withdraw their occupation forces from Korea as early as practicable;

(4) *Resolves* that, as a means to the full accomplishment of the objectives set forth in the resolution of 14 November 1947, a Commission on Korea consisting of Australia, China, El Salvador, France, India, the Philippines and Syria shall be established to continue the work of the Temporary Commission and carry out the provisions of the present resolution, having in mind the status of the Government of Korea as herein defined, and in particular to:

(a)   Lend its good offices to bring about the unification of Korea and the integration of all Korean security forces in accordance with the principles laid down by the General Assembly in the resolution of 14 November 1947;

(b)   Seek to facilitate the removal of barriers to economic, social and other friendly intercourse caused by the division of Korea;

(c)   Be available for observation and consultation in the further development of representative government based on the freely-expressed will of the people;

(d)   Observe the actual withdrawal of the occupying forces and verify the fact of withdrawal when such has occurred; and for this purpose, if it so desires, request the assistance of military experts of the two occupying Powers;

(5) *Decides* that the Commission:

(a)   Shall, within thirty days of the adoption of the present resolution, proceed to Korea, where it shall maintain its seat;

(b)   Shall be regarded as having superseded the Temporary Commission established by the resolution of 14 November 1947;

(c)   Is authorized to travel, consult and observe throughout Korea;

(d)   Shall determine its own procedures;

(*e*)   May consult with the Interim Committee with respect to the discharge of its duties in the light of developments, and within the terms of the present resolution ;

(*f*)   Shall render a report to the next regular session of the General Assembly and to any prior special session which might be called to consider the subject-matter of the present resolution, and shall render such interim reports as it may deem appropriate to the Secretary-General for distribution to Members ;

(6) *Requests* that the Secretary-General shall provide the Commission with adequate staff and facilities, including technical advisers as required ; and authorizes the Secretary-General to pay the expenses and *per diem* of a representative and an alternate from each of the States members of the Commission ;

(7) *Calls upon* Member States concerned, the Government of the Republic of Korea, and all Koreans to afford every assistance and facility to the Commission in the fulfilment of its responsibilities ;

(8) *Calls upon* Member States to refrain from any acts derogatory to the results achieved and to be achieved by the United Nations in bringing about the complete independence and unity of Korea ;

(9) *Recommends* that Member States and other nations, in establishing their relations with the Government of the Republic of Korea, take into consideration the facts set out in paragraph (2) of the present resolution.

UN Official Records of the Third Session of the General Assembly, Resolutions, Part I, 21 September–12 December 1948, Document No. A/810, pp. 25-7.

16   28 *July* 1949

SUMMARY, ANALYSIS AND CONCLUSIONS OF THE REPORT OF THE UNITED NATIONS COMMISSION ON KOREA

(A) EFFORTS OF THE COMMISSION TO IMPLEMENT THE GENERAL ASSEMBLY RESOLUTION OF 12 DECEMBER 1948.

I. Unification

(*a*)   Efforts of the Commission to gain access to the north;

(1)   The Commission was no sooner established in Seoul than it began to consider means of obtaining access to the north. For that purpose, it sought to obtain the good offices of the Union of Soviet Socialist Republics ; it addressed a letter to General Kim Il Sung by various routes ; it made repeated broadcast appeals to the north

for facilities to permit a visit. All its efforts have met with failure, because until now there has been no response to these attempts of the Commission to contact the north.

(*b*)   Korean proposals for unification ;

(2) The Government of the Republic has proposed that the Commission approach the USSR to urge it to withdraw its troops from North Korea, to disband the North Korean régime and security forces, and to allow the Government of the Republic to assert jurisdiction in the northern zone. The accomplishment of the foregoing would be followed by elections in North Korea under the observation of the Commission.

Persons outside the Government have presented to the Commission suggestions in various forms for the initiation of discussions between representatives of north and south looking to unification. No suggestions for the solution of the practical questions involved in the initiation of such discussions have been put forward. Moreover, all such suggestions have been opposed by the Government of the Republic. The Commission has limited itself to a public expression of its readiness to assist in any discussions initiated by representatives of north and south under conditions offering assurance that they would be meaningful.

(3) All proposals emanating from the north concerning ways of achieving the unification of Korea have been based on principles inconsistent with the General Assembly resolutions of 14 November 1947 and 12 December 1948, and, procedurally, have involved the exclusion of the United Nations from any part in their realization. The question of action by the Commission in respect of such suggestions has not arisen.

II. *Integration of Security Forces*

(4) In view of the inability of the Commission to make progress in the performance of its duties on the political level, it has not been possible to seek to bring about accord in respect of the integration of the security forces of north and south.

III. *The 38th Parallel—A Barrier to Friendly Intercourse*

(5) The Commission has been unable to set on foot measures to facilitate a reduction of barriers to the beneficial exchange of goods and services and to other friendly intercourse between north and south because of the suspicion which prevails between their respective régimes. The Government of the Republic has now outlawed trade as an instrument of subversive propaganda and an exchange of views with the north on this or any other subject has not been possible.

(6) The border is becoming the scene of increasingly frequent exchanges of fire and of armed raids along the 38th parallel. According to information received from United States military authorities, some of the raids from the north were set on foot for the purpose of introducing groups of trained saboteurs into the territory of the Republic.

(7) The People's Republic has been recognized by the USSR with which it maintains diplomatic relations. Much publicity has been given to a recent visit of General Kim Il Sung to Moscow and to the evidences of esteem shown him. It is reported that an agreement for economic aid and cultural exchange was concluded in the course of this visit.

(8) All these events have tended to fortify the 38th parallel in its character as a barrier to the friendly intercourse of the people of Korea with each other.

IV. Further Development of Representative Government

(9) The Commission has held itself available to the Government of the Republic of Korea for consultation in the further development of representative government. The Government of the Republic, which takes the view that the Commission's functions in this regard have relevance only north of the 38th parallel, has not required the Commission's services in this respect in the south. The Commission has, however, studied the problems of representative government in the Republic and has heard the views of Government officials, experts and organizations on the subject. It has also made enquiries concerning the structure of government in the north and the means of extending representative government there.

V. Withdrawal of Occupation Forces

(10) The Commission has fulfilled, in respect of the occupation forces of the United States of America, the duty laid upon it by paragraph 4 (d) of the General Assembly resolution of 12 December 1948 to observe the withdrawal of the occupation forces of the occupying Powers. The withdrawal of United States occupation troops was completed on 29 June 1949, under the observation of the Commission, which has since verified the fact of their withdrawal. While unable to verify the disposition made of the military equipment belonging to the United States, which was not withdrawn with its troops, the Commission is satisfied that all of this has been transferred to the Korean security forces and that none of it remains under the control of the United States.

(11) The Commission has signified to the USSR, through the Secretary-General of the United Nations, its readiness to carry out

in respect of the occupation forces of that Power the duties imposed by paragraph 4 (*d*) of the General Assembly resolution of 12 December 1948. The Commission has received no reply to the message transmitted to the USSR on its behalf.

(B) FACTORS AFFECTING THE IMPLEMENTATION OF THE GENERAL ASSEMBLY RESOLUTION OF 12 DECEMBER 1948.

(12) The Temporary Commission, in the second part of its report to the General Assembly, had expressed a doubt whether the developments which it reported constituted a progress in the situation which existed on 14 November 1947, when the General Assembly adopted its first resolution on the Korean problem, and on 26 February 1948, when the Interim Committee made its recommendations. Of these developments, the chief one was the establishment of rival political régimes in the two zones into which Korea is divided. The Temporary Commission had stressed the urgent need for setting up some procedure for peaceful negotiations before military evacuation of the occupying forces had abandoned Korea to the arbitrary rule of rival political régimes whose military forces might find themselves driven to internecine warfare. The Commission had refrained from going further and defining methods for peaceful relations between the governments of North and South Korea, because that task was believed to be futile so long as the opposing ideologies and policies to which those governments subscribed continued in opposition to each other with ever-increasing violence in all parts of the world where they confronted each other. The Commission looked to the General Assembly for an answer to this basic difficulty.

(13) The Temporary Commission, in the first part of its report, declared that it had concluded that the holding of elections in the southern zone of Korea would be a step in the re-establishment of the independence of Korea, and reported that the elections held on 10 May were a valid expression of the free will of the electorate in those parts of Korea which were accessible to the Commission and in which the inhabitants constituted approximately two-thirds of the people of all Korea.

(14) The General Assembly approved the conclusions of the Temporary Commission, both those offered in the first part and those stated in the second part of the report. It recorded its concurrence in the conclusions stated in the first part of the report by declaring that there had been established a lawful government (the Government of the Republic of Korea), having effective control and jurisdiction over that part of Korea where the Temporary Commission was able to observe and consult and in which the great majority

of the people of all Korea resided ; that this Government was based on elections which were a valid expression of the free will of the electorate of that part of Korea and which were observed by the Temporary Commission ; and that this was the only such government in Korea (paragraph 2 of the resolution of the General Assembly of 12 December 1948).

(15) The General Assembly gave effect to the conclusions stated in the second part of the report by establishing the present Commission. It charged the Commission to 'have in mind the status of the Government of the Republic of Korea as defined by the General Assembly' ; at the same time that it was to 'lend its good offices to bring about the unification of Korea'.

(16) In the opinion of the present Commission, its predecessor had not misread the omens. The problem of Korean independence and unification has been increasingly prejudiced by the consolidation of the rival political régimes which had emerged when the Temporary Commission reported last year.

(17) The Government of the Republic of Korea had just come into being when the Temporary Commission finished its principal labours in Korea. The present Commission, however, found a Government actively administering its territory in full awareness of its independent sovereign status.

(18) That Government had informed the Korean public, even before the Commission came to Seoul, that the resolution represented an acknowledgement of the claims made by the Government's representative at the first part of the third regular session of the General Assembly in Paris. The Commission saw no need to engage in discussion with the Government over the question whether the General Assembly had approved the claim of the Government to be the lawful authority of all Korea, or of only that part lying south of the 38th parallel. This could only have added to the difficulties of the Government, without evident advantage to the cause in which the Commission was labouring.

The Government has not abated in any respect the claims which it put forward at Paris. It has maintained inflexibly the contention that the northern régime has been outlawed by the General Assembly and that the Commission, like the Government, ought therefore to refrain from dealing with it. It has insisted that the Commission was authorized to deal only with the USSR in respect of North Korea in order to persuade the Soviet Union to dissolve the northern régime and to permit the Government of the Republic to hold elections in the northern zone under the supervision of the Commission.

(19) The form in which the Commission's powers were cast did not strengthen its position *vis-à-vis* the Government. The

Commission was 'to lend its good offices'; it was 'to be available for observation and consultation'; it was to 'seek to facilitate'; all attributes of an intermediary, who cannot function in the absence of demands for the services authorized to be performed. It has been noted elsewhere in the present report that the Government of the Republic has not recognized that paragraph 4(c) of the General Assembly resolution had any application to itself, and for that reason has not called on the Commission for help of any kind in meeting the developing problems of representative government. It has not called on the Commission for assistance in initiating or conducting negotiations or, indeed, any preliminary exchange of views with North Korean leaders. It has not required the services of the Commission for the purpose of exploring the practical possibilities of a reduction of other than political barriers. In the absence of an initiative from the Government, the Commission has had no opportunity to open the armoury of its own powers.

(20) In barring *ab initio* any idea of discussion with northern leaders of the basis for the creation of an all-Korean régime, the Government has indicated that in its view the Commission had been sent to Korea for the sole purpose of lending its good offices to the Government of the Republic of Korea in vindication of the latter's claims. Acceptance of that view would have made it impossible for the Commission to have undertaken the role which the Temporary Commission had in mind in pressing urgently for the institution by the General Assembly of machinery of negotiation between the rival political régimes and which the General Assembly assigned to the Commission in December 1948.

The differences with the Government have not alone, or even chiefly, been at the root of the lack of achievement which the Commission is obliged to report. The problems created by the differences between the Government and the Commission never became real, because the Commission was unable to establish contact with the north.

(21) From north of the parallel the Commission has been a target of defamation and inflammatory attacks, which have not been without effect and counterpart in the south. The most courteous appeals for facilities that would permit a visit to the north and allow the initiation of preliminary and tentative exploration of the subject of unification have been ignored. Every channel of communication has been employed without avail. The USSR, requested through the Secretary-General to lend its good offices to establish contact between the Commission and the north, has not acknowledged the communication. Transmission of a message directly to General Kim Il Sung through shipping channels *via* Hong Kong has

been without result. Transmission of the Commission's request through a weekly mail exchange between north and south has elicited no response. Repeated radio broadcast appeals have been equally without reply, unless the systematic vituperation of the Pyongyang radio was such.

(c) PRESENT STATUS OF THE KOREAN PROBLEM

I. Fervent Desire for Peaceful Unification

(22) The Government has not only made clear that it would not participate in official discussions with the north looking to unification, but has also indicated that it frowned on unofficial efforts in this behalf. It has made clear that it views any suggestions for north-south discussion, even of an unofficial and most tentative kind, as a form of disloyalty. In the face of this attitude, the Commission has not felt free to encourage extra-governmental efforts of contact.

(23) The Commission, moreover, has not felt that the proposals of the extra-legislative opposition to the Government led by Mr Kim Koo and Mr Kimm Kiusic for the initiation of north-south discussions in a conference, or by some other means, merited encouragement. Consistently with the view they took when the question of participation in the 10 May 1948 elections was under consideration, the leaders of the opposition are not deterred by the results of these elections from favouring new elections in the north and south. The Government has always regarded the conference proposal as a communist trick designed to bring about public discord and confusion. The experience of the so-called 'North-South Conference' of last year certainly goes far to confirm this belief. The suggestions which the Commission has heard from those who favour a new conference have impressed it as vague and wishful. The difficult questions involved in such a conference have either not been faced or have found no answer. The means of making such a conference truly representative, the status of the participants, the questions with which they would deal, the procedure to be employed for giving effect to any agreement that might be reached, all these problems have been evaded by those who advocated such a conference.

(24) Despite the failure of the 'North-South Conference' of April 1948, the idea of a renewed attempt in this direction still persists in some quarters. The Government appears to have underestimated the hold on the imagination of the people of Korea of the idea that Korea's difficulties could be overcome if leaders of north and south would sit down together and seek a common answer to its problems. The propaganda agencies of the northern régime have been able

to make much political capital by appropriating the idea of a conference. It is they who have been able to make play with the slogans of the 'people's democracy', the 'fatherland front', a 'conference' of delegates from political parties and social organizations of South and North Korea. The latest move in that direction from the north has been a 'Manifesto' of the Democratic Front for the Attainment of Unification for the Fatherland.

(25) The Republic still labours under the disadvantage of political division, which began with the difference of view over the question of the 10 May 1948 elections. The Government has made no effort to heal this breach. Instead of mobilizing the strength of the patriotic opposition behind itself and presenting to the north the spectacle of a vigorous and united Republic, it faces the 38th parallel at the head of a divided people.

II. Lack of a Spirit of Compromise

(26) The Republic is a result of free elections and the expression of a people's will. Psychologically, if not materially, the activities of the north have compelled the Republic to go on a war footing, and this spiritual mobilization has to some extent brutalized the conduct of government and engendered suspicion of those who remain independent and critical of spirit. This comes at a time when the feeling for freedom in the sense of the association of liberty with responsibility has hardly broken through the millennial tradition of government from above, or else has not advanced beyond the level of licence. The north has troubled the relative calm which is needed for the psychological and social translation of the laws of liberty into the practice of freedom through a careful nurture of procedural and institutional growth.

(27) The failure of the north to respond to the Commission's appeals is only one sign of its contempt for the international community's efforts to obtain a peaceful solution of the Korean problem on the basis of the principles announced in the two General Assembly resolutions.

The northern régime is the creature of a military occupant and rules by right of a mere transfer of power from that Government. It has never been willing to give its subjects an unfettered opportunity, under the scrutiny of an impartial international agency, to pass judgement upon its claim to rule. The claims to be a 'people's democracy' and its expressions of concern for the general welfare are falsified by this unwillingness to account for the exercise of power to those against whom it is employed.

Professions of devotion to Korea and of a desire for unity are many, but are belied in action. The cutting-off of electric power had grave effects on the morale and economy of the south. The armed attacks along the border serve no legitimate purpose and are unfortunate, since the people on both sides of the parallel are Korean. The activities of the north reach deep into the territory of the Republic to mislead those whose grievances are legitimate enough into struggling for ends which they do not understand and which have nothing in common with their own purposes. To provoke small groups of harassed people into taking up hopelessly crude arms against those in authority in the hope of ending their troubles is utterly irresponsible.

(28) The suspicion engendered by mutual rivalry and conflicting claims to supremacy has not only pinioned the spiritual freedom of the Korean people, it has also resulted in the blocking up of the normal channels of trade for fear that previous experience would be repeated and that along them would flow not only goods, but propaganda. In this respect, also, the objectives of the General Assembly have been defeated. The Commission must report that until now it has met opposition from the Government of the Republic to suggestions for a renewal of economic exchange, while it has never been given an opportunity of making proposals to that end to the north. Hence, it has been able only to make public an expression of its readiness to assist in a resumption of legitimate trade on a trial basis.

III. Growing Military Strength in North and South

(29) There is much military posturing on both sides of the parallel. This holds a serious danger of provoking open military conflict. Military conflict in Korea would mean the most barbarous civil war. The USSR continues to refuse to have any dealing with the Commission ; it lends countenance to northern leaders in bellicose utterances and in a refusal to consider ways of adjusting existing differences on any plane of relations between north and south. In this connexion, note should be taken of the fact that the North Korean régime has recently concluded a treaty with the USSR. It is reported that an agreement for military aid has been concluded between North Korea and the Chinese communist forces in Manchuria.

Border raids from the north are frequently reported and are said to be increasing in intensity. The Commission, on one occasion, has itself seen a contest for hills in the vicinity of the parallel. The scale of such conflicts is small. The Commission is not in a position to judge what they portend, though it can testify that they upset the peaceful routine of the countryside and cause unnecessary loss of life. The propaganda efforts of dissension and subversion have been stepped up.

(30) All this induces equal and opposite reactions in the south. The Government is hastening the pace of its military preparations and is pressing the United States for military aid beyond that already received. United States military personnel advise and assist in the training of the Republic's forces, as on the other side of the parallel military personnel of the USSR reportedly perform like services for the northern forces.

IV. International Political Climate

(31) Running through the diverse opinions concerning the solution of the problem of Korea which the Commission has heard is a general belief that the USSR and the United States are responsible for the present plight of the country and have left it in the lurch. An equally general opinion is that the problem cannot be solved until the two Powers take steps in concert to lift the barrier at the 38th parallel and restore to Korea the independence and unity which were promised at the Moscow Conference of Foreign Ministers in December 1945.

The Government of the Republic claims that the USSR still exercises decisive control over the régime in the north. It has expressed the opinion that the problem of Korea can be solved if the USSR will withdraw its protection from the northern régime and allow the people of North Korea to give expression to their hidden loyalty to the Republic. From the United States, the Government of the Republic expects, as a matter of obligation, military and economic aid for defence against the menace of aggression and invasion from the north.

(32) Recent events in Asia have induced nervousness in the territory of the Republic, and emboldened propaganda from the north. These events have been cited by the Government of the Republic as a reason why the defence of the Republic should become a United States commitment. The Korean Press carries frequent reports from Washington of requests by the Government of the Republic for arms and other military aid from the United States. In June and July many mass meetings and parades were held to protest against the withdrawal of American troops and to demand arms for defence. The President of the Republic has on several recent occasions insisted that the United States had a responsibility for the future of the Republic and should assist the countries of the Pacific to close ranks in a Pacific Pact against the dangers that threaten them.

(33) Underlying the prevalent belief that the Korean problem cannot be solved without prior accord between the USSR and the United States is a general scepticism concerning the ability of the

United Nations to find a solution to the Korean problem, although this by no means signifies that the presence of the Commission is not found useful in other respects. In appraising the reasons for its own failure to accomplish the task with which it had been charged, the Commission may take note of factors having a decisive bearing on that lack of success. Among these, the relations between the USSR and the United States continue to be the largest single, and perhaps decisive, factor contributing to the growing hardening of relations between north and south.

(D) CONCLUSIONS

(34) The people of Korea are remarkably homogeneous. Ethnically and culturally they are one. They have a passionate longing for unity and independence and have a profound desire for the peaceful unification of their country.

The division of Korea has resulted in adverse economic consequences in the south, the only part of Korea to which the Commission has had access. The aftermath of the Second World War would have made the need for outside aid urgent in any case. But if the country were united, the south would not require such aid in the same degree and would be able to stabilize its economy more easily and at a higher level.

The division of Korea has caused bitterness, frustration and mutual distrust among its people. The frequent raids along the 38th parallel have further accentuated these feelings. The division of Korea was caused by the exigencies of the Second World War. There is no justification for the continued separation of the two parts of the country.

The Republic of Korea looks to the United Nations for the solution of many of its problems, for it feels that the Republic is in some sense a creation of the United Nations. In the opinion of the Government, as evidenced by its request that the stay of the Commission in Korea be prolonged for another year, the presence of the Commission has been a stabilizing factor in the situation.

(35) Bearing in mind these fundamental considerations underlying the Korean problem, the United Nations Commission on Korea has reached the following conclusions:

(i) The embittered propaganda and hostile activities which now mark the relations between the two parts of Korea render the prospect of unification more and more remote.

(ii) As long as the opposition of the Union of Soviet Socialist Republics to the efforts of the United Nations Commission to achieve the objectives of the General Assembly resolution of 12 December 1948 continues, neither a relaxation of hostile propaganda nor any other measure can facilitate to a substantial degree the achievement of unification.

(iii)   The world-wide antagonism between the Union of Soviet Socialist Republics and the United States of America continues to be, as it was when the Temporary Commission was in Korea, one of the basic factors underlying the present difficulties. Without a new effort by those Powers to reach agreement on the question of Korea, no substantial progress towards the achievement of unification on the basis of the principles approved by the General Assembly can be made.

(iv)   From its very inception, the newly formed Republic of Korea has been confronted with many difficulties. It faced insurgent uprisings from within and was menaced by continuous clashes on the 38th parallel. While making due allowance for these factors, the Commission believes that a broadening of the Government's political base would allow it to meet these difficulties more success-fully and so enable it to play a more effective part in achieving unification.

(v)   The present Commission, like its predecessor, must place on record an acknowledgement that the situation in Korea is now no better than it was at the beginning, and that it has not been able to facilitate the achievement of the objectives set by the General Assembly.

Report of the United Nations Commission on Korea, Vol. I, Chapter IV, General Assembly Official Records ; Fourth Session, Supplement No. 9 (A/936), pp. 30-4.

III   KOREAN EFFORTS FOR A UNITED KOREA

17   23 *April* 1948

MESSAGE   OF   THE   UNITED   CONFERENCE   OF
REPRESENTATIVES   OF   NORTHERN   AND   SOUTHERN
KOREA   TO   THE   GOVERNMENTS   OF   THE   USSR
AND   THE   USA   ON   THE   WITHDRAWAL   OF   FOREIGN
TROOPS   FROM   KOREA

We the representatives of fifty-six political parties and social organizations of northern and southern Korea, with a membership of over ten million, having assembled at a united conference and discussed the political situation in the country, address the following message to the Governments of the Union of Soviet Socialist Republics and of the United States of America :

It will soon be three years since the day when, through the efforts of the Allies, Korea was liberated from the half-century-long oppression of the Japanese imperialists. Emancipated from colonial slavery and from the tyranny of the Japanese enslavers the Korean people were jubilant and rejoiced, believing that at last the long-awaited freedom had come and Korea would be an independent, sovereign democratic state. However, the aspirations and hopes of the Korean people to see their country established as a sovereign democratic state have not been realized. To this day our country remains artificially divided into two parts, which has a pernicious effect upon the entire political, economic and cultural life of the Korean people.

An analysis of the political situation that has now been created in Korea brings us to the unanimous conclusion—and we consider it our duty to say it plainly—that the responsibility for the intolerable situation created in Korea rests squarely on the ruling circles of the United States of America, who intend to hold separate elections in southern Korea with the aim of perpetuating the existing temporary division of Korea and retarding the country's unification and the re-establishment of its independence.

The united conference of representatives of political parties and social organizations of northern and southern Korea, fully conscious of its responsibility, declares that the Korean people will never agree to the holding of separate elections in the South and will hinder it by all the means at their disposal. On behalf of the twenty-seven million people of Korea we protest against the holding of separate elections in the South, we protest against the unlawful decisions of the General Assembly and the Interim Committee of the United Nations Organization, which were adopted without the participation and against the wishes of the Korean people. We demand the immediate removal of the United Nations Temporary Commission from Korea, because it is being employed for the splitting of Korea.

The Korean people both in the North and in the South are striving for unity and democracy. The Korean nation is capable of creating by itself a single democratic government without foreign interference. It is our profound conviction that, under the conditions now created, the simplest, most reasonable and correct solution of the Korean question would be to carry out the proposal of the Soviet Union for the simultaneous withdrawal of foreign troops from Korea and for leaving it to the Korean people themselves to decide their domestic affairs.

The united conference addresses the request to the Governments of the USSR and the USA that they should simultaneously withdraw their troops from Korea and enable our people—freely, according to their own wishes and without foreign interference—to hold general elections for a National Korean Democratic Government and to create a single independent democratic state, so that our country may thus obtain real national independence and join the family of the freedom-loving nations of the world as a member on a footing of equality.

The Soviet Union and the Korean Question, pp. 66-7.

18   7 *May* 1948

REPLY OF THE SOVIET GOVERNMENT TO THE MESSAGE OF THE UNITED CONFERENCE OF RE-PRESENTATIVES OF NORTHERN AND SOUTHERN KOREA ON THE WITHDRAWAL OF FOREIGN TROOPS FROM KOREA

The Soviet Government has received the message of the united conference of political parties and social organizations of northern and southern Korea to the Governments of the USSR and USA with the request that they should simultaneously withdraw their troops from Korea and enable the Korean people—freely and without foreign interference—to hold general elections, form a National Democratic Government and create a single independent democratic state.

The Soviet Government well understands and sympathizes with the aspiration of the Korean people to unite their country and create an independent democratic state of Korea. It was for this very reason that at the second session of the United Nations General Assembly the Soviet delegation objected to the attempt to settle the Korean question without the participation of representatives of the Korean people and without regard for its national interests.

The Soviet Government insisted that the American and Soviet troops must be simultaneously withdrawn from Korea, considering this an essential requisite for the free expression of the will of the Korean people. It will be remembered that already in September 1947 the Soviet delegation made a proposal to this effect in the USSR-US Joint Commission, suggesting that a definite date should be appointed for the withdrawal of the troops—in the beginning of 1948. This proposal was repeated by the Soviet delegation at the session of the United Nations General Assembly in October 1947. However, this proposal of the Soviet Government was not accepted.

The Soviet Government is as heretofore prepared immediately to withdraw its troops from Korea on condition that the USA troops are withdrawn from Korea simultaneously.

The Soviet Union and the Korean Question, pp. 68-9.

19   30 *April* 1948

DECLARATION OF THE KOREAN UNITY CONFERENCE
AGAINST SEPARATE ELECTIONS IN SOUTH KOREA

As the result of detailed and comprehensive discussion, an understanding has been reached on the following questions :

(1) Under present conditions the immediate and simultaneous withdrawal of foreign troops from the territory of our country in conformity with the Soviet Union's proposal is the only correct and just solution of the Korean problem. All those who desire the unity of democratic Korea should support this reasonable proposal.

Since the expulsion of the Japanese, our people have matured sufficiently to be perfectly capable of settling its State affairs without outside interference. Our country possesses quite enough trained personnel for this purpose. The United States must accept this fair proposal of the Soviet Union and withdraw its Army from South Korea, thus solving the problem of Korea's independence in practice.

(2) The leaders of parties and public organizations of North and South Korea declare that after the withdrawal of foreign troops they will never permit an outbreak of civil war or any disturbances which militate against the Korean's desire for unity. The people's indomitable desire to achieve the unity of the nation, and the understanding reached between the biggest parties of North and South, constitute a reliable guarantee of full order in the country.

(3) After the withdrawal of foreign troops, the parties and organizations listed below will immediately, at an all-Korean political conference, form a democratic government representing all sections of the Korean people, and this will assume power in the country and responsibility for economic, political and cultural life.

It will be the most urgent task of this government to hold a really free general election, with direct, equal and secret vote, of a single legislative body for Korea, which will then set up a single democratic government and adopt a new constitution.

(4) Inasmuch as the separatist elections in South Korea are opposed by political parties and public organizations of North and South

with a membership of more than ten million, which constitutes an absolute majority of citizens entitled to vote, these elections, even if they are held, can never reflect the will of our people. They can be nothing but sham elections, and it is not accidental that they are being prepared in an atmosphere of gross coercion and terror.

In view of the above, the leaders of the political parties and public organizations who have signed the present communiqué will not recognize the results of these elections or support any separatist government which may be set up after the elections.

[The communiqué was signed by the leaders of 15 political parties and public organizations of North Korea and of 26 parties and organizations of South Korea.]

Documents on International Affairs, 1947-8, Royal Institute of International Affairs, pp. 701-2.

20   25 *August* 1948

DECLARATION AFFIRMING THE COMMUNIQUE OF THE JOINT CONFERENCE OF NORTH AND SOUTH KOREAN LEADERS AND DENOUNCING ALL ACTIVITIES CONTRARY TO ITS PROVISIONS

The independence of Korea which was promised by the Allied Powers—the United States, the Soviet Union, China, and Great Britain—appears to become more remote with the passage of time. The division of the nation is intensified by the occupation of American and Soviet troops.

Motivated by the belief that our unification and national independence should be accomplished in accordance with the principle of self-determination, we advocated a joint conference of the leaders of North and South Korea. This conference was held in Pyongyang in April 1948. The political leaders of North and South Korea reached complete accord regarding the establishment of a central government and national unification. The following joint communiqué was declared on 30 April :

(1) A nation-wide political conference shall be held following the withdrawal of Soviet and American troops.

(2) A unified provisional central government shall be formed.

(3) A nation-wide election shall be held.

(4) The Constitution shall be enacted.

(5) A formal central government shall be formed.

The North Korean leaders however, have convoked the so-called second joint conference of North and South Korean political leaders, in contradiction to the firm and solemn agreement previously made, in order to establish a People's Republic in North Korea, and adopted a resolution which is contrary to the Joint Communiqué issued at Pyongyang on 30 April 1948. The so-called Constitution of the People's Republic has been promulgated and the North Koreans are trying to enforce an election in order to establish a government.

The undersigned political parties declare :

(1) That the so-called Second Joint Conference of North and South Korean Political Leaders is illegal.

(2) We have despatched no representatives to the so-called Second Joint Conference of North and South Political Leaders.

(3) We denounce all the other activities and trend of events that have taken place in North Korea which are contrary to the provisions of the Joint Communiqué formulated on 30 April. We, hereby, make this firm and solemn declaration at home and abroad.

(signed) :
(1) National Independence Federation.
(2) Korean Independence Party.
(3) Democratic Independence Party.
(4) New Progressive Party.
(5) Korean Farmers' Party.
(6) Sam Il Colleagues' Society.
(7) Independent Women's League.
(8) Patriotic Youths Colleagues' Group.
(9) Youth Society for Founding a Nation.
(10) Repatriates' Association.
(11) Korean Students' Federation.
(12) National Construction Students' Federation.
(13) North West Students' Federation.
(14) North West Union of Christian Endeavour Society.
(15) Patriotic Colleagues' Society.
(16) Patriotic Old Men's Society.
(17) League of Patriots for the Independence.
(18) First Hwanghae Province Youth Corps.
(19) Korean New Civilization Party.
(20) Revolutionary Colleagues' Youth Society.
(21) Korean Inventors' Association.
(22) Canton and Hongkong Society.
(23) Christian New Democratic Society.
(24) Industrial Rehabilitation Association.
(25) South Korea Chun Do Kyu Youth Friends' Party.

Korea 1945 to 1948, pp. 113-14.

IV DEMOCRATIC REPUBLIC OF KOREA (SOUTH)

21   31 *May* 1948

SYNGMAN RHEE'S ADDRESS TO THE FIRST
CONGRESS OF THE REPUBLIC OF KOREA

Today we are assembled here to open the first Congress of the Republic of Korea. For this day we must first thank Almighty God ; secondly, the patriotic men and women who sacrificed their lives ; and thirdly, our friendly nations, particularly the United States and the United Nations, for their great contributions which made this occasion possible. As members of the Legislative Assembly elected by, for, and of the people of Korea, we are here to assume the authority and responsibility as their representatives in adopting a national constitution and re-establishing an independent democratic government. As the chairman of this great Assembly, I have the honour to formally declare to the world that this day the Republic of Korea is born again and further declare that this Assembly is the sole representative body of this nation.

On 1 March 1919, the representatives of the 13 provinces gathered in Seoul organized the great National Assembly and declared to the nations of the world the establishment of the independent Republic of Korea and organized the provisional government of this republic, thus laying the foundation of the democratic principle for our nation. Unfortunately, due to the world situation, we were unable to achieve our aim. Our people, both at home and abroad, however, supported that government, giving up their lives and shedding their blood in order to uphold the principle and spirit of that memorable day of 1 March 1919. Logically enough, this Congress which we open today is the successor of that great General Assembly and the government which we are to organize will be the successor of that provisional government established in Seoul at that time. Therefore, we hereby confirm that this is the day when that Republic of Korea is reborn after 29 years of our revolution. It is appropriate and proper to continue to hold that historical year of 1919 as our epochal national year and this Assembly as our National Congress representing the entire nation, consequently the government of the entire nation.

We deeply regret that our brethren of the five provinces in the North were not able to elect their representatives to participate with us in this Assembly. However, four and a half million refugees from the North participated in the national election, and some of them have been elected as members of this House. Moreover, we have reserved a certain number of seats for the representatives freely elected by our people in the North to come and occupy them so that they will fully share the responsibilities and privileges with the rest of us. In this we count on the support of the United States and the United Nations so as to achieve our common objective as speedily as possible. We hereby reassert that it is our firm unanimous determination that our people will either live together or die together in our struggle for the complete restoration of our country and that we will not yield one foot or one inch of our land to any nation or any group of nations.

The main objectives of this Congress, as already made known, are to adopt a constitution based on democratic principles and to establish a government according to that constitution and to form a national defence force for the security and defence of our country and provide for the relief of our suffering people. We will regulate the prices of rice and other necessary commodities, put into effect a land reform programme with fairness to all, protect individual freedom and equal rights regulated by law, protect the lives and rights of our people residing overseas through international negotiations, promote the interest of public education, develop our industries, endeavour to open commercial relations with other nations on a fair and equal basis, safeguard the freedom of speech, Press, assembly, and religion, promote the peace of the world through friendly relations with other Powers, attempt to open direct friendly negotiations with the Soviet Union for a just solution of the critical common problems of the two nations, and to settle the political, economical, and other urgent problems with Japan through negotiations whenever possible.

The duties and responsibilities of every member of this Congress are heavy and urgent and we cannot afford to indulge ourselves in petty discussions and unnecessary debates on minor detail matters tending to waste valuable time ; we must first take up the main problems as announced in our programme and take action on one after another after due and full discussion of them.

When we have set up our government, the American Military Government will withdraw for the Military Government authorities are fully ready to turn the administration over to our government. We hope our government will request the Government of the USA to let us retain some of our American friends who have been serving in the central administration as well as those in the provincial governments who can be helpful to us either as advisers or technicians. The American forces of occupation, we hope, will remain for security purposes until our government has organized our own security force. However, the United States will act in this matter in accordance with the decision of the United Nations. Therefore, in co-operation with the United States and the United Nations, we shall act according to our common understanding and agreement. The only point which must be clearly understood is that the remaining of the security forces shall not interfere with the exercise of our sovereign rights. There is no doubt that whenever we request the withdrawal of the American forces they will evacuate at once. It is a well-known fact that the United States has no political or territorial interest in any part of the world. America's interest is in the establishment of democratic governments wherever possible for the sake of world peace and of commercial relations for mutual benefit. Therefore, what America expects from us is nothing more than the goodwill of our people. Although American forces may remain for the time being due to international circumstances, they will leave Korea without delay whenever the Korean Government formally requests their withdrawal.

To the Korean Communists we are willing to offer another and last opportunity to repent and join hands with us in our common efforts towards the complete restoration of our nation. If they accept this opportunity and sufficiently demonstrate their desire to co-operate in our national programme, we shall forgive and forget the past and regard them just as we do the rest of our loyal citizens in both the North and South. If, however, they fail to utilize this opportunity and insist on their unpatriotic efforts to affiliate our nation with any of the foreign powers and continue to murder, burn, and destroy, in order to carry out that unpatriotic proposition, we shall have to deal with them strictly and sternly according to the law. They must realize that from now on no foreign influence can help them to secure pardon or release from due punishment for their crimes.

Any violator of law and order will have to pay the full penalty for his crimes. In order to live and let live and to enjoy the blessings of freedom and prosperity, they must observe law and justice ; otherwise they will not be allowed to enjoy the privileges of democracy.

To all my fellow citizens, I wish to give the advice that if they are misled into believing that the establishment of the Congress and of the government will bring every individual citizen all that they need without work on their part, then they will soon be disappointed and disillusioned. Under the old monarchical system the people left all the affairs of the nation entirely in the hands of those in the government without any participation in it. But under a democratic government, the people are rulers of the nation, and, if the rulers neglect their duties, the nation will again fall into jeopardy. From now on, every citizen, man or woman, must realize that he or she has an equal share of the responsibility, authority, and power, and must exert all of their energy to work and struggle to consolidate and strengthen the foundation of the state which in turn will safeguard his or her individual rights and privileges, so as to make steady progress towards the prosperity of our nation. There should be no one, regardless of sex or age, who has no work or duty to perform, and, if there are any unpatriotic and subversive elements who try to obstruct or destroy the progress of our nation, they should be strictly dealt with according to the law so that no loyal law-abiding citizen may suffer. People and government must strive together in carrying out the determination to stamp out all the evils of corruption and profiteering. We must disclose and purge all such practices which sap the vitality of the nation, and whoever is proven guilty either within or without the government should be rigorously punished. I request every individual and organization to do their utmost for the solution of this most urgent question for the sake of all.

Henceforth the destiny of our Republic and the welfare of our people will be entirely in the hands of the individual citizens of Korea. If we fail, we shall suffer and have only ourselves to blame. If we succeed, we shall enjoy all the benefits and blessings thereof and all our friendly nations will willingly give us their warm and sympathetic support. I trust all the members of this Assembly will heartily join me in the full measure of devotion to the cause of our nation. I know that all our people will revive the self-sacrificing patriotic spirit of 1919. Let us recall the solemn vow made in the Declaration of Independence and renew our determination 'to continue our struggle to the last man and to the last moment'. With this determination, let us pledge ourselves to the great tasks before us in the presence of Almighty God and of our 30,000,000 fellow citizens.

Korea 1945 to 1948, pp. 73-7.

22   12 *June* 1948

RESOLUTION OF THE SOUTH KOREAN NATIONAL
ASSEMBLY ON ELECTION OF REPRESENTATIVES
FROM NORTH KOREA

Adopted 12 June 1948

To Our Fellow Countrymen in North Korea :
Thanks to the blood of our martyrs and the spirit of our patriots, our independence movement conducted since 1919 finally resulted in international promises of independence at Cairo and Potsdam.

The task of the US-USSR Joint Commission which was organized by the Moscow agreement, however, contradicted the will of the 30 million Korean people and, therefore, the Commission finally broke up.

International justice expressed by the resolution of the General Assembly of the United Nations on 14 November 1947, brought UNTCOK* into Korea, and the May 10 general elections were held in a free atmosphere in the area where it was possible, according to the resolution of the UN Little Assembly on 27 February 1948. We, the members elected by the free will of the nation, held a solemn opening ceremony of the National Assembly before the eyes of the world, and we are proceeding to the great task of establishing a complete sovereign government. We deeply regret that our fellow countrymen in North Korea did not have the opportunity to hold a general election as we did because the USSR boycotted the UN resolution.

Therefore, we, the members of the National Assembly, resolve to express our sincerest desire to our fellow countrymen in North Korea, as follows :

We hope you, our fellow countrymen in North Korea, will hold a general election soon in a free atmosphere in accordance with the UN resolutions as we did, elect true representatives of the people, and send them to the National Assembly to sit with us.

Korea 1945 to 1948, p. 78.

* United Nations Temporary Commission on Korea.

23   12 *July* 1948

CONSTITUTION OF THE DEMOCRATIC
REPUBLIC OF KOREA (SOUTH)

Preamble

We, the people of Korea, with a glorious tradition and history from time immemorial, following the indomitable spirit of independence, as manifested in the establishment of Tai Han Republic in the course of the Sam-il independence movement,

Now at this time engaged in reconstructing a democratic, independent country, are determined :

To consolidate national unity by justice, humanity, brotherly love and the elimination of all kinds of social evils,

To offer equal opportunities to every person,

To provide for the fullest development of the equality of each individual in all fields of political, economic, social and cultural life,

To permit every person to discharge his duties and responsibilities,

To promote the welfare of the people, to maintain permanent international peace, and thereby to assure Security, Liberty and Happiness of ourselves and our posterity,

Do hereby ordain and establish this Constitution on the 12th day of July in the year One Thousand Nine Hundred and Forty-Eight in the National Assembly composed of our freely and duly elected representatives.

Ch. I. General Provisions

Article 1.   The Republic of Korea shall be a democratic republic.

Article 2.   The sovereignty of the Korean Republic shall reside in the people as a whole. All state authority shall emanate from the people.

Article 3.   The requirements for Korean citizenship shall be determined by law.

Article 4.   The territory of the Republic of Korea shall consist of the Korean Peninsula, and its accessory islands.

Article 5.   The Republic of Korea shall guarantee liberty and equality and the initiative of each individual in the fields of political, social and economic life. It shall be responsible for their protection and adjustment for the promotion of the public welfare.

Article 6.   The Republic of Korea shall denounce all aggressive wars. The mission of the national military forces shall be to perform the sacred duty of protecting the national territory.

Article 7.   The duly ratified and published treaties and the generally recognized rules of international law shall be valid as a binding constituent part of the law of Korea. The status of aliens shall be guaranteed within the scope of international law and international treaties.

Ch. II. Rights and Duties of Citizens

Article 8.   All citizens shall be equal before the law. No discrimination, in any field of political, economic and social life, derived from sex, religion, or social position shall exist. Privileged status shall not be recognized, nor shall it ever be established in the future. The bestowment of badges, medals and other decorations shall confer to the bearer only personal honours and no privileged status shall be established.

Article 9.   All citizens shall have personal freedom and no citizen shall be arrested, detained, searched, tried, punished, or subject to compulsory labour unless according to law. No citizen shall be arrested, detained or searched except by warrant of a judge. In case a person is apprehended *flagranto delicto* or in case of danger that a person under suspicion may escape or destroy evidence, the detecting authority may ask for an *ex post facto* warrant of arrest in accordance with the provisions of law. The right to receive assistance from counsel and the right to request the court for examination of the legality of an apprehension shall be guaranteed.

Article 10. All citizens shall be free from 'limited residence', restrictions on domicile or restrictions on change of domicile, trespasses upon and the searching of private premises other than specified by law.

Article 11. The privacy of correspondence of all citizens shall remain inviolate and shall not be interfered with except in accordance with law.

Article 12. All citizens shall enjoy freedom of religion and conscience. No state religion shall exist. Religion shall be independent from politics.

Article 13. Citizens shall not be subjected to any restrictions on the freedom of speech, Press, assembly and association except as specified by law.

Article 14. All citizens shall have freedom of science and art. Rights of authors, inventors, and artists, shall be protected by law.

Article 15. The right of property shall be guaranteed. Its nature and restrictions shall be defined by law. The exercise of property rights shall conform to the public welfare. Expropriation, use or restriction of private property for public purposes shall be accompanied by due compensation in accordance with the provisions of law.

Article 16. All citizens shall be entitled to equal opportunity for education. At least elementary education shall be compulsory and free of charge. The educational system shall be determined by law and all educational institutions shall be placed under the supervision of the state.

Article 17. All citizens shall have the right and duty to work. The standards of the conditions of labour shall be determined by law. Special protection shall be extended to the labour of women and children.

Article 18. Freedom of association, collective bargaining and collective action of labourers shall be guaranteed within the limits of the law. Workers employed in profit making private enterprises shall be entitled to share in the profits of such enterprises in accordance with the provisions of law.

Article 19. Citizens who are incapable of making a living because of old age, infirmity or incapacity to work shall be entitled to protection by the state in accordance with the provisions of law.

Article 20. Marriages shall be based on the equality of men and women. The purity of marriage and the health of the family shall receive the special protection by the state.

Article 21. All citizens shall have the right to submit written petitions to each government agency and the government shall be obliged to examine such petitions.

Article 22. All citizens shall have the right to be tried in accordance with the law by judges whose status has been determined by law.

Article 23. No citizen shall be prosecuted for a criminal act unless such act constituted a crime prescribed by law at the time at which it was committed nor shall he be placed in double jeopardy.

Article 24. All defendants in criminal cases shall have the right to be tried in public without delay unless there is proper reason for not doing so. When a defendant in a criminal case who has been detained is found not guilty he may in accordance with the provisions of law request compensation from the government.

Article 25. All citizens shall have the right to elect government officials in accordance with the provisions of law.

Article 26. All citizens shall have the right to assume public office in accordance with the provisions of law.

Article 27. Public officials shall be the trustees of the sovereign people and shall at all times be responsible to the people. All citizens shall have the right to petition for the removal of public officials who acted unlawfully. Citizens who suffered damages by unlawful acts of public officials in the exercise of their official duties may request compensation from the government or the public corporate bodies concerned, provided that the civil or criminal liability of the public officials concerned shall not be exempted thereby.

Article 28. Liberties and rights of the people shall not be ignored for the reason that they are not enumerated in this Constitution. A law imposing restrictions upon the liberties and rights of citizens shall be enacted only where such law is deemed necessary for the maintenance of public order and welfare of the community.

Article 29. All citizens shall have the duty to pay taxes in accordance with the provisions of law.

Article 30. All citizens have the duty to defend the national territory in accordance with the provisions of law.

Ch. III. *National Assembly*

Article 31. The legislative power shall be exercised by the National Assembly.

Article 32. The National Assembly shall be composed of members elected by universal, direct, equal and secret votes.

The details for the election of the members of the National Assembly shall be determined by law.

Article 33. The term of the members of the National Assembly shall be four years.

Article 34. The National Assembly shall convene each year on twentieth day of December. Should that day fall on a public holiday, the National Assembly shall assemble on the following day.

Article 35. In case of an extraordinary necessity the Speaker of the National Assembly shall summon a special session of the National Assembly upon the request of the President or upon the request of not less than one-fourth of the members of the National Assembly. The National Assembly shall convene immediately if there should arise a cause requiring the election of the President or Vice-President during a recess of the National Assembly.

Article 36. The National Assembly shall elect its Speaker and two Vice-Speakers.

Article 37. Unless otherwise provided in this Constitution or the rules of the National Assembly attendance of a majority of the members duly qualified and seated and the vote of a majority of the members present shall be necessary for acts of the National Assembly. The Speaker shall have the right to participate in voting and to break a tie vote.

Article 38. The proceedings of the National Assembly shall be open to the public but a closed session may be held by a resolution of the National Assembly.

Article 39. Bills may be introduced by the members of the National Assembly or the government.

Article 40. Bills passed by the National Assembly shall be sent to the government and the President shall, within 15 days, promulgate the law. In case of objection the President shall return the bill to the National Assembly for reconsideration with a statement of the reasons of his objections. If, in the presence of two-thirds of the members duly elected and seated the bill is confirmed on reconsideration by two-thirds of the members present, such bill shall be determined to be a law. If a bill is not returned within fifteen days after it has been presented to the government, the same shall become law. The President shall have the duty to proclaim without delay a law which has been determined under the foregoing paragraph. A law shall be effective twenty days after the date of proclamation unless otherwise stipulated.

Article 41. The National Assembly shall consider and decide upon budgets.

Article 42. The National Assembly shall have the right to consent to treaties concerning international organizations, peace treaties, treaties pertaining to mutual aid, commercial treaties, treaties financially incumbent on the state or the people, treaties related to legislative affairs, and declare war against a foreign state.

Article 43. The National Assembly shall demand, if necessary, documents, subpoena witnesses and receive testimonies or opinions for purposes of supervision and inspection.

Article 44. The Prime Minister, ministers and their representatives shall be authorized to attend, state their opinion, and answer questions at the meetings of the National Assembly. Whenever requested by the National Assembly, the Prime Minister, ministers and their representatives are obliged to attend a meeting of the National Assembly and to answer questions.

Article 45. The National Assembly shall investigate the qualifications of its members, establish its own rules of procedure and decide on disciplinary punishments of its members. The concurrence of two-thirds of the members duly qualified and seated shall be necessary for the expulsion of a member of the National Assembly.

Article 46. In the event the President, Vice-President, ministers, the Head of the Board of Audit, judges and other public officials as determined by law violate in the exercise of their official duties provisions of this Constitution or other laws the National Assembly may resolve to impeach them. A motion for impeachment shall be signed by no less than 50 members of the National Assembly. Attendance of two-thirds of the members of the National Assembly duly elected and seated and the vote of two-thirds or more of the members present shall be necessary to institute impeachment.

Article 47. An Impeachment Court shall be established by law for the purpose of hearing impeachment cases. The Impeachment Court shall be presided over by the Vice-President and five justices of the Supreme Court and five members of the National Assembly shall serve as associate judges. When the President or Vice-President is tried the Chief Justice shall preside. The concurrence of two-thirds of the judges is required for impeachment. A judgement in case of impeachment shall not extend further than removal from office; but the party convicted shall not be exempted from civil or criminal responsibility.

Article 48. No member of the National Assembly can be a member of any provincial council.

Article 49. When the National Assembly is in session no member of the National Assembly shall be arrested or detained without the consent of the National Assembly except when apprehended *flagrante delicto*. In case the apprehension of a member has been made before the convocation of the National Assembly, such member shall be released during the session in case the National Assembly so requests.

Article 50. No member of the National Assembly shall be held responsible to anyone outside of the Assembly for any statement or vote occurring within the Assembly.

Ch. IV. Government.

SECTION I—PRESIDENT

Article 51. The President of the Republic shall be the head of the executive branch of the government and shall represent the Republic *vis-à-vis* foreign Powers.

Article 52. In case the President is unable to execute his office for any reason, the Vice-President shall act for him and in case both the President and Vice-President are unable to perform their duties, the Prime Minister shall act for the President.

Article 53. The President and Vice-President shall be elected by the National Assembly by secret ballot. The election of the President and Vice-President shall be determined by the concurring vote of two-thirds of the members of the National Assembly in the presence of two-thirds of the members duly elected and seated. In case no candidate receives two-thirds of the votes a second ballot shall be taken. In case no candidate receives two-thirds of the votes in the second ballot a run-off balloting shall be conducted between the two candidates who received the highest number of votes and the candidates who received the plurality of the votes in the run-off balloting shall be elected.

Article 54. Before the President assumes his office he shall take the following oath :

I do solemnly swear before the nation that I shall observe the Constitution, promote the welfare of the people, defend the state and shall faithfully execute the office of President.

Article 55. The President and Vice-President shall hold office for four years. Consecutive re-election shall be permissible for one time only. The term of office of the Vice-President shall begin and end simultaneously with that of the President.

Article 56. The election for the President and Vice-President shall be held not later than 30 days before the expiration of the term of the preceding President and Vice-President. The vacancy of the President or Vice-President shall be filled without delay by election in the National Assembly.

Article 57. When in time of civil war, or in a dangerous situation arising from foreign relations, or in case of a national calamity, or on account of a grave economic or financial crisis it is necessary to take urgent measures for the maintenance of public order and security, the President shall have the right to issue orders having the effect of law or to make necessary financial dispositions, provided, however, that the President shall exercise such powers exclusively if time is lacking for the convocation of the National Assembly.

Such orders or dispositions shall be reported without delay to the National Assembly for confirmation. If confirmation of the National Assembly is not obtained, such orders or dispositions shall lose their effect thereupon, and the President shall announce it without delay.

Article 58. The President may issue orders within the framework of the powers delegated to him and orders necessary for the enforcement of laws.

Article 59. The President shall conclude and ratify treaties, declare war, make peace, and receive and accredit diplomatic representatives of foreign countries.

Article 60. The President may address the National Assembly or express his opinion on important national affairs by written messages.

Article 61. The President shall be the Commander-in-Chief of the National Military Force.

The organization and formation of the National Military Force shall be determined by law.

Article 62. The President shall appoint and remove government officials in accordance with the Constitution and the law.

Article 63. The President shall have the power to grant pardons, mitigation of punishment and restoration of rights, in accordance with the provisions of law.

The granting of an amnesty shall require the consent of the National Assembly.

Article 64. The President shall proclaim a state of siege in accordance with the provisions of law.

Article 65. The President shall confer decorations and extend other honours or awards.

Article 66. The acts of the President pertaining to state affairs shall be executed in written documents and all such documents shall be countersigned by the Prime Minister and the minister concerned.

The foregoing paragraph applies equally to acts of the President pertaining to military affairs.

Article 67. The President shall not be charged with criminal offence during his tenure of office except in case of treason.

Section II—State Council

Article 68. The State Council shall act as a collegiate body. It shall be composed of the President, the Prime Minister and other ministers and shall decide on important national policies which come within the scope of the powers of the President.

Article 69. The President shall appoint the Prime Minister with the consent of the National Assembly. When the National Assembly convenes after a general election the appointment of the Prime Minister shall be confirmed by the National Assembly. The ministers shall be appointed by the President. The total number of ministers shall not be more than 15 and not less than 8. No military personnel shall be appointed Prime Minister or minister unless he has resigned from active service.

Article 70. The meetings of the State Council shall be presided over by the President.

The Prime Minister shall assist the President and shall be the Vice-Chairman of the State Council.

Article 71. The decisions in the meetings of the State Council shall be by majority vote. The President shall have the right to vote and to break a tie vote.

Article 72. The following matters shall be referred to the State Council for decision :

(1) Fundamental plans and policies concerning national affairs ;

(2) Proposed treaties, declaration of war, conclusion of peace, and other important foreign policy ;

(3) Proposed amendments to the Constitution, bills and orders of the President ;

(4) Proposed budgets, reports to the Board of Audit, urgent financial dispositions, and the defrayment of the reserve fund ;

(5) Matters pertaining to the request of convening the National Assembly for an extraordinary session ;

(6) Proposed proclamation and termination of a state of siege ;

(7) Important military affairs ;

(8) Conferment of honours and grant of pardon, mitigation of punishment or restoration of rights ;

(9) Matters referring to the liaison between departments of the executive branch and determination of their jurisdiction ;

(10) Examination of petitions submitted or referred to the government ;

(11) Appointment and removal of justices of the Supreme Court, Procurator General, the Head of the Board of Audit, the President of the National University, Ambassadors, Ministers, the highest ranking officer of the National Military Force, the Chief of Staff and other public officials and the managers of important national enterprises designated by law ;

(12) Establishment and operation of important policies of the various branches of the executive branch of the government ;

(13) And other matters presented by the Prime Minister or the ministers.

Section III—Executive Departments

Article 73. The heads of the departments of the executive branch shall be appointed by the President from among the ministers.

The Prime Minister shall, under the orders of the President, control and supervise the heads of the departments ; he shall take charge of administrative affairs not assigned to any particular department.

Article 74. The Prime Minister and the head of each executive department may, by virtue of their implied authority or by special delegation, issue 'Orders of the Prime Minister' or Department Orders respectively, concerning affairs in their agencies.

Article 75. The organization and function of each department of the executive branch shall be determined by law.

Ch. V. Courts

Article 76. The judicial power shall be vested in the courts composed of judges. The organization of the Supreme Court and the lower courts shall be determined by law. The qualification of judges shall be determined by law.

Article 77. The judges of the court shall judge independently in accordance with the Constitution and the law.

Article 78. The Chief Justice of the Supreme Court shall be appointed by the President with the consent of the National Assembly.

Article 79. The tenure of the judges shall be ten years and the judges may be reappointed in accordance with the law.

Article 80. Judges shall not be dismissed, suspended from office or have their salaries reduced except by impeachment or criminal or disciplinary punishment.

Article 81. The Supreme Court shall have jurisdiction to decide finally whether administrative orders and regulations, and dispositions, are consistent with the Constitution and the law.

Whenever the decision of the case depends on the determination of the constitutionality of a law, the court shall proceed in accordance with the decision of the Constitution Committee. The Vice-President shall be the Chairman of the Constitution Committee and five justices of the Supreme Court and five members of the National Assembly shall serve as members of the Constitution Committee. A decision holding that a law is unconstitutional requires a two-thirds majority of the Constitution Committee.

The organization and the rules of procedure of the Constitution Committee shall be determined by law.

399

Article 82. The Supreme Court may establish internal regulations of the court and rules pertaining to routine matters.

Article 83. The trial and the announcement of judgement shall be open to the public but may be closed to the public by a decision of the court when it is considered to disturb public peace and order or to be dangerous to public morals.

Ch. VI. *Economy*

Article 84. The principle of the economic order of the Republic of Korea shall be to realize social justice, to meet the basic demands of all citizens and to encourage the development of a balanced economy.

Within the limits of the foregoing paragraph the economic freedom of each individual shall be guaranteed.

Article 85. Mines and other important mineral resources, marine resources, water power and natural powers which may be utilized economically shall be owned by the State. In order to utilize and develop such resources, licences shall, in case of public necessity, be granted for a limited period to private persons in accordance with the provisions of law and shall be cancelled in accordance with the provisions of law.

Article 86. Farmland shall be distributed to self-tilling farmers. The method of distribution, the extent of possession, and the nature and restrictions of ownership shall be determined by law.

Article 87. Important transportation and communication enterprises, financial and insurance institutions, electricity, irrigation, water supply, gas and any enterprises having public character, shall be managed by the government or by juridical persons of public law. When required by public necessity such enterprises shall be licensed to private individuals in accordance with the provisions of law and licences shall be cancelled in accordance with the provisions of law.

Foreign trade shall be under the control of the government.

Article 88. In order to meet urgent necessities of national defence or national life private enterprises shall be transferred to state or public ownership, or their management shall be placed under control or supervision of the state or juridical persons of public law, when it is deemed urgently necessary in accordance with provisions of law.

Article 89. Art. 15, par. 2 of this Constitution shall be applicable to the cancellation of a licence, the expropriation, use or restriction of property as provided in Arts. 85-8.

Ch. VII. *Finance*

Article 90. The items and rates of all taxes shall be determined by law.

Article 91. The Government shall submit to the National Assembly at the beginning of each annual meeting for decision a budget covering all revenues and expenditures for the fiscal year. In case a special disbursement covers a period of more than one year, such disbursement shall be established by the National Assembly as a continual fund.

The National Assembly shall neither increase items of expenditure, nor establish new items of expenditure without the concurrence of the government.

Article 92. The raising of a national loan or the conclusion of any contract incumbent upon the National Treasury outside the national budget shall be subject to a decision of the National Assembly.

Article 93. The creation of a reserve fund for unforeseen expenditures outside of the budget, or for any disbursement in excess of the budget, shall be decided by the National Assembly in advance ; the disbursement of the reserve fund shall be confirmed by the subsequent session of the National Assembly.

Article 94. The National Assembly shall enact the annual budget before the beginning of the fiscal year. In case the budget cannot be enacted in time on account of unavoidable reasons, the National Assembly shall establish a temporary budget for a period not exceeding the first month of the fiscal year and the regular budget shall be enacted within this period.

Article 95. The counts of revenue and disbursement of the state shall be investigated annually by the Board of Audit.

The Government shall submit to the National Assembly, in session the following year, a statement of accounts together with the auditing report of the Board of Audit.

The organization and functions of the Board of Audit shall be determined by law.

Ch. VIII. *Local Autonomous Organizations*

Article 96. Local autonomous organizations shall manage their property and perform their administration within the framework of laws and orders and shall perform such additional tasks as are delegated to them by law.

Local autonomous organizations may establish self-governing regulations within the framework of laws and orders.

Article 97. The organization and operation of local autonomous organizations shall be determined by law. There shall be a Board or Council set up in each local autonomous organization.

The organization and authority of the local councils and the election of its members shall be determined by law.

Ch. IX. Amendment to the Constitution

Article 98. A motion to amend the Constitution shall be introduced either by the President or by one-third or more of the members of the National Assembly duly elected and seated.

Proposed amendments to the Constitution shall be announced by the President to the public.

The period for an announcement as prescribed in the foregoing paragraph shall not be less than 30 days.

The decision on the amendment to the Constitution requires the concurrence of more than two-thirds of the members of the National Assembly duly elected and seated.

When an amendment to the Constitution has been adopted the President shall promulgate it immediately

Ch. X. Supplementary Rules

Article 99. This Constitution shall be in effect from the date of its promulgation so declared by the Speaker of the National Assembly which enacted this Constitution. However, those provisions which can be made effective only after the enactment of supplementary laws shall become effective from the date at which such a supplementary law becomes effective.

Article 100. Existing laws and ordinances shall be in effect to the extent that they do not conflict with this Constitution.

Article 101. The National Assembly which enacted the Constitution may establish a special law dealing with the punishment of malicious anti-national acts committed prior to 15 August 1945.

Article 102. The National Assembly which enacted this Constitution shall exercise the powers of the National Assembly as prescribed in this Constitution ; the terms of its members shall be two years from the date of the convocation of the National Assembly.

Article 103. Government officials who are holding positions at the effective date of this Constitution shall continue their duties until such time as their successors shall be elected or appointed according to this Constitution.

Korea 1945 to 1948, pp. 78-95.

ADDRESS BY SYNGMAN RHEE ON INAUGURATION
AS FIRST PRESIDENT OF THE REPUBLIC OF KOREA

Honoured by the nation to be its first President, I now stand here deeply moved with feelings of gratitude on one hand and on the other with anxieties of heavy responsibilities that are to rest with me.

It has been often said that when joy reaches beyond the limit, laughs turn into tears. How I experienced the truth of the saying, 'Men and women who come to congratulate turn away their heads to hide their tears.' Congratulatory telegrams from various parts of the country express the same emotions. Self-trained as I am not to be carried away by feelings, nor to show them in public, I myself cannot help being shaken to the core with emotions, being only human after all. For the independence we lost 40 years ago is found again ; the nation known to be dead and buried has come to its life anew. On this solemn occasion, I vow before my God and my fellow countrymen to carry out my responsibilities to the limit of my ability and strength. You, too, I ask, dear fellow countrymen, to take a vow in your secret hearts to put the national interest before your own and thus perform your glorious and sacred duties as citizens of Korea. The responsibilities you delegate to me cannot be carried out successfully by any one man. I dare undertake them not on the strength of my own ability but in the sole trust that the concerted efforts of my patriotic countrymen will enable me to discharge them.

It was the solidarity of the people that made the election a complete success to the marvel of our friendly neighbours. The consequent national legislature is truly democratic in character, including several parties of different shades, even a few leftists. Experience disposed some to expect that it would not work, torn by violent dissensions. True, there were heated debates. But not one when the constitution and the government organization's law were enacted by the majority vote. Feelings subsided, leaving no ill will behind. This is how the momentous decisions were made in the shortest possible time. The devotion shown by the representatives and the expert commissioners is truly worthy of all praise.

Naturally I am disabled by this inauguration to retain the chairmanship of the national legislature. But the vacancy will be filled when the other seats probably made vacant by the present occupants accepting positions in the Cabinet or any other positions are filled by by-elections. Meantime the Vice-chairmen will do the presiding as they have often done for me in the past, for which I thank them.

Rumours are rife as to who will be the Prime Minister, who the Cabinet members. You need not pay much heed to them. When everything is made known, they will prove mere surmises, quite beside the mark.

Two considerations are preponderant in organizing the government : in the first place, to make it an efficiently working organization; and, in the second place, to make it stand on a firm foundation, not easily to be shaken. Therefore, regardless of party affiliations or personal relations, men best able and best united to administer the enacted laws in accordance with the wishes of the people will be chosen to governmental positions. A man may be either too big or too little for a place. But a truly great man is able not only to cover a big thing but also a small one and, above all, not to be ashamed of doing a small thing well. With su~h truly great souls coming forward to fill a place with a will, whether it be high or low, the attainment of our ultimate objects will be made possible. Such men of genuine character alone will make the government work like a clock, achieving wonders within and enhancing confidence in us abroad. This government shall thus be representative of the whole nation, not limited to one locality. As often emphasized in the past, the nation will be endangered, if the administrative power is monopolized by one party or one group of politicians. Every citizen must do his part well, loving and guarding the government he helps set up. Failing to do this, we shall again have to suffer aliens to take over what is our due. Our bitter experiences in the past 40 years are enough to drive this truth home.

Good citizens must be protected, while bad ones curbed. Selfishness must make room for justice. Formerly the state used to decline by the monarchs upholding the unworthy and estranging the wise. But in these times when it is the people that elect their own officers, it is up to them to exercise the judgement to distinguish between the good and bad, between the competent and incompetent.

As regards our recognition, since it lies with our neighbours, not ourselves, nothing definite can be said now ... The great task before us is rather to lay the national foundation firm and strong, without troubling about how we shall be received by the world. If we acquit ourselves well and rise to their expectation, they will of themselves recognize and assist us without our asking. So everything depends upon ourselves.

To the United Nations General Assembly to be held at Paris in the coming September, we shall be represented by a delegation composed of men of diplomatic ability. Though it is yet too early to give out their names, the question is almost settled who they shall be. In this connexion, a word of thanks is due to Miss Louisa Yim, who worked for us so hard at Lake Success, despite the fact that we were not able to support her financially or even to correspond with her to any sufficient extent. Her services will be long remembered.

A word for the Communists among our northern brethren in the Soviet zone. Those who want to sell their country to a foreign Power in the name of Communism, undoing their own nation, cannot but be condemned as traitors by the whole people. I earnestly appeal to them to stop their traitorous activities and come back to the unified national fold, ready to conform to the form of government the people will decide in the democratic way, whatever shape it may take. We are not so much against Communism as against the treason of its devotees. Let me once more urge them to come back repenting their past ill conduct and peacefully unite the bisected country into one so that they, too, may share the blessings therefrom. If they should persist, however, in their mistaken path, their doom is unavoidable both before man and God.

In international relations we will uphold peace, parity, amity, free commerce on principles of equality and co-prosperity. If there be any differentiation of attitude on our part, it will be because it was forced upon us. To a friendly neighbour, we will require their friendliness with our own. But from an unfriendly one, we shall be compelled to hold ourselves aloof.

For the past 40 years we simply did not exist in the eyes of the world. The world judged us by what others said about us, not by anything we did. But now when we are being helped to our feet by our well-meaning neighbours, we can have our own say, and show to them what we are doing. We should like to ask our neighbours, from now on, to weigh us not by what they hear about us but by what they see we are doing.

To make much of the impression we make on the outside world, to make actual facts known as they exist here to all the peace-loving free individuals abroad is not for pushing our own interests alone, but also as a means of safeguarding world peace.

To build up a new nation, a new constitution, a new government is, of course, necessary but what is far more needed is a new people. We cannot make a holy state out of a corrupt people. With a rejuvenated national spirit blasting away all the old corrupt practices, we can possibly make up for the last 40 years, catching up with the times. My beloved 30 million brethren, let us all strive to be worthy members of the new rising nation whose foundation should be on the rock of ages never to be washed away by the torrent of world events.

Korea 1945 to 1948, pp. 95-8.

V PEOPLE'S REPUBLIC OF KOREA (NORTH)

25   *May* 1948

KIM SUNG'S REPORT ON PROGRESS OF THE KOREAN DEMOCRATIC PEOPLE'S REPUBLIC (NORTH) TO THE KOREAN UNITY CONFERENCE

Delegates,

Before making a report on the situation in Northern Korea I should like to say a few words regarding the political significance of this conference.

This conference is of significance not only from the standpoint of Korea, but also internationally.

The significance of this conference lies in the fact that representatives of all political parties and social organizations both in Southern and Northern Korea have met together here for the first time since the liberation of our fatherland from Japanese imperialism.

And this conference is significant, on the other hand, because it has been convened particularly at this juncture when our fatherland is confronted with the danger of a split, when the attempt by American imperialists to colonize Southern Korea is becoming more and more candid, and when the crisis confronting our fatherland to-day is very serious—the worst of this kind ever experienced by our fatherland since liberation.

Such being the case, this joint conference should discuss, straightforwardly and rightly, the political situation both in Southern and Northern Korea and work out fundamental measures to cope with the national crisis with which our fatherland is confronted.

Delegates,

At present the political situation of our fatherland is very complicated and tense. The reason for this is, on the one hand, that American imperialists backed by the former pro-Japanese collaborators and national traitors, are manoeuvring to split us thirty million Korean people and colonize our land. With the object of realizing this dark ambition, they, under the subterfuge of the United Nations Korean Commission, are attempting to enforce separate elections in Southern Korea for the establishment of a so-called 'unified national government'.

Our fatherland is confronted with crisis. Before us thirty million Korean people the danger of enslavement has arrived again.

And the reason the political situation of our fatherland is very complicated and tense is, on the other hand, that the colonial policy of American imperialists today towards our fatherland has brought a life and death struggle to the Korean people. For the entire Korean people, who have risen in protest to the policy of American imperialists to colonize and enslave our fatherland, are opposing the election comedy in Southern Korea. And this resistance movement is greatly helping unite all democratic forces throughout Korea, crying for the establishment of a united, democratic, independent Korea.

We thirty million Koreans are a nation of a single identity which has enjoyed unity throughout its history of fifty centuries. Notwithstanding this, however, our fatherland is artificially divided across the 38th Parallel. This is a peculiarity of the political situation of our fatherland.

The division between South and North has compelled the Korean people to fight for the glory, liberty and democratic independence of our fatherland.

The people in Northern Korea, under genuine and friendly support of the Soviet Union, have achieved great results in connexion with the historical work of democratic reconstruction of our fatherland.

But the people in Southern Korea are groaning under the severe rule of these reactionary elements who are piloted by the US Army as they did under the rule of Japanese imperialists. As a matter of fact, they are now in straitened conditions, politically and economically. This fact has been known through publications in Southern Korea and even through American publications.

In order to analyse this complicated political situation in our fatherland it is necessary to view the issue historically.

We groaned under the colonial régime of Japanese imperialists for thirty-six years. These thirty-six years marked a miserable period of unjust oppression upon and enslavement of our nation. Japanese imperialists built in Korea not for the prosperity of our fatherland or for the future development of our nation, but as preparations to launch their beastly aggressive war in Eastern Asia.

We Korean people were offered as a slave labour power for the colonial robber of Japanese imperialism.

The Japanese colonial robbers looked down upon us Korean people as an inferior nation, thus excluding Koreans from the work of directing industrial undertakings or state institutions.

Only a small minority of pro-Japanese collaborators and national traitors who had been isolated from the people turned into loyal hounds of Japanese imperialism, and served for Japanese imperialists.

With the aim of blunting the awakening of the Korean people, the Japanese imperialists endeavoured to erase our national cultures with a long history of fifty centuries by forcing us to speak

Japanese, adopt Japanese customs, and worship Japanese literature and the so-called Japanese religion—Shintoism.

In August 1945 the Red Army drove away the Japanese army from the soil of our country. And the Red Army entered into our country as they liberated freely the Korean people. Thus, the Korean people was enabled to put an end to a bitter era of humiliation and enslavement of the Korean people. At the same time, the bright path of regeneration of the Korean people had been opened.

Even our descendants for ever will remember the glorious service rendered by the Red Army which heroically fought at the sacrifice of lives.

The US Army landed on Southern Korea after the termination of the war without using a single bullet. Under the war-time arrangement between the US and Soviet Governments, the area north of the 38th Parallel was temporarily assigned for occupation by the Red Army and that south of the 38th Parallel by the US Army. As such, the 38th parallel became a temporary line between the Soviet and US Armies.

But this 38th Parallel line, as everyone of you well knows, has actually become a frontier rather than a temporary line, thereby artificially dividing our fatherland between South and North, despite the fact that our fatherland is a single piece of land. The fact that the Red Army occupied the area north of the Parallel line and the US Army that south of it, caused both Southern and Northern Korea to pursue opposite directions.

As everyone of you well knows, both the Soviet Union and the United States towards the end of 1945 signed the Moscow Decisions regarding Korea.

I am refraining from making any detailed remarks on this issue. What I want to point out here is only the fact that the Red Army in occupation of Northern Korea has been constantly pursuing the path leading to the realization of the Moscow Decisions whereas the US Army in occupation of Southern Korea has been pursuing the path leading to disrupting these Decisions. With regard to the actual situation in Southern Korea I believe all the delegates from Southern Korea will make detailed reports based on innumerable facts they have to date witnessed with their own eyes. But allow me to point out only one fact.

Shortly after the liberation of our fatherland from the colonial rule of Japanese imperialism people's committees began to be created in every part of Southern Korea and Northern Korea. The fact that these committees came into being was mainly due to people's creative initiatives, and in many cases spontaneously. This phenomenon was nothing more or less than a manifestation of justifiable desire on the part of the Korean people to organize autonomous organs with their own hands for their liberated fatherland so as to stabilize the people's livelihood and preserve peace and order as speedily as possible. And it is a well known fact that an all-Korea conference of people's committees thus organized was scheduled to be convened in Seoul.

But a trend such as this entirely was far from suitable to the taste of American imperialists. To those American imperialists who attempted to realize their gruesome scheme to enslave our fatherland, it was their desire to see political power fall not into the hands of the people, but into the hands of those national traitors and reactionary elements who could faithfully put into force their plot by selling down the river their fatherland and people.

Therefore, American imperialists dissolved the people's committees in Southern Korea by resorting to ruthless methods which are beyond description.

And thus, the American Military Government seized the entire political power in its hands and left no stone unturned to disrupt the Moscow Decisions instead of putting them into force.

Southern Korea, instead of being enabled to reconstruct our fatherland democratically and establish a people's régime by a great spontaneous movement of a liberated nation, has turned out to be what a member of the so-called United Nations Korean Commission describes as a 'police state'.

The situation in Northern Korea is different fundamentally from that in Southern Korea, the cause for it being that the Red Army in occupation of Northern Korea enforced from beginning to end the Moscow Decisions on Korea and granted freedom of a wide scope to the people of Northern Korea.

Thus, the people in Northern Korea were enabled to organize institutions of a régime with their own hands.

The people's committees in Northern Korea, instead of being dissolved like in Southern Korea, enjoyed freedom of action, and were able to preserve order in the country and stabilize security of the people's livelihood.

And these autonomous organs directed the magnificent work of reconstructing the state by restoring industries, transportation, communications and commerce which was launched by the people in Northern Korea.

Through this magnificent state reconstruction work the people's committees already achieved great results in 1945 and 1946, thus enjoying high prestige among the wide masses of the people.

New leaders, who emerged from the people, have been trained through the process of actual works carried out by organs of the people's régime, various political parties and social organizations in Northern Korea.

Many of those who directly participated in activities at the time the people's committees were brought into being are today known as prominent leaders of the people's régime. That the form of the people's régime is most suitable to development of our fatherland is clearly attested to by the fact that the prestige of the people's committees is growing day by day, for it has been examined through actual works carried out amidst most complicated circumstances under which the administrative institutions of Japanese imperialism had to be replaced by new ones.

As the political, economic and cultural life of Northern Korea grew day by day, the people in Northern Korea, with the object of legally preserving this form of régime, carried out elections for the people's committees in provinces, cities and counties towards the end of 1946, and for the people's committees in hamlets (Myon) and villages towards the beginning of 1947.

These elections for the people's committees of all ranks were carried out under democratic principles of a wide scope and in accordance with the universal, equal, direct, and secret vote.

This means that for the first time in Korean history democratic elections were held, for through the medium of this event the people were able to express their views most widely and freely. In the work of preparing for, and enforcing these elections, representatives of people of every strata and walks of life, and those representing all political parties and social organizations took part with greatest enthusiasm. For example, at the time of elections for the people's committees in provinces, cities and counties, 80,470 persons participated in election committees.

Of these 9 per cent were women, this being the first time for Korean women to participate in state work. Those who were not capable of participating in the first elections in accordance with election rules numbered only 4,380 ; they were the proven former pro-Japanese collaborators and insanes, or those who had been deprived of their election rights as a result of public trials.

This number represented only one-thousandth of the total voters. The elections were enforced amidst an overflowing political enthusiasm demonstrated by the entire voters. The elections for the people's committees of all ranks were participated in by 99·6 per cent of the total voters.

This bears witness to the fact that the prestige of the people's committees has been uplifted among the masses of the entire people.

As the result of elections for the people's committees in provinces, cities, counties, hamlets (Myon), and villages, 70,217 members were elected. This figure frankly shows how widely the masses of the people in Northern Korea are taking part in organs of the régime.

The people's committees are composed of those representing peasants, workers, clerks, intelligentsia, business men, industrialists, religionists, and all walks of life and strata.

The people's committees are composed of those representing all democratic political parties and social organizations in Northern Korea ; of those elected as members of the people's committees, 13·1 per cent represent women.

In February 1947 a convention of the people's committees was held. On the occasion, the Northern Korea Supreme People's Assembly, highest organ of the Northern Korea people's régime, was brought into being. Like the people's committees this assembly is also composed of those representing people of all walks of life and strata, as well as of those representing all political parties and social organizations in Northern Korea. As such, elections for the people's committees were completed from bottom to top, and these elections for the people's committees legally consolidated the new form of the people's régime.

Since then, one year has already elapsed.

During the past one year the people's committees have become organizations stronger than ever. And leaders of the people's régime have gained great experience through democratic construction, demonstrated their excellent capabilities as they put into execution various measures, and at the same time demonstrated their wonderful abilities to solve the most complicated problems in connexion with the political, economic, and cultural life of our fatherland.

This is a stern fact smashing to pieces vicious propaganda being carried on by those American imperialists who look down upon the Korean people, saying in derision that the Korean people are still far from capable of constructing their own state with their hands.

In all directions the people's committees have achieved great results, the most important of all being various great democratic reforms which have been enforced in Northern Korea.

Particularly what I want to point out here is that these great democratic reforms were enthusiastically supported by the masses of the people since they were enforced for the interest of the people.

Democratic reforms uplifted the patriotic enthusiasm of the masses of the people in Northern Korea, for the people once more firmly recognized the fact that the people's committees, which they had created with their own hands, most faithfully are enforcing aspirations and expectations of the people. Through actual works of the people's committees the people have been convinced of this fact ... (Section on economic and educational reforms omitted.)

Towards the beginning of this year (1948) the Northern Korea Supreme People's Assembly organized a Constitution Enactment Committee, decision having been reached to put to discussion by the people a provisional Korean constitution drafted by this committee. In fact, discussion is being carried on regarding the draft of the provisional Constitution, the most important phenomenon being that an absolute majority of the people not only in Northern Korea but in Southern Korea as well are enthusiastically supporting the draft of the Provisional Korean Constitution.

Of course, this is by no means an accident.

For this Constitution has contributed to strengthen all the democratic reforms already enforced in Northern Korea, and at the same time the path the entire Korean people shall follow has been clearly shown by it.

To date, the Constitution Enactment Committee has received 55,000 letters of gratitude along with documents containing decision in favour of the draft of the Constitution as well as recommendations regarding the draft of the Constitution. This bears witness to the fact that the entire Korean people are greatly interested in adopting a genuine democratic Constitution.

The fact that the entire Korean people are supporting the draft of the Provisional Korean Constitution must be considered as their supporting all those great democratic reforms that have been put into force throughout Northern Korea. In other words, this means that the entire Korean people are wholeheartedly supporting the works of the Northern Korea People's Committee.

Delegates !

In order to rightly evaluate the actual situation in Northern Korea I cannot help but relate how the people in Northern Korea are being united in their struggle to construct a democratic, autonomous, independent state.

The unity of the people in Northern Korea has a firm foundation. That is to say, the entire people in Northern Korea have been united on the foundation of supporting the people's committees which are an agency of political power of their own, as well as on the foundation of supporting all those democratic reforms which have been enforced in Northern Korea for the interests of the masses of the people. The crystallization of unity of the people in Northern Korea is the Northern Korea Democratic National Front, which embraces all political parties and social organizations, as well as a wide scope of the masses of the people representing all strata and walks of life throughout Northern Korea.

At present there are 3 big political parties, 16 social organizations and 17 trade unions under the leadership of the Northern Korea Democratic National Front.

All the political parties and social organizations in Northern Korea are holding identical views and opinions regarding the political issues. For they are supporting the people's committees and democratic reforms, and are active in the struggle to construct a united, democratic, autonomous, independent state. The Northern Korea Democratic National Front is embracing 6 million persons as its organized forces ; its strength and unity having already been demonstrated.

This was clearly shown by the fact that the wide masses of the people enthusiastically supported the candidates recommended by the Northern Korea Democratic National Front at the time elections were held for the people's committees.

All this magnificent strength shows that it is possible to mobilize the entire people in Northern Korea to participate in the struggle to construct a democratic, independent state of Korea.

Delegates !

The actual situation in Northern Korea can be briefly evaluated as follows.

Firstly, the political power in Northern Korea has fallen into the people's hands, for the people have become complete masters in every field of political, economic and cultural life. Taking advantage of the free conditions created by the Red Army, the people in Northern Korea have created an agency of political power of their own in the form of the people's committees, strengthened and developed it.

Secondly, in Northern Korea democratic reforms suitable to the interests of the wide masses of the people have been enforced, with the result that the leadership of the masses of the people in every field of political, economic and cultural life has been guaranteed. On the other hand, the foundation of reactionaries has been fundamentally uprooted. In other words, the enforcement of democratic reforms has prevented the reactionary elements in Northern Korea from holding any foundation of their own whatever.

Thirdly, the enforcement of democratic reforms in Northern Korea has created very favourable conditions for future restoration and development of the people's economy. At the same time, by achieving great results in restoring and developing the people's economy the democratic reforms have constantly elevated the material and cultural standard of the masses of the people.

Fourthly, all these great achievements in Northern Korea have been seized by us through our struggle. Moreover, these achievements have become a firm material foundation on which the entire people in Northern Korea are united like steel around the people's committees, an agency of political power of their own.

Contrary to this, the situation in Southern Korea, a half of the territory of our fatherland, is entirely different. In Southern Korea the US occupation army has grabbed the entire political power in its hands, thereby preventing the Korean people from controlling and administering their country with their own hands. Democratic reforms still remain to be enforced in Southern Korea, with the result that centuries-old aspirations of the Korean people have not yet been realized. Lately reactionary publications in Southern Korea widely talk about the enforcement of 'land reform'. This so-called 'land reform' is intended not only to deceive the Korean peasants in Southern Korea but also this scheme is, in actuality, nothing but an insult to those Korean peasants in Southern Korea who are being oppressed.

The material situation of the masses of the people in Southern Korea is deteriorating more and more, which fact is admitted even by the reactionary elements in Southern Korea. And the reactionary elements in Southern Korea, under the aegis of the American military government, are cudgelling their brains in working out all sorts of traitorous and anti-popular measures to suppress the democratic forces in Southern Korea.

Consequently, Southern Korea of today has been transformed into a state of anarchy where terrorism is rampant in the broad daylight.

And yet the Americans, notwithstanding they have made such a mess out of Southern Korea, are still far from satiated as they are indulged in wild dreams for a world domination ; they are actually scheming to permanently enslave Southern Korea.

At present our fatherland is confronted with a grave national crisis where our fatherland is likely to fall victim to the aggressive policy of American imperialism. Therefore, we people in Northern Korea are seriously worried about the destiny of our compatriots, our parents, our brothers and sisters in Southern Korea south of the 38th Parallel. At the same time, we are sending our warmest encouragement and support to those compatriots in Southern Korea who are now carrying on a patriotic struggle for the glory, dignity and freedom of our fatherland against the enslavement policy of American imperialists. And we are united with our fighting compatriots in Southern Korea in our common struggle to construct an independent state.

Delegates !

From the first day of their landing on the soil of our fatherland the American imperialists have been uninterruptedly enforcing their crafty aggressive policy.

The conference of the foreign ministers of the Soviet Union, the United States and the United Kingdom, held in Moscow in December 1945, adopted decisions on Korea.

These historical decisions adopted by the Moscow conference foresaw reconstructing Korea as an autonomous independent state on the foundation of democracy. But these decisions could not be realized. Every one of you is well aware of the main reasons for it. The Soviet-US joint conference was held on two different occasions to come to an agreement for the enforcement of the decisions, only to prove in vain.

We Korean people are well aware of the causes for the failure of the task of the Soviet-US joint conference ; we know who is to blame. The task of the Soviet-US conference having thus resulted in failure, the Soviet Government on 26 September 1947 proposed simultaneous withdrawal of both the Soviet and US occupation forces from Korea towards the beginning of 1948, so that the Korean people themselves could settle their own problems. In other words, had this proposal been put into execution, the Korean people could have autonomously elected a supreme legislative organ, established a united democratic government, formed a national army, and reconstructed the political and economic life of our fatherland on the foundation of democracy without intervention or pressure from any foreign country.

This proposal by the Soviet Government was enthusiastically supported by the entire Korean people who were determined to solve the Korean unification issue with their hands by causing the Soviet and US occupation forces to withdraw from the soil of Korea. But a handful of pro-Japanese collaborators, national traitors and reactionaries in Southern Korea were opposed to this proposal. Why ? Because these traitorous elements feared they could no longer continue their treacherous acts against the interest of the people in the event the US occupation forces withdrew from Southern Korea.

Syngman Rhee and his traitorous gang came out in opposition to the withdrawal of the US occupation forces from Southern Korea. This act disclosed in broad daylight the true feature of those treasonous reactionary elements.

And this crime by these treacherous elements once more demonstrated before the Korean people that Syngman Rhee and his gang were loyal hounds of American imperialism selling our fatherland and the interest of our nation to the American imperialists.

The proposal by the Soviet Government also caused pandemonium even among the American imperialists. In point of fact, the US Government rejected it, for the withdrawal of its troops from Southern Korea entirely runs counter to aggressive schemes of the American imperialists. The Korean issue was part of the whole issues outstanding between the Soviet and US Governments which could be settled only through the good offices of the two governments. In other words, the Korean issue was entirely out of the scope of the United Nations. Notwithstanding this, the US Government illegally brought it up at the UN General Assembly and attempted to cause the Korean issue to be solved favourable to it. The US Government, taking advantage of those automatic hand-raising machines created within the United Nations which are politically and economically enslaved to the American monopoly capitalists, caused the UN General Assembly to reject the Soviet proposal and adopt instead tricky decisions based upon military and political schemes of the American imperialists.

As every one of you well knows, the so-called United Nations Korean Commission, in accordance with the decision of the UN General Assembly, was formed, its function being to supervise the enforcement of elections and the establishment of a Korean government as well as of a Korean national army.

The Korean people refused to recognize this decision of the UN General Assembly. Towards the end of last year (1947) when this decision was adopted by the UN General Assembly, they carried out solemn demonstrations and held mass rallies in every nook and corner of Southern and Northern Korea in protest against this decision.

The Korean people believed that the UN General Assembly would, as a matter of course, invite their representatives to discussions on the Korean issue and that discussion could be held only under participation by the Korean representatives.

At the UN General Assembly the Soviet delegation proposed inviting the representatives of the Korean people, and this proposal was supported by the representatives of many democratic countries.

But the UN General Assembly refused to invite the Korean representatives. This was purely due to a high-handed demand by the US delegation who feared that the Korean representatives would expose before the eyes of the world the colonial policy now being enforced by the American imperialists in Southern Korea.

This measure taken by the UN General Assembly was a ruthless and insulting act trampling under foot even the elementary rights of the Korean people.

We Korean people could not permit the UN General Assembly to determine our destiny without participation by our representatives. Therefore, the Korean people resented the act of the UN General Assembly in discussing the Korean issue in such a way—so much so that they were compelled to carry out a nation-wide strong protest movement against the UN decision.

The trouble lies not only in the fact that the UN General Assembly discussed the Korean issue in an unreasonable method, but also in the fact that it, in accordance with the high-handed demand from the American imperialists, adopted decisions detrimental to the interests of the Korean people. Why is it that the Korean issue has been settled in this way?

Why is it that the UN General Assembly rejected the most legitimate proposal to let the Korean people establish their own government with their hands, but that it adopted the proposal to organize the so-called UN Korean Commission which is antagonistic towards the Korean people?

That is because the UN General Assembly is being gradually transformed into a tool of the expansion policy of American imperialism and because those countries economically enslaved to the United States are dancing to the tune of the American imperialists. More than that, this is because the withdrawal of US troops from the soil of Korea runs counter to the scheme of the colonial plunderers of American imperialism. The American imperialists are manœuvring to establish a separate government in Southern Korea by partitioning our fatherland. Herein lies the objective of aggressive schemes of the American imperialists.

In order to split our fatherland the American imperialists are causing the so-called UN Korean Commission to play a Herculean role.

The UN Korean Commission is nothing but a tool whereby individual actions of the US Government in Southern Korea and the US policy to split our fatherland can be legalized and whereby with the aim of establishing a separate government in Southern Korea an election comedy is to be performed.

We Korean people are well aware of the political significance of the UN Korean Commission as well as of its schemes. Therefore, the entire Korean people are openly antagonistic towards the UN Korean Commission, for they consider it as nothing but a scheme to intervene in Korean internal affairs. And the Korean people are demanding the speedy withdrawal of the UN Korean Commission from our fatherland.

We demand that the Korean people be granted the right and possibility of independently establishing a united democratic people's government without interference from the outside.

The UN Korean Commission, after having sized the fact that the entire Korean people are dead set against the establishment of a separate government in Southern Korea, asked the UN General Assembly for instructions for its future activity, so that it might avoid the responsibility for splitting Korea.

In accordance with the recommendations by the UN Korean Commission that elections be permitted to be held even in Southern Korea alone and in accordance with insistent demand by the American imperialists, the UN 'little assembly' adopted a decision to hold separate elections in Southern Korea so as to establish a separate government.

This decision was adopted by 31 countries against 2 countries which opposed it and 11 others which waived the right to vote. The United States had expected that its proposal would be absolutely supported because of the absence of the delegates of the Soviet Union and all other Eastern European democratic countries, and it had actually left no stone unturned for this purpose.

But the UN Little Assembly failed to come to a unanimous decision.

At the time the decision on the Korean issue was being discussed at the UN Little Assembly, the Swedish and Norwegian delegates were opposed to enforcing separate elections in Southern Korea.

The Swedish delegate held the view that he was opposed to enforcing elections only in Southern Korea, not only because of lack of official data regarding the actual situation in Southern Korea, but because of the fact that the United Nations was not brought into being as an instrument to discuss the post-war mediation issues.

On the other hand, the Norwegian delegate declared that by adopting the US decision the UN Little Assembly was abusing the right accorded it by the UN General Assembly.

Besides this, it must be pointed out that even a member of the so-called UN Korean Commission admitted the fact that those supporting the establishment of a separate government in Southern Korea were only the faithful servant of the American imperialists, Syngman Rhee, and the Korean Democratic Party composed of the pro-Japanese collaborators, big landlords and industrialists under the leadership of Kim Sung Soo.

The said delegate also confessed that not only the leftists and the middle-of-the-roaders, but also even many of the rightist leaders were opposed to enforcing separate elections under the subterfuge of establishing a 'national government', for they realized that separate elections in Southern Korea would split Korea permanently.

418

Even within the so-called UN Korean Commission 4 out of 8 members voted in favour of enforcing separate elections in Southern Korea, but 2 others voted against it while 2 others waived the right to vote.

But the US delegate, who acted as the master of the UN Little Assembly, trampled under foot this legitimate opposition by the delegates of many countries. At the UN Little Assembly the American imperialists candidly unmasked themselves and brought pressure to bear upon the UN Little Assembly to adopt their decision guaranteeing their administration in Southern Korea.

At present, the American military government, under the subterfuge of the so-called UN Korean Commission, is preparing for separate elections in Southern Korea.

What attitude are the entire Korean people both in Southern and Northern Korea taking regarding separate elections in Southern Korea ?

In order to answer this question, we must clarify what the entire Korean people want, how they are fighting against the colonial policy of the American imperialists, and what must be done.

We Korean people are well aware of the fact that the purpose of separate elections to be enforced in Southern Korea on 10 May 1948 is to split Korea permanently, so that the American imperialists may convert Southern Korea into a US colony as well as into their political and military base.

We are a nation with a history of 50 centuries. How can we tolerate the realization of such a reactionary and anti-popular scheme of the American imperialists aiming at splitting our people ?

Therefore, the entire Korean people throughout Korea are strongly demanding that outside intervention in internal affairs of our fatherland be terminated and that the UN Korean Commission withdraw from the soil of our fatherland.

In protest against the UN Korean Commission in numerous factories workers and clerks throughout Southern Korea are carrying on strikes, which started on 8 January 1948—the first day the UN Korean Commission set foot on the soil of our fatherland.

As every one of you well knows, 8 January 1948 all factory workers and clerks in Seoul struck.

Towards the beginning of February a magnificent strike was carried out by communication and factory workers throughout Southern Korea.

According to reports of the Korean News Agency in Seoul, this general strike completely paralysed Southern Korea.

The strikers demanded of Lieutenant-General John R. Hodge, commander of the US occupation forces in Southern Korea, that the UN Korean Commission and the US occupation troops be withdrawn from the soil of Korea.

Even American newsmen stationed in Seoul reported that masses of the people demonstrating in protest against the UN Korean Commission came into bloody clashes with police.

These strikes are still going on. This fact the delegates from Southern Korea know more than anyone else.

It is not only the workers in Southern Korea but also the peasants in Southern Korea who in co-operation with the entire workers and people are carrying on a heroic struggle for the unification of our fatherland and the establishment of a united democratic government.

Delegates from Southern Korea !

The entire people in Northern Korea are wholeheartedly supporting your sacrificial and heroic struggle against the split of our fatherland. The entire people in Northern Korea are absolutely behind you with national enthusiasm and brotherly encouragement.

The people in Northern Korea are in conditions entirely different from those in which the people in Southern Korea find themselves. The people in Northern Korea have become the masters of their land. In the hands of the people in Northern Korea there are land, political power and industry.

As already mentioned above, the people in Northern Korea have carried out great historical democratic reforms.

But Korea still remains to be unified, and because our fatherland has not as yet been unified under a united democratic government, the democratic reforms are not capable of attaining greater achievements. Every one of us well knows this.

The people in Southern Korea are determined to share life or death, or comfort and hardship with our parents, brothers and sisters in Southern Korea, regardless of what conditions and environment we may find ourselves in, until the unification of our fatherland against its split is assured.

We know that splitting our fatherland will once more impose the painful yoke of colonial enslavement upon the 30 million Korean people.

Therefore, the people in Northern Korea will deal with any kind of separate government with antagonism and undauntedly advocate unifying Southern and Northern Korea, and continue to fight for the attainment of this object.

The people in Northern Korea consider it the most urgent task to present a nation-wide united front with their compatriots in Southern Korea—the descendants of the same blood—in their common struggle to frustrate the aggressive scheme of the American imperialists to split Korea.

The people in Northern Korea have—through demonstrations, rallies, protests, decisions, and manifestoes—demonstrated their definite political attitude against criminal activities being perpetrated by the so-called UN Commission on Korea as well as against foreign intervention in the Korean question.

The masses of the people in Northern Korea are appealing to the people in Southern Korea that they rise like one man and participate in our common struggle for freedom and independence of our fatherland by extricating ourselves from the complicated political situation created in our country.

The masses of the people in Northern Korea are encouraging the people in Southern Korea to carry out all the more positively and decisively their struggle to boycott separate elections which will ruin our country.

It is the biggest political task for the entire Korean people to boycott and frustrate the Southern Korea separate elections which are against the interest of the people and which will ruin our country.

You, representatives from Southern Korea, can firmly believe that your compatriots in Northern Korea will share life and death or happiness and hardship with our compatriots in Southern Korea and fight, to the bitter end, against the separate elections in Southern Korea as well as against the establishment of a separate government in Southern Korea.

Those who are, at this moment of today, supporting the enforcement of separate elections in Southern Korea are nothing but national traitors whose treason is worse than that committed by Song Byung Choon and Lee Wan Yong, the two worst traitors the Korean people ever had for fifty centuries of their national life. We have already mentioned the traitor Syngman Rhee.

Everyone of the entire Korean people well knows that Syngman Rhee is the most despicable traitor of the Korean people. And everyone of the entire Korean people well knows that Syngman Rhee is a hound of the American imperialists, as it is a common knowledge that he has been raised by the American imperialists for the past forty years.

He is willing to do whatever his American masters dictate. But we don't talk about only Syngman Rhee himself. For we consider as a traitor anyone who supports separate elections in Southern Korea, no matter who he may be.

We must expose such traitors of the Korean people, we must isolate and ostracize them from the people, and we must cause the entire people to spit on them, hate them, and deal with them with antagonism. At the same time, we must clearly interpret to the masses of the people the significance of the aggressive scheme behind the Southern Korea separate elections.

Every true Korean patriot must realize that these separate elections will inevitably lead Southern Korea to the abyss of ruin, thereby transforming Southern Korea into a US colony.

Therefore, any who truly loves his fatherland must boycott these separate elections, no matter who he may be.

In this nationwide struggle, regardless of party, religion, and political views, the entire Korean patriots throughout the country must be united.

Unity alone is the prerequisite to our victory. Therefore, this conference must work out measures how to all the more strengthen our unity and to what direction we should lead this united strength for the attainment of the supreme cause of the Korean people in connexion with our great historic work of unifying our fatherland and establishing a united democratic government.

The political situation in Northern Korea as well as the most basic and characteristic feature of the political life of our fatherland can be briefly summarized something as follows :

As every one of you can realize, this conference has been convened under such a complicated environment of our fatherland as well as under conditions embracing various difficult problems. Therefore, at this conference we must frankly and without reservation, discuss the political situation created in our fatherland, and work out the only and common measure to fight against the split of our fatherland, manœuvres of the UN Commission on Korea, and the Southern Korea separate elections.

We must disrupt aggressive schemes of the American imperialists.

We must carry out a struggle to unite our fatherland as an autonomous, independent state and establish our united government on the wide democratic basis.

At this grave moment our fatherland is confronted with a crisis ; we must be united, we must repulse the danger of splitting our fatherland, and smash the scheme of the American imperialists to colonize Southern Korea. If we fail to work out this great measure for the salvation of our fatherland, we must bear in mind that we are going to commit a sin against the entire Korean people as well as against our coming descendants—a sin which can't be wiped out for centuries to come.

The most fundamental political conclusion which starts from the prevailing political situation created in our fatherland is as follows :

Long live a united democratic Korea !

The UN Commission on Korea must leave the soil of our fatherland!

May those truly Korean patriots who are carrying on sacrificial struggle against the colonial aggressors of American imperialism have victory and glory!

Long live the great democratic reforms enforced in Northern Korea!

Tewksbury, Donald G., *Source Material on Korean Politics and Ideologies* (Mimeographed), International Secretariat, Institute of Pacific Relations, New York, 1950, pp. 98-114.

26   *3 September* 1948

CONSTITUTION OF THE DEMOCRATIC PEOPLE'S REPUBLIC OF KOREA (EXCERPT)

Ch. I. Fundamental Principles

Article 1. Our country is the Korean People's Democratic Republic.

Article 2. The Sovereignty of the Korean People's Democratic Republic is in the people. The people shall exercise their Sovereignty through the people's committees, the new form of the state Sovereignty, which was brought into existence in accordance with the free will of the people simultaneously with the 15 August Liberation of 1945.

Article 3. All the organs representing the Sovereignty shall be elected from the *ri* (or village) people's committee up to the supreme people's committees. Elections for the organs of the Korean People's Democratic Republic shall be held on the basis of the principles of general, equal and direct elections.

Article 4. Representatives and committee members of all the organs of the Sovereignty shall hold themselves responsible for their works and activities before their voters. In the event any representative or committee member of the organs of the Sovereignty loses confidence from the voters, the voters can recall him even before his tenure of office has expired.

Article 5. Natural resources buried underground, forests, rivers, portations, communications, broadcasting stations, banks, hydroelectricity, water works, mineral fountains, natural energies, the properties formerly owned by the Japanese, and all the properties of Korean national traitors shall belong to the entire people, i.e., to the State. Foreign trade shall be conducted by the State and also under the supervision of the State.

Article 6.   The former landownership by the Japanese State and by the Japanese subjects, that by Korean landlords, and the tenancy system shall permanently be abolished. Land can be had only by one who tills it. No one can own land beyond what is stipulated by the law. The scope of land one can own shall separately be stipulated by the law. Landownership by the individuals as well as by the State and the co-operative organizations shall be granted. The area of land to be owned by the State as well as by the co-operative organizations shall be limitless. The State shall grant special protection to the interests of the toiling peasants, and assist them by various methods as permitted by its economic policy.

Article 7.   For those areas within Korea where land reform has not yet been enforced, the land reform shall be enforced on the date to be fixed by the Supreme People's Assembly. Land reform for these areas shall be enforced on the basis of the ordinances regarding the land reform carried out in Northern Korea.

Article 8.   Individual ownership of land, trucks, farming tools, other means of production, middle and small commercial organs, raw materials, manufactured goods, houses, all other auxiliary household equipments, household utensils, incomes, and savings shall be protected by the law. The inheritance right of individual ownership shall be guaranteed by the law. Initiative of individual management shall be encouraged.

Article 9.   The State shall encourage development of the people's co-operative organizations. The ownership by the co-operative organizations shall be protected by the law.

Article 10.   With the object of reasonably utilizing all economic resources as well as all the potential economic resources in the country for the interests of the people, the State shall draw up a single people's economic plan, and at the same time shall direct economic and cultural recovery and development in the country on the basis of this people's economic plan. In enforcing this people's economic plan the State shall permit the branch of individual economy to participate in this plan on the basis of the ownership by the States and the co-operative organizations.

Tewksbury, Donald G., *Source Materials on Korean Politics and Ideologies*, pp. 119-20.

PART TWO

I RELATIONS WITH UNITED STATES

27   11 *August* 1948

LETTER FROM PRESIDENT SYNGMAN RHEE TO GENERAL HODGE ON TRANSFER OF GOVERNMENTAL FUNCTIONS TO THE GOVERNMENT OF THE REPUBLIC OF KOREA

I have the honour to inform you that, in consequence of the deliberations and acts of the Korean National Assembly, which was constituted as a result of the election held on 10 May 1948 under the observation of the United Nations Temporary Commission on Korea, there was formed as of 5 August 1948 the Government of the Republic of Korea. In accordance with paragraph 3 of resolution II of the United Nations General Assembly Resolutions on Korea of 14 November 1947, the United Nations Temporary Commission on Korea was notified on 6 August 1948 of the formation of this government.

In furtherance of the United Nations General Assembly resolutions on Korea, particularly paragraph 4 of resolution II, I have the honour further to inform you that the Government of the Republic of Korea, after consultation with the United Nations Temporary Commission on Korea, will be prepared to take over the functions of government. To that end your co-operation and assistance are requested in transferring to the Government of the Republic of Korea all such functions now exercised by you as Commanding General, United States Army Forces in Korea, including the direction of all police, coast guard, and constabulary units now in being.

The Government of the Republic of Korea recognizes that it will be necessary for you to retain control over areas and facilities of vital importance to you (such as ports, camps, railways, lines of communications, airfields, etc.), as you deem necessary in order to accomplish the transfer of authority to the Government of the Republic of Korea and the withdrawal of United States occupation forces from Korea in accordance with the United Nations General Assembly resolutions on Korea. During this period, the personnel of your command, both military and civilian, including their dependents, shall remain under your exclusive jurisdiction.

In the interest of providing a progressive and orderly transfer of full governmental responsibility and authority from the United States Army Forces in Korea to the Government of the Republic of Korea and to accomplish the purposes set forth above, I am prepared to name Mr Lee Bum Suk, Mr Yun Tchi Young, and Mr Taik Sang Chang to consult with representatives of your command.

Korea 1945 to 1948, pp. 98-9.

28   11 *August* 1948

LETTER FROM GENERAL HODGE TO PRESIDENT RHEE ON TRANSFER OF GOVERNMENTAL FUNCTIONS

I have the honour to acknowledge Your Excellency's note of 9 August 1948 in which you informed me of the fact that, in accordance with the United Nations General Assembly resolution II of 14 November 1947 the United Nations Temporary Commission on Korea was notified on 6 August 1948 of the formation of the Government of the Republic of Korea, and in which you requested my co-operation and assistance in transferring to that government the functions of government now exercised by me as Commanding General of the United States Army Forces in Korea.

I am pleased to note that the Government of the Republic of Korea recognizes that it will be necessary for me to retain control over areas and facilities of vital importance (such as ports, camps, railways, lines of communication, airfields, etc.) as I deem necessary in order to accomplish the transfer of authority to the Government of the Republic of Korea and the withdrawal of United States occupation forces from Korea in accordance with the United Nations General Assembly resolutions on Korea. Furthermore, I note that the Government of the Republic of Korea recognizes my exclusive jurisdiction over the personnel of my command, both military and civilian, including their dependents.

I shall be pleased to co-operate with you in arranging a progressive and orderly transfer of governmental functions, and including the assumption of responsibilities for the direction of all police, coast-guard, and constabulary units now in being, leading to the withdrawal of United States forces from Korea and the termination of the United States occupation. To this end, and for the purpose of facilitating arrangements for the withdrawal of the forces under

my command, I have appointed Maj.-Gen. Charles G. Helmick and
Mr Everett F. Drumright to consult with Your Excellency's
representatives Mr Lee Bum Suk, Mr Yun Tchi Young, and
Mr T. S. Chang.

Korea 1945 to 1948, pp. 99-100.

29   12 *August* 1948

STATEMENT OF THE UNITED STATES GOVERNMENT
ON RECOGNITION OF THE SOUTH KOREAN
GOVERNMENT

In the Joint Declaration issued at Cairo on 1 December 1943,
the three subscribing Powers—the United States, China, and Great
Britain—expressed their determination 'that in due course Korea
shall become free and independent'. This determination was reaffirmed in the Potsdam Declaration of 26 July 1945 with which
the Soviet Union associated itself upon its declaration of war against
Japan on 8 August of that year. On 27 December 1945 in Moscow
the Foreign Ministers of the Soviet Union, the United States, and
Great Britain concluded an agreement, later adhered to by the
Government of China, designed to re-establish Korea as an
independent state.

Although the annexation of Korea by Japan was effectively
terminated with the occupation of that country by the armed forces
of the Soviet Union and the United States in August and September
1945, the freedom and independence of Korea so solemnly pledged
by the four Powers have proved slow of realization. After nearly
two years of painstaking but unavailing effort to give effect to
those pledges through negotiations with the other occupying
Power, the United States Government, on 17 September 1947, laid
the problem of Korean independence before the General Assembly
of the United Nations. The will of an overwhelming majority of
that body was expressed in two resolutions adopted by it on 14
November 1947, the purpose of which was to make it possible
for the Korean people to attain their long-sought freedom and
independence through the holding of free and democratic elections
and the establishment, on the basis thereof, of a national government.

In pursuance of those resolutions, elections were held in Korea
on 10 May of this year, under the observation of the United Nations
Temporary Commission on Korea, for the purpose of electing

427

representatives to a National Assembly which might in turn form a national government. The National Assembly so elected convened on May 31 and has proceeded to form a government—a government in which it is hoped that the people of north Korea, who were prevented from participating in the 10 May elections by the refusal of the Soviet Union to permit the implementation of the General Assembly resolutions in its zone of occupation, will be free in due course to assume their rightful role. Notification of the formation of the new government was communicated to the United Nations Temporary Commission on Korea on 6 August 1948.

It is the view of the United States Government that the Korean Government so established is entitled to be regarded as the Government of Korea envisaged by the General Assembly resolution of 14 November 1947. Pending consideration by the General Assembly at its forthcoming Third Session of the report of the United Nations Temporary Commission on Korea, the United States, pursuant to its responsibility as occupying Power, is sending to Seoul a special representative who will be authorized to carry on negotiations with that Government, in consultation with the United Nations Temporary Commission on Korea, concerning the implementation of the further provisions set forth in paragraph 4 of the second of the General Assembly resolutions of 14 November 1947. As such special representative the President has named John J. Muccio of Rhode Island, who will have the personal rank of Ambassador.

Korea 1945 to 1948, pp. 100-1.

30   24 *August* 1948

AGREEMENT BETWEEN THE UNITED STATES AND THE REPUBLIC OF KOREA ON TRANSFER OF JURISDICTION OVER SECURITY FORCES

The negotiation of the first of several agreements for the transfer of authority from the United States authorities to the Government of the Republic of Korea has been completed in an atmosphere of mutual understanding. This agreement, regarding security forces, was signed today. Dr Syngman Rhee, President of the Republic of Korea and by constitution Commander-in-Chief of Korean Armed Forces, and Lt.-Gen. John R. Hodge, Commanding General, United States Army Forces in Korea, were the signatories.

This is an interim agreement and provides for the progressive turning over to the Korean Government of jurisdiction over and command of all Korean security forces (police, constabulary, and coast-guard) as rapidly as is possible, consistent with the common security of the Republic of Korea and the United States Army Forces in Korea. During the period of the agreement the United States Army will continue to assist the Korean Government in the training and equipment of the constabulary and coast-guard. It also provides for the use of those areas and facilities essential for the maintenance of the United States troops until the withdrawal from Korea is completed as visualized in paragraph 4 of resolution II of the United Nations General Assembly, 14 November 1947.

The agreement is effective only until the United States troops have withdrawn from Korea.

Korea 1945 to 1948, pp. 103-4.

31   11 *September* 1948
AGREEMENT BETWEEN THE UNITED STATES AND THE REPUBLIC OF KOREA ON INITIAL FINANCIAL AND PROPERTY SETTLEMENT

Preamble

The Government of the United States of America and the Government of the Republic of Korea, in view of the note of 9 August 1948 from the President of the Republic of Korea to the Commanding General, United States Army Forces in Korea, the note of 11 August 1948 from the Commanding General, United States Army Forces in Korea, to the President of the Government of the Republic of Korea, and in view of the desirability of concluding an initial financial and property settlement between the governments of the undersigned, being duly authorized by their respective governments for that purpose, agree as follows :

Article 1. The Government of the United States of America hereby transfers to the Government of the Republic of Korea all right, title, and interest held by the United States of America to all property classified as national property in the land and buildings ledgers, and map books of the district tax offices and the land and buildings registers of the courts, together with all improvements and additions to such property, all cash and bank deposits of the United States Army Military Government in Korea and of the South

429

Korean Interim Government, all equipment, supplies, and other property held by the departments, offices, and agencies of the United States Army Military Government in Korea and of the South Korean Interim Government, including all relief and rehabilitation supplies heretofore furnished to the Korean economy by the Government of the United States of America. Military property of the Government of the United States of America furnished to the Korean constabulary, police, or coast-guard will be transferred to the Government of the Republic of Korea from time to time as authority for such transfer is given by the Government of the United States of America to its representative in Korea. Such transfers of military property shall be accomplished through the Office of the Foreign Liquidation Commissioner of the United States Department of State and in accordance with separate agreements to be entered into between said Government of the Republic of Korea and the Foreign Liquidation Commissioner. The Government of the Republic of Korea agrees that property retained for use by or under the control of the United States Army Forces in Korea during the period of troop withdrawal shall be made available for the use of the Government of the United States of America and maintained without charge to the Government of the United States of America during the period of troop withdrawal. The Government of the Republic of Korea agrees that properties specified in Exhibit A shall be made available for the temporary use of the Government of the United States under free leaseholds, and further agrees that it will bear all costs in Korean currency for the repair and maintenance of such properties. The Government of the Republic of Korea hereby assumes and relieves the Government of the United States of America of all liability for the South Korean Interim Government overdraft account at the Bank of Chosun, commitments under loans guaranteed by the United States Army Military Government in Korea, its agencies and instrumentalities, and by the South Korean Interim Government, and all other obligations incurred by the United States Army Military Government in Korea and by the South Korean Interim Government, including present and future claims of every kind and description.

This section shall be effective until an agreement comes into effect between the Government of the United States of America and the Government of the Republic of Korea on aid to the Government of the Republic of Korea. To the extent that relief and rehabilitation supplies still on hand or hereafter received are transferred to the Government of the Republic of Korea by the Government of the United States of America, such transfer shall be made in a progressive and orderly manner, and the Government of the

Republic of Korea shall assume responsibility for the receipt, allocation, distribution and accounting of American-financed supplies. Net *Won* proceeds and accounts receivable derived from the sales of relief and rehabilitation supplies by the United States Military Government in Korea or by the South Korean Interim Government shall be turned over to the Government of the Republic of Korea. The Government of the Republic of Korea agrees to deposit these proceeds in a special account in its name in the Bank of Chosun. The Government of the Republic of Korea further agrees to deposit in this special account the proceeds of all sales of relief and rehabilitation supplies which have been or may be transferred by the Government of the United States of America to the Government of the Republic of Korea. Disbursement from this special account will be made only for such purposes as are agreed upon between the senior representative of the Government of the United States of America and the Government of the Republic of Korea.

Net proceeds in Korean currency and accounts receivable derived from sales of certain property declared surplus to the Office of the Foreign Liquidation Commissioner of the United States Department of State and heretofore furnished to the Korean economy are hereby transferred to the Government of the Republic of Korea.

Article 2. The Government of the United States of America agrees to effect settlement for all imports from Japan for the Korean economy delivered between 9 September 1945, and the effective date of this agreement, less the value of Korean exports shipped to Japan during such period.

Article 3. The Government of the United States of America hereby transfers from its custody to the custody of the Government of the Republic of Korea any property in Korea which may have been owned or controlled, directly or indirectly, in whole or in part, on or since 9 August 1945, by Germany or by any German nationals, corporations, societies, associations, or any other German organization. The Government of the Republic of Korea agrees to take all necessary measures to facilitate such transfers of German assets in Korea as may be determined by the United States of America in consultation with the Republic of France and the United Kingdom of Great Britain and Northern Ireland.

Article 4. The Government of the United States of America hereby transfers to the Government of the Republic of Korea the Korean foreign-exchange bank shares presently owned and held by the United States Army Military Government in Korea, together with all the assets and liabilities of said bank. The Government of the United States of America hereby transfers to the Government of the Republic of Korea the net residual balances of foreign exchange now standing to the credit of the South Korea Interim Government in said bank, subject to allocations and use only after consultation with and concurrence of the senior representative in Korea of the Government of the United States of America. Pending further agreement between the Government of the Republic of Korea and the Government of the United States of America, existing foreign-exchange controls shall be retained by the Government of the Republic of Korea.

Article 5. The Government of the Republic of Korea recognizes and ratifies such disposition of former Japanese public and private property vested under Ordinance No. 33 of the United States Army Military Government in Korea as has already been effected by the United States Army Military Government in Korea. Except for reservations in respect to the acquisition and use of property by the Government of the United States of America contained in Articles I and XI of this agreement, the remaining vested but unsold property, the net unexpended proceeds from rentals and sale of vested property, together with all accounts receivable and sales contracts, shall be transferred to the Government of Republic of Korea in the following way :

(*a*) All cash, bank deposits, or other liquid assets are hereby transferred as of the effective date of this agreement ;

(*b*) All other vested property that is to be transferred, together with all available inventories, maps, deeds, or other evidences of ownership, will be turned over progressively to the Government of the Republic of Korea, supported by balance sheets, operating statements, and other financial records relating to vested property, as rapidly as an orderly transfer can be effected. The Government of the Republic of Korea agrees to establish a separate governmental agency to receive and administer for the benefit of Korean people the property, heretofore vested under Ordinance No. 33, which is or will be transferred to the Government of the Republic of Korea under the provisions of this article.

The Government of the Republic of Korea will respect, preserve, and protect the rights and interests, direct or indirect, of nationals of countries at war with Japan, in former Japanese property in Korea acquired by the Government of the Republic of Korea in accordance with this Article provided such rights and interests were legally acquired by *bona fide* transfer prior to the effective date of Ordinance No. 33.

The Government of the Republic of Korea hereby relieves the United States of America of all liability, including all current and future claims arising out of the vesting, administration, and disposal of the property referred to in this Article.

Article 6. Property in Korea of United Nations nationals, which was seized, confiscated, or sequestered by the Imperial Japanese Government under its war-time regulations, together with property in Korea of other persons which was treated by the Imperial Japanese Government as enemy property and which is transferred to the Government of the Republic of Korea under the provisions of Article V will be protected and preserved by the Government of the Republic of Korea pending its return to its rightful owners, provided such owners request the return of the property within a reasonable period. The Government of the Republic of Korea undertakes to return all such identifiable property, if not otherwise provided for by mutual agreement between the owner and the Government of the Republic of Korea. Continuing the policy initiated by the United States Army Military Government in Korea, the Government of the Republic of Korea undertakes to compensate the owners for damage or loss to such property during the period that it was not under the control of such owners, to the same degree as compensation is paid by the Government of the Republic of Korea for loss or damage to Korean property seized, confiscated, or sequestered for war purposes by the Imperial Japanese Government, its agencies, instrumentalities, or its nationals. The Government of the Republic of Korea hereby relieves the Government of the United States of America from liability for any claim arising out of the administration of property referred to in this Article prior to the effective date of this agreement.

Article 7. The Government of the United States of America and the Government of the Republic of Korea agree to collaborate in arranging a satisfactory settlement of any unpaid debt owing to the Soviet authorities in Korea for power furnished for the Korean economy from 9 September 1945 to the effective date of this agreement. The Government of the United States of America further agrees to liquidate this debt, whenever a fair value of the unpaid debt has been agreed upon by the representatives of the Soviet and United States authorities.

Article 8. The Government of the United States of America, through the United States Army Military Government in Korea, has reimbursed Korea at a fair dollar value for all goods, services, and facilities provided for and to the United States Army Forces in Korea from the Korean economy for the period from 9 September 1945, through 30 June 1948, inclusive ; and for all claims of every kind and description against the Government of the United States of America, its officials, employees, or agencies and instrumentalities, raised or which may be raised by the Government of the Republic of Korea, its nationals, or other individuals and organizations, as a result of the occupation of Korea by the United States Army Forces in Korea during such period.

The Government of the Republic of Korea agrees that this payment constitutes full, final, and complete settlement for all goods and services used by or provided to the United States Army Forces in Korea during the aforementioned period, and for all claims of every kind and description against the Government of the United States of America, its officials, employees, or agencies and instrumentalities, raised or which may be raised by the Government of the Republic of Korea, its instrumentalities, nationals, or other individuals or organizations as a result of the occupation of Korea by the United States Army Forces for the period from 9 September 1945, through 30 June 1948. The Government of the Republic of Korea further discharges and agrees to save harmless the Government of the United States of America, its officials, employees, or agencies and instrumentalities, its nationals or other individuals and organizations, from all claims of every kind and description arising as a result of the occupation of Korea by the United States Army Forces in Korea during the period prior to 1 July 1948. The Government of the Republic of Korea hereby recognizes and ratifies the agreement under which the above-mentioned payment to Korea was effected.

The Government of the Republic of Korea also assumes and relieves the Government of the United States of America of all liability for funds used from the overdraft account at the Bank of Chosun entitled 'United States Army Military Government in Korea Funding Account'. The Government of the Republic of Korea agrees that the Commanding General, United States Army Forces in Korea, shall continue to draw *Won* from the overdraft account at the Bank of Chosun presently entitled 'United States Army Military Government in Korea Funding Account No. 2', and the Government of the United States of America hereby agrees to pay to the Government of the Republic of Korea in dollars or other United States assets the fair dollar value of all goods and services procured in the Korean economy with *Won* drawn from such account.

Article 9. (a) In consideration for certain property heretofore furnished to the Korean economy by the Government of the United States of America through the Office of the Foreign Liquidation Commissioner of the United States Department of State and the United States Army Military Government in Korea, including the net proceeds in Korean currency arising from the sale of such property, the Government of the Republic of Korea agrees to pay to the Government of the United States of America in the manner provided in section (b) and (d) of this Article, the fair value of said property, not to exceed the equivalent of $25,000,000, as shown on the records of said Foreign Liquidation Commissioner, covering the transfer of such property to the United States Army Military Government in Korea. Interest shall accrue at the rate of $2\frac{3}{8}$ per centum per annum from 1 July 1948, on the unpaid balance of the total fair value of said property and shall be due and payable in Korean currency on 1 July of each year, the first payment to be made on 1 July 1949.

(b) At such time and in such amounts as shall be specified by the Government of the United States of America, the Government of the Republic of Korea shall pay in Korean currency all or part of the balance then due under the indebtedness set forth in this Article, including interest due and unpaid, if any, less any credits made for property as provided in paragraph (d) of this Article, and the Government of the United States of America shall credit the balance due under such indebtedness with the United States dollar equivalent of such currency. Any currency so received by the Government of the United States of America shall be used in accordance with the provisions set forth in paragraph (c) of this Article.

(c) The Government of the United States of America and the Government of the Republic of Korea agree that the Korean currency to be received by the Government of the United States of America as provided in paragraph (b) of this Article, as well as the Korean currency to be received by the Government of the United States of America's interest provided in paragraph (a) of this Article, shall be expended in Korea and may be used for the payment of any or all expenditures in Korea of the Government of the United States of America, including expenditures for :

(1) Such educational programmes as may be mutually agreed upon by the two governments ; and

(2) The acquisition of property located in Korea, either real or personal, tangible or intangible, including improvements to any property in which the Government of the United States of America has an interest.

Such property shall include initially the property listed in the supplement to this agreement.*

(d) At the request of the Government of the United States of America the Government of the Republic of Korea shall deliver title to such property as may, by mutual agreement, be acquired by the Government of the United States of America in accordance with the terms of this Article.

* Supplement (not printed) contains list of buildings to be transferred to the Government of the United States for the use of the mission.

Upon delivery of title to such property by the Government of the Republic of Korea to the Government of the United States of America, the Government of the United States of America shall credit the account of the Government of the Republic of Korea under this Article with the agreed-upon fair dollar value of such property.

(*e*) Except as may be provided by special agreement between the two governments, the Government of the United States of America shall not request the Government of the Republic of Korea to make payment in Korean currency or to deliver title to property located in Korea, as provided in paragraphs (*b*) and (*d*) of this Article, the combined total amount of which exceeds in any single fiscal year beginning 1 July, the equivalent value of $5,000,000 plus interest due and payable as provided in paragraph (*a*) of this Article.

(*f*) The *Won* equivalent of the dollar obligations assumed by the Government of the Republic of Korea under the terms of this agreement shall be calculated by mutual agreement between the Government of the Republic of Korea and the Government of the United States of America, such calculations to be made immediately prior to each payment. The *Won* equivalent in any case shall be no less favourable to the Government of the United States of America than the conversion rate legally available to any third party at the time of each transaction.

Article 10. The Government of the Republic of Korea hereby agrees that it will not permit the re-export or diversion of equipment, supplies, and other property furnished to it by the Government of the United States of America under the terms of this agreement unless such re-export or diversion is approved by a duly authorized representative of the Government of the United States of America.

Article 11. The Government of the Republic of Korea agrees to continue in full force and effect all existing laws, ordinances, public acts, and regulations of the United States Army Military Government in Korea and/or of the South Korean Interim Government until repealed or amended by the Government of the Republic of Korea.

Article 12. Pending negotiation of mutually satisfactory treaties of amity and commerce, it is agreed by the contracting parties that the rights and privileges now enjoyed by the United Nations nationals and firms engaged in lawful pursuits in Korea shall be respected and affirmed.

Article 13. Administrative control over the accounts, properties, and operating facilities transferred to the Government of the Republic of Korea under the terms of this agreement shall be turned over in a progressive and orderly manner to the authorized officials of the Government of the Republic of Korea within 30 days from the effective date of this agreement, or as rapidly as the Government of the Republic of Korea is prepared to assume such operations and responsibilities, except that administrative control over vested properties and over relief and rehabilitation supplies shall be turned over not later than 90 days from the effective date of this agreement, or as rapidly as the Government of the Republic of Korea is prepared to assume such operations and responsibilities.

Article 14. Until such time as the United States Army Forces in Korea are withdrawn from Korea, the Government of the United States of America and the Government of the Republic of Korea agree that they shall be bound by, and shall respect, all agreements previously made between the United States Army Forces in Korea and the several departments of the United States Army Military Government in Korea concerning the use of certain transportation, communication, and other facilities and services by the United States Army Forces in Korea.

The present agreement shall become effective with the formal notification to the Government of the United States of America that the Korean National Assembly has consented to this agreement.

Korea 1945 to 1948, pp. 104-12.

32   20 *September* 1948

STATEMENT OF THE UNITED STATES POSITION ON
WITHDRAWAL OF OCCUPATION FORCES FROM
KOREA

It has been the consistent view of this government that the best interests of the Korean people would be served by the withdrawal of all occupying forces from Korea at the earliest practicable date. This same view was embodied in the United Nations General Assembly resolution of 14 November 1947, in which provision was made for such withdrawal as soon as practicable after the establishment of the Korean Government which it was the intention of that resolution to bring into being. Had the Soviet Union co-operated in carrying out the provisions of the resolution of 14 November 1947, the question of troop withdrawal from Korea would doubtless have been already resolved.

The United States Government regards the question of the withdrawal of occupying forces as but one facet of the entire question of the unity and independence of Korea. The General Assembly of the United Nations has taken cognizance of this larger question as evidenced by the resolution referred to above, and it may be expected to give further consideration to the matter at its forthcoming meeting.

Korea 1945 to 1948, p. 116.

33   *7 June* 1949

PRESIDENT TRUMAN'S MESSAGE TO US CONGRESS
ON AID TO KOREA

To the Congress of the United States :

I recommend that the Congress authorize the continuation of economic assistance to the Republic of Korea for the fiscal year ending 30 June 1950.

The United States is now providing relief and a small amount of assistance in rehabilitation to the Republic of Korea under Public Law 793—Eightieth Congress. The continuation of that assistance is of great importance to the successful achievement of the foreign policy aims of the United States. The authority of the present act extends only until 30 June 1949. For this reason legislation is urgently needed and I am hopeful that the Congress may give it early consideration.

The people of the United States have long had sympathetic feelings for the Korean people. American missionaries, supported by American churches of many denominations, brought spiritual guidance, education and medical aid to the Korean people during their forty years of Japanese bondage. All Americans who have come to know the Korean people appreciate their fierce passion for freedom and their keen desire to become an independent nation.

Early in the war with Japan, it was resolved that Korea should be liberated. In the Cairo Declaration of December 1943, the United States joined with the United Kingdom and China to express their determination that in due course Korea should become free and independent. This pledge was reaffirmed in the Potsdam Declaration of 26 July 1945, with which the Soviet Union associated itself upon its entrance into the war against Japan in the following month.

438

With our victory over Japan, it was hoped that the Korean nation would be reborn. Unfortunately, however, only the people south of the Thirty-Eighth Degree Parallel have thus far attained their freedom and independence.

The present division of Korea along the Thirty-Eighth Parallel was never intended by the United States. The sole purpose of this line along the Thirty-Eighth Degree Parallel was to facilitate acceptance by the Soviet and United States forces of the surrender of Japanese troops north and south of that line. Immediately after the completion of the Japanese surrender, the United States through direct negotiations with the Soviet Union sought to restore the unity of Korea.

For two years these efforts were rendered unavailing by the attitude of the Soviet Union. When it became apparent that further delay would be injurious to the interests of the Korean people, the United States submitted the matter to the General Assembly of the United Nations, in the hope that the United Nations could assist the people of Korea to assume their rightful place as an independent, democratic nation.

By vote of an overwhelming majority, the General Assembly adopted a resolution on 14 November 1947 calling for an election, under the observation of a United Nations temporary commission on Korea, to choose a representative national assembly for the purpose of drafting a democratic constitution and establishing a national government.

The Soviet Union refused to permit the United Nations Commission to enter its zone. Consequently, the right of the Korean people to participate in a free election to establish a free government was confined to South Korea. As a result of this election, the Government of the Republic of Korea was inaugurated 15 August 1948.

The General Assembly of the United Nations at its next session considered the report of its commission and in December 1948 adopted a resolution holding the Government of the Republic of Korea to be the validly elected, lawful government of the area in which elections were held under the commission's observation— and the only such government in Korea. The General Assembly established a reconstituted commission to consult with the occupying Powers on the withdrawal of their forces and to continue to work for the unification of Korea under representative government.

The United States terminated its military government in Korea upon the inauguration of the Government of the Republic of Korea and recognized the new Government on New Year's Day, 1949.

The December 1948 resolution of the General Assembly called on the occupying Powers to withdraw their forces as soon as practicable.

The United States has thus far retained a small number of troops in Korea at the request of the Government of the republic to give the republic an opportunity to establish forces adequate to protect itself against internal disturbances and external attacks short of an aggressive war supported by a major Power. A military advisory group requested by the Korean Government for training purposes will be retained in Korea after the withdrawal of United States troops.

The debilitated state in which the Korean economy was left by the Japanese has been accentuated by the separation of the hydro-electric power, coal and metal and fertilizer industries of the north from the agricultural and textile industries of the south and by the effects of continuing Communist agitation.

The United States has furnished the people of South Korea with basic relief during the period of military government. Despite such assistance however, the republic is still far short of being able to support itself, even at the present modest standard of living of its people. It is in urgent need of further assistance in the difficult period ahead until it can stand on its own feet economically.

The aid now being provided to Korea is essentially for basic relief. Without the continuation of such relief, its economy would collapse—inevitably and rapidly. Bare relief alone, however, would not make it possible for the republic to become self-supporting. The republic would remain dependent upon the continuation of relief from the United States at a costly level into the indefinite future—and subject to the same inevitable collapse at any time the relief should be withdrawn. For these reasons the aid granted should be not for mere relief but for recovery. The kind of programme which is needed is the kind which the Congress has authorized for the countries of Western Europe and under which those countries have achieved such rapid progress towards recovery during the past year.

Full advantage should be taken of the broad and successful ex-perience in Western Europe by continuing responsibility for the administration of the Korean aid programme in the Economic Co-operation Administration, which has been administering aid to Korea since 1 January of this year.

Prior to 1 January of this year, aid to Korea was administered by the Army as a part of its programme for government and relief in occupied areas. The budget which I submitted to the Congress in January contemplated that economic assistance to Korea would be continued outside of the Army's programme for government and relief in occupied areas.

The needs of the Republic of Korea for economic assistance have been carefully studied in the light of the latest available information. I am convinced that the sum of $150,000,000 is the minimum aid essential during the coming year for progress towards economic recovery.

Such a recovery programme will cost only a relatively small amount more than a bare relief programme. Yet a recovery programme—and only a recovery programme—will enable the Republic of Korea to commence building up the coal production, electric power capacity and fertilizer production which are fundamental to the establishment of a self-supporting economy and to the termination of the need for aid from the United States. Aid in the restoration of the Korean economy should be less costly to the United States in the end than a continued programme of relief.

The recovery programme which is recommended is not only the soundest course economically but also the most effective from the standpoint of helping to achieve the objectives of peaceful and democratic conditions in the Far East.

Korea has become a testing ground in which the validity and practical value of the ideals and principles of democracy which the republic is putting into practice are being matched against the practices of communism which have been imposed upon the people of North Korea. The survival and progress of the republic towards a self-supporting, stable economy will have an immense and far-reaching influence on the people of Asia.

Such progress by the young republic will encourage the people of Southern and Southeastern Asia and the islands of the Pacific to resist and reject the Communist propaganda with which they are besieged. Moreover, the Korean Republic, by demonstrating the success and tenacity of democracy in resisting communism, will stand as a beacon to the people of Northern Asia in resisting the control of the Communist forces which have overrun them.

The Republic of Korea, and the freedom-seeking people of North Korea held under Soviet domination, seek for themselves a united, self-governing and sovereign country, independent of foreign control and support and with membership in the United Nations. In their desire for unity and independence, they are supported by the United Nations.

The United States has a deep interest in the continuing progress of the Korean people towards these objectives. The most effective, practical aid which the United States can give towards reaching them will be to assist the republic to move towards self-support at a decent standard of living. In the absence of such assistance, there can be no real hope of achieving a unified, free and democratic Korea.

If we are faithful to our ideals and mindful of our interest in establishing peaceful and prosperous conditions in the world, we will not fail to provide the aid which is so essential to Korea at this critical time.

HARRY S. TRUMAN

Department of State Bulletin, Washington D.C., 19 June 1949, pp. 781-3.

II RELATIONS WITH THE SOVIET UNION

34   10 *September* 1948

MESSAGE OF THE SUPREME PEOPLE'S ASSEMBLY OF KOREA (NORTH) TO THE GOVERNMENTS OF THE SOVIET UNION AND THE UNITED STATES ON THE WITHDRAWAL OF TROOPS FROM KOREA

Three years have elapsed since the day when by the efforts of the Allies Korea was liberated from the protracted colonial oppression of Japanese imperialism.

Delivered from Japanese colonial slavery, the Korean people hoped that, with the help of the great Allied Powers, it would succeed in quickly re-establishing its national independence and constituting its own independent democratic state. However, these cherished hopes and aspirations of the entire Korean people have not been realized to this day.

There are still American and Soviet troops on Korean territory, and, owing to this, Korea still remains divided along the 38th parallel into two parts—in spite of the fact that Korea represents a single and indivisible organism both as regards the national composition of her population and as regards her economic structure.

The agricultural South, where the American troops are stationed, has been artificially cut off from the industrial North, where Soviet troops are present.

Entirely different social and economic conditions and political régimes have been created in North and South Korea.

This division of Korea, a country which represents a single unit nationally and economically, greatly hinders and retards her economic, political and cultural regeneration.

The continued presence of foreign troops in Korea and her division into two parts not only causes enormous economic damage to the Korean people, but harbours a great political danger.

442

Anti-popular pro-Japanese elements, various political adventurers and charlatans from the camp of Korean reaction are seeking, in furtherance of their sordid, selfish political aims, to take advantage of the presence of American and Soviet troops on Korean territory in order to foment hostility between the USA and USSR and also to foment antagonism and enmity between the population of northern and southern Korea.

It goes without saying that this only increased the political tension in the Far East and contains elements of a threat to world peace and the security of nations.

The Korean people could understand the presence of American and Soviet troops on Korean territory in the first months after the end of the second world war, inasmuch as those troops were responsible for the disarmament of the Japanese army and for the enforcement of the other terms of Japan's unconditional surrender on Korean territory.

But today, three years after the disarmament of the Japanese army in Korea and Japan's surrender, there is no explanation, nor, still less, any justification, for the continued presence of foreign troops on Korean territory.

Since the first day of their liberation from colonial bondage to Japan, the Korean people have been working self-sacrificingly for the creation of an independent democratic state of their own.

Since the implementation of the Moscow Decision on Korea has been thwarted, the fundamental and main slogan of this nation-wide effort is the demand for the immediate withdrawal of all foreign troops from Korea and for affording the Korean people the opportunity to decide their future themselves, without foreign interference.

The demand for the immediate withdrawal of all foreign troops from Korea and for the reunion of Korea in a single state has the active and determined support of the overwhelming majority of Korean political parties and social organizations of various political trends, and of the absolute majority of the Korean nation as a whole.

For the speediest reunion of Korea in a single independent democratic state, elections were held in South and North Korea in August 1948. These elections, in which the voters freely expressed their will, demonstrated the unbending determination of the entire Korean people in its struggle for the unity and independence of their country.

In North Korea 99·97 per cent, and in South Korea 77·52 per cent of the entire electorate—in other words, 85·2 per cent of the electorate of all Korea—took part in the election of deputies to the Supreme People's Assembly of Korea.

The deputies elected to the Supreme People's Assembly of Korea represent all the major Left, Right and Centrist parties of the North and the South and all social strains of the population of Korea.

By their widespread and unanimous participation in the Elections to the Supreme People's Assembly of Korea, the Korean people have thus once again clearly and convincingly demonstrated their refusal to recognize the unlawful elections held in South Korea on 10 May 1948 under the supervision of the United Nations so-called Temporary Commission on Korea, and also their refusal to recognize, and their universal boycott of, the 'National Assembly' and 'Government' set up in South Korea on the basis of those elections.

The Supreme People's Assembly of Korea is the truly national and only lawful highest legislative body in Korea, inasmuch as it has been set up on the basis of the free expression of the will of the Korean people.

Expressing the wishes and firm will of the entire Korean nation, the Supreme People's Assembly of Korea approaches the Government of the United States and the Government of the Soviet Union with the urgent request that they should immediately and simultaneously withdraw their troops from Korea, inasmuch as this is the prime and indispensable condition for the reunion of Korea, for her economic, political and cultural revival and progress, and for the establishment of a peace-loving democratic Korean state. In the three years that have passed since Korea's liberation from colonial dependence on Japan, the Korean nation has produced its own political, technical and cultural forces capable of promoting by their own efforts the economic, political and cultural development of an independent Korean democratic state.

The talk to the effect that the simultaneous withdrawal of all foreign troops from Korea might cause public disorder or even civil war is absolutely groundless and an insult to the national dignity of the Korean people.

The fact that a Supreme People's Assembly of Korea has been created, that this Assembly has set up a single Korean Government of representatives of various political trends in North and South Korea, that there is political co-operation among the major Left, Right and Centrist Korean political parties and social organizations, and that there is political unity among the absolute majority of the population of North and South Korea is a guarantee that complete order and public peace will reign throughout Korea during and after the withdrawal of the foreign troops from Korea.

In addressing this letter to the Government of the great Soviet Union, the Supreme People's Assembly of Korea takes the occasion to express on behalf of the entire Korean nation its sincere gratitude for having, already on the 26th of September 1947, made its proposal for the simultaneous withdrawal of Soviet and American troops from Korea, and for having since repeatedly confirmed its readiness immediately to withdraw its troops from Korea if the USA Government also withdraws its troops from Korea at the same time.

The Supreme People's Assembly of Korea hopes that the USA Government too, out of respect for the national interests of the Korean people and in the endeavour to consolidate tranquillity, peace and friendship among nations, will meet this request of the Korean people and will consent to withdraw its troops from Korea simultaneously with the withdrawal of the Soviet troops.

The Soviet Union and the Korean Question, pp. 72-5.

35   18 *September* 1948

REPLY OF THE PRESIDIUM OF THE SUPREME SOVIET OF THE USSR TO THE MESSAGE OF THE SUPREME PEOPLE'S ASSEMBLY OF KOREA ON THE WITHDRAWAL OF TROOPS FROM KOREA

Mr Kim Doo Bong,
President of the Presidium
of the Supreme People's Assembly of Korea,

The Presidium of the Supreme Soviet of the USSR has received the message of the Supreme People's Assembly of Korea of 10 September with the request for the simultaneous and immediate withdrawal of the Soviet and the American troops from Korea.

The Presidium of the Supreme Soviet of the USSR has taken note of the statement of the Supreme People's Assembly of Korea that the fact that a Supreme People's Assembly of Korea has been set up and that this Assembly has formed a single Korean Government from representatives of various political trends of North and South Korea, representing the will of the overwhelming majority of the population of northern and southern Korea, is a guarantee that during and after the withdrawal of foreign troops from Korea complete order and public peace will prevail throughout Korea.

After examining the message of the Supreme People's Assembly of Korea, the Presidium of the Supreme Soviet of the USSR has found it possible to meet the wish expressed in that message and has given appropriate instructions to the Council of Ministers of the USSR to evacuate the Soviet troops from northern Korea and to complete the evacuation by the end of December of this year.

At the same time the Presidium of the Supreme Soviet of the USSR has expressed the hope that the USA Government will also agree to evacuate the American troops from southern Korea by the same date.

N. SHVERNIK
President of the Presidium of the Supreme Soviet of the USSR

A. GORKIN
Secretary of the Presidium of the Supreme Soviet of the USSR

The Soviet Union and the Korean Question, pp. 76-7.

36   20 *September* 1948

STATEMENT OF THE MINISTRY OF FOREIGN AFFAIRS OF THE USSR ON THE EVACUATION OF SOVIET TROOPS FROM KOREA

On 10 September the Supreme People's Assembly of Korea adopted the text of a message to the Government of the Soviet Union and of the United States of America with a request for the simultaneous withdrawal of American and Soviet troops from Korea. It also stated that the fact that a Supreme People's Assembly of Korea had been set up and that this Assembly had formed a single Korean Government of representatives of various political trends of North and South Korea, representing the will of the overwhelming majority of the population of northern and southern Korea, was a guarantee that during and after the withdrawal of foreign troops from Korea complete order and public peace would prevail throughout Korea.

It is known that in the autumn of 1945 Soviet troops, after smashing the Japanese Kwantung Army, liberated Korea from the Japanese invaders and, on the basis of an agreement among the Allies, remained in Korea north of the 38th parallel, while American troops remained on Korean territory south of the 38th parallel. While remaining in northern Korea the Soviet forces afforded the Korean population the full opportunity of setting up democratic administrative bodies and invariably rendered friendly assistance in the national regeneration of Korea. At the same time the number of Soviet troops in northern Korea was being gradually reduced.

In September 1947 the Soviet Government proposed to the Government of the United States of America that the Soviet and the American troops should be simultaneously withdrawn from Korea. After that it has time and again confirmed its readiness immediately to withdraw the Soviet troops from northern Korea, if the Government of the United States of America simultaneously withdrew the American troops from southern Korea, to which, however, the Government of the United States of America has so far not given its consent.

The question put by the Supreme People's Assembly of Korea about the simultaneous withdrawal of Soviet and American troops from Korea was submitted by the Soviet Government to the Presidium of the Supreme Soviet of the USSR which examined the above-mentioned message of the Supreme People's Assembly of Korea and found it timely to evacuate the Soviet troops from northern Korea, expressing the hope that the USA Government would also agree to evacuate the American troops from southern Korea, in accordance with the wish expressed by the Supreme People's Assembly of Korea.

In fulfilment of the decision of the Presidium of the Supreme Soviet of the USSR, the Council of Ministers of the USSR has decided :

(1) To evacuate to Soviet Union territory the Soviet troops remaining on the territory of northern Korea.

(2) To instruct the Ministry of the Armed Forces of the USSR to begin the evacuation of Soviet troops from northern Korea not later than in the second half of October this year and to complete it by 1 January 1949.

The Soviet Union and the Korean Question, pp. 78-9.

37   *8 October* 1948

LETTER FROM THE CHAIRMAN OF THE MINISTERIAL CABINET OF THE KOREAN PEOPLE'S DEMOCRATIC REPUBLIC KIM SUNG TO THE CHAIRMAN OF THE COUNCIL OF MINISTERS OF THE USSR J. STALIN ON THE ESTABLISHMENT OF DIPLOMATIC RELATIONS BETWEEN THE USSR AND KOREA

Mr J. V. Stalin,
Chairman of the Council
of Ministers of the USSR,

On behalf of the Government of the Korean People's Democratic Republic I have the honour to address this letter to you, Highly

Esteemed Mr Chairman, and to convey to you the following wish of my Government.

In the three years that have elapsed since the liberation of Korea from prolonged colonial oppression by Japanese imperialism, profound changes have taken place in the life of the Korean people which are of immense significance to the historical destiny of our country. All over Korea popular elections have been held to a single national legislative body—the Supreme People's Assembly of Korea. Following on these elections a Government of the People's Democratic Republic was formed, which is composed of representatives of all social strata of the population of North and South Korea, and which has received the warm approval and unanimous support of the entire Korean people. The Government of the Korean People's Democratic Republic has entered on the performance of its duties and has begun its activities for the benefit of the Korean people.

Expressing the unanimous aspiration of the Korean people, and on behalf of my Government, I request you, and through you the Government of the USSR, to establish diplomatic relations with the Korean People's Democratic Republic and to exchange ambassadors. I also request the Government of the USSR, parallel with the establishment of diplomatic relations, to establish close economic relations between the two States for the common benefit of our peoples.

I am profoundly convinced that the establishment of diplomatic relations between the Korean People's Democratic Republic and the USSR will contribute to the strengthening of friendly relations between our peoples and serve the cause of peace and security in the Far East.

With deep esteem,

KIM SUNG
*Chairman of the Ministerial Cabinet of the
Korean People's Democratic Republic*

The Soviet Union and the Korean Question, pp. 82-3.

38   12 *October* 1948

LETTER FROM THE CHAIRMAN OF THE COUNCIL OF
MINISTERS OF THE USSR J. STALIN TO THE
CHAIRMAN OF THE MINISTERIAL CABINET OF THE
KOREAN PEOPLE'S DEMOCRATIC REPUBLIC KIM
SUNG ON THE ESTABLISHMENT OF DIPLOMATIC
RELATIONS BETWEEN THE USSR AND KOREA

I acknowledge the receipt of your letter of October 8 in which
you state that the Government of the Korean People's Democratic
Republic has entered on the performance of its duties, and propose
the establishment of diplomatic relations with the USSR and
exchange of ambassadors, as well as the establishment of corresponding economic relations between our two States.

The Soviet Government, which unswervingly upholds the right
of the Korean people to create their united independent State,
welcomes the formation of the Korean Government and wishes it
success in its activities in behalf of the national resurgence and
democratic development of Korea. The Soviet Government expresses
its readiness for the establishment of diplomatic relations between
the USSR and the Korean People's Democratic Republic and
exchange of ambassadors, and parallel with this, for the establishment of corresponding economic relations.

The Soviet Union and the Korean Question, p. 84.

39   17 *March* 1949

AGREEMENT ON ECONOMIC AND CULTURAL CO-
OPERATION BETWEEN THE USSR AND THE
PEOPLE'S REPUBLIC OF KOREA (NORTH)

The Presidium of the Supreme Soviet of the Union of Soviet
Socialist Republics and the Presidium of the Supreme National
Assembly of the Korean People's Democratic Republic, striving
for the further promotion and strengthening of economic and
cultural relations between the USSR and the Korean People's
Democratic Republic, convinced that the consolidation and promotion of these ties meets the vital interests of the peoples of both
countries and will in the best way facilitate their economic and
cultural development, have decided to conclude to these ends the

present agreement and to appoint as their plenipotentiary representatives :—

The Presidium of the Supreme Soviet of the Union of Soviet Socialist Republics—Andrei Yanuarovich Vyshinsky, Minister of Foreign Affairs of the USSR ;

The Presidium of the Supreme National Assembly of the Korean People's Democratic Republic—Kim Ir Sen, Chairman of the Council of Ministers of the Korean People's Democratic Republic,

Who upon exchange of their credentials, found to be in proper order, have agreed upon the following :—

Article 1.—The contracting parties will in every way promote and consolidate trade relations between them on the basis of co-operation, equality and mutual benefit. The Governments of both contracting parties will from time to time conclude agreements determining the volume and composition of mutual deliveries of goods for yearly as well as longer periods and other conditions ensuring uninterrupted and increasing trade turnover between both countries in accordance with the requirements for developing the national economy of each of them.

Article 2.—The contracting parties shall grant each other the right to reciprocal most-favoured-nation treatment with respect to all matters relating to commerce and navigation between both countries, as well as with regard to the activity of physical and juridical persons of one contracting party on the territory of the other party.

Article 3.—The contracting parties shall in every way promote and consolidate the relations established between them in the fields of culture, science and art.

Accordingly, the Governments of the contracting parties shall enter into negotiations with the object of concluding corresponding agreements. In so doing both Governments shall be guided by their aspirations further to consolidate these relations.

Article 4.—The contracting parties shall facilitate the exchange between both countries of experience in the field of industry and agriculture through the despatch of experts, the rendering of technical aid, the organization of exhibitions, the exchange of specimens of seeds and plants, as well as in other ways.

Article 5.—The present agreement is concluded for a period of ten years.

The agreement shall be ratified in the shortest possible time and shall come into force as from the day of the exchange of ratification instruments, which shall be effected in Pyong-Yang.

Unless either of the contracting parties gives notice in writing one year prior to the expiration of the said ten-year term of its intention to renounce the agreement, the latter will remain in force for one year as from the day when the agreement may be renounced by either of the contracting parties.

In witness whereof the plenipotentiary representatives of both contracting parties have signed the present agreement and affixed their seals thereto.

Done in Moscow on 17 March 1949 in two copies in the Russian and Korean languages, both texts being equally valid.

Upon the authorization of the Presidium of the Supreme Soviet of the Union of Soviet Socialist Republics, A. Y. Vyshinsky.

Upon the authorization of the Presidium of the Supreme National Assembly of the Korean People's Democratic Republic, Kim Ir Sen.

Tewksbury, Donald G., *Source Materials on Korean Politics and Ideologies*, pp. 127-8.

JAPAN

JAPAN

INTRODUCTION

AFTER HER DEFEAT in the Second World War Japan came under
Allied occupation with American troops being mainly responsible
for the carrying out of the occupation. General MacArthur was
named the Supreme Commander for the Allied Powers (SCAP) to
implement the objectives of the Allied Powers. The authority of the
Emperor and the Japanese Government was made subject to the
Supreme Commander. The goal of Allied occupation was the reconstruction of a peaceful and democratic Japan. On 29 August
1945 the State-War-Navy-Co-ordinating Committee sent to the
Supreme Commander, General MacArthur, a general statement of
US occupation policy on the basis of which he could make his
plans. This policy was the basis of a much more detailed and
technical directive, known as the Basic Post-Surrender Policy
Directive, which was forwarded to the Supreme Commander on 26
June 1947. The Directive laid down that the ultimate objective of
the Allied Powers was to assure that Japan would not again become
a menace to the peace and security of the world, and that a democratic and peaceful government would be established as early as
possible. To achieve this objective Japan was to be completely disarmed and demilitarized and the existing economic basis of Japanese
military strength was to be destroyed and not to be permitted to
revive.

Two international bodies were set up by the Foreign Ministers'
Conference at Moscow in December 1945 to supervise the occupa-
tion of Japan. One was a top-level policy-making body called the
Far Eastern Commission, consisting of representatives of the
USSR, United Kingdom, United States, China, France, Netherlands, Canada, Australia, New Zealand, India, the Philippines,
Pakistan, and Burma. Sitting at Washington, its main responsibility
was to formulate the policies, principles and standards by means of
which Japan could fulfil its obligations under the surrender terms.
The second body was the Allied Council of Japan consisting of four
members representing the United States, the Soviet Union, China
and a Commonwealth group composed of the United Kingdom,
Australia, New Zealand, India and Pakistan. It sat in Tokyo for the
purpose of consulting with and advising the Supreme Commander
on the implementation of the terms of surrender, the occupation

and control of Japan, and the occupation directives. The Supreme Commander, however, remained the sole executive authority for the Allied Powers.

The twofold task of the occupation was the elimination of aggressive and ultra-nationalistic influences and the establishment of a framework of democratic structure. A SCAP directive of 4 January 1946 required the Japanese Government to order the dissolution and prohibition of ultra-nationalistic and militaristic institutions and societies. Some 1300 organizations were dissolved and banned in accordance with this directive. The directive also required the Japanese Government to remove from public office or position of influence all those persons who had been promoters of ultra-nationalistic ideas or aggressive acts towards foreign countries. Persons so removed could not be employed anywhere in the Government service, national, prefectual or local. Nearly 200,000 persons were purged from public life under this directive and the purge programme was completed by the middle of 1948.

Among the major objectives of the Allied Powers in Japan were the reorganization of political life by modifying the feudal and authoritarian tendencies, the elimination of the political power of the Emperor, the establishment of a legislative body and making the executive responsible to such a legislative body, and the development of political parties. In order to eliminate the political power of the Emperor, a new constitution was drafted, which was promulgated on 3 November 1946 and which went into effect on 3 May 1947. The Constitution established the parliamentary system of government as in England, and incorporated principles of popular sovereignty, fundamental human rights and freedom, and renunciation of war. Two houses of legislature, the House of Councillors and the House of Representatives, were created, both the houses being elected. The Diet, consisting of the two houses, became the highest organ of the state, representing the sovereign will of the people. The executive power of the state was vested in the Cabinet which was composed of the party or parties commanding a majority in the Diet. The executive power of the Cabinet is discharged by the different organs of administration which are governed by the National Government Organization Law, promulgated on 5 July 1948. This law contains the general principles applicable to all branches of administration.

The bureaucracy and the police were two integral parts of the military state structure of Japan before the end of the Second World War. An essential task in the process of democratization of Japan was the reform of the bureaucracy and the police. The first National Diet passed laws for the amendment of the Civil and

Criminal Codes, the National Public Service Law and the Police Law. The reforms prescribed in the National Public Service Law, passed on 21 October 1947, aimed at the weakening of the previous power of the bureaucracy by introducing more democratic methods of employee selection and improvement in the promotion and administration of the civil service under the supervision of a National Personnel Authority which was given wide discretionary powers of employment and dismissal. The Police Law, passed on 8 December 1947, had as its objective the decentralization and democratization of the police force by creating local police units under the authority of locally elected commissions.

In the economic field, the Basic Post-Surrender Policy Directive stipulated as the Allied objective the destruction of the existing economic basis of Japanese military strength and the reorganization of the economic structure on peaceful and democratic lines so as to permit a wide distribution of income and ownership of the means of production. To achieve this the Directive called for a programme of dissolution of the large industrial and banking combinations which had exercised control of a great part of Japan's trade and industry. The programme for the democratization of Japanese industry, trade and finance, known as the 'Zaibatsu Programme', aimed at the elimination of the economic and political power of the great Zaibatsu combines and leaders mainly through the dissolution of the Zaibatsu holding companies and removal of the Zaibatsu family members and their principal designees, the dissolution of or reorganization of individual operating concerns which restricted competition, prevention of the revival of private monopoly, and the disposal to new owners of securities taken over by the government. A number of measures were taken to deprive the Zaibatsu, and the system of holding companies they had organized, of their great power over Japanese economic life.

SCAP issued a directive to the Japanese Government on 23 July 1946 requiring it to take action to prevent members of Zaibatsu families from holding positions of responsibility in any company and to forbid interlocking directorates and intercorporate security ownership. A Holding Company Liquidation Commission was established to dispose of the securities held by the Zaibatsu members and the holding companies listed for dissolution. In April 1947 the Diet passed the Anti-Monopoly Law, prohibiting inter-corporate stockholding, multiple directorships, unfair pricing and other competitive practices, participation in international cartels, etc., and in December 1947 the 'Law for the Elimination of the Excessive Concentrations of Economic Power' was put on the statute book, requiring the dissolution of large corporations which hampered the

growth of a competitive economy. By the end of 1949 the former
83 Zaibatsu holding companies had been broken up and dissolved
and 56 Zaibatsu family members purged from positions of responsibility in public or business life. Some 1200 'restricted concerns'
had been divested of their inter-corporate security holdings and
nearly 30 large concerns charged as 'excessive concentrations of
economic power' were being divided into smaller companies or
undergoing other structural changes.

Reforms were also undertaken in the field of labour with a view
to promoting the development of an independent trade union movement on democratic lines. It was recognized that a strong trade
union movement would be a foil to the Zaibatsu elements which had
a large hand in the pursuit of aggressive policies. The Trade Union
Law, the Labour Standards Law, which banned involuntary servitude and provided for the establishment of minimum standards of
work for the industrial workers of Japan, the Workmen's Compensation
Insurance Law, and the Labour Relations AdjustmentLaw were passed
for the regulation of relations between employers and employees and
for the growth of strong labour organizations on a democratic basis.

The reform measures, particularly the 'Zaibatsu Programme',
aroused strong criticism in Congressional and business circles of the
United States who feared that the reform programme was too drastic
and might impair the recovery of Japanese economy and hamper
foreign business activity in Japan. The programme for deconcentration had to be modified to meet this growing criticism. Moreover,
with the development of the cold war, America began increasingly to
look upon Japan as an ally and a valuable base in East Asia and
therefore the dominant motive of American policy towards Japan
changed from a punitive one to one of guidance along the paths to
revival. The first clear indication of the change came from Kenneth
Royall, Secretary of the Army, who declared in a speech at San
Francisco on 7 January 1948 that the aim of American policy was
to develop a self-sufficient democratic Japan, able to stand as a
deterrent to any future totalitarian war threats.

The change in American objectives was reflected by the shift in
the attitude towards reparations and deconcentration. In 1946 the
Far Eastern Commission had accepted an American proposal about
interim removal of equipment, as reparations, which was regarded
as obviously in excess of the peace-time needs of Japan. In the
spring of 1947 the American Government authorized removals up to
30 per centof the obvious excess level, to be distributed among China,
Great Britain, the Netherlands, and the Philippines. In the meantime, however, SCAP (Supreme Commander for the Allied Powers)
invited a group of engineering and accounting firms known as Overseas

Consultants Incorporated to make a survey of Japanese industry and determine the 'excess' equipment which could be removed as reparations. Its report which was published on 2 March 1948 made a drastic revision in the proposed removals, from the earlier value of Y. 990 million to a total of Y. 172 million—at 1939 prices. The reduction was suggested in order to facilitate Japan's economic recovery with a view to making it self-sufficient. This mission was followed in March 1948 by another mission consisting of American businessmen and headed by Mr P. H. Johnston, Chairman of the Chemical Bank and Trust Company, which undertook a fresh survey of Japan's economic situation and prospects. This mission came to the conclusion that the capacity that could be spared without affecting Japan's useful peace-time productivity was not great. The Johnston Report of 26 April 1948 accordingly recommended a further revision in the 'excess' total bringing it down to Y. 102,247 and in the 'primary war facilities' total slashing it from Y. 1·64 million to Y. 662,000. It was obvious that the United States favoured the ending of any substantial removals for reparations in the interests of the industrial recovery of Japan which was now America's primary objective.

An inevitable result of the new policy was the reconsideration of the programme of deconcentration of Japanese industry, in fact of the whole Zaibatsu programme. The programme had come in for sharp criticism in the United States as too severe. It was feared that it was injuring Japanese recovery and obstructing legitimate foreign business activity in Japan. The Zaibatsu programme was relaxed in 1948 and 1949. All but 30 of the 325 concerns listed for investigation were released without action. In June 1949 some of the more stringent provisions of the Anti-Monopoly Law were amended. The Zaibatsu continued to maintain their hold on the financial life of the country because the big banks were not touched and their controlling network was not disturbed. The change of emphasis in American policy was confirmed by a statement of the American Government to the Far Eastern Commission in December 1948. The statement claimed that the major provisions of the deconcentration programme as directed by the Far Eastern Commission had already been carried out and that the Commission should therefore cease consideration of the matter. The Russian member of the Far Eastern Commission had proposed on 23 September 1948 that all restrictions on Japanese peace-time industries be removed but with a provision, in a treaty for Japan, which would give the right of international supervision to the interested Powers so as to prevent any revival of Japanese capacity to make war. The Soviet proposal was unacceptable to the Far Eastern Commission.

One of the chief aims of the Allied Powers was to reorganize the political structure and bring governmental powers and functions under the control of the Japanese people. Japan had its first free election based on universal adult franchise on 10 April 1946. There were four main political parties in the field : the Liberal Party, the Progressive Party (later known as the Democratic Party), the Social Democratic Party, and the Communist Party. The first two parties, despite their nomenclature, were really conservative parties, and all the four parties had their roots in the pre-war era. No party gained an absolute majority and Shigeru Yoshida, leader of the Liberal Party, formed a conservative coalition with the Progressive Party. The government proved ineffectual and there was serious labour trouble during its short and unhappy span of existence. SCAP had to intervene in early 1947 to prevent a threatened general strike. As a result of this situation, and in view of the fact that the Constitution was to come into effect in May, General MacArthur ordered new elections which were held on 25 April 1947. The Social Democratic Party gained a plurality of seats but failed to get an absolute majority. Their leader Tetsu Katayama formed a coalition Cabinet with the Democratic Party (formerly called the Progressive Party).

It was a coalition at cross purposes in which the Socialists had continually to modify their stand in order to retain the support of the Democrats. Katayama resigned in February 1948. The same Coalition formed another Cabinet but with the Premiership going to the Democratic Party leader, Hitoshi Ashida. The Ashida Government proved to be another weak and divided coalition régime and throughout his period of office Ashida was faced with the general opposition of organized labour. The economic situation of Japan gave serious cause for anxiety. The most urgent problem was to increase substantially agricultural and industrial production and control inflation. By the end of 1947 industrial production stood at only 45 per cent of the 1930-34 average level. The note issue had risen from 30 billion yen at the time of surrender to 220 billion yen and the wholesale prices were ten times higher than at the beginning of 1946. Japan had a heavy trade deficit which came to about 300 billion dollars and which was being borne by the United States. These trends continued in 1948 during the period of the ineffectual government of Ashida. Although industrial production had risen to 62 per cent of the pre-war average, the note issue had further increased and moreover there was a rise in prices. Japanese economy was being saved from collapse by American aid. There was a mounting budget deficit and an increasing inflation.

The worsening economic situation hit the working classes very hard and this fact found expression in frequent and widespread strikes and in other labour demonstrations for higher wages and a change in the economic philosophy of the government. The Communists were very active in organizing the vocal expression of labour's discontent and took full advantage of the situation. SCAP had to intervene in early 1948 to prevent a paralysis of communications and transport through strikes in these state-operated concerns. This extreme political leadership to legitimate economic grievances gave rise to a dangerous situation. On 22 July 1948 General MacArthur in a letter to Prime Minister Ashida recommended the amending of the National Public Service Law so as to prevent state employees from resorting to strike action. The purported amendments produced consternation among government employees and there were loud protests from labour against this restriction on trade union activity. However, the government was determined to curb it and on 30 November the Japanese Diet adopted the amendments which denied the right of collective bargaining and strike to certain categories of public servants. On 11 December, the Diet passed the Public Corporation Law which set up public corporations for railway workers and for those in the government monopolies of salt, camphor and tobacco. Their employees were granted the right of collective bargaining but not that of strike.

In early 1949 the Diet passed amendments to the Trade Union Law of December 1945, to prevent the seizure of power in the trade unions by Communist minorities, and the Labour Relations Adjustment Law of September 1946, granting the government the power to impose compulsory mediation for a month in case of a threatened strike in an industry which it considered one of public welfare.

The deteriorating economic situation was a source of great concern to the American authorities. It was obvious that the United States could not go on supporting Japan's economy indefinitely. In May 1948 the American Government sent to Japan an economic and financial mission headed by Mr R. A. Young of the Federal Reserve Board. The Young Mission's findings were confidential but the Mission reportedly recommended a general programme of economic stabilization through effective control over wages and prices, reduction in government expenditure and reform of taxation. However, the Ashida Government was a weak government and was afraid of introducing such drastic reforms which would initially be very unpopular. After a series of political scandals implicating senior Cabinet members, including Ashida himself, the government collapsed in October 1948 and Yoshida of the Liberal Party formed a caretaker government, until new elections were held in January 1949 which returned Yoshida's party with an absolute majority.

461

Since verbal representations regarding the economic situation were having little effect on the Japanese Government, the United States decided to employ compulsion in order to move the Japanese Government. On 10 December 1948, the American Government issued an interim directive to General MacArthur asking him to direct the Japanese Government to adopt immediately a programme of fiscal, monetary, price and wage stability. The nine measures listed in the Directive were transmitted by General MacArthur to the Japanese Government on 19 December and came to be known as the Economic Stabilization Programme.

The Economic Stabilization Programme resulted in large-scale personnel reduction with all its attendant hardships. There was disquiet and unrest among both the labouring and the white-collar classes, particularly among those who were directly affected by the Programme. The Communist Party waged a bitter struggle to prevent the implementation of the Programme, but the government, backed by SCAP, was determined to see it through and hit back with great force. The retrenchment programme was also used to get rid of the Communists and other trouble-makers in the government and industrial enterprises. Moreover, the militant and violent tactics of the Communists turned many of their adherents among the working class and the lower middle class away from them.

The successful implementation of the Stabilization Programme led to improvement in the economic situation in 1949. The Japanese budget for the fiscal year 1949-50 was brought into balance. A single general rate of exchange for the year was introduced in April 1949. There was a 20 per cent reduction in the note-issue from the post-war peak. The consumer prices and wages were only slightly above the level established in early 1949. However, inflationary tendencies arising from food, clothing and other necessaries of life remained and called for continued price and distribution controls. It was stabilization at a high level rather than deflation. The note issue was 363 billion yen on 31 December 1949, compared with 355 billion yen at the end of 1948. The economy was still held by the margin of American aid.

The political scene continued to be dominated by the four main political parties, but there were indications of the strengthening of the Right as well as the Left at the expense of the Centre. The 'caretaker' government of Mr Yoshida, which was formed in October 1948, held the general election in January 1949. There was general public disgust over the ineptness and corruption of the previous Socialist and Democratic-led coalitions. In the 1949 election the Liberals increased their strength from 132 to an absolute majority of 264. The Democrats' strength fell from 126 to 68 and that of the

Socialists from 143 to 49. Communist representation rose from 4 to 35.

The Liberal Party is one of the most conservative of all the political parties in Japan. Its chief support comes from business and middle class groups in the cities and from rural areas which generally vote conservative. The party subscribes to the classical liberal concepts of 'individualism', 'free enterprise', and 'limited government' and its policy has been directed towards growth of private enterprise, relaxation rather than expansion of governmental economy and limited expenditure for social welfare measures. The Liberals also stand for a strongly pro-American foreign policy and consider that Japanese security can be safeguarded only through joining the Western bloc.

Another conservative party in the field is the Democratic Party. Starting out as one of the leading parties in the country, the Democratic Party survived as a minor force in the elections of 1949. Ever since its inception the Party has gone through a series of crises and more and more of its adherents have been deserting its ranks and skipping over to the Liberal Party. Theoretically, the Democrats advocate a policy of reformed capitalism. They have made a vain bid to set themselves up as a progressive 'third force' between unreformed capitalism and full-fledged socialism. The differences between the two conservative parties stem not so much from basic policies as from personal differences between the leaders of the two parties.

Drawing its inspiration largely from the British Labour Party, the Socialist Party stands for the elimination of the capitalist system through an evolutionary process and the maintenance of parliamentary institutions. The Socialist Programme includes the nationalization of basic industries, the broadening of the land reform programme, and encouragement of the co-operative movement. Although capable of presenting a direct appeal to the masses, the Socialist Party is a house divided against itself. Much of its weakness is due to the threefold split in the Party. The Left wing wants to pursue the path of neutrality in the cold war while the Right wing would emulate its counterparts in Europe. The Centrists adopt a middle position and put their faith in the United Nations.

The fourth party of national significance is the Communist Party of Japan. Communist influence in Japan had been on the increase in 1947, 1948 and 1949. It increased its representation in the House of Representatives from 4 in 1947 to 35 in 1949. The Communists exercise their greatest influence in student and labour circles, with a sprinkling of intellectual and diverse support. The Communist Party in its 1949 election programme demanded the ending of

American occupation, a 'democratic peace treaty', including the Soviet Union and New China, giving no nation preferential treatment in military and economic matters, and friendship and trade with New China.

The 1949 elections showed some polarization of power at the two extremes of the Japanese political spectrum. On the extreme Right was the Liberal Party and on the extreme Left an increasingly strong and militant Communist Party. It was feared that if the Right failed to achieve economic stability, there might be a swing to the other extreme.

The occupation of Japan was not intended to last so long. When the Allied Powers formulated their basic policies for Japan, it was hoped that the occupation of Japan under American auspices would be for the purpose of breaking up the military-state structure of Japan and effecting democratic reforms with a view to setting Japan on the path of peaceful democratic progress, and that it would be terminated as early as possible after the Allied Powers had devised the terms of a peace treaty for Japan. Unfortunately the Allied Powers fell out and there was no agreement on the terms of a peace treaty, with the result that the occupation had to be unduly prolonged. In 1949 the prospects of an early agreement were still remote, but the United States showed a growing impatience with the delay in arriving at a peace treaty and took steps to relax the control of SCAP and give more freedom to Japanese Government as well as to promote Japan's return to normal intercourse with the outside world. In May 1949 General MacArthur told the Japanese people that the continuation of the occupation was due to international factors but he assured them that the policy of relaxation of occupation controls would be further extended.

JAPAN

POLITICAL, CONSTITUTIONAL AND ECONOMIC DEVELOPMENTS

Section Four
Political Developments

Section Five
Economic Stabilization

Section Six
Selected Speeches and Messages of General MacArthur

I CONSTITUTIONAL DEVELOPMENTS

3 *November* 1945

BASIC INITIAL POST-SURRENDER DIRECTIVE TO
SUPREME COMMANDER FOR THE ALLIED POWERS
FOR THE OCCUPATION AND CONTROL OF JAPAN

(1)   *The Purpose and Scope of This Directive.*

(a)   This directive defines the authority which you will possess
and the policies which will guide you in the occupation and control
of Japan in the initial period after surrender.

(b)   Japan, as used in this directive, is defined to include : The
four main islands of Japan : Hokkaido (Yezo), Honshu, Kyushu and
Shikoku and about 1,000 smaller adjacent islands including the
Tsushima Islands.

(c)   This directive is divided in Part I : General and Political ;
Part II : Economic and Civilian Supply and Part III : Financial.

Part I—General and Political

(2)   *The Basis and Scope of Military Authority.*

The basis of your power and authority over Japan is the directive
signed by the President of the United States designating you as
Supreme Commander for the Allied Powers [SWNCC 21/6(JCS
1467)] and the Instrument of Surrender [SWNCC 21/6 (Annex ' 4 ' to
JCS 1380/5)], executed by command of the Emperor of Japan
[SWNCC 21/6 (Annex 'B' to JCS 1380/5)]. These documents, in
turn are based upon the Potsdam Declaration of 26 July 1945
[SWNCC 149/1 (Annex 'C' to JCS 1380/5)], the reply of the Secretary of State on 11 August 1945 to the Japanese communication of
10 August 1945 [SWNCC Memo for Info. No. 19 (Annex 'E' to
JCS 1380/5)], and the final Japanese communication on 14 August
1945 [SWNCC Memo for Info. No. 19 (Annex 'F' to JCS 1380/5)].
Pursuant to these documents your authority over Japan, as Supreme
Commander for the Allied Powers, is supreme for the purpose of
carrying out the surrender. In addition to the conventional powers
of a military occupant of enemy territory, you have the power to
take any steps deemed advisable and proper by you to effectuate
the surrender and the provisions of the Potsdam Declaration. It is
contemplated, however, that unless you deem it necessary, or are
instructed to the contrary, you will not establish direct military
government, but will exercise your powers so far as compatible with
the accomplishment of your mission through the Emperor of Japan
or the Japanese Government. In the exercise of your powers you
will be guided by the following general principles.

(3) *Basic Objectives of Military Occupation of Japan.*

(*a*) The ultimate objective of the United Nations with respect to Japan is to foster conditions which will give the greatest possible assurance that Japan will not again become a menace to the peace and security of the world and will permit her eventual admission as a responsible and peaceful member of the family of nations. Certain measures considered to be essential for the achievement of this objective have been set forth in the Potsdam Declaration. These measures include, among others, the carrying out of the Cairo Declaration and the limiting of Japanese sovereignty to the four main islands and such minor islands as the Allied Powers determine ; the abolition of militarism and ultra-nationalism in all their forms ; the disarmament and demilitarization of Japan, with continuing control over Japan's capacity to make war ; the strengthening of democratic tendencies and processes in governmental, economic, and social institutions ; and the encouragement and support of liberal political tendencies in Japan. The United States desires that the Japanese Government conform as closely as may be to principles of democratic self-government, but it is not the responsibility of the occupation forces to impose on Japan any form of government not supported by the freely expressed will of the people.

(*b*) As Supreme Commander for the Allied Powers your mission will be to assure that the surrender is vigorously enforced and to initiate appropriate action to achieve the objectives of the United Nations.

(*c*) This directive does not purport finally to formulate long-term policies concerning the treatment of Japan in the post-war world, nor does it seek to prescribe in detail the measures which you are to take throughout the period of your occupation of Japan in the effort to give effect to the surrender and the Potsdam Declaration. Those policies and the appropriate measures for their fulfilment will in large measure be determined by developing circumstances in Japan. It is, therefore, essential that surveys dealing with economic, industrial, financial, social and political conditions in Japan be constantly maintained by you and made available to your government. These surveys should be developed in such a manner as to form the basis for effecting modifications in the initial measures of control set forth herein as well as for the progressive formulation of policies to promote the ultimate objectives of the United Nations. Supplemental directives will be issued to you through the Joint Chiefs of Staff as may be required.

(4) *The Establishment of Military Authority over Japan.*

(*a*) Immediately upon the surrender of Japan you will require the Emperor, the Japanese Government and the Japanese Imperial

General Headquarters to issue orders to all the armed forces of Japan and all armed forces under Japanese control to cease hostilities and to surrender their arms and to issue such other orders as may be required to give effect to the instrument of surrender and the policies set forth in the Potsdam Declaration. You will require the Emperor and the Japanese Government to take all necessary steps to assure that all orders issued to effectuate the objectives of your mission are promptly and fully complied with by all persons in Japan.

(b) You will occupy the Imperial capital of Tokyo, and the capitals of such prefectures as you deem necessary in order to facilitate your control over the Japanese Government. You will also occupy such strategic places as you may deem necessary. Otherwise you should not occupy any part of Japan unless it becomes essential to impose direct military government therein. However, you may temporarily utilize your forces in any area of Japan as may be required for the fulfilment of your mission. Subject to the provisions of sub-paragraph 4(c) below, you will take prompt action to assure the restoration and maintenance of law and order by Japanese authorities or by your forces, if necessary.

(c) Where action is necessary in order to carry out the surrender, you have the right to act directly from the outset. Otherwise, subject always to your right as the Supreme Commander to take direct action in the event of the unwillingness or failure of the Emperor or other Japanese authority to act effectively, you will exercise your supreme authority through the Emperor and Japanese governmental machinery, national and local. The policy is to use the existing form of government in Japan, not to support it. Changes in the direction of modifying the feudal and authoritarian tendencies of the government are to be permitted and favoured. In the event that the effectuation of such changes involves the use of force by the Japanese people or government against persons opposed thereto, you as Supreme Commander should intervene only where necessary to ensure the security of your forces and the attainment of all other objectives of the occupation. You may, as circumstances require, exercise your supreme power and authority in the fullest measure including the imposition of direct military government. If it becomes necessary to impose direct military government in any part of Japan, you will immediately thereafter advise the Joint Chiefs of Staff. You will not remove the Emperor or take any steps towards his removal without prior consultation with and advice issued to you through the Joint Chiefs of Staff.

(d) You will take appropriate steps in Japan to effect the complete governmental and administrative separation from Japan of (i) all Pacific islands which she has seized or occupied under mandate or otherwise since the beginning of the World War in 1914, (ii) Manchuria, Formosa and the Pescadores, (iii) Korea, (iv) Karafuto, and (v) such other territories as may be specified in future directives.

(e) By appropriate means you will make clear to all levels of the Japanese population the fact of their defeat. They must be made to realize that their suffering and defeat have been brought upon them by the lawless and irresponsible aggression of Japan, and that only when militarism has been eliminated from Japanese life and institutions will Japan be admitted to the family of nations. They must be told that they will be expected to develop a non-militaristic and democratic Japan which will respect the rights of other nations and Japan's international obligations. You will make it clear that military occupation of Japan is effected in the interests of the United Nations and is necessary for the destruction of Japan's power of aggression and her war potential and for the elimination of militarism and militaristic institutions which have brought disaster on the Japanese. With this end in view, and to ensure the security of the troops, a policy of non-fraternization may be applied in Japan if and to the extent that you may deem it to be desirable. Your officers and troops, however, should so treat the Japanese population as to develop confidence in the United States and the United Nations and their representatives.

(f) You will require the Emperor to abrogate all laws, ordinances, decrees and regulations which would prejudice the achievement of the objectives set forth in the Potsdam Declaration or which conflict with the instrument of surrender or with directives which may be issued to you through the Joint Chiefs of Staff. You will, in particular, assure the abrogation of all laws, orders and regulations which established and maintained restrictions on political and civil liberties and discriminations on grounds of race, nationality, creed or political opinion. Agencies or parts of agencies charged specifically with the execution of legislation abrogated or to be abrogated shall be abolished immediately.

(g) You will establish such military courts as may be necessary with jurisdiction over offences against the forces of occupation and over such other matters as are consistent with the implementation of the surrender. You will, however, except as otherwise deemed necessary by you, ensure that Japanese courts exercise an effective jurisdiction over cases not of direct and predominant concern to the security of your troops.

(h) Representatives of civilian agencies of the United States Government or of other United Nations governments shall not participate in the occupation or function independently within Japan except upon your approval, and subject, as to purpose, time and extent, to decisions communicated to you by the Joint Chiefs of Staff.

(5) Political and Administrative Reorganization.

(a) Local, regional and national agencies of governmental administration, excluding those with functions and responsibilities inconsistent with the purposes of the occupation will be permitted to continue to function after the removal of officials who are unacceptable as described in paragraph 5 (h) below, or who are ascertained to be unreliable. Such agencies and their personnel will be held responsible for the administration of government and will be charged with the execution of your policies and directives. At all times, however, and in all circumstances you are empowered yourself to take direct action if and to the extent that Japanese authorities fail satisfactorily to carry out your instructions.

(b) Except as indicated in paragraph 7 (c) below, in no circumstances will persons be allowed to hold public office or any other positions of responsibility or influence in public or important private enterprise who have been active exponents of militant nationalism and aggression, who have been influential members of any Japanese ultra-nationalistic, terroristic or secret patriotic society, its agencies or affiliates, who have been influential in the activities of the other organizations enumerated in paragraph 5 (g) below, or who manifest hostility to the objectives of the military occupation.

(c) You will assure that at all times, so long as the present form of government is retained, the posts of Lord Privy Seal, Privy Council, Prime Minister and Cabinet members are held only by persons who may be relied upon to further the purposes of your mission. You will require the immediate abolition of the Ministry of Greater East Asia but may retain such of its machinery and personnel as may be necessary to carry out the separation of colonies provided for by paragraph 4 (d) above. You will progressively disband and eliminate the Ministries of War, Navy, and Munitions during the process of disarmament and demobilization.

(d) Local responsibility for the local enforcement of national policy will be encouraged.

(e) Ordinary criminal and civil courts in Japan will be permitted to continue to function subject to such regulations, supervision and control as you may determine. As rapidly as possible, judges and other court personnel who are unacceptable under the provisions of paragraph 5 (b) above will be removed. Such officials will be replaced with acceptable and qualified successors. Full power of review will be retained by you over all courts which are allowed to function. You will veto all decisions which are inconsistent with the purpose of your mission. You will take all practicable measures to cause the release of persons held in custody solely under laws or regulations of the type to be abrogated under paragraph 4 (*f*) above.

(*f*) Criminal and ordinary police agencies, and such others as you may consider proper to be retained under appropriate supervision, must be purged of undependable and undesirable elements, in particular, of members of ultra-nationalistic, terroristic and secret patriotic societies.

(*g*) Throughout Japan you will assure the dissolution of the Political Associations of Great Japan, the Imperial Rule Assistance Association (Taisei Yokusankai), the Imperial Rule Assistance Political Society (Taisei Seijikai), their affiliates and agencies or any successor organizations, and all Japanese ultra-nationalistic, terroristic and secret patriotic societies and their agencies and affiliates.

(*h*) You will direct the Japanese Government to recall such Japanese diplomatic and consular officials and other agents abroad as the Department of State may request through the Joint Chiefs of Staff. You will also direct the Japanese Government to arrange for the turning over to the custody of properly accredited representatives of the Allied governments of archives and property of Japanese diplomatic and consular establishments for the purposes of effectuating the surrender.

(*i*) All property, real and personal, owned or controlled by any of the organizations referred to in paragraph 5 (*g*) above, should be considered public property. If there is any doubt as to the public status of any property (e.g., property of quasi-official companies or of private companies in which the Japanese Government or the Japanese Imperial Household has an important interest), it should be considered public property. Imperial Household property shall not be excepted from any action necessary to carry out the objectives set forth in this directive.

(6) *Demilitarization*.

(*a*) You will assure that all units of the Japanese armed forces including the Gendarmerie (Kempei) but not the civil police, Civilian Volunteer Corps, and all para-military organizations are promptly disarmed. Personnel of such units will not be held as prisoners of war, but as disarmed units under their own officers and will be demobilized in accordance with directives issued or to be issued by you. You will require that provision be made against any inequitable treatment of or disabilities against any member of the Japanese armed forces taken as a prisoner of war who is returned to Japan.

(*b*) You will provide for the permanent dissolution of all military and para-military organizations, including the Supreme Military Council, the Board of Field Marshals and Fleet Admirals, the Imperial General Headquarters, the Army and Navy General Staffs, the Army, Navy, Civilian Volunteer Corps and Gendarmerie, together with all reservists and other militaristic associations which might serve to keep alive the military tradition in Japan. You may, however, for a brief period of time, utilize military and naval agencies, including those enumerated above, for the limited purpose of giving effect to the surrender with particular reference to demobilization. All military and para-military training on land and sea and in the air will be prohibited.

(*c*) In accordance with the provisions of the directive already issued you,* you will seize or destroy all arms, ammunition, naval vessels, and implements of war, including aircraft designed for civil use, and stop the production thereof.

(*d*) You will take proper steps to destroy the Japanese war potential, as set forth in Parts II and III in this directive.

(7) *Arrest and Internment of Japanese Personnel.*

(*a*) The following will be arrested as rapidly as practicable and held as suspected war criminals, pending further instructions concerning their disposition :

(i) All members of the Supreme Military Council, the Board of Field Marshals and Fleet Admirals, the Imperial General Headquarters, and the Army and Navy General Staffs ;

(ii) All commissioned officers of the Gendarmerie (Kempei), and all officers of the Army and Navy who have been important exponents of militant nationalism and aggression ;

(iii) All key members of ultra-nationalistic, terroristic and secret patriotic societies ; and

(iv) All persons who you have reason to believe are war criminals or whose names or descriptions are contained in lists of suspected war criminals which have been or may be furnished to you.

(*b*) All persons who have played an active and dominant governmental, economic, financial or other significant part in the formulation or execution of Japan's programme of aggression and all high officials of the Political Association of Great Japan, the Imperial Rule Assistance Association, the Imperial Rule Assistance Political Society and their agencies and affiliates or successor organizations will be interned pending further disposition. You may intern other civilians as necessary for the achievement of your mission.

* SWNCC 58/9 (JCS 1328/5).

(c) You may, however, for a brief period of time, utilize the closely supervised services of those persons within the categories enumerated in sub-paragraphs 7 (a) (i) and (ii) above, who are absolutely required by you to ensure the demobilization of the Japanese armed forces.

(d) You will receive further instructions concerning your responsibility with relation to war criminals, including those who have committed crimes against peace and crimes against humanity.

(e) No differentiation shall be made or special consideration be accorded to civilian or military personnel arrested as war criminals either as to manner of arrest or conditions of detention, upon the basis of wealth, or political, industrial, or other rank or position.

(f) All nationals of countries except Japan with which any of the United Nations are or have been at war in World War II (Bulgaria, Finland, Germany, Hungary, Italy, Roumania, and Thailand) will be identified and registered and may be interned or their activities curtailed as may be necessary under the circumstances. Diplomatic and consular officials of such countries will be taken into protective custody and held for further disposition.

(g) Property, real and personal, owned or controlled by persons who have been detained or arrested under the provisions of paragraph 7 will be taken under your control pending directions as to its eventual disposition.

(8) *Prisoners of War, United Nations Nationals, Neutrals, and Other Persons.*

(a) You will ensure that prisoners of war and displaced persons of the United Nations are cared for and repatriated.

(b) Nationals of neutral countries will be required to register with the appropriate military authorities. They may be repatriated under such regulations as you may establish. However, all nationals of neutral nations who have actively participated in any way in the war against one of the United Nations will be arrested for disposition in conformity with later instructions. Nationals of neutral nations will be accorded no special privileges of communications or business relationships with their home countries or people resident outside Japan. The persons, archives and property of diplomatic consular officials of neutrals will be accorded full protection.

(c) All civilians who are nationals of the United Nations, resident or interned in Japan will be identified, examined closely, and if you deem it advisable, may be placed in custody or restricted residence. All such nationals who fall within the provisions of paragraph 7 (b) above shall be arrested and held as suspected war criminals. All other United Nations nationals who have actively participated in any way in the war against one or more of the United Nations will be arrested and held for later disposition. Thereafter, they will be dealt with in accordance with instructions to be furnished you. In general, practical measures will be taken to ensure the health and welfare of United Nations nationals.

(d) You will treat Formosan-Chinese and Koreans as liberated peoples in so far as military security permits. They are not included in the term 'Japanese' as used in this directive but they have been Japanese subjects and may be treated by you, in case of necessity, as enemy nationals. They may be repatriated, if they so desire, under such regulations as you may establish. However, priority will be given to the repatriation of nationals of the United Nations.

(e) Within such limits as are imposed by the military situation, you should take all reasonable steps necessary to preserve and protect the property of the United Nations and their nationals.

(9) *Political Activity.*

(a) The dissemination of Japanese militaristic and ultra-nationalistic ideology and propaganda in any form will be prohibited and completely suppressed. You will require the Japanese Government to cease financial and other support of National Shinto establishments.

(b) You will establish such minimum control and censorship of civilian communications including the mails, wireless, radio, telephone, telegraph and cables, films and Press as may be necessary in the interests of military security and the accomplishment of the purposes set forth in this directive. Freedom of thought will be fostered by the dissemination of democratic ideals and principles through all available media of public information.

(c) You will immediately place under control all existing political parties, organizations and societies. Those whose activities are consistent with the requirements of the military occupation and its objectives should be encouraged. Those whose activities are inconsistent with such requirements and objectives should be abolished. Subject to the necessity of maintaining the security of the occupying forces, the formation and activities of democratic political parties with rights of assembly and public discussion will be encouraged. Free elections of representative local governments should be held at the earliest practicable date, and at the regional and national levels as directed, after consideration of your recommendation, through the Joint Chiefs of Staff. Your action in connexion with the programme referred to in this sub-paragraph should be taken in the light of one of the ultimate objectives of the occupation, the establishment, in accordance with the freely expressed will of the Japanese people, of a peacefully inclined and responsible government.

(*d*) Encouragement will be given to the development of democratic organizations in labour, industry and agriculture.

(*e*) Freedom of religious worship shall be proclaimed promptly by the Japanese Government. To the extent that the security of your military occupation and the attainment of its objectives are not prejudiced and subject to paragraph 9 (*a*) and (*c*) above, you will insure freedom of opinion, speech, Press, and assembly.

(10) *Education, Arts and Archives.*

(*a*) As soon as practicable, educational institutions will be re-opened. As rapidly as possible, all teachers who have been active exponents of militant nationalism and aggression and those who continue actively to oppose the purposes of the military occupation will be replaced by acceptable and qualified successors. Japanese military and para-military training and drill in all schools will be forbidden. You will assure that curricula acceptable to you are employed in all schools and that they include the concepts indicated in paragraph 3 (*a*) above.

(*b*) You should cause to be preserved for your information and use the records of all governmental and quasi-governmental, important private financial, industrial, manufacturing and business concerns, and the Japanese organizations referred to in paragraph 5 (*f*) above.

(*c*) You will, so far as practicable, cause to be protected and preserved, all historical, cultural and religious objects, against depredations by the occupational forces, or others.

Part II—A. *Economic*

Objectives and General Basic Principles.

(11) The policies of the American Government in regard to the economic affairs of Japan during the period of occupation are intended simultaneously to accomplish the following purposes :

(*a*) To eliminate existing specialized facilities for the production of arms, munitions, or implements of war of any kind.

(*b*) To destroy the economic ability of Japan to create or support any armaments dangerous to international peace.

(*c*) To execute such programme of reparations and restitution as may be decided upon by the appropriate Allied authorities.

(*d*) To encourage the development within Japan of economic ways and institutions of a type that will contribute to the growth of peaceful and democratic forces in Japan.

(*e*) To supervise and guide the operation of Japanese economic arrangements and operations to assure that they conform to the general purposes of the occupation, and make possible the eventual readmission of Japan to the ranks of peaceful trading nations.

The instructions composing the economic part of the directive are intended to advance these objectives during the first and immediate period of occupation that lies ahead ; they will be subject to addition and revision in the light of circumstances which you encounter and the conduct of the Japanese people.

(12) Your supreme authority as Supreme Commander for the Allied Powers in Japan will extend to all matters in the economic sphere. In the exercise of that authority, to the extent that the accomplishment of your objectives permits, you will use the services of the Emperor and the machinery of the Japanese Government to accomplish your objectives. You will require them to carry out your orders, and to make such changes in the administrative organization of those branches of government concerned with economic matters as may seem to you necessary to carry out your objectives. You should act directly :

(*a*) If, because of the very nature of the task, action through Japanese authorities will not effectively accomplish your economic objectives.

(*b*) In the event that operation through the Japanese Government clearly fails in any particular phase of your operations to prove a satisfactory method.

In acting directly, you will establish administrative machinery independent of and superior to the Japanese officials and agencies to execute or assure the execution of the economic measures contained in this directive until such time as you may deem that the tasks can be satisfactorily assigned to the Japanese Governmental authorities.

(13) You will not assume any responsibility for the economic rehabilitation of Japan or the strengthening of the Japanese economy. You will make it clear to the Japanese people that :

(*a*) You assume no obligations to maintain, or have maintained, any particular standard of living in Japan, and

(*b*) That the standard of living will depend upon the thoroughness with which Japan rids itself of all militaristic ambitions, redirects the use of its human and natural resources wholly and solely for purposes of peaceful living, administers adequate economic and financial controls, and co-operates with the occupying forces and the governments they represent.

It is not the policy of the United States to prevent the eventual achievement by Japanese working effort and resources of conditions of life in Japan consistent with objectives specified in paragraph 11.

479

Economic Disarmament.

(14)   In order to effect the economic disarmament of Japan :

(*a*)   You will stop immediately and prevent the future production, acquisition, development, maintenance, or use of all arms, ammunitions, and other implements of war ; naval vessels ; all types of aircraft including those designed for civilian use ; and all parts, components, and materials especially designed for incorporation in any of the foregoing.

(*b*)   You will take such measures as you deem necessary to safeguard the facilities used or intended for use in the production or maintenance of any of the items above mentioned. Pending further instructions as to their ultimate disposition such facilities are not to be destroyed except in emergency situations.

(*c*)   You will not postpone the enforcement of the prohibitory programme specified in sub-paragraph (*a*) or carrying out instructions that you will receive pursuant to sub-paragraph (*b*) without specific approval through the Joint Chiefs of Staff. Should you, however, find that production of any of the items enumerated in sub-paragraph (*a*) is essential to meet your requirements for military operations, the occupying forces, or temporary military research, you will make suitable recommendations to the Joint Chiefs of Staff ; and pending the decision of the Joint Chiefs of Staff, you are authorized to make arrangements for production to the minimum extent necessary therefore.

(15)   Instructions which will be subsequently transmitted to you for carrying out programmes for economic disarmament, reparations and restitution will involve the reduction or elimination of certain branches of Japanese production, such as iron, steel, chemicals, non-ferrous metals, aluminium, magnesium, synthetic rubber, synthetic oil, machine tools, radio and electrical equipment, automotive vehicles, merchant ships, heavy machines, and important parts thereof.

Pending, however, final and specific decision on these matters, you will permit continued production in those industries and the repair of production facilities to the minimum extent required to meet the needs of the occupation forces, and the minimum peaceful requirements of the population.

You will make clear to the Japanese that any permission to continue production or to repair production facilities is granted without prejudice to final decisions, as to either the limitations that may be imposed upon any branch of the Japanese economy or deliveries which may be required as reparations or restitution.

(16)   You may also permit the conversion of plant and equipment, including those types mentioned in paragraphs 14 and 15, to the

production of essential consumer goods. You will satisfy yourself that any such conversion undertaken is a genuine move towards a peaceful economy and not a disguised attempt to preserve capacity to produce for military purposes.

You will also make clear to the Japanese that any such permission to convert is granted without prejudice to subsequent decisions as regards removal of plant or equipment on account of reparations or restitution or scrapping for security reasons under paragraph 11.

(17) You will :

(a) Immediately establish a system of inspection, and control to ensure that production of the type forbidden in paragraphs 14 and 15 is not undertaken in concealed or disguised form.

(b) Have prepared as rapidly as possible inventory reports upon all significant facilities that have been producing or are intended to produce the products covered in paragraph 14, and in all the industries specifically mentioned in paragraph 15. These reports should specify the condition and capacity of plant and equipment and the extent of raw materials stocked, finished goods, and goods in process. You will also inventory the Japanese merchant fleet.

In order to furnish the information necessary for further decisions concerning economic policy you will communicate those reports to the Joint Chiefs of Staff.

(c) Develop and recommend to the Joint Chiefs of Staff controls which will prevent Japanese rearmament after termination of your occupation.

(18) You will ensure that all laboratories, research institutes, and similar technological organizations are closed immediately except those you deem necessary to the purposes of the occupation. You will provide for the maintenance and security of physical facilities thereof when deemed necessary, and for the detention of such personnel as are of interest to your technological or counter-intelligence investigations. You will at once investigate the character of the study and research conducted in such closed organizations and as rapidly as possible permit the resumption of those forms of study and research that have an obviously peaceful purpose under appropriate regulations which (i) define the specific type of research permitted, (ii) provide for frequent inspection, (iii) require free disclosure to you of the results of the research, and (iv) impose severe penalties, including permanent closure of the offending institution whenever the regulations are violated.

The Operation of the Japanese Economic System.

(19) The Japanese authorities will be expected to develop and effectively carry out programmes of working activity that will enable

them out of their own resources and labour to accomplish the following :

(*a*)   To avoid acute economic distress.

(*b*)   To assure just and impartial distribution of available supplies.

(*c*)   To meet your demands for the needs of the occupying forces.

(*d*)   To meet the requirements for such reparations deliveries as may be agreed upon by the Allied Governments.

In order to achieve these aims, the Japanese authorities will have to make the utmost effort to maximize production of agricultural and fishery products, coal, charcoal, housing repair materials, clothing and other essentials. In the event that they fail to do so, you will direct them to take such measures as in your judgement are necessary.

(20)   You will require the Japanese authorities to provide goods and services to meet the needs of the occupying forces to the extent that this can be effected without causing starvation, widespread disease and acute physical distress.

(21)   The Japanese authorities shall be permitted on their own responsibility to establish and administer any controls over economic activities that are appropriate or necessary in order to achieve the economic ends specified in paragraph 19. Both the policy and the administration of these controls shall be subject to your approval and supervision particularly in so far as they may conflict with paragraph 15. This paragraph shall not preclude your taking direct action as provided in paragraph 12.

(22)   Serious inflation will substantially retard the accomplishment of the ultimate objectives of the occupation. You will, therefore, direct the Japanese authorities to make every feasible effort to avoid such inflation. However, prevention or restraint of inflation shall not constitute a reason for limiting the removal, destruction, or curtailment of productive facilities in fulfilment of programmes for reparations, restitution, demilitarization, or economic disarmament.

Elimination of Certain Elements in the Japanese Economic System.

(23)   You will prohibit the retention in or selection for positions of important responsibility or influence in industry, finance, commerce, or agriculture of all persons who have been active exponents of militant nationalism and aggression, of those who have actively participated in the organizations enumerated in paragraph 5 (*g*) (above, Political and General Part) of this directive, and of any who do not direct future Japanese economic effort solely towards peaceful ends. (In the absence of evidence, satisfactory to you, to the contrary, you will assume that any persons who have held key

positions of high responsibility since 1937, in industry, finance, commerce or agriculture have been active exponents of militant nationalism and aggression.)

(24) You will require the protection from destruction and the maintenance for such disposition as may be determined by this and other directives of all plants, equipment, patents, books and records and all other significant property of the large Japanese industrial and financial companies and trade and research associations that have played an important part in the Japanese war effort or economy.

Democratization of Japanese Economic Institutions.

(25) It is the intent of the United States Government to encourage and show favour to :

(a) Policies which permit a wide distribution of income and of ownership of the means of production and trade.

(b) The development of organizations in labour, industry, and agriculture organized on a democratic basis. Accordingly, you will :

(i) Require the Japanese to establish a public agency responsible for reorganizing Japanese business in accordance with the military and economic objectives of your government. You will require this agency to submit, for approval by you, plans for dissolving large Japanese industrial and banking combines or other large concentrations of private business control.

(ii) Establish and maintain surveillance, until satisfactory plans for reorganization have been approved, over the Japanese businesses described in sub-paragraph (i) above in order to ensure conformity with the military and economic objective of your government.

(iii) Dissolve the Control Associations. Any necessary public function previously performed by these associations should be transferred to public agencies, approved and supervised by you.

(iv) Abrogate all legislative or administrative measures which limit free entry of firms into industries to be reorganized where the purpose or effect of such measures is to foster and strengthen private monopoly.

(v) Terminate and prohibit all Japanese participation in private international cartels or other restrictive private international contracts or arrangements.

(vi) Require the Japanese to remove, as rapidly as practicable, war-time controls over labour and reinstate protective labour legislation.

(vii) Require the removal of all legal hindrances to the formation of organizations of employees along democratic lines, subject to any necessary safeguards to prevent the perpetuation of militaristic influences under any guise or the continuation of any group hostile to the objectives and operations of the occupying forces.

(viii)   Prevent or prohibit strikes or other work stoppages only when you consider that these would interfere with military operations or directly endanger the security of the occupying forces.

Foreign Economic Transactions.

(26)   You will establish controls over all Japanese foreign trade in goods and services. Such controls should be so operated as to give effect during the initial period to the following policies :

(*a*)   Exports shall not be approved if such goods are clearly needed to meet minimum domestic requirements.

(*b*)   No exports of plant and equipment shall be permitted until determination has been made as to whether they may be required for reparation or restitution.

(*c*)   Exports other than those directed to be shipped on reparation account or as restitution may be made only to those recipients who agree to provide necessary imports in exchange or agree to pay for such exports in foreign exchange.

(*d*)   All proceeds of exports shall be controlled by you and made available in the first place for the payment for approved imports. No person, corporation or organization in Japan shall be permitted to acquire foreign assets of any kind except with your special approval.

(*e*)   Approval should be given only to imports which are clearly in accord with the economic policies elsewhere set down in this directive.

(*f*)   Neither the need for imports or exports (including exports that might be made on reparations account) shall be deemed a reason for requiring or permitting any branch of Japanese industry to be restored or developed to an extent that might significantly contribute to Japan's war-making potential, or promote dependence by other countries on Japan for strategic products.

(27)   The Japanese authorities are to enter into no economic agreements of any kind with foreign governments or interests except after prior consultation with you by your express approval. Any such proposed agreements should be submitted to the Joint Chiefs of Staff for their consideration.

Reparations and Restitutions.

(28)   You will assure the execution of programmes of reparations in kind and of restitution of identifiable looted property in accordance with decisions of the appropriate Allied authorities transmitted to you by the Joint Chiefs of Staff. Reparations will be accomplished :

(*a*) Through the transfer of Japanese property located outside of the territories to be retained by Japan ;

(*b*) Through the transfer from Japan of goods, existing plant, equipment, and facilities that are not necessary to the operation of a peaceful Japanese economy, or the supplying of the occupying forces.

All requests received by you for reparations or restitution from the United Nations which have been victims of Japanese aggression will be reported with your recommendations to the Joint Chiefs of Staff.

B. *Civilian Supply and Relief*

Civilian Supply Policy and Standard of Provision.

(29) (*a*) You will assure that all practicable economic and police measures are taken to achieve the maximum utilization of essential Japanese resources in order that imports into Japan may be strictly limited. Such measures will include production and price controls, rationing, control of black markets, fiscal and financial controls and other measures directed towards full employment of resources, facilities and means available in Japan.

(*b*) You will be responsible for providing imported supplies only to supplement local resources and only to the extent supplementation is needed to prevent such widespread disease or civil unrest as would endanger the occupying forces or interfere with military operations. Such imports will be confined to minimum quantities of food, fuel, medical and sanitary supplies and other essential items, including those which will enable local production of such supplies which you would otherwise have to import.

(*c*) Supplies necessary to be imported under paragraph 29 (*b*) above will be obtained to the extent possible from surpluses available from other Asiatic and Pacific Ocean areas. To the extent that such surpluses are available in areas under the jurisdiction of other United States commanders, arrangements may be made by you directly with such other commanders. To the extent that such surpluses are available in areas under the jurisdiction of governments other than the United States, or the military commanders of such governments, negotiations necessary to obtain such surpluses will be conducted by or with the approval of local United States diplomatic representatives in the areas in question. In the event such diplomatic representatives are not available, you will report the situation, with your recommendations, to the Joint Chiefs of Staff.

(*d*) If you deem that you should assume responsibility for additional imports to accomplish the objectives of your occupation, you will submit your recommendations to the Joint Chiefs of Staff.

Methods and Conditions of Distribution.

(30) You will require that all practicable steps be taken to assume the fair and equitable distribution of supplies under uniform ration scales.

(31) To the maximum extent consistent with military expediency, import supplies for the civilian population should, in so far as practicable and desirable, be delivered to such Japanese public supply agencies or other consignees as are acceptable to you and under your direct supervision or control. Whenever possible, such deliveries will be at ports of entry, but if necessary, deliveries may take place at appropriate inland centres of distribution.

(32) You may make sales directly to wholesalers or other commercial dealers in the event that no satisfactory public supply agency exists or that operational or other reasons render distribution of civilian supplies through such an agency impracticable. In order to limit direct provision and distribution of supplies by you to the civilian population, you should assure that the Japanese do not unnecessarily involve the occupying forces in such responsibility. Such direct sales by you as are necessary will be paid for by the purchaser in local currency at prices determined by you to be consistent with the internal economy.

(33) Supplies delivered to supply agencies or other consignees will be sold by them through distribution channels and in accordance with distribution policies satisfactory to you and at prices determined by you to be consistent with the internal economy. When military necessity requires, civilian supplies may be made the subject of direct relief issue by you or by supply agencies under your supervision or control.

Part III. *Financial*

(34) In the financial field you will make full application of the principles stated elsewhere in this directive, acting through the Japanese Government to the extent that effective execution of the policies and programmes hereinafter enumerated will permit, but establishing administrative machinery not dependent upon Japanese authorities and agencies to the extent necessary to execute or assure the effective execution of such policies and programmes. You are specifically directed to establish such independent administrative machinery in order to execute or assure the effective execution of the provisions of paragraphs 40, 41, 45, 46, and 47 of this directive.

(35) Japanese financial organizations and the public finance system will be expected to function on the basis of Japanese resources. You will take no steps designed to maintain, strengthen,

or operate the Japanese financial structure except in so far as may be necessary for the purposes specified in this directive.

(36) You may authorize or require the Bank of Japan or any other bank or agency to issue bank notes and currency which will be legal tender ; without such authorization no Japanese governmental or private bank or agency will be permitted to issue bank notes or currency.

(37) You will require the Japanese authorities to make available to you legal tender yen notes or yen credits free of cost and in amounts sufficient to meet all expenses of your forces including the costs of your military occupation.

(38) (a) In the event that for any reason adequate supplies of regular legal tender yen notes are not available you will use supplemental military yen (Type 'B') issued pursuant to military proclamation. Supplemental yen will be declared legal tender and will be interchangeable at par without distinction with other legal tender yen currency.

(b) Regular yen currency will include currencies which are now legal tender in the area.

(c) Japanese military yen issued for circulation in territories occupied by the Japanese will not be legal tender and will not be acceptable nor interchangeable with supplemental yen or regular yen currencies.

(39) You will not announce, establish or permit the use or publication, until receipt of further instructions, of any general rate of exchange between the Japanese yen on the one hand and the US dollar and other currencies on the other. However, a rate of conversion to be used exclusively for pay of military and naval personnel and for military and naval accounting purposes, namely 15 regular or supplemental yen equal one US dollar, has already been communicated to you.

(40) You will remove and exclude from positions of important responsibility or influence in all public and private financial institutions, agencies or organizations all persons who have been active exponents of militant nationalism and aggression or who actively participated in the organizations enumerated in paragraph 7 of this directive. It may be generally assumed in absence of evidence to the contrary that any persons who have held key positions in any such institutions, agencies, or organizations are active exponents of militant nationalism and aggression. You will also prevent the retention in or selection for places of importance in the financial field of individuals who do not direct future financial effort solely towards peaceful ends.

(41) You will close and not allow to reopen banks and other financial institutions whose paramount purpose has been the

financing of war production or the mobilization or control of financial resources in colonial or Japanese occupied territories. These include :

(a) The War-time Finance Bank;

(b) The National Financial Control Association and its member control associations;

(c) Offices, in the area, of the Bank of Chosen and the Bank of Taiwan;

(d) The various banks and development companies whose fields of operation have been outside Japan proper such as the Southern Development Company, the Southern Development Company Bank and the Tokyo offices of the Central Bank of Manchou, Bank of Mongolia, Federal Reserve Bank of China, and Central Reserve Bank of China. You will take custody of all the books and records of these banks and other institutions.

(42) You are authorized to take such financial measures as you may deem necessary to accomplish the objective of your military occupation, specifically including, without limitation, the following :

(a) Close banks, other than those indicated in paragraph 41 above, only where clearly necessary for the purposes of introducing satisfactory control, removing objectionable personnel and taking measures to effectuate the programme for the blocking of certain accounts and transfers or the determination of accounts to be blocked or for other reasons of military necessity. You should reopen any banks so closed except those indicated in paragraph 41 above, as promptly as is consistent with the accomplishment of the foregoing purposes ;

(b) Prohibit or regulate transfers or other dealings in private or public securities or real estate or other property ;

(c) Establish a general or limited moratorium or moratoria only to the extent clearly necessary to carry out the objectives of your military occupation ;

(d) Close stock exchanges, insurance companies and similar financial institutions for such periods as you deem appropriate.

(43) You will prohibit the payment of :

(a) All military pensions, or other emoluments or benefits, except compensation for physical disability limiting the recipient's ability to work, at rates which are no higher than the lowest of those for comparable physical disability arising from non-military causes ;

(b) All public or private pensions or other emoluments or benefits granted or conferred :

(i) By reason of membership in or services to the Political Association of Great Japan, the Imperial Rule Assistance Association (Taisei Yokasankai), the Imperial Rule Assistance Political Society

(Taisei Seijikei), their affiliates and agencies or any successor or similar organizations, and all Japanese nationalistic, terroristic and secret patriotic societies and their agencies and affiliates.

(ii) To any person who has been removed from an office or position in accordance with paragraphs 5 or 40 of this directive.

(iii) To any person interned in accordance with paragraph 7 of this directive, during the term of his internment, or permanently in case of his subsequent conviction.

(44) (a) Any laws, ordinances and regulations or practices relating to taxation or other fields of finance which tend to discriminate for or against any person because of nationality, race, creed or political opinion will be amended, suspended or abrogated to the extent necessary to eliminate such discrimination. The collection of contributions of any kind for nationalistic, imperialistic, militaristic, or anti-democratic societies of any kind will be prohibited.

(b) You will ensure that Japanese public expenditure is consistent with the objectives stated elsewhere in this directive.

(45) You will impound or block all gold, silver, platinum, currencies, securities, accounts in financial institutions, credits, valuable papers and all other assets within the categories listed below :

(a) Property owned or controlled directly or indirectly, in whole or in part, by any of the following :

(i) The Japanese national, prefectural and local governments, or any agency or instrumentality of any of them, including all utilities, undertakings, public corporations or monopolies under the control of any of the above ;

(ii) The Governments, nationals, or residents of Germany, Italy, Bulgaria, Rumania and Hungary, including those of territories formerly occupied by them and by Japan ;

(iii) The Japanese Imperial Household ;

(iv) The Political Association of Great Japan, the Imperial Rule Assistance Association, the Imperial Rule Assistance Political Society, their affiliates and agencies or any successor or similar organizations, and all Japanese nationalistic, terroristic and secret patriotic societies, agencies and affiliates and their officials, leading members and supporters ;

(v) The National Shinto ;

(vi) All organizations, clubs or other associations prohibited or dissolved by you ;

(vii) Absentee owners of non-Japanese nationality including United Nations and neutral governments and Japanese outside of Japan ;

(viii) Any person or concern in any area under Japanese control at any time since 1894, except the islands of Honshu, Hokkaido,

Kyushu, Shikoku and whatever minor islands are left to Japan ;

(ix)   Persons subject to internment under provisions of paragraph 7, and all other persons specified by Military Government by inclusion in lists or otherwise.

(b)   All Japanese (public and private) foreign exchange and external assets of every kind and description located within or outside Japan.

(c)   Property which has been the subject of transfer under duress, wrongful acts of confiscation, dispossession or spoliation, whether pursuant to legislation or by procedure purporting to follow forms of law or otherwise.

(d)   Works of art of cultural or material value of importance, regardless of ownership.

You will take such action as will ensure that any impounded or blocked assets will be dealt with only as permitted under licenses or other instructions which you may issue. In the case particularly of property blocked under (a) (i) above, you will proceed to adopt licensing measures which while maintaining such property under surveillance would permit its use by you or by the licensees in consonance with this directive. In the case of property blocked under (c) above, you will institute measures for prompt restitution, in conformity with the objectives of this directive and subject to appropriate safeguards to prevent the cloaking of militaristic and other undesirable influence.

You will require from the Japanese Government such reports as you deem necessary to obtain full disclosure of all assets mentioned in (b) above.

(46)   You will seek out and reduce to the possession or control of a special agency established by you within your command all Japanese (public and private) foreign exchange and external assets of every kind and description located within or outside Japan.

(47)   All foreign exchange transactions, including those arising out of exports and imports, will be controlled with the aim of preventing Japan from developing a war potential and of achieving the other objectives set forth in this directive. To effectuate these purposes, you will :

(a)   Prohibit, except as authorized by regulation or license, all dealings in gold, silver, platinum, foreign exchange, and all foreign exchange transactions of any kind.

(b)   Make available any foreign exchange proceeds of exports for payment of imports directly necessary to the accomplishment of the objectives of this directive, and authorize no other outlay of foreign exchange assets without specific approval of your government through the Joint Chiefs of Staff.

(c) Establish effective controls with respect to all foreign exchange transactions, including :

(i) Transactions as to property between persons inside Japan and persons outside Japan ;

(ii) Transactions involving obligations owed by or to become due from any person in Japan to any person outside Japan ; and

(iii) Transactions involving the importation into or exportation from Japan of any foreign exchange asset or other form of property.

(d) You will provide full reports to your government with respect to all Japanese foreign and external assets.

(48) No extension of credit to Japan or Japanese by any foreign person, agency or government will be permitted except as may be authorized by your government through the Joint Chiefs of Staff upon your recommendations.

(49) It is not anticipated that you will make credits available to the Bank of Japan or any other bank or to any public or private institution. If, in your opinion, such action becomes essential, you may take such emergency actions as you may deem proper, but in any such event, you will report the facts to your government through the Joint Chiefs of Staff.

(50) You will maintain such accounts and records as may be necessary to reflect the financial operations of your military occupation and you will provide the Joint Chiefs of Staff with such information as it may require, including information in connexion with the use of currency by your forces, any governmental settlements, occupation costs, and other expenditures arising out of operations or activities involving participation of your forces.

Political Reorientation of Japan, September 1945 to September 1948, Report of Government Section Supreme Commander for the Allied Powers, US Government Printing Office : 1949-819337, Appendix A :13, pp. 428-39.

2   Promulgated 3 *November* 1946
                                      Became effective 3 *May* 1947

THE CONSTITUTION OF JAPAN

We, the Japanese people, acting through our duly elected representatives in the National Diet, determined that we shall secure for ourselves and our posterity the fruits of peaceful co-operation with all nations and the blessings of liberty throughout this land, and resolved that never again shall we be visited with the horrors of war through the action of government, do proclaim that sovereign power resides with the people and do firmly establish this Constitution. Government is a sacred trust of the people, the authority for which is derived from the people, the powers of which are exercised by the representatives of the people, and the benefits of which are enjoyed by the people. This is a universal principle of mankind upon which this Constitution is founded. We reject and revoke all constitutions, laws, ordinances, and rescripts in conflict herewith.

We, the Japanese people, desire peace for all time and are deeply conscious of the high ideals controlling human relationship, and we have determined to preserve our security and existence, trusting in the justice and faith of the peace-loving peoples of the world. We desire to occupy an honoured place in an international society striving for the preservation of peace, and the banishment of tyranny and slavery, oppression and intolerance for all time from the earth. We recognize that all peoples of the world have the right to live in peace, free from fear and want.

We believe that no nation is responsible to itself alone, but that laws of political morality are universal ; and that obedience to such laws is incumbent upon all nations who would sustain their own sovereignty and justify their sovereign relationship with other nations.

We, the Japanese people, pledge our national honour to accomplish these high ideals and purposes with all our resources.

Ch. I. The Emperor

Article 1. The Emperor shall be the symbol of the State and of the unity of the people, deriving his position from the will of the people with whom resides sovereign power.

Article 2. The Imperial Throne shall be dynastic and succeeded to in accordance with the Imperial House Law passed by the Diet.

Article 3. The advice and approval of the Cabinet shall be required for all acts of the Emperor in matters of state, and the Cabinet shall be responsible therefor.

Article 4. The Emperor shall perform only such acts in matters of state as are provided for in this Constitution and he shall not have powers related to government.

The Emperor may delegate the performance of his acts in matters of state as may be provided by law.

Article 5. When, in accordance with the Imperial House Law, a Regency is established, the Regent shall perform his acts in matters of state in the Emperor's name. In this case, paragraph one of the preceding article will be applicable.

Article 6. The Emperor shall appoint the Prime Minister as designated by the Diet.

The Emperor shall appoint the Chief Judge of the Supreme Court as designated by the Cabinet.

Article 7. The Emperor, with the advice and approval of the Cabinet, shall perform the following acts in matters of state on behalf of the people :

Promulgation of amendments of the constitution, laws, cabinet orders and treaties.

Convocation of the Diet.

Dissolution of the House of Representatives.

Proclamation of general election of members of the Diet.

Attestation of the appointment and dismissal of Ministers of State and other officials as provided for by law, and of full powers and credentials of Ambassadors and Ministers.

Attestation of general and special amnesty, commutation of punishment, reprieve, and restoration of rights.

Awarding of honours.

Attestation of instruments of ratification and other diplomatic documents as provided for by law.

Receiving foreign ambassadors and ministers.

Performance of ceremonial functions.

Article 8. No property can be given to, or received by, the Imperial House, nor can any gifts be made therefrom, without the authorization of the Diet.

Ch. II. *Renunciation of War*

Article 9. Aspiring sincerely to an international peace based on justice and order, the Japanese people forever renounce war as a sovereign right of the nation and the threat or use of force as means of settling international disputes.

In order to accomplish the aim of the preceding paragraph, land, sea, and air forces, as well as other war potential, will never be maintained. The right of belligerency of the state will not be recognized.

Ch. III. *Rights and Duties of the People*

Article 10. The conditions necessary for being a Japanese national shall be determined by law.

Article 11. The people shall not be prevented from enjoying any of the fundamental human rights. These fundamental human rights guaranteed to the people by this Constitution shall be conferred upon the people of this and future generations as eternal and inviolate rights.

493

Article 12. The freedoms and rights guaranteed to the people by this Constitution shall be maintained by the constant endeavour of the people, who shall refrain from any abuse of these freedoms and rights and shall always be responsible for utilizing them for the public welfare.

Article 13. All of the people shall be respected as individuals. Their right to life, liberty, and the pursuit of happiness shall, to the extent that it does not interfere with the public welfare, be the supreme consideration in legislation and in other governmental affairs.

Article 14. All of the people are equal under the law and there shall be no discrimination in political, economic or social relations because of race, creed, sex, social status or family origin.

Peers and peerage shall not be recognized.

No privilege shall accompany any award of honour, decoration or any distinction, nor shall any such award be valid beyond the lifetime of the individual who now holds or hereafter may receive it.

Article 15. The people have the inalienable right to choose their public officials and to dismiss them.

All public officials are servants of the whole community and not of any group thereof.

Universal adult suffrage is guaranteed with regard to the election of public officials.

In all elections, secrecy of the ballot shall not be violated. A voter shall not be answerable, publicly or privately, for the choice he has made.

Article 16. Every person shall have the right of peaceful petition for the redress of damage, for the removal of public officials, for the enactment, repeal or amendment of laws, ordinances or regulations and for other matters ; nor shall any person be in any way discriminated against for sponsoring such a petition.

Article 17. Every person may sue for redress as provided by law from the State or a public entity, in case he has suffered damage through illegal act of any public officials.

Article 18. No person shall be held in bondage of any kind. Involuntary servitude, except as punishment for crime, is prohibited.

Article 19. Freedom of thought and conscience shall not be violated.

Article 20. Freedom of religion is guaranteed to all. No religious organization shall receive any privileges from the State, nor exercise any political authority.

No person shall be compelled to take part in any religious act, celebration, rite or practice.

The State and its organs shall refrain from religious education or any other religious activity.

494

Article 21. Freedom of assembly and association as well as speech, Press and all other forms of expression are guaranteed.

No censorship shall be maintained, nor shall the secrecy of any means of communication be violated.

Article 22. Every person shall have freedom to choose and change his residence and to choose his occupation to the extent that it does not interfere with the public welfare.

Freedom of all persons to move to a foreign country and to divest themselves of their nationality shall be inviolate.

Article 23. Academic freedom is guaranteed.

Article 24. Marriage shall be based only on the mutual consent of both sexes and it shall be maintained through mutual co-operation with the equal rights of husband and wife as a basis.

With regard to choice of spouse, property rights, inheritance, choice of domicile, divorce and other matters pertaining to marriage and the family, laws shall be enacted from the standpoint of individual dignity and the essential equality of the sexes.

Article 25. All people shall have the right to maintain the minimum standards of wholesome and cultured living.

In all spheres of life, the State shall use its endeavours for the promotion and extension of social welfare and security, and of public health.

Article 26. All people shall have the right to receive an equal education correspondent to their ability, as provided by law.

All people shall be obligated to have all boys and girls under their protection receive ordinary education as provided for by law. Such compulsory education shall be free.

Article 27. All people shall have the right and the obligation to work.

Standards for wages, hours, rest and other working conditions shall be fixed by law.

Children shall not be exploited.

Article 28. The right of workers to organize and bargain and act collectively is guaranteed.

Article 29. The right to own or to hold property is inviolable.

Property rights shall be defined by law, in conformity with the public welfare.

Private property may be taken for public use upon just compensation therefor.

Article 30. The people shall be liable to taxation as provided by law.

Article 31. No person shall be deprived of life or liberty, nor shall any other criminal penalty be imposed except according to procedure established by law.

495

Article 32. No person shall be denied the right of access to the courts.

Article 33. No person shall be apprehended except upon warrant issued by a competent judicial officer which specifies the offence with which the person is charged, unless he is apprehended, the offence being committed.

Article 34. No person shall be arrested or detained without being at once informed of the charges against him or without the immediate privilege of counsel ; nor shall he be detained without adequate cause ; and upon demand of any person such cause must be immediately shown in open court in his presence and the presence of his counsel.

Article 35. The right of all persons to be secure in their homes, papers and effects against entries, searches and seizures shall not be impaired except upon warrant issued for adequate cause and particularly describing the place to be searched and things to be seized, or except as provided by Article 33.

Each search or seizure shall be made upon separate warrant issued by a competent judicial officer.

Article 36. The infliction of torture by any public officer and cruel punishments are absolutely forbidden.

Article 37. In all criminal cases the accused shall enjoy the right to a speedy and public trial by an impartial tribunal.

He shall be permitted full opportunity to examine all witnesses, and he shall have the right of compulsory process for obtaining witnesses on his behalf at public expense.

At all times the accused shall have the assistance of competent counsel who shall, if the accused is unable to secure the same by his own efforts, be assigned to his use by the State.

Article 38. No person shall be compelled to testify against himself.

Confession made under compulsion, torture or threat, or after prolonged arrest or detention shall not be admitted in evidence.

No person shall be convicted or punished in cases where the only proof against him is his own confession.

Article 39. No person shall be held criminally liable for an act which was lawful at the time it was committed, or of which he has been acquitted, nor shall be he placed in double jeopardy.

Article 40. Any person, in case he is acquitted after he has been arrested or detained, may sue the State for redress as provided by law.

Ch. IV. The Diet

Article 41. The Diet shall be the highest organ of state power, and shall be the sole law-making organ of the State.

Article 42. The Diet shall consist of two Houses, namely the House of Representatives and the House of Councillors.

Article 43. Both Houses shall consist of elected members, representative of all the people.

The number of the members of each House shall be fixed by law.

Article 44. The qualifications of members of both Houses and their electors shall be fixed by law. However, there shall be no discrimination because of race, creed, sex, social status, family origin, education, property or income.

Article 45. The term of office of members of the House of Representatives shall be four years. However, the term shall be terminated before the full term is up in case the House of Representatives is dissolved.

Article 46. The term of office of members of the House of Councillors shall be six years, and election for half the members shall take place every three years.

Article 47. Electoral districts, method of voting and other matters pertaining to the method of election of members of both Houses shall be fixed by law.

Article 48. No person shall be permitted to be a member of both Houses simultaneously.

Article 49. Members of both Houses shall receive appropriate annual payment from the national treasury in accordance with law.

Article 50. Except in cases provided by law, members of both Houses shall be exempt from apprehension while the Diet is in session, and any members apprehended before the opening of the session shall be freed during the term of the session upon demand of the House.

Article 51. Members of both Houses shall not be held liable outside the House for speeches, debates or votes cast inside the House.

Article 52. An ordinary session of the Diet shall be convoked once per year.

Article 53. The Cabinet may determine to convoke extraordinary sessions of the Diet. When a quarter or more of the total members of either House makes the demand, the Cabinet must determine on such convocation.

Article 54. When the House of Representatives is dissolved, there must be a general election of members of the House of Representatives within forty (40) days from the date of dissolution, and the Diet must be convoked within thirty (30) days from the date of the election.

When the House of Representatives is dissolved, the House of Councillors is closed at the same time. However, the Cabinet may in time of national emergency convoke the House of Councillors in emergency session.

Measures taken at such session as mentioned in the proviso of the preceding paragraph shall be provisional and shall become null and void unless agreed to by the House of Representatives within a period of ten (10) days after the opening of the next session of the Diet.

Article 55. Each House shall judge disputes related to qualifications of its members. However, in order to deny a seat to any member, it is necessary to pass a resolution by a majority of two-thirds or more of the members present.

Article 56. Business cannot be transacted in either House unless one-third or more of the total membership is present.

All matters shall be decided, in each House, by a majority of those present, except as elsewhere provided in the Constitution, and in case of a tie, the presiding officer shall decide the issue.

Article 57. Deliberation in each House shall be public. However, a secret meeting may be held where a majority of two-thirds or more of those members present passes a resolution therefor.

Each House shall keep a record of proceedings. This record shall be published and given general circulation, excepting such parts of proceedings of secret session as may be deemed to require secrecy.

Upon demand of one-fifth or more of the members present, votes of the members on any matter shall be recorded in the minutes.

Article 58. Each House shall select its own president and other officials.

Each House shall establish its rules pertaining to meetings, proceedings and internal discipline, and may punish members for disorderly conduct. However, in order to expel a member, a majority of two-thirds or more of those members present must pass a resolution thereon.

Article 59. A bill becomes a law on passage by both Houses, except as otherwise provided by the Constitution.

A bill which is passed by the House of Representatives, and upon which the House of Councillors makes a decision different from that of the House of Representatives, becomes a law when passed a second time by the House of Representatives by a majority of two-thirds or more of the members present.

The provision of the preceding paragraph does not preclude the House of Representatives from calling for the meeting of a joint committee of both Houses, provided for by law.

Failure by the House of Councillors to take final action within sixty (60) days after receipt of a bill passed by the House of Representatives, time in recess excepted, may be determined by the

House of Representatives to constitute a rejection of the said bill by the House of Councillors.

Article 60. The budget must first be submitted to the House of Representatives.

Upon consideration of the budget, when the House of Councillors makes a decision different from that of the House of Representatives, and when no agreement can be reached even through a joint committee of both Houses, provided for by law, or in the case of failure by the House of Councillors to take final action within thirty (30) days, the period of recess excluded, after the receipt of the budget passed by the House of Representatives, the decision of the House of Representatives shall be the decision of the Diet.

Article 61. The second paragraph of the preceding article applies also to the Diet approval required for the conclusion of treaties.

Article 62. Each House may conduct investigations in relation to government, and may demand the presence and testimony of witnesses, and the production of records.

Article 63. The Prime Minister and other Ministers of State may, at any time, appear in either House for the purpose of speaking on bills, regardless of whether they are members of the House or not. They must appear when their presence is required in order to give answers or explanations.

Article 64. The Diet shall set up an impeachment court from among the members of both Houses for the purpose of trying those judges against whom removal proceedings have been instituted.

Matters relating to impeachment shall be provided by law.

Ch. V.   The Cabinet

Article 65. Executive power shall be vested in the Cabinet.

Article 66. The Cabinet shall consist of the Prime Minister, who shall be its head, and other Ministers of State, as provided for by law.

The Prime Minister and other Ministers of State must be civilians.

The Cabinet, in the exercise of executive power, shall be collectively responsible to the Diet.

Article 67. The Prime Minister shall be designated from among the members of the Diet by a resolution of the Diet. This designation shall precede all other business.

If the House of Representatives and the House of Councillors disagree and if no agreement can be reached even through a joint committee of both Houses, provided for by law, or the House of Councillors fails to make designation within ten (10) days, exclusive of the period of recess, after the House of Representatives has made designation, the decision of the House of Representatives shall be the decision of the Diet.

Article 68. The Prime Minister shall appoint the Ministers of State. However, a majority of their number must be chosen from among the members of the Diet.

The Prime Minister may remove the Ministers of State as he chooses.

Article 69. If the House of Representatives passes a no-confidence resolution, or rejects a confidence resolution, the Cabinet shall resign *en masse*, unless the House of Representatives is dissolved within ten (10) days.

Article 70. When there is a vacancy in the post of Prime Minister, or upon the first convocation of the Diet after a general election of members of the House of Representatives, the Cabinet shall resign *en masse*.

Article 71. In the cases mentioned in the two preceding Articles, the Cabinet shall continue its functions until the time when a new Prime Minister is appointed.

Article 72. The Prime Minister, representing the Cabinet, submits bills, reports on general national affairs and foreign relations to the Diet and exercises control and supervision over various administrative branches.

Article 73. The Cabinet, in addition to other general administrative functions, shall perform the following functions :

Administer the law faithfully ; conduct affairs of state.

Manage foreign affairs.

Conclude treaties. However, it shall obtain prior or, depending on circumstances, subsequent approval of the Diet.

Administer the civil service, in accordance with standards established by law.

Prepare the budget, and present it to the Diet.

Enact cabinet orders in order to execute the provisions of this Constitution and of the law. However, it cannot include penal provisions in such cabinet orders unless authorized by such law.

Decide on general amnesty, special amnesty, commutation of punishment, reprieve, and restoration of rights.

Article 74. All laws and cabinet orders shall be signed by the competent Minister of State and countersigned by the Prime Minister.

Article 75. The Ministers of State, during their tenure of office, shall not be subject to legal action without the consent of the Prime Minister. However, the right to take that action is not impaired hereby.

Ch. VI. Judiciary

Article 76. The whole judicial power is vested in a Supreme Court and in such inferior courts as are established by law.

No extraordinary tribunal shall be established, nor shall any organ or agency of the Executive be given final judicial power.

All judges shall be independent in the exercise of their conscience and shall be bound only by this Constitution and the laws.

Article 77. The Supreme Court is vested with the rule-making power under which it determines the rules of procedure and of practice, and of matters relating to attorneys, the internal discipline of the courts and the administration of judicial affairs.

Public procurators shall be subject to the rule-making power of the Supreme Court.

The Supreme Court may delegate the power to make rules for inferior courts to such courts.

Article 78. Judges shall not be removed except by public impeachment unless judicially declared mentally or physically incompetent to perform official duties. No disciplinary action against judges shall be administered by any executive organ or agency.

Article 79. The Supreme Court shall consist of a Chief Judge and such number of judges as may be determined by law ; all such judges excepting the Chief Judge shall be appointed by the Cabinet.

The appointment of the judges of the Supreme Court shall be reviewed by the people at the first general election of members of the House of Representatives following their appointment, and shall be reviewed again at the first general election of members of the House of Representatives after a lapse of ten (10) years, and in the same manner thereafter.

In cases mentioned in the foregoing paragraph, when the majority of the voters favours the dismissal of a judge, he shall be dismissed.

Matters pertaining to review shall be prescribed by law.

The judges of the Supreme Court shall be retired upon the attainment of the age as fixed by law.

All such judges shall receive, at regular stated intervals, adequate compensation which shall not be decreased during their terms of office.

Article 80. The judges of the inferior courts shall be appointed by the Cabinet from a list of persons nominated by the Supreme Court. All such judges shall hold office for a term of ten (10) years with privilege of reappointment, provided that they shall be retired upon the attainment of the age as fixed by law.

The judges of the inferior courts shall receive, at regular stated intervals, adequate compensation which shall not be decreased during their terms of office.

Article 81. The Supreme Court is the court of last resort with power to determine the constitutionality of any law, order, regulation or official act.

Article 82. Trials shall be conducted and judgement declared publicly.

Where a court unanimously determines publicity to be dangerous to public order or morals, a trial may be conducted privately, but trials of political offences, offences involving the Press or cases wherein the rights of people as guaranteed in Chapter III of this Constitution are in question shall always be conducted publicly.

Ch. VII. Finance

Article 83. The power to administer national finances shall be exercised as the Diet shall determine.

Article 84. No new taxes shall be imposed or existing ones modified except by law or under such conditions as law may prescribe.

Article 85. No money shall be expended, nor shall the State obligate itself, except as authorized by the Diet.

Article 86. The Cabinet shall prepare and submit to the Diet for its consideration and decision a budget for each fiscal year.

Article 87. In order to provide for unforeseen deficiencies in the budget, a reserve fund may be authorized by the Diet to be expended upon the responsibility of the Cabinet.

The Cabinet must get subsequent approval of the Diet for all payments from the reserve fund.

Article 88. All property of the Imperial Household shall belong to the State. All expenses of the Imperial Household shall be appropriated by the Diet in the budget.

Article 89. No public money or other property shall be expended or appropriated for the use, benefit or maintenance of any religious institution or association, or for any charitable, educational or benevolent enterprises not under the control of public authority.

Article 90. Final accounts of the expenditures and revenues of the State shall be audited annually by a Board of Audit and submitted by the Cabinet to the Diet, together with the statement of audit, during the fiscal year immediately following the period covered.

The organization and competency of the Board of Audit shall be determined by law.

Article 91. At regular intervals and at least annually the Cabinet shall report to the Diet and the people on the state of national finances.

Ch. VIII.   Local Self-Government

Article 92.   Regulations concerning organization and operations of local public entities shall be fixed by law in accordance with the principle of local autonomy.

Article 93.   The local public entities shall establish assemblies as their deliberative organs, in accordance with law.

The chief executive officers of all local public entities, the members of their assemblies, and such other local officials as may be determined by law shall be elected by direct popular vote within their several communities.

Article 94.   Local public entities shall have the right to manage their property, affairs and administration and to enact their own regulations within law.

Article 95.   A special law, applicable only to one local public entity, cannot be enacted by the Diet without the consent of the majority of the voters of the local public entity concerned, obtained in accordance with law.

Ch. IX.   Amendments

Article 96.   Amendments to this Constitution shall be initiated by the Diet, through a concurring vote of two-thirds or more of all the members of each House and shall thereupon be submitted to the people for ratification, which shall require the affirmative vote of a majority of all votes cast thereon, at a special referendum or at such election as the Diet shall specify.

Amendments when so ratified shall immediately be promulgated by the Emperor in the name of the people, as an integral part of this Constitution.

Ch. X.   Supreme Law

Article 97.   The fundamental human rights by this Constitution guaranteed to the people of Japan are fruits of the age-old struggle of man to be free ; they have survived the many exacting tests for durability and are conferred upon this and future generations in trust, to be held for all time inviolate.

Article 98.   This Constitution shall be the supreme law of the nation and no law, ordinance, imperial rescript or other act of government, or part thereof, contrary to the provisions hereof, shall have legal force or validity.

The treaties concluded by Japan and established laws of nations shall be faithfully observed.

Article 99.   The Emperor or the Regent as well as Ministers of State, members of the Diet, judges, and all other public officials have the obligation to respect and uphold this Constitution.

Ch. XI.   Supplementary Provisions

Article 100. This Constitution shall be enforced as from the day when the period of six months will have elapsed counting from the day of its promulgation.

The enactment of laws necessary for the enforcement of this Constitution, the election of members of the House of Councillors and the procedure for the convocation of the Diet and other preparatory procedures necessary for the enforcement of this Constitution may be executed before the day prescribed in the preceding paragraph.

Article 101. If the House of Councillors is not constituted before the effective date of this Constitution, the House of Representatives shall function as the Diet until such time as the House of Councillors shall be constituted.

Article 102. The term of office for half the members of the House of Councillors serving in the first term under this Constitution shall be three years. Members falling under this category shall be determined in accordance with law.

Article 103. The Ministers of State, members of the House of Representatives and judges in office on the effective date of this Constitution, and all other public officials who occupy positions corresponding to such positions as are recognized by this Constitution shall not forfeit their positions automatically on account of the enforcement of this Constitution unless otherwise specified by law. When, however, successors are elected or appointed under the provisions of this Constitution, they shall forfeit their positions as a matter of course.

Political Reorientation of Japan, Appendix C:21, pp. 671-7.

II POLITICAL 'DEMOCRATIZATION'

3   19 *March* 1947
THE DIET LAW*

Ch. I.   Convocation and Opening Ceremony

Article 1. An Imperial rescript convoking the Diet shall be promulgated, setting the date for assembling.

An Imperial rescript convoking an ordinary session shall be promulgated at least twenty (20) days in advance.

* The Diet Law was enacted 19 March 1947. The Law Amending the Diet Law was enacted 5 July 1948. The original law and the amendments are contained herein; changes and additions are in italics and deletions are in square brackets. Paragraph headings and the numbers of articles are italicized in any case.

An Imperial rescript convoking an extraordinary session or a special session under Article 54 of the Constitution of Japan need not be bound by the provision of the preceding paragraph.

Article 2. An ordinary session shall be convoked annually within the first ten days of December. The date of convocation, however, must be such that the term of office of Diet members will not expire during an ordinary session.

Article 3. A demand for convocation of an extraordinary session must be submitted in writing jointly by one-fourth or more of all members of either House to the Cabinet through the President of the House.

Article 4. A demand for an emergency session of the House of Councillors, with date for assembling stipulated, must be made to the President of that House by the Prime Minister.

Article 5. Diet members must assemble at their respective Houses on the date designated by the Imperial rescript of convocation.

Article 6. On the date of assembling, each House shall elect a President and Vice-President, or both, if the offices are vacant.

Article 7. Pending the election of the President and Vice-President, the Secretary-General shall act in the capacity of President.

Article 8. An Opening Ceremony shall be held at the beginning of each session.

Article 9. The President of the House of Representatives shall preside at the Opening Ceremony.

In case the President of the House of Representatives is absent or incapacitated, the President of the House of Councillors shall preside.

Ch. II. *Term of Session and Recess*

Article 10. The term of an ordinary session shall be one hundred and fifty (150) days.

Article 11. The term of either an extraordinary session or a special session shall be determined by decision of the Houses.

Article 12. The term of a Diet session may be extended by decision of the Houses.

Article 13. If the Houses disagree on the matters under the two preceding Articles, the decision of the House of Representatives shall prevail.

Article 14. The term of a Diet session shall be counted as from the date of convocation.

Article 15. A recess of the Diet shall require the decision of both Houses, but either House acting alone may recess for a period not to exceed [seven (7)] *ten (10)* days.

During a recess of the Diet or of a single House, a plenary session of either House may be called when the President of the House deems it urgent or when one-fourth or more of all members of the House demand it.

Ch. III. *Officers and Expenditures*

Article 16. The officers of each House shall be as follows :
(1) President.
(2) Vice-President.
(3) President *pro tem*.
(4) Chairmen of Standing Committees.
(5) Secretary-General.

Article 17. There shall be one President and one Vice-President for each House.

Article 18. The term of office for the President and for the Vice-President of each House shall coincide with their term of office as Diet members.

Article 19. The President of each House shall maintain order in the House, adjust its proceedings, supervise its business, and represent it.

Article 20. The President of each House may attend and address committee meetings.

Article 21. When the President of either House is absent or the office is vacant, the Vice-President shall perform the functions of the President.

Article 22. When both the President and the Vice-President of either House are absent or incapacitated, a President *pro tem*. shall be elected by the House to perform the functions of the President.
The House may entrust the President with the selection of the President *pro tem*.

Article 23. When in either House the office of President or Vice-President, or both, become vacant, elections shall be conducted immediately to fill them.

Article 24. When a President *pro tem*. is to be elected, and no officer is present to perform the functions of the President in conducting the elections prescribed in the preceding Article, the Secretary-General shall perform the functions of the President.

Article 25. Chairmen of Standing Committees shall be elected in each House from among the membership of the respective Standing Committees.

Article 26. Each House shall have one Secretary-General, Secretaries, and other necessary personnel.

Article 27. The Secretary-General shall be elected in each House from among non-Diet members. Secretaries and other personnel shall be appointed or dismissed by the Secretary-General with the consent of the President *and the approval of the Standing Committee for House Management.*

Article 28. The Secretary-General shall, under the supervision of the President, administer the affairs of the House and sign official documents.

The Secretaries shall, by order of the Secretary-General, administer the affairs of the House.

Article 29. If the Secretary-General is absent or incapacitated, or the office is vacant, a Secretary who has been previously designated shall perform the functions of the Secretary-General.

Article 30. Officers can resign with permission of the House. During adjournment, permission for resignation of officers may be given by the President.

30-2. If either House finds it specially necessary, by decision of the House a Standing Committee Chairman may be relieved of his post.

Article 31. Officers shall not hold, concurrently, a government office.

Article 32. Expenditures of each House shall be appropriated independently in the national budget.

The above appropriation shall include a contingent fund.

Ch. IV.   Members

Article 33. No member of either House shall be arrested without the consent of the House concerned during the term of a session unless he is apprehended while committing a crime outside the Diet.

Article 34. During an emergency session of the House of Councillors, no member of the House of Councillors shall be arrested without the consent of the House, unless he is apprehended while committing a crime outside the Diet.

A member of the House of Councillors who is arrested before the opening of an emergency session of that House must be freed during the term of the session upon demand of the House.

34-2. Under the provisions of Articles 33 and 34, in asking the consent of the House concerned for the arrest of a member, the Cabinet shall submit a copy of the written request presented by the court or the judge to the Cabinet prior to issuance of the warrant of arrest.

Article 35. Members shall each receive an annual allowance not less in amount than the highest pay for government officials in general.

Article 36. Members shall receive a retirement allowance, according to provisions separately made.

Article 37. Members may travel without charge on State railways during a session and at any other time on official business, according to regulations separately made.

Article 38. Members shall receive allowances, as fixed separately, for posting official documents and for communications of official character during the term of a session.

[*Article 39.* Members cannot, during the term for which they are elected, be appointed as officials of the Government or of a local public entity, unless stipulated by law.]

[Members cannot, during the term for which they are elected, be appointed as members of committees, advisers, non-official staff (Shokutaku), or other similar offices under the various administrative branches of the Government, unless such an appointment is fixed by law or provided for by decision of the Diet.]

Article 39. No member, during his term of office, shall be appointed concurrently as an official of the Government or of a local public entity, except as Prime Minister, other Cabinet Ministers, Secretary-General of the Cabinet, Vice-Minister of each Ministry, or offices otherwise positively stipulated by law; provided, however, that with the approval of the Diet, members may be appointed, during their term of office, as commissioners, advisers (komon), councillors (sanyo), or as other corresponding officials of the executive branch of the Government.

Ch. V.   Committees and Committee Members

Article 40.   In each House there shall be Standing Committees and Special Committees.

Article 41.   Standing Committee members shall be selected by each House at the beginning of the first session of their term of office as Diet members and shall serve during their term.

[Each member shall be selected to serve on at least one Standing Committee but cannot serve concurrently on more than three Standing Committees.]

Every member shall serve on at least one Standing Committee; however, he shall not serve on more than two Standing Committees concurrently. If he serves on two Standing Committees, one of the two shall be limited to the Standing Committee for Budgets, Audit, House Management, Disciplinary Measures, or Library Management.

Article 42.   Standing Committees of each House shall be as follows, and they shall examine the bills, petitions, representations, and other items which come under their respective spheres of work.

(1)   *Standing Committee for Administrative Research and Civil Service.*

(2)   Standing Committee for [Public Safety and Local Government] *Local Administration.*

(3)   *Standing Committee for Economic Stabilization.*

(4)   Standing Committee for [Judicial Affairs] *Attorney General's Office.*

(5)   Standing Committee for Foreign Affairs.

(6)   Standing Committee for Finance.

(7)   Standing Committee for Education.
[Standing Committee for Culture].
(8)   Standing Committee for Welfare.
(9)   Standing Committee for Commerce *and Industry.*
[Standing Committee for Mining and Industry, Standing Committee for Electricity].
(10) Standing Committee for Agriculture and Forestry.
(11) Standing Committee for Fisheries.
(12) Standing Committee for Transportation.
(13) Standing Committee for Communications.
(14) Standing Committee for Labour.
(15) *Standing Committee for Construction.*
[Standing Committee for National Land Planning].
(16) Standing Committee for Budgets.
(17) Standing Committee for Audit.
(18) Standing Committee for House Management.
(19) Standing Committee for Disciplinary Measures.
(20) Standing Committee for Library Management.

[Each House can increase, decrease, or combine the Standing Committees above mentioned, upon recommendation of the Legislative Committee of the Houses.]

Either House may establish Standing Committees other than those listed in the preceding paragraph or may combine those mentioned above if a national administrative organ is newly established or abolished, or upon recommendation of the Legislative Committee of the Houses, or if deemed especially necessary by the House. However, the Houses shall have identical Committees.

[*Article 43.* Each Standing Committee shall be provided with at least two qualified specialists, who are not Diet members, and an adequate number of secretarial assistants, all of whom shall be permanent staff. However, qualified specialists and secretarial assistants shall not be appointed when the House deems them unnecessary.]

[Qualified specialists above mentioned shall receive adequate remuneration and shall not be otherwise employed. They cannot occupy any post in the administrative branches of the Government for two (2) years following their resignation from a Standing Committee.]

Article 43. Each Standing Committee shall have at least two non-Diet member specialists (called Qualified Specialists, 'senmonin'; Research Secretaries, 'chosain'; and Research Clerks, 'chosa-shuji') as permanent staff of the Committee, unless the House deems their appointment unnecessary.

Qualified Specialists shall receive adequate compensation and shall not hold any other post concurrently.

Qualified Specialists shall not take any post in the executive branch of Government for one (1) year following resignation from their posts.

Article 44. A Standing Committee of one House may hold a joint hearing with a Standing Committee of the other House if they so agree.

Article 45. Members of a Special Committee shall be elected by each House in order to examine specially designated matters which do not come within the jurisdiction of any Standing Committee, and they shall serve until the matter they are entrusted with is decided upon by the House.

The Chairman of a Special Committee shall be elected by a majority vote of the Committee from its membership.

Article 46. Membership on Standing Committees and Special Committees shall be allotted in proportion to the numerical strength of political parties or groups in the respective Houses.

46–2. *After appointment of Committee members in compliance with the preceding paragraph, the President may, notwithstanding the provision of Article 41, paragraph 1, change committee membership with the approval of the Standing Committee for House Management when it becomes necessary to reallocate members as the result of a shift in the numerical strength of parties or groups in the House.*

Article 47. Standing Committees and Special Committees shall examine matters entrusted to them only during the term of a session.

During adjournment, however, Standing Committees and Special Committees may, by decision of each House, examine matters especially entrusted to them.

Article 48. The Chairman of each Committee shall adjust its proceedings and maintain order in the Committee.

Article 49. A Committee may not open deliberations and transact business unless one-half or more of its members are present.

Article 50. The proceedings of a Committee shall be decided by majority vote of the members present. In case of a tie, the Chairman shall make the decision.

Article 51. A Committee may conduct open hearings on important questions of popular concern or public interest in order to hear the views of interested parties or persons of learning and experience.

Such hearings must be held on the general budget and on important revenue bills.

Article 52. A Committee may be attended by Diet members and the general public as authorized by the Chairman. However, a Committee may hold secret meetings if it so decides.

The Chairman of a Committee may cause non-committee members to leave a meeting so as to maintain order.

510

Article 53. The Chairman must report the proceedings and results of his Committee to the House.

Article 54. A minority opinion rejected in Committee may be reported to the House by members of the minority following the Chairman's report.

The President may place a time limit on the minority report. When an adequate summary of the minority report is presented to the President, it shall be entered in the Record of Proceedings, together with the Committee's report.

Ch. VI. *Plenary Sessions*

Article 55. The President of each House shall fix the calendar of proceedings and give advance notice of it to the House.

If the President deems it urgent, he may hold a plenary session after merely notifying members of the date and time of such session.

55–2. Concerning the order of proceedings and other matters which the President deems necessary, he may consult only with a sub-committee selected by the Standing Committee for House Management ; however, the President shall not be bound by their opinions if they fail to agree.

Article 56. Any member may introduce a bill.

When a bill is introduced, the President shall assign it to the appropriate Committee for examination, after which it shall be placed on the agenda in plenary session. However, when considered urgent, Committee examination may be omitted by decision of the House.

A bill which the Committee decides not to submit to a plenary session of the House shall not be submitted. However, when demanded by twenty (20) or more members within seven (7) days (not counting the period of recess) from the date of the Committee decision, it must be submitted to a plenary session.

If no such demand is made, the bill is rejected.

The two preceding paragraphs shall not apply to bills transmitted from the other House.

56–2. Concerning any bill introduced in the House, an explanation of its purport will be heard in plenary session if deemed specially necessary by the Standing Committee for House Management.

56–3. Each House may request a Committee to make an interim report on a matter pending in the Committee if the House deems it specially necessary.

If deemed of urgent necessity by the House, a time limit may be placed upon Committee deliberations after an interim report, as provided in the preceding paragraph, has been made, or it may deliberate the case in a plenary session.

If a time limit has been placed upon Committee deliberations and such deliberations have not been completed within the time limit, deliberations shall be made in plenary session. However, the House may extend the term for deliberation at the request of the Committee.

Article 57. A motion to amend a Bill, in order to be placed before a plenary session, requires the support of twenty (20) or more members.

Article 58. A Bill submitted by the Cabinet to one House shall be sent to the other House for preliminary examination within five (5) days [following its submission] *from the date of its presentation* to one House.

Article 59. The Cabinet may not amend or withdraw a Bill already on the agenda of the House or of a Committee without consent of the House.

Article 60. The Committee Chairman, his proxy, or the proposer of a Bill that has been passed by one House may explain the Bill when it is presented in the other House.

Article 61. The President of each House may limit time for interpellations, debate, or other utterances, unless [otherwise decided by] the House *has previously decided otherwise.*

If one-fifth or more of the members object to the time limit placed by the President, he shall consult the House.

The part of a member's speech omitted because of the time limit may be entered in the Record of Proceedings to such an extent as considered suitable by the President, unless otherwise decided by the House.

Article 62. Upon motion by the President or by ten (10) or more members, the proceedings of each House may be closed to the public by a vote of two-thirds or more of the members present.

Article 63. Parts of the Record of Proceedings of a secret session which have been voted upon as specially requiring secrecy may not be made public.

Article 64. When the office of Prime Minister becomes vacant or when the Prime Minister tenders his resignation, the Cabinet shall immediately so notify both Houses.

Article 65. When Bills requiring the decision of both Houses are passed, or when the decision of the House of Representatives becomes the final decision of the Diet, those Bills requiring promulgation shall be reported to the Throne through the Cabinet by the President of the House of Representatives, while other Bills shall be sent to the Cabinet.

Nomination of a Prime Minister shall be communicated by the President of the House of Representatives to the Throne through the Cabinet.

Article 66. A law must be promulgated within thirty (30) days from the date of its submission to the Throne.

Article 67. A special law applicable only to a single local public entity shall, after approval by the Diet, be submitted to a vote of the people of the local public entity concerned, as provided separately by law, and when approved by the majority of the voters of that local public entity shall become law.

Article 68. Any matter not decided during a session shall not be carried over to the following session, *excepting the case prescribed in Article 47, paragraph 2.*

Ch. VII. *Minister of State and Representatives of the Government*

Article 69. The Cabinet may, with the approval of the Presidents of the Houses, appoint representatives of the Government to assist Ministers of State in the Diet.

Article 70. A Minister of State and a representative of the Government, when desiring to speak at a House or Committee meeting, must notify the President or the Chairman of the Committee concerned.

Article 71. A Committee may, through the President, request the presence of a Minister of State or a representative of the Government at its meeting.

Article 72. A Committee may, through the President, request the presence of *and explanation by* the President of the Board of Audit and auditors at its meeting.

With the consent of a Committee, the Chief Justice of the Supreme Court or a deputy designated by him may, upon his request, attend Committee meetings to offer explanations.

Article 73. Reports of proceedings of the Diet and of Committee meetings shall, simultaneously with their distribution to Diet Members, be delivered to Ministers of State and representatives of the Government.

Ch. VIII. *Interpellations and Free Discussion*

Article 74. A member of each House desiring to interpellate the Cabinet must obtain the approval of the President.

A brief statement of the purport of an interpellation shall be presented to the President.

When a member objects to the President's disapproval of his interpellation, the President must submit the matter to a decision of the House.

If demanded by the member, the President shall have entered in the Record of Proceedings a brief statement of the purport of the member's disapproved interpellation.

Article 75. The President of each House shall transmit to the Cabinet a brief statement of the purport of an approved interpellation.

The Cabinet must make a reply within seven (7) days of receipt of an interpellation. When a reply is not made within the specified period, the reason for the delay shall be clearly stated.

Article 76. When an interpellation is urgent, it may be made orally if the House so decides.

Article 77. The Cabinet reply to an interpellation may be put to debate, and also to a vote of the House, upon motion of a member.

Article 78. Each House must, during the term of a session, meet at least once every [two (2)] *three* (3) weeks for the purpose of conducting free discussion [of national affairs] *in relation to government* by its members.

A subject under free discussion may be put to a vote of the House upon motion of a member.

A time limit for speeches during free discussion shall be set by the President, unless otherwise decided by the House.

Ch. IX. Petitions

Article 79. A person desiring to petition either House shall present a written petition to the House through a member.

Article 80. Adoption of a petition shall be by decision of either House after examination by the appropriate Committee.

A petition deemed by the Committee to be unnecessary for submission to the House shall not be submitted. However, when demanded by twenty (20) or more members, a petition must be presented to the House.

Article 81. Petitions adopted by either House and deemed appropriate for Cabinet action shall be transmitted to the Cabinet.

The Cabinet must, every year, report to the House concerned the particulars of the disposal of petitions mentioned in the preceding paragraph.

Article 82. Each House independently shall receive and dispose of petitions without interference from the other House.

Ch. X. Relations Between the Houses

Article 83. When a matter requiring a decision of the Diet has been passed or amended by House A, the said matter shall be transmitted to House B, when such matter has been rejected by House A, the notification of rejection shall be made to House B.

When House B has agreed to or rejected a matter transmitted from House A, notification of agreement or rejection shall be made to House A.

When House B has amended a matter transmitted from House A, it shall be referred to House A.

When House A has agreed or has not agreed to a matter referred thereto by House B, notification of agreement or disagreement shall be made to House B.

Article 84. When the House of Representatives has not agreed to a legislative Bill referred thereto by the House of Councillors, or when the House of Councillors has rejected a legislative Bill transmitted thereto by the House of Representatives or has not agreed to a legislative Bill referred thereto by the House of Representatives, the House of Representatives may request a meeting of a Joint Committee of the Houses.

In spite of the preceding paragraph, the House of Councillors may, with its notification of disagreement, request a meeting of a Joint Committee of the Houses, only when the House of Councillors has not agreed to a legislative Bill referred thereto by the House of Representatives. However, on this occasion, the House of Representatives may refuse the request for a meeting of a Joint Committee of the Houses.

Article 85. In connection with budget estimates or treaties receiving prior consideration by the House of Representatives, when the House of Representatives has not agreed to a matter referred thereto by the House of Councillors, or when the House of Councillors has rejected a matter transmitted thereto by the House of Representatives, the House of Representatives must request a meeting of a Joint Committee of the Houses.

In connection with treaties receiving prior consideration by the House of Councillors, when the House of Councillors has not agreed to a matter referred thereto by the House of Representatives, or when the House of Representatives has rejected a matter transmitted thereto by the House of Councillors, the House of Councillors must request a meeting of a Joint Committee of the Houses.

Article 86. When either House has decided upon the nomination of the Prime Minister, the other House shall be so notified.

When the Houses disagree upon the nomination of the Prime Minister, the House of Councillors must request a meeting of a Joint Committee of the Houses.

Article 87. Except for the provisions in the three preceding Articles, in connection with matters requiring Diet decision, when the House exercising posterior consideration disagrees with the decision of the House exercising prior consideration, the latter may request a meeting of a Joint Committee of the Houses.

Article 88. When either House has requested a meeting of a Joint Committee of the Houses, the other House cannot refuse, except as provided in Article 84, paragraph 2.

Article 89. A Joint Committee of the Houses shall consist of twenty (20) members, ten (10) of whom shall be elected by each House.

Article 90. A meeting of a Joint Committee of the Houses shall be presided over alternately by a Chairman elected by and from each House's membership on the Joint Committee. The Chairman for the initial meeting shall be chosen by lottery.

Article 91. A meeting of a Joint Committee of the Houses cannot open proceedings or make any decision unless two-thirds or more of the Joint Committee-men respectively of each House are present.

Article 92. A Joint Committee of the Houses shall decide upon a definitive draft only when two-thirds or more of the members of the Joint Committee present have voted for it.

The proceedings of a Joint Committee of the Houses shall, except as provided in the preceding paragraph, be determined by a majority vote of the members of the Joint Committee present ; in case of a tie, the decision shall be made by the Chairman.

Article 93. A definitive draft prepared by a Joint Committee of the Houses shall be considered first by the House which requested the meeting and then by the other House.

A definitive draft shall not be subject to further amendment.

Article 94. When a definitive draft cannot be agreed upon by a Joint Committee of the Houses, the Chairmen of the Joint Committee must so notify their respective Houses.

Article 95. The President of either House may be present and express his views at a meeting of a Joint Committee of the Houses.

Article 96. A Joint Committee of the Houses may demand the presence at its meeting of Ministers of State and representatives of the Government.

Article 97. Other than those specified in the two preceding Articles, only committee members shall be permitted to attend a meeting of a Joint Committee of the Houses.

Article 98. Rules concerning a Joint Committee of the Houses, other than those provided for in this law, shall be prescribed by decision of the Houses.

Ch. XI. *Legislative Committee of the Houses*

[*Article 99.* The Legislative Committee of the Houses shall make recommendations to the Houses and the Cabinet concerning the introduction of new legislation, existing law, and Cabinet orders ; it shall also investigate and study the Diet Law and other regulations of the Houses and make recommendations to the Houses for their revision.]

Article 99. *The Legislative Committee of the House shall perform the following functions : (1) to single out specific problems relating to government and to make recommendations thereon to the Houses ; (2) to make recommendations to the Houses for new legislation or concerning existing laws and Cabinet orders ; (3) to investigate and study the laws and regulations pertaining to the Diet and to make recommendations to the House for their revision.*

The Legislative Committee of the Houses shall, before the end of every session, submit to the President of each House a report on the matters listed in the preceding paragraph.

[*Article 100.* The Legislative Committee shall consist of eighteen (18) members, of whom the House of Representatives shall elect ten (10) and the House of Councillors elect eight (8). The Chairman of the Committee shall be elected by majority vote of the Committee from among its members.]

Article 100. *The Legislative Committee of the Houses shall consist of ten (10) members of the House of Representatives and eight (8) members of the House of Councillors, elected by the respective Houses. Meetings shall be presided over alternately by Chairmen elected respectively by the Committee members of each House. The Chairman for the initial meeting shall be decided by lottery.*

The term of office of Committee members shall be the same as that of members of the Houses.

Article 101. The Legislative Committee cannot hold a meeting while the Diet is not in session, unless otherwise decided by the Diet.

Article 102. Additional provisions governing the Legislative Committee shall be decided by the Houses.

Ch. XII. *Relations Between the Diet, the General Public, and Public Offices*

Article 103. Each House may dispatch its members for examination [and investigation] *of bills and other matters, for investigations in relation to government, or for any other purpose deemed necessary by the House.*

Article 104. The Cabinet, the Government, and public offices must comply with requests of each House for submission of necessary reports and documents for investigation.

[*Article 105.* The Cabinet and the Ministries must send copies of their publications to the Diet Library.]

[When deemed necessary, the Standing Committees for Library Management, jointly or separately, may cause the Cabinet and Ministries to send their publications to Diet Members.]

Article 106. When witnesses are called to testify in connection with legislative matters and the investigation of national affairs, each House shall, according to regulations separately made, provide them with travel expenses and daily allowances.

Ch. XIII. *Resignation, Retirement, Vacancies, and Qualifications*

Article 107. Each House may authorize resignations of its members. When the House is adjourned, the President may authorize resignations.

Article 108. A member becomes retired when he is elected to the other House or when he is appointed to an office which, according to law, he cannot occupy concurrently as a Diet member.

Article 109. A member becomes retired when he loses eligibility for Diet membership.

Article 110. The President of the House concerned must notify the Election Administration Management Commission of the existence of a Diet vacancy.

Article 111. When a litigation occurs concerning a member's qualifications, the House concerned will offer a resolution after the completion of the Committee's examination.

The above-mentioned litigation shall be presented in written form to the President by a member of the House concerned.

Article 112. When a litigation concerning a member's qualifications has been initiated, the member may employ one or two attorneys, but only one at State expense.

Article 113. A member will maintain his membership and authority connected with it in the House until he has been disqualified. However, he may defend himself but cannot vote in a meeting in which a litigation concerning his qualifications is pending.

Ch. XIV. *Discipline and Police*

Article 114. In order to maintain discipline during sessions the President of each House shall exercise police power within the Diet in accordance with this Law and the regulations prescribed by each House.

The preceding paragraph shall be applied *mutatis mutandis* during an emergency session of the House of Councillors.

Article 115. The Cabinet shall dispatch, upon request of the Presidents of the Houses, an adequate police force for the Diet. The police will be superintended by the Presidents.

Article 116. During a plenary session, when a member acts contrary to this Law or rules of proceedings, or is guilty of disorderly conduct, or injures the dignity of the House, the President shall warn or restrain him or cause him to retract his words. When a member disobeys an order, the President may silence him until the end of the meeting or cause him to leave the chamber.

Article 117. The President may recess or adjourn a meeting in case it becomes too disorderly to control.

Article 118. A visitor who obstructs the progress of business in the House may be ordered to leave the House by the President or may be placed in custody of the police, if necessary.

The President may order all visitors to leave in case the gallery becomes disorderly.

Article 119. No insulting language shall be used and no remarks concerning the private affairs of another member shall be made in the House.

Article 120. A member insulted during a plenary session or in committee may appeal to the House for action against the guilty members.

Ch. XV. *Disciplinary Measures*

Article 121. The President shall refer a disciplinary case occurring in the House to the Standing Committee for Disciplinary Measures for examination, and he shall pronounce the sentence passed by the House.

A Committee Chairman shall report a disciplinary case occurring in a Committee to the President for necessary action.

A motion for disciplinary action, initiated by twenty (20) or more members, shall be presented within three (3) days after a disciplinary case occurs.

Article 122. Disciplinary action shall be as follows :
(1) Admonition in a meeting open to the public.
(2) Address of apology in a meeting open to the public.
(3) Suspension of attendance in the House for a certain period.
(4) Expulsion.

Article 123. Neither House shall refuse to seat a member who has been re-elected following his expulsion.

Article 124. The President shall refer to the Standing Committee for Disciplinary Measures a case of a member who fails to attend the House without justification within seven (7) days after the member received an invitation which the President specially sent to him because, (a) the member did not attend the Diet without a justifiable reason within seven (7) days after the date of convocation, (b) the member was absent from a plenary session or a committee meeting without a justifiable reason, (c) the period of leave of absence expired.

519

Ch. XVI. Court of Impeachment

Article 125. Impeachment against judges shall be conducted by the Court of Impeachment, composed of an equal number of judges elected by the respective Houses from among their members.

The Presiding Judge of the Court of Impeachment shall be elected by majority vote of the Court from among its members.

Article 126. Removal proceedings against judges shall be instituted by the Proceedings Committee composed of members elected by the House of Representatives.

The Chairman of the Proceedings Committee shall be elected by majority vote of the Committee from its membership.

Article 127. A judge of the Court of Impeachment shall not become concurrently a member of the Proceedings Committee.

Article 128. When the judges are elected in each House and the Proceedings Committee members are elected in the House of Representatives, alternate members for these positions shall be elected.

Article 129. Matters relating to the Court of Impeachment and the Proceedings Committee, other than those provided for in this Law, shall be determined by law.

Ch. XVII. [Diet Library and Members' Club]

National Diet Library, Legislative Bureau, and Members' Club.

Article 130. The *National* Diet Library shall be established *in the Diet as Provided by law* to help members with investigations and research.

The *National* Diet Library may be used by the public.

[*Article 131.* Each House shall have a legal department to expedite the drafting of legal measures by members.]

Article 131. A Legislative Bureau shall be established in each House for the purpose of aiding Diet members in drafting legislation.

The Legislative Bureau of each House shall have a Director, Secretaries, and other necessary personnel.

The Director shall be appointed or dismissed by the President, with the approval of the House. However, the President may accept the resignation of the Director during adjournment of the Diet.

The Director shall administer the business of the Legislative Bureau under the supervision of the President.

Secretaries and other personnel of the Legislative Bureau shall be appointed or dismissed by the Director with the consent of the President and the approval of the Standing Committee for House Management.

Secretaries shall administer their business under the direction of the Director.

Regulations necessary for administering the business of the Legislative Bureau shall be approved by the Standing Committee for House Management.

Article 132. A Members' Club, where office rooms and one (1) secretary [clerical assistant] for each member shall be provided, shall be established to facilitate members' business.

Supplementary Provisions

This Law shall come into force from the day of the enforcement of the Japanese Constitution.

The present Law of the Houses shall be repealed.

Until an election for the President and Vice-President of the House of Representatives is held according to this Law, the President and Vice-President who hold office when this Law comes into force shall remain in their respective offices.

Until an election for the Secretary-General of each House is held according to this Law, the Chief Secretary of the House of Representatives and of the House of Peers who hold office when this Law comes into force shall continue to hold their respective offices as Secretary-General.

Until the House of Councillors adopts its House regulations, the regulations for the House of Representatives shall be followed with respect to procedures and regulations for meetings or other matters in the first session of the House of Councillors.

Supplementary Provisions of Amendment Law (5 July 1948).

(*a*) *This Law shall come into force as from the day of its promulgation, provided however, that the revised provisions of Article 41, paragraph 2, and Article 42 shall be enforced as from the date of convocation of the Third Session of the Diet.*

(*b*) *A part of the Law concerning the Temporary Appointment of Parliamentary Vice-Ministers (Law No. 26 of 1948) shall read as follows :*

Article 3. Deleted.

Article 8. The provisions of Article 1 and Article 2 of this Law shall become invalid as from the date of the enforcement of the National Government Organization Law.

(*c*) *'Vice-Minister of each Ministry' in the amended provision of Article 39 shall read as 'Parliamentary Vice-Ministers' until the date of the enforcement of the National Government Organization Law.*

Political Reorientation of Japan, Appendix H : 19, pp. 968-76.

NATIONAL PUBLIC SERVICE LAW

Ch. I.   General Provisions

Article 1.   (Object of this Law) The object of this Law is to assure the people democratic and efficient administration of their public affairs by establishing basic standards which shall be applicable to all official positions and places of employment in the national public service (the national public service as defined in this law does not include members of the Diet) and by providing that personnel shall be so selected and directed in a manner consistent with democratic practices as to promote maximum efficiency in the performance of public duties.

Article 2.   (Regular and Special Government Service) The national public service shall be divided into the regular government service and the special government service.

The regular government service shall be comprised of all positions in the national public service other than those in the special government service.

The special government service shall be comprised of the following types of positions :

(1)   The Prime Minister.

(2)   Ministers of State.

(3)   Director-General of the Cabinet Secretariat.

(4)   Deputy Director-General of the Cabinet Secretariat.

(5)   Director-General of the Bureau of Legislation.

(6)   Parliamentary Vice-Minister of each Ministry.

(7)   Vice-Minister of each Ministry.

(8)   Counsellor of each Ministry.

(9)   President of the Construction Board and President of the Central Liaison Office.

(10)   Confidential Secretaries to the Prime Minister (not exceeding three in number) and other Confidential Secretaries (one for each Minister of State or head of agency included in the special government service).

(11)   Positions the appointment to which requires an election, resolution or consent of one or both Houses of the Diet.

(12)   Personnel of Government enterprises, 'Kodan' and others similar thereto as designated by law or rules of the National Personnel Commission.

(13)   Advisers, Consultants, Committee-men and other personnel similar thereto as designated by law or rules of the National Personnel Commission.

(14) Employees engaged in common labour.

(15) Grand Steward, Grand Chamberlain, Chamberlains and other personnel of the Imperial House Office as designated by law or rules of the National Personnel Commission.

(16) Ambassadors and Ministers.

(17) Judges, one Confidential Secretary to the Chief Justice of the Supreme Court and Judicial Research Officials.

(18) Employees of the Diet.

The provisions of this Law shall apply specifically to all positions in the regular government service (to be hereinafter referred to as the service and persons holding positions therein as personnel).

The provisions of this Law shall not apply to positions in the special government service unless specifically provided by an amendment to this Law.

Ch. II. The National Personnel Commission

Article 3. (Installation) In order to ensure the thorough-going enforcement of this Law and attain its objectives, the National Personnel Commission shall be set up under the jurisdiction of the Prime Minister.

The Commission shall take charge of the following matters:

(1) Integration and co-ordination of position classification, appointments and dismissals of personnel of the service, their compensation, pension and other personnel administration matters;

(2) Matters concerning examination of personnel;

(3) Other matters placed under its jurisdiction on the basis of law.

Article 4. (Personnel) The Commission shall have the following personnel:

Chairman.

Commissioners . . . . Three.

Executive Director . . . . One.

Other personnel provided by Cabinet Order.

Article 5. (Commissioners of the Commission) Commissioners of the Commission (to be hereinafter referred to as Commissioners) shall be appointed, with the consent of the Diet, by the Cabinet from among persons 35 years old or more, who are of highest moral character and integrity, in known sympathy with the democratic form of government and efficient administration therein based on merit principles, and possessing a wide range of knowledge and sound judgment concerning personnel administration.

In case the House of Councillors does not consent to the appoint-ment of the Commissioner despite the consent of the House of

Representatives, the consent of the House of Representatives shall be taken as the consent of the Diet in the same manner as provided by Paragraph 2 of Article 67 of the Constitution of Japan.

The appointment and dismissal of a Commissioner shall be attested by the Emperor.

No person falling under one of the following specifications shall be appointed as Commissioner :

(1)   A person who has been adjudicated incompetent, quasi-incompetent, or bankrupt and has not yet been rehabilitated ;

(2)   A person who has been sentenced to a penalty heavier than imprisonment without hard labour by the criminal court or who has been punished upon conviction of an offence prescribed in Chapter IV ;

(3)   A person who falls under one of the specifications mentioned in Item 3 or Item 5 of Article 38.

No person shall be eligible for appointment as a Commissioner who has been a candidate for national or prefectural elective public office or who is or has been an officer of a political party within one year previous to the proposed date of appointment, as provided by rules of the Commission.

With respect to the appointment of Commissioners, no two persons among them shall be members of the same political party or graduates of the same professional sub-division of the same department of the same university or high school (in universities where there is no professional sub-division, graduates of the same department).

Article 6.   (Oath Taking and Performance of Duties) After he has been appointed as a Commissioner, the new incumbent shall not exercise the powers pertaining to his office until he has signed a written oath before the Chief Justice of the Supreme Court, as provided by rules of the Commission.

The provisions of Section VII of Chapter III shall apply correspondingly to Commissioners.

Article 7.   (Term of Office) The term of office of a Commissioner shall be four years. However, a Commissioner who is appointed to fill a vacancy shall remain in office during the unexpired portion of the term of his predecessor.

A Commissioner may be reappointed. However, he shall not remain in office continuously for a period exceeding 12 years.

A person who has been a Commissioner shall not be eligible to appointment to any position in any agency of the National Government other than the Commission for one year after the termination of his service as Commissioner. Exceptions, however, may be authorized by rules of the Commission.

Article 8. (Retirement and Removal from Office) A Commissioner shall automatically retire from office when he falls under one of the following specifications :

(1) When he has come under one of the instances mentioned in Paragraph 4 of Article 5 ;

(2) When his removal from office is affirmed on public impeachment proceedings based on charges filed by the Prime Minister ;

(3) When he has been continuously in office as a Commissioner for 12 years.

The causes for impeachment prescribed in Item 2 of the preceding paragraph shall be as follows :

(i) When he is mentally or physically incompetent to perform official duties ;

(ii) When he has acted contrary to the duties of his position or is guilty of such malfeasance as to render himself unfitting to be Commissioner.

In cases when two persons or more among Commissioners have come to belong to the same political party, all except one person shall be removed from office, with the consent of the Diet, by the Cabinet. However, in cases specifically provided by rules of the Commission, a Commissioner may be immediately removed by the Cabinet.

The provision of the preceding paragraph shall not jeopardize the position of a Commissioner who has not changed his political status in regard to party affiliations.

The provision of Paragraph 2 of Article 5 shall apply correspondingly to the instances specified in Paragraph 3.

Except the cases mentioned in Paragraph 3, no commissioner shall be removed from office against his will.

Article 9. (Impeachment of Commissioner) Proceedings for impeachment of a Commissioner shall be conducted by the Supreme Court.

When the Prime Minister intends to bring impeachment action against a Commissioner, he shall file charges in writing setting forth the alleged offence, both in general and particular, and submit them to the Supreme Court.

In the case of the preceding paragraph, the Prime Minister shall forward a copy of the charges mentioned in the same paragraph to the accused Commissioner.

The Supreme Court shall set a date for hearing not less than thirty days and not more than ninety days after the filing of the charges mentioned in Paragraph 2, and notify the Prime Minister and the accused Commissioner at least thirty days in advance of the date set for hearing.

The Supreme Court shall announce its findings within one hundred days after the original date of hearing.

The proceedings for impeachment of Commissioners shall be provided by rules of the Supreme Court.

Costs of hearings shall be borne by the national treasury.

Article 10. (Salary) A Commissioner shall be paid a salary corresponding to that of a Minister of State.

Article 11. (Chairman of the Commission) The Chairman of the Commission (to be hereinafter referred to as the Chairman) shall be appointed by the Prime Minister from among Commissioners.

The Chairman shall preside over the affairs of the Commission and represent the Commission.

When the Chairman is unable to be attached to his duties or if his post is vacant, a senior Commissioner shall act for the Chairman in the performance of his duties.

Article 12. (Commissioners' Conference) In the Commission there shall be set up a Commissioners' Conference which is composed of the Commissioners. The Executive Director of the Commission shall be present at the Commissioners' Conference as Executive Secretary.

When exercising the powers enumerated below, the Commission shall require a resolution of the Commissioners' Conference :

(1) The enactment, amendment, or abrogation of rules of the Commission ;

(2) Recommendations to the head of the appropriate agency of government as specified in Article 22 ;

(3) Submitting opinions of the Commission to the Prime Minister as specified in Article 23 ;

(4) Report to the Prime Minister as specified in Article 24 ;

(5) Drafting of a position classification plan as specified in Article 29 ;

(6) Determination of standards for evaluation and designation of an evaluating body as specified in Article 36 (including cases to be correspondingly applied in Article 37) ;

(7) Designation of examining bodies as specified in Article 48 ;

(8) Approval of temporary employment and its renewal, restriction of number of personnel for temporary employment and determination of their qualifications, and cancellation of temporary employment as specified in Article 60 ;

(9) Drafting of a pay plan as specified in Article 63 ;

(10) Preparation of revisions of the pay plan as specified in Article 67 ;

(11) Recommendations to the head of an appropriate agency of government, and drafting plans concerning recognition for efficient

performance or measures for correcting failure to perform efficiently as specified in Article 72 ;

(12)   Evaluation of a case as specified in Article 87 ;

(13)   Evaluation of action and submitting a report to the Prime Minister as specified in Article 92 ;

(14)   Drafting of important matters concerning compensation as specified in Article 95 ;

(15)   Evaluation of a protest as specified in Article 103 ;

(16)   Drafting of important matters concerning pension as specified in Article 108 ;

(17)   Other matters which, by a resolution of the Commissioners' Conference, require a resolution of the same conference.

Regular meetings of the Commissioners' Conference shall, as a rule, be held at least once a week at a fixed place, as provided by rules of the Commission.

Proceedings at a meeting of the Commissioners' Conference shall be recorded in its minutes.

The minutes specified in the preceding paragraph shall be prepared by the Executive Secretary.

Necessary determinations concerning the proceedings of the Commissioners' Conference shall be provided by rules of the Commission.

Article 13.   (Secretariat of the Commission and Other Agencies) The Commission shall have a Secretariat, which shall take charge of general affairs concerning matters under the jurisdiction of the Commission.

The Commission may establish local offices with the approval of the Diet.

Article 14.   (Executive Director of the Commission) The Executive Director of the Commission shall, under the direction and supervision of the Chairman, take charge of the affairs of the Secretariat, and act as the Executive Secretary of the Commissioners' Conference and Chairman of the National Personnel Council.

Article 15.   (Prohibition of Personnel of the Commission from Holding Concurrent Positions) No Commissioner and Executive Director shall hold any concurrent position in the service other than that in the Commission.

Article 16.   (Rules of the Commission) The Commission shall, with the approval of the Prime Minister, make rules concerning matters necessary for the execution of this Law.

Rules of the Commission shall be published by the Prime Minister in the *Official Gazette*.

Article 17.   (Investigation) The Commission, or any person or persons designated by the Commission may conduct investigations of an employment situation involving personnel of the service, the condition of personnel management and other matters related to personnel administration.

The Commission, or person or persons designated in accordance with the provision of the preceding paragraph, may, when necessary in conducting the investigations specified therein, subpoena witnesses or demand the presentation of books and records or copies thereof pertinent or alleged to be pertinent to any investigation or hearing.

Article 18. (Control of Delivery of Compensation) The Commission shall control delivery of compensation to personnel of the service.

Article 19. (Personnel Records) The Commission shall administer matters concerning personnel records relating to personnel of the service.

The Commission shall prescribe that the Prime Minister's Office and any ministries or agencies of government prepare and maintain personnel records inclusive of all particulars relating to personnel of the agencies of government concerned.

The particulars to be entered in personnel records, the form thereof, and other necessary determinations concerning personnel records shall be provided by rules of the Commission.

Where it is deemed that the personnel records prescribed in Paragraph 2 are contrary to the rules of the Commission, the Commission may order revisions and such other steps as may be called for.

Article 20. (Statistical Reporting) The Commission shall, as provided by rules of the Commission, prescribe and administer a system of statistical reporting concerning employment in the service.

When it is necessary in connection with the statistical reporting mentioned in the preceding paragraph, the Commission may require any appropriate agency of government to give required information on request or at specified time and in specified form.

Article 21. (Delegation of Functions) Of the functions prescribed in this Law, the Commission may delegate unimportant functions to other agencies of government. Even in these cases, the Commission shall not be free from responsibility in regard to the exercise of such functions.

Article 22. (Recommendations for Improvement of Personnel Administration) The Commission may make recommendations to any appropriate minister or head of other agency of government concerning improvements of personnel administration.

The Commission may make recommendations to any appropriate minister or head of another agency of government concerning the change of placement and transfer of personnel between the various ministries or agencies of the National Government so as to contribute to the improved efficiency of administrative operations throughout the Government.

In the cases of the preceding two paragraphs, the Commission shall submit a due report thereon to the Prime Minister.

Article 23. (Advice on Enactment, Amendment or Abrogation of Laws and Orders) If, in order to assure the realization of the objective of this Law, the Commission has opinions concerning the enactment, or amendment or abrogation of laws and orders, it shall submit them to the Prime Minister.

Article 24. (Report on Business) The Commission shall, as provided by the Prime Minister, make an annual report to the Prime Minister of its activities and accomplishments covering each fiscal year of operation.

The Prime Minister shall publish the report mentioned in the preceding paragraph.

Article 25. (Directors of Personnel) In the Prime Minister's Office, the various ministries and other agencies of the government designated by rules of the Commission, there shall be, as a member of its staff, a Director of Personnel.

The Director shall be head of a bureau or division in charge of business pertaining to personnel functions, and assist the head of the agency of government concerned by taking charge of business pertaining to personnel functions.

Article 26. (National Personnel Council) In order to ensure close contact and mutual co-operation concerning the enforcement of this Law between the Commission and the Prime Minister's Office, the various ministries and other agencies of government, there shall be set up in the Commission a National Personnel Council.

The National Personnel Council shall be composed of a Chairman and members.

The Chairman shall be the Executive Director and members shall be the Directors specified in the preceding Article.

The National Personnel Council may submit recommendations to the President on important matters relating to personnel administration.

Except as prescribed in the preceding four paragraphs, necessary determinations concerning the National Personnel Council shall be provided by rules of the Commission.

Ch. III.   Standards for the Service
SECTION I.   GENERAL RULES

Article 27. (Principles of Equal Treatment) In the administration of this Law, all of the people shall be accorded equal treatment and shall not be discriminated against by reason of race, religious faith, sex, social status or family origin.

Article 28. (Principle of Meeting Changing Conditions) The standards concerning compensation, hours of work and other working conditions to be established under this Law may from time to time be changed to meet changing conditions under procedures to be determined by the Diet.

SECTION II. POSITION CLASSIFICATION PLAN

Article 29. (Establishment of Position Classification Plan) The position classification plan shall be prescribed by law.

The Commission shall develop a position classification plan whereby all positions in the service are classified by classes determined according to the kinds of duties and by grades according to the degrees of complexity of duties and responsibilities involved.

In the position classification plan, classification of positions shall be so effected that the same qualifications may reasonably be required for and the same schedules of basic pay may be applied equitably to all positions in the same grade and class.

The plan as provided in the preceding three paragraphs shall be submitted to the Diet for approval before the enforcement of this Law.

Article 30. (Enforcement of the Position Classification Plan) The position classification plan shall be gradually enforced, commencing first with segments where it is practicable.

Except as prescribed in this Law, determinations necessary for the enforcement of the position classification plan shall be provided by rules of the Commission.

Article 31. (Allocation of Positions) In the event of enforcing the position classification plan, the Commission shall, as provided by rules of the Commission, allocate to one of the grades of a class of the position classification plan every position to which such plan is applicable.

The Commission shall, as provided by rules of the Commission, review at any time the allocations prescribed in the preceding paragraph, and revise them, where deemed necessary.

Article 32. (Prohibition of Classification of Positions by other than the Position Classification Plan) In regard to positions to which the position classification plan is applicable, no classification of positions on any basis other than the position classification plan shall be made as the basis for the development and application of qualification standards for employment and the payment of compensation.

Section III. Examination, Appointment and Dismissal

Article 33. (Basic Standard for Appointment and Dismissal) Appointment and dismissal of a person in the service shall be made entirely on the basis of the result of his examination and the merit of his performance of duties or other demonstrated abilities.

Except as prescribed in this Law, determinations necessary for enforcing the basic standard mentioned in the preceding paragraph shall be provided by rules of the Commission.

Part 1. General Rules

Article 34. (Definition of Employment, Initial Appointment, Promotion, Demotion and Transfer) Employment as referred to in this Law is defined as the appointment of any person to any position in the service by any of the following means : initial appointment, promotion, demotion and transfer.

An initial appointment as referred to in this Law is defined as an appointment of a person to any position in a class by any means other than by promotion, demotion or transfer.

A promotion as referred to in this Law is defined as the assignment of a person to a position in the same class in a grade higher than he is holding.

A demotion as referred to in this Law is defined as the assignment of a person to a position in the same class in a grade lower than he is holding.

A transfer as referred to in this Law is defined as the assignment of a person to a position in the same grade and class in a different subdivision of the same organization or a different organization in the service.

Article 35. (Method of Filling Vacancies) When a vacancy occurs in the service, an appointing officer, except as specially provided by law or rules of the Commission, may appoint a person by any one of the following means : transfer, initial appointment, promotion or demotion. This shall not, however, apply to cases where the Commission recognizes the special necessity and designates the method of employment.

Article 36. (Method of Initial Appointment) Initial appointment of personnel shall be by competitive examination. However, in cases where, with respect to a grade or grades of a class or classes of positions prescribed by rules of the Commission, the approval of the Commission has been obtained, this provision shall not preclude such initial appointment by means of an evaluation of demonstrated abilities other than by competitive examination.

The evaluation specified in the proviso of the preceding paragraph shall be conducted by the Commission or an evaluating body appointed by the Commission in accordance with standards established by the Commission.

Without prejudice to the provisions of the preceding two paragraphs, initial appointments of personnel to a position may be made from among persons who have previously held a position of the same or higher grade in the same class, as provided by rules of the Commission.

Article 37. (Method of Promotion) Promotion of personnel shall be by competitive examination (to be hereinafter referred to as examination) among incumbents of positions in the next lower grade of the same class to which the promotional position under consideration belongs. This provision shall not, however, preclude the Commission from restricting the scope of persons to be examined, at the request of an appointing officer, to employees under his jurisdiction.

In cases where, in view of the duties and responsibilities of the position to which appointment is to be made, the Commission deems it impracticable to hold an examination among the incumbents concerned, promotion may be made by means of an evaluation based on the past service record of such incumbents.

The provision of Paragraph 2 of the preceding Article shall apply correspondingly to the instances of the evaluation under the preceding paragraph.

Article 38. (Provisions for Disqualification) No person falling under one of the following types of cases shall be eligible to appointment in the service, except as provided by rules of the Commission or quasi-incompetent.

(1) A person who has been adjudicated incompetent or quasi-incompetent;

(2) A person who has been sentenced to a penalty heavier than imprisonment without hard labour by the criminal court, and on whom the execution of the sentence has not been completed or who has not yet ceased to be amenable to the execution of the sentence;

(3) A person who was dismissed by disciplinary decision and of whom a period of two years has not expired since the date of dismissal;

(4) A Commissioner or Executive Director who has committed a crime prescribed in Article 109, Item 3 of Article 110 and has been convicted;

(5) A person who, on or after the date of the enforcement of the Constitution of Japan, formed or belonged to a political party or association which advocated the overthrow by force of the Constitution of Japan or the Government existing thereunder.

Article 39. (Prohibition of Illegal Acts concerning Personnel Matters) No person shall, for the purpose of realizing any one of the items mentioned below, pay or receive or offer or solicit or promise to pay or receive money or other benefit, or use threat, coercion or other similar method, or, directly or indirectly, use or offer or demand or promise to use public office or be in any way concerned with such acts.

(1) Resignation, temporary retirement or failure to accept appointment ;

(2) Withdrawal of his application for examination or appointment, or suspension of competition for appointment ;

(3) Effecting or recommending employment, promotion, retention in employment or other advantage in the service.

Article 40. (Prohibition of Acts of Fraud concerning Personnel Matters) No person shall make any false or dishonest statement, record, certificate, mark rating, evaluation or report with regard to any examination, evaluation, personnel record or appointment.

Article 41. (Prohibition against Obstructing the Right to Examination of Appointment and Furnishing of Information) No person belonging to any examining body or other personnel in the service shall obstruct any person in his right to examination or appointment or furnish any special or secret information for the purpose of favourably affecting or discriminating, against the rights or prospects of any person with respect to examination or appointment in the service.

Part 2. *Examination*

Article 42. (Instances of Holding Examination) Examination shall be held, as provided by rules of the Commission, according to grade or grades of a class or classes of position.

Article 43. (Disqualifications for Examination) Persons who are ineligible to appointment for reasons other than those specified in Article 44 shall not compete in an examination.

Article 44. (Prerequisites of Eligibility for Examination) For persons intending to compete in an examination, objective and uniformly applicable qualifications which constitute a minimum essential to the performance of the duties of a grade or grades of a class or classes of positions involved, shall be determined as prerequisites by rules of the Commission.

Article 45. (Content of Examination) Each examination shall have as its object the accurate measurement of the relative abilities of the persons examined to perform the duties of the grade and class of positions concerned, and shall be practical in character.

Article 46. (Entrance Examination to be Open and Equal) Entrance Examination shall be open and on equal terms to any citizen who possesses the minimum qualifications determined as prerequisites by rules of the Commission.

Article 47. (Announcement of Entrance Examination) Announcement of entrance examinations shall be given publication by means of Official Notification.

The announcement of examination of the preceding paragraph shall set forth the duties and responsibilities of the grade and class of positions for which examination is to be held, the rates of pay, the prerequisites of eligibility, the subjects of examination and the individual weights thereof, the time and place of examination and where, when and how necessary application forms may be secured and filed and other qualifying procedure observed and such other information as the Commission may deem pertinent.

The Official Notification prescribed in Paragraph 1 shall, as provided by rules of the Commission, be given publicity in such a way that all pertinent details relating to the examination in view may unfailingly become known to all persons presumably qualified for such examination.

The Commission shall at all times exercise diligence in the efforts to secure adequate participation of presumably qualified persons in examinations.

Article 48. (Examining Bodies) Examinations shall, as provided by rules of the Commission, he conducted only by examining bodies determined by the Commission.

Article 49. (Time and Place of Examination) The time and place of examinations shall be so decided that they may be reasonably accessible to any qualified citizen in the country.

Part 3.   Employment Eligible Lists

Article 50. (Preparation of Eligible List) In regard to employment of personnel by examination, employment eligible lists (entrance eligible lists and promotional eligible lists) shall be prepared by grade and class of positions, as provided by rules of the Commission.

Article 51. (Persons to be entered in Entrance Eligible List) The names and examination scores of those who have achieved the qualifying score or better under entrance examination shall be entered in the entrance eligible list in the precise order of their examination scores as eligible to appointment to the appropriate positions in the grade and class covered by the list.

Article 52. (Persons to be entered in Promotional Eligible List) The names and examination scores of those who have achieved the qualifying score or better in promotion examinations shall be entered

534

in the promotional eligible list in the precise order of their examination scores as eligible to promotion to the appropriate positions in the grade and class covered by the list.

Article 53. (Inspection of Eligible List) Employment Eligible Lists shall be at all times open to inspection of the persons examined, appointing agencies of government and other interested parties upon demand.

Article 54. (Cancellation of Eligible List) The Commission may, at its discretion, cancel, either in whole or in part, eligible lists which have been in use for over one year or at any time for one of the causes prescribed by the Commission.

Part 4. Employment

Article 55. (Appointing Officer) Appointment to a position in the service, whether as the result of entrance examination, promotion examination, or other qualifying procedure, shall be made only by an appointing officer.

Except as specifically prescribed by Law, the appointing power shall be vested with the Cabinet, the Prime Minister, various ministers, heads of other administrative agencies of government according to the grades of positions provided by Cabinet Order.

The appointing officer who is the head of an administrative agency of government prescribed in the preceding paragraph may delegate such appointing power only to a high official of such agency, as provided by Cabinet Order.

Article 56. (Method of Appointment from Entrance Eligible List) Initial appointment from an entrance eligible list shall be made from amongst the top five names on such list for each vacancy to be filled.

Article 57. (Method of Promotion from Promotional Eligible List) Promotion of personnel from a promotional eligible list shall be made from amongst the top five names on such list for each vacancy to be filled.

Article 58. (Recommendation of Eligibles for Employment) In cases where the appointing officer desires to fill an authorized vacancy by initial appointment or promotion and makes due application therefor, the Commission shall, as prescribed by rules of the Commission, submit the required number of eligibles prescribed in the preceding two Articles for the employment in view from among those entered in the appropriate employment eligible lists.

Article 59. (Conditional Period of Initial Appointment) Any initial appointment to the grade or class prescribed by rules of the Commission shall be considered conditional and shall become regular only after the appointee shall have served in the position concerned a period of not less than six months during which he shall have performed satisfactorily the duties of that position.

Necessary determinations concerning conditional initial appointment shall be provided by rules of the Commission.

Article 60. (Temporary Employment) An appointing officer, as provided by rules of the Commission, may effect, with the approval of the Commission, temporary appointments each not to exceed six months in duration, in emergencies, to positions of an essentially temporary and transitory nature or in instances when an eligible list has not been established by the Commission. In such cases, temporary appointment may, with the approval of the Commission, be renewed once for an additional period of six months, as provided by rules of the Commission, but not more than once.

The Commission may, with respect to temporary appointment, limit by grade and class of positions the number of such appointments and specify qualifications of personnel so employed.

The Commission may cancel any temporary appointment which violates provisions of the preceding two paragraphs.

Temporary appointment shall not in any way confer the right to or preference in selection for permanent employment.

Except as prescribed in the preceding four paragraphs, this Law, Cabinet Orders issued thereunder and rules of the Commission shall apply to temporary appointees.

Part 5. *Temporary Retirement, Reinstatement, Retirement and Dismissal*

Article 61. (Temporary Retirement, Reinstatement, Retirement and Dismissal) The temporary retirement, reinstatement, retirement and dismissal of personnel of the service shall be effected by the appointing officer.

SECTION IV. COMPENSATION

Article 62. (Basic Standard for Compensation) Personnel of the service shall be compensated on the basis of the duties and responsibilities of their positions.

The purport of the provision of the preceding paragraph shall be achieved as quickly as possible and in so far as practicable giving due consideration to existing practices.

Part 1. *Pay Plan*

Article 63. (Delivery of Compensation under Pay Plan) The Compensation to personnel of the service shall be effected under a pay plan prescribed by law, and, unless provided therein, no money or valuable thing of any kind may be given as compensation.

The Commission shall conduct necessary investigations and studies and, as a result thereof, draft and submit to the Prime Minister a pay plan conforming to the position classification plan.

Article 64. (Compensation Schedule) A compensation schedule shall be provided in the pay plan.

In the compensation schedule, there shall be clearly specified by a fixed range of variation the amount of pay for each grade, which shall be determined after taking into consideration the cost of living, prevailing wage rates and other pertinent factors.

Article 65. (Matters to be provided in Pay Plan) In addition to the compensation schedule of the preceding Article, the following items shall be provided in the pay plan. Matters concerning :

(1)   Standards for an increase of pay within a same grade ;

(2)   Compensation of positions upon the initial application of the position classification plan ;

(3)   Compensation for overtime, night and holiday work ;

(4)   Allowances for service in specially designated areas, for hazardous jobs and other extraordinary services ;

(5)   Adjustments of compensation by the Commission in regard to positions not requiring full-time service, those for which the facilities necessary for living are wholly or partly supplied at official expense, and others with special working conditions.

The standards of Item 1 of the preceding paragraph shall be determined after taking into consideration length of service, efficiency of service and such other service connected factors.

Article 66. (Determination of Amount of Compensation) Each person in the service shall be paid at one of the rates set forth in the pay plan for the grade and class of the position in which he is employed.

In determining the basic pay plan, no discrimination of any kind shall be made by non-service connected factors.

Article 67. (Revision of Pay Plan) The Commission shall at all times conduct necessary investigations and studies concerning the pay plan and shall, as frequently as it deems such action necessary, prepare and submit to the Prime Minister any revisions, either upward or downward, of the compensation schedules.

Part 2.   *Delivery of Compensation*

Article 68. (Payroll) A person or persons who deliver compensation of any kind to personnel of the service shall first prepare a payroll in regard to a recipient or recipients.

Payrolls shall be kept available for examination by personnel of the Commission at any time.

537

Except as prescribed in the preceding two paragraphs, necessary determinations concerning payrolls shall be provided by Cabinet Order and rules of the Commission.

Article 69. (Auditing of Payroll) Where it is necessary to ensure that delivery of compensation is conducted in compliance with law, order or rules of the Commission, the Commission may audit payrolls or order corrections when it is deemed necessary.

Article 70. (Action against Illegal Payment) In case it is discovered that compensation is paid contrary to law, order or rules of the Commission, the Commission besides taking appropriate steps in regard to the matters under its own jurisdiction, shall, if it is deemed necessary, according to its nature report the case to the Board of Audit or the public procurator for action.

SECTION V. EFFICIENCY

Article 71. (Basic Standard for Efficiency) Personnel of the service shall have their efficiency fully developed and increased.

Except as prescribed in this Law, determinations necessary for enforcing the basic standard of the preceding paragraph shall be provided by rules of the Commission.

The Commission shall conduct necessary investigations and studies concerning programmes which will develop and increase the efficiency of personnel of the service and take appropriate steps to assure the installation of such programmes.

Article 72. (Evaluation of Work Performance) The performance on duty of personnel of the service shall be periodically evaluated by the head of the administrative agency of government where they are employed who shall take such appropriate action as the result of valuation may call for.

The Commission shall have the power of making necessary determinations concerning the evaluation mentioned in the preceding Article and records thereof and of recommending to the head of the appropriate administrative agency such action consistent with this Law as may be calculated to develop and improve the efficiency of the personnel of the service.

The Commission shall draw up plans concerning recognition for efficient performance and measures for correcting failure to perform efficiently, and submit them to the Prime Minister.

Article 73. (Programmes for Improving Efficiency) For the purpose of developing and improving the efficiency of persons in the service, the Commission and the head of the appropriate administrative agency involved shall formulate and exercise diligence in administering programmes concerning :

(1) Education and training of personnel ;

(2)   Health of personnel ;
(3)   Recreation of personnel ;
(4)   Safety of personnel ;
(5)   Welfare of personnel.

In regard to the formulation and administration of the programmes of the preceding paragraph, the Commission shall be responsible for their overall planning, their integration and co-ordination with the appropriate agencies involved and surveillance over such agencies.

Section VI. Status, Disciplinary Punishment and Guarantee

Article 74. (Basic Standard for Status, Disciplinary Punishment and Guarantee) In regard to their status, disciplinary punishment and guarantee, personnel of the service shall be treated equitably.

Except as prescribed by this Law, determinations necessary for enforcing the basic standard mentioned in the preceding paragraph shall be provided by rules of the Commission.

Part 1. Status

Article 75. (Guarantee of Status) Personnel of the service shall not, against their will, be demoted or be temporarily retired or be dismissed, unless they come under one of the causes provided by law.

Personnel of the service shall suffer reduction of pay grade when they come under one of the causes prescribed by rules of the Commission.

Article 76. (Forfeiture of Office due to Disqualification) When a person in the service falls under one of the cases as specified in Article 38, he shall automatically forfeit his office, except as provided by rules of the Commission.

Article 77. (Removal from Office by Impeachment) Provisions for impeachment of persons in the service shall be prescribed by law.

Article 78. (Instances of Demotion and Dismissal against his Will) In cases where a person in the service falls under one of the following cases, he may be demoted or dismissed against his will, as provided by rules of the Commission :

(1)   When his performance on duty fails to show any merit ;
(2)   When due to mental or physical debility, he has difficulty or is incompetent to perform official duties ;
(3)   When otherwise he lacks the qualifications for fitness required for positions of a grade or grades or a class or classes.

Article 79. (Instances of Temporary Retirement against his Will) In cases where a person in the service falls under one of the following cases, he may be temporarily retired against his will.

(1)   When he requires a prolonged period of rest due to mental or physical debility ;

(2)   When he is prosecuted with respect to a criminal case.

Article 80.   (Effect of Temporary Retirement) The period of temporary retirement in any case as specified in Item 1 of the preceding Article shall be one year ; if the debility ceases to exist during the period of temporary retirement, the reinstatement shall be ordered forthwith, while a person who still remains temporarily retired on the expiration of the prescribed period shall automatically be treated as retired.

The period of temporary retirement in any case as specified in Item 2 of the preceding Article shall be the same as the inherence of the case in question with the law court concerned.

While still retaining his status in the service, a person who is temporarily retired does not attend to his official duties. During his temporary retirement, he shall receive one-third of his pay.

Article 81.   (Exceptions to Application) In regard to the status of personnel mentioned below, the provisions of Article 75, Article 78 to the preceding Article inclusive and Articles 89 to 92 inclusive shall not apply :

(1)   Temporary personnel ;

(2)   Personnel in conditional period of initial appointment ;

(3)   Personnel who become supernumeraries or whose positions are abolished due to an amendment or abrogation of the law concerning the official organization or of the fixed number of personnel or as a result of a reduction in budget ;

(4)   Persons who, in consequence of a revision of the allocation of positions by the classification plan, suffer the same result as a reduction of pay grade or demotion.

In regard to the status of personnel enumerated in various items of the preceding paragraph, necessary determinations may be provided by rules of the Commission.

As to which of the persons enumerated in Item 3 of Paragraph 1 shall be demoted, or be temporarily retired or dismissed, the decision shall be made on the basis of the merit of their performance on duty and other demonstrated abilities.

Part 2.   *Disciplinary Punishment*

Article 82.   (Instances of Disciplinary Punishment) When he falls under one of the following cases, a person in the service may, as disciplinary punishment, be dismissed, suspended from duty, suffer reduction in pay or administration of a reprimand :

(1)   When he has acted contrary to this Law or rules of the Commission ;

(2) When he has acted contrary to the duties of his position or has neglected his duties ;

(3) When he is guilty of such malfeasance as to render himself unfitting to be a servant of the community.

Article 83. (Effect of Disciplinary Punishment) The period for suspension of duty shall range from one month to one year.

While still retaining his status in the service, a person who is suspended from duty does not attend to his official duties. While he is suspended from duty, he shall receive one-third of his pay.

In case of reduction in pay, less than one-third of his pay shall be deducted for a period ranging from one month to one year.

Article 84. (Administrator of Disciplinary Punishment) Disciplinary punishment shall be administered by an appointing officer.

Article 85. (Relations with Criminal Court) While a case which is to be subjected to disciplinary punishment is in the criminal court, no disciplinary proceedings may be taken on the same case.

Part 3. Guarantee

DIVISION 1. APPLICATION FOR ADMINISTRATIVE ACTION ON WORKING CONDITIONS

Article 86. (Application for Administrative Action on Working Conditions) Personnel of the service may present application to the Commission relative to salary, wages, or any of the working conditions, and ask that they be accorded appropriate administrative action by the Commission or the head of an employing agency of government.

Article 87. (Review and Evaluation of Case) When the application specified in the preceding Article is received, the Commission shall conduct such investigations, hearings or other fact-finding operations as may in its direction be necessary, and evaluate the situation with due regard to fairness to the public and all persons concerned and in terms of maintaining and improving the efficiency of personnel of the service.

Article 88. (Action to be taken as a Result of Evaluation) When the Commission considers action necessary in regard to working conditions on the basis of the evaluation specified in the preceding Article, it shall take its own action on the matters under its jurisdiction, and recommend to the head of an appropriate agency of government to take action in regard to other matters.

DIVISION 2. REVIEW OF DISADVANTAGEOUS ACTION TAKEN AGAINST THE WILL OF PERSONNEL

Article 89. (Delivery of Written Statement of Charges for Reduction of Pay Grade, etc., taken against the Will of Personnel)

When a person in the service, against his will, has his pay grade reduced, or is demoted, temporarily retired, dismissed or otherwise subjected to greatly disadvantageous action, or is about to be administered disciplinary punishment, he shall at the time of such action be given by the officer taking such action a written statement of charges fully setting forth the reasons therefor.

In cases where a person in the service considers that he has been subjected to greatly disadvantageous action specified in the preceding paragraph, he may demand delivery of the written statement of charges mentioned in the same paragraph.

Article 90. (Appeal for review) The employee subject to the action specified in Paragraph 1 of the preceding Article may, within thirty days after he has received the written statement of charges, appeal to the Commission for review thereof.

Article 91. (Investigation) On receipt of the appeal specified in the preceding Article, the Commission, or an agency or agencies designated by the Commission, shall promptly investigate the case.

In the cases specified in the preceding paragraph, if the employee subject to the action demands a hearing, such hearing shall be accorded. If requested by the employee concerned, the hearing shall be a public hearing.

The officer who took the action or his representative and the employee subject to the action may appear at all hearings, be represented by counsel of their own choosing, be heard and present witnesses, books, records and any pertinent facts and data.

Persons other than those mentioned in the preceding paragraph may present to the Commission any facts and data concerning the case.

Article 92. (Action to be taken as a Result of Investigation) If, as a result of the investigation specified in the preceding Article, the validity of the charges is established, the Commission shall confirm the action of the employing agency of government.

If, as a result of the investigation specified in the preceding Article, it is established that the action taken is at variance with the facts or otherwise is not justified, the Commission shall, in regard to the cancellation or revision of the original action, the restoration of employment rights to the person involved, the correction of any injustice that may have been done him by reason of such inaccurate accusation, and the reimbursement of any compensation lost by reason of such inaccurate accusation, take its own action for the matters under its jurisdiction, and shall, in regard to others, submit a report to the Prime Minister giving its views thereon.

Upon receipt of the report specified in the preceding paragraph, the Prime Minister shall, in compliance with such report, take such appropriate action as to give necessary direction, etc., to the head of the employing agency of government to which the employee involved is attached.

Division 3. Compensation for Injury and Disease Incurred in Line of Duty

Article 93. (Compensation for Injury and Disease Incurred in Line of Duty) In case a person in the service dies, is injured or incurs disease in line of duty or dies as the result thereof, a system of compensating the employee concerned and his immediate dependents for damage resultant of any such incident, shall be established and enforced.

The compensation system specified in the preceding paragraph shall be provided by law.

Article 94. (Matters to be provided in Law) In the compensation system mentioned in the preceding Article, the following matters shall be provided :

(1) Protection of the employee concerned against economic distress during periods of incapacity resultant of injury or disease incurred in line of duty ;

(2) Compensation of the employee for permanent or prolonged damage to his earning capacity resultant of injury or disease incurred in line of duty ;

(3) In the event of the death of the employee resultant of injury or disease incurred in line of duty, compensation for damage sustained by the surviving members of his family or those who maintain their living by an income of the employee at the time of his death.

Article 95. (Responsibility of the Commission for Drafting Compensation System) The Commission shall conduct essential studies in regard to the compensation system as soon as practicable, and submit its recommendations thereon to the Prime Minister.

Section VII. Performance on Duty

Article 96. (Basic Standard for Performance on Duty) Any person in the service, as a servant of the community, shall attend to his duties in the interest of the public, and exert his utmost in the performance of his duties.

Except as prescribed in this Law, determinations necessary for enforcing the basic standard specified in the preceding paragraph shall be provided by rules of the Commission.

Article 97. (Subscription to Oath) Personnel of the service shall subscribe to the oath of office, as provided by rules of the Commission.

Article 98. (Duty to Obey Laws and Orders and Orders of Superiors) Personnel of the service in the performance of their duties shall comply with laws and orders and observe the orders of their superiors on matters pertaining to the performance of their official duties. They may, however, express their opinions regarding the orders of their superiors.

Article 99. (Prohibition of Acts Causing Loss of Credit) No person in the service shall act in such a way as to cause the loss of credit of his position or reflect adversely on the national public service.

Article 100. (Duty to Preserve Secrecy) A person in the service shall not divulge any secret which may have come to his knowledge in the performance of his duties. This shall also apply after he has retired from office.

In case a person in the service is to make a statement concerning any secret in respect of his duties as a witness or an expert witness prescribed by law or order, he shall require the permission of the head of his employing agency of government (or in the case of a retired employee, the head of the agency of government having jurisdiction over the position he held at the time of retirement or any position similar thereto).

The permission referred to in the preceding paragraph shall not be refused, except under conditions and procedures provided by law or rules of the Commission.

Article 101. (Undivided Attention to Duty) Personnel of the service, except in cases authorized by the head of their employing agency of government because of special circumstances, shall give their full working time and occupational attention to the duties of their public position.

Article 102. (Restriction of Political Activities) No person in the service shall solicit, or receive, or be in any manner concerned in soliciting or receiving any subscription or other benefit for any political party or political purpose.

No person in the service shall be a candidate for elective public office in cases provided by rules of the Commission.

No person in the service specified by law or rules of the Commission shall be an officer of any political party or political organization.

Article 103. (Exclusion from Private Enterprise) A person in the service shall not concurrently hold a position therein and a position of an officer, adviser or councillor in any company or other organization established for the purpose of carrying on any commercial, industrial or financial or other private enterprise aiming at pecuniary gain (to be hereinafter referred to as profit-making enterprise), nor shall he carry on, on his own account, any enterprise which aims at pecuniary gain.

No person who was in the service shall, for a period of two years after leaving the service, accept an appointment involving representation of a profit-making enterprise which is closely connected with the duties of the public position he held for two years prior to retirement.

The provisions of the preceding two paragraphs shall not apply to cases wherein approval is given by the Commission on the recommendation of the head of the employing agency of government, as provided by rules of the Commission.

With respect to a profit-making enterprise, when a person in the service holds stocks, shares or other interests therein to such a degree as to be in a position to participate in the management of such enterprise, the Commission may call upon such employee to submit a report regarding his holdings of stocks, shares and other interests, as provided by rules of the Commission.

When the Commission, on the basis of the report specified in the preceding paragraph, considers it inappropriate for the person concerned to continue the holdings in question in the performance of his duties, it may serve notice to the employee to the same effect, as provided by rules of the Commission.

Upon receipt of the notice mentioned in the preceding paragraph, if the employee concerned has objection to the substance thereof, he may file a protest with the Commission within thirty days after he has received the said notice.

The provisions of Paragraphs 2 and 3 of Article 91 shall apply correspondingly to the instances of protest as specified in the preceding paragraph.

An employee who has not filed any protest as specified in Paragraph 6 and an employee whose protest has not been sustained as the result of investigation by the Commission shall divest himself of his holdings either in whole or in part within a period provided by rules of the Commission or relinquish his position, as provided by rules of the Commission.

Article 104. (Restriction of Participation in Other Undertaking or Business) If a person in the service is, in consideration of an honorarium, concurrently to hold a position therein and a position of an officer, adviser or councillor in any undertaking other than a profit-making enterprise, or to engage in any other undertaking or to carry on business, the permission of the head of the employing agency of government shall be required.

Article 105. (Scope of Duties of Personnel) Apart from taking charge of duties prescribed by law or order, personnel of the service as such shall assume no other obligation whatever.

Article 106. (Conditions of Work) Necessary determinations concerning conditions of work and other matters pertinent to the performance of duties may be provided by rules of the Commission.

The rules of the Commission mentioned in the preceding paragraph shall be consistent with the purport of this Law.

SECTION VIII. PENSION TO RETIRED EMPLOYEES

Article 107. (Basic Standard for Pension to Retired Employees) Persons in the service who have faithfully served for a reasonable period of time and retired shall be given a pension.

Necessary determinations concerning the pension mentioned in the preceding paragraph shall be provided by law.

Persons who retire as the result of injury or disease incurred in line of duty or the surviving members of those who die in line of duty may be given a pension as provided by law.

Article 108. (Object of the Pension System) The pension system shall have as its object the provision for each person, after retirement, of an income adequate to sustain him and his immediate dependents at the time of retirement or death in manner dignified and appropriate to the circumstances of retirement or death.

In the cases of Paragraph 3 of the preceding Article, due adjustments with the compensation system specified in Article 93 shall be effected.

The pension system shall be designed on a sound basis and administered by the Commission.

The Commission shall conduct essential studies in regard to the pension system as soon as practicable and submit its recommendations thereon to the Prime Minister.

Ch. IV. Penal Provisions

Article 109. A person who violates the prohibition prescribed in Article 39 shall be sentenced not to exceed three years in penal servitude or fined not to exceed ten thousand yen.

Money or other benefit given or received by the person mentioned in the preceding paragraph shall be confiscated. When it is not possible to collect such amount either in whole or in part, its value shall be sought and collected.

Article 110. A person falling under one of the following cases shall be sentenced not to exceed one year in penal servitude or fined not to exceed five thousand yen.

(1) A person who has been subpoenaed as a witness in accordance with the provision of Paragraph 2 of Article 17 and has made a false statement;

(2) A person who has been ordered to produce books, records or copies thereof in accordance with the provision of Paragraph 2 of Article 17 and has produced false books, records or copies thereof ;

(3) A person who violates the prohibition prescribed in Article 40 or Article 41 ;

(4) A person who violates the prohibition prescribed in Paragraph 2 of Article 103.

Article 111. A person who has been subpoenaed as a witness in accordance with the provision of Paragraph 2 of Article 17 and has not responded, except for just cause, or who, in accordance with the provision of the same paragraph, has been ordered to produce books, records or copies thereof and has not complied with such order without any just cause shall be fined not to exceed three thousand yen.

Supplementary Provisions

Article 1. In this Law the provision of Article 2 of the Supplementary Provisions shall be enforced from 1 November 1947, and other provisions from 1 July 1948.

The Commission shall be set up not later than 1 January 1949.

In this Law provisions other than those concerning the establishment of the Commission and the Performance on Duty (inclusive of the supplementary provisions related thereto) may be gradually applied as practicable, as provided by law or rules of the Commission.

Article 2. A Temporary National Personnel Commission (to be hereinafter referred to as the Temporary Commission) shall be set up under the jurisdiction of the Prime Minister.

The Temporary Commission shall have the power of investigating positions, employment situations and other matters pertaining to personnel administration in general and making other preparations in so far as are necessary for the enforcement of this Law.

The Temporary Commission shall exercise the powers of the Commission as provided in this Law from 1 July 1948, up to the installation of the Commission. In this case, 'the Commission' in this Law shall be taken to read 'the Temporary Commission' and 'Commissioners' shall be taken to read 'members of the Temporary Commission'.

The Temporary Commission shall be composed of a chairman and two members.

The chairman and members of the Temporary Commission shall retire upon the installation of the Commission. In this case the chairman of the Temporary Commission shall promptly hand over charge to the Chairman of the Commission.

The provisions of Paragraph 1 of Article 5, Paragraphs 3 to 5 inclusive of the same Article and Paragraph 2 of Article 11 shall apply correspondingly in respect of the chairman and members.

The Temporary Commission shall have a Secretariat.

In the Secretariat of the Temporary Commission there shall be one Executive Director and necessary personnel prescribed by Cabinet Order.

Necessary determinations concerning the implementation of the powers of the Temporary Commission may be provided by Cabinet Order until 1 July 1948, after which time such determinations shall be provided by law or rules of the Commission.

Article 3. In Paragraph 6 of Article 5, the department of the university or high school shall include the department of the universities under the 'University Ordinance', the high schools under the 'High School Ordinance' or the colleges under the 'College Ordinance'.

Article 4. Of Commissioners who are appointed at the outset, the term of office of two shall, without prejudice to the provision of Paragraph 1 of Article 7, be five years for one and three years for the other. In this case, which Commissioner shall have which term of office shall be decided by the Prime Minister.

Article 5. In case Commissioners other than the Chairman are simultaneously appointed from the outset, in applying the provision of Paragraph 3 of Article 11, 'a senior Commissioner' shall be taken to read 'a Commissioner on a longer term of office'.

Article 6. Dismissals by disciplinary decision referred to in Item 3 of Article 38 shall include those effected under the provisions heretofore in force.

Article 7. The temporary retirement or disciplinary punishment of a person who, under the regulations heretofore in force, has been ordered to be temporarily retired or has been under disciplinary proceedings or has been subjected to disciplinary action shall be the same as heretofore.

Article 8. The provision of Item 2 or Item 3 of Article 82 shall also apply to acts committed before the application of the provisions of the same Article.

Article 9. On a date to be later established by the Commission, persons actually holding positions designated by the Commission shall, as provided by rules of the Commission, be regarded as having qualified themselves in the examination or the evaluation based on this Law or otherwise as having possessed the qualifications necessary for the grade and class to which the positions involved belong and held the latter under the procedure based on this Law. This provision shall not, however, apply to persons specified in Article 11 of the Supplementary Provisions.

Article 10. In cases of the designation of positions specified in the preceding Article, an appointing officer may, with the approval of the Commission, extend beyond the limits specified in Paragraph 1 of Article 60 temporary employment to the positions designated in the preceding Article for a period not to exceed three years from the dates as specified in the preceding Article.

Article 11. Persons actually holding, on a date to be later established by the Commission, such positions as heads and assistant heads of external and internal bureaus of the Prime Minister's Office, the various ministries, and agencies specified by the Commission and other positions of organizational level in the service, similar to the foregoing, as designated by the Commission, shall, as provided by rules of the Commission, be deemed on that date as having received temporary employment prescribed in the preceding Article ; such temporary employment, however, shall not exceed three years from 1 July 1948.

In regard to the positions as specified in the preceding paragraph, it shall be the duty of the Commission by greatest diligence to make allocations of positions and administer the necessary examinations or evaluations under this Law within two years after 1 July 1948.

Article 12. The provision of Article 100 shall also apply to former personnel who had retired before the enforcement of the provision of the same Article.

Article 13. In case it is necessary to make exceptions to this Law on the basis of the special nature of the duties and responsibilities of any positions in the regular government service, such as diplomatic and consular officials, other personnel stationed abroad, school-teachers, court officials or public procurators, such exceptions may be separately provided by law or rules of the Commission. These exceptions shall not, however, be contrary to the spirit of Article 1 of this Law.

Article 14. Interim exceptions and other matters necessary for the revision or abrogation of the provisions of the laws and orders concerning personnel which are actually valid at the time of enforcing or applying the various provisions of this Law, and for applying the provisions of this Law to persons subject to those of such laws and orders shall be provided by law or rules of the Commission.

Political Reorientation of Japan, Appendix H:21, pp. 1022-35.

GENERAL MACARTHUR'S LETTER TO PRIME MINISTER
KATAYAMA CONCERNING POLICE REFORM AND
REORGANIZATION OF THE JUSTICE MINISTRY

Dear Mr Prime Minister :

I have given careful consideration to your letter of 3 September and to the plan for the reorganization of the police system submitted therewith. I fully understand your difficulty in reaching an acceptable compromise between the two divergent schools of thought of which you speak—a compromise which will prove adequately effective to meet the requisites for the preservation of law and order within Japan, and yet at the same time not impinge upon the ideal of human liberty to which the people of Japan are now committed, nor upon that fundamental principle indispensable to a democratic society so aptly stated in the Preamble of the Constitution of Japan, 'Government is a sacred trust of the people, the authority for which is derived from the people, and the benefits of which are enjoyed by the people'.

I am in full accord with the proposition that the realities of the situation require the maintenance of a national rural police unit to maintain law and order in the rural areas and available to the National Government to meet emergency conditions with which police forces available to the several local governments may be unable adequately to cope, and your suggested increase in the overall authorized police strength to 125,000 men, to provide for such a national rural police meets with my full approval. I am not in accord, however, with the idea of, nor the necessity for, delaying the decentralization of the police power now existing, as I feel that the preservation of that power in its present centralized form is wholly incompatible with the spirit and intent of the new Constitution and inimical to democratic growth.

It has been a dominant characteristic of modern totalitarian dictatorships, as it was in Japan's feudalistic past, to establish and maintain a strongly centralized police bureaucracy headed by a chief executive officer beyond the reach of popular control. Indeed, the strongest weapon of the military clique in Japan in the decade prior to the war was the absolute authority exercised by the national government over the thought police and the Kempei Tai, extending down to prefectural levels of government. Through these media, the military were enabled to spread a network of political espionage, suppress freedom of speech, of assembly, and even of thought, and by means of tyrannical oppression to degrade the dignity of the individual. Japan was thus in the fullest sense a police state.

It is in recognition of this condition that the police system must be so reorganized as to provide what you so clearly describe in your letter as a 'fundamental remedy of the misuse of the police by the state power as in the past'. In the achievement of this objective, the potentiality of a police state inherent in centralized control must scrupulously be avoided. It should never again be possible for anti-democratic elements, either of the extreme right or the extreme left, to enmesh the freedom of the people in a web of police terrorism.

This basic objective can best be accomplished by the thorough decentralization of the police system in accordance with the principle of local autonomy embodied in the Constitution. Each city and town should be responsible for the preservation of law and order within its boundaries through its own local police system independent of the central government and headed by a police chief to be appointed and removable by a commission composed of three civilian members appointed by the mayor of the city or town with the consent of the local assembly and holding office for a fixed term of years. At the prefectural level there should also be a corresponding commission similarly appointed which will exercise operational control over the national rural police operating within the boundaries of that prefecture, reserving to the national government administrative authority over such national rural police wherever stationed.

Such a reformation of the Japanese police system would be in consonance with the general pattern of the reorganization of the Japanese governmental structure, integrating police officials and services as agencies of the people at the appropriate levels of government. Action towards such end should proceed immediately upon enactment of the appropriate statute.

The national government should allocate the necessary funds until such time as local financing is possible. So long as it is necessary for the national government to make allocations of funds, the strength of the police in the various localities should remain fixed at the present number, but after provisions have been made for the localities to assume the financial burden, the responsibility for determining the necessary numbers within their respective borders should belong to the cities and towns, in accordance with local requirements.

The necessary legislation should, of course, be enacted at the present session of the Diet. If vigorously prosecuted, I believe that completion of the plan may be accomplished within a period of ninety days thereafter.

As to an appropriate organization on the national level, I believe that there should be created directly under the authority of the Cabinet a Public Safety Commission composed of five members who have not been career officials, either in the police or the civil service.

Such commission should be appointed by the Prime Minister, with the consent of the Diet, and should hold office for a fixed term of years.

To prevent the resurgence in disguised form of a centrally controlled national police network no channel of command should exist between the national rural police unit and the local police forces, but technical channels of communication should, of course, be permitted in the interest of overall efficiency and to facilitate a relationship of mutual assistance, liaison and co-ordination. The intervention by the national government into control over prefectural or local police affairs should temporarily be provided for, however, in the event of a national emergency when, upon the recommendation of the National Public Safety Commission, the Prime Minister might assume operational control over prefectural units of the national rural police force, subject to ratification by the Diet within twenty days. In this way the authority of the prefectural governor may be protected against arbitrary police interference by the national government, at the same time affording adequate safeguard for the national interest.

In the past, one of the ill-conceived aspects of the Japanese police system was the exercise by police officials of numerous administrative functions not related to the task of investigation and apprehension of criminals or the preservation of public order. All such functions should be exercised by non-police representatives of the particular ministry having responsibility for such matters, and wherever proper should be decentralized to local public entities in accordance with the provisions of the Constitution conferring upon such entities 'the right to manage their property, affairs, and administration'.

Closely related to the law enforcement process is, as you have specifically pointed out in your letter, the subject of reform in the judicial administrative system. Under the Constitution of Japan, the Supreme Court is now vested with the administration of judicial affairs and the rule-making power. With the establishment of an independent judiciary, the Ministry of Justice no longer is responsible for the determination of rules of procedure and of practice, the internal discipline of the courts, or other attributes of the judicial process. Moreover, with the diminution of the role of the procurators in the administration of justice and their subordination to the rule-making power of the Supreme Court, the basic attributes of the procuratorial system under the Ministry of Justice have been radically revised.

On the other hand, to the Cabinet, as the executive branch of the government, is expressly delegated the responsibility for executing the provisions of the Constitution and of the laws enacted by the National Diet, as well as for determining questions of amnesty, commutation of punishment, and restoration of rights. To reflect adequately this constitutional separation of powers, it would seem desirable that the Ministry of Justice, within which authority over adjudicative functions has been traditionally intermingled with executive power, be replaced by an Attorney-General, sitting in the Cabinet as a Minister of State and serving as the chief legal adviser to the executive branch of the government.

To administer the laws effectively requires the closest co-ordination between police officials charged with the apprehension of offenders against the national laws, and public attorneys charged with the prosecution thereof. The establishment of an Attorney-General's Office with the responsibility of conducting all litigation, criminal and civil, in which the government has a direct interest, and of furnishing all legal advice to the Prime Minister and other Ministers of State in the discharge of their duties, would I believe provide a mechanism for such close co-ordination, facilitate the faithful execution of the laws, and support the independence of the judiciary as the bulwark of the liberties of the people. Consistent with this concept of an Attorney-General, the present Legislative Bureau of the Cabinet can be dispensed with in the interest of governmental efficiency and economy.

Within the framework of the plan outlined in your letter, modified in the manner I have indicated, I feel confident that a law enforcement system may be evolved in Japan which will satisfy all requirements of public safety, which will provide for the definitive separation of the administrative from the judicial process, and which at the same time will comply meticulously with the underlying principles of the Constitution. In this connexion it should be borne in mind that, in the final analysis, police power in the preservation of law and order in a democratic society does not attain its maximum strength through oppressive controls imposed upon the people from above, but rather does it find infinitely greater strength in the relationship of servant of, and answerable directly to, the people. Thereby, and thereby alone, may it encourage respect for the people's laws through confidence and paternalistic pride in the police as the law enforcement agency of the people themselves.

I am hopeful that the legislation necessary to give effect to these programmes in the reorganization of government can be completed in time for consideration at the current session of the National Diet. To such end do not hesitate to call upon this headquarters for any assistance which you believe would be helpful.

Sincerely yours,

The Prime Minister,   DOUGLAS MACARTHUR
Tokyo, Japan.

Political Reorientation of Japan, Appendix D:7, pp. 705-6.

POLICE LAW

In conformity with the Constitution of Japan which preserves the ideal of human liberty for the nation and with a view to furthering the principle of Local Autonomy, the National Diet, for the purpose of maintaining order, strengthening the enforcement of statute, securing the maximum of human dignity through recognition of individual and communal responsibility, and establishing systems of democratic authority vested in the people to safeguard the rights and liberties of the individual, does enact the Police Law as follows :

Ch. I. General Provisions

Article 1. The police shall have charge of protecting lives, persons and properties of the people, detecting crimes, apprehending suspects and maintaining public safety.

Activities of the police shall be strictly limited to the extent mentioned in the preceding in any way such as to interfere with the civil liberties and rights of the individual, as guaranteed in the Constitution of Japan.

Article 2. The term 'administrative control' as used in the present Law shall comprehend all matters relating to the organization and budget of the police as well as to personnel affairs of its officials.

The term 'operational control' as used in the present Law shall comprehend the matters relating to the following affairs :

(1) Maintenance of public order ;
(2) Protection of life and property ;
(3) Prevention and suppression of crimes ;
(4) Detection of crimes and apprehension of suspects ;
(5) Control of traffic ;
(6) Serving of warrants of arrest and of detention and other affairs ordered by the Court, Judge or Public Procurator and provided for by law.

The term 'crimes' as used in the present Law shall include violations of economic laws and ordinances, but shall not be limited thereto.

Article 3. The oath of office taken by all categories of personnel subject to this Law shall include the obligation to defend and uphold the Constitution and the laws of Japan.

Ch. II. National Rural Police

SECTION 1. NATIONAL PUBLIC SAFETY COMMISSION

Article 4. There shall be established under the jurisdiction of the Prime Minister a National Public Safety Commission and a

National Rural Police Force not to exceed 30,000 of police personnel in strength, the expenses of which shall be borne by the National Government.

The National Public Safety Commission shall take charge of the following affairs :

(1)   Matters concerning the maintenance and control of the police communication system (except systems connecting the headquarters of the police of autonomous entities with lower organizations within their jurisdiction), provided that the police of autonomous entities shall have access to police communication systems for the purpose of communicating with other police of autonomous entities and with the National Rural Police ;

(2)   Matters concerning the maintenance and control of criminal identification facilities ;

(3)   Matters concerning the maintenance and control of police education and training facilities ;

(4)   Other matters concerning the administrative control of the National Rural Police ;

(5)   Matters concerning criminal identification and criminal statistics ;

(6)   Matters concerning the preparation and execution of plans for integrating the police to cope with a state of national emergency ;

(7)   Matters concerning the control of the Imperial Guard, and policing of those buildings and facilities occupied by the Diet, Cabinet Ministries (including the Prime Minister's Office and Attorney-General's Office), Board of Audit and the Supreme Court within the Metropolis upon request of the agencies concerned.

Article 5.   The National Public Safety Commission shall be composed of five members.

Members of the Commission shall be appointed by the Prime Minister with the consent of both Houses of the Diet from among persons who have not been in the police service or who have not the career of public servants in the Government or public offices (except those who have been either elected or appointed through the public election or the election or resolution of one or both Houses of the Diet or of the Assemblies of local autonomous entities subsequent to 2 September 1945).

If, in regard to the appointment of a member of the Commission, the House of Representatives consents, but the House of Councillors does not, the consent of the House of Representatives shall be the consent of the Diet in conformity with the instance mentioned in Article 67, Paragraph 2 of the Constitution of Japan.

A person falling under any of the following numbered items shall not be able to become a member of the Commission :

(1)   An incompetent or quasi-incompetent person, or a bankrupt who has not been rehabilitated ;

(2)   A person who has been sentenced to imprisonment or a heavier punishment ;

(3)   A person who, on and after the day of enforcement of the Constitution of Japan, has organized or joined a political party or any other organization advocating destruction by violence of the Constitution of Japan or the Government formed thereunder.

The appointment of members of the Commission shall not result in three or more of them belonging to the same political party.

Article 6.   The provisions of Section 7 of Chapter III of the National Public Service Law shall apply *mutatis mutandis* to members of the Commission.

Members of the Commission shall not become officers of a political party or any other political organization.

Article 7.   The term of office of members of the Commission shall be five years, provided that a member filling a vacancy shall remain in office during the rest of the term of office of his predecessor.

Members of the Commission may be reappointed. .

Article 8.   In case a member of the Commission has come to fall under any of the items of Article 5, Paragraph 4, he shall *ipso facto* be relieved of his office.

The Prime Minister may, in case he considers that a member of the Commission has been incapacitated from performing his duties on account of a mental or physical defect or that he has violated his official obligations or committed a misconduct ill befitting a member of the Commission, dismiss him with the consent of both Houses of the Diet.

The Prime Minister shall dismiss the following members of the Commission with the consent of both Houses of the Diet :

(1)   All except two of such members of the Commission as have simultaneously come to belong to the same political party to which none of the members have belonged ;

(2)   All except one of such members of the Commission as have come to belong to a political party to which one of the members of the Commission has already belonged.

The provisions of Article 5, Paragraph 3, shall apply *mutatis mutandis* to the cases mentioned in the preceding two paragraphs.

The Prime Minister shall immediately dismiss a member of the Commission who has come to belong to a political party to which two members of the Commission have already belonged.

Except in the cases mentioned in Paragraphs 2 and 3 and the preceding Paragraph, no member of the Commission shall be dismissed against his will.

Article 9. Members of the Commission shall receive a salary similar to that of the Procurator-General.

Article 10. There shall be a chairman of the Commission who shall be selected and appointed through co-optation by its members. The term of office of the chairman shall be one year, provided that he may be reappointed.

The chairman shall preside over the affairs of the National Public Safety Commission.

Section 2. Executive Office of the National Public Safety Commission

Article 11. There shall be established in the Public Safety Commission as its executive office a headquarters of the National Rural Police to deal with affairs concerning matters within the authority of the National Public Safety Commission.

Article 12. There shall be appointed a Director-General in the Headquarters of the National Rural Police.

The Director-General shall be appointed, and dismissed for cause, by the National Public Safety Commission in accordance with the provisions of the National Public Service Law.

Article 13. The Director-General shall be subject to the direction and supervision of the National Public Safety Commission and control the affairs of the Headquarters of the National Rural Police.

Article 14. In the Headquarters of the National Rural Police, there shall be no more than five divisions, comprising in them General Affairs Division, Police Affairs Division and Criminal Investigation Division.

There shall be attached to the Headquarters of the National Rural Police a Police College.

The Police College shall train the pre-service and in-service police personnel of the National Rural Police and also, upon request of the police of autonomous entities, may train such personnel thereof.

Article 15. In the Headquarters of the National Rural Police, there shall be an Assistant-Director, not more than five Chiefs of Divisions and police personnel, other necessary subordinate personnel and subordinate organs as provided for by the National Public Safety Commission.

The personnel mentioned in the preceding paragraph shall be appointed, and dismissed for cause, by the Director-General of the Headquarters of the National Rural Police in accordance with the provisions of the National Public Service Law.

Article 16. The whole country shall be divided into six Police Regions and there shall be established in each Police Region a Headquarters of the Police Region as a local office of the National Rural

Police to take charge of the assigned affairs of the Headquarters of the National Rural Police.

The area and name of each Police Region and the location and name of the Headquarters of each Police Region shall be in accordance with the appended list.

Article 17. In the Headquarters of each Police Region, there shall be a Director, Police personnel and other necessary personnel and organs as provided for by the National Public Safety Commission.

The organization shall follow the pattern as established for the National Rural Police Headquarters.

The personnel provided for in the preceding paragraph shall be appointed, and dismissed for cause, by the Director-General of the Headquarters of the National Rural Police in accordance with the provisions of the National Public Service Law.

Article 18. The Directors of the Headquarters of Police Regions shall be subject to the direction and supervision of the Director-General of the Headquarters of the National Rural Police, deal with the affairs of the Headquarters of Police Regions and administratively co-ordinate and promote the uniformity of the National Rural Police of To, Do and Prefectures under their jurisdiction.

The Directors of the Headquarters of Police Regions and Public Safety Commissions of To, Do and Prefectures shall maintain close liaison and adequately co-operate with each other in regard to police matters.

Article 19. There shall be attached to the Headquarters of each National Rural Police Region a Regional Police School.

The Regional Police School shall train the pre-service and in-service police personnel of the National Rural Police and also, upon request of the police of autonomous entities, may train such personnel thereof.

The Regional Police Schools and the Police College shall be maintained and operated by the National Rural Police.

Section 3. Public Safety Commission of To (Metropolis), Do (Hokkaido) and Prefectures

Article 20. There shall be established under the jurisdiction of the Governors of To, Do and Prefectures Public Safety Commissions of To, Do and Prefectures.

The Public Safety Commissions of To, Do and Prefectures shall exercise operational control over the National Rural Police of To, Do and Prefectures.

Article 21. The Public Safety Commissions of To, Do and Prefectures shall each be composed of three members.

Members of the Commission shall be appointed by the Metropolitan, Hokkaido or Prefectural Governor with the consent of the Metropolitan, Hokkaido or Prefectural Assembly from among persons of the respective Metropolitan, Hokkaido or Prefectural Assembly and who have not been in the police service or have not the career of public servants in the Government or public office (except those who have been either elected or appointed through the public election or the election or resolution of one or both Houses of the Diet or of the Assemblies of local autonomous entities subsequent to 2 September 1945).

A person falling under any of the following items shall not become a member of the Commission :

(1)   A bankrupt who has not been rehabilitated ;

(2)   A person whose sentence of imprisonment or a heavier punishment has been executed ;

(3)   A person who, on and after the date of enforcement of the Constitution of Japan, has organized or joined a political party or any other organization advocating destruction by violence of the Constitution of Japan or the Government formed thereunder.

The appointment of members of the Commission shall not result in two or more of them belonging to the same political party.

Article 22.   Members of the Commission shall not be able to become concurrently members of the Assemblies or salaried personnel of the Metropolis, Hokkaido, Prefectures, Special Wards, cities, towns or villages, or officers of a political party or any other political organization.

In addition to the preceding paragraph, matters concerning the performance of duties of members of the Commission shall be fixed by Metropolitan, Hokkaido or Prefectural Regulations in line with the provisions of Section 7 of Chapter III of the National Public Servants Law. However, the restrictions provided for in Articles 103 and 104 of the same Law shall not apply except in case the Governors of To, Do and Prefectures consider that a member of the Commission has been incapacitated from his service ; and with regard to the service of members of the Commission it shall be fixed by the Public Safety Commission of To, Do and Prefectures.

Article 23.   The term of office of members of the Commission shall be three years, provided that a member filling a vacancy shall remain in office during the rest of the term of office of his predecessor.

Members of the Commission may be reappointed.

Article 24.   In case a member of the Commission falls under any of the following items, he shall *ipso facto* be relieved of his office :

(1)   In case he has come to fall under any of the Items of Article 21, Paragraph 3 ;

(2) In case he has ceased to have the right to be elected as a member of the respective Metropolitan, Hokkaido or Prefectural Assembly.

The provisions of Articles 86, 87 and Article 88, Paragraph 2 of the Local Autonomy Law shall apply *mutatis mutandis* to the request of dismissal of a member of the Commission provided that 'more than one-third of the total number of persons' used in Article 86, Paragraph 1 of the same Law shall read 'more than one-third of the total number of persons who have the right to vote within the jurisdiction of respective National Rural Police of To, Do and Prefectures'.

The Governors of To, Do and Prefectures may, in case they consider that a member of the Commission has been incapacitated from performing his duties on account of a mental or physical defect or that he has violated his official obligations or committed a misconduct ill befitting a member of the Commission, dismiss him with the consent of the Assemblies of To, Do and Prefectures.

In case two or more members of the Commission have come to belong to the same political party, such members except one of them shall be dismissed by the Governors of To, Do and Prefectures with the consent of the Assemblies of To, Do and Prefectures, provided that the Governors of To, Do and Prefectures shall immediately dismiss the members of the Commission who have come to belong to a political party to which one of the members of the Commission has already belonged.

Except in the cases mentioned in the preceding two Paragraphs, no member of the Commission shall be dismissed against his will.

Article 25. To, Do and Prefectures shall provide members of the Commission with remuneration and compensation for such expenses as they may require for performing their duties.

In regard to the remuneration and compensation of expenses mentioned in the preceding Paragraph, the provisions of Article 203, Paragraph 3 and Article 206 of the Local Autonomy Law shall apply.

Article 26. There shall be a chairman in each of the Public Safety Commissions of To, Do and Prefectures who shall be selected through co-optation by the members. The term of office of the chairman shall be one year, provided that he may be reappointed.

The chairman shall preside over the affairs of the Public Safety Commission of the respective To, Do and Prefectures.

SECTION 4. NATIONAL RURAL POLICE OF TO (METROPOLIS), DO (HOKKAIDO) AND PREFECTURES

Article 27. The National Rural Police of To, Do and Prefectures shall, within the boundaries of the respective To, Do and Prefectures (except the areas under the jurisdiction of the police of autonomous entities), carry out those functions as listed in Article 2, Paragraph 2.

Article 28. There shall be established not more than one To or Prefecture headquarters of the National Rural Police within each To and Prefecture at the places where the Governments of To and Prefectures are situated. In Do (Hokkaido) there shall be established not more than 14 headquarters of the National Rural Police in the administrative sub-divisions, one of which shall be at the place where the Government of Do (Hokkaido) is situated.

The area under the jurisdiction of the National Rural Police of To, Do and Prefectures shall be divided into Police Districts, and there shall be established a police station for each Police District.

The area of each Police District and the location, name and jurisdiction of each police station shall be determined by the National Rural Police.

There shall be established police boxes or police sub-stations as lower organizations of police stations.

Article 29. There shall be established branches of the National Rural Police of To, Do and Prefectures at necessary places to have charge of liaison between the National Rural Police of To, Do and Prefectures and the police of autonomous entities and the maintenance and control of the police communication systems under the jurisdiction of the National Rural Police.

Article 30. The Chiefs of the Headquarters of the National Rural Police of To, Do and Prefectures (hereinafter to be called the Chief of Police of To, Do and Prefectures) shall be appointed, and dismissed for cause, by the Directors of the Headquarters of Police Regions with the consent of the Director-General of the Headquarters of the National Rural Police in accordance with the provisions of National Public Service Law.

Article 31. The Chiefs of Police of To, Do and Prefectures shall be subject to the operational control of the Public Safety Commissions of To, Do and Prefectures and subject to the administrative control of the Directors of Police Regions.

Article 32. The Chiefs of Police of To, Do and Prefectures shall control the police communication systems under the jurisdiction of the National Rural Police which are within the boundaries of the respective To, Do and Prefectures.

Article 33. There shall be established in the National Rural Police Headquarters of To, Do and Prefectures necessary divisions and sections (including structures concerning criminal identification and criminal statistics).

Article 34. There may be attached to the National Rural Police of To, Do and Prefectures :

The Police Schools of To, Do and Prefectures shall train the pre-service and in-service police personnel of the National Rural Police and also, upon request of the police of autonomous entities, may train such personnel thereof.

Article 35. In the National Rural Police of To, Do and Prefectures, there shall be police personnel who are Superintendents, Inspectors, Assistant Inspectors, Sergeants and Policemen, and other necessary personnel, in addition to the Chief of Police.

Ranks of police personnel shall be Chief of Police, Superintendent, Inspector, Assistant Inspector, Sergeant and Policeman.

Police personnel shall take charge of police affairs subject to the direction and supervision of their superiors.

Article 36. The personnel mentioned in the preceding Article, Paragraph 1 shall be appointed, and dismissed for cause, by the Chiefs of Police of To, Do and Prefectures in accordance with the provisions of the National Public Service Law, provided that no such personnel shall be placed on duty with the National Rural Police until he has undergone a course of basic police training.

Necessary matters concerning the oath, training and education, formality and uniform of police personnel shall be determined by the National Public Safety Commission.

Article 37. The chiefs of police stations shall be Superintendents or Inspectors.

The chiefs of police stations shall be subject to the direction and supervision of the Chiefs of Police of To, Do and Prefectures, execute police affairs within their jurisdiction and direct and supervise the personnel of police stations.

Article 38. The chiefs of police sub-stations shall be Inspectors or Assistant Inspectors.

The chiefs of police sub-stations shall be subject to the direction and supervision of the Chiefs of Police of To, Do and Prefectures, execute the affairs provided for in Article 29 and direct and supervise the personnel of police sub-stations.

Article 39. Detailed matters concerning the organs and officials of the National Rural Police of To, Do and Prefectures shall be fixed by the National Public Safety Commission.

Ch. III. Police of Autonomous Entities

SECTION 1. GENERAL PROVISIONS

Article 40. Cities or urban communities having five thousand population or over (hereinafter called cities, towns and villages) shall be responsible for the maintenance of police and enforcement of law and order within their boundaries.

The urban communities provided for in the preceding paragraph shall be given public notice by the Cabinet Order in accordance with the population based on the latest census announced in the Official Gazette.

Article 41. The police of cities, towns and villages shall perform all functions in matters listed in Article 2, Paragraph 2.

Article 42. Expenses necessary for the police of autonomous entities shall be borne by the respective cities, towns and villages.

SECTION 2. PUBLIC SAFETY COMMISSIONS OF CITIES, TOWNS AND VILLAGES

Article 43. There shall be established under the jurisdiction of the mayors of cities and headmen of towns and villages Public Safety Commissions of cities, towns and villages to control the police within the boundaries of the respective city, town and village.

Article 44. In regard to the organization and operation of the Public Safety Commissions of cities, towns and villages and the qualification, appointment, prohibition of the concurrent holding of other offices, performance of duties, term of office, retirement, dismissal, remuneration and compensation of expenses of members of such Commissions, the provisions of Articles 21 to 23 inclusive, Article 24, Paragraphs 1, 3 to 5 inclusive, Articles 25 and 26 shall apply *mutatis mutandis*, provided that in case a member of the Commission is to be dismissed in consequence of the request of dismissal in accordance with the provisions of the Local Autonomy Law, he shall lose his office irrespective of the provisions of Article 24, Paragraph 5. And 'To, Do and Prefectures' as used in Articles 21 to 26, inclusive, shall read 'cities, towns and villages', 'Governors of To, Do and Prefectures' as used herein shall read 'mayors of cities and headmen of towns and villages' and 'regulations of To, Do and Prefectures' as used therein shall read 'regulations of cities, towns and villages'.

SECTION 3. POLICE OF CITIES, TOWNS AND VILLAGES

Article 45. There shall be established one or more police stations in each city, town and village.

Where there are two or more police stations, there shall be established a Headquarters of the Police of cities, towns and villages.

The location, name and jurisdiction of each police station and the name and organization of the Headquarters of the Police of cities, towns and villages shall be determined by By-laws of cities, towns and villages after consulting with the Public Safety Commissions of cities, towns and villages.

Article 46. In the police of cities, towns and villages there shall be a Chief of Police and police personnel of the ranks necessary and consistent with efficient policing in accordance with the provisions of this Law.

The provisions of Article 35, Paragraphs 2 and 3 shall apply *mutatis mutandis* to the police personnel of cities, towns and villages referred to in the preceding paragraph.

The fixed number of police personnel of cities, towns and villages shall be determined by the local entities under by-laws in accordance with local requirements, and shall not exceed 95,000, provided that until such time as local autonomy in financial matters has been established, the fixed number of police personnel of cities, towns and villages shall be in accordance with the standards fixed by Cabinet Order. Such standards shall be fixed according to the population of cities, towns and villages and according to the ranks of police personnel necessary for efficient policing, administration of police and supervision of police. Such standards shall also specify the numbers and types of professional, technical, clerical and maintenance employees necessary for efficient policing in accordance with city, town and village population. Readjustment in the allocation of the total personnel strength of 95,000 shall be made only through legislation enacted by the Diet after such time as local autonomy in financial matters has been established.

Article 47. The Chiefs of Police of cities, towns and villages shall be appointed, and dismissed for cause, by the Public Safety Commissions of cities, towns and villages in accordance with by-law.

Article 48. The Chiefs of Police of cities, towns and villages, in accordance with the standards fixed by the Public Safety Commission, shall appoint, and dismiss for cause, the police personnel of the respective city, town and village. They shall also direct and supervise such personnel.

Article 49. The chiefs of police stations shall be police personnel not lower than Assistant Inspectors. However, the Chiefs of Police of cities, towns and villages may hold such offices concurrently.

The chiefs of police stations shall be subject to the direction and supervision of their superiors, execute police affairs within their jurisdiction and direct and supervise the personnel subordinate to them.

Article 50. The appointment and dismissal, allowance, performance of duties and other matters of police personnel shall be fixed by by-laws of cities, towns and villages in line with the spirit of the National Public Service Law, provided that such persons as have not undergone a course of basic police training shall not be placed on duty with the police of cities, towns and villages except as temporary personnel thereof.

Necessary matters concerning the oath, education and training, formality and uniform of municipal police personnel shall be fixed by municipal regulations in line with the regulations to be determined by the National Public Safety Commission as provided for in Article 36, Paragraph 2, provided that the uniform shall be easily distinguishable from that of the National Rural Police.

SECTION 4. SPECIAL PROVISIONS CONCERNING SPECIAL WARDS

Article 51. In areas where special wards exist, the wards shall be collectively responsible for police within the areas of such wards.

Article 52. For such special wards there shall be established one Special Ward Public Safety Commission corresponding to Public Safety Commissions of cities, towns and villages, under the jurisdiction of the Governor of To, and members thereof shall be selected and appointed by the Governor of To with the consent of the Metropolitan Assembly.

Article 53. Except the matters provided for in the preceding two Articles, areas where special wards exist shall be considered as a city so far as the Municipal Police in such areas is concerned, and the provisions concerning the Municipal Police shall apply *mutatis mutandis.*

Ch. IV. Relationship between the National Rural Police and the Police of Autonomous Entities, and Relationship among the Police of Autonomous Entities

Article 54. There shall exist neither administrative nor operational control by the National Rural Police over the police of cities, towns and villages. These police shall be obligated to co-operate with each other.

Article 55. The police personnel of the National Rural Police may, at the request of the Public Safety Commissions of cities, towns and villages for assistance, exercise their authority in the area of the respective city, town and village under the operational control of the Public Safety Commission of the city, town or village which made the request for assistance.

Article 56. The Chiefs of Police of To, Do and Prefectures shall maintain close liaison with the Chiefs of Police of cities, towns and villages within To, Do and Prefectures.

Ch. V. Exercise of Authority Outside of Jurisdiction

Article 57. The National Rural Police and the Police of cities, towns and villages shall, in regard to a crime committed in an area within five hundred metres outside of the boundaries of the jurisdiction of the respective National Rural Police of To, Do and Prefectures or the Police of cities, towns and villages, exercise their authority also in that area.

Article 58. The National Rural Police and the Police of cities, towns and villages may, with regard to specific individual cases of criminal operations which have been conducted within the area under their jurisdiction (including here and hereinafter in this Article any area within five hundred metres outside of the boundaries of their jurisdiction) or originated in, or extended their authority beyond the boundaries of their jurisdictions for the suppression and detection of such operations and apprehension of suspects.

Article 59. In those cases where the National Rural Police maintain facilities within the autonomous entities and in those cases where the autonomous entities maintain facilities within areas outside their boundaries, the National Rural Police and Police of such autonomous entities respectively shall exercise police power and jurisdiction over such facilities.

Ch. VI. *Criminal Statistics and Criminal Identification*

Article 60. The Chiefs of Police of cities, towns and villages shall on forms and in the manner provided for by the National Public Safety Commission make reports of criminal statistics and of criminal identification consisting of evidence, photographs, finger-prints, physical description and criminal characteristics of suspects and arrested individuals to the Director-General of the Head-quarters of the National Rural Police, through the Chiefs of Police of To, Do and Prefectures.

Article 61. There shall be established facilities for criminal identification in the Headquarters of the National Rural Police, and the Headquarters of the National Rural Police of To, Do and Prefectures.

Ch. VII. *Special Measures in a State of National Emergency*

Article 62. If deemed especially necessary for the maintenance of peace and order in a state of national emergency the Prime Minister may, upon the recommendation of the National Public Safety Commission, issue a proclamation of a state of national emergency in respect of the country as a whole or any part of it.

The proclamation mentioned in the preceding paragraph shall set forth the area, outline of the situation and date of the effectuation of the proclamation.

Article 63. When the proclamation mentioned in the preceding Article has been issued, control over the whole police shall be temporarily assumed by the Prime Minister in accordance with the provisions of the present Law. In this case the Director-General of the Headquarters of the National Rural Police or the Director of the Headquarters of the Police Region shall give necessary order to, or direct, the Chiefs of Police of To, Do and Prefectures or the Chiefs of Police of cities, towns and villages within the area set forth in the proclamation.

Article 64. The Prime Minister may order the National Rural Police or the Police of cities, towns and villages outside of the area set forth in the proclamation to despatch to necessary areas the whole or a part of police personnel for assistance.

The police personnel despatched in accordance with the provisions of the preceding paragraph may perform their duties also in the area to which they have been despatched during the period of their mission there.

Article 65. The proclamation of a state of national emergency by the Prime Minister according to Article 62 must be ratified by the Diet within twenty days of the date of the proclamation. If the House of Representatives is dissolved, such ratification shall be obtained from the House of Councillors convoked in emergency session provided for in Article 54 of the Constitution of Japan.

If no ratification of the proclamation of a state of national emergency has been made according to the provisions of the preceding paragraph within the period mentioned therein or if the ratification has been rejected, the proclamation of a state of national emergency shall lose its effect for the future.

Article 66. The Prime Minister shall, in case he has proclaimed a state of national emergency, promptly proclaim the rescission of the former proclamation when he deems that its necessity has ceased to exist. He must do so if the Diet so directs.

In regard to the proclamation of the rescission mentioned in the preceding paragraph and other duties of the Prime Minister provided for in the present Law, the National Public Safety Commission shall always give necessary advice to the Prime Minister.

Ch. VIII. *Miscellaneous Provisions*

Article 67. The relationship between the Public Safety Commissions of cities, towns and villages and police personnel on the one hand and the Public Procurators on the other shall be otherwise determined by Law.

The National Public Safety Commission shall constantly maintain close liaison with the Procurator General.

Article 68. In case an alteration has taken place in the area which shall be under the jurisdiction of the National Rural Police of To, Do and Prefectures and the area which shall be under the jurisdiction of the Police of cities, towns and villages, or in case an area which shall be under the jurisdiction of the Police of one city, town or village, or two or more cities, towns and villages has been divided into areas which shall be under the jurisdiction of the Police of two or more cities, towns and villages or has become an area which shall be under the jurisdiction of the Police of one city, town or village, measures consequent upon the alteration of jurisdiction shall be completed not later than fifty days from the day the alteration has become necessary.

Until the measures mentioned in the preceding paragraph have been completed, the former police jurisdiction shall prevail in the area concerned. In the case of the latter part of the preceding paragraph, duties of the former mayor of a city or headman of a town or village shall be performed by mayors of cities and headmen of towns and villages of two or more areas through mutual consultation or by the mayor of a city or the headman of a town or village.

Supplementary Provisions

Article 1. The date of enforcement of the present Law shall be fixed by Cabinet Order in respect of each provision within a period not exceeding ninety days of the day of its enactment.

Article 2. The term of office of the members of the National Public Safety Commission to be appointed for the first time after the enforcement of the present Law shall be one year for one of the five members, two years for one member, three years for one member, four years for one member, and five years for one member.

The term of office for each member provided for in the preceding paragraph shall be determined by the Commission by lot.

Article 3. The term of office of the members of the Public Safety Commissions of To, Do and Prefectures and the Public Safety Commissions of cities, towns and villages to be appointed for the first time after the enforcement of the present Law shall be one year for one of the three members, two years for another and three years for another.

The term of office for each member provided for in the preceding paragraph shall be determined by the respective Commission by lot.

Article 4. The National Public Service Law shall be considered as already in effect within the extent necessary for the application of the present Law.

In the case mentioned in the preceding paragraph, the authority of the National Personnel Commission shall, pending its establishment as provided for in the National Public Service Law, be exercised by the Temporary National Personnel Commission in conformity with the instance mentioned in Article 2 of the Supplementary Provisions of that Law.

Article 5. During one year after the enforcement of the present Law, the personnel in charge of the National Rural Police or the police of autonomous entities may, in case there exists no list of candidates for appointment or in case there is especial necessity, be temporarily appointed from among the persons who have qualifications necessary for such officials of the central government or the local governments as are corresponding to the respective personnel in accordance with the existing laws and orders.

Article 6. The appointment and dismissal, allowances and performance of duties of the police personnel of the National Rural Police and other necessary matters concerning such personnel shall still conform for the time being to existing instances of the police personnel of the Metropolitan Police Board and Prefectures, pending the establishment of rules of the National Personnel Commission concerning police personnel or the determination by the National Public Safety Commission in accordance with provisions of Article 36, Paragraph 2.

Article 7. In case an official of the National Government who is in the service of the Metropolitan Police Board or the Hokkaido or Prefectural Police Division at the time of the enforcement of the present Law has consecutively become a member of the personnel of the Municipal Police, he shall be considered as being in service with the same status as before, and the provisions of the Pension Law shall apply to him *mutatis mutandis* for the time being. In case this member of the personnel of the Municipal Police has become a member of the personnel of the National Rural Police, his tenure of office as a member of the personnel of the Municipal Police shall be added to the years of his service as a public servant.

In case an official of the Metropolis, Hokkaido or a Prefecture who is in the service of the Metropolitan Police Board or the Hokkaido or Prefectural Police Division has consecutively become a member of the personnel of the National Rural Police, his tenure of office as an official of the Metropolis, Hokkaido or Prefecture shall be added to the years of his service as a public servant so far as the application of the Pension Law is concerned.

Article 8. Expenses necessary for the Police of cities, towns and villages shall be borne by the National Treasury and the Metropolis, Hokkaido and Prefectures as provided for by Cabinet Order until such time as local autonomy in financial matters has been established.

Expenses necessary for the National Rural Police shall be borne by the National Treasury and the Metropolis, Hokkaido and Prefectures until the time mentioned in the preceding paragraph.

In regard to the appointment of police expenses to the National Treasury and to the Metropolis, Hokkaido and Prefectures, existing instances shall still be followed until the time mentioned in Paragraph 1.

Article 9. In cases where municipalities newly assume responsibility for police on or after the enforcement of the present Law, State property and Metropolitan or Prefectural property or the goods owned by the State, Metropolis, Hokkaido or Prefectures which is or are actually being used for police and surplus to the needs of National Rural Police shall, if needed by the Municipal Police, be transferred without compensation to the respective municipality ; provided that, in case there is a debt pertaining to such property or goods, the disposition of them shall be determined by mutual consultation.

Article 10. Criminal identification facilities, police communication systems and police education and training facilities under the control of the Metropolitan Police Board or the Police Division of Do, and Prefectures at the time of the enforcement of the present Law shall be maintained and controlled by the National Rural Police except the Training Schools at Atago-cho, Minato-ku, Tokyo-to and in the Palace grounds of the present Metropolitan Police Board which shall be transferred to the municipal police of Special Wards of Tokyo-to.

Article 11. All Affairs Unions and Office Affairs Unions of towns and villages existing at the time of the enforcement of the present Law shall be considered as a town or a village so far as the application of the provisions of the present Law is concerned.

Article 12. 'The respective administrative organ' as used in Articles 1 and 2 of the Administrative Enforcement Law shall mean 'the chiefs of police stations as used in Articles 37 and 49', and 'the respective administrative organ' as used in Articles 3 to 5 inclusive and 'the administrative organs' as used in Article 6 of the above mentioned Law shall include 'the chiefs of police stations' as used in Articles 37 and 49.

Article 13. Municipalities shall assume responsibility for police within their boundaries in accordance with the provisions of Article 40, Paragraph 1, as from the day the Public Safety Commission has been formed and necessary police personnel have been appointed in the respective municipality by the application of the provisions of the present Law concerning the Police of Autonomous Entities provided that the day shall not be later than ninety days after the enactment of the present Law.

Article 14. In cases where municipalities have come to assume responsibility for police within their boundaries in accordance with the provisions of the preceding Article, the Metropolitan Police Board or the Hokkaido or Prefectural Police Division shall perform its duties as the National Rural Police until the provisions of the present law concerning the National Rural Police have taken effect.

Article 15. Part of the Local Autonomy Law shall be amended as follows :

In Article 13, Paragraph 2, 'members of an electoral administration committee or inspection commissioners' shall read 'members of an electoral administration committee, inspection commissioners or members of a public safety commission of city, town or village'.

In Article 21, Paragraph 2, 'a police officer' shall read 'a member of the national police force', and 'a member of a public safety commission of an ordinary local public body and a member of a municipal police force' shall be added next to 'a revenue officer'.

In Article 86, Paragraph 1, and Article 88, Paragraph 2, 'electoral administration committee or inspection commissioner' shall read 'electoral administration committee, inspection commissioners or members of a public safety commission of city, town or village'.

In Article 121, 'an inspection commissioner' shall read 'an inspection commissioner and member of a public safety commission'.

In Article 125, 'or its inspection commissioners' shall read 'its inspection commissioners or the public safety commission of the city, town or village concerned'.

In Article 130, Paragraph 1, 'a police officer' shall read 'a police officer with competent jurisdiction'.

In Article 158, Paragraph 1, 'matters relating to police' and 'police Division' shall be deleted.

In Article 160, Paragraph 2, 'a police officer' shall read 'a police officer with competent jurisdiction'.

In Article 173, Paragraph 1, 'educational officials or police officials' shall read 'educational officials', and the same Article, Paragraph 5 shall be deleted.

In Article 277, 'Article 145' shall read 'Article 121, Article 145'.

The proviso of Article 1 of the Supplementary Provisions shall be deleted.

In Article 4 of the Supplementary Provisions, '(excluding the Metropolitan Police Board, same hereinafter)' shall be deleted.

Article 7 of the Supplementary Provisions shall be amended as follows : Article 7 (deleted).

Article 16. Part of the Law concerning the Election of the Members of the House of Representatives shall be amended as follows :

In Article 9, 'and a police officer' shall read 'a member of the national police force, a member of the public safety commission of the Metropolis, district, urban or rural prefecture, city, town or village and a member of a municipal police force'.

571

In Article 40, 'a police officer' shall read 'a police officer with competent jurisdiction'.

In Article 41, 'a police officer' shall read 'a police officer with competent jurisdiction'.

In Article 112, Paragraph 2, and Article 113, Paragraph 2, 'a police officer' shall read 'a member of the public safety commission of the Metropolis, district, urban or rural prefecture, city, town or village or a member of the national police force or a member of a municipal police force' and 'the Metropolis, district, urban or rural prefecture concerned' shall read 'the areas concerned'.

In Article 121, Paragraph 2, 'a police officer' shall read 'a police officer with competent jurisdiction'.

In Article 124, 'a police officer' shall read 'a police officer with competent jurisdiction'.

Article 17. A part of the Law concerning the Election of the Members of the House of Councillors shall be amended as follows :

In Article 7, 'and a police officer' shall read 'a member of the national police force, a member of the public safety commission of the Metropolis, district, urban or rural prefecture, city, town or village and a member of a municipal police force'.

Article 18. Part of the Law concerning People's Examination of Supreme Court Judges shall be amended as follows :

In Article 44, Paragraph 2, 'a police officer' shall read 'a member of the public safety commission of the Metropolis, urban or rural prefecture, city, town or village, a member of the national police force, or a member of a municipal police force' and 'the Metropolis, district, urban or rural prefecture concerned' shall read 'the areas concerned'.

Article 19. Provisions in other laws and ordinance relating to a police officer shall be deemed to refer to a police official with competent jurisdiction.

Political Reorientation of Japan, Appendix H : 30, pp. 1062-71.

7   *26 December* 1947

LAW ABOLISHING THE HOME MINISTRY

The Ministry for Home Affairs shall be abolished as of 31 December 1947. For this purpose, the following Imperial Ordinances shall be repealed :

Imperial Ordinance concerning the Regulations governing the Organization of the Ministry for Home Affairs.

Imperial Ordinance concerning the Regulations governing the Temporary Establishment of the Investigation Bureau in the Ministry for Home Affairs.

Imperial Ordinance concerning the Regulations governing the Organization of the Reconstruction Board.

Imperial Ordinance concerning the Regulations governing the Temporary Establishment of the Special Construction Bureau in the Reconstruction Board.

Supplementary Provisions

Functions which will remain as the responsibility of the Ministry for Home Affairs at the date of its abolition shall be handled by an Office of Domestic Affairs belonging to the jurisdiction of the Prime Minister.

Such organization and personnel of the Ministry for Home Affairs as may be needed for the conduct of the business mentioned in the preceding paragraph may be transferred as provided for by Cabinet Order.

The post of the head of the Office of Domestic Affairs may be filled by a Minister of State.

The Office of Domestic Affairs shall be of temporary character and will cease to function and exist when its functions have been transferred to other agencies or eliminated as provided by law.

The Office of Domestic Affairs may not exist in any event more than 90 days as from the day of its establishment.

Political Reorientation of Japan, Appendix H : 34, p. 1089.

8   5 *July* 1948

NATIONAL GOVERNMENT ORGANIZATION LAW

Article 1. (General Provisions) The object of this Law is to regulate the national government organization which is necessary for the efficient prosecution of national administrative affairs by establishing standards for the organization of administrative organs under the control and jurisdiction of the Cabinet.

Article 2. The national government organization shall, under the control and jurisdiction of the Cabinet, be systematically constituted of a system of administrative organs having a well-defined scope of authority and responsibility and specific functions for which they are responsible.

The national administrative organs shall, under the control and jurisdiction of the Cabinet, maintain liaison with one another so that they may consummate their administrative functions as an organic whole.

Article 3. (Establishment and Abolition of Administrative Organs, their Specific Functions, etc.) The national government organization shall be determined by this Law.

For the purpose of administrative organization the national administrative organs shall be comprised of an Office on ministerial level, Ministry, Commission or Agency. The establishment or abolition of such administrative organs shall be provided for by separate law.

Commissions and Agencies shall be those set up as independent organizations of the Prime Minister's Office, the Attorney-General's Office or each Ministry.

Administrative organs set up as provided for in Paragraph 2 shall be enumerated in the Appendix to this Law.

Article 4. The scope of authority and responsibility of administrative organs referred to in the preceding Article and specific functions for which they are responsible shall be provided for by separate law.

Article 5. (Heads of Administrative Organs) The head of the Prime Minister's Office, the Attorney-General's Office, and each Ministry shall be, respectively, the Prime Minister, the Attorney-General and a Minister of each Ministry (to be hereinafter referred to as 'each Minister'), who, as a competent Minister referred to in the Cabinet Law, shall have charge and control of their respective administrative affairs.

The Attorney-General shall be appointed by the Prime Minister from among the persons most fitted for the post. He shall be a Minister of State.

Ministers of various Ministries shall be appointed by the Prime Minister from among Ministers of State. This shall not, however, preclude the Prime Minister from assuming in person any of those posts.

Article 6. The head of a Commission shall be Chairman, and of an Agency, Director.

Article 7. (Internal Subdivisions and Organs) For the purpose of administering their respective specific functions, an Office on ministerial level and a Ministry shall have the internal subdivisions enumerated below :

Secretariat
Bureaux
Sections

574

For the purpose of administering their respective specific functions an Agency shall, as a rule, have the internal subdivisions enumerated below :

Secretariat

Divisions

Sections

Of the subdivisions referred to in the preceding two paragraphs, the establishment of the Secretariat, Bureau and Division, and the scope of affairs under their respective charge shall be provided for by law, while the creation of a Section and the scope of affairs under its respective charge shall be determined by each Minister or the head of an independent organization within the limits of the pertinent law. However, in the case of creating a Section budgetary procedure shall be accompanied therewith.

The Commission shall have a Secretariat. The provisions of the preceding two paragraphs shall apply correspondingly to the internal organization of the Secretariat.

Article 8. In addition to the internal subdivisions referred to in the preceding Article, in case there is special necessity within the scope of specific functions as provided for by law, Councils or Committees (to be taken to embrace all those of an advisory or investigational nature, etc. other than Commissions provided for in Article 3), Experimental Stations or Laboratories, Research Institutes, Educational Facilities, Medical Facilities and other organs may be set up as provided for by law.

In case the organs referred to in the preceding paragraph are to be established in local areas, the same shall be subject to the provisions of Article 156 of the Local Autonomy Law (Law No. 67 of 1947).

Article 9. In case it is necessary to make them administer its specific functions, each administrative organ referred to in Article 3 may, as provided for by law, establish local branch offices.

Article 10. (Authority and Responsibility of the Heads of Administrative Organs) Each Minister, a Chairman of each Commission, or Director of each Agency shall preside over the affairs of his organ and control and supervise its personnel in regard to the performance of their duties.

Article 11. When each Minister deems it necessary to enact, amend, or abrogate any law or cabinet order in respect to administrative affairs under his charge, he shall submit a draft to the Prime Minister and ask for a cabinet conference.

Article 12. Each Minister may issue an ordinance for his respective office (an ordinance of the Prime Minister's Office, an ordinance of the Attorney-General's Office or a ministerial ordinance)

575

for the purpose of implementing any law or cabinet order in respect to administrative affairs under his charge or as specially authorized by law or cabinet order.

The head of an independent organization may submit to the respective competent Minister a draft of the ordinance referred to in the preceding paragraph in respect to the affairs under the jurisdiction of his organ and ask for its issuance.

Unless authorized by law, no penal clause nor any provision which imposes obligations or restricts rights of individuals may be included in the ordinance referred to in the preceding two paragraphs.

Article 13. The head of each independent organization may, as provided for by separate law, issue on his own accord rules and special orders other than cabinet orders or the orders as prescribed in Paragraph 1 of the preceding Article.

The provision of paragraph 3 of the preceding Article shall apply correspondingly to the orders referred to in the preceding paragraph.

Article 14. In case it is necessary to make any public announcement in respect to the affairs under the jurisdiction of his organ, each Minister or the head of each independent organization may issue a notification.

For the purpose of giving orders or conveying directions in respect to the affairs under the jurisdiction of his organ, each Minister or the head of each independent organization may issue instructions or circular notices to the organizations and personnel under his jurisdiction consistent with the provisions of the National Public Service Law (Law No. 120 of 1947) and rule issued thereunder.

Article 15. With respect to affairs under his charge each Minister may direct and supervise the heads of local public entities in respect to national administrative affairs which they execute as provided for in Article 150 of the Local Autonomy Law. If the control or execution of national affairs that falls within the sphere of competence of the governor of the metropolis, district or urban or rural prefecture in his capacity as a national official is deemed to be contrary to the provisions of law or order or to the action of each competent Minister, or if he is negligent in the control or execution of such national affairs, each competent Minister may, as provided for in Article 146 of the Local Autonomy Law, order matters which such governor is to be compelled to carry out, ask for a trial by a law court, or proceed, after court determination, to execute the matters involved on behalf of the said government, or the Prime Minister may remove him from office as provided for in the same Article.

In case the removal from office has been effected under the provision of the preceding paragraph, the Prime Minister shall take steps to announce the reasons for such action and to make them known to the residents of the said metropolis, district or urban or rural prefecture, as provided for by cabinet order.

Article 16. If an ordinance of an Office on ministerial level, or ministerial ordinance, or an order or direction issued by each Minister to the head of a local public entity or his other act on the basis of his authority for directing or supervising the latter as provided for in the preceding Article is deemed to be contrary to the primary object of local autonomy, the said head of a local public entity may make due representation to that effect to the Prime Minister. In such a case, if the representation is deemed to be well-founded on reason, the Prime Minister shall make investigation within thirty days, direct the Minister involved or take such other steps as may be considered justified ; and in case the Prime Minister finds that the representation is not justified, he shall notify the head of the local public entity concerned with the reasons therefor.

The representation referred to in the preceding paragraph shall not thereby affect the validity of an order, direction, or other act of the Minister concerned.

Article 17. (Positions in Administrative Organs) Each Ministry shall have one Vice-Minister, which position shall be in the special government service.

The Vice-Minister shall assist the Minister, participate in the formation of policies and programme planning, regulate the ministerial affairs, and shall act for the Minister in his absence.

Article 18. The Prime Minister's Office shall have two Confidential Secretaries, and the Attorney-General's Office and various Ministries shall each have one Confidential Secretary.

Confidential Secretaries shall deal with confidential matters under orders of the respective Minister or temporarily assist in the affairs of any subdivision by his order.

Article 19. The fixed number of positions for each administrative organ shall be provided for by law.

Article 20. Each administrative organ referred to in Article 3 shall, as a rule and in conformity with its internal subdivisions as specified in Article 7, have the following positions as the respective head thereof :

Chiefs of Bureau
Chiefs of Division
Chiefs of Section

The scope of specific functions and the authority and responsibility involved in the positions referred to in the preceding paragraph shall be classified in accordance with the provisions of the National Public Service Law.

Article 21. (Special Provision for Administrative Organ of Government Enterprises) In regard to an administrative organ of government enterprises, the same may be otherwise provided for specifically by law regardless of the provisions of Article 7 and of the preceding Article.

Article 22. ('Kodan') The public corporation 'Kodan' shall be deemed an administrative organ of the national government, whose establishment or abolition shall be provided for by separate law.

'Kodan' shall be enumerated in the Appendix to this Law.

Supplementary Provisions

Article 23. The present Law shall come into force on and after 1 January 1949. However, the provision of Article 27 shall come into force as from the day of its promulgation.

Article 24. In addition to administrative organs referred to in Paragraph 2 of Article 3, in case there is special necessity, a Board with the Prime Minister as its head may be set up provisionally as provided for by separate law.

Unless otherwise prescribed by law, the provisions in this law concerning an Office on ministerial level and a Ministry shall apply correspondingly to a Board.

Article 25. Of the provisions of Article 19, those on positions shall become applicable from such a date as the position classification plan is determined and becomes effective under the National Public Service Law, and until that date the types of personnel for administrative organs and the specific matters for which they are responsible shall, unless otherwise provided for by law or cabinet order, be in accordance with the Common Rules concerning Personnel heretofore in force, and those on their fixed number shall come into force as from 1 January 1949.

Until the date as specified in the preceding paragraph, Vice-Ministers shall be first class officials, and Confidential Secretaries shall be second class officials, while Directors of an Agency, unless otherwise prescribed, shall be first class officials.

Article 26. Necessary details for implementing this law shall be provided for by cabinet order unless otherwise prescribed.

Article 27. The Appendix to this law provided for in Paragraph 4 of Article 3 and in Paragraph 2 of Article 22 shall be consolidated and attached only after the laws as required under the provisions of Article 3 and Article 22 are enacted, but not later than 1 January 1949.

Political Reorientation of Japan, Appendix H: 40, pp. 1151-3.

9   24 *July* 1948

GENERAL MACARTHUR'S LETTER TO PRIME MINISTER
ASHIDA CONCERNING REVISION OF THE
NATIONAL PUBLIC SERVICE LAW

I have reviewed the conclusions drawn from the joint studies conducted between representatives of your government and this headquarters into the adequacy of the National Public Service Law as a solution to the problems now existing with respect to the public service of Japan. I am in general accord with these conclusions as to existing inadequacies which must be corrected.

It was the purpose of the National Public Service Law to provide for the installation of a democratic and efficient public service in the Government of Japan. The plan envisioned a modern type of personnel system which recruits public employees from the entire public by competitive test and promotes them on the basis of merit, providing scientific supervision over their classification, compensation, training, evaluation, health, safety, welfare, recreation and retirement.

The system provides a grievance procedure for employees and assures them fair and equitable treatment in administration. Enforced by a quasi-judicial administrative authority and supplemented by emergency provisions aimed at immediate reform where urgency demands it, it constitutes a constructive programme for dealing with the hazards which old bureaucratic practices present to the success of democracy in Japan.

The pattern of personnel administration as here inaugurated views the entire people as exercising sovereignty and control over employees of government through the National Diet which, functioning through a National Public Service Authority, applies principles of scientific personnel management and standardizes the public service, its recruitment, compensation, discipline, benefits and other factors incident to employment.

Such a system in accordance with democratic concepts, is designed to regard the faithful administration of the law and the efficient conduct of the government's business as a prime duty without yielding to the pressure of politics or privilege.

The studies, now completed, of various laws relating to this subject matter, reveal omissions to deal adequately with the situation.

They fail to afford positive safeguards against minority pressure upon the authority and integrity of government and they fail to apply the law to many classifications of governmental employees who clearly are entitled to civil service benefits and protection and subject to its restrictions. Throughout there is a noticeable failure to distinguish between employee relationships in government and labour relations in private enterprise.

The rapid and unprecedented gains labour has made in Japan during the Occupation attest my own awareness of the vital importance of trade unionism in modern life and of the historical significance of the trade union movement throughout the world in correcting many of the abuses associated with modern industrial economy.

In government, however, this movement has but limited application and cannot substitute for or challenge duly constituted executive, judicial and legislative agencies exercising the sovereign power.

At the start of the industrial era, the tendency existed to treat labour as a commodity, without voice in the price to be paid or the conditions of its employment.

As the technology of mass production developed, however, workers had a better opportunity to organize for their mutual benefit and through long and arduous struggle secured the economic power of bargaining collectively through representatives of their own choice for an improved standard of life, a betterment in working conditions and some degree of social security.

This right of association with its inherent power of compulsion had progressively developed in the trade union movement an economic power which has brought to bear an increasingly potent influence upon industrial economy. Such influence in democratic society has in turn been translated into political power through the support it has given to political parties, but it would be violative of the democratic concept for the trade union movement to usurp the function of the duly elected representatives of the people as a whole by superimposing union judgement upon legislation and administration.

It is true that in all industrialized countries specific pressure groups exist, representing not only the interests of labour but also those of business, finance, agriculture, and the professions.

Although such pressure groups contend for power and influence in a democracy, they are transcended by the fundamental concept of national unity. The 'public' is not considered merely the residual members of the community who do not belong to such specific pressure groups, but consists of all the people and the 'public interest' is synonymous with the general welfare.

The significance of this concept is as well understood in Japan as in any Western democracy. The Constitution of Japan itself recognizes the 'unity of the people' and the 'will of the people with whom resides sovereign power'; the Constitution itself affirms the principle that 'the freedoms and rights guaranteed to the people by this Constitution shall be maintained by the constant endeavour of the people' who, 'shall always be responsible for utilizing them for the public welfare'; and the Constitution itself envisages a National Diet as 'the highest organ of state power' which shall be 'representative of all the people'.

If this fundamental concept of the Constitution declaring the unity of the people and the supremacy of the public interest is to be preserved inviolate, no part of the power of government can be delegated to or usurped by any private group whatsoever.

Were the contrary true the 'responsible government' for Japan contemplated by the Potsdam Declaration and created by the Constitution could not exist. For it is axiomatic that a government which abdicates its sovereign power is no longer responsible.

By its very nature, as a private entity the labour union does not possess the attributes of government. Wherever it has flourished, the strength of free trade unionism has always sprung from its independence of government and its freedom from domination by government in the pursuit of its lawful and legitimate objectives.

Having experienced the suppression which was an attribute of totalitarian Japan, Japanese labour since the Occupation has in general understood this principle and chosen the path of free trade unionism, eschewing those reckless policies the inevitable effect of which would be to provoke severe repressive measures in safeguard of the general welfare.

It has recognized that free workers in free private enterprise cannot exercise sovereign power except in their capacity as free men at free elections. Indeed, because it upholds the dignity of the individual and of his labour, free trade unionism in the pursuit of labour's legitimate objectives constitutes one of the strongest bulwarks of democracy.

There is, however, a sharp distinction between those who have dedicated their energies to the public service and those engaged in private enterprise. The former are the very instruments used for the exercise by government of the people's sovereign power, and as such owe unconditional allegiance to the public trust imposed by virtue of their employment. For upon them rests, in the words of the late President of the United States, Franklin D. Roosevelt, a foremost exponent of the rights of labour, the obligation to serve the whole people, whose interests and welfare require orderliness and continuity in the conduct of Government activities.

This obligation is paramount. Since their own services have to do with the functioning of the government, a strike of public employees manifests nothing less than an intent on their part to prevent or obstruct the operations of government until their demands are satisfied. Such action, looking towards the paralysis of government by those who have sworn to support it, is unthinkable and intolerable.

I am in full accord with this view. No person holding a position by appointment or employment in the public service of Japan or in any instrumentality thereof should resort to strike or engage in delaying or other dispute tactics which tend to impair the efficiency of governmental operations.

I feel that any person, holding such a position, who resorts to such action against the public of Japan thereby betrays the public trust reposed in him and forfeits all rights and privileges accruing to him by virtue of his employment.

For as President Roosevelt further stated, all government employees should realize that the process of collective bargaining, as usually understood, cannot be transplanted into the public service. It has its distinct and insurmountable limitations when applied to public personnel management. The very nature and purposes of government make it impossible for administrative officials to represent fully or to bind the employer in mutual discussions with government employee organizations.

The employer is the whole people, who speak by means of laws, enacted by their representatives of Congress. Accordingly, administrative officials and employees alike are governed and guided, and in many instances restricted, by laws which establish policies, procedures, or rules in personnel matters.

It must be clearly understood, however, that this concept does not mean that public servants are deprived of the untrammelled right individually or collectively, personally or by chosen representatives, freely to express their views, opinions or grievances for the purpose of seeking a betterment of their conditions of public employment.

Such rights are inherent in a democratic society and inalienable and I believe are adequately provided for in the proposed revision of existing law.

Moreover, the special restrictions which protection of the national interest impose upon the employees of government make it at all times incumbent upon government to provide adequate safeguards to the welfare and interests of such employees. Indeed, so completely is this concept understood and followed in democratic society that the opportunity for public service with the added dignity, prestige and permanence of such a status, is universally regarded and sought as a desirable privilege.

So far as the railways, salt, camphor, and tobacco activities presently under government ownership are concerned, I believe that employees thereof might well be excepted from the regular civil service.

In this event, however, public corporations should be established by appropriate action to manage and operate these activities. Proper provision should be made for standards, policies, and procedures of employment and while substituting mediation and arbitration measures for the protection accorded others under the civil service, safeguards should be provided to the public interest against any interruption of operations resulting from failure of employees faithfully to discharge their responsibilities of employment.

Moreover, in the interest of efficiency, I believe that a complete reorganization of the Ministry of Communications is desirable, with the separation of the postal services of the government from the other functions of that Ministry and the establishment of two Cabinet agencies in lieu thereof.

The National Public Service Law was initially conceived in recognition of the fact that a complete reform of the Japanese bureaucracy is essential to the success of democratic institutions in Japan, as such institutions, whether political, economic or social, will inevitably find strength or weakness in direct proportion to the efficiency of the governmental services and the vigorous leadership which government, as organized to safeguard the public interest and advance the general welfare, is capable of extending to the sovereign people from whom its powers are derived. The success of this reform is accordingly no less a primary objective of the Occupation than it is prerequisite to the future well-being of the people of Japan.

In the solution of this problem the paramountcy of the public interest is therefore of foremost consideration and a corollary thereto is the need that a safeguard be erected to ensure that the lawful authority of the government as the political instrument to enforce the people's will, as expressed in the body of public law, be only challengeable at the polls as provided under well established democratic practice.

To hold otherwise would be to subvert the public interest by rendering government subservient to a primacy of the special privilege of minority groups, a condition which inevitably leads to anarchy, insurrection and destruction. This is a rule fundamental to the very existence of a democratic society, and yet its enforcement in the great Western democracies has only recently necessitated the full application of the police power of the State involving the employment of the armed forces as well as the civil police.

In Japan, where the maintenance of armed forces is renounced by constitutional mandate, such application of police power can, however, only be supported by the civil police. This renders it all the more necessary here than elsewhere that the law carefully define and make unmistakably clear the authority of government and provision for the firm preservation of its integrity and dignity.

It is to this end that I feel that a comprehensive revision of the National Public Service Law to bring the same within the framework of the concepts herein discussed should be undertaken immediately. To assist you in this matter this headquarters will continue to be available for advice and consultation.

Sincerely yours,

(Signed) DOUGLAS MACARTHUR

Contemporary Japan, Tokyo, Vol. XVII, Nos. 7-12, July-December 1948, pp. 404-9.

III ECONOMIC 'DEMOCRATIZATION'

10   1 *April* 1947

LABOUR STANDARD LAW

Ch. I. General Provisions

Article 1. (Principle of Working Condition) Working condition must be that which should meet the need of the worker who lives a life worthy of a human being.

The standard of working condition affixed by this Law is the minimum. Therefore parties of labour relations must not reduce the working condition with excuse of this standard and, instead, should endeavour to raise the working condition.

Article 2. (Decision of Working Condition) Working condition should be decided by the worker and employer on an equal basis.

The worker and employer must abide by the collective agreement, rule of employment and labour contract, and must discharge their respective duties faithfully.

Article 3. (Equal Treatment) No person shall discriminate against or for any worker by reason of nationality, creed or social status, in wages, working hours and other working conditions.

Article 4. (Equal Wages for Men and Women) The employer shall not discriminate women against men concerning wages by reason of the workers being women.

Article 5. (Prohibition of Forced Labour) The employer shall not force workers to work against their will by means of violence, intimidation, imprisonment, or any other unfair restraint on the mental or physical freedom of the workers.

Article 6. (Expulsion of Intermediate Exploitation) Unless permitted based on the Law, no person shall obtain profit as a vocation by intervening in the employment of others.

Article 7. (Guarantee for the Exercise of Civil Right) The employer shall not refuse when the worker requires necessary time to exercise franchise and other civil right or to execute public duty during working hours. However the employer may change the required time as far as the change does not hinder the exercise of the right or the execution of public duty.

Article 8. (Scopes of Applicable Enterprises) This Law applies to each of the items of enterprises and offices listed below. However, it does not apply to any enterprise or office employing only those relations living with the employer as family members nor to domestic employees in the household.

(1) Enterprises engaged in the manufacture, rebuilding, improving, repairing, cleaning, sorting, packing and decoration of goods, finishing, tailoring for the purpose of selling, destruction or breaking up, and alteration of material. (This includes industries which generate, transform, and transmit electricity, gas and various forms of power and also waterworks.)

(2) Mining, sand mining, stone cutting and other extraction of gravel or minerals.

(3) Engineering, construction, and building, remodelling, maintenance, repairing, renovation, wrecking, dismantling of structure and those enterprises engaged in preparatory work for the above enterprises.

(4) Enterprises engaged in the transportation of freight and passengers by roads, railroads, streetcar lines, cable lines, vessels and airplanes.

(5) Enterprises handling freight at docks, on vessels, at jetties, piers, railway stations, and warehouses.

(6) Enterprises engaged in the cultivation of land or reclamation of waste land, planting, cultivating, harvesting of crops, timber cutting, and other agricultural and forestry enterprises.

(7) Enterprises engaged in the breeding of animals, catching, gathering and breeding of marine animals and seaweed, and other enterprises such as livestock raising, sericulture and fisheries.

(8) Enterprises engaged in the selling, delivery, storing and lending of commodities and barber-shop.

(9) Banking, insurance, agency, brokerage, bill collection, information and advertising enterprises.

(10) Motion-picture production and showing cinematography, stage and other show enterprises.

(11) Postal, telegraph, and telephone services.

(12) Enterprises engaged in education, research and investigation.

(13) Enterprises engaged in the treatment and care of the sick and feeble, and other hygiene and sanitation.

(14) Hotel, restaurant, snack bar, service trade, and recreation hall enterprises.

(15) Enterprises engaged in incineration, cleaning and butchery.

(16) Governmental and other public office which do not come under any of the foregoing items.

(17) Other enterprises or offices defined by Ordinance.

Article 9. (Definition) In this Law, the worker is defined indiscriminately of the kinds of occupation as one who is employed in the above-mentioned enterprises or offices (hereinafter called enterprise simply) and receives a wage therefrom.

Article 10. In this Law, the employer is defined as the owner or manager of the enterprise or any other person who acts on behalf of the owner of the enterprise in matters concerning the workers of the enterprise.

Article 11. In this Law, the wage is defined as the wage, salary, allowance, bonus and every other payment to the worker from the employer as remuneration for labour under whatever name they may be called.

Article 12. In this Law, the amount of the average wage is defined as the quotient obtained by dividing the total amount of wages for a period of three months preceding to the day on which the calculation of average wage became necessary by the number of all days during the period. However, the amount of the average wage shall not be less than the amount computed by one of the following methods.

(1) In case the wage is computed by the labour days or labour hours, or defined by piece-rate or other contract price, 60 per cent of the quotient obtained by dividing the total sum of wages by the number of the labour days during that period.

(2) In case a part of the wage is defined by month, week, or any other fixed period, aggregate of the quotient obtained by dividing the total sum of those parts by the number of all days during that period and the sum computed by the foregoing method.

When there is a fixed day for closing the wages account, the period of the preceding paragraph shall be calculated from the last fixed day.

If the period mentioned in the two preceding paragraphs includes any of the following periods the days and wages in that period shall be excluded from the days and total amount of wages above-mentioned.

(i) Days of rest for medical treatment caused by injury or illness while on duty.

(ii) Days of rest before and after childbirth according to the stipulation of Article 65.

(iii) Days of rest caused by reason for which the employer is responsible.

(iv) Probation period.

The total amount of wages of Paragraph 1 does not include extraordinary wages, wages which are paid periodically with more than three months period and wages which are paid by anything other than money that is not within a certain scope.

In case the wage is paid in anything other than money, the scope to be included in the total sum of wages under Paragraph 1 and the method necessary for the reckoning of the cost shall be defined by the ordinance.

For a worker who has been employed for less than three months, the period of Paragraph 1 shall be the period of his or her employment.

The average wages of daily workers shall be fixed by the authoritative minister according to the kind of the industry or the occupation.

In case the average wage cannot be computed by Paragraph 1 to Paragraph 6 inclusive the methods will be defined by the competent Minister of Labour.

Ch. II. Labour Contract

Article 13. (Contract Violating This Law) Labour contract which defines working conditions inferior to the standard of this Law is invalid so far as such conditions are concerned ; in this case those conditions which become invalid are replaced by the condition of this Law.

Article 14. (Period of Contract) Labour contracts, excluding those without any set period, shall not be concluded for a period longer than one year except those requiring a definite period for the completion of a project.

Article 15. (Clarification of Labour Contract) In making a labour contract, the employer must clarify the wages, working hours and other working conditions to the worker.

When the working conditions clarified under the preceding paragraph are different from the real fact, the workers may cancel the labour contract without notice.

In the case aforesaid, the employer must bear the necessary travelling expense for workers who have changed residence for the work when they return home within 14 days after cancellation.

Article 16. (Ban on Contract of Indemnity) The employer is prohibited from making a contract which fixes in advance either the sum payable to the employer for breach of contract, or the amount of indemnity for damage.

Article 17. (Ban on Deduction for the Payment of Advanced Money) The employer must not deduct wages to collect advanced money or other claim advanced on condition of labour.

Article 18. (Compulsory Deposit) The employer must not make a deposit contract or a contract to keep the savings-note, concomitant with the labour contract.

To keep the deposit committed by free will in custody, the employer must define the method of keeping and releasing and must obtain the sanction of the administrative office.

Article 19. (Restriction Concerning the Dismissal of Workers) The employer shall not dismiss a worker injured or taken ill while on duty during the period of medical treatment and 30 days thereafter; nor shall he discharge a woman pregnant or who has given childbirth during the period of vacation stipulated in Article 65 and for 30 days thereafter. However, this shall not apply when the employer pays expiry compensation stipulated in Article 81 or when the continuance of the enterprise is made impossible by reason of some natural calamity or other inevitable cause.

In case of the latter part of the foregoing proviso to the preceding paragraph the employer must obtain the approval of the administrative office to the reason.

Article 20. (Dismissal Notice) When the employer wishes to cancel the labour contract he must give at least 30 days' advance notice. An employer who does not give 30 days' notice in advance shall pay money equivalent to the 30 days' average wages. This does not apply when the continuance of the enterprise is made impossible by reason of some natural calamity or other inevitable cause, or when the employer dismisses the worker by reason for which the worker is responsible.

The number of days of notice under the preceding paragraph may be reduced in case the employer pays the average wages for the number of the reduced days.

In case of the proviso to Paragraph 1 of the preceding Article, Paragraph 2 of the said Article shall apply.

Article 21. The preceding Article shall not apply to those workers who come under any one of the following :

(1) Workers who are employed daily.

(2) Workers who are employed for a period not longer than two months.

(3) Workers who are employed in a seasonal work for a period not longer than four months.

(4) Workers on probation.

The preceding paragraph shall not apply when a worker who comes under item 1, is employed for more than a month consecutively, or when a worker who comes under item 2 or 3 is employed for more than the period fixed by each item, or when a worker who comes under item 4 is employed for more than 14 days.

Article 22. (Certificate of Employment) When a worker on the occasion of retirement requests a certificate stating the period of employment, the kind of occupation, the position in the enterprise and wages, the employer shall present him one without delay.

The employer shall not insert in the certificate what the worker does not require.

The employer in conspiracy with others shall not send any communication concerning nationality, creed, social status or the union activity of the worker with the will to impede the employment of the worker nor tack on any secret sign on the certificate mentioned in Paragraph 1.

Article 23. (The Return of Money and Other Valuables) Upon a worker's death or his dismissal, the employer shall complete the payment of wages, and return whatever reserves, bonds, savings and other funds and valuables belonging to the worker, within 7 days of the claimant's request.

If the claims to the wages and valuables described in the preceding paragraph are disputed, the employer shall pay or return the amount remaining undisputed within the period fixed in the same paragraph.

Ch. III. Wages

Article 24. (Payment of Wages) Wages must be paid in cash and in full directly to the workers. However, when otherwise stipulated by the Law, or by collective agreement, the employer can deduct a part of the wage or pay not in cash.

Wages must be paid at least once a month at a definite date. However this does not apply to extraordinary wages, bonus and the like which will be defined by ordinance.

Article 25. (Emergency Payment) When the worker requires to appropriate money for emergency use such as child-birth, disease, accident and other cases which will be defined by ordinance in detail, the employer shall pay the accrued wages before the day of payment.

Article 26. (Rest-day Allowance) For the rest-day caused by reason for which the employer is responsible, the employer shall pay allowance equivalent to 60 per cent of the worker's average wage.

Article 27. (Guarantee in Piece Work System) When the worker is employed by piece rate or at contract wage the employer must assure the worker of a fixed sum of wage proportionate to the working hour.

Article 28. (Minimum Wage) When the competent office considers it necessary it can fix a minimum wage for workers employed in certain enterprises or in certain occupations.

Article 29. Central Wage Boards and Local Wage Board shall be established for the purpose of investigating matters pertaining to wages.

In case of necessity, a special committee may be established regarding certain enterprise or occupation in the Wage Board.

The members of the Wage Board shall be appointed by the competent office in the same number from among the representatives of labour and management, and the public. The representatives of labour and management shall be appointed upon the basis of the recommendation of both parties.

Necessary matters except the stipulation of this Law pertaining to the Wage Board will be stipulated by ordinance.

Article 30. When the competent office wishes to fix the minimum wages, it must first apply for the investigation and recommendation of the Wage Board thereupon.

In the foregoing case the Wage Board shall recommend to the competent office an amount of minimum wages for workers who are employed in certain enterprises or in certain occupations.

The competent office shall hold a public hearing on the foregoing recommendation, and then based on the recommendation and public opinion, shall fix the minimum wage.

When the local administrative office wishes to fix minimum wages it must obtain the approval of the competent Minister after it has finished the procedure of the three foregoing paragraphs.

When the Wage Board thinks it necessary, it can recommend matters pertaining to wages to administrative offices concerned.

Article 31. When the minimum wage is fixed, the employer shall not employ a worker at less wage than the fixed minimum wage. However, this shall not apply to the following cases :

(1) In case the employer obtains the approval of the administrative office concerning a worker whose efficiency is remarkably low on account of a mental or physical handicap.

(2) In case the worker does not work for the fixed period of time by reason for which the worker is responsible.

(3) In case the employer has obtained the sanction of the administrative office with regard to the worker on probation or worker whose work schedule is remarkably short.

Ch. IV. *Working Hours, Recess, Holidays and Annual Vacation with Pay*

Article 32. (Working Hours) The employer shall not employ the worker more than 8 hours a day excluding a recess or forty-eight hours a week.

In case the employer stipulates by the rules of employment or by other stipulation, he may employ the worker according to the stipulation more than eight hours on a special day or forty-eight hours in a special week when the average working hours of four weeks do not exceed forty-eight hours in a week.

Article 33. The employer may extend the working hours described in the preceding Article or in Article 40 under the sanction of the administrative office in case of accidents and other unavoidable temporary need within the limit of the necessity. However, when the necessity is so urgent that there is not time enough to obtain the sanction of the administrative office, the employer must report to that effect *ex post facto* without delay.

When the administrative office considers the extension of the working hour to be illegal in the foregoing case, it is authorized to order the employer to give the worker a recess or holiday corresponding to the prolonged hour.

In case there is temporary necessity to transact the official business, the Government official, municipal official and other public official employed in the enterprise of Article 8 item 16 may be employed longer than the working hours described in the preceding Article or in Article 40 regardless of the stipulation of Paragraph 1, or may be employed on rest days stipulated in Article 35.

Article 34. (Recess) The employer shall provide recess totalling at least forty-five minutes for those who have worked more than six hours, and at least one hour for those who have worked more than eight hours.

The forementioned recess must be given to all workers at the same time. However, this provision shall not apply when the employer receives sanction from the administrative office.

The employer shall allow the workers to use the recess described in Paragraph 1 as they please.

Article 35. (Rest Days) The employer must provide at least one rest day per week to the worker.

The stipulation in the foregoing paragraph does not apply to employers who provide four or more rest days during four weeks.

Article 36. (Overtime Working and Working on Rest Days) Regardless of the respective Articles, the employer may extend the working hours stipulated in Article 32 and Article 40 or employ workers on rest days stipulated in the preceding Article if he reaches an agreement with the trade union when there is a union which is composed of the majority of the workers at the working place, or with persons representing the majority of workers when there is not such a union and submits the written agreement to the administrative office. However, in case of underground labour or other jobs injurious to health as specified by ordinance the extension shall not exceed two hours per day.

Article 37. (Increased Wages for Overtime Work, Work on Rest Days and Midnight Labour) When the employer extends the working hour or employs the worker on a rest day under the stipulations of Article 33 or of the preceding Article or employs the worker between 10 p.m. and 5 a.m. (when the competent Minister of Labour deems it necessary he may change these hours from 11 p.m. to 6 a.m. specifying the area or the season), he shall pay for the labour of the hour or the day an increased rate of wages by at least 25 per cent of the normal wages.

Family allowance, commutation allowance and other wages stipulated by ordinance are excluded from the normal wage upon which an increased rate of wages should be computed.

Article 38. (Computation of Working Time) The working hours as stipulated by this Law shall be summed up regardless of change in working places.

In underground labour the whole period from the time the worker enters into the pit-mouth to the time the worker goes out of the pit-mouth including recess is deemed as working hours. In this case, the stipulation concerning recess in Article 34, Paragraphs 2 and 3, shall not apply to underground labour.

Article 39. (Annual Vacation with Pay) The employer shall grant six days annual vacation with pay consecutively or separately to the workers who have been employed continuously for a year and were present over eighty per cent of the whole working days.

The employer shall grant an increased annual vacation with pay amounting to one day per one continued year in addition to the annual vacation specified in the foregoing paragraph to workers who have worked continuously for two or more years. However, in case the total vacation with pay exceeds 20 days, the employer need not give a vacation with pay so far as the excess is concerned.

The employer shall grant the vacation stipulated in the two preceding paragraphs in the season the worker requires, and shall pay the worker the average wages during the period. However, when it prevents the normal operation of the enterprise to give the vacation in the required season, the employer is authorized to change the season.

Days of rest for medical treatment caused by injury or illness while on duty and the days of rest before and after child-birth according to the stipulation of Article 65 shall be deemed to be present in applying paragraph 1.

Article 40. (Special Ordinance of Working Hours and Recess) In certain occupations or enterprises which come under Article 8, item 4, item 5 and item 8 to item 17 inclusive, in which it is essential to avoid inconvenience to the public or the like or in which there is other special need, a special ordinance concerning the working hours of Article 32 and the recess of Article 34 may be issued within the limit that is unavoidable.

The special ordinance stipulated in the preceding paragraph shall conform as closely as possible to the standards of this Law and shall not be detrimental to the health and welfare of the employees.

Article 41. (Exception of Application) Stipulations of this Chapter and Chapter VI concerning working hours, recess and holidays shall not apply to the following items :

(1) Persons engaged in an enterprise which comes under items 6 and 7 of Article 8.

(2) Persons holding positions of supervision of management, or persons employed in confidential capacity whatever the enterprise may be.

(3) Persons engaged in intermittent labour and approved by the administrative office.

Ch. V.   Safety and Sanitation

Article 42. (Prevention of Accident and Disease) The employer must take necessary measures to prevent accident resulting from machinery, tools and other equipment or, gas, steam, dust and other material.

Article 43. With regard to the establishment or an annex where the workers are accommodated the employer must take necessary means for ventilation, lighting, illumination, heating, damp-proofing, rest, emergency escape, cleanliness, and other facilities necessary for the maintenance of health, good morale, and life of the workers.

Article 44. Workers shall observe necessary rules for the prevention of danger and injury.

Article 45. The standard of means to be taken by the employer in accordance with Article 42 and Article 43 and the rules which the workers should observe under the preceding Article shall be stipulated by ordinance.

Article 46. (Safety Equipment) Machinery and tools requiring dangerous work shall not be transferred, rented, or installed unless they are fitted up to a certain standard or safety equipments are installed.

Machinery and tools which require particularly dangerous work, shall not be manufactured, altered or installed unless special permission of the administrative office is given in advance.

The kind of machinery and tools, and the standard of the safety equipment prescribed in the two foregoing paragraphs shall be defined by ordinance.

Article 47. (Efficiency Test) The machinery and tools mentioned in paragraph 2 of the foregoing Article must not be operated unless they pass the efficiency test given by the administrative office after the lapse of the period specified by ordinance.

The efficiency test of the foregoing paragraph may be trusted to others than the administrative office of the same paragraph whom the competent Minister of Labour designates.

Article 48. (Ban on Manufacture of Harmful Products) Yellow phosphorus matches and other harmful products determined by ordinance must not be manufactured, sold, imported, or kept in possession for the purpose of sale.

Article 49. (Restriction on Dangerous Work) The employer shall not allow an inexperienced worker to clean, oil, examine, or repair the dangerous part of any machinery or transmission apparatus in motion, or to put on or to take off the driving belts or ropes of any machinery or transmission apparatus in motion, or to handle a derrick driven by power, or to perform any other dangerous work.

The employer shall not allow a worker who has not the necessary skill to engage in a specially dangerous work.

The scope of work, experience and skill in the two foregoing paragraphs shall be decided by ordinance.

Article 50. (Safety and Sanitation Education) On employing a worker the employer shall equip him with the necessary health and safety education for the operation concerned.

Article 51. (Ban on the Employment of Sick Persons) The employer shall stop the work of workers who have contracted a contagious disease, mental disease, or are taken ill in case the labour aggravates the condition.

The kind and degree of sickness which should be banned by the preceding stipulation shall be determined by ordinance.

Article 52. (Physical Examinations) Any employer engaged in a certain enterprise shall give workers physical examinations at the time of employment and also at fixed periods.

The worker who does not desire to undergo the diagnosis of the doctor nominated by the employer must undergo the diagnosis of another doctor and submit a document which proves the result of the diagnosis to the employer.

Based on the results of the physical examination described in the preceding two paragraphs, the employer shall take necessary measures to preserve the workers' health such as shifting a worker to another job, or shortening his work hours.

The kind and scale of the enterprise and the frequency of the physical examination shall be defined by ordinance.

Article 53. (Safety Supervisor and Health Supervisor) Any employer engaged in certain enterprises shall appoint a safety supervisor and a health supervisor.

The kind and scale of the enterprise and the qualification and duties of the safety supervisor and health supervisor shall be determined by ordinance.

The administrative office is authorized to order an increase in the number of, or to discharge the safety and health supervisors when they deem it necessary.

Article 54. (Supervisory Administrative Method) When an employer who employs more than ten workers usually, or who employs the workers in hazardous or injurious enterprise defined by ordinance decides to construct, move, or remodel the building, dormitory and other annex and installation, he must make a plan which complies with the standard of safety and health defined by ordinance issued under Article 45 or Article 96 and submit it to the administrative office fourteen days prior to the start of the project.

The administrative office is authorized to stop the start of the work or to order a change in the project when it recognizes the project as being inferior to the necessary standard of safety and health.

Article 55. The administrative office is authorized to order the employer to stop the use of part or the whole of, or to alter, the building, dormitory and other annex, installation and material, and to make other necessary changes to prevent accidents if it regards those as violating safety standards.

In case of the foregoing paragraph the administrative office is authorized to order the workers necessary matters concerning matters it has ordered the employer.

Ch. VI. *Women and Minor Workers*

Article 56. (Minimum Age) Minors under full 16 years of age shall not be employed as workers. However, this does not apply to minors who are over full 14 years old and have completed the course of compulsory education prescribed by ordinance or the course equivalent to or higher than that.

Regardless of the provision of the preceding paragraph, children above full 12 years old may be employed in certain occupations in enterprises which come under Article 8, item 6 to item 17 inclusive, in light labour which is not injurious to the health and welfare of the children, outside of the school hours of the children and under the permission of administrative office. However children under full 12 years old may be employed in motion picture productions and dramatic performance enterprises under same condition.

Article 57. (Certificate of Minors) The employer shall keep a census register which proves the age of the minors under full 18 years old at the working place.

Concerning the children who come under Paragraph 2 of the preceding Article, the employer shall keep a certificate issued by the schoolmaster to prove that the employment does not hinder the schooling of the children, and a document to prove the consent of the parents or the guardian at the working place.

Article 58. (Labour Contracts of the Minor) The parent or the guardian shall not make a labour contract in place of the minors.

The parent or the guardian and the administrative office are authorized to cancel the contract for the future if they consider it unfair to the minor.

Article 59. The minor has the right to receive wages independently, the parent or the guardian shall not receive as proxy the wage earned by the minor.

Article 60. (Working Hours and Rest Days of Minors) Article 32, Paragraph 2, Article 36 and Article 40 shall not apply to minors under full 18 years old.

Concerning children who come under Article 56, Paragraph 2, the working hours of Article 32, Paragraph 1, are replaced as seven hours a day, forty-two hours a week, including school hours.

Regardless of Article 32, Paragraph 1, working hours for minors above full 15 years old (including minors above full 14 years old who come under the proviso of Article 56, Paragraph 1) and under full 18 years old, may be extended to 10 hours a day, in case the employer reduces the working hours of one day in a week to 4 hours and the total working hours of a week do not exceed 48 hours.

Article 61. (Working Hours and Rest Days of Women) The employer shall not employ women above full 18 years old, overtime more than 2 hours a day, 6 hours a week, and 150 hours a year, nor employ them on rest days even though the employers reach agreement under Article 36.

Article 62. (Midnight Labour) The employer shall not employ minors under full 18 years, or women, between the hours of 10 p.m. and 5 a.m. However this shall not apply when a male over full 16 years of age is employed by rotating shift system.

When the competent Minister of Labour deems it necessary, he may change the hours of the preceding paragraph from 11 p.m. to 6 a.m. specifying the area and the season.

When work is done in rotating shifts, the employer may employ these workers till 10.30 p.m. regardless of the provisions of the 1st paragraph or from 5.30 a.m. regardless of the stipulation of the preceding paragraph under the sanction of the administrative office.

The three foregoing paragraphs shall not apply when the employer extends the working hour by the stipulation of Article 33, nor to those enterprises which come under items 6, 7, 13, 14 of Article 8 nor to the telephone system. However, this shall not apply to minors under full 18 years old employed in the enterprise of item 14.

In applying paragraph 1 to children who come under Article 56, paragraph 2, principal clause, the hour of paragraph 1 is replaced as from 8 p.m. to 5 a.m. and in applying paragraph 2 as from 9 p.m. to 6 a.m.

Article 63. (Restrictions on Dangerous and Harmful Jobs) The employer shall not allow minors under full 18 years and women to engage in the dangerous jobs specified in Article 49, nor in jobs which require the conveyance of heavy weight goods specified by ordinance.

The employer shall not employ minors under full 18 years of age in work involving the handling of poisons, powerful drugs or other injurious substances, or explosive, combustible or inflammable goods, or in work in places where dust and powder, or harmful gas and radial rays are generated, in places of high temperatures and pressures, or other places which are dangerous or injurious to the health and welfare of the minor.

The preceding paragraph may be applied by ordinance to women over full 18 years of age who are engaged in certain jobs specified in the same paragraph.

The scope of the work described in Paragraph 2 and the scope of application by the preceding paragraph will be decided by the competent Minister.

Article 64. (Ban on Underground Labour) The employer shall not employ minors under full 18 years of age or women in underground labour.

Article 65. (Before and After Child-birth) The employer shall not employ a woman for 6 weeks before child-birth when she requests rest days during that period.

The employer shall not employ women within 6 weeks after child-birth. However, when the woman requests employment after 5 weeks, it is permissible to assign her to a job that the doctor pronounces unharmful to her.

When the pregnant woman requires, the employer shall change her to a lighter job.

Article 66. (Nursing Period) When nursing a baby less than one year old the woman may obtain nursing time, twice a day, each thirty minutes during working hours, besides the recess mentioned in Article 34.

The employer shall not work the woman during the nursing time mentioned in the preceding paragraph.

Article 67. (Menstruation Leave) The employer shall not keep working a woman who suffers heavily from menstruation nor women employed in jobs injurious to menstruation if she request a menstruation leave.

The scope of the job mentioned in the preceding paragraph will be determined by ordinance.

Article 68. (Fare for Returning Home) The employer shall bear the necessary fare in case minors under full 18 years of age or women wish to return home within 14 days after dismissal. However, this does not apply if minors under full 18 years of age or women were dismissed for a reason for which they are responsible and if the employer receives authorization from the administrative office after explaining the grounds for dismissal.

Ch. VII.   *Training of Skilled Labourer*

Article 69. (Expulsion of Evils of the Apprentice) The employer shall not exploit the apprentice, pupil, student or other workers under whatever name he may call them, on the score of the worker purporting to learn the skill.

The employer shall not employ a worker who purports to learn the skill in a job which has no relation to learning the skill.

Article 70. (Training of the Skilled Labourer) When there is necessity to train a skilled labourer who requires the training for a certain long period in the course of labour, a special ordinance will be issued which stipulates matters pertaining to the method of training, the qualification of the employer, period of contract, working hours and wages necessary for the training of the skilled labourer.

In case of the foregoing paragraph, the special ordinance may stipulate, concerning the period of contract under Article 14, payment of wages under Article 24, minimum wages under Article 31, and restriction on employment in dangerous or injurious labour under Article 49 and Article 63, other than the standard of this Law within the limit of necessity.

Article 71. The employer who wants to employ a labourer in accord with the preceding Article must fix the number of the labourers, method of indoctrination, period of contract, working hours, wage standard, and method of payment, and obtain the permission of the administrative office thereupon.

When the employer employs a labourer based upon the permission of the preceding paragraph, he must report it to the administrative office and receive a certificate of being the worker to learn the skill which (certificate) he shall have to keep at his working place.

Article 72. For minors who are employed under the two preceding Articles, 12 working days shall be given as the annual holidays with pay stipulated in Article 39, Paragraph 1.

Article 73. When employers who have employed workers to whom the stipulations of Article 70 and Article 71 apply, lose their qualification or violate the terms of the authorization, the administrative office may cancel the authorization mentioned in the Article 71.

Article 74. The special ordinance stipulated in Article 70 shall be defined after consultation with the Committee for the Training of Skilled Labourers.

The members of the Committee for the Training of Skilled Labourers shall be appointed in the same number from the representatives of labourers and employers concerned and the representatives of the public by the competent Minister of Labour.

Matters pertaining to the Committee for the Training of Skilled Labourers other than the stipulation in the two foregoing paragraphs shall be defined by ordinance.

Ch. VIII. *Accident Compensation*

Article 75. (Medical Compensation) In case a worker is injured or falls ill because of duty, the employer shall furnish necessary medical treatment, or bear the expenditure for necessary medical treatment.

The scope of illness contracted because of duty and the necessary medical treatment as stipulated in the preceding paragraph shall be decided by ordinance.

Article 76. (Non-Duty Compensation) For a worker who is unable to work because of the medical treatment described by the stipulation of the previous Article, and who does not get paid, the employer shall pay non-duty compensation equivalent to 60 per cent of the worker's average wages during the period of the worker's medical treatment.

Article 77. (Compensation for Physical Handicaps) For a worker who is injured or falls ill because of duty and is physically handicapped when he recovers, the employer must pay handicap compensation according to the extent of the worker's handicap ; the amount of which shall be the amount of the average wage multiplied by the number of days fixed in the annex table No. 1.

Article 78. (Exceptions to Non-Duty and Physical Handicap Compensations) For a worker who is injured or falls ill because of duty, because of some serious personal fault, the employer is not obligated to pay the non-duty and physical handicap compensation when he receives the approval of the administrative office on the fact.

Article 79. (Compensation for Bereaved Families) When a worker dies because of duty the employer shall pay compensation equivalent to 1,000 days' average wage of the worker to the bereaved families or persons who were dependent on the worker's income at the time of the worker's death.

Article 80. (Expense of Funeral Rites) When a worker dies because of duty the employer shall pay the expense of funeral rites equivalent to 60 days' average wage of the worker to the person handling the funeral rites.

Article 81. (Expiry Compensation) In case a worker who receives compensation by Article 75 fails to recover from the injury or illness in three years from the date of his first medical treatment, the employer may discontinue the compensation prescribed in this Law after paying an expiry compensation equivalent to 1,200 days' average wage of the worker.

Article 82. (Compensation Payable in Instalment Plan) In case the employer gets the consent of the recipient of the compensation after proving an ability to meet payments, he can make annual payments every year, for a period of 6 years, of an amount of the average wage multiplied by the number of the days fixed in the attached table No. 2, instead of the compensation stipulated in Article 77 and Article 79.

Article 83. (Compensation Rights) Compensation rights shall not be changed by the labourer's resignation.

Compensation rights shall not be transferred or forfeited.

Article 84. (Relation to Other Laws) The employer is exempted from compensation obligation when he receives for the same accident benefit corresponding to the compensation of this Law from the Workman's Accident Compensation Insurance Law as far as the sum of benefit is concerned, or when he is eligible for compensation for the same accident corresponding to the compensation of this Law based on other laws or ordinances designated by ordinance.

When the employer pays compensation of this Law he is exempted within the limit of the amount from the damage indemnity under the Civil Code.

Article 85. (Investigation and Arbitration) Persons who have objections concerning the recognition of the injury, illness, or death on duty, the method of medical treatment, the amount of compensation or other matters pertaining to the compensation may require the investigation and arbitration thereabout of the administrative office.

When the administrative office deems it necessary, it may investigate or arbitrate in the case by the authority.

The administrative office is authorized to require a medical examination or autopsy when the office deems it necessary for the investigation or the arbitration.

The requirement of investigation and arbitration under Paragraph 1 and the beginning of investigation and arbitration under Paragraph 2 are deemed as request in the judicial court, concerning the interruption of prescription.

Article 86. (Appeal Board of Workmen's Accident Compensation) Those who are not satisfied with the result of the investigation and arbitration under the preceding Article can require the investigation and arbitration of the Appeal Board of Workmen's Accident Compensation.

Those who wish to sue civil action concerning the matters pertaining to the compensation under this Law must go through the investigation and arbitration of the Appeal Board of Workmen's Accident Compensation.

The members of the Appeal Board of Workmen's Accident Compensation shall be appointed in the same number from the representatives of labourers and employers and the representatives of the public by the Administrative Office.

Matters pertaining to the Appeal Board of Workmen's Accident Compensation other than those stipulated in the three foregoing paragraphs will be stipulated by ordinance.

Article 87. (Exception of Contracting Enterprise) When the enterprise is carried on under several times contracts, the original contractor is deemed as employer as far as accident compensation is concerned.

In the case of the foregoing paragraph, if the original contractor makes a contract in writing that the subordinate contractor should be responsible for compensation, the subordinate contractor is also deemed as employer. However, the original contractor shall not make more than one contract concerning the same enterprise that the subordinate contractor should be responsible for compensation.

In the case of the preceding paragraph, when required for compensation the original contractor may ask the worker to require the payment from the subordinate contractor first. However, this shall not apply in case the subordinate contractor becomes bankrupt or disappears.

Article 88. (Details on Compensation) Details concerning compensation payment other than those described in this Chapter shall be decided by ordinance.

Ch. IX.   Rule of Employment

Article 89. (Responsibility of Drawing Up and Submitting the Rule of Employment) Employers who employ more than ten workers continuously shall draw up a Rule of Employment on the following items and submit it to the administrative office. This is the same when they alter the Rule of Employment.

(1) The time to begin and end the work, recess, holidays, vacations, and matters pertaining to the change of the shift when the workers are employed in two or more shifts.

(2) The method of decision, computation and payment of wages, date of closing the account and payment of wages, and matters pertaining to the promotion in wages.

(3) Matters pertaining to retirement.

(4) When there is stipulation concerning retirement allowance and other allowance, bonus, minimum wage, matters pertaining to such items.

(5) When there is stipulation to make the workers bear the cost of food, working equipment and other expense, matters pertaining to such times.

(6) When there is regulation concerning safety and sanitation, matters pertaining to the regulation.

(7) When there is regulation concerning accident compensation, and relief for injury and illness suffered not from duty, matters pertaining to the regulation.

(8) When there is stipulation concerning official compensation and sanctions, matters pertaining to the kinds and degree of them.

(9) When there is other stipulation which is applicable to all workers, matters pertaining to such regulation.

When the employer deems it necessary, he may separate the regulation concerning wages, safety and sanitation, and accident compensation and relief for injury and illness suffered not from duty and make respective rules of them.

Article 90. (Procedures of making Rule of Employment) In making a Rule of Employment, the employer shall ask the opinion of the trade union which is composed of the majority of the workers when there is one at the working place concerned and not a person representing the majority of the workers.

The employer must attach a document to prove the opinions mentioned in the preceding paragraph to the Rule of Employment when he submits it in accordance with Paragraph 1 of the preceding Article.

Article 91. (Restrictions on Sanitation) When decrease of wage is to be stipulated as sanctioned in the Rule of Employment the amount of decrease shall not exceed half of one day's average wage for a single violation and shall not exceed ten per cent of the total wages for all violations during a payment period.

Article 92. (Relation with Laws and Ordinances or Labour Agreement) The Rule of Employment must not infringe on any law and ordinance or on Labour Agreement applicable to the working place.

The administrative office is authorized to order changes in the Rule of Employment if it is not in accord with laws and ordinances or Labour Agreement.

Article 93. (Validity) Labour contracts which stipulate conditions inferior to the standard fixed in the Rule of Employment are invalid as far as such conditions are concerned. In this case conditions which became invalid are replaced by the standard fixed in the Rule of Employment.

Ch. X. Dormitory

Article 94. (Autonomy of the Dormitory Life) The employer shall not infringe on the freedom of the private life of the workers in a dormitory attached to the enterprise.

The employer shall not interfere in the selection of the dormitory leader, room leader, and other leaders necessary for the autonomy of the dormitory life.

Article 95. (Order of Dormitory Life) The employer shall make a Rule of Dormitory attached to the working place covering the following items and submit it to administrative office. This is the same when he alters the Rule of Dormitory.

(1) Matters pertaining to arising, retiring, leaving the premises, and staying out overnight.

(2) Matters concerning daily functions.

(3) Matters concerning meals.

(4) Matters related to safety and health.

(5) Matters concerning the management of buildings and equipment.

The employer must obtain the consent of the representative of the majority of the workers living in the dormitory concerning matters which come under items 1 to 4 of the preceding paragraph.

The employer shall attach a document to prove the above-mentioned consent when he submits it in accord with Paragraph 1.

The employer and the workers who live in the dormitory must abide by the Rule of Dormitory.

Article 96. (Equipment, Safety and Sanitation of the Dormitory) Concerning the dormitory attached to the enterprise, the employer must take necessary means for ventilation, lighting, heating, damp-proofing, cleanliness, emergency escape, maximum accommodations, sleeping facilities, and other things necessary for the prevention of accident, good morale and sanitation.

The standard of means to be taken by the employer in accordance with the preceding paragraph will be stipulated by ordinance.

Ch. XI. Inspection Organization

Article 97. (Inspection Organization) For the enforcement of this Law, a Labour Standard Bureau in the competent Ministry of Labour, a Labour Standard Office in each prefecture and a Labour Standard Inspection Office within the scope of the prefecture shall be established.

When the competent Minister of Labour deems it necessary, a Regional Labour Office may be established which supervises several Prefectural Labour Standard Offices.

The Regional Labour Office, the Prefectural Labour Standard Office, and the Labour Standard Inspection Office shall be under the direct control and supervision of the competent Minister of Labour.

The number of officials of the Labour Standard Bureau, the location, name, administrative scope, and the number of officials of the Regional Labour Office, the Prefectural Labour Standard Office, and the Labour Standard Inspection Office shall be defined by ordinance.

Article 98. A Committee of Labour Standard shall be established in the competent Ministry of Labour and in the Prefectural Labour Standard Office to investigate matters pertaining to the enforcement and improvement of this Law.

The Committee of Labour Standard can recommend administrative offices concerned with labour standard of its own will even when it is not consulted by the competent Ministry of Labour or by the Prefectural Labour Standard Office.

The members of the Committee of Labour Standard shall be appointed in the same number from the representatives of labourer and employer and public by the administrative office.

Necessary matters except the three preceding paragraphs pertaining to the Committee of Labour Standard shall be defined by ordinance.

Article 99. Labour standard inspectors and other necessary officials defined by ordinance shall be installed in the Labour Standard Bureau, the Regional Labour Offices, the Prefectural Labour Standard Office, and in the Labour Standard Inspection Offices.

Chiefs of the Labour Standard Bureau, the Regional Labour Office, the Prefectural Labour Standard Office, and Chiefs of the Labour Standard Inspection Offices shall be appointed from among the inspectors.

Matters pertaining to the qualification, appointment and dismissal of a Labour Standard Inspector, shall be stipulated by ordinance.

In order to dismiss a Labour Standard Inspector, the competent Minister must obtain the concurrence of the Limitation Committee for Labour Standard Inspectors which shall be established by ordinance.

Article 100. The Chief of the Labour Standard Bureau under the supervision of the competent Minister of labour shall direct and supervise the Chief of the Regional Labour Bureau and the Chief of the Prefectural Labour Standard Office, and administer matters concerning the establishment or revision of the laws and ordinances concerning the labour standard, the appointment, dismissal and training of labour standard inspectors, establishment and co-ordination of the method of inspection, compilation of inspection year book, matters pertaining to the Committee of Labour Standard, the Committee for the Training of Skilled Labourers, the Limitation Committee for Labour Standard Inspectors and the Central Wage Board, and other matters pertaining to the enforcement of this Law, and shall direct and supervise officials who belong to the Bureau.

The Chief of the Regional Labour Office, under the direction and supervision of the Chief of the Labour Standard Bureau, shall direct and supervise the Chiefs of Prefectural Labour Standard Offices within the scope of the supervision and shall supervise matters pertaining to the co-ordination of the method of inspection and shall direct and supervise officials who belong to the office.

The Chief of the Prefectural Labour Standard Office under the direction and supervision of the Chief of Labour Standard Bureau, or the Chief of Regional Labour Office administer the direction and supervision of Chiefs of Labour Standard Inspection Offices within his scope, matters pertaining to the coordination of methods of inspection, matters pertaining to the Committee of Labour

Standard, the Appeal Board of Workmen's Accident Compensation and the Local Wage Board and other matters pertaining to the enforcement of this Law, and shall direct and supervise officials who belong to the office.

The Chief of the Labour Standard Inspection Office shall, under the direction and supervision of the Chief of the Prefectural Labour Standard Office, administer inspection, inquiry, approval, authorization, sanction, investigation, arbitration and other administrations based on this Law, and shall direct and supervise the officials who belong to the office.

The Chief of the Labour Standard Bureau, and the Chief of the Regional Labour Office or Chief of Prefectural Labour Standard Offices have the right to enforce the right which belongs to the chief of subordinate offices by themselves, or to let the Labour Standard Inspector who belongs to them enforce it.

Article 101. (Authority of the Labour Standard Inspectors) The Labour Standard Inspector is authorized to inspect working places, dormitories and other attached buildings, and examine records and documents, and question the employer or the workers.

A Labour Standard Inspector who is a doctor is authorized to make a medical examination of the worker who seems to be afflicted with disease which obliges the employer to ban the job of the worker.

The labour standard inspector may collect without cost such amount of samples or ingredients of the manufactures or materials as is necessary for the examination of injurious matter.

Article 102. In regard to violation of this Law, the Labour Standard Inspector is authorized to exercise the powers of a judicial police officer according to the Criminal Procedure Law.

Article 103. When the establishment, dormitory and other annex in which the workers are working, or the equipment or materials are below the standards of safety and health and when there are imminent threats to the safety and health of the workers, the Labour Standard Inspector can immediately exercise the authority vested in the administrative office under Article 55.

Article 104. (Report to the Inspection Organization) In case there is a fact inferior to the standard of this Law, at the working place, labourers may report to the administrative office or to the Labour Standard Inspector to that effect.

The employer shall not dismiss or discriminate against the workers who reported the fact according to the preceding paragraph by reason of their doing so.

Article 105. (Reponsibilities of the Labour Standard Inspector) The Labour Standard Inspector must not reveal any secret he learns

606

in the course of his duty. This applies even after the inspector resigns from his position.

Ch. XII. Miscellaneous Regulations

Article 106. (Dissemination of Law and Regulations) The employer shall inform the workers of the gist of this Law and ordinances based on this Law, and the rule of employment, by displaying or posting them in conspicuous places throughout the working place and by other means.

The employer shall inform workers living in the dormitory of the provisions concerning the dormitory of this Law and ordinances based on them and the rule of the dormitory, by displaying or posting them in conspicuous places in the dormitory and by other means.

Article 107. (Workers' Roster) The employer shall prepare a workers' roster for each worker (except daily worker) at each working place and must enter the worker's name, date of birth, personal history, and other matters as prescribed by ordinance.

Where there is any change in the matters to be entered by the stipulation of the preceding paragraph, the employer must revise it without delay.

Article 108. (Wage Ledger) The employer shall prepare a wage ledger at each working place and must enter the basic facts for the calculation of wages, the amount of wages, and other matters prescribed by ordinance at each payment without delay.

Article 109. (Preservation of Records) The employer shall keep the roster of workers, wage ledgers and important records of employment, dismissal, accident compensations, wages and other important matters concerning labour relations for a period of three years.

Article 110. (Reporting) When required by the administrative office or by the Labour Standard Inspector concerning the execution of this Law, the employer or the worker must report or appear without delay.

Article 111. (Free Proof of the Census Registers) Workers or worker aspirants may obtain proof of their census register from registration officials or their alternates free of cost. The same applies when the employer wishes to obtain a proof of the census register of workers or worker aspirants.

Article 112. (Application to Government and Public Organizations) This Law and ordinances based upon this Law are defined to apply to government, prefectures, cities, towns, villages, and other corresponding bodies.

Article 113. (Enactment of Ordinance) Ordinances based upon this Law shall be enacted after listening to the opinion of the representatives of both labour and employer and the public on the draft of them at the public hearing meeting.

Article 114. (Additional Payment) The law court is authorized by the request of the worker to order the employer who violated the stipulation of Article 20, Article 26, Article 31, or Article 37, or the employer who did not pay the average wage stipulated in Article 39, Paragraph 3, to pay the same amount of additional payment in addition to the unpaid money which the employer should have paid under these Articles.

Article 115. (Prescription) Wages, accident compensation, and other claims based on the stipulation of this Law shall become extinctive by prescription if they are not executed for two years.

Article 116. (Seamen) This Law shall not apply to seamen under Seamen's Act except Article 1 to Article 11 inclusive, Article 117 to Article 119 inclusive, and Article 120.

Ch. XIII. Penalty

Article 117. Any person who violates the stipulation of Article 5 shall be punished with penal servitude of not less than 1 year and not exceeding ten years, or with a fine of not less than 2,000 yen and not exceeding 30,000 yen.

Article 118. Any person who violates the stipulations of Article 6, Article 48, Article 56, or Article 64 shall be punished with penal servitude not exceeding one year or with a fine not exceeding 10,000 yen.

Article 119. Any person who corresponds to one of the following items shall be punished with penal servitude not exceeding 6 months or with a fine not exceeding 5,000 yen.

(1) A person who violates the stipulations of Article 3, Article 4, Article 7, Article 16, Article 17, Article 18, Paragraph 1, Article 19, Article 20, Article 22, Paragraph 3, Article 31, Article 32, Article 34, Article 35, Article 36, proviso clause, Articles 37, 39, 42, 43, 46, 47, Paragraph 1, Articles 49, 51, 60, Paragraph 2 or Paragraph 3, Article 61 to Article 63 inclusive, Articles 65, 66, 72, 75, to Article 77 inclusive, Articles 79, 80, 94, Paragraph 2, Article 96 or Article 104, Paragraph 2.

(2) A person who violates the order under Article 33, Paragraph 2, Article 54, Paragraph 2 or Article 55, Paragraph 1.

(3) A person who violates the stipulation of ordinance issued under Article 40.

(4) A person who violates the number of workers, method of indoctrination, period of contract, working hours, wage standard or method of payment, permitted under Article 71, Paragraph 1.

Article 120. A person who corresponds to one of the following items shall be punished with fine not exceeding 5,000 yen.

(1) Any person who violates the stipulation of Article 14, Article 15, Paragraph 1 or Paragraph 3, Article 22, Paragraph 1 or Paragraph 2, Articles 23 to 27 inclusive, Article 33, Paragraph 1, proviso clause, Articles 44, 50, 52, Paragraph 1 or Paragraph 2, Article 53, Paragraph 1, Article 54, Paragraph 1, Articles 57 to 59 inclusive, Articles 67, 68, 71, Paragraph 2, Articles 89, 90, Paragraph 1, Articles 91, 95, Paragraph 1 or Paragraph 2, or Article 105 to Article 109 inclusive.

(2) A person who violates the method of keeping and releasing sanctioned under Article 18, Paragraph 2.

(3) A person who violates the order under Article 53, Paragraph 3, Article 35, Paragraph 2, or Article 92, Paragraph 2.

(4) A person who refuses, impedes, or evades the inspection, medical examination, or collection of samples by the Labour Standard Inspector based on the stipulation of Article 101, or person who refuses to reply or makes mendacious reply to the inquiry of the Labour Standard Inspector, or person who does not offer records and document or who submits mendacious record or document to the Labour Standard Inspector.

(5) A person who does not report or submits mendacious report, or did not appear when required by the administrative office or by the Labour Standard Inspector based on Article 110.

Article 121.   In case a person who perpetrated the violation of this Law is a deputy hired person or other employee who acts on behalf of the owner of the enterprise, in matters concerning the workers of the enterprise, the owner of the enterprise shall be also fined by the stipulation in each Article in addition to the perpetrator. However, in case the owner of the enterprise (when the owner is a corporation, its representatives, when the owner is a minor who is not given equal right as the adult concerning the enterprise, or a person adjudged as incompetent, the legal representatives of them, are deemed as the owner of the enterprise; this term is used in the same meaning hereafter in this Article) took necessary measures to prevent the violation, the owner shall not be fined by the stipulation of each Article.

The owner of the enterprise who has known the plan of violation and has not taken necessary measures to prevent the violation, or who has known the violation and has not taken necessary measures to correct the violation, or who instigated the violation shall be subject to punishment as the perpetrator.

Supplementary Provisions

Article 122.   The date for the enforcement of this Law shall be fixed by Imperial Ordinance.

Article 123. Factory Law, Minimum Age for Industrial Employment Law, Workmen's Accident Relief Law, Shop Law, Prohibition Laws of Yellow Phosphorus, Match Manufacturing, and No. 87 Laws of 1939, are abolished.

Article 124. Mining Law is revised as follows : Article 71 item 2, Article 75 to Article 80-4 inclusive and Article 97, item 3 and item 4 are abolished.

Article 125. Sand Mining Law is revised as follows : Articles 76 to 79 inclusive in Article 23, Paragraph 1, and Paragraph 2 of the same Article are abolished.

Article 126. Trade Union Law is revised as follows : Article 32 is abolished.

Article 127. The stipulations of Article 18, Paragraph 2, Article 49, Article 57, Article 60, Article 63 inclusive, Article 89, Article 95, Articles 106 to 108 inclusive shall not apply for six months after the date of the enforcement of this Law.

Concerning those matters which have been prohibited or restricted by the old laws and which correspond to the provisions of the preceding paragraph the stipulations of the old laws still hold good for that period.

Article 128. In case the employer who employs children above full 12 years old at the time of enforcement of this Law, employs those children continuously, the stipulation of Article 56 shall not apply to the person for six months after the date of enforcement of this Law.

In case the employer who employs men above full 16 years old at the time of enforcement of this Law employs them continuously, the stipulation of Article 64 shall not apply to the persons for one year after the date of enforcement of this Law.

Article 129. Concerning the accident compensation for the injury, illness, or death because of duty which occurred before the date of enforcement of this Law, the stipulation of relief in the old laws still hold good.

Article 130. Concerning the application of penalty to the act perpetrated before the enforcement of this Law, the old Acts still hold good.

ATTACHED TABLE No. 1
Chart of Compensation for Damages and the Classification of Physical Handicaps

Classification		Compensation for damages
1	....	1,340 days
2	....	1,190 ,,

Classification   Compensation for
                                            damages

3	....	1,050 days
4	....	920 ,,
5	....	790 ,,
6	....	670 ,,
7	....	560 ,,
8	....	450 ,,
9	....	350 ,,
10	....	270 ,,
11	....	200 ,,
12	....	140 ,,
13	....	90 ,,
14	....	50 ,,

ATTACHED TABLE No. 2

Chart of Payments for Compensation for Damages

Classification   Compensation for
compensation   damages
for injury

1	....	240 days
2	....	213 ,,
3	....	188 ,,
4	....	164 ,,
5	....	142 ,,
6	....	120 ,,
7	....	100 ,,
8	....	80 ,,
9	....	63 ,,
10	....	48 ,,
11	....	36 ,,
12	....	25 ,,
13	....	16 ,,
14	....	9 ,,
Compensation for bereaved family	....	180 ,,

Political Reorientation of Japan, Appendix H: 9, pp. 872-84.

II   31 *July* 1948

CABINET ORDER BANNING COLLECTIVE BARGAINING
BY GOVERNMENT EMPLOYEES

I hereby promulgate the Cabinet Order concerning the Temporary Measures to be taken in consequence of the letter of the Supreme Commander for the Allied Powers to the Prime Minister dated 22 July 1948 under the Imperial Ordinance No. 542 of 1945 concerning the Orders to be issued in pursuance of the Acceptance of the Potsdam Declaration.

Signed: HIROHITO, Seal of the Emperor.
This thirty-first day of the seventh month of the twenty-third year of Showa (31 July 1948).

Prime Minister,
ASHIDA HITOSHI

Cabinet Order No. 201

Cabinet Order concerning the Temporary Measures to be taken in consequence of the letter of the Supreme Commander for the Allied Powers to the Prime Minister dated 22 July 1948.

The Cabinet hereby establishes the Cabinet Order concerning the temporary measures to be taken in consequence of the letter of the Supreme Commander for the Allied Powers to the Prime Minister dated 22 July 1948 under the Imperial Ordinance No. 542 of 1945 concerning the Orders to be issued in pursuance of the Acceptance of the Potsdam Declaration.

Article 1. (1) Those persons who hold positions as employees of the national government or local public entities, regardless of whether they are appointed or employed (hereinafter referred to as public employees and the Temporary National Personal Commission has the authority to determine whether certain positions are in public service or not when there is doubt) shall not have the right, to be exercised against the national government or local public entities, of collective bargaining as usually understood with its coercive character supported by the strike threat. Public employees or their organizations, however, may not be denied the freedom, within the restriction of the present Cabinet Order, to negotiate with the appropriate agency of the national government or local public entity in the sense of being able freely to present individually or collectively, through their representatives, their complaints, opinions, desires and grievances and to support the same by adequate opportunity for discussion and the submission of evidence.

(2) All acts heretofore taken by the national government or local public entities in personnel matters affecting public servants will be valid so long as they do not violate the spirit of the limitations imposed by the present Cabinet Order or were not taken in contravention of such limitations.

(3) All mediation proceedings now pending in which the national government or local public entities are parties will be suspended. The National Personnel Authority will hereafter be the agency charged with the protection of the interests of public servants.

Article 2. (1) No public employees may resort to strike or engage in delaying or other dispute tactics which tend to impair the efficiency of operation of national government or local public entities.

(2) Those who act in violation of the provisions of the preceding paragraph, regardless of their status of being public employees, may not assert their rights derived from such appointment or employment against the national government or local public entities.

Article 3. Those who act in violation of Paragraph 1 of Article 2 shall be liable to penal servitude not exceeding one year or a fine not exceeding 5,000 yen.

Supplementary Provisions

(1) The present Cabinet Order shall come into force as from the day of its promulgation.

(2) The present Cabinet Order shall be effective until the legislation by the Diet concerning the amendment of the National Public Service Law mentioned in the letter of the Supreme Commander for the Allied Powers to the Prime Minister dated 22 July 1948 and other measures which may be deemed necessary are undertaken and come into force.

Text Supplied by the Japanese Government Overseas Agency, New Delhi, August 1948.

12   1 *February* 1948

GENERAL MACARTHUR'S REPLY TO CRITICISM OF ECONOMIC POLICY

(*The following was sent as a letter to Mr J. H. Gipson, The Caxton Printers, Ltd., Caldwell, Idaho, under date of 24 January 1948 ; permission for release to the press was given on 1 February 1948.—Ed.*)

Thank you so much for sending me the extract of comments on Japan from the December release of the Committee for Constitutional

Government in New York, with your letter of 27 December which has just reached me.

I have never heard of this Committee and know nothing about its purpose or composition, but its estimate of the situation here is amazing in its complete inaccuracy. The existing Government of Japan is fully representative of the popular will, elected under thoroughly democratic processes in accordance with the provisions of a constitution patterned in essential respects after our own. The only 'private enterprise' which has heretofore existed in Japan was neither free nor competitive—two fundamental qualifications of American economic philosophy which it is my firm purpose to see entrenched in the Japanese system before the Occupation withdraws.

Japan has long had a system of 'private enterprise'—but one which permitted ten family groups comprising only fifty-six Japanese families to control, directly or indirectly, every phase of commerce and industry ; all media of transportation, both internal and external; all domestic raw materials ; and all coal and other power resources. The 'private enterprise' was thus limited to a few of feudal lineage, who exploited into virtual slavery the remainder of the Japanese people, permitted higher standards of life to others only through sufferance, and in search of further plunder abroad furnished the tools for the military to embark upon its ill-fated venture into world conquest. The record is thus one of economic oppression and exploitation at home, aggression and spoliation abroad. As early as 1930, these Japanese industrial combines veered in the direction of armaments production and geared the country for war. This portrays the private enterprise to which the Committee refers.

As you will see, the very start towards free enterprise is dependent upon tearing down so abnormal a structure. For, so long as it remains undisturbed, it is a standing bid for State ownership, and a fruitful target for Communist propaganda and collectivist purposes. The Japanese people, with the exception of those who covet the opportunity to exploit this situation for ideological purposes, and those who have been entrenched within its orbit of political and economic power, are overwhelmingly in favour of destroying such a system, and unless its destruction is effected peacefully and in due order under the occupation, there is little doubt but that if necessary the way would be found even through the violence of revolutionary means once the occupation is withdrawn.

In all of these measures in the reformation of Japan, it must be clearly understood that we are here dealing with fundamental realities. It does not suffice merely to issue an edict that there shall be no socialism, or that there shall be no advance of communism or other ideologies opposed to the one in which we ourselves firmly believe. For the strength of such an edict would find its measure in the power of Allied bayonets alone. The need has called for positive action which, while we yet have time, will superimpose here upon a decadent and discredited past a system of government and economics which, because their very processes generate a more healthy and virile society will even after our controls are lifted stand as an invincible buttress against the inroads of any conflicting philosophies of life.

In the accomplishment of this purpose, two difficult barriers have stood out to bar any progress. The one has dealt with the feudalistic system of land ownership under which practically all agricultural land has been owned by a relatively few persons of feudal heritage, with all agrarian workers exploited under conditions of practical serfdom. This archaic system of land ownership is being torn down in order that through sale in small lots those who long have worked the soil may have the opportunity substantially to profit from their toil. Thereby there will emerge in Japan, from a field heretofore fertile to the spread of communism, a new class of small capitalistic landowners which itself will stand firm against efforts to destroy the system of capitalistic economy of which it will then form an integral part. Needless to say, the communists and the land barons alone oppose this reform.

The other barrier is the one which I have heretofore described, popularly known as the Zaibatsu, and in neither case, even despite war enrichment at the sacrifice of American blood, has there been any confiscation of property, as the principle of just compensation throughout has governed, with untrammelled recourse left to judicial appeal in the Japanese courts. The effect of its dissolution will be to transform a small number of monopolistic combines into numerous competing units and to bring about widespread ownership of the instruments of production and trade, thereby erecting a solid bulwark against the spread of ideologies and systems destructive of both free enterprise and political freedom under democratic capitalism. Otherwise, if business in Japan were allowed to continue with its concentration of economic power, it would lead to concentration of power in government, and from there the transition to socialism of one form or another would be natural, easy of accomplishment, and inevitable.

The statement of the Committee that 'prominent leaders including many outstanding friends of freedom, have been ousted from the control of industry and their places have been taken by incompetent visionaries' finds no basis in fact. Apart from action taken with respect to the Zaibatsu, wherein the family members and their appointees are removed from positions of influence in the identical enterprises they have heretofore controlled, there have been in all less than two hundred and fifty persons removed under Allied policy from positions in the economy under the purge programme. The removal of these persons was due to their close identity with the causes which led to war. In the implementation of this phase of the occupation programme, I have in the exercise of the normal discretion accorded a field commander, pursued far less drastic measures than were called for by my policy directives from the Allied Powers, shifting the emphasis from punitive action to action merely designed to provide for a more healthy leadership and one unattained by war responsibility. Even in those cases of persons removed from positions of power, involving the most aggravated circumstances, I have, against strong Allied opposition, permitted no property confiscation, no deprivation of liberty, no forfeiture of political rights, and where restriction upon future economic activity is involved embracing but a relatively few persons, I have ensured that policy-makers rather than technicians were affected, and have left undisturbed a broad field of economic activity in which even they might continue to engage without the slightest restriction. If within this small group of persons affected, there are any outstanding 'friends of freedom', they are unknown to this headquarters, and all have had the opportunity through exhaustively fair hearings before screening committees of the Japanese Government and on appeal, to prove any such contentions. The statement that the places of those few removed have been taken by incompetent visionaries is absurd. Such places have in all cases been filled by junior executives of long service in the enterprises concerned, who have moved up into opportunities which otherwise would not have been available to them.

The Committee's statement that 'the government has been flooded with a horde of bureaucrats', not unlike the situation in other capitals, is probably true. Even so, on the national level of government there are less than 350,000 persons so employed, which is not disproportionate to Japan's population of seventy-eight million, should standards elsewhere be accepted as a general guide. It is not the quantity, however, which has given me most concern, but the quality and the inordinate power which the bureaucracy traditionally has arrogated to itself in Japan. To cope with this evil, we are now in the process of assisting the Japanese Government towards a civil service reform. The pattern already has been set through wise and farsighted legislation, the implementation of which will be completed within the present year. The basic purpose and effect of this reform is to require that all public officials justify

616

the trust of public responsibility and answer for their acts directly to the people.

The general statement that the money is unsound, that foreign trade is restricted by a maze of regulations, and that production is paralysed is wholly misrepresentative in its failure to recognize the following fundamental and controlling facts, i.e., (1) that Japan is a totally defeated nation, still technically at war with the Allied Powers and under the controls of military occupation ; (2) that a primary objective of war and cause of defeat was the destruction of Japan's industrial capacity to wage war and ability to transport its sinews on the high seas ; (3) that Japan has always been dependent for the bulk of the raw materials essential to sustain the industrial capacity upon procurement from abroad, now denied by the economic blockade inherent in the present situation ; (4) that Japan's shipping afloat has been destroyed, and Manchuria, Formosa and Korea, former sources of direct procurement of essential raw materials, have been taken away ; and (5) that Japanese money, not unlike that even of all of the victor nations, is suffering the severe strain of war-caused economic dislocations.

Finally, the statement that 'the net result has been so to paralyse production as to leave the Japanese people on the verge of starvation, and that the Americans are now called upon to furnish hundreds of millions of dollars to relieve the hunger for which our representatives are primarily responsible' is completely lacking in realism and false as an indictment. The wonder is that despite the lack of needed raw materials, widespread destruction of plant facilities, and seizures under Allied policy for reparation payments, the industrial output has risen from complete paralysis at war's end to over 40 per cent of pre-war levels. It must be understood that the Japanese people before the war suffered a deficiency in indigenous food resources which compelled the importation from abroad of approximately 20 per cent of food requirements. Add to this natural deficiency the fact that over six million Japanese citizens have been repatriated to the home islands, with none permitted to leave during the Occupation, while Manchuria, Korea and Formosa have been removed as sources of food supply, and you can understand the actualities which exist. During the Occupation we have contributed food partially to cover this deficiency, but such contribution has not even approximated to the importations required during the pre-war era when industry was at full capacity and there was a smaller population to feed. Such action has not been entirely altruistic as under Japan's present status the Japanese people are in all practical aspects our prisoners of war, and as such entitled to our protection under the international conventions which we ourselves historically have never failed to respect. Even so, the Japanese people have made diligent effort themselves to solve this deficiency problem, and once a healthier economic structure has been erected, there will be seen, through the release of long suppressed energies of a people enslaved, the building of that higher productivity which alone comes from a people who are free.

The foregoing will give you the facts as they exist for comparison with those stated by the Committee, which you have been good enough to quote. The prescription for Japan's economic ills is as crystal clear as it is simple—a structural redesign to make possible the emergence of an economic system based not solely upon the formula of 'private enterprise' to which the Committee alludes, but to *free* private *competitive* enterprise which Japan has never before known, and which alone will maximize the energies of the people. Even more, the conclusion of a treaty of peace which would permit the reopening of the channels of trade and commerce to make available essential raw materials to feed the production lines, world markets to absorb the finished products, and food to sustain working energy.

DOUGLAS MACARTHUR

Political Reorientation of Japan, Appendix F : 42, pp. 780-82.

13   19 *May* 1948

JOHNSTON COMMITTEE REPORT (SUMMARY)

In Japan General MacArthur, Supreme Commander for the Allied Powers, is administering the Occupation of the four main islands which have a population of nearly 80,000,000.

The Committee has been greatly impressed with the complete demilitarization of Japan and with the progress made in developing representative government in that formerly feudalistic country. A thoroughly democratic constitution has been adopted and an elected Diet, or Parliament, is actively functioning. Unlike the situation in Germany and Korea, Japan is not cut up in separate zones of occupation, and a Japanese Government is actively dealing with the daily problems of its people. The Japanese people themselves seem to be fully co-operating with the Occupation authorities. These are outstanding achievements.

Although two and one-half years have passed since the surrender, no treaty of peace has yet been signed. The United States has been paying the military costs of occupation and in addition, under its international law obligation as occupying Power to prevent disease and unrest, has been furnishing food and other relief supplies to keep the Japanese people alive. Those relief costs run to nearly $400,000,000 a year. In our opinion the United States must now face squarely the problem of assisting the Japanese people to become self-supporting.

Japan has been shorn of its empire and no longer has under its control resources of food and raw materials which formerly contributed to its prosperity. It has been expelled from China, Manchuria, Korea and Formosa, southern Sakhalin, the Kurile, Marshall and Mariana groups of islands. It grows only 80 per cent of its minimum food requirements. Its population is increasing a million a year. It must produce and export industrial products in large volume to live. It is short of natural resources and raw materials.

The Committee believes that the United States should now assist the recovery of Japan. Japan's industrial products are needed throughout the Far East, whose countries also need Japan as a market for their potential exportable production—their tin, rubber, copra, wool, cotton, iron ore, bauxite, sugar and rice. Japanese industry is operating at a very low level—less than 45 per cent of the 1930-34 average. Shortage of needed raw materials is a major reason. However, despite the upheaval of war and defeat and the changing social outlook, the traditional will to work of the Japanese people themselves is still in evidence. Food production and coal production have been rising, although both are far below minimum needs. Food collections are better than at any time since the occupation—in fact rice collections reached 100 per cent of this year's quota while the Committee was in Japan.

The reparations issue has not been settled. The Japanese do not yet know which plants and which equipment will be left to them, so, within industries thought to be subject to reparations, incentive to restore and reconstruct is suppressed. Plants which are needed in bringing about the recovery of Japan should be retained and only excess capacity removed. Otherwise the United States, which is now extending relief to Japan, would in reality be paying the reparations bill. In our opinion, the capacity that can be spared without affecting Japan's useful peace-time productivity is not great. It is most important that the present uncertainty be removed and the reparation issue be finally settled.

Japanese exports have been growing and reached $172,000,000 last year. Most of these exports, however, were made possible only by a special scheme of American assistance—particularly in cotton manufacture. A beginning has been made, nothing more. Total exports will have to increase to eight to nine times present levels to provide payment for the imported food and raw materials needed to sustain a reasonable standard of life in Japan. In our opinion, it should be possible to accomplish this if tranquillity is restored throughout the Far East, if present restrictions in Japanese trade and travel are lessened, and if help is given to import raw materials and get production going. An eventual shift in Japanese food and other imports from the dollar area to the sterling and Far Eastern areas, with compensation in Japanese industrial exports, is essential to any permanent Far Eastern recovery.

The Japanese merchant marine has been reduced by war losses to 20 per cent of its pre-war size. Most of the larger ocean-going Japanese ships have been lost with the bulk of the remaining fleet consisting of small coastal and fishing vessels. Payment to non-Japanese shipping of present-day inflated freights on essential imports is a large factor in Japan's foreign trade deficit. We believe that Japan should be encouraged to increase its merchant shipping both by new building and by bareboat chartering of available vessels.

Principal among Japan's internal problems is the inflationary spiral resulting from the extreme scarcity of raw materials and consumer goods, the constant upward pressure of wages and other costs, and the heavy budgetary deficit. The internal cost of the occupation adds to this problem. Until this inflation problem can be solved by greater production, increased tax revenues, and more rigid control of governmental expenditures, the establishment of a stable foreign exchange rate, and even of a stable internal economy, can hardly be achieved. Here again, the importation of greater amounts of raw materials and the resulting increased production will assist in a solution.

Drastic and continuing efforts by the Japanese themselves are necessary to balance the national budget. Self-help and self-sacrifice in clarifying and controlling internal price and wage relationships, in reducing national expenditures and increasing tax revenues, expanding domestic production of food, coal and products from other Japanese resources, are essential to proper use of any American assistance and, of course, to economic recovery itself. The Japanese people will have to work hard and long, with comparatively little recompense for many years to come, in order to survive and support their growing population.

In conclusion the Committee agrees with General MacArthur and the Department of the Army that industrial recovery of Japan on a peaceful basis is necessary to bring about a self-supporting economy ; that this programme has now properly become a primary objective of the occupation; and that the American Government in the national interest should support a reasonable recovery programme.

In Korea the problem is complicated by the artificial division of the country into two zones of military occupation. The Koreans are eager for the independence to which our Government is committed. It has been impossible so far to hold elections throughout all Korea, but an election is soon to be held in the South Korean (American) zone, under the auspices of the United Nations. After the election and the establishment of a representative government it is proposed under the United Nations resolution to work out arrangements for the withdrawal of occupation troops.

Korean food production is improving and South Korea should eventually be able to supply its own food requirements if fertilizer requirements can be met. Other problems, however, are most acute. Lack of raw materials is greater even than in Japan. South Korea is dependent on North Korea for most of its electric power supply. The Korean rail-roads would stop if coal supplied by our Occupation authorities in Japan were cut off. The industries which Japan developed during 40 years of Japanese control are operating at only about 20 per cent of capacity. South Korea is short of raw materials, and equally short of management and technical supervision formerly supplied by the Japanese. As in Japan, the United States has been supplying food, fertilizer, and petroleum products to keep the economy from collapse and to prevent widespread disease and unrest.

Here again the Committee believes, with General Hodge, our Military Commander, that reasonable assistance should be given to finance importation of agricultural and industrial goods. An interim aid programme, not limited solely to relief, should give a new Korean Government, when it is formed under the supervision of the United Nations, the needed help to establish the stable economic conditions so necessary to encouraging the development of free democratic government.

Finally, our Committee has examined the proposed recovery programme prepared by the Department of the Army and supported by the State Department. The programme would provide a total of $220,000,000 for a twelve-month period for raw materials and other recovery items for Japan, Korea, and the Ryukyu Islands. We believe such a recovery programme essential in order to reduce and eventually eliminate spending in these areas for relief.

As an occupying Power we have accepted a flag responsibility. We believe the United States can discharge this responsibility better, and end it earlier, by concentrating on economic recovery and by gradually reducing relief. Our Committee therefore recommends approval and execution by our Government of the suggested recovery programme at the earliest possible date.

Contemporary Japan, Vol. XVII, Nos. 4-6, April-June 1948, pp. 211-14.

14   23 *September* 1948

STATEMENT OF THE SOVIET REPRESENTATIVE ON
THE FAR EASTERN COMMISSION ON THE LEVEL OF
ECONOMIC LIFE IN JAPAN AND THE POLICY
TOWARDS JAPANESE INDUSTRY

The question of the level of industrial development for Japan is one of the most important questions requiring settlement. The determination of the level for the development of Japanese industry will predetermine the future economic development of Japan.

However, while considering this question it is necessary to understand clearly what industry is to be developed. Industry may work to meet the peaceful requirements of the country. But it is also known that industry may work for the purpose of military preparation, as was the case earlier in Japan.

Therefore, from the very beginning it is necessary to clarify this question and then to determine one's attitude toward one or another proposal concerning the level of the future industrial capacity of Japan. Besides, it should be remembered that Japan will have to satisfy legitimate claims for reparations on the part of those states which suffered from Japanese aggression.

The Soviet Government does not consider it reasonable to require limitations of the level of the development of Japan's peaceful industry for the future. Such a requirement could find no justification whatsoever. It would meet neither the interests of the Japanese people, nor the interests of other countries, and, first of all, of Asiatic countries which are in need of economic ties with Japan.

A high level of industrial development of Japan will not in itself be dangerous if Japan is not permitted to revive her war industry and militarism. Japanese industry in the past served as an economic basis for Japanese aggression, not because it had reached a comparatively high level of development, but because of the fact that its development had been subordinated to the needs of war.

Japanese militaristic circles, acting contrary to the vital interests of the Japanese people, directed the development of the country's industry as well as of the economy as a whole in such a way that it was adapted to meet the needs of the army and navy, i.e., it worked for the preparation of war.

Such a situation suited the interests of aggressive Japanese circles, which set themselves the purpose of enslaving other countries and peoples in alliance with Hitlerite Germany. However, it goes without saying that this should not be repeated, since militaristic Japan was defeated and there is an opportunity to direct the development of Japan along democratic and peace-loving lines. Now measures must be taken to prevent the revival of Japanese militarism and the conversion of Japan once again into a hotbed of war danger.

In order to ensure the settlement of this problem, the development of Japanese industry should have as its sole purpose the satisfaction of the peaceful needs of the Japanese people. If we proceed from this, the only correct basis, the unfoundedness of demands to limit the development of peaceful Japanese industry will become self-evident.

The development of peaceful Japanese industry to the level of 1930-34 or to a higher level will contribute to the improvement of the physical well-being of Japan's population, which continues to suffer serious after-effects of the criminal and adventurous policy of the Japanese militarists.

Such a development of industry will broaden the possibilities of Japanese export, will contribute to the strengthening of Japan's economic independence and will lighten the dependence of Japan's national economy on external factors which are alien to her interests.

Besides this, the export of Japanese industrial goods would contribute to the satisfaction of appropriate needs, for example, of certain Asiatic countries, and would thus serve for Japan as a basis for the import of raw materials needed by her, and of other goods necessary to satisfy the peaceful needs of the Japanese people.

It follows from the above that the objective of the Allied Powers should be, not limitation of the development of Japan's peaceful industry, but prevention of the development in Japan of war industry, as well as prevention of the creation of conditions under which Japanese militarism and Japanese aggression can revive.

Naturally, the question arises as to how this objective could possibly be attained. The Soviet Government considers that this objective can be attained if an appropriate control is established in Japan for a certain period in order to prevent the revival or creation of Japanese war industry. All peace-loving nations should be interested in the establishment of such a control.

Such a control, established for a period of several years and exercised by the Powers most interested in preventing a new Japanese aggression, should be provided for in the Peace Treaty with Japan, the preparation and conclusion of which is long overdue.

In accordance with the position which I have stated, I propose on the instructions of the Soviet Government that the following decisions be adopted :—

(1) No limitations should be imposed upon the restoration and development of peaceful Japanese industry which seeks to satisfy the needs of the Japanese population, nor upon the development of export in accordance with the needs of Japan's peaceful economy.

(2) The revival and creation of Japanese war industry should be prohibited and there should be established, for a period of several years, a control over the fulfilment of this decision, to be exercised by those Powers most interested in preventing a new Japanese aggression.

USSR Information Bulletin, Washington, 6 October 1948.

15   9 *December* 1948

STATEMENT BY GENERAL FRANK Mc COY, UNITED STATES REPRESENTATIVE ON THE FAR EASTERN COMMISSION, ON UNITED STATES POLICY TOWARDS JAPANESE INDUSTRIAL DECONCENTRATION

Some months ago, my Government suspended its participation in discussions in the Far Eastern Commission of a United States policy proposal which was then under active consideration in the Commission. This proposal, designated as FEC 230, presented an extremely detailed plan for the implementation of a general policy which already had been stated in existing directives to the Supreme Commander. That policy, which called for the dissolution of certain Japanese combines and a widening in the distribution of the income and ownership of Japanese industry, was then and continues to be, in the view of my Government, a fundamental objective of the Occupation.

The action of the United States in suspending consideration of its proposal, however, has led to certain questions among the members of this Commission and among the Japanese people. The purpose of this statement is to clarify the position of the United States with respect to FEC 230.

Since the very first week of the Occupation, the Supreme Commander has devoted a considerable part of the time and resources of his staff to the problem of reorganizing the financial and industrial institutions of Japan. This program, which has been based upon the Post-Surrender Directive issued 6 December 1945 and on the Far Eastern Commission's own Basic Post-Surrender policy for Japan, was designed to make possible the early development of democratic and peacefully-inclined economic institutions in Japan. To bring about the result, plans were immediately developed and put into effect to dissolve the control of Japanese finances and industry which rested in the hands of a few powerful Japanese families.

As a part of this programme, the Supreme Commander directed the Japanese Government to adopt various laws and to create certain governmental bodies charged with the responsibility of undertaking a major reorganization of the ownership and control of Japanese industry. In the brief span of three years substantial progress has been made by these bodies. The assets of the fifty-six persons who comprised the heads of the ten major Zaibatsu families and the assets of the eighty-three holding companies controlled by these persons have been acquired by the Government and are in process of being sold to the Japanese public. A much larger number of companies have been compelled to divest themselves of holdings in and control over smaller enterprises. Such control was exercised through intercorporate stockholdings, interlocking directorates and similar devices. Contractual arrangements to which these Japanese enterprises were parties which had the effect of placing the control of production or trade in the hands of such enterprises have been declared void. The innumerable Control Associations through which Japanese enterprises exercised their collective authority are being liquidated. Action is being taken and is well-advanced towards reorganization of former savings banks, trust companies and governmental banking institutions, making possible the emergence of a significant number of new commercial banks, to compete with and supplement the few large banking combines which formerly dominated Japanese credit sources. Finally, some scores of Japanese companies whose present state may constitute a threat to competitive enterprise are being scrutinized, one by one. Where necessary, these combines will be subjected to such reorganization as may be required to remove the existing threat.

To insure that the dispersion of economic control which is developing from these measures will not likely be reversed in the years to come, substantial revisions have been effected in the basic economic legislation of Japan. To begin with, an Anti-Trust Law has been adopted and a fair Trade Commission set up to enforce the Law. In general the Law seeks to restrain the development of new combines, excessively large or powerful, by outlawing agreements which restrain production or trade, by placing limitations upon intercorporate stockholdings, interlocking directorates, and similar devices for the concentration of corporate control, and by setting up procedures and penalties for the enforcement of these provisions. Other legislation now requires Japanese corporations to make considerably more information available to their stockholders and the public than heretofore has been the case and generally requires the management of corporations to adhere to much higher standards of public responsibility in the managements of their enterprise.

Moreover, many existing laws which tended to centralize the control of Japanese industry within a small group have been abrogated outright. Others have been modified drastically. The Fair Trade Commission and other Government agencies are analysing still other Japanese laws to eliminate provisions which confer special privilege or tend to restrain or eliminate competition. Various laws relating to the conduct of Japanese banking have been placed under particularly careful scrutiny. One of the principle objectives of the revision of Japanese banking laws is to create a climate in which the undesirable pre-war concentration of Japanese credit in a few hands could not recur.

In all this, the Japanese Government has demonstrated a commendable ability to comprehend Allied objectives and has co-operatively fulfilled its obligations. The Japanese Fair Trade Commission has prosecuted a significant series of cases against Japanese businessmen who were violating one provision or another of the statutes which seek to prevent new concentrations of Japanese industry. The Japanese Holding Company Liquidation Commission has made a careful study of the structure of the larger Japanese combines and, in close co-operation with the Supreme Commander, is currently developing plans for such reorganization of these combines as may be needed.

As the occupation and the economic situation have developed, there has been a corresponding evolution in the deconcentration programme. For example, it has proved possible and desirable to dissolve most of the war-time control associations. As new sources of credit have been created through the conversion of other financial institutions to commercial banks, it has been possible to reconsider the need for the actual dissolution, once believed necessary, of Japan's biggest banks, which under earlier circumstances had dominated the credit structures of Japan.

With the daily growth of indication that the Japanese propose to enforce their trade laws vigorously and effectively, it has been possible to reconsider the standards to be used in the dissolution of some of the combines still existing. These changes in emphasis have been responsive to changing circumstances and have represented relatively minor alterations in a programme which basically remains unchanged. That programme, adhering to the broad purposes of the directive of the Far Eastern Commission, seeks to achieve in Japan an economic climate conducive to the development of a democratic society. It seeks to prevent the resurgence of economic power in the hands of a few who recognize no responsibility to the Japanese people or the world at large.

When the United States suspended its participation in the discussion of FEC 230 in the Far Eastern Commission, that decision was based upon the growing realization that the guidance for the Supreme Commander and the Japanese envisaged therein had largely been overtaken by events. The major points of procedure set out in that document already had been implemented in Japan. Other details believed necessary to the accomplishing of the major objectives either had been faithfully adopted or had become unnecessary or inappropriate. Useful as the paper might have been at an earlier stage of the Occupation, that usefulness no longer appeared to exist.

That the paper has become outmoded in so brief a period is a singular tribute to SCAP and the Japanese Government. Procedures which it was thought would take years to carry out in many cases have been accomplished in a matter of months. Major technical obstacles have been overcome and the demonstrated determination of the Supreme Commander to carry the programme through has elicited a gratifying degree of co-operation from the Japanese themselves. Accordingly, upon a careful re-survey of the deconcentration programme now well advanced in Japan, the United States now believes that, as a practical matter, there is no need to lay down policies for the guidance of the Supreme Commander, with respect to any remaining significant aspect of the programme. Indeed, to do so in the outmoded terms in which FEC 230 is cast might well do more harm to the programme than good. Hence, the United States has withdrawn its support of FEC 230 as a proposal upon which the Far Eastern Commission could act with benefit to the Occupation.

This does not mean that the deconcentration programme has been completed. Considerable amounts of securities still remain in the hands of the Government and must be disposed of. Ingenuity and vigour must be brought to this task. Existing banking legislation will undoubtedly be elaborated and refined in consonance with the objectives of this programme. Those remaining Japanese combines whose existence may constitute a threat to competitive enterprise will, where necessary, be reorganized as required to remove such threat. But these programmes no longer call for the development of policy. They call largely for a practical application of judgement,

energy and enterprise in implementing a programme whose philosophy
and objectives are clearly understood by the Supreme Commander
and the Japanese Government, as they have already convincingly
demonstrated.

Documents on International Affairs, 1947-8, Royal Institute of International Affairs,
London, 1952, pp. 725-8.

IV POLITICAL DEVELOPMENTS

16   1 *June* 1947

PRIME MINISTER TETSU KATAYAMA'S STATEMENT
ON THE POLICY OF HIS COALITION CABINET

In accordance with the stipulations of the new Japanese Constitution, I was nominated as the Prime Minister in the National Diet on
23 May, and since that time I have devoted my efforts towards the
formation of a national coalition Cabinet. I have today completed
the formation of a new Cabinet through a coalition of three parties—
the Social Democratic Party, the Democratic Party and the People's
Co-operative Party.

I sincerely regret that we could not gain the participation in the
Cabinet of the Liberal Party, the third ranking party in the House
of Representatives. However, the new Cabinet intends to observe
the spirit of the policy agreement reached among the four parties,
including the Liberal Party, on 16 May, to adopt a middle course
without leaning towards either the extreme right or the extreme left
and especially to demarcate a clear line *vis-à-vis* communism. It is
hoped, therefore, that the Liberal Party on its part will co-operate
with the new Cabinet from the outside.

The duties of the newly-born coalition Cabinet are very heavy.
Before anything else, it must surmount the economic crisis at present
confronting Japan, rehabilitate production and place Japan's
economy on the road to recovery. For this purpose, necessary democratic controls must be enforced in economy and at the same time
for the purpose of economic rehabilitation all the people must share
equally in making sacrifices and give their earnest co-operation.

Next, the new Cabinet must put into practice the various democratic principles which permeate the new Constitution and must
guide the Japanese people so that Japan will become a truly democratic and peace-loving nation.

The road that lies ahead for Japan is full of difficulties, but I am
confident that with the united co-operation of the Japanese people

and the kind assistance of the Allied Powers, Japan will definitely be able to overcome the difficult situation.

I believe that democratic government must be permeated by a spirit of Christian love and humanism. Hitherto, government in Japan created the impression that it was apt to be motivated by falsehood and intrigue, but I believe that government in the future must be guided by a Christian spirit of morality. A government founded on moral ethics and based on humanism has been my long-cherished faith, and at the same time it was the guiding spirit of the Social Democratic Party which I lead.

As the Prime Minister of the first democratic government chosen under the new Constitution, I express on behalf of the people of Japan my deepest gratitude to General MacArthur, the Supreme Commander for the Allied Powers, who has extended his assistance to the democratization of Japan. Today, Japan has taken the first step towards her revival as a democratic and peaceful nation.

The Japanese people, viewing their bright hopes for the future and extending their united co-operation in order to surmount the present difficult situation, are eagerly looking forward to the day when they will take their place with the nations of the world as a truly peaceful and democratic people.

It is my fervent hope that the democratic people throughout the world will give their unbounded assistance to the people of a new Japan.

Contemporary Japan, Vol. XVI, Nos. 4-6, April-June 1947, pp. 227-8.

17   1 *January* 1948

PRIME MINISTER KATAYAMA'S NEW YEAR STATEMENT

The First National Diet, in accordance with the spirit of the new Constitution, realized the reorganization of the nation's police system for the democratization of the political and social fields, the democratization of the nation's judicial courts, the revision of the feudalistic family systems and others. In the economic field, the Diet approved such measures as the Economic Power Deconcentration Law, the Farmland Reform programme, the Agricultural Co-operative Union Law and a series of other democratic legislations are to bring about a social revolution in Japan. The task confronting us, indeed, is a difficult one.

In other words, we are faced with the task of accomplishing a historic work—that of realizing a democratic revolution. I always hope that we would be able to accomplish this great revolution peacefully through a bloodless revolution.

I wish that the people of Japan will rule the National Diet from the viewpoint of freedom and equality, clearly recognizing the fact that the people are neither a third party to the Government nor cold critics of it, but are directly concerned with it.

I hope to strengthen the tie between the National Diet and the people and bring about an organic relation between them so that the will of the people may be directly reflected in the National Diet. This is the task entrusted to the political parties.

I earnestly wish to enact a Political Party Law and revise the Election Law, because I hope that the political parties may see a healthy development and fulfil their duty in reflecting the will of the people upon the National Diet. I desire this deeply for the cause of democratic politics.

I wish the people of Japan would fully understand what social democracy in this country means. It is reported that the projected new conservative party will adopt the platform of anti-communism, and other minor parties and factions are expected to join the projected party for the cause of anti-communism.

However, it is social democracy, instead of capitalism, that is opposed to communism and is in a most vigorous conflict with it on all affairs.

Theoretically, and also in practice, social democracy is fighting communism, as can be easily understood by observing the actual situation in Europe.

This is apparent in the history of Japan's social movements. It is most difficult for capitalism to expel communism from the nation's politics and industry. Attempts by new conservative parties to subdue communism is something like licking honey through a cleft stick. Only social democracy is capable of pointing out the weaknesses of communism and denounce its existence, although time does not permit me here to dilate on what social democracy proposes to do and why.

Since the formation of my Cabinet, however, I consistently have stuck to this line. Not only in the past but in the future as well, I am determined to keep faith in this fact and expel capitalism and oppose communism with a view to fostering social democracy. I earnestly wish that the entire people thoroughly understand social democracy and, on the basis of this understanding, proceed with their efforts to reconstruct their country.

I hope that labour achieve a healthy development of the union movement and play an important role in efforts to increase production. It is my ultimate political wish to stabilize the nation's livelihood. But prior to reaching this goal there are a number of things to be done.

I wish that labour rationally adjust itself so that the people in general recognize its demands as essential to the development of industry and the rise of national economy. It is earnestly hoped that the workers during this year demonstrate to the people through their union movements that they are shouldering the burden of recovering production and reconstructing industry.

Contemporary Japan, Vol. XVII, Nos. 1-3, January-March 1948, pp. 98-100.

18   6 *January* 1948

SPEECH BY KENNETH C. ROYALL, SECRETARY OF THE US ARMY, TO THE COMMONWEALTH CLUB, SAN FRANCISCO, ON AMERICAN POLICY TOWARDS JAPAN

To many American citizens—including myself—the most surprising development—and one of the most disappointing aspects of our victory over Germany and Japan has been the responsibility and cost which have been placed upon us in the matter of occupation. There were few who originally recognized the extent of this burden. And today every citizen of our country is justified in asking the 'what' and the 'why' of our occupation policies.

On this occasion I will speak specifically of Japan. Immediately after the surrender, the objectives of our policy were stated to be, first, 'to insure that Japan will not again become a menace to the peace and security of the world', and, second, 'to bring about the earliest possible establishment of a democratic and peaceful government which will carry out its international responsibilities, respect the rights of other states, and support the objectives of the United Nations'.

The underlying idea was the prevention of future Japanese aggression—direct prevention by disarmament, and indirect prevention by creating a type of government unlikely to develop again the spirit of aggressive war. The real well-being of Japan—or her strength as a nation—was decidedly a secondary consideration—secondary to protection of ourselves against Japan, and secondary to payment of reparations to the victorious Allies for the damages inflicted upon them.

This attitude is clearly shown by the emphasis in the original directive, which stated in part : 'Japan shall be permitted' (not encouraged but permitted) 'to maintain such industries as will sustain her economy and permit the exaction of reparations . . . but not . . . enable her to rearm . . . Access to, as distinguished from control of, raw materials shall be permitted. Eventual Japanese participation in world trade . . . shall be permitted.'

It is clearly understandable—and it was fully in accord with the then feelings and opinions of our people—that in 1945 the main purpose of occupation should be protection against an enemy which had viciously attacked us and which had committed brutal atrocities against our troops and our private citizens.

Since then new conditions have arisen—in world politics and economics, in problems of national defence, and in humanitarian considerations. These changes must now be fully taken into account in determining our future course, but it should be remembered that these developments arose in large part after the original policies were set.

These original policies were promptly carried out. Within a few months after the end of hostilities, all Japanese tactical units had been dissolved and all implements of war destroyed or insulated. The top Japanese military organizations, as well as the infamous secret and terroristic societies, were abolished. Those who formulated the Japanese policies of conquest and aggression were removed from important political and economic positions.

War-making industries were marked for removal and reparation. This included arsenals, private munitions plants, aircraft factories, military research laboratories, synthetic rubber and oil plants, ship-building installations, and certain chemical, machine tool, precision bearing, thermo-electric, and metal factories, non-ferrous and others. Commitments were made to other nations for payment of reparations with those plants.

Other steps followed, including those leading to the dissolution of concentrations of property ownership and economic power. At the end of the war—and for a long period before the war—land ownership had been in the hands of a comparatively small part of the population. The system was analogous to the feudal system of past centuries, and in Japan the 'land barons' used their power to encourage war.

In the business field, the Zaibatsu, or 'money cliques,' dominated completely and ruthlessly the Japanese economy—through holding companies and monopolies. A dozen families controlled over 75 per cent of the country's commerce, industry and finance.

The influence over the Japanese Government of these and other monopolies was almost unbounded, and they were linked inseparably with the militarists. This joint group over a course of years—and particularly in the year and a half before Pearl Harbour—encouraged Japan toward war and destruction.

Steps were taken to break both types of concentrations. Under a directive issued by the Supreme Allied Commander, the Japanese Diet enacted in the Fall of 1946 a Land Reform Law under which, through local land commissions, the 5½ million Japanese farm families could acquire land from the present owners at a reasonable price and pay for it over a period of years. This programme will be completed by the end of 1948. Just as in America the small landowner is symbolically and factually democracy in practice, so we expect that in time the strength of Japanese democracy will find roots in similar soil.

Action against the Zaibatsu has proceeded vigorously, and its control has now been virtually abolished. Sixty-seven holding companies with 4,000 subsidiaries and affiliates, have been marked for liquidation. The two largest holding companies—Mitsubishi and Mitsui—have been closed. Others of the larger ones have been almost wholly liquidated.

The Japanese Government has been directed to prepare legislation prohibiting international cartels. Stringent anti-trust and deconcentration legislation has been prepared and passed in part. A Holding Company Liquidation Commission has been established and is functioning in the supervision of the entire programme.

While these various steps were being taken, new developments were arising, and old factors were changing in importance. Japan had never been able to provide all of its own food—nor to produce enough of many other necessities of life. Seventy-eight million Japanese occupy an area smaller than California, and of that area only 16 per cent is capable of cultivation.

The population is still growing at an enormous rate. It is expected to reach 84 million by 1951. The current troubled condition in Asia leaves practically no food available for import into Japan, even if the currency and Japanese exports situation would make food purchases possible—which they would not.

And yet without food and other necessities, Japan would be faced with widespread starvation and disease—would seethe with unrest and disorder and hopelessness. Even aside from the simple principles of humanity, we could not, under such conditions, accomplish our original objective of a peaceful Japanese government. Nor could we hope that Japan would be other than susceptible to totalitarian demagogues from within and without. Without help the country would become a prey to non-democratic ideologies of aggression.

To meet this situation America has supplied Japan with food and other necessities. This assistance has given the country a base upon which to build, and it has been possible to supplant totalitarianism and Shintoism with democracy, to begin to replace educational regimentation with academic freedom, and to build the foundations for a peace-loving government of the people.

For this and other achievements in Japan, great credit must be given to General MacArthur and his staff. America was indeed fortunate that for this vital task it had an outstanding leader who could bring the Japanese to a complete realization of their defeat and at the same time obtain their full co-operation in forming a free and stable government.

But the Department of the Army and the Department of State— which shares the policy responsibility of occupation—both Departments realize that for political stability to continue and for free government to succeed in the future, there must be a sound and self-supporting economy, and General MacArthur in command of the occupation can be depended upon to implement these policies.

We also realize that the United States cannot forever continue to pour hundreds of millions of dollars annually into relief funds for occupied areas, and that such contributions can end without disaster only when the occupied countries can pay for their own necessities with their own production and exports.

These factors have resulted in efforts to improve in many fields the economic situation in Japan. And with this increasing economic approach there has arisen an inevitable area of conflict between the original concept of broad demilitarization and the new purpose of building a self-supporting nation.

In the case of agriculture the two purposes do happen to run practically parallel. The breaking down of feudal holdings has ended a war-making influence. At the same time the wider division of lands tends to produce incentive on the part of the larger number of land-owners and thereby to increase overall production.

But it is a different situation with manufacturing. The destruction of synthetic rubber or shipbuilding or chemical or non-ferrous metal plants will certainly destroy the war potential of Japan, but such destruction may also adversely affect the peace potential.

The dissolution of the Zaibatsu may present in itself no serious economic problem, but at some stage extreme deconcentration of industry, while further impairing the ability to make war, may at the same time impair manufacturing efficiency of Japanese industry—may, therefore, postpone the day when Japan can become self-supporting.

Such is our dilemma. It is clear that Japan cannot support itself as a nation of shopkeepers and craftsmen and small artisans any more than it can exist as a purely agricultural nation. We can expect a continuing economic deficit in Japan, unless there is at least some degree of mass industrial production.

Another borderline situation between demilitarization and economic recovery is presented in the case of personnel. The men who were the most active in building up and running Japan's war machine—militarily and industrially—were often the ablest and most successful business leaders of that country, and their services would in many instances contribute to the economic recovery of Japan.

What should we do about them now? We cannot afford to leave the Japanese war system intact nor forget that there is danger in retaining in power leaders whose philosophy helped bring on World War II. On the other hand we cannot afford to sterilize the business ability of Japan.

Nor can we believe without qualification individual Japanese protestations of war innocence or of peacetime reformation. One Senator said to me in Germany shortly after VE Day: 'I have inquired everywhere, and I have not yet found a single Nazi in Germany,' to which could perhaps now be added, 'nor a war-lord in Japan.'

All these matters present questions of degree, and the decisions are matters of judgement. These decisions are not difficult at a cocktail party or from an easy chair or on a rostrum, if made by those who have no responsibility for the decisions or their results. It is somewhat different when you must live and suffer with any errors that you might make.

The Departments of State and Army are trying to draw the lines in the right place. And in doing so they are giving—and will give—full weight to the changes in political and military and economic considerations which have occurred since the initial days of occupation.

We realize that deconcentration must stop short of the point where it unduly interferes with the efficiency of Japanese industry. Earlier programmes are being re-examined—as for example the details of the programme stated in the paper submitted some months ago to the Far Eastern Commission, and recently given wide publicity as FEC 230.

We are not averse to modifying programmes in the interests of our broad objectives. A bill recently submitted to the Japanese Diet setting up procedure for deconcentration of excessive economic power was changed before its final enactment—changed with a view to giving added weight to the economic needs of Japan.

In the case of plant dismantling and reparations—in addition to the matter of disarmament—we are bound by certain agreements with other nations—agreements which must be carried out unless breached by those others or altered by consent. However, since last summer we have had a competent group of industrial engineers in the Pacific selecting the specific plants which, consistent with our obligations, can be dismantled with the minimum of detriment to Japanese economic recovery. The report and recommendations of this committee should reach the Department of the Army during this month.

I would not leave the impression that questions of demilitarization or reparation or deconcentration or disqualification of personnel are the most immediate obstacles to Japanese recovery. The principal difficulties arise from the destruction which war brought to Japan and to the chaotic condition which has existed in the Far East since VJ Day.

The flimsy nature of Japanese construction and the concentrated population centres made these islands most vulnerable targets for our incendiary and other missiles. Even aside from the effects on Hiroshima and Nagasaki of the atomic bombs, many Japanese cities were largely destroyed. I believe that on a percentage basis greater Tokyo—with about 7 million people as of 1940—was as badly damaged as any enemy city in the entire world.

Japan has long been dependent on the rest of Asia not only for foodstuffs but for raw materials needed in their manufacturing and business life, and it has relied largely on general commerce with China and other neighbours. With the war and its aftermath these sources of import and export are largely non-existent.

Many affirmative steps have been and are being taken to meet these and other difficulties—and to promote recovery and thereby hasten the day when Japan will cease to be a financial burden to the United States. I wish that time permitted me to discuss in detail our activities in many fields, including those of finance and credit and foreign trade.

Some results of our efforts are apparent. Overall Japanese industrial production has risen from 18 per cent of the 1930-34 level in January 1946 to 40 per cent in August 1947. In the case of coal—basically needed for business recovery—the present production is 86 per cent of the 1930-34 level. Fertilizer has increased fourfold during occupation. One-fourth of the war-destroyed houses in Tokyo and vicinity have been replaced. Six hundred thousand acres of land have been reclaimed for cultivation, and a million more should be added by 1950.

In this whole picture of Japan do not forget that we are supervising an entire Government—and one disorganized by an unsuccessful war. We have all the many normal policy and operating problems of a stable and successful Government plus the added ones produced by the unusual and distressing conditions peculiar to present-day Japan.

The differences from our own country are such that we cannot expect to impose on the Japanese people an exact reproduction of American democracy. It follows that often there is no precise precedent for our problem, and the Departments must do as our forefathers did in the early days of our own government—reach the best results we can by trial and error.

The lines to be drawn are, of course, not always easy to draw, and as in the case of all decisions of importance one cannot be too dogmatic. There can be—and are likely to be—differences of opinion among sincere and informed people. Nor do I have any illusion that everything we do will be perfect.

But I can assure you that our decisions will be made with realism and with a firm determination of doing all possible to prevent Japan from again waging unprovoked and aggressive and cruel war against any other nation. We hold to an equally definite purpose of building in Japan a self-sufficient democracy, strong enough and stable enough to support itself and at the same time to serve as a deterrent against any other totalitarian war threats which might hereafter arise in the Far East.

Documents concerning the Allied Occupation and Control of Japan, Vol. II (*Political, Military and Cultural*), pp. 4-10, compiled by the Division of Special Records, Foreign Office, Japan, 1949.

19   22 *January* 1948

ADMINISTRATIVE POLICY SPEECH BY PRIME MINISTER KATAYAMA TO THE SECOND SESSION OF THE NATIONAL DIET

I

On the occasion of the opening of the Second Session of the Diet, I desire to give on behalf of the Government an outline of its general policies of administration and to clarify its attitude in dealing with the current situation.

The year 1948 is going to be a historic year for Japan. It is in this year that we must make a positive progress towards national reconstruction and lay down a firm economic foundation for the bloodless democratic revolution of our country.

During the past eight months since its formation, the present Cabinet has instituted emergency measures of various kinds aimed principally at solving the immediate economic problems confronting the nation. Now in the coming year, the Government intends to embark upon the execution of a permanent reconstruction programme, and make this a year of economic reconstruction and industrial rehabilitation. For it is through the accomplishment of this task that we can build up a nation of peace and democracy.

It is only through the establishment of an economic foundation for democratization that we may hope to be readmitted into the comity of nations both in name and in fact. In this sense, the Government wishes to make this a significant year of reconstruction and production expansion, and is resolved afresh to do everything in its power in the face of the difficult situation of today.

The present economic condition of our country is still precarious. However, there are a number of very hopeful developments in recent weeks which will affirm my faith that Japan will in the near future realize genuine economic stability. In other words, being convinced that production expansion, rehabilitation and reconstruction constitute the bulwark against inflation, the Government has decided to make production expansion the central policy for 1948 and to draw up a positive programme.

Our rehabilitation and construction programme has to be a long-range plan, sound and rational. During 1948, the first year, we intend to put into effect production expansion plans by putting priorities on the basic industries and on expedient industries. The figures the Government has in mind relating to the first year's production goal are in round figures as follows :

Coal	36,000,000 tons
Electric power	31,600,000,000 kilowatt hours
Iron & steel (ordinary steel & steel material)	1,000,000 tons
Ammonium sulphate	900,000 tons
Cement	2,000,000 tons
Cotton yarn	480,000,000 pounds

By bringing up production to the above figures, the Government expects to realize roughly more than a 40 per cent increase over 1947.

As regards rice, wheat and other staple foodstuffs, we count upon every farmer-household being able to increase production by 10 per cent over the normal annual yields.

The Government wishes that this programme will be studied and established not only by the Diet but also by the entire nation. We are planning to call a meeting of experts representing various circles for a conference on the ways of facilitating economic reconstruction. We confidently expect that the objectives of the programme will be confirmed to coincide with the objective of all those attending the conference.

Especially with respect to coal, the Government has always laid stress upon its production expansion. Now it intends to administer effectively the Temporary Coal Mine Control Law passed by the first Diet session so as to leave nothing to be desired for actuating the 'Production First' principle. At present the mining of coal is being gradually put on the right track. Last December, we were able to set a post-war record of 2,960,000 tons. Of course, we will not rest content with this, but go on increasing the output further under the five-year plan to be established.

With respect to electric power, the Electric Power Crisis Surmounting Measure which was announced some time ago will be pushed vigorously forward to increase the capacity for power generation.

The replenishment of transportation capacity, which is inseparably bound up with production expansion, will be carefully studied and planned in view of the serious deterioration and destruction of both land and marine equipment. This solution of coal and power problems is expected to bring about substantial production increases in all lines of mining and manufacturing industries. On the other hand, the Government plans to consolidate the foundation for the promotion of export industries, and to increase also to a degree the production of domestic consumption goods.

For the expansion of agricultural production, the Government will do all in its power. That is to say, the Government will bring about an improvement of farm management through the agricultural co-operatives and make it the foundation for building a greater production power. A measure looking to rationalization of the delivery quota system will be speedily instituted. The farmer will be made to hold himself responsible for the delivery of his rice quota, while the Government will hold itself responsible for the rationing of tools and materials and premiums. We hope to solve the food problem through division of responsibility in this manner. The Government feels keenly the urgent necessity of revising fundamentally the system of food delivery. We are grateful that the rice delivery for 1947 is progressing favourably through the efforts of all concerned. A bill for establishing a system for responsible delivery will soon be submitted to the present session of the Diet.

Now let me say a few words regarding small and medium enterprises. Small and medium industries are to constitute hereafter the mainstay of Japan's export industries. Moreover, from the existing economic state of the country a tendency is seen toward a steady growth of the population that must perforce depend upon these enterprises for a living. The promotion of small and medium enterprises, therefore, forms the control theme in the nation's economic reconstruction, and the Government will adopt suitable measures to that end.

II

It is the policy of the government to check inflation and to promote recovery during this year through such plans for production, expansion and industrial reconstruction as I have just outlined. But in order to put such plans into practice and to achieve the production goal, it is necessary to institute a fixed counter-measure against inflation.

I need scarcely tell you that the direct cause of inflation lies in an over-issue of currency. In order to put a check upon currency issue, the Government must curtail disbursements, suppress loans to enterprises and at the same time make the people pay more taxes and deposit more money in their banks. Of course, the expenditures we must properly bear as a defeated nation amount to huge sums. Moreover, if we withheld unduly industrial capital, it would mean lowering of production, and there are limits to taxation. But in spite of all these considerations, the inflationary trend of currency, if allowed to continue indefinitely, is bound to bring on the danger of a débâcle. We must at all costs slow down the march of inflation and finally stop it altogether.

For this purpose, we shall have to effect a substantial restoration of financial balance by retrenchment of disbursements coupled with increase of revenues. Accordingly the government policy underlying the 1948-9 budget is to match the scope of national finances to the actual strength of national economy. That is to say, expenditures are limited to items truly indispensable and for the building of a democratic state. At the same time, the Government proposes to reduce the costs of administration through administrative reform, retrenchment, etc., and to ensure the balance between incomes and outlays throughout the year, and furthermore to effect periodical adjustments of the budget.

On the side of revenues, while the tax rates have already risen rather high, the taxes in arrears and outstanding add up to a colossal sum. In view of this current situation, the Government, in accordance with the resolution of the first Diet session relating to the 'Full Tax Payment Campaign', is planning to launch a nation-wide campaign with the Diet as the nucleus in order to arouse the people thoroughly to the sense of obligation for tax payment so that they will pay on their own accord for the sake of national reconstruction.

On the other hand, the Government itself will seek to expand and strengthen the tax collection machinery and to renovate the method of handling taxation affairs. The treatment of tax officials will be rationally improved ; their sense of responsibility aroused, and strict discipline enforced.

With respect to the so-called inflation, profiteers guilty of tax evasion will be ferreted out as an enemy of the people. We have already adopted the policy under which tax evaders of a vicious character are made subject to penal servitude, and we are considering a water-tight system including the organization of 'Tax Evasion Prevention Corps' and the utilization of information by third parties. With regard to the reform of the taxation system, it is our intention to submit a concrete plan to the present session of the Diet. However, we intend to adopt measures in this connexion which conform with the changes in the actual conditions of the people's income and in the economic situation and which also fully take into consideration the position of the working masses. As our general policy, we propose to lighten the income tax for the workers during the 1948-9 fiscal year.

With respect to industrial loans, which are liable to lead to currency inflation, the Government will make every effort to prevent loose-lending by tightening its supervision over the loans made by the Rehabilitation Financing Fund, and by tying up more closely the allocation of commodities with the issuance of loans besides applying the method of controlling loans under the Loan Issuance Control Regulations. However an indiscriminate suppression of loans such as may impede wholesome industrial activities should be absolutely avoided. The Government, adhering rigidly to its stand that 'Banking organs shall be servants of industry' is determined to maintain 'sound banking'.

Finally, it goes without saying that in order to prevent inflation from bringing on a débâcle it is necessary to foster confidence in currency. In this sense, I wish to reiterate here the declaration of the Government that there shall be absolutely no freezing of the new yen.

III

In the last analysis, the principal objective of all anti-inflation measures comes to the establishment of stability in price and wages, and the elimination of deficits from the household account.

For this purpose the Government will strive to replenish the real wages of the worker, to say nothing of preserving the actual living standards of the people in general. By shattering the vicious price-wage circle and at the same time by expanding production, we hope to stabilize as soon as possible the people's livelihood and especially the household economy of the worker.

The Government, with the view of setting up an economic structure under which an honest worker is sure of earning his livelihood, intends to take the following steps for replenishing the real wages. Firstly, with regard to staple food, the existing system for the extra rice rations to workers will be studied thoroughly from a new angle ; the rationing standards will be rationalized and the rationing method renovated within the limits that it does not interfere with the general rationing programme. Through an efficient and effective handling of the system in accordance with the amounts of actual work, the necessary rations of food for each kind of labour according to its nature will be assured. Besides, as far as permitted by the technique of rationing operations, the quality and quantity of extra rations will be rationalized by putting rice, wheat, barley, etc. under a graded priority system, and care will be taken to see that no delay or no default occurs in rationing.

Secondly, with regard to fish and vegetables and other perishable foods, the link system currently in force will be strengthened on a priority basis so as to keep production under planned control, so as to realize marked increases in the regular rations. Moreover, with regard to foodstuffs, clothing, fuel, and other necessaries for workers, their supply will be ensured for the maintenance of the minimum living standard of the people.

Additional rations for workers are planned by increasing the supplying capacity and the Government is considering a system of priority rationing. For this purpose, the Government will duly operate the various Kodan (public corporations) and other distribution agencies for a sure and swift rationing. Livelihood co-operatives by area and by occupation will be promoted and encouraged. Besides the Government is thinking of adopting a new and especially powerful rationing formula for securing the rationing of the workers' necessaries.

By such methods as I have described it is intended to increase as much as possible the distribution of commodities at fixed prices, to banish black-market expenditures from household economy, and to replenish the real wage of the worker, and thereby bring about the stabilization of prices and wages. It is the policy of the Government to apply its major efforts to the replenishment of real wages but to avoid any formula of merely raising the currency wages, which results in price rise and sets in motion the interminable price-wage race. The present price structure will be carefully studied also from this angle.

If the said base needs to be revised, we must be on guard lest we commit any error as regards the time and the mode of such revision. The Government will act properly from the standpoint of truly protecting the interests of the workers. I hope that the workers will understand the intentions of the Government and that they will be generous enough to afford positive co-operation to the Government in carrying out its measures for price and wage stabilization and to wait a little while and watch for the results.

I am delighted at the rapid strides the labour movement has been making of late among the workers. Here we may see at long last a hopeful sign of the rebirth of the Japanese race. I confidently hope that through the good sense and sound judgement of these workers who really have at heart the future welfare of our people and country, certain unwholesome elements who plot for the destruction of national economy and the disturbance of social order will soon be eliminated.

IV

The Government is resolved to carry out an administrative reform programme for the furtherance of efficiency and the democratization of officialdom and thereby to set an example to private enterprises in general for putting themselves in a good state of health. The programme aims at the simplification and rationalization of governmental machinery and the reduction, rebuilding and reorganization of government business.

Special efforts will be made to wipe out bureaucratic tendencies in the central government, and to do away with the reduplication of authority among various offices, to define and clarify the responsibility of each official. Furthermore, in consonance with the spirit of local self-government the authority of the central organs relating to local affairs will be transferred as far as possible to the local governments, and the local agencies of the central organ will be liquidated to the greatest possible extent. Under this programme the various ministries and boards will find it necessary to reduce their personnel.

By putting efficiency before number, the Government hopes to effect personnel reduction both in budget and in organization. The treatment of officials will be improved as much as possible while on the other hand strict discipline will be enforced. In order to execute such a bold and fundamental reform, the Government will appoint a council for the reform of administrative organs and obtain its report at an early date.

It is anticipated that a certain amount of unemployment will be unavoidably caused by personnel reduction under the proposed programme. Appraising the general unemployment situation the Government will take the necessary counter-measures by appropriating the maximum sum that the national finances can spare for that purpose. Needless to say, it will not do just to let the ranks of recipients of unemployment doles swell. We must provide opportunity of employment and seek to absorb and utilize the surplus labour power.

Parallel with the plan to increase production mentioned previously the Government is drawing up plans also for the stabilization of the people's occupation. Taking into consideration the fact that agriculture has little room left for absorbing surplus population, it is planned to develop mining, manufacture, and export industries, and solve the problem of unemployment through the increase of production capacity in these lines of industry.

V

Furthermore, for the construction of a new Japan, the Government proposes to adopt cultural measures and steps for the improvement of livelihood and to seek the promotion of such measures from all angles.

For the renovation and advancement of education, the Government will proceed with the installation of the 6-3 system as far as the treasury permits. It is planned to open a new system for high schools, including night schools for working youths, and to institute compulsory education for the deaf and dumb. For democratizing educational administration, or encouraging science and arts, and for raising the cultural standards of the people, we will formulate concrete plans adaptable to a peace-loving nation.

Especially for the promotion of scientific research and the advancement of technology, the Government will carry out the necessary measures, while paying due regard to the independent views of the researchers and technicians. Again, housing programmes will be speeded in order to provide living quarters to the masses and to the workers in vital industries. It is the intention of the Government to amplify the Livelihood Protection Law and bring about an early rehabilitation of war-devastated cities.

There are today approximately 750,000 of our compatriots who still remain abroad, especially in Soviet territory. The Government has expressed its deepest sympathy for these people and the members of their families who are waiting their return, and it has made every effort to hasten their repatriation. However, it is deeply regretted that these efforts have not lived up to expectations. The Government intends hereafter to continue to devote its utmost efforts in this connexion by seeking the assistance of the various authorities concerned.

The Government is most anxious to see that the Election Law is revised with a view to establishing a system of State-managed elections which cost nothing to candidates. We believe it is of the utmost importance for new Japan that elections are held in a clean auspicious atmosphere.

VI

The Government hopes that the peace conference will be convened very soon. However, the most important thing in this connexion is that we Japanese do first what is required of Japan. Our obligations are not confined to political reforms alone, but we must accomplish what we should in the field of economic reconstruction for national recovery as well. It would be idle just to go on begging the world for pity. We would never get anything anywhere that way. The Government will go forward to complete the democratization of the nation, and at the same time to rehabilitate and rebuild the country, so that we may be prepared for the peace conference at any time.

In conclusion I desire to speak through the Diet a few words to all workers and farmers of Japan. The success of national economic reconstruction depends solely upon you. I know you will never countenance any such schemes as are designed to bring disorder to society and destruction to industry. Let me appeal to your sound judgement and good sense and express my fervent hope that through your efforts our national goal will be achieved for production expansion and economic reconstruction. As regards your constructive movements, the Government wishes you swift progress and is glad to extend whole-hearted support.

Now let me turn and speak to the people of all Japan. I believe the ultimate objective of the Government to be the stabilization of people's livelihood. To that end is dedicated all my energy. Unless we work for economic recovery of our land before any and everything else, we shall not be able to achieve the objective of the Government. And it is with your co-operation alone that we may hope to accomplish the task of economic reconstruction. It goes without saying that lofty political and moral ideals are needed for the reconstruction of our country. But I believe that it requires in addition an attitude on the part of the people to pool what little they have and to combine their talents and abilities and co-operate for the common cause of economic reconstruction. Through this second session of the Diet I ask you all for co-operation and collaboration.

Contemporary Japan, Vol. XVII, Nos. 1-3, January-March 1948, pp. 100-07.

10 *February* 1948

PRIME MINISTER KATAYAMA'S STATEMENT
ON THE RESIGNATION OF HIS CABINET

In view of the prevailing situation, I have decided today on the resignation of the Cabinet. I believe this is a large manifestation of the difficulties of the internal situation of political parties into which it is easy to fall, particularly in the case of a coalition Cabinet, and I further believe that this is one historical phase which is difficult to avoid under Japan's present situation. This was indeed a great test for myself and for the political parties. If democratic government in Japan is enabled to develop soundly with this as one forward step, it would be most fortunate for our country. The decision to resign without resorting especially to dissolving the National Diet at this time is due to a serious consideration for the existing situation both within and outside the Cabinet.

If I am to speak frankly on this occasion, Japan, as a defeated nation, is endeavouring to rehabilitate the nation's shattered economy while at the same time accomplishing a democratic revolution without resort to violence, but she cannot do this through half-hearted efforts. The reason we asked the people to persevere under hardships and suffering was solely for the sake of our country's revival. And for this purpose, I believe that Japan's democratic revolution cannot be accomplished unless the extremes of the right and the left are rejected and a middle course followed. That is to say, until the time that a party having an absolute majority comes into being, a coalition Cabinet is still necessary. I think this is one form of a middle-of-the-road government. I have constantly pursued this course during the little more than eight months that have passed, and it is my conviction that by this means alone can our economy be rehabilitated and international trust and confidence in us be enhanced.

The record of our achievements may not necessarily have been spotless but I do believe that we have been able to live up in some measure to the expectations of the people because some hope at least has been extended to us in solving the basic issues of Japan's economic recovery, such as the questions of food, increased coal production and the introduction of foreign credits, and because marked progress has been made in our democratization in all fields, politically, economically and socially. I have great hopes that the fruits of these measures shall be crowned with success in the near future.

Contemporary Japan, Vol. XVII, Nos. 1-3, January-March 1948, pp. 107-8.

PRIME MINISTER HITOSHI ASHIDA'S STATEMENT ON THE POLICY OF HIS CABINET

In announcing the policy of the new Cabinet I wish to point out first of all, that true democratization of Japan is the most important prerequisite for the spiritual and economic reconstruction of Japan.

The Japanese people, having repudiated militarism once and for all, are now trying to erect an edifice of democracy on the ruins of war. With the eyes of the world focussed upon her, a new Japan is in the making—a nation which is dedicated to peace, a nation which is to deserve the world's trust and confidence. As Premier of this new Japan I pledge my utmost efforts to faithful observance of the Potsdam Declaration, which calls for the revival and strengthening of democratic tendencies among the Japanese people. The best endeavours of the government will be directed to that end.

The grave political situation of today does not permit any alternative for us but to adhere to a firm 'middle-of-the-road' policy. I am resolved to combat both extremes, the right and the left. It is my conviction that radical ideologies are inimical to the healthy growth of democracy. In view of the fact that certain elements are exerting baneful influences abetting labour disputes, and causing social unrest and disruption of industry, determined steps will be taken to counter their activities.

The economic outlook of post-war Japan is none too bright. How to restore her finance and industry to normal ; how to stabilize the people's livelihood—these are stupendous problems that must be faced and solved. The crusade against inflation will be continued and intensified. Increased production shall be our watchword. To attain this goal, measures will be taken to give priority to key industries, with special emphasis laid upon the development of hydro-electric power. At the same time, every encouragement will be extended to small and medium-size enterprises in an all-out effort to stimulate export and tourist trades.

The rapid growth of the labour movement in our country is most gratifying, and the Government will give it full support to accelerate its sound progress. On the other hand, it will be absolutely imperative that just and equitable relations are maintained between capital and labour, without which all hope would be lost for an early reconstruction of our national economy.

Finally, I desire to express the nation's profound gratitude to the Supreme Commander for the Allied Powers. The occupation policy has been executed with a spirit of benevolence and generosity unparalleled in history. We are all fully aware that no matter what we ourselves may do, a speedy recovery of Japan would be impossible without continued Allied assistance, moral as well as material. And I hope and trust that this assistance will be granted in the crucial years to come.

Contemporary Japan, Vol. XVII, Nos. 1-3, January-March 1948, pp. 110-11.

22

20 *March* 1948

PRIME MINISTER ASHIDA'S ADMINISTRATIVE
POLICY SPEECH IN THE NATIONAL DIET

The task of forming a new cabinet has fallen on me by designation of the National Diet. I feel deeply indeed my heavy responsibilities to the State and to the nation. I am firmly resolved to devote myself, body and soul, to the performance of the duties of my office.

Both internationally and internally, numerous difficulties beset the path of Japan's recovery. Unless they are successfully surmounted, the future of our race will be dark. And there exists no other means by which we Japanese can save ourselves but to unite as one man and overcome those difficulties. Japan finds herself today in a predicament as of a ship in distress, floundering in a stormy sea. The only way to save the ship is for both the crew and the passengers to unite their efforts, everybody doing what he can for the safety of the ship. So it is with our nation. It is not the moment for us to waste time in bootless arguments, being preoccupied only in the furtherance of party interests.

That is why my party has always advocated a political truce and the people's unity for overcoming the national crisis. That is why, at the time of the formation of the Katayama Cabinet, we joined in the four-party policy agreement and I did my utmost to facilitate the smooth functioning of government through a spirit of mutual concession. When organizing the present Cabinet, I requested the various parties for co-operation with the purpose in view of bringing about the suspension of political wars and the consolidation of the nation's total strength. I regret that I have not succeeded in realizing my aim fully, possibly because of the existence of some differences in the way of looking at the present crisis. But we have by no means given up our hopes in this respect. We will strive resolutely to consolidate the total power of the nation, and to stabilize both the people's livelihood and the political situation. To that end, the

Government will listen to the voice of the people with an open mind and act always in the spirit of mutual concession and conciliation.

The supreme objective which the new Cabinet seeks to attain is the establishment of a world of peace, liberty and justice. It is with this ideal in view that we shall undertake our domestic recovery ; and it is with this spirit that we shall handle our external affairs. The new Constitution which was promulgated in the year before last declares definitely the establishment of peace and freedom.

I firmly believe that only by pursuing and realizing the ideals of peace, liberty and justice can the Japanese people show themselves to be worthy of a place in history. In this sense, our new Constitution is indeed a great manifesto of national renaissance. It is all too evident that we must not permit it to remain a mere declaration on paper, but must make every effort to put it into practice at home and abroad.

Such being the supreme objective of the new Cabinet, it will most naturally adhere to the middle-of-the-road policy. For an extremist ideology, either of the right or of the left, will never serve the cause of peace. In a nation's transitional period such as ours today when we are undergoing the so-called 'bloodless revolution', the people are liable to be swept off their proper course. But one-sided ideologies and extremist political actions will in the end only lead to the danger of a revolution by violence. Certainly, they do not open the way to peace.

In this sense, we reject liberty unaccompanied by responsibility. We also reject egoism masquerading in the garb of justice. We will ever follow democracy and steer a middle course. And under the principle of social solidarity and national co-operation we will seek the simultaneous realization of increased production and equitable distribution.

It is the fervent desire of all Japanese that our country rejoin the family of peaceful nations at the earliest possible date. At the present time, it cannot be predicted when a peace conference will be held, but we will prepare for such a conference from now and direct our utmost efforts towards enhancing the world's trust and confidence placed in Japan. I believe that we can win the trust of other Powers in us only by loving liberty and cherishing justice and by demonstrating our determined will to contribute, materially and spiritually, to world culture.

The substance of the peace treaty is, of course, a matter to be determined by the Allied Powers. But so long as our actions conform to the principles of peace, liberty and justice, we may surely expect the peace terms to be such as will in no way impair Japan's independence and survival.

We are now living under military occupation. It is universally recognized that the control exercised by the Occupation Forces is one of fairness and tolerance unparalleled in history. To this generous Occupation policy, our people have responded with an attitude of genuine co-operation. It is under this auspicious circumstance that we have been able already to resume many of our normal activities of life though a peace treaty is yet to be concluded. In dealing with any phase of internal administration at this juncture, the Government will direct special attention to its bearing on Japan's international relations.

Now, turning to the subject of economic measures, I shall confine myself to two or three points, since my colleagues are to explain them in detail later.

Needless to say, any government in Japan today must give priority to the task of overcoming inflation. Nor will anybody dispute the fact that the basic measure for checking inflation is to expand production. In order to bring about an increase in production, it will be of the utmost importance that a rational harmony is effected between labour and management and especially that the working masses, awakened to the consciousness of their solemn responsibilities, give willing co-operation. From this standpoint, the Government earnestly desires to see a healthy growth of labour unions. However, those lacking in the co-operative spirit that is so essential to community life should be rejected absolutely, whether they be on the side of capital or on the side of labour. For, in the final analysis, they are inimical to the interests of the general masses of the country.

The absorption of floating purchasing power is a most urgent measure to combat inflation. In this connexion, the Government is now preparing concrete measures and intends to submit them to the National Diet in the near future. However, in undertaking these measures which touch upon circulation, the Government will pay due attention to the maintenance of public confidence in the currency, which is a matter of vital importance.

The accumulation of capital is another important problem, Japan having lost one-third of her national wealth as a result of the war. However, today when a great majority of the people have come to join the ranks of the working class, it will be all the more necessary to collect capital from these wide circles of society. Ways must be devised to minimize the risks of investment in order to protect the interests of the public.

The rationalization of industrial management is the next problem. Without rationalizing industry and increasing efficiency to the maximum, there can be obviously no increase in national wealth.

Again, the key to the development of our foreign trade after Japan has been permitted to enter the international market in the future lies in industrial rationalization. In this connexion, it will be necessary to improve our production technology. I regret to say that in production technique, Japan has of late fallen far below the world level. The Government will take all possible measures to bring about improvements in industrial technology.

In discussing economic measures, I would like to speak of one or two points I have in mind. In the first place, in a country like Japan with a peculiar topography, I believe that we must find out and develop those industries best suited to the land. For example, the development of hydro-electric power will be of urgent necessity in order to offset the shortage of coal, and the Government may have to consider the question of providing funds for the construction of large-scale power plants. With regard to the food problem, recent deliveries of rice have registered a phenomenal success, one hundred per cent deliveries of the allotted quotas having already been completed. This is due entirely to the crystallization of the patriotic spirit of the farming population, and I wish to take this opportunity to express to them our profound gratitude. However, numerous measures, such as the thorough implementation of the second agricultural reform programme and the improvement of the rice delivery system, are still necessary for the increased production of food. The Government intends to take up concrete studies of these questions.

Furthermore, the rehabilitation of the damages caused by the flood last year is a matter of great urgency, and the Government is now preparing all possible measures to meet this problem. Then, I believe the rolling hill country covering approximately 3,000,000 *chobu*, situated between the plains and the mountains, should be developed, since this would be an effective measure for increasing production of food and for relieving unemployment.

With regard to the basic policy for economic recovery, it is felt that there may arise divergencies in basic concepts among the various political parties and groups. However, in view of the situation in which Japan is placed now, the measures to meet the immediate needs should be evident to all. That is why even a capitalistic party which places the ultimate objective of economy in free enterprise considers a certain measure of controls as being absolutely necessary under the existing circumstances of extreme shortages of goods. The long-range production programme which will soon be announced by the Government anticipates the time when, with an increase in production, controls will be removed, to be replaced by a rational economic structure.

The foregoing has been a brief outline of the measures planned by the Government for the increase of production. Some time will be required, however, before they bear fruit to the fullest measure. In the meantime, there lurks the danger of an acceleration of the inflationary spiral and of a breakdown in our economy. The urgent task of the moment parallel with the increase of production, lies in tiding over the current emergency through importation of scarce commodities.

The importation of the vital commodities which Japan sorely lacks depends solely upon the friendly assistance of the Allied Nations. It is most gratifying to us all that the situation is taking a turn for the better, and prospects of our procuring increasingly large amounts of commodities are brightening.

It is reported that in some quarters in the United States a plan is under consideration to restore Japanese economy to 125 per cent of the 1930-34 level by 1954.

For a time following the surrender, Japan's economy fell to rock-bottom. But thanks to the energetic efforts of the people and to the supply of materials by the Allied Powers, there is no doubt that, slowly but surely, it is making progress toward recovery, and that in spite of the advance of inflation, the livelihood of the people has actually been improved. If material assistance by the Allied Powers is forthcoming at this time, the inflationary trend will be greatly weakened, and our economic recovery can be laid on a firm foundation. Thus can we for the first time entertain hopes of extricating ourselves from the life of poverty we have endured for so long. Naturally, in order to obtain Allied assistance, we must deserve it.

As clear proof that the people of Japan will not betray the trust placed in them by foreign countries, we are resolved not only to observe strictly the terms of the Potsdam Declaration but also to hasten the democratization of our country and direct all our efforts to the building up of Japan as a nation of culture. Furthermore, in order to facilitate the introduction of foreign capital, it is necessary to eliminate the many existing bottlenecks and to perfect such conditions as will induce foreign capitalists to invest gladly in Japan's industries. The Government intends to submit plans for improvements to the Diet.

Since the war's end, law and order has been maintained far better than one might have expected in a defeated nation. However, it is most deplorable that as a result of the war, culture and morality have been permitted to deteriorate and there is still no appreciable decrease in crimes. The question of eradicating brutality from Japanese character is largely a matter of stabilizing livelihood and an educational programme for raising moral standards. The Government, gravely concerned, is determined to seek a speedy solution of this question.

The system of local self-government, under the new Constitution, is now being put to a test. In view of the fact that the local self-government system constitutes one of the key factors of democracy, we hope that the right spirit of self-government will manifest itself and that our programme of decentralization of authority will be carried out both in name and in fact. I believe that the police forces which have been transferred to local governments will hereafter play their role as true friends of the people. At the same time, however, I sincerely hope that the public will extend full co-operation towards the prevention of crimes.

Furthermore, with regard to the elevation of public morals, we will undertake appropriate measures speedily for the sake of our national honour. The spirit of upholding justice without fear and of the love for our fellow countrymen had long been our cherished tradition. Only by retrieving this tradition can we make Japan a truly good country to live in.

With this spirit as the keynote, the Government will devote further efforts to the promotion of education and adhere strictly to the policy hitherto pursued by the former Cabinet in connexion with the implementation of the new 6-3 school system.

I should like to say a few words at this point concerning the repatriates from overseas and the war-sufferers, who are placed in the most miserable circumstances. A great number of these people are without clothing and homes, but the Government pledges to exert its earnest endeavours to provide State relief for these people as far as possible.

The rehabilitation of war-devastated cities is another problem which is of great urgency. The Government intends to mobilize experts in the field and to expedite this work in accordance with their plans. Particularly with regard to the housing programme, we will study what has been done in the Western countries ; and by adopting whatever methods we find suitable, we will carry out our project at the earliest possible date.

Finally, let me speak a few words on the deep concern we feel over the current international situation.

We Japanese know only too well what calamities the late Great War has brought upon mankind. A great many nations are now suffering in the grip of hunger and destitution, confusion and chaos. And in spite of it all, the spectre of another world cataclysm—a third Great War—haunts sorely afflicted humanity. Such is the condition today.

The opportunity has not yet arrived for Japan to join the United Nations, and we are not in a position to have a voice in the organization of peace. However, with our very existence and independence so closely bound up with the world condition, it is impossible for us to remain indifferent to any international development that threatens peace. We are especially perturbed at the persistent political instability in our neighbour nations of the Far East, which constitutes a great stumbling block to the economic recovery of our country.

Japan's resolve to renounce war by abandoning all forms of armament is written large in our new Constitution. I fervently hope that the lofty ideal will guide all nations along with us on the road to peace. It is under the banner of that ideal that we are determined to march on and contribute our share to the construction of a world of peace, liberty and justice.

Such is the general outline of the views and policies of the new Cabinet. I have spoken of our aims, material and spiritual, in the present stage of our political situation, and of our formulas for surmounting the current economic crisis. It is on the basis of such fundamental concepts as I have stated that the Government will seek to consolidate the constructive forces in the country, and to achieve political stabilization and economic recovery through joint efforts with the entire nation.

Today, when peoples everywhere are suffering from want, we have no intention of assuming such a cowardly attitude as dependence on outside help alone for our salvation. In the matter of food supply or production of goods, we should first be up and doing our best to achieve self-supply and self-sufficiency. It is in such terms as these that a nation's characteristic trait of not expecting help from outside without first helping itself is revealed most unmistakably. Today, in adversity, we Japanese have a fine opportunity, I believe, of demonstrating our mettle before the world.

While the present crisis confronting Japan is not totally blocking our path of progress, to surmount it is indeed a stupendous task. The Government can accomplish this task only with the wholehearted support and co-operation of the entire nation as well as of the National Diet.

The new Cabinet will keep an open mind, listen always to public opinion, and pay careful attention to all constructive views in and out of the Diet, so that it may faithfully and successfully fulfil the duties to the nation.

Contemporary Japan, Vol. XVII, Nos. 1-3, January-March 1948, pp. 111-17.

23   4 *April* 1949

PRIME MINISTER SHIGERU YOSHIDA'S ADMINISTRATIVE POLICY SPEECH IN THE FIFTH NATIONAL DIET

The outcome of the last general elections has clearly demonstrated that the Japanese people were eager to have the political situation stabilized and that they wanted to put their Government in the hands of robust conservative parties.

My Government, brought into being by an overwhelming popular support, is now prepared to put its convictions into deeds and pursue vigorously its policies for national reconstruction. For only by so doing can the Government meet the people's expectations and trust and make Japan deserving of the generous assistance of the Allied Powers.

The reckless warfare of ten years has left this country in a condition of indescribable destruction and confusion. In order to clear the war's aftermath and to rebuild our country, we must squarely face the realities of the situation. We should boldly plan and embark upon a long-range programme with a united and determined will.

This point was strongly emphasized in General MacArthur's letter to me of 19 December 1948 concerning the Nine-Point Economic Stabilization Programme and also in the more recent statement of Mr Dodge. I myself am convinced that without such a programme there will be no reconstruction.

The budget about to be submitted to you is one which the Government has compiled on its own responsibility, but which accepts and embodies the substance of the Dodge statement as well as the Nine Principles. Resolved to achieve true economic independence and reconstruction, the Government has first of all drawn up a balanced budget in the face of serious difficulties. It is a matter of grave concern that because of our stringent post-war economy and because of the exhaustion of resources our people are made to shoulder heavy taxes and suffer unparalleled hardships. The Government proposes, therefore, to carry out drastic administrative reforms and effect improvements in the taxation system and the method of tax collection in the coming months, while on the side of expenditures, further cuts will be made. It is planned to dispose of Government properties to lighten the people's tax burden. Accordingly, as these plans materialize the Diet will be convoked in extraordinary session to take the necessary legislative action.

True economic stability and progress depend upon the disposition of national problems under sound fiscal and currency policies.

Therefore, it is important that all policy decisions are linked to the national budget.

It is the Government which has been chiefly responsible for the aggravation of inflation in the past. Unless the Government now takes the steps to curb inflation, the country will be ruined. It is indeed very hard for the Government to cut down subsidies, investments and general expenses, but it must be done.

It is true our production index has risen with the large progressive increases in American aid funds. Export is expanding but import grows more rapidly so that our unfavourable balance of trade is increasing from year to year. And we are barely covering the deficits with American money. Obviously this situation cannot be allowed to continue indefinitely.

In order to stabilize our national economy permanently to end inflation for all time, and to make the country self-supporting and prosperous, a drastic measure must be adopted even if it hurts. Japan's ailing economic body requires a major surgical operation. And we will courageously and patriotically endure the pain.

We are all very grateful for the sympathetic understanding and bounteous aid of the Allied Powers—especially of the United States of America. However, what is important is that we should as soon as possible become self-supporting and be able to get along without outside help. I earnestly hope that all Japanese will resolve to achieve national reconstruction without depending on Allied munificence alone but by dint of their spirit of self-reliance and by their willingness to submit to austerity and hard work. In this respect I believe we should do well to emulate the British people who are so solidly united in their gallant struggle for economic independence.

I hope the strong and responsible policies the Government proposes to pursue will meet with whole-hearted support and co-operation on the part of the entire nation.

I should like to add here a word with reference to the single exchange rate which is, needless to say, indispensable for the promotion of trade and the induction of foreign capital. Japanese economy today appears on the surface to have attained a measure of stability. But this stability rests upon American aid, and there lurks within it many a factor tending towards instability. We must first of all regain a healthy economic power. Otherwise, we shall not be able to maintain a single exchange rate even if one is established. Nor may we hope to attract foreign investments to our shores.

The Government's other programmes for national reconstruction include :

Promotion of export industries.

Promotion and improvement of agriculture.

Unemployment counter-measures.

Disaster relief measures.

Renovation of education; advancement of science; and enhancement of morality.

With respect to these individual programmes, the respective competent minister concerned will give you detailed explanations in due course.

As Foreign Minister, I want to speak concerning the repatriation of overseas Japanese nationals. So far, more than six million have been brought home, but I regret to say that there still remain more than 400,000 of our compatriots who are compelled to pass their fourth winter in cold countries.

I desire to express my sincere sympathy for them and their families and friends at home. Thanks to the kind and tireless endeavours of the Allied headquarters, an understanding seems to have been obtained from the Government concerned, so that I believe we may expect the repatriation completed by the end of this year.

I avail myself of this occasion to touch on a subject of general concern. Rumours of various kinds are being circulated concerning the dangers involved in Japan's international position. Such is a usual phenomenon which arises in the wake of a great war. But the memory of the last war is still too fresh in the minds of all nations, and no country wants war. I sincerely hope that our people will not be misled by such rumours emanating from abroad. On the other hand, it is most gratifying that Japan is coming to be invited to participate in international conferences in the field of science, religion, the Red Cross and labour, and she is being permitted to despatch trade missions to various quarters of the world.

We hear frequently nowadays of the 'extreme right' or the 'extreme left'. But these epithets are used mostly by those who have an axe to grind. I am confident that a vast preponderant majority of Japanese strongly desire the economic reconstruction and rehabilitation of the country and are determined to work and co-operate towards that end. However, there are those, though a very small minority, who not only obstruct national reconstruction but are also scheming to bring destruction and chaos upon the country. The existence of this latter group, regrettable as it is, is a fact which we must recognize.

To conclude, the budget we are submitting represents the obligation which the government of post-war Japan should have carried out, but which has happened to be neglected until this day. Japan at this juncture needs unity. She needs economic patriotism. I fervently hope the nation will unite in an all-out effort to observe the Nine Principles as fully and faithfully as any other obligations imposed upon her by the Allied occupation policy. That is the only way to win our goal of democratic government and of economic independence, so that Japan may be welcomed back by other Powers as an active member in the society of nations.

Contemporary Japan, Vol. XVIII, Nos 4-6, April-June 1949, pp. 256-9.

24   8 *November* 1949

PRIME MINISTER YOSHIDA'S ADMINISTRATIVE POLICY
SPEECH IN THE SIXTH NATIONAL DIET

It is scarcely necessary for me to say that the most fervent wish of our nation is the conclusion of Japan's peace treaty at the earliest possible date. And what we must do to that end is to demonstrate to the world that we are a truly civilized people worthy of a place of honour in the community of nations.

It is most gratifying that of late we are receiving more and more invitations to send observers to international conferences on trade, labour and scientific problems; that the restrictions on foreign travel are being gradually relaxed ; and that we are achieving the restoration in fact of our foreign intercourse through participation in various international agreements and trade pacts.

The question of atomic energy that has recently come to the fore is causing us deep concern over the future of our national security. Under the new constitution we solemnly declared ourselves an unarmed nation, by voluntarily renouncing war and abandoning all forms of armament. Relying on world public opinion wedded to peace, we mean to contribute to the concord and prosperity of mankind.

Let us show more clearly than ever this firm resolve on our part and let the world understand and appreciate our position. That will be I believe, the best guarantee of security for our nation. Let us remember that it was reliance upon imperfect armament, coupled with ignorance of world conditions and trends, that spelled the ruin of our country and brought upon us an unparalleled calamity as well as condemnation by the whole world.

Being unarmed, I am convinced, is something in which we may well take pride, and which really assures our security and well-being. I earnestly hope you will all be brought round thoroughly to this way of thinking.

As you all know, the Government has set up this year the first consolidated balanced budget since the war's end, and has pursued a vigorous policy of economic stabilization on the basis of Joseph

Dodge's recommendations. Thanks to the benevolent assistance of the United States as well as to the efforts of our nation, inflation has been so far successfully checked. With our national economy being stabilized and normalized, we are entering upon a stage of real and positive recovery.

Then, the Supreme Commander for the Allied Powers sent me a letter, advising tax reforms on the basis of a report of the Shoup Mission, which had been prepared after arduous and intensive study of Japan's taxation system. In compliance with this letter of Gen. MacArthur the Government is now working on a bill for establishing a comprehensive and rational taxation system adapted to the current situation of the country.

Government starts with taxation, while taxes are levied on the basis of government expenditure. An equitable tax system and tax collection method befitting the capacity of the people to pay will alone bring forth good government and stabilize the national life. Unfortunately in our country the requirements of the army and navy and the exigencies of war over the long years past have warped and twisted our taxation system, and given rise to improper and inequitable practices in tax collection. These evils cannot be eradicated in a short space of time ; both the Government and the people must unite and co-operate to rectify the situation.

To lighten the tax burden of the people and to restore the disastrous damages is the urgent task of the day. In the execution of the budget of the current year the Government intends to reduce administrative expenditures and cut down the price-difference compensation and other forms of subsidy. By curtailing Government spending to the utmost, we plan to apply the money so saved during this fiscal year to the reduction of certain taxes to be announced later, as well as to the rehabilitation of devastated areas.

Furthermore, it is our intention so to control Government expenditures as to be able to adjust and modify various taxes in the coming fiscal year.

The successive storms and floods in the past months have put an immense stumbling block in our programme for economic reconstruction. The afflicted areas deserve every sympathy. The damage is of course partly due to abnormal rainfalls, but it is also unmistakably attributable to the neglect of afforestation and riparian works since the pre-war years. By formulating an overall land development programme including afforestation, flood control, irrigation and exploitation of electric power resources, and appropriating the necessary funds therefor, the Government will vigorously push it forward with a view to letting it contribute also to the solution of the unemployment problem.

To consolidate the foundation of our educational system for the proper training of our growing generation is a vital task attending Japan's national reconstruction. The Government will pay special attention to primary schools in order to foster common sense and sound thoughts among the young, and will take whatever steps are possible and are within our means with respect to physical facilities as well as curriculum and method of instruction.

The personnel reduction programme of the Government, which was completed at the end of last September, has resulted in the saving of 20,000 million yen in administrative expenditure. But we are determined to go a step further. We will re-examine the country's entire administrative systems, both central and local, and try to contrive a truly rational and compact government machinery.

We will effect further retrenchment in the number of organs and personnel through abolition or adjustment of various economic controls. We will pare off gradually the various Government subsidies as a measure to promote self-supporting economy. While curtailing expenditures as much as possible, we will provide appropriations, wherever necessary, as far as our finances will permit. By adhering thus to a really sound and balanced fiscal policy, we aim to lay a firm foundation of national economy.

It may be said that in every age and in every country, the government is always the biggest spendthrift. It is amazing how government money is squandered. In these days when we must economize on expenditures by all means for the sake of post-war reconstruction I regret to note the persistence of the demands for additional appointments, or for more subsidies and aid funds.

Again, it is an undeniable fact that there are not a few among those in Government service, who, abusing their authority, impose hardships and needless red tape upon the public. But with respect to this matter as well as administrative economy and simplification, the Government must ask for vigilance and co-operation on the part of the public, without which the desired reforms are impossible.

In the face of dire commodity shortages following the war's end control was unavoidable. But thanks to American aid and our production recovery, we have now reached a stage where there exists a number of things on which control is unnecessary, or even harmful. The Government has, therefore, been endeavouring to readjust or remove such controls. This year we have succeeded in lifting control from vegetables, coal, copper, non-ferrous metals, firewood, aquatic products and other items. Consequently, we are planning to carry out the reorganization, or abolition as the case may be, of various Government corporations involved.

The single exchange rate of the yen, which was fixed some time ago at a level lower than anticipated, has been conducive, as you know, to the promotion of our foreign trade. Now with the devaluation of the pound it is feared our export trade might encounter some difficulties. But you should remember that when the rate of 360 yen to the dollar was fixed, there were those who advocated a rate of 330 yen, or even 300 yen, to the dollar. The low yen rate was adopted by considering the world fiscal trends and taking future contingencies into account.

The Government will, therefore, hold fast to the 360 yen rate, and rely for export promotion on the lowering of production cost and the improvement of equality through tax reduction, rationalization of enterprises and application of advanced scientific technologies.

If the Government were to fail at this juncture to stick to the current yen rate and the traders at home and abroad were to look for devaluation, that would not only really hurt our export but also jeopardize the country's economy which has just begun to be stabilized. It is through non-devaluation of the yen that we can procure food and industrial raw materials at cheapest prices, reduce production cost, and ultimately realize the expansion of our export trade. The fact that in certain quarters in England the devaluation of the pound is being criticized as a premature scheme, should, I believe, serve us a warning.

The Government will, of course, continue to do everything in its power to promote foreign trade through such measures as the securing of export funds, normalization of exchange transactions, conclusion of trade agreements, relaxation of trade control and supervision, and placing trading activities under a free system.

It goes without saying that we should fulfil our foreign obligations and enhance our credit abroad. I desire to avail myself of this opportunity to reiterate that we are preparing for the resumption of our foreign loan services which have been suspended for these past years since the outbreak of the Pacific War.

Under the Agricultural Land Reform our rural communities have been remodelled on the owner-farmer basis. The Government will pursue comprehensive and appropriate policies so as to enable farming operation to adapt itself to the changes in the international situation as well as in domestic conditions, and to stabilize and put on a solid foundation the agricultural industry of Japan.

Just now the revision of the pay base for public service personnel is being debated here and there. But any change in the pay schedule affects the commodity price immediately, and there is the danger of setting the vicious price-wage cycle in motion. The Government desires to avoid a base-pay revision, but to secure the livelihood of

Government employees by raising their real wage through tax reduction, increased allowances and welfare measures.

The greatest asset left to post-war Japan is to be found in her workers, numbering tens of millions. We rejoice at the present trend of our labour movement which is taking a wholesome and constructive course, resulting in the enhancement of labour productivity. On the other hand, the administrative adjustment and the rationalization of enterprises are inevitably swelling the ranks of unemployed, which is a source of grave concern.

As counter-measures for the present the Government will on the one hand, expand its public works programmes and absorb as large numbers as possible into such channels as rehabilitation of devastated areas, land development and opening of natural resources; and, on the other hand, protect the jobless through proper operation of the emergency unemployment relief enterprises and the unemployment insurance system. But a positive solution of the unemployment problem is to be sought in the creation of fresh demand for labour through the promotion of industries and trade, to which, as I have stated before, the Government will give full attention.

As regards the repatriation of our nationals abroad, thanks to the extraordinary efforts of the Allied Headquarters, more than six million were returned from various areas before the end of last year while some 85,000 have come back this year from the end of June to date. But the fact that a great many are still detained in Siberia and China is a cause for profound anxiety. In order to speed their return the Government will redouble its efforts, maintaining close contact with the Allied authorities concerned.

Now there are other matters such as measures relating to medium and small enterprises, agriculture and forestry, aquatic industry protection, transportation and communication renovation, social safeguard system and local finances, all of which are important affairs of state. The policies and programmes of the Government concerning these will be presented to you respectively by the competent Ministers concerned.

Under the National Public Service Personnel Law we have recently promulgated regulations prescribing the scope of political activities by Government officials. It is a proper and necessary measure. We are convinced that a Government official, who is to serve the people as a whole, should in the public interest naturally submit to certain restraints so that he may preserve his unbiased position, as is provided for by the Constitution.

It is a universal post-war phenomenon that social unrest, attending hard living, invites the infiltration of radical foreign ideologies, and attempts are made at bringing destruction and confusion to the country.

I regret we have also certain terroristic and destructive minority elements who ignore the importance of liberty and the dignity of the individual and have more than once tried to plunge the country into chaos and obstruct the progress of national recovery.

However, a great majority of our people are, needless to say, possessed of common sense, judgement, and the courage of conviction. They desire sincerely the rehabilitation of Japan. Rejecting any malcontent outright, they will devote themselves, heart and soul, to the task of national reconstruction. Even those who harbour extremist notions will, I believe, be restored to patriotic national consciousness some day as economic conditions improve, as wholesome thoughts come to prevail and as the international atmosphere clears up.

Let me conclude by saying that with the co-operation of the people, the Government is prepared to take all possible measures in order to ensure peace and order throughout the land.

Contemporary Japan, Vol. XVIII, Nos 10-12, October-December 1949, pp. 567-72.

V ECONOMIC STABILIZATION

25   23 *May* 1948

REPORT ON THE ECONOMIC CONDITION OF JAPAN
BY THE ECONOMIC STABILIZATION BOARD

The former Cabinet published an economic report on 4 July 1947 and made it clear that the post-war economy of Japan was in a critical condition by an extraordinary under-production and the mounting inflation. Ten months have since passed. In this report we shall try to trace the progress of Japanese economy since that time and to describe the general outlook of its future development. Compared with ten months ago, the living conditions of the people are just as hard as ever but, due to the increased production of coal and to the prospect of increasing economic aids from Allied Powers, the outlook of economic rehabilitation has become brighter. Food condition is also expected to improve owing to the accomplishment of the full quota delivery by our supply. Furthermore the tempo in advance of prices has somewhat slowed down since last autumn and a hopeful outlook as to the prevention of critical inflation has come to be entertained.

On the other hand the war damages of our economy are serious and the post-war problems of production, foreign trade and inflation are full of difficulties. Unstinted efforts of the whole nation are required to be made for a long time before the realization of a self-supporting economy and prosperity. The present Report tries to make clear the actual condition of Japanese economy and to provide our people with a clue to reconstruction so that they may exert themselves with full understanding of the actual economic conditions.

We shall clarify some of the fundamental conditions of post-war Japanese economy. We shall make a general survey of the present economic conditions and then describe the present status of production, foreign trade, prices, money and finance, wage, family expenditure, etc.

The post-war economy of our country is fundamentally different in many respects from the pre-war one, its principal differences being loss of property, reduction of foreign trade, rapid increase of population, etc. As a result of researches conducted chiefly by the Economic Stabilization Board since the summer of last year, a report on the war damages of our economy has recently been made. According to that report the total sum of the properties (excluding weapons, aeroplanes, war-vessels, and other military properties) lost in the homeland by air raids and other warlike operations amounts to 49,673,611,000 in terms of the price level at surrender time and 1,383·4 billion in terms of official price at the end of last year, or 20 per cent of the total domestic assets in pre-war days. In addition to the above there are indirect losses due to depreciation of assets which were not repaired and replaced, to the forceful demolition of houses and others for dispersion purpose, to the dilapidation of peacetime industry equipments, and the losses due to reparations removal, loss of assets abroad, etc. Our national income in 1935 was 14·5 billion, of which, 2·2 billion (or in terms of price level at surrender time 6·5 billion) was turned to new investment.

Therefore, even with the economic capacity of 1935, it will take nearly 10 years to make up for the above direct losses. With the economic power at present when population is 115 per cent and real income is less than 60 per cent of those days, recovery would take still longer time. We can, of course, shorten the period necessary for recovery by saving consumption, increasing accumulation and by obtaining monetary aids from foreign countries. But it is by no means an easy task to repair and restore worn-out facilities of transportation, housing, factories, etc., and to rehabilitate the long un-attended rivers, roads, forests, etc.

Furthermore the loss of assets does not end in itself. It constitutes a major factor in retarding the post-war economic recovery by contracting the production basis. For example the shortage of houses and the dilapidation of transport facilities lead to a lower labour efficiency and the deterioration of transportation, electricity, communications and other facilities worsens the productive condition of industries. The post-war economy has so far left such losses of assets to continue and expand rather than make up for them.

The second condition in our post-war economy is the difficulties in foreign trade. In order that the 80 million Japanese attain a living standard of 1930-34, it will be necessary to make an import of about $2 billion and to make a corresponding export. But the post-war foreign trade has been inactive owing to the existence of manifold difficulties. In the last year actual import was 25 per cent while export was less than 10 per cent respectively of the figures mentioned above. In view of the fact that our country has to depend upon the import of various goods, such as foodstuffs, textiles, industrial raw materials, etc., reduction of foreign trade means a lowering of living standard and the inactivity of industries.

Owing to the political and economic instability prevailing in the East Asiatic countries which used to be our major markets and sources of supply, we have chiefly to rely upon USA for imports, thus turning the trade balance *vis-a-vis* USA extremely unfavourable to us. This has been remedied to some extent by monetary aids from USA but is difficult of fundamental solution until the import and export capacities of East Asiatic countries are restored.

The third condition is the rapid increase of population. According to the census held on 1 October 1947, the total population of our country was 78·62 million, which shows an increase of around 6·6 million since the surrender. The above increase is mainly attributable to the repatriation which amounted to 5·77 million at the end of October 1947. The increase of population means an increase of productive labour and serves to the rehabilitation of economy but on the other hand means an increased consumption of food and other goods and serves to aggravate the import burden and unemployment problem.

As is clear from the foregoing it is extremely difficult to recover in a short period the Japanese economy to the pre-war level. The self-supporting economy and the improvement of living standard can be achieved only through nation-wide savings and hard work.

Under the above-mentioned fundamental conditions, post-war production, particularly that of industries, has remarkably decreased. On the other hand the release of purchasing power accumulated during the war, and the subsequent over-expenditure in public finance and deficit financing to enterprises had rapidly accelerated in inflation and the prices had kept on rising. Industrial production, which had declined immediately after the surrender to about 10 per cent of the pre-war 1930-34 level, recovered in autumn of 1946 to nearly 40 per cent but thereafter with ups and downs had shown no noticeable increase. Tempo of inflation stepped up from the end of 1946 to the spring of 1947 and prices rose by 10-15 per cent every month. Inflation was expected to enter a catastrophic stage before long.

Therefore the preceding Cabinet, immediately after its formation in June 1947, took up the economic problem and put into practice a series of counter-measures, such as the publication of economic emergency measures, revision of price level, food emergency measures, etc. By making public the serious condition of Japanese economy it appealed to the nation to put up with an austere life and to co-operate.

These measures, not necessarily without some defects when they were put into effect, were supposed to have served, judging from the subsequent economic development, as a basis for the recovery of production and for arresting inflation and as a starting point in improving, though gradually, the national living condition.

As regards the mining and manufacturing industries, production declined temporarily during the summer and autumn of 1947 owing to the seasonal shortage of electricity supply, unsmooth import of raw cotton, etc., but the average production in the 1947 fiscal year reached the level of 43·1 per cent of that in 1930-34 or 21 per cent increase as compared with that in the preceding fiscal year. Especially since last December production has been improving and the production indices of December, January, February, and March in terms of the 1930-34 basis were 44·8 per cent, 41·9 per cent, 45·5 per cent and 49·0 per cent respectively in spite of the dry season.

As regards coal, production began to increase in the latter half of 1947 and a yearly output of 29·32 million tons was secured in the 1947 fiscal year, or 97·7 per cent of the 30 million ton target. The above production increases may be regarded to have been achieved as a result of the priority given to coal production since the beginning of 1947 and the unusual combined efforts exerted by the Government and the people for the attainment of that target. Thus, the total production of coal has increased by 30 per cent and coal for mining and manufacturing uses has increased by 46 per cent respectively, as compared with that in the preceding fiscal year, thereby supplying the motive power for production recovery.

As regards electricity, its irregular supply has greatly hampered the industries in 1947 in spite of the fact that the total generated power was 85 per cent over and above that in 1930-34, demonstrating a remarkable increase of electricity consumption as compared with the meagre industrial production. This is mainly due to the shortage of coal, petroleum, and other fuels but there seems to exist some room for further nationalization of electricity consumption. In fact the mining and manufacturing industries have as stated above increased their production by 21 per cent in the 1947 fiscal year, while their consumption of electricity in the same period has increased only by 4 per cent.

As regards manufacturing industry, its production in the 1947 fiscal year rose to a level of 35·8 per cent of that in 1930-34 or 20 per cent increase over the preceding fiscal year. As is shown in the following table, generally speaking, the production recovery in basic capital goods was noticeable of which the production of consumer goods remained stagnant.

	A	B
Textile industry	19·8[%]	121[%]
Metal industry	39·7	171
Machinery industry	47·0	112
Chemical industry	49·8	131
Food Processing industry	43·4	81

Note : (A) Production in the fiscal year 1947; 1930-34 = 100.
       (B) Percentage against preceding year.

The production target of mining and manufacturing industries for the 1947 fiscal year was fixed by the former Government at a level 40 per cent above that of the last fiscal year. In view of the fact that the recovery of production is the most important problem in our post-war economy, and that unless a speedy increase of production of basic materials is achieved, such factors as the exhaustion of stock materials, the progressing deterioration of industrial equipments and devastation of national land, etc., would make our economic recovery ever harder, we have to make every possible effort to attain production increase.

Of course, many difficulties are expected to arise in respect of transportation and other fields, but judging from the bright prospect of increased import of industrial raw materials for the manufacture of export goods as well as for the production of basic materials for domestic use, the attainment of the said target will not necessarily be impossible.

However, we should not neglect the possible adverse effect of mounting inflation on production. In the present fiscal year substantial increase of production mainly in export goods and basic capital

goods can be expected, while much production increase in consumer
goods for domestic consumption which are most effective in arresting
the present inflationary trend cannot be expected. Furthermore, a
speedy recovery of production will require a huge outlay of funds.
Therefore, we have to endeavour to attain the above target of production increase while arresting inflation by absorbing as much
purchasing power as possible through the encouragement of savings
and the increase of national revenues.

As regards agricultural production, in spite of the shortage of
fertilizers, flood damages and other adverse conditions, the rice crop
in 1947, favoured with good weather, was a bumper one with a net
production of 59·67 million 'koku' which is close to the 61·38
million 'koku' in 1946. Rice delivery proceeded smoothly and the
delivery target of 30·55 million 'koku' was accomplished in the
middle of March this year, thereby contributing largely to the
amelioration of food conditions this year.

The target of agricultural production for the present fiscal year
is set at a level of 10 per cent over that of the last fiscal year. In
case it is fully achieved, food conditions after the coming autumn
will be somewhat ameliorated, thereby contributing greatly to the
improvement of general economic conditions.

As regards transportation, marine transportation fulfilled the
10·68 million ton target for the fiscal year of 1947 which is an 88
per cent increase over that of the preceding year. Railroad transportation in the fiscal year of 1947 was 112 million tons, or a 12 per
cent increase over the preceding year, but the above tonnage was
only 85 per cent of the required transportation and constituted an
important bottleneck in production recovery.

The transportation problem is expected to continue as the greatest
bottleneck in production recovery this year as well. Inasmuch as
many difficulties are expected even in the attainment of the 130
million ton goal which is 6 per cent above the level of the preceding
year, an all-out effort must be made for the increase of transportation capacity through improvement of operation efficiency, repair
and replacement of worn-out facilities and rolling stock.

In foreign trade of the last calendar year, import was $526 million
while export was $174 million, i.e., a sizeable increase over the respec-
tive level in the preceding year. In imports, items for the prevention
of hunger and disease occupied 68 per cent of the total amount while
the import of raw materials for export and basic materials necessary
for economic rehabilitation remained rather small. Unfavourable
balance of trade amounted to $352 million. Thus the total post-
surrender unfavourable balance amounted to $530 million. The
economy of Japan is thus sustained by such huge foreign aid.

668

This year it is expected that the productive activities will be enhanced through the increase of import funds in various forms and through the subsequent substantial increase of industrial raw material imports. It is our responsibility to make the greatest effort for the increase of export, to reduce the burden of the Allied Powers, and to expedite the realization of the self-supporting economy.

Let us now consider the impact of inflation upon monetary condition. In the first half of 1947 official prices rose slightly but black-market prices and effective prices rose rapidly and almost doubled by July. Owing to the subsequent revision of the price level, official prices rose substantially during the latter half but black-market prices and effective prices rose considerably less rapidly.

The bank note issue increased by 103·9 billion during the fiscal year 1947. The increase was marked particularly in the October-December period and the amount of bank notes at the end of last year amounted to 219·1 billion. Through January and February this year, however, the bank notes kept on decreasing and the amount at the end of March was 218·7 billion which is less than at the end of last year. The above recent trend is regarded as having been brought about by the acceleration of financial revenues, the restriction of financial expenditure, the regulation of industrial finance, the encouragement of savings, etc. In view of the fact, however, that there are strong factors at work which are conducive to inflation, such as the increasing stringency of industrial finance, gradual rise of the wage level, below-cost official prices, etc., we are not yet in a stage to envisage the final solution of inflation.

Let us analyse the causes of currency expansion in the 1947 fiscal year. As against the total fund requirements of 232·3 billion to be divided into 64·8 billion for the expenditures of the national treasury in excess of its revenues and 167·5 billion of the industrial funds, the net increase of savings has amounted to only 125·5 billion with the remaining balance of 103 billion being financed by the expansion of issue of the Bank of Japan notes.

As regards public finance, the General Account for the 1947 fiscal year managed to maintain its balance by dint of the tax collection campaign since last January, and the strict restriction on Government expenditures. However, in the Special Accounts the borrowings and the net increase of Government bonds have amounted to 66·5 billion of which 58·4 billion has been undertaken by the Bank of Japan, a principal source of currency expansion attributable to the public finance.

In view of the fact that on the revenue side such incomes as are difficult to catch have greatly increased as a result of the inflation, it is an urgent necessity to catch such incomes to the maximum through the strengthening of the tax collecting function. Furthermore, inasmuch as the tax burden on the low income earners is heavy, it is regarded as necessary to revise the tax system in this respect.

On the expenditure side a virtual reduction of outlay has been effected through price-rises, but we must further reduce the expenditures through the distribution on priority basis of appropriations and the enforcement of surveillance on expenditures.

Most deficits in the Special Accounts are attributable to the Railway and Communications Special Accounts, and 16·9 billion and 6·7 billion of deficit are shown in the balance of each of these Special Accounts respectively. Some steps will have to be taken in this connexion.

In the industrial finance, the restriction of lendings through the enforcement of finance regulations served to arrest the currency expansion and the price rises. On the other hand a credit expansion has to be made in order to maintain the activities of important productive enterprises. Particularly the amount financed through the Reconstruction Finance Bank during a year ending on 31 March increased by 53·5 billion which is 32 per cent of the total increased lendings in that period. The RFB has played an important part in the maintenance of the important basic industries through the inflationary period. But taking into consideration the fact that the deficit finance occupies a substantial portion and that it is difficult to dispose of the Reconstruction Finance Bonds, it is desirable to make a proper selection of borrowers and a systematic enforcement of supervision in accordance with the actual circumstances in industries.

As to enterprises, they appear to be gradually losing the flexibility of management. However, as it is expected that the economy will generally turn to normalcy and participate in the international economy, inefficient enterprises may be gradually liquidated. Under the post-war economic condition where there are shortages of fuel and power and raw materials, deterioration of equipment, austerity of living conditions, etc., it is inevitable that there may be some over-employment compared with the pre-war period. But we must raise labour productivity as quickly as possible by overcoming these adverse conditions.

As to wages and family expenditures, the former kept on rising by nearly 10 per cent per month in the latter half of last year and the overall monthly average wages of the factory workers rose from 1,834 in July to 3,224 in March this year. The wage rise in and after the latter half of last year was greater than the price rise and the real wages in January-March this year were about 20 per cent above those in the corresponding period of last year.

Family expenditures increased rapidly in the first half of last year but in the latter half the increase rate became less rapid owing to the improvement of staple food rations and to the slow-down of black market price rise. Due to the fact, however, that the improvement of non-staple food distribution was insufficient, that the consumption level has gradually been raised, etc., the household deficit has not been written off. In proportion to the improvement of food condition this year, the balance between wages and household expenditures will be improved to some extent compared with last year.

The present real wages and real family expenditures in urban areas are around 30 per cent and 40 per cent respectively of those in the pre-war period. The unbalance between the two percentages constitutes a fundamental cause of the household deficit. It is to be noticed, in particular, that the tax burden occupies nearly 10 per cent of the family expenditure of workers.

The supplies of necessaries, such as clothing, fuel, daily necessaries, etc., did not show any noticeable improvement compared with the preceding year. In view of the fact that emphasis is placed on the recovery of basic industries and the increase of export in this year, no sizeable increase in the supply of consumer goods can be expected. But the amelioration of food condition and the general increase of production will, though gradually, improve the living standard of our people.

As is clear from the foregoing, the economy of our country is beginning to show some signs of improvement, such as increase in production, particularly that of coal, increase of raw material imports, amelioration of food condition, slow-down of inflationary trend, etc. However, there is a considerable amount of foreign trade deficit, and furthermore worn out facilities, damaged rivers, devastated forests, etc., are still unattended. In order to make up for extensive war damages, modernize production facilities, increase export, and to attain a self-supporting economy, we shall have to make a further great effort hereafter.

As has been made clear in the foregoing, Japanese economy faces an important cross-road this year ; three years since the termination of the war have seen the continuation of emergency measures under the pressure of the hard-pressed economic situation. The situation at home as well as abroad seems to encourage us to make this year the first one for the real reconstruction of peace-time economy. We are required to place our economy on a self-supporting basis and thus minimize the burden on the part of the Allied Powers and further contribute to the reconstruction and prosperity of this part of the world with maximum industrial recovery and export increase.

How can we answer the requirement ? What is most essential is to promote maximum recovery of production while arresting the advance of inflation as much as possible, and furthermore, to try to improve our economy to run with highest possible efficiency. For the implementation of this objective it is essential that an economic rehabilitation programme be drafted on an objective basis, indigenous resources utilized to the full, technical standard raised and higher efficiency attained in the respective fields of public administration, enterprise management and labour.

It is further required that the minimum living of the people be guaranteed by way of promoting equitable distribution of necessary goods and at the same time luxurious consumption be, of course, restricted and present extremely short supply of internal capital accumulated and restored ; to be invested in useful productive fields accelerating economic recovery.

The future of our economy depends upon whether the problems which are mentioned above will be solved or not, and we should not forget that the outside assistance of constructive nature will come only when the Japanese people themselves endeavour to utilize their available resources to the maximum extent.

Contemporary Japan, Vol. XVII, Nos. 4-6, April-June 1948, pp. 214-22.

26   18 *December* 1948

PROGRAMME TO ACHIEVE ECONOMIC STABILIZATION

The Departments of State and Army announced today that the Supreme Commander for the Allied Powers will direct the Japanese Government to carry out an effective Economic Stabilization Programme calculated to achieve fiscal, monetary, price and wage stability in Japan as rapidly as possible, as well as to maximize production for export. The action of the Supreme Commander will be taken pursuant to an interim directive issued to him by the United States Government which is in accord with the terms of reference of the Far Eastern Commission.

Economic stability is a most urgent requirement for assuring the continuation of Japan's economic recovery and to ensure the maximum effect from use of US appropriated funds. General MacArthur and responsible officials in Washington have been encouraged by the marked general recovery in Japanese industrial production through 1948 (with November at 62 per cent of the 1930-34 average and 47 per cent above a year ago) and by the anticipated increase in exports this year to about $260,000,000, 48 per cent above 1947. General price and monetary inflation have continued, however, with the consumer price level and increasing 60 per cent over the period between November 1947 and November 1948. The retarding effects of this general and continuing inflation, together with the dangers to the gains already achieved, have made apparent the necessity for more resolute and intensive action by the Japanese.

Improvements in the Japanese general standard of living will be contingent on the degree to which the Japanese give whole-hearted support to the achievement of economic stabilization and recovery. Their performance in carrying out their programme will be weighed in connexion with future requests for appropriated funds for Japan.

Countries which are recipients of US assistance under the Economic Co-operation Act of 1948 have also undertaken certain measures similar to those specified in this programme. These include financial and monetary measures necessary to stabilize their currencies, to establish or maintain valid rates of exchange, to balance their budgets as soon as practicable and generally to maintain confidence in their monetary system. The action in Japan is in line with the efforts of the US in other parts of the world to contribute to general economic recovery.

The necessity for such a programme was recognized by General MacArthur in July 1948 when he urged upon the Japanese Government a programme which was substantially that which he has now directed they carry out. The specific objectives of the programme are :

(a) Achieving a true balance in the consolidated budget at the earliest possible date by stringent curtailing of expenditures and maximum expansion in total governmental revenues, including such new revenue as may be necessary and appropriate.

(b) Accelerating and strengthening the programme of tax collection and ensuring prompt, widespread and vigorous criminal prosecution of tax evaders.

(c) Assuring that credit extension is rigorously limited to those projects contributing to the economic recovery of Japan.

(d) Establishing an effective programme to achieve wage stability.

(e) Strengthening and, if necessary, expanding the coverage of existing price control programmes.

(f) Improving the operation of foreign trade controls and tightening existing foreign exchange controls, to the extent that such measures can appropriately be delegated to Japanese agencies.

(g) Improving the effectiveness of the present allocation and rationing system, particularly to the end of maximizing exports.

(*h*)   Increasing production of all essential indigenous raw material and manufactured products.

(*i*)   Improving efficiency of the food collection programme.

The above plans will be developed to pave the way for the early establishment of a single general exchange rate.

Department of the US Army, *Press Release*, 18 December 1948.

27   19 *December* 1948

GENERAL MACARTHUR'S LETTER TO PRIME MINISTER YOSHIDA REGARDING THE ECONOMIC STABILIZATION PROGRAMME

I am just in receipt of an interim directive from the Government of the United States forwarded to me in accordance with the terms of reference of the Far Eastern Commission. This directive establishes a series of objectives designed to achieve fiscal, monetary, price and wage stability in Japan as rapidly as possible, as well as to maximize production for export. Such objectives, which are listed as an enclosure to this letter are clear and explicit, and as pointed out in the public release of the United States State and Army Departments follow an objective pattern, the general aspects of which have heretofore been communicated to the Japanese Government as a means towards the ultimate desired stability.

The directive proceeds from the premises that the prompt economic stabilization of Japan is a primary objective common both to the Allied Powers and the Japanese people ; that the American people so long as called upon to underwrite existing deficits in the indigenous resources required to sustain Japanese life are entitled to the maximized industry of the Japanese people and the minimized loss incident to a maldistribution of available resources or failure vigorously to produce native raw products or curb extravagance and waste in the operation of government and industry ; and that by positive Allied intervention may obstructions incident to improvidential political conflicts, unobjective labour strife, and destructive ideological pressures best be avoided.

The fundamental objective of this action, reduced to language which all may understand, is the prompt achievement of that degree of economic self-sufficiency which alone can justify and ensure political freedom. For there can be no political freedom so long as a people's livelihood is dependent upon the largess of others. Nor may a people

674

fully mobilize the collective will as an impregnable barrier against evil and destructive ideological pressures and as an irresistible force towards progressively improved living standards, if lacking in that resolute dignity which alone springs from mastery over its own deficiencies.

Necessarily, the action of the United States is tied in to the problem of relief and recovery appropriations, which may be expected in future only in ratio to progress made through the combined efforts of the Japanese people towards achievement of the stated objectives. This will call for a reorientation of Japanese thought and action, with both subordinated to a primary purpose common to all of the people. It will call for increased austerity in every phase of Japanese life and for the temporary surrender of some of the privileges and immunities inherent in a free society.

There will be no place for interference by management or labour with the acceleration of production, for the burden will be shared by every segment of Japanese society. There will be no place for political conflict over the objectives to be sought as these objectives are stated with crystal clarity. Nor will there be any place for ideological opposition as the purpose to be served is common to all of the people, and any attempt to delay or frustrate its accomplishment must be curbed as menacing the general welfare.

In keeping with my long established policy, in so far as is possible, I shall look to the Japanese Government and people for the vigorous and faithful fulfilment of this stabilization programme. I have faith in their ability, however stern the requirement and great the personal sacrifice, to achieve so worthy a national goal. The course ahead may well prove difficult but its impact upon individual life will be minimized if the burden is equalized among all of the people.

It is my earnest hope and indeed my confident expectation that all Japanese men and women will rally with vigour and determination to the challenge of this objective. If they do, Japan will evolve a pattern of progressive stability for all of strife-torn Asia to emulate. If they do not, Japan may perish.

Contemporary Japan, Vol. XVII, Nos. 7-12, July-December 1948, pp. 434-5.

ANNOUNCEMENT BY GENERAL HEADQUARTERS, THE
SUPREME COMMANDER FOR THE ALLIED .POWERS,
CONCERNING FOREIGN BUSINESS AND INVESTMENT
ACTIVITIES IN JAPAN

Foreign Business and Investment Activities in Japan

(1) Rescission and Reference.

(*a*) Rescission. Paragraph 3(*b*), Circular 17, General Headquarters,
Supreme Commander for the Allied Powers, 2 June 1948.

(*b*) Reference. Circular 1, General Headquarters, Supreme Commander for the Allied Powers, 14 January 1949.

(2) Purpose. The purpose of this circular is to establish the
conditions under which non-Japanese nationals and foreign controlled
firms and their authorized agents may conduct business and investment activity in Japan.

(3) Definitions.

(*a*) A 'foreign controlled firm', for the purpose of this circular, is defined as a corporation, institution, or other organization wholly owned
or controlled, directly or indirectly, by non-Japanese nationals.

(*b*) 'Business activity in Japan', for the purpose of this circular,
is defined as commercial or financial transactions or industrial
operations other than those conducted solely for the occupation
forces.

(4) Entry. As indicated in referenced circular, (1) (*b*) above, and
under conditions set down therein, persons with a trade, business,
or investment interest in Japan who have been sponsored by Allied
or neutral governments are permitted entry into Japan.

(5) Permission to do business.

(*a*) Military personnel and personnel attached to or accompanying
the occupation forces, including their dependents, are prohibited
from engaging in business or investment activity in Japan, except as
specifically licensed by General Headquarters, Supreme Commander
for the Allied Powers. Employment of dependents by private
commercial concerns engaged in international trade is authorized
provided this employment does not involve dependents serving on
their own behalf or as agents to make sales to or purchases from
Japanese agencies or individuals.

(*b*) Non-Japanese nationals who have been in continuous residence
in Japan since 2 September 1945, or who have been permitted entry
by the Supreme Commander for the Allied Powers for the purpose
of establishing permanent residence in Japan, and firms wholly

owned or controlled by them are permitted to engage in business transactions in Japan on a non-discriminatory basis with Japanese nationals, except as provided in paragraph (8) below.

(c) Effective the date of this circular, Allied and neutral nationals or firms who are entitled to claim restoration or restitution of properties or contract rights held prior to 7 December 1941 are permitted to resume their pre-war business activities in Japan on a non-discriminatory basis with Japanese nationals, except as provided in paragraph (8) below.

(d) In all other cases, effective the date of this circular, non-Japanese nationals and foreign controlled firms and their authorized agents are permitted to engage on a non-discriminatory basis with Japanese nationals, except as provided in paragraph (8) below, in international trade and in those specific business activities in Japan which positively aid in Japanese economic rehabilitation, or provide a source of foreign exchange for Japan or are otherwise in furtherance of occupation objectives. Application to secure permission for engaging in specific activities other than international trade will be made to General Headquarters, Supreme Commander for the Allied Powers.

(e) Notwithstanding the provisions of sub-paragraphs (a) and thru (d) above, persons and firms engaged in business involving the receipt of foreign exchange in Japan ; the importation or dissemination of educational, informational or cultural materials from abroad ; or other activities which may hereafter be designated, are required to be licensed by the Supreme Commander for the Allied Powers. Persons and firms now operating under licence by the Supreme Commander for the Allied Powers, which are not required to be licensed by this sub-paragraph, may request termination of such licences if they so desire.

(6) Compliance with Regulations of the Supreme Commander for the Allied Powers and Japanese Law. All permission to engage in international trade and other business activity granted by the above paragraph is contingent upon compliance with regulations of the Supreme Commander for the Allied Powers and Japanese Law, including applicable economic control regulations. Violations thereof will constitute grounds for termination of permission to do business and for deportation. Laws particularly relevant in this connexion are the Price Control Ordinance, the Temporary Demand and Supply Adjustment Law (governing allocations of critical industrial materials) and Japanese tax laws.

(7) Critical shortages in the Japanese economy. At the present time Japan is suffering from critical shortages of materials, facilities and services. Business and industrial operations conducted by non-

Japanese nationals and firms may be handicapped by such shortages and are hereby so informed. The permission to do business granted by or pursuant to paragraph (5) in no way constitutes grounds for any special claim on materials, facilities and services necessary to carry out the contemplated business operations or continue present business operations. Non-Japanese nationals or firms wishing to engage in business in Japan which would require Japanese materials, facilities or services are advised to inquire of the Japanese Government Economic Stabilization Board as to the prospective availability of such materials, facilities and services and to guide themselves accordingly.

(8) Acquisition of Properties and Rights.

(a) Effective the date of this circular non-Japanese nationals and foreign controlled firms permitted to do business by Paragraph (5) above and their authorized Japanese agents are authorized to acquire or lease properties and rights in Japan in accordance with Japanese law, except that acquisition of property interests and rights in the following categories from Japanese nationals, from firms in which Japanese nationals or firms have a proprietary interest and from Japanese Government agencies will be void unless validated by the Japanese Government and the Supreme Commander for the Allied Powers :

(i) Acquisition of title to stocks and shares or of an interest in the profits of an enterprise.

(ii) Acquisition of title to land and/or residence for business purposes, and to commercial and industrial buildings and installations, and plant and facilities attached thereto. (Land and residences reasonably required by an individual signatory to the contract for his full or part-time residence are not business properties ; all other land and residences are business properties and subject to the provisions of this sub-paragraph.)

(iii) Leases for periods in excess of five years, mortgages or other hypothecations, and arrangements for or options to future acquisition of properties in the categories indicated in sub-paragraphs (i) and (ii) above.

(iv) Acquisition of patents of Japanese origin and rights thereunder.

(v) Acquisition of rights to a proportion of the output or sales of an enterprise for a period in excess of one year.

(b) Applications for validation as required by sub-paragraph above will be submitted to the appropriate agency of the Japanese Government as designated.

(c) Real properties acquired or leased by non-Japanese nationals and foreign controlled firms are subject to requisition by the occupation forces on the same basis as Japanese properties. Non-Japanese nationals and foreign controlled firms contemplating acquisition or lease of real properties may secure information from General Headquarters, Supreme Commander for the Allied Powers, as to whether there is a foreseeable occupation requirement for the properties involved.

(d) The requirements for validation established in this paragraph shall not apply to restoration or restitution of properties to pre-war owners by the Japanese government under supervision of the Supreme Commander for the Allied Powers nor shall anything in this paragraph be construed as validating any acquisition or lease of properties or rights which was made before the date of the circular and which was contrary to existing laws or regulations of the Supreme Commander for the Allied Powers or otherwise invalid at the time made.

(9) Remittances. Except as provided by special licence by the Supreme Commander for the Allied Powers, conversion of yen into foreign currency or exchange and agreements or arrangements involving conversion are prohibited.

Contemporary Japan, Vol. XVIII, Nos. 1-3, January-March 1949, pp. 140-43.

29   15 *January* 1949

ANNOUNCEMENT BY THE SUPREME COMMANDER FOR
THE ALLIED POWERS ON MINIMUM STANDARDS FOR
BUSINESS AND INVESTMENT ACTIVITIES OF
NON-JAPANESE IN JAPAN

The Supreme Commander for the Allied Powers has announced the following standards and criteria for validation of acquisition of Japanese properties and rights by non-Japanese during the Occupation.

PURPOSE: The minimum standards which follow have been established in order to guide and encourage acquisition of and investment in Japanese properties and rights by non-Japanese nationals and foreign controlled firms in such manner as to:

(1) Assist in and promote the rapid rehabilitation of the Japanese economy to the end of ensuring self-support and national independence.

(2) Protect the Japanese people and economy in the conservation of their national resources during a period of military occupation.

(3) Stimulate the restoration of sound international peacetime economic relationships as between Japan and the rest of the world.

STANDARDS: Detailed criteria of standards for investment for approval for validation under the provisions of Circular No. 2, SCAP, 1949 are as follows:

(1) Application must demonstrate that the investment or acquisition of property is necessary:

(a) To carry on present business activities in the case of persons continuously resident in Japan since 2 September 1945 or

(b) To resume a specific pre-war activity in the case of those with a legitimate restitution claim or •

(c) To carry on a new activity which will improve Japan's foreign exchange position, or positively aid in Japanese economic rehabilitation or otherwise further a specifically expressed SCAP objective.

(2) Application must demonstrate that alternative means, such as short-term lease or rental, purchase of bonds, expansion of non-Japanese enterprises, acquisition from non-Japanese, etc., are not practicable to achieve the purpose desired.

(3) If yen is to be used for investment purposes, the application must show that yen was legally obtained from foreign exchange after the date of Circular No. 2 or that yen funds to be used for such acquisition were acquired by business operations in Japan during the Occupation and were not excessive in view of the goods or services furnished in connexion with the acquisition thereof or yen acquired in lieu of restitution.

(4) An application for acquisition must show that the property or right will be used in a manner that will add constructively to the Japanese economy.

(5) Acquisition will not be validated where there is reasonable ground for belief that it is being acquired on behalf of a foreign government.

(6) Acquisition of property interest or right in the following will not be validated:

(a) An enterprise a material amount of the assets of which have been or are likely to be designated for reparations removals, until such removal has been effected.

(b) An enterprise which is or is considered by competent authority to be subject to dissolution, liquidation or reorganization under the economic reform programme until the final adjudication of such dissolution, liquidation or reorganization.

(7) The terms of any contract for acquisition must be fair to the Japanese seller or, in the case of a share of an enterprise or of its profits, production or sales, fair to the Japanese enterprise or its Japanese shareholders.

(8) Investment in existing Japanese enterprises may only be made if the investment creates additional assets for the Japanese enterprise in contradistinction to the purchase of stocks or securities from other investors.

(9) Notwithstanding paragraphs 1-8 above, acquisition of properties or rights by those receiving yen in lieu of restitution of property which was formerly owned by them and was treated as enemy property under Japanese war-time regulations will be validated automatically, providing only :

(a) Total yen expended in each case under this exception does not exceed yen received in lieu of restitution.

(b) Property or right acquired is similar in nature to formerly owned property.

(10) Transactions will not be validated where there are reasonable grounds for suspecting fraud, duress or undue influence.

Contemporary Japan, Vol. XVIII, Nos. 1-3, January-March 1949, pp. 143-5.

30   *4 April* 1949

ADDRESS TO THE FIFTH EXTRAORDINARY SESSION
OF THE NATIONAL DIET BY THE DIRECTOR OF THE
ECONOMIC STABILIZATION BOARD ON THE FUTURE
ECONOMIC POLICY OF JAPAN

After four years of difficult travel in the post-war period, the Japanese economy has at last come to show some signs of stabilization as evidenced by the gradual rise in production, slowing down of inflation, gradual rise in real income of workers. This has been made possible thanks to the sympathetic assistance and guidance of the Allied Powers and to the efforts and co-operation of the whole nation for rehabilitation, demonstrated in delivery of foodstuffs, increased production of coal and in other fields of economy, for which I take this opportunity to express my warm thanks.

On the other hand, however, a careful scrutiny of our national economy will reveal that it still harbours not a few unhealthy elements, the worst of which being the foreign aid amounting to several hundred million dollars per year. We must not forget that the stabilization signs of our economy are based on the support of the citizens and enterprises of USA. The production equipments of enterprises are getting worn out and their real capital is getting fast depleted. Enterprises depend for their questions on huge amounts of price adjustment subsidy, and deficit financing for them is accumulating, thus losing their soundness and independence.

In other words, the present Japanese economy must be said to be operating in excess of its real capacity by the subsidies and American aids. In case the present trend is left unchecked, an insecure economic prosperity will be built upon the precarious basis. It is, therefore, my conviction that the future economic policies must be geared to the real stabilization of economy.

The Nine-Point Economic Directive issued by SCAP in December last year clearly points to this direction and shows that the Allied policy towards Japan has reached the stage where it demands the stabilization and self-supporting of Japan's economy. With a view to establishing a self-supporting economy, the Nine-Point Programme aims at vigorously enforcing stabilization measures and carrying on a thoroughly rational operation of economy. For this purpose it purports to implement a nine-point measure as a preparation for the establishment of a single exchange rate.

I am convinced that the reconstruction of our country will not be achieved unless we achieve, despite difficulties, the economic stabilization which constitutes the first step towards economic self-support along the nine-point directive. In this belief the Government will execute various economic measures by requesting enterprises to carry out forceful rationalization measures and by asking our people to put up with strict austerity.

The true balance of the consolidated budget referred to in the nine-point directive means a thorough elimination of inflationary factors on the side of public finance. For that purpose it becomes necessary to secure a real balance of consolidated revenues and expenditures inclusive of general and special accounts and other Governmental agencies. In formulating the balanced budget all sorts of economic requirements compete each other on the budget and the Government had to work very hard in adjusting them. On the expenditure side the Government had to slash the badly need-ed public works expenditure, enforce administrative adjustment, rationalization of special accounts, and reduce other expenditures. As regards the price adjustment expenditure which is needed for price stabilization, the items to be subsidized have been reduced and unit subsidy has been drastically curtailed, thus making it necessary for enterprises to enforce drastic rationalization. Import subsidies have also been reduced to the minimum which business accounting and household budgets permit.

As regards national revenues, there is no alternative but to collect and secure tax revenues to realize a true balance in the consolidated budgets and the Government is determined to make every effort to secure as much tax revenue as possible under the current taxation system. The Government is, of course, well aware of the fact that the current tax burden is by no means light and is determined to double its efforts to improve the method of taxation in the course of the year so as to make the tax burden more equitable on one hand and to minimize the actual spending of the appropriation, to sell State properties, etc., on the other in order to alleviate the people's burden. But, at the same time, it is requested that the people will positively co-operate for securing tax revenues which are indispensable for putting Japan's economy on a self-supporting basis.

Regarding the US aid appropriations for Japan's economy, inasmuch as they have been heretofore used without restriction their original purport has not been fully realized. Therefore, the Government intends to specify in the budgets such aid in terms of Yen in order to put the aid to the most effective use. That is to say, the Government will put all the aids in a special account called US Aid Counterpart Fund for Japanese Stabilization and to put them to the most proper and effective use, that is, to economic rehabilitation, redemption of Government bonds, etc.

In connexion with the problem of financing, the Government wishes to make it clear to establish and carry out a sound financial policy. That is to say, along the principle that sources of funds should be found in the accumulated capital, the people are requested to minimize their personal expenditure and to maximize their savings, and enterprises are requested to procure their necessary funds through their own production efforts and capital accumulation within the framework of the so-called 'Three Principles of Enterprises'.

Thus, the Government tried to eradicate all potential inflationary factors both in public and private finances.

It goes without saying, however, that even under such sound financial policy as stated above the Government has to see to it that funds really essential for the maintenance of production activities and for economic rehabilitation be fully secured. Inasmuch as a substantial portion of the US aid has been made available for construction and rehabilitation purposes and for general industries through the redemption of Government bonds, RFB bonds, etc., the industrial funds estimated to be available for the 1949 fiscal year both for equipments and for operation are not considered necessarily insufficient in total for the maintenance of estimated business activities. However, in proportion as the function of the Reconstruction Finance Bank is reduced and the relative importance of general financial institutions increases in consequence of their enlarged cash in hand through the redemption of Government bonds, RFB bonds, etc., it becomes absolutely necessary to obtain their voluntary co-operation to secure necessary funds for such fields as deemed essential from the standpoint of national economy.

The Government wishes to take some proper steps regarding fund control with due regard to future changes in situation and to promote the sound development of security market with a view to promoting self-procurement of capital. Furthermore, such measures as will enable a rational amortization are under consideration in order to prevent any further depletion of capital.

Next is the price policy at the present stage. The point at issue here is to stabilize prices at a low level corresponding to the afore-stated sound financial policy and to make domestic price level approach the international level now that we are expected to parti-cipate in the international economy with the establishment of a single exchange rate, thereby paving the way towards stabilization of well-balanced economy. The current price structure established in June last year has been distorted due to subsequent economic changes to the detriment, in some respects, of reasonable operation of economy. Necessary adjustment will be made to remedy the situation. Overall raise of price level will, however, in so far as possible be avoided at this time. In particular, freight transportation charges and the prices of stabilization-bond materials will be main-tained at the current level and prices of consumption goods of which production conditions have improved will be reduced in order to contribute to the stabilization of household budget and balancing of price structure.

Substantial amount of price adjustment subsidies is included in the proposed budget in order to stabilize prices at low level. Funda-mentally such subsidies are not desirable from the standpoint of rationalization of economy and independence of enterprises. However to abolish all subsidies at one stroke at this moment is merely to cause unnecessary disturbance in our vulnerable economy. The amount of subsidies as appropriated is deemed to be the necessary minimum. We will see to it that the amount of subsidy per unit be slashed, that subsidy payment be cut down through rationalization of enter-prises, and that no unnecessary and unjustifiable subsidies be paid out.

With regard to the problem of eliminating the discrepancies between domestic and international prices and adjusting the impact of exchange rate upon domestic price structure, it is urgently neces-sary for the normal development of our economy in the future that the domestic price structure which has long been secluded from international economy develop into a reasonable and natural one as an integral part of international economy. That is to say, we have first to endeavour to align our price structure to the international one in order that the Japanese economy gains self-support in the international economy.

On the other hand, violent impact of the establishment of a single exchange rate and the alignment of domestic and international prices upon enterprises and household budget should be avoided as far as possible for stabilization of price level. The Government will, therefore, pay import subsidies as a transitional measure in order to mitigate such undesirable impact. It is needless to say that the import subsidy payment be minimized through the reduction of production costs.

In spite of the aforestated price policy aimed at stabilization at low level, it is unavoidable to raise consumer's price of staple foods on account of the rise in agricultural parity indices, passenger fare and communication charges for the realization of financial independence in Special Accounts. Again some price revision of consumer goods is necessary in consequence of the abolition of some of the import subsidies. However, saving of consumption and accumulation of capital is indispensable for the self-support of national economy. The reconstruction of the Japanese economy can be attained only through saving and austerity on the part of the State, enterprises and household. It is sincerely requested that the people will bear the unbearable to overcome an austere living which we have to get through.

It is needless to say that the basic measures to really stabilize our economy lie in securing increasing production. It is for this reason that the Government calls for all-out efforts on the part of management and labour. The increase in production, however, can serve as a basis for sound economic development only when it is based on rational production management. It is in this respect that the Government has clearly established the ' Three Principles of Enterprises' and is prepared to carry out appropriate measures in conformity with the Nine Objectives in order to enforce rationalization of enterprises and to encourage introduction of private foreign capital on thus stabilized economy.

That is to say, the basic industries, such as coal-mining and electricity enterprises, are requested to operate profitably within the framework of the current price structure through rationalization of management. The policy with regard to such industries has tended to be based on a production-increase-first-principle, with the result that they have depended too much upon generous assistance of the Government, such as subsidy payment and deficit financing. Various unreasonable and unsound elements have, therefore, remained in these industries.

685

As regards export industries, in particular, the rationalization of which is urgently called for in order to compete with foreign enterprises in the international market, the Government has set the maximum export price ratio at Y425 on and after 1 April as another step towards the establishment of a single exchange rate, and will strongly promote their rationalization with the idea that export subsidies will entirely be abolished when a single exchange rate is established.

As to the effect which the condition of fund supply has upon enterprises, enforcement of a strict sound financial policy as stated above will mean that the industrial fund has to be financed generally from accumulated capital. Enterprises, therefore, are requested to rationalize themselves through reduction of production costs. The Government on its part intends to take necessary measures to secure necessary funds.

Such is the general policy towards enterprises. The Government is concerned about the possible effects of the enforcement of such policy upon medium and small enterprises. The Government is convinced that as long as medium and small enterprises endeavour to rationalize themselves in accordance with the Nine Objectives in cognizance of the part they play in the development of the Japanese economy. The Government will endeavour to nurture such medium and small enterprises.

As the aforementioned policy of economy stabilization will be carried out rigorously, rise in real wages in future can be attained only through combined efforts on the part of capital and labour for the increase of production. It is needless to say that the Government will renew its efforts to stabilize the living of workers through the establishment of distribution order and securing of living necessaries in cognizance of the fact that the working population bear the brunt of reconstruction. If an economy spoiled by deficit financing, subsidy payment, price raising, etc., be continued to be spoiled, inflation will proceed indefinitely and the national economy will never attain self-support and stabilization. The living of the working population will constantly be threatened. The Government is convinced that such is not in the interests of the working population. The Government is determined to take really constructive measures even though they might not be palatable. It is desired that enterprises as well as workers co-operate with the Government in full understanding of the fact that the Japanese economy will be reconstructed and the living standard of the Japanese people raised only after we have overcome a severe trial now confronting us through our sweat and tears.

With regard to unemployment which may arise in consequence of the enforcement of the aforementioned policies, the Government will do its best to absorb them in industries which will expand in future, such as export industries, in particular, as well as in new enterprises to be financed from foreign assistance fund. Insurance and other unemployment measures will be extended as far as permitted by the national economy.

At this critical juncture of the Japanese economy, the Government is desirous of seeing sound development of labour unions and relies upon the consciousness and all-out effort of the working population.

Now I am going to explain about problems concerning agriculture. The production increase in agriculture is of fundamental importance to the present Japanese economy from the standpoint of firmly establishing the basis for economic rehabilitation as well as of reducing the importation of foodstuffs. In view of the above fact, I request the farmers to make further efforts towards the production increase of foodstuffs at this critical moment. The fact that the food crisis our nation suffered in the post-war period has been finally overcome is largely attributable to the efforts made by the farmers, for which I do not know how to thank them. The Government has decided to take measures designed to have the rice quota system operated more efficiently and more fairly than ever, for which purpose nothing will be left untried to secure 100 per cent production and delivery by the farmers of the pre-planting delivery quota allocation for 1949 which has already been decided, while the production and delivery of foodstuffs over and above said allocation will be tried by all means.

As for the improvement in production conditions indispensable for the strengthening of agricultural production capacity such as land reform, the Government will undertake to make efforts at expediting the said improvement as much as the national economy permits. At the same time the Government will minimize through the aforementioned maintenance of the present price structure financial burdens on the farmers both in agricultural management and household budget while taking measures to supply as much fertilizer and other reproduction materials as possible. As for the price of rice, wheat, barley, etc., back payment for the increase of agricultural parity index since the price revision in 1948, will be made along the policy determined by the Government to secure agricultural reproduction. On the part of farmers, however, I believe they must refrain from depending wholly upon measures to be taken by the Government, and minimize consumption and accumulate capital by their own hands through their own organization so as to invest it in agriculture so that the farmers themselves may open the way for the expansion of agricultural production.

The next problem is about measures for export promotion. I have so far dwelt on the measures to stabilize domestic economy. In view of the present conditions of Japanese economy, that is, having a colossal population of 80,000,000 on a limited territory with poor natural resources, and barely maintaining the present production and living standard by the support of huge amounts of funds and materials extended by the USA, it is most urgent to promote export thereby enlarging the scope of economic circulation in order to secure the self-support and rehabilitation of economy.

For the purpose of wiping out the ill-fame of 'economy stilts' and of achieving economic rehabilitation by our own efforts, the Government has determined to reduce domestic requirements as much as possible, to make efforts for the reduction of production cost and to develop and promote export as well as to increase invisible export. To realize the above, the Government has established the principle of top priority to export, along which efforts are being made for the preferential procurement of materials for export industries, smooth operation of trade financing, etc. In addition, the Government is trying hard to simplify the trade procedures and enlarge export and import on the private basis to the end of returning to normal trade while requesting GHQ for the adjustment of external relations such as the positive development of export markets and the improvement of trade terms.

The Government has adopted the Export-First Policy mentioned above and is going to exert its utmost effort to execute it successfully. However, the export encouragement measure by grant of export subsidy is not acceptable for international considerations. Therefore, it has become absolutely necessary for the Japanese economy to effect the rigid rationalization of enterprises and to improve technical level by developing scientific technique in order to secure a footing in the international competitive economy. Those who are engaged in export industries are hereby specially requested to do their best.

In view of the expected decline in effective demand and general purchasing power, which will be brought about by rigorous execution of rationalization programme and austere national life, and the gradually improving demand-supply situation of materials, the economic control of material such as allocation and rationing of materials and price control will be simplified as far as possible and be strengthened in effectiveness of the enforcement in the reduced scope of control, thus contributing to the establishment of order in the distribution field. In promoting the rationalization of enterprises mentioned above, restoration of initiative and profitability of enterprises are required first of all. From this point of view, it is intended to abolish such control as requires unnecessarily complicated procedure and to devise strong measures to introduce the principle of competition in case necessary controls are enforced. It is for this purpose

688

that it is intended to readjust the distribution Kodans system, to reduce items of designated production materials and to abolish rationing control of fresh vegetables at this time. Furthermore as regards the pending reopening of restaurants practical measures commensurate with realities will be taken.

When we rigorously execute the domestic economic stabilization measures in accordance with the Nine Objectives and promote economic rehabilitation through developing our export on the stabilized economy, the establishment of a single exchange rate will be realized at an early date, the induction of foreign private capital will be encouraged in expectation of maintenance of the exchange rate, employment will be increased, living standard will be improved. Thus it is believed that self-support of Japanese economy will be realized. It is my belief that only by realizing the above, will Japan be recognized as a welcome member of international society and the way will be open for independence and peace.

Contemporary Japan, Vol. XVIII, Nos. 4-6, April-June 1949, pp. 259-66.

31   12 *May* 1949

ANNOUNCEMENT BY GENERAL FRANK Mc COY, US
REPRESENTATIVE TO THE FAR EASTERN COMMISSION
CONCERNING THE SUSPENSION OF ADVANCE
TRANSFER PROGRAMME

The Japanese reparations problem has been one of the most important and pressing questions with which the Far Eastern Commission and its member countries have had to deal. The United States, on its part, has taken a long and continuing interest in this problem and has been keenly aware of the interest of the other FEC countries in finding a reasonable solution to it. It is to be regretted that this controversial issue which for such a long time has proved incapable of solution by this Commission continues to retard the achievement of economic self-support by Japan, which is so greatly in the interest of our common objectives with respect to that country.

In our discussions of the matter here in the Commission we have proceeded from the agreement contained in the Potsdam Declaration that reparations would be exacted from Japan and they should be in a form which would not impair the ability of the Japanese people to support themselves. From the earliest days of the Far Eastern Commission the United States has been guided by a desire

that the victims of Japanese aggression receive as reparations such
of Japan's resources as was possible without jeopardizing Japan's
ability to meet its own peaceful needs. The United States has felt,
further, that in order that the nations devastated by Japan might
receive reparation while their need was greatest, in order that there
might be removed from the mind of the Japanese Government and
people uncertainty regarding the reparations question, and in order
that as many as possible of Japan's post-war obligations might be
disposed of during the period of the occupation, a reparations programme should be worked out and put into effect at the earliest
practical moment.

These factors led the United States Government to take the initiative in making a number of policy proposals to the Far Eastern
Commission. In April 1946, the United States submitted to the
Far Eastern Commission a pattern of proposals providing that there
should be made immediately available for reparations designated
quantities of industrial facilities which were at that time considered
to be clearly surplus to Japan's peaceful needs. Between May and
December of that year the Commission adopted a series of Interim
Reparations Policy decisions based upon these US proposals, but
the subsequent inability of the Commission to agree on a schedule
of shares for division of the facilities among the claimant countries
prevented implementation of the decisions. In April 1947 the US
Government offered further proposals, which would have had the
effect of making known to Japan precisely, and on a final basis, what
industrial capacity should be considered by that country to be im-
mune from removal as reparations and what should be eligible for
removal. In the same month, the US because of its desire to work
towards a settlement of this matter issued an Advance Transfers
interim directive, under authority granted in Paragraph III 3, of
the Terms of Reference of the Far Eastern Commission, instructing
the Supreme Commander to effect delivery to four of the FEC
countries of 30 per cent of the facilities which the Far Eastern Commission itself had previously determined in the Interim Removals
decisions to be available for reparations removal. Issuance of this
directive was motivated in part by a desire to assist those countries
which had in the course of fighting against Japan's aggression
on their own territories suffered most grievously, but it was also
motivated by a reparations programme from which all eleven
countries might benefit.

In November 1947, the United States Government took the
initiative once more in an effort to end the stalemate within the
Commission on the question of reparations shares, a stalemate which
continued to make it impossible for any of the Commission's

decisions on reparations problem to take practical effect. This US proposal contained the provision that if the Far Eastern Commission countries would accept the schedule of percentages which had been worked out by the US Government—on the basis of prolonged exchanges of views among Commission members as to the equities involved—the US Government, on its part, would make available an important part of its own share for distribution among the countries which could accept the US proposals as a whole. Sixteen months have passed and this proposal has not been accepted by the Commission.

I should like to emphasize at this point that the action of my Government, and, it is assumed, of the other Member Governments, in participating in the policy decisions which have been taken by the Commission on the question of reparations was predicated upon two basic assumptions, namely, that the resources to be removed from Japan as reparations were clearly excess to the peaceful needs of a self-supporting Japanese economy, and that there would be a shares schedule acceptable to and agreed upon by the Far Eastern Commission countries which would determine in what proportions available reparations should be divided.

As I have already stated, and as the Commission well knows, the second of these assumptions has not been realized and there seems little prospect of its being realized. As regards the first assumption, that reparations removals should be limited to facilities clearly excess to the needs of a self-supporting Japanese economy, successive studies during the past eighteen months of Japan's future industrial requirements have necessitated progressive upward adjustments of earlier estimates of these requirements. The first of these studies was that of Overseas Consultants Incorporated, whose report was made available to the Commission on 2 March 1948, and the second was that of the so-called Johnston Committee, whose report was made available to the Commission on 19 May 1948. Both of these reports came to the conclusion that the quantity of capital equipment in Japan which could be properly considered in excess of Japan's peaceful needs had been greatly overestimated. Both reports indicated that for a variety of reasons the Japanese economy was continuing to operate at a heavy deficit even though living standards remained at a minimum level, and that the end to these deficits is not in sight. The evidence contained in these reports, and the common knowledge of all Far Eastern Commission countries leads to the inescapable conclusion that the Japanese economy can be made to bear additional economic burdens, beyond those directly related to meeting its own requirements, only by prolonging or increasing the staggering costs borne by the American taxpayer.

The United States has, since the time of the Japanese surrender, carried the burden of preventing such disease and unrest in Japan as might jeopardize the purposes of the occupation. The critical economic conditions with which, it is now apparent, Japan is faced, and the prospect of continuing deficits in Japan's international payments for some years to come, render measures of Japanese economic recovery of utmost importance. It is inescapable that if the basic purposes of the occupation are to be achieved, the Japanese people must be enabled to support themselves at a tolerable standard of living. No one could reasonably suggest that Japan should be abandoned to economic despair. So to abandon Japan would be to undo the costly victory in the Pacific.

I am sure that other Commission countries agree with my Government that the Japanese people themselves must exert maximum efforts for the attainment of recovery. For some months the US Government has explored means whereby this objective could best be achieved. In issuing its directive of 10 December 1948 regarding Japan's economic stabilization, the US Government took a major step towards requiring the Japanese people to exert their utmost energies in stabilizing their economy and reducing their dependence for subsistence on foreign subsidy. Under present circumstances in Japan the cost of dismantling, packing, and transporting reparations facilities would conflict with the programme of Japan's economic stabilization and would constitute an additional financial burden upon the US Government. I do not wish to emphasize this point unduly, but the US Government would be lacking in candour if it did not point out that the resources at its disposal to meet demands from all parts of the world are limited.

It is now apparent to the US Government that the first as well as the second of the two basic assumptions mentioned earlier, assumptions which underlay the policy decisions of the FEC having to do with reparations and which are a precondition for an FEC reparations programme, has not been realized. This fact has led my Government to several conclusions. Before stating them, however, I wish to emphasize that the US Government maintains fully and categorically its support of the principle adopted by the Far Eastern Commission that Japan's war-making capacity should be eliminated. As you know, all of Japan's specialized war-making facilities have been destroyed. The US Government believes that all other equipment used for war purposes in the past should, if retained in Japan, be fully converted to the purposes of and utilized in Japan's peaceful economy. Where this cannot be done, the US Government believes that such equipment should be scrapped. The US will not permit difficulties in reaching a solution of the reparations problem to be a means whereby Japan's war capacity might re-emerge.

It may not be amiss at this point to recall that Japan has already been deprived not only of all of its overseas territorial possessions, but also of substantial quantities of real property of Japanese ownership and origin in the former possessions and elsewhere abroad. This property constitutes a large payment which the Japanese have already made towards satisfaction of their reparations obligations. Unfortunately, from the standpoint of equity, some countries have benefited more than others in the reparations that they have obtained in this form. However, from the standpoint of Japan, the loss of these properties, whatever the proportions in which they happen to have been distributed, drastically reduces Japan's ability to support even at a minimum level the needs of its people.

In view of the above considerations, the United States is forced to the following conclusions :

(a) The deficit Japanese economy shows little prospect of being balanced in the near future and, to achieve eventual balance, will require all resources at its disposal.

(b) The burden of removing further reparations from Japan could detract seriously from the occupation objective of stabilizing the Japanese economy and permitting it to move towards self-support.

(c) There is little or no prospect of the Far Eastern Commission agreement on a reparations shares schedule despite the repeated initiatives by the United States over the past three years to assist the Commission in reaching such an agreement. Without agreement on a shares schedule the existing Far Eastern Commission policy decisions regarding reparations are incapable of implementation.

(d) Japan has already paid substantial reparations through expropriation of its former overseas assets and, in smaller degree, under the Advance Transfer Programme.

In the light of these conclusions the United States Government is impelled to rescind its interim directive of 4 April 1947 bringing to an end the Advance Transfer Programme called for by that directive. It is impelled also to withdraw its proposal of 6 November 1947 on Japanese reparations shares, and I am so informing the Secretary-General. Finally, the US Government takes this occasion to announce that it has no intention of taking further unilateral action under its interim directive powers to make possible additional reparations removals from Japan.

I earlier stated my Government's belief that maximum efforts should be exerted by the Japanese themselves for their economic recovery. It is the view of the United States that all facilities, including so-called 'primary war facilities', presently designated as available for reparations which can contribute to Japanese recovery should be utilized as necessary in Japan's peaceful economy for recovery purposes.

With regard to 'primary war facilities', all of which as I earlier stated were some time ago stripped of their special purpose equipment and thus of their 'war facilities' characteristics, it is the view of the US that SCAP, under the authority granted in Paragraph 10 of the FEC decision on Reduction of Japanese Industrial War Potential, should as rapidly as practicable require the dismantlement, dispersion or other action for the utilization in Japan's peaceful economy of such of these facilities as are required to meet the needs of the occupation, which needs prominently include economic recovery. Remaining 'primary war facilities' should continue to be protected, in the sense of preventing loss or scrapping of individual items, pursuant to the above-mentioned FEC decision requiring their 'impounding'. Impounding does not, however, include the requirement that the facilities be kept in their present locations or that the Japanese devote resources to preserve their value or maintain them in working order.

The United States, it will be recalled, has repeatedly clarified its understanding that the 'level of industry' proposals before the Commission, excepting those levels which will lapse by FEC decision on 1 October 1949, had application only to the question of the quantities of industrial facilities which could be spared for reparations, and had no bearing on the matter of future levels of industrial capacity in Japan. Turning now to this latter question, I have already emphasized my Government's support of the principle that Japan's capacity to make war should not be permitted to re-emerge. It is the considered view of the United States Government that this objective does not require that Japan's production for peaceful purposes be limited or that limitations be imposed on levels of Japanese productive capacity in industries devoted to peaceful purposes. This belief, coupled with the evidence of Japan's present economic plight and the difficult problems Japan will face in future in attaining levels of industrial production and foreign trade sufficient to support its people even at minimum levels, render it clearly advisable in my Government's view that Japan be permitted to develop its peaceful industries without limitation. The problem facing us is not one of limitation of Japan's peaceful industries but of reviving these industries to provide the people's barest wants.

The US Government plans shortly to submit to the FEC for its consideration proposals for the rescission or amendment of existing and pending FEC reparations and level of industry policy papers so as to bring FEC policies on these matters, should the proposals be approved by the Commission, into conformity with the position which I have set forth. My Government earnestly hopes that the other Member Governments will appreciate the considerations underlying this position and will be able to concur in the new United States proposals.

Documents Concerning the Allied Occupation and Control of Japan, Vol. III (*Financial, Economic and Reparations*), pp. 294-300, Compiled by Section of Special Records, Foreign Office, Japan, 1949.

32   26 *August* 1949

RECOMMENDATIONS OF THE SHOUP MISSION ON THE REFORM OF JAPAN'S TAXATION SYSTEM

The recommendations of the tax mission cover four general topics. First, the total amount of taxation assumed to be necessary for the next fiscal year, 1950-51, and the proportions to be raised by the national government and the local governments. Second, the major changes in the structure of the tax system, as for example, the part of the national total that is recommended to be raised by the personal income tax. Third, the changes to be made within each tax, as for instance, the way in which members of a co-living family shall be treated under the income tax. Fourth, some administrative considerations, such as methods of inducing taxpayers to comply with the law, and of allowing them to appeal against reassessments, and the role, if any, that business associations should be allowed to play in getting the income tax assessed and collected.

The report will present in detail not only the recommendations, but the reasons why they were reached. It is hoped that through the publication of this report an intelligent discussion of the Japanese tax system will develop, in the Press, in national and local tax offices throughout the country, in business circles, in women's organizations, and in the universities and secondary schools.

The total amount of tax revenue to be collected during the fiscal year 1950-51 is assumed to be only slightly less than during the current fiscal year. This is partly because the danger of further inflation has not yet disappeared, and partly because the local governments need more tax revenue of their own, if the programme of local autonomy is to be maintained. However, these remarks do not include the so-called voluntary contributions collected in most localities, often to erect school buildings, or to supply other local services. It is expected that these local contributions will decrease greatly next year, if the local governments have adequate tax sources of their own. If the voluntary contributions are counted in with taxes, as indeed for most purposes they should be, the programme recommended by the tax mission assumes an appreciable, but not a substantial, reduction in total revenue.

Moreover, the determination of the total amount of tax revenue to be raised is not the primary responsibility of the tax mission, for that amount depends partly on the amount of government expenditures and the extent to which the government debt should be retired. The policy on these two issues must continue to be that formulated under the Dodge Stabilization Plan, namely, continued reduction in national government expenditures, chiefly through the reduction of price subsidies, and continued debt retirement.

The assumptions made are that the total national government revenue from taxes in 1950–51 will be 576 billion yen, compared with 635 billion yen budgeted for the current year. It is also assumed that in 1951–2 the national government's need for tax revenue will be somewhat lower than for 1950–51, owing to continued retrenchment in expenditures.

Both of these totals of tax revenue include 120 billion yen profit from the government tobacco monopoly. In addition, the national government's general account is assumed to receive about 70 billion yen from miscellaneous receipts, the same amount as budgeted for this year.

The total of local tax revenue is assumed to rise from 150 billion yen this year to 190 billion yen in 1950–51, if the voluntary contributions are not counted. If they are counted, it is difficult to express the result in figures, since the total amount of such contributions is not known, but if, as seems possible, they are as much as 40 billion yen this year, and if they decline to 10 billion yen next year, the total of local government taxes and contributions rises only slightly, from 190 billion yen this year to 200 billion yen next year. The local governments are also expected to continue to receive 25 billion yen a year from rents, fees, and other miscellaneous sources. 'Miscellaneous' does not include borrowed money.

Total taxes, national and local, are therefore assumed a total 766 billion yen in 1950–51, compared with a budgeted amount of 785 billion yen for 1949–50, a decrease of about 20 billion yen, if voluntary contributions are not taken into account. If they are included, the tax total declines from about 825 billion yen to about 776 billion yen, though both these totals are conjectural owing to lack of information on contributions.

The tax mission recommends that the personal income tax continue to be the major source of revenue for the national government, but that the revenue from this source be decreased slightly next year, to about 290 billion yen from the 310 billion yen budgeted for the current year. The decrease in rates and increase in exemptions is considerably greater than this small decline would suggest. This is possible partly because it is expected that taxable personal incomes will be somewhat greater in 1950 than in 1949, even if business activity merely levels off, and assuming no rise in prices. Another reason why so much can be expected from the personal income tax in 1950–51 is that collections of back taxes will still be large, in view of the assessments made at the high rates in force the present year. Ultimately, the personal income tax yield would be expected to level off at about 278 billion yen, if business activity and the price level did not change, and if there were no improvement in the degree of taxpayers' compliance with the law, and in the efficiency of the tax administration. Actually, it is expected that the lower rates and higher exemptions recommended by the mission would have a favourable effect on both these factors. The yield might therefore be expected to level off at a somewhat higher figure, but, in order to take no chances with the nation's economic stability, it is best not to count on those factors for the immediate future.

The mission recommends that, with respect to the small number of well-to-do-persons, the present very high top rates of the income tax be replaced by a tax on the net fortune, or net worth, of these individuals. Under this recommendation, an individual with three dependents and a large income would pay only 55 per cent income tax on all that part of his income in excess of 360,000 yen, but he would also pay an annual low-rate property tax on his net worth (his total assets, minus his total liabilities). The rate would start at ½ of 1 per cent on that part of his net worth that is in excess of 5 million yen. The rate would rise, until it reached 3 per cent on that part of the net worth in excess of 50 million yen. In general, at these rates, it would not be a paying proposition for the wealthy tax-payer to try to hide his wealth in the form of bank notes or precious stones instead of leaving it where it could earn interest and dividends. The tax would yield only 2 billion yen, but it is also true that the very top rates of the income tax do not add much to revenue, at least under present conditions, where the number of wealthy taxpayers is small. The mission points out, however, that the fact that a certain group of taxpayers is small in number is no reason for excusing them from paying their fair share of the tax bill.

The role of the income taxes on corporations decreases under the tax mission's recommendations, provided all the other recommendations of the mission regarding ways to stop evasion and avoidance of the personal income tax by well-to-do investors are adopted. It is recommended that the excess profits tax be repealed, effective 1 January 1950; it is too complicated a tax to be satisfactory during peacetime, at least under present conditions in Japan. The corporation tax rate remains at 35 per cent, but there is a 6 per cent tax on the increase in book value of assets that occurs under the revaluation of assets that is recommended by the mission. The net result of these corporate tax recommendations is that corporations are estimated to pay considerably more next year than the budget estimate of 27 billion yen for this year. Actually, it appears that collections this year may reach nearly 50 billion yen, and it is approximately this amount which is expected from corporations under the recommendations for next year. Repeal of the excess profits tax, and allowance of extra depreciation that will result from the revaluation of assets, will lose about 30 billion yen of revenue next year, but the revaluation tax will bring in about 30 billion yen. The total yield of the revaluation tax might be as much as 60 billion yen, but the mission recommends that only half the tax be paid next year. One-quarter would be due in 1951–2 and one-quarter in 1952–3. In later years, after the revaluation tax had been paid in full, but while the effect of the higher depreciation and the repeal of the excess profits tax was still being felt, the yield of the corporation tax would drop back to 20 billion yen or 30 billion yen annually.

In the opinion of the tax mission, profits earned in the corporate form should not be taxed more heavily merely because they arise under that form. On the other hand, use of the corporation as a means of avoiding the personal income tax, or postponing payment of that tax for a long period, should not be permitted.

Taxes on gifts during life-time and on descendants' estates are estimated to yield only 2 billion yen this year. The mission recognizes that this tax is not likely to be a major source of revenue, but it recommends a substantial change in the manner of imposing the tax, which should eventually increase the yield and also make the tax more equitable.

No change in the role of the tobacco monopoly, which contributes 120 billion yen profit to the general account, is recommended.

The mission believes that the present rates of the liquor taxes were put at too low a level when they were decreased in the spring of 1949, in what was said to be an effort to maximize revenue. It is recommended that the rates be increased, in the expectation that the liquor tax revenue would rise to at least 80 billion yen next year and probably to higher levels.

698

Complete repeal of the textile taxes is recommended by the mission. For the most part, these are taxes on necessaries of life. Some part of the expenditures on textiles are of a somewhat luxury nature, but it is difficult to isolate and measure that part ; moreover, the producers of silk are undergoing a severe readjustment and should not be further imperilled by a continuance of the 40 per cent tax on silk. The tax is recommended for repeal as of 1 March 1950, except that the 40 per cent rate should be cut to 10 per cent as soon as possible, to lessen the transitional effect that may be caused as silk merchants try to keep inventories at a minimum in anticipation of the forthcoming tax decrease. The textile tax is estimated to yield 17 billion yen in 1949–50.

The commodity taxes, or excise taxes, which are estimated to yield 27 billion yen this year, are recommended for continuance at the same level of yield next year. They are, in general, taxes on luxuries, and as such are needed at the present time. Some minor changes are recommended.

The mission recommends that the transactions tax be repealed, but only if the expenditures of the national government, aside from debt reduction and grants to the localities, are reduced next year to 450 billion yen or less. Otherwise revenue needs dictate maintaining the transactions tax. In any event, a certain minimum amount of reduction in the personal income tax, and the repeal of the textile taxes are given priority over any reduction or repeal of the transactions tax. However, the transactions tax is not a desirable kind of tax, in the opinion of the mission, and it should in no case be increased from the present 1 per cent level. Its yield for the present fiscal year is estimated at 45 billion yen.

Other internal revenue taxes of a minor nature total 22 billion yen in this year's budget, and no substantial changes are recommended for the present in this area, hence about the same yield is expected next year.

At the local level, the mission recommends that the prefectures get about the same amount of money from their own taxes next year as they are scheduled to receive this year (about 70 billion yen). However, it is recommended that this money come chiefly from three taxes, each of them to be solely the property of the prefectures, in place of the present system, whereby the prefectures share with the cities, towns, and villages the proceeds from seven important taxes.

Under the plan of the tax mission, the prefectures would obtain between 40 and 50 billion yen from the enterprise tax, which at present yields 26 billion yen to the prefectures and another 26 billion yen to the municipalities. Thus the enterprise tax would decline slightly in importance. It is also recommended that the base of the tax be changed from profits to a broader base, known as 'value-added', to be explained below.

The prefectures would get another 10 billion yen from the admissions tax and slightly more than this from the amusement taxes. It is recommended that the rate of the admissions tax be reduced from the present 150 per cent to 100 per cent, whereby the yield would drop from its current estimated level of 14 billion.

A few miscellaneous taxes would bring the prefectures another 5 billion yen.

The mission recommends that the real property acquisition tax be repealed. This tax hinders the transfer of property, thus preventing it from being put to its best use. The tax is also too great a capital charge on the building of a new structure.

Also recommended for repeal is the local tax of 5 per cent on retail sale of liquor, in view of the recommendation for strengthening the liquor tax at the national level.

The tax mission recommends that the cities, towns, and villages be given additional taxing power sufficient to raise their revenue from the nearly 80 billion yen estimated for the current year to nearly 120 billion yen for the year 1950–51. The mission expresses the opinion that the need for further financial support for local autonomy is acute in the municipalities, rather than in the prefectures.

The 120 billion yen would come almost entirely from two major taxes, the inhabitant's tax and the land and house tax. The municipalities would have exclusive use of these taxes, instead of sharing the proceeds with the prefectures as at present. On the other hand, the municipalities would no longer get a share in the enterprise tax, the admissions tax, or the amusement taxes, and would lose their current revenue from the real property acquisition tax and the liquor consumption tax, owing to the repeal of these levies.

The land and house tax, under the mission's recommendations, would be extended to become a tax on all real estate and depreciable property, and the current rate would be raised, so that the yield would increase from the 14 billion yen estimated for the current year, to slightly more than 50 billion yen.

Miscellaneous taxes would account for 7 billion yen for the municipalities instead of 11 billion yen as at present.

The tax mission recommends a large number of changes in the definition of the tax base, and in the tax rates. The more important of those recommendations are given here.

For the personal income tax, the mission recommends :

(1) An increase in the personal exemption, from 15,000 yen a year to 24,000 yen. Part of this increase, as explained below, represents

a combining of part of the present earned income credit with the personal exemption.

(2) A change in the dependant credit, equivalent to an increase. At present, the tax-payer is allowed a credit against the tax, a credit of 1,800 yen per dependant. It is recommended that this allowance be changed to a deduction from income, and set at 12,000 yen per dependant. The present credit against the tax adds 9,000 yen to the exemption level for the first two dependants and slightly less than 9,000 yen for the third and following dependants.

(3) An absorption of part of the present earned income credit into the personal exemption, so that the only part of the present 25 per cent earned income credit that continues to appear as a distinct item on the return is a 10 per cent allowance. In this way, 15 per cent out of the present 25 per cent allowance is in effect extended to farmers and businessmen, indeed, to every one. The mission believes that the present 25 per cent difference between the wage or salary earner and the small businessman or farmer is too great. In principle, this could be altered by keeping the full 25 per cent credit for the wage and salary earner and extending a 15 per cent credit to the farmer and small businessman. This is in fact just what is recommended for the balance of the present year, from 1 October 1949 to 31 December 1949. But as a permanent method, it is undesirable because it runs contrary to simplification of the tax-return form. Consequently, instead, the personal exemption is increased, in the mission's plan, much more than would otherwise have been recommended. This means that 15 per cent out of the present 25 per cent credit is extended even to investors who have no true earned income, but this is a slight defect that is permitted in order to gain greater simplicity of the tax-return form ; that form will then need to have only one line for earned income credit (10 per cent for wage and salary earners) instead of two lines (25 per cent for wage and salary earners and 15 per cent for farmers and other unincorporated business). Maximum earned income credit is limited to 20,000 yen.

(4) A lowering of the schedule of income tax rates. A copy of the schedule recommended by the mission is given below :

Taxable Income Bracket						Rate
0 — 50,000	..	..	..	..	..	20%
50,000 — 80,000	..	..	..	..	..	25
80,000 — 100,000	..	..	..	..	..	30
100,000 — 120,000	..	..	..	..	..	35
120,000 — 150,000	..	..	..	..	..	40
150,000 — 200,000	..	..	..	..	..	45
200,000 — 300,000	..	..	..	..	..	50
over 300,000	..	..	..	..	..	55

The most striking feature of the rate scale is that the top rate is only 55 per cent. This 55 per cent rate applies to that part of a taxpayer's income that exceeds 300,000 yen. The tax mission is of the opinion that unduly harmful economic effects can be avoided if the top rate imposed on the well-to-do taxpayers with incomes over 300,000 yen is limited to 55 per cent. This recommendation is dependent on the enactment of a net worth tax described in 6, below.

(5) A few illustrations will indicate the extent of the tax reduction recommended under 1 to 4, above. A married man with two dependent children, whose income is from an unincorporated business or a farm, with a net income of 100,000 yen before deducting the personal exemption or the allowance for dependants, will pay 8,000 yen income tax, instead of 17,850 yen as at present. This is the type of tax-payer who receives the largest percentage tax relief, under the mission's proposals. Such taxpayers have been discriminated against in recent years, because of the unduly large differential in favour of workers through the earned income credit and the relatively small allowance for dependants. A tax-payer with the same family, but an income of 200,000 yen would have his income tax reduced from 58,850 yen to 38,500 yen. If his income is 1,000,000 yen, the tax falls from 567,000 yen to 467,000 yen ; but such a tax-payer would probably have a net worth of more than 5,000,000 yen and hence also pay something under the net worth tax.

A married man with two dependent children who earns 100,000 yen as wages or salary would find his tax reduced from 9,600 yen to 6,000 yen. At a 200,000 yen salary his tax would fall from 42,100 yen to 30,500 yen. At 1,000,000 yen salary the tax falls from 541,350 yen to 456,000 yen. This million-yen individual might own little or no property, hence not be subject to the net worth tax.

For single persons with no dependants the effect of the tax reduction is less marked ; having no dependants, they do not get the benefit of the increase in the dependants allowance. If the net income is from farming or unincorporated business and is 100,000 yen, the decline in income tax is from 23,250 yen to 16,500 yen. If the net income is 200,000, the tax falls from 64,250 yen to 54,200 yen. At 1,000,000 income the tax falls from 573,000 yen to 486,800 yen, but this individual is likely to be subject to the net worth tax.

A single wage or salary earner with no dependants, net income 100,000 yen, would have his tax reduced from 15,000 to 14,000 yen. This relatively smaller reduction reflects the tax mission's view that compared with other types of income tax payers, the single wage earner with no dependants has been given rather favourable treatment under the present law. Moreover, the mission recommends the repeal of the present provision that requires all members of a co-living family to file a joint return. This recommendation gives relief to many single taxpayers, a relief not reflected in the example just stated. At 200,000 yen net income the reduction in tax is from 47,500 yen to 45,200 yen. At 1,000,000 yen the tax falls from 546,750 yen to 475,800 yen.

The mission warns against placing too much emphasis on these comparisons of national income tax alone. On the one hand, the increase recommended in the local inhabitant's tax makes the total income tax reduction less than the national figures alone indicate. On the other hand, the effect of the mission's plan on the low-income taxpayers must take into account the recommendation that the textile tax be repealed, that the rate of the admissions tax be lowered, and that, if government expenditures drop to a specified level, the transactions tax be repealed. The mission emphasizes that each one of its recommendations is related to all the others. 'What we are recommending is a tax system, not a number of isolated measures having no connexion with one another.'

A number of other changes are recommended for the income tax including : a liberalized definition of a dependant ; a provision for averaging the income from author's royalties and other irregular income so that the taxpayer will not be unfairly pushed up into the higher rate brackets ; a special additional exemption of 12,000 for the blind and others with extreme physical handicaps ; and deduction of medical expenses and loss of property due to accident or theft, to the extent that the total of such expenses and losses exceeds 10 per cent of the net income. The mission recommends full inclusion of capital gains in taxable income, not merely 50 per cent as at present with the following provisions : full deduction of capital losses ; the gains and losses to be averaged forward over five years to keep the taxpayer from being pushed up into the higher rate brackets ; and no gains or losses to be taken into account if they result under a fluctuation of the price level of more than 15 per cent, so that mere paper gains will not be taxed, and mere paper losses not allowed. The mission emphasizes that full inclusion of capital gains and losses, with those qualifications, is an essential part of its plan to prevent the double taxation of corporation income and the avoidance of personal income tax through retention of earnings in a corporation. If capital gains and losses were only partly taken into account, or were ignored, the whole structure of corporation and individual income taxation would have to be changed, and harsher and less fair measures would have to be imposed.

With respect to foreign nationals, the mission believes that the top rate of 55 per cent (plus a few points under the inhabitant's tax) should not prove an important barrier to their activity in Japan. The net worth tax would apply to foreign nationals only in exceptional cases, and, depending on the degree of encouragement that is desired to be accorded them, they might or might not be exempted entirely from the net worth tax. The mission recommends, moreover, that when adequate experience has been obtained with the net worth tax to show that it is a reliable source of revenue, the top rates of the income tax should then be further reduced to 50 per cent or even 45 per cent.

(6) The net worth tax is recommended at rates which will enable this tax to be paid out of income. The specific rates recommended for 1950-51 are as follows :

Net worth up to 5,000,000 yen is exempt.

Individuals with net worth of more than 5,000,000 yen would pay, on that part of the net worth in excess of 5,000,000 yen, but not in excess of 10 million yen, 0·5 per cent (one half of one per cent) on that part. For the 10 million yen to 20 million yen bracket the rate would be 1·0 per cent ; for the 20 million to 50 million bracket, 2·0 per cent ; for the part above 50 million, 3·0 per cent.

At these rates it would hardly ever pay the taxpayer to try to evade the tax by hiding his assets in a non-income producing form, as in bank notes or precious stones. In the first place, he would almost surely be found out sooner or later, since the income tax assessor has an interest in checking on the taxpayer's net worth, to find out if he has reported his income correctly, from dividends, interest, and rentals ; when the taxpayer gives a gift or leaves an estate at death, a similar rechecking occurs ; when he sells an asset and is taxed on the gain or wants a deduction for the loss, he is checked again. And his holdings of real estate will be subject to check under the local house and land tax. The four taxes (income tax, net worth tax, tax on gifts and bequests, and land and house tax) so interlock that any attempt at evasion would become quite hazardous for the taxpayer.

In the second place, the mission points out, if the wealthy individual is willing to put his wealth where it will earn a good return, the combined burden of the income tax and the net worth tax will still leave him something, whereas if he hoards his wealth he gets zero income from it. An investor subject to the top rate of 55 per cent, and getting 10 per cent on his investment, will lose 15 yen a year on each 1,000 yen of capital if he hoards his wealth in non-income-producing form, even if he successfully and illegally evades the net worth tax at the top (3 per cent) rate. And if his hoard is discovered and assessed, he would have lost 45 yen a year by hoarding. If he pays net worth tax at only the 0·5 per cent rate, he obtains no income if he hoards, but if he invests at 10 per cent he would obtain, after paying the income and net worth taxes, a net return of 40 yen on each 1,000 yen of capital.

For the corporation income tax, in addition to the changes already noted earlier, the mission recommends that the present 20 per cent withholding rate on dividends be repealed, since the 35 per cent tax on corporate profits is itself to be considered a withholding tax. The stockholder receiving the dividend is given a credit against his individual tax of 25 per cent of dividends he receives, to compensate for the 35 per cent tax paid by the corporation. Still personal income tax can be indefinitely postponed by the corporation's retaining earnings instead of distributing them promptly as dividends ; so, to compensate the government for the loss of interest it suffers from such postponement of personal tax payment, it is recommended that the corporation pay an interest surcharge levy of 1 per cent a year on the earnings that it retains. This applies only to earnings made in 1950 and later years, not to the surplus already accumulated before 1950.

A number of problems common to the corporation income tax and the personal income tax are treated by the mission.

First, the essential steps in the recommended programme for revaluation of assets are given in the main report, and full details in an appendix to the report, both of which will be published shortly.

Second, it is recommended that the special 65 per cent tax on inventory profits be repealed except where the rise in inventory is due to a price rise following the abolition of subsidies.

Third, net losses should be carried over to other years to be offset against the income of those years, and, in the opinion of the mission, there should be a limited carry-back as well as a carry-forward.

Fourth, an option to the taxpayer to use any one of several methods of accounting for inventory and for depreciation, under proper safeguards, is recommended.

Fifth, stricter enforcement of the provisions against deducting capital outlays all in one year is urged, as also disallowance of heavy entertainment expenses now commonly deducted as business expenses.

For the rest of the national taxes, the statements made earlier in the report indicate the changes recommended by the mission.

Among the local taxes, it is recommended that the inhabitant's tax contain simply the flat *per capita* element and an income element, not a property element, in view of the taxation of property recommended under the new house and land tax and the net worth tax. The municipalities could levy the income element either as a percentage of the national personal income tax, or as a percentage of the income (after exemptions) used in computing the national tax, or as a percentage of the income left after deducting both the national tax and the personal exemptions. The tax could be either flat-rate or progressive. Maximum rates would be 10 per cent, 15 per cent, and 20 per cent, respectively, for the three methods.

The land and house tax, under the mission's recommendations, is transformed into a tax on the capital value of land, buildings, and other depreciable property, not including stock in trade, securities, cash, and other non-depreciable assets. An appraisal at current values is recommended, except that farm land is to be valued at the official price, multiplied by an adjustment factor designed solely for the purposes of this tax; this factor is not to exceed 25, and is to be reduced if the official price of farm land rises.

The enterprise tax is recommended for revision, by enlarging the tax base from profits to 'value-added'. The tax would be imposed on gross receipts minus the cost of everything bought from other business firms, including capital equipment like buildings and machinery. There would therefore be no depreciation accounting involved, and no inventory accounting. Another way of defining the new tax base is to say it is the sum of profit, interest paid, rental paid, and payrolls. This base is chosen because it is economically neutral. It does not favour the vertically integrated concern, and does not discriminate against the use of machinery and other capital equipment. Farmers would be exempt from the tax.

The mission places great emphasis on the need for greatly improved administration of the tax laws. Its recommendations for a fair and economically beneficial tax system cannot be of practical significance unless taxpayers are willing to comply with the law, and tax administrations are able and determined to enforce the law fully and not arbitrarily. Much more improvement along these lines is needed, in the opinion of the mission, although a good start has been made at the national level with the recent establishment of the Tax Administration Agency, the National Tax Inspectors, and the National Tax Investigators. The mission recommends that the number and the quality of national tax personnel be increased well above the levels resulting from the recent 20 per cent decrease in number of authorized personnel. At the local level, too, increases in number and quality are deemed necessary.

The scope of the mission's task did not extend to all matters of detail in administration, but the mission's report does present, in a separate chapter, a number of specific recommendations for improving the processes of assessment, appeal, and litigation under the national income tax. Among these recommendations are the following: that business associations be not allowed to have

706

anything to do with determining the amount of income tax their members pay; that a special group of officials in the national tax offices serve as a Conference Group to confer with the taxpayer when he cannot reach agreement with the official who made the original reassessment; that a special 'blue return' form be available to businessmen and farmers under the personal income tax if they keep books in accordance with standards laid down by the Ministry of Finance, and those who met the requirements for filing on such a return be assured that they will not be reassessed without examination of their books; that most farmers be relieved of the necessity of filing declarations of estimated income, and be required to pay at the time they receive money from the sale of crops, by a system of withholding at the source on payments made to them by government bodies for their crops, and that this be coupled with a much closer approximation to each farmer's actual income as shown by production records and other data relating to him, in place of using average data for an area; that a special tax court be set up to handle tax cases; and that the role of the certified public accountant be greatly expanded.

A change in the fiscal relations on the national, prefectural, and municipal governments is recommended by the mission. In place of many of the specific grants (subsidies) now made, a general equalizing fund is recommended; also a new body, a Local Finance Commission, designed to implement the new inter-governmental relations.

The Tax Mission is composed of seven members, who spent four months of the summer in Japan. The director of the mission is Professor Carl S. Shoup, of the School of Business and the Graduate Faculty of Political Science at Columbia University, New York City. The other members of the mission and their professional connexions are:

Dean Howard R. Bowen, College of Commerce and Business Administration, University of Illinois.

Prof. Jerome B. Cohen, Department of Economics, College of the City of New York.

Rolland F. Hatfield, Director of Tax Research, Department of Taxation, St. Paul, Minnesota.

Prof. Stanley S. Surrey, School of Jurisprudence, University of California, Berkeley, California.

Prof. William C. Warren, School of Law, Columbia University, New York City.

Prof. William Vickrey, Graduate Faculty of Political Science, Columbia University, New York City.

Contemporary Japan, Vol. XVIII, Nos. 7-9, July-September 1949, pp. 386-98.

VI SELECTED SPEECHES AND MESSAGES OF GENERAL MACARTHUR

33   1 *January* 1948

GENERAL MACARTHUR'S NEW YEAR MESSAGE
TO THE JAPANESE PEOPLE

The design of a remodelled and reconstructed Japan is nearing completion. The pattern has been etched, the path has been laid. The development now lies largely in your own hands. Success or failure will depend upon your ability to practise the simple yet transcendental principles which modern civilization demands.

No Occupation, however benevolent and beneficial, can substitute for the spiritual uplift which alone can lead to an invincible determination to build a future based upon the immutable concepts of human freedom—a social status under which full consciousness of individual responsibility must ever remain the keystone to the arch of success and progress.

Individual hardship is inevitable. Your economy, due to the disastrous war decisions of your past leaders, is now impoverished. This can only be relieved by employment to the maximum of the energies of your people, by wisdom and determination on the part of your leaders, and by the restoration of peace with its removal of existing limitations upon international trade. So long as your needs continue to be greater than your productive capacity, controls upon your internal economy will be essential lest the weaker segments of your population perish. Such controls must, however, only be temporary and subject to ultimate removal in favour of free enterprise.

Economically, allied policy has required the breaking up of that system which in the past has permitted the major part of the commerce and industry and natural resources of your country to be owned and controlled by a minority of feudal families and exploited for their exclusive benefit. The world has probably never seen a counterpart to so abnormal an economic system. It permitted exploitation of the many for the sole benefit of the few. The integration of these few with government was complete and their influence upon governmental policies inordinate, and set the course which ultimately led to war and destruction. It was indeed so complete a monopoly as to be in effect a form of socialism in private hands. Only through its dissolution could the way be cleared for the emergence of an economy conducive to the well-being of all the people—an economy embodying the principle of private capitalism based upon free competitive enterprise—an economy which long experience has demonstrated alone provides the maximum incentive to the development of those fundamental requirements to human progress—individual initiative and individual energy.

Politically, progress towards reform has been equally encouraging. Your new constitution is now in full effect, and there is increasing • evidence of a growing understanding of the great human ideals which it is designed to serve. Implementing laws have reoriented the entire fabric of your way of life to give emphasis to the increased responsibility, dignity and opportunity which the individual now holds and enjoys. Government has ceased to be totalitarian and has become representative, with its functions decentralized to permit and encourage a maximum of individual thought and initiative and judgement in the management of community affairs. Control of every political segment has been shifted to permit the selection of a new leadership of your free choice capable of advancing democratic growth.

Socially, many of the shackles which traditionally have restricted individual thought and action have been severed and action has been taken to render the exercise of police power a matter for individual and community, rather than national, responsibility. The judicial system has been freed from executive and legislative controls, and laws have been enacted to temper inordinate bureaucratic power by requiring all public officials to justify the trust of public responsibility and answer for their acts directly to the people.

Every Japanese citizen can now for the first time do what he wants, and go where he wants, and say what he wants, within the liberal laws of his land. This means that you can select your own work, and when you have completed it you can choose your own method of relaxation and enjoyment, and on your day of rest you can worship as you please, and always you can criticize and express your views on the actions of your Government. This is liberty. Yet inherent in it are its obligations to act with decorum and self-restraint, and become acutely conscious of the responsibilities which a free society imposes upon its every segment.

The future therefore lies in your hands. If you remain true to the great spiritual revolution which you have undergone, your nation will emerge and go on—if you accept only its benefits without its obligations, it will wither and go under. The line of demarcation is a simple one, understandable to all men—the line between those things which are right and those things which are wrong. The way is long and hard and beset with difficulties and dangers, but it is my hope and belief and prayer on this New Year's Day that you will not falter.

Political Reorientation of Japan, Appendix F: 39, p. 776.

34   3 *May* 1948

GENERAL MACARTHUR'S MESSAGE ON THE
FIRST ANNIVERSARY OF THE ENFORCEMENT
OF THE NEW CONSTITUTION

One year ago your new Constitution became the supreme law of the land, and the cause of human freedom advanced as a mantle of personal dignity thereby fell upon every Japanese citizen. The people turned their eyes towards the dawn of a higher concept of life, heralded by a charter which provides the design for a political and social edifice resting upon the pillars of liberty and justice.

Adapted from the experience of the ages, this charter embodies the most enlightened advances in the concept of human relationship which civilization thus far has been able to evolve, and as it now stands it lags behind none in form, in substance, or in progressive thought. But the written word alone gives only indirect protection to the rights and privileges which it ordains. Such protection resides actually in the resolute will of the people in whom the sovereign power dwells. And no man is entitled to the blessings of freedom unless he be vigilant in its preservation and vigorous in its defence.

It is for the people, therefore, as empowered by its terms, to translate this charter into living and resourceful actuality, that the new Japanese way of life may be fashioned according to its general design, a workable and beneficent way of life which while fundamentally in complete harmony with Japanese character and culture and basic needs, yet overlooks no gain elsewhere made towards advancing human welfare. For the course of civilization is not static, and it is therefore for the Japanese people in shaping their own free destiny carefully to scrutinize the lessons history has taught in other lands and search for weak practices as well as strong failure as well as success, in order that the way may be oriented to the best that experience provides. The concept of human freedom is immutable but its translation into living actuality is subject to progressive advance as the minds of men find reorientation with enlightened knowledge and changing conditions with which society must cope.

Today great ideological issues are stirring mankind. These issues are clearly defined as between democracy and despotism—freedom and slavery. While the great majority of the peoples of the earth seek freedom, the forces of despotism, composed of wilful minorities, are on the march in every land. Whether they be of the extreme left or of the extreme right makes little difference, for their purpose is to destroy freedom, and the two often exert pressure in common accord in the effort to achieve this purpose. While only minorities compose these pressure groups, they garner support from the ignorant, the gullible, and the weak-minded. Their fundamental aim is to destroy the highly developed moral concepts of the modern world and to superimpose upon the ashes thereof a social system which experience has shown to be barren of truth and light, without hope or promise and bereft of faith, a system under which the masses of men are denied the fruits of their toil and the benefits of their skill to enrich a ruling few, neither responsible to the popular will nor dedicated to the public good. Defence against such minority pressure lies more than all else in the spiritual strength of the people and the unyielding firmness of their chosen leaders. For the lessons of contemporary history make it unmistakably clear that when peoples or their leaders shrink or yield before such pressure or permit invisible controls to be superimposed upon representative government by any minority groups whatsoever, governments fall and freedom perishes.

The past year has witnessed notable progress in the reshaping of Japanese life to conform to Japan's constitutional mandates. The entire body of Japanese law has now been modified and the structure of government redesigned to render it a thoroughly democratic instrument, truly representative of the popular will. The highly centralized controls previously existing have been severed, with each community within the broad outline of the charter left the untrammelled right and fixed responsibility to manage its own affairs, exercise its own police power, and resolve its own peculiar social problems.

The very essence of democracy lies in the reservation of the maximum of political power in the people for exercise up through the smallest political sub-divisions of government. Its antithesis lies in the concentration of the political power in the hands of a few for exercise down to the smallest political sub-divisions of government. Japan, traditionally governed under the latter, is now fully oriented towards the former, as all segments of Japanese life, freed from arbitrary and oppressive centralized control, are becoming welded into strong and purposeful communities, which in common cause and for the common benefit will give vitality to a free nation. Ceaseless vigilance must be maintained to ensure that the maximum of local autonomy is preserved if democracy, now firmly planted, is to survive.

The Japanese people are coming to understand, apply and cherish the rights and privileges conferred by their new constitution. It is encouraging to note that care is being exercised to avoid the perversion of grants of liberty into seeming grants of licence, and that there is a growing understanding that with every right and privilege conferred there is a corresponding obligation imposed—an obligation to exercise that right and privilege in such manner as to avoid violence to the rights and privileges of others. Every segment of Japanese society will find its authority for advance within the provisions of this great charter, and yet unrelaxed vigilance is necessary to ensure that by operation of government no one segment advances at the expense of any other. Thus you will find that if you avoid conferring special privilege upon any one segment you will confer equal privilege upon all and the Constitution will thereby serve its avowed purpose of providing that equal protection shall be extended to every citizen of the land.

You have reoriented your economy towards a system based upon the principles of free private competitive enterprise, and with it are reorganizing the concentration of economic power which long has suppressed any possibility for equality of opportunity, one of the great pillars to democratic life. And by wise and advanced laws you have safeguarded against any reversion to monopolistic control. If this course be firmly held and unceasing vigilance be maintained to hold to a minimum the burden of the expense of government upon the individual you will leave unimpaired the incentive to maximized initiative and energy and the assumption of reasonable risks inherent in economic adventure, all essential to progress in a free economy.

It is heartening to observe a growing consciousness of public responsibility on the part of the people, as increasingly is heard the expression of public opinion. For the most effective curb upon excesses or corruption in government or any segment of Japanese life lies in an informed public opinion and its vigorous and fearless defence against threat to the public interest. An informed public opinion is dependent in turn upon a free, responsible and courageous Press, and it is gratifying that the Japanese Press during the past year has shown great progress in the development of those qualities. It appears increasingly to understand that in the constitutional guarantee of a free Press, a responsible Press is intended—a Press which will play a vital role in the orientation of public opinion by propagating the truth in order that the people wherein sovereignty rests may make sound political decisions with minds uncorrupted by slanted, distorted or false propaganda.

The past year has witnessed impressive gains in the enhanced dignity and improved working conditions of labour. And both labour and management in the social struggles inherent in a society which is free are displaying a growing awareness of the fact that labour-management disputes involve triangular rather than bilateral interests, with the public interest by far the predominant one. In Japan with its economy of scarcity resulting from war and destruction no segment of society is without want and consequently many demands are understandably motivated by the wish for more of the fundamentals of life, but if a sound course is to be charted, each segment must realistically assess the resources available and measure its demands to correspond to its fair share. This necessitates more than all else responsible leadership and, on the part of the rank and file, ceaseless vigilance to ensure that Japan's already meagre resources be not imperilled by irresponsible action.

Japan today is a land of relative calm and purposeful effort in a turbulent and confused surrounding. That it is so reflects great credit upon the stamina, resiliency and determination of its people. So it must remain. For such a Japan with all effort dedicated to building a new and impregnable citadel of democracy in the East will provide its people with the blessings of a truly free way of life and thereby prove a factor for stability in a world torn by the uncertainties of confusion and fear.

Political Reorientation of Japan, Appendix F : 48, pp. 788-9.

35   1 *January* 1949

GENERAL MACARTHUR'S NEW YEAR MESSAGE
TO THE JAPANESE PEOPLE

To the People of Japan :

The period just concluded has been of great historical significance to Japan and to the other nations of the world. For in this period mankind has been groping for the solution to many ills which have beset the human race since the dawn of time. Steps have been halting and uncertain due to the confusion still engendered in the aftermath of war by the clash of opposed ideologies and the ambitions of selfish men who seek advantage from the universal will for peace. Encouragement is seen, however, from the fact that thinking men of all nations and all races, in increasing numbers, are firmly facing the historical realism that war, long tried, has never been and never will be a panacea for human ills, and are diligently searching for other means to orient mankind towards that human progress which alone can come from the abolition of war and the peaceful solution of issues between nations and men. Thus, on balance, definite progress is being made in mobilizing the full power of world opinion in support of the general welfare of all mankind.

In Japan, despite freedom's convulsions on the Asiatic mainland, the situation has continued calm and well ordered as you have worked to lay imperishable foundation stones in the political mould of freedom and dignity and peace. You have established here a truly representative government in accordance with and responsive to the will of the majority. In no land anywhere are men more free or more safe and secure, and men here live in greater peace and greater tranquillity than do many of your neighbours. A serenity of calm has indeed enveloped your Island for which every law-abiding citizen fully shares in the credit.

The period we now enter will test the invincibility of your will and the wisdom and capacity of your endowment to erect upon that political base an edifice of economic security, cast in the enlightened experience of time, which will fully support and preserve it. For political freedom and economic self-sufficiency are inseparable and of mutual support, as each is dependent for survival upon the spiritual strength of the other. Much that you have done in the fashioning of a strong and durable political base has earned the approval of other peoples, but now that the emphasis has shifted from political to economic reconstruction a world awaits with critical but not unfriendly eye your mastery of the problem. For as I pointed out in my letter of 19 December last to your Prime Minister, in which I set forth the intermediate objectives prerequisite to the attainment of your economic self-sufficiency, political freedom is impossible of achievement so long as your daily livelihood is dependent in any degree upon the beneficent energies of others. Furthermore, in the past I repeatedly have affirmed to my own government that your will and your industry were such that given a reasonable opportunity for trade you could fully establish a self-supporting economy, producing for others no less than you received from others, and that this alone was the opportunity you asked and which you sought. You now have that opportunity. It is for you in gearing the forces of internal production to demonstrate the justification for my faith.

Your immediate response to the challenge of these objectives has been most encouraging. On the labour front where the heavy burden of individual toil necessarily must fall there has emerged a high type of labour statesmanship, which has seen and fully accepted the need temporarily to lay aside some of labour's energies in support of the national objective. In the ranks of management, too, the response has been similarly encouraging. Those who till Japan's soil, by their skill and industry already in the past have won my sincere admiration, but even they are gearing themselves for renewed and greater effort to maximize Japan's indigenous food resources. And with the rapid and determined mobilization of Japan's public opinion now under way under the leadership of a sound and patriotic Press, there is no room for doubt that these economic objectives progressively will be achieved.

This does not mean that the difficulties ahead will be light as the emphasis shifts from political to economic concern, but the measure of the individual burden to be borne will lie in the number of citizens who rally to assume their full share of the responsibility. And any who fail resolutely to do so must feel the full weight of an aroused public approbrium. For none of right may shirk his equitable share of this, a whole people's burden.

The general election just ahead will test your wisdom in the selection of a leadership to whom you will in this crucial period entrust the sovereign power. The times require great dignity and capacity for wise statesmanship and such should be the measure of your choice—men capable of elevating your national legislative forum to the standard set by the finest of your traditions. Thereafter the issue will rest squarely upon the type of leadership they bring to the country and the resolute will by which each among your citizenry acquits his individual responsibility in the great task of ensuring that Japan may live. I have left this largely to your implementation without the slightest reservation of doubt concerning your ability to master its attending responsibility.

To enhance the spiritual strength necessary to carry on in the pattern which your general welfare now demands and in recognition of those advances you have heretofore made in establishing the sturdy base for a free political destiny, I now restore to you the unrestricted use and display of your national flag within your country's territorial limits. And I do so with the fervent hope that this flag shall ever stand in future before the world as a symbol of peace based upon those immutable concepts of justice and freedom universally sought by the human race ; that it shall stand a firm advocate for a concept of nationalism ever subordinate to the higher duty of obedience to the universal laws, written and unwritten, which establish the mutual obligations and responsibilities among peoples within the family of nations ; and that it shall serve as a shining beacon to summon every Japanese citizen resolutely to the duty of building Japan's economic stature to ensure and preserve Japan's political freedom.

Contemporary Japan, Vol. XVIII Nos. 1-3, January-March 1949, pp. 126-8.

GENERAL MACARTHUR'S STATEMENT ON THE
OCCASION OF AMERICA'S INDEPENDENCE DAY

July 4th in this as in every year is a day for deep and inspirational reflection by every American whether at home or abroad. Not only does it register another anniversary in the life of our great American Republic—another milestone in the evolution of what we ourselves proudly term the concepts of Americanism—but of yet deeper significance it provides a traditional opportunity for Americans of each successive generation to assay the manner in which they themselves have discharged the stewardship of America's free institutions passed on in sacred trust by the generation just gone.

At this distant point of observation that opportunity is particularly arresting. For we stand here, abreast of the threatening sweep of Communistic forces over the heart of Asia, among a proud race of people, bereft of faith in past concepts which brought them to disaster, who avidly seek knowledge and understanding of those concepts of Americanism which have been triumphant in the struggle of mankind for a betterment of life. It is a point of vantage from which to view the beneficial impact of those concepts upon other peoples of the world, for the contraction of distance by the accelerating speed of communication has rendered the freedom of others strategically interwoven with the preservation of that of our own.

Here in Japan the norm of American democracy has thus faced two challenging tests : its adaptability where tradition, culture and custom have been evolved under political, economic and social concepts irreconcilable with the concept of human freedom ; and its power of resistance, despite conditions of political instability, economic impoverishment and social unrest, to the appeal of the Communist propaganda. Both tests have shown conclusive results. The concepts of Americanism have found no barrier to their assimilation in Oriental culture or custom and the resulting blend between the best of the East and the best of the West is proving an impregnable front against Communism's most aggressive assaults.

The results are as conclusive as the reasons are sound. All segments of the human race, regardless of ethnological, geographical or cultural considerations, are fundamentally alike in the universal longing for high personal dignity, and broader individual opportunity— qualities which find the means of development only in a society which is free. All segments recoil from submitting their lives to the despotic rule of force and want instead to live by rules founded upon moral standards and spiritual ethics. All reject despotism in any form, unless and until it is forced upon them.

The evolution of Communism within the present century gives the measure of its own weakness and forecast of its ultimate universal rejection as a philosophy or pattern of life. Originating in the doctrine of extreme Marxian socialism, which advocated overthrow of the economic system based upon capitalistic management through abolition of both private property and individual profit by the exercise of the political power, it was early found that its adherents could not command the political power required to implement the programme through the normal, peaceful or constitutional process. For the innate common sense of the human race proved an effective barrier to the peaceful and successful propagation of the Marxian doctrine. To breach this defence a merger consequently was effected with the terroristic concept known as nihilism which sought the destruction of existing governments by assassination and other violence as the means to seize the political power. Communism as presently advanced, however, neither is based upon political philosophy or economic doctrine, nor any serious pretence thereof. It has emerged as an instrument of force and intimidation to permit minority elements by stealth, infiltration and deceit to seize the political power from the majority ruling under constitutional process. Atheistic in conception, it repudiates the existence of an omnipotent Providence and rejects the moral precepts and theological teachings which support the higher sensibilities of the human race. As befits the character of its leadership, its sole underlying motive is to serve the lust for personal power. To such end it has become the rallying media for the malefactor, the corruptible and the fool, and it welds these subnormal elements of society into an organized, disciplined and effective force in order by the spread of confusion, unrest and violence to disrupt the cohesion and strength in an otherwise orderly society. Communism thus has emerged as a movement of national and international outlawry without a due philosophic basis which offers nothing but ultimate enslavement to those segments of the human race which become its prey. That it should continue to advance its treacherous purposes behind the shield of those very freedoms which to succeed it must destroy is one of the paradoxes of this age and poses the question as to whether such movements should longer be accorded the validity, the sanction and the protection of law.

Here in Japan the great masses of the people are unmoved by the line of Communist propaganda for they fully comprehend the incipient threat of the Communist movement. They are, and will remain, an effective bulwark to stem its advance east and discourage its advance south. The American people may feel assured, moreover, that those immutable concepts of American democracy offered here as the means to the betterment of individual life and a truly worthwhile collective peace will be cherished, preserved, and advanced as the Japanese people march towards a higher and a more objective destiny within the fellowship of man.

Contemporary Japan, Vol. XVIII, Nos. 7-9, July-September 1949, pp. 383-5.

37   *2 September* 1949

GENERAL MACARTHUR'S STATEMENT ON THE FOURTH ANNIVERSARY OF THE RETURN OF PEACE

Today marks the fourth anniversary of that historic event on the battleship Missouri in Tokyo Bay when the warring nations of the Pacific entered into solemn covenants designed to restore the peace. The four years since passed have been fruitful years here in terms of human progress, as the Japanese people have fully and faithfully observed their surrender commitments and advanced steadily and progressively along the road of spiritual regeneration and physical reconstruction. Today, Japan might, indeed, be viewed as a symbol of hope for less fortunate peoples overwhelmed by the despotic rule of coercive force. For, despite the continued presence on Japan's soil of an occupation force from beyond the seas, the Japanese people in their enjoyment of full personal freedom know that by their skill and their industry they serve no other cause but their own. They, themselves, plot the ultimate course of Japan's destiny within the family of free nations.

The past year has witnessed accelerated progress in every phase of Japan's reconstruction. True, as elsewhere, there have been assaults upon the integrity of the democratic process by the small existent Communist minority, but these assaults were effectively repulsed—not by the repressive force of police power—but by the weight of an increasingly informed and active Japanese public opinion aroused to meet the threat to their free institutions. As a result, the threat of Communism as a major issue in Japanese life is past. It fell victim to its own excesses. The Japanese mind penetrated the hypocrisy supporting its position. This test of strength, while disturbing to orderly progress, served to bring to light for the first time the full latent power of the Japanese devotion to the concepts of freedom and the integrity of their constitutional processes.

Therein lies encouragement for Japan's potential strength as a bulwark of human freedom.

Politically, progressive gains have been made in the fabrication of a system of government truly representative in character. The lines of separation between the three great branches, executive, legislative and judicial, as provided by the constitutional design, have found strength in healthy public discussion of the vital issue of constitutional interpretation, and as a result the affairs of government have advanced with a minimum of overlapping friction and increasing inter-branch co-operation.

The development of the desired autonomous responsibility in the conduct of local affairs has been retarded somewhat by the need for rationalization in the field of government finance to permit local revenues to support local government. A remedy for this difficulty is now being evolved, providing hope that the coming year will produce the legal basis fully to sustain the severance of pre-existing centralized controls and support the development of a political and social system resting upon interrelated and self-sustaining segments at the community level from which the national government may draw its power and direction. Therein will lie the safeguard against the re-emergence of autocracy as the prevailing philosophy of government in Japan.

Probably the most significant political development of the past year has been the growing consciousness of individual responsibility in the conduct of public affairs. This has been given emphasis by a popular demand for higher standards of public morality keynoted by action of the electorate in rejecting for return to elective office public officials whose public record was compromised by the exposure of corruption in government. Administrative and judicial action in the investigation of the stewardship of public responsibility and vigorous prosecution, without fear or favour, of violators of the public trust not only have served to safeguard the public interest, but have given vital reality to the constitutional assurance of 'equality before the law'. There is thus rapidly taking form the ethical base upon which the pillars of a free, responsible and representative government safely may rest.

Socially, the Japanese people are wearing well their constitutional mantle of personal liberty and individual dignity. Apart from the growing consciousness of individual responsibility in the conduct of public affairs, there has been a sharp revulsion against persons who have failed to abide by the law, with a resulting decisive drop in the incidence of private crime. The basic causes of social unrest throughout Asia have largely been eradicated in Japan by a redesign of the social structure to permit the equalization of individual opportunity and personal privilege. This is having a profound influence upon the economic potential, thereby fortifying the spirit against radical designs of either extreme to suppress freedom.

Substantial progress has been made in the building of an effective police system based upon the statutory principle of decentralization in the exercise of the police power. Increasingly, the Japanese people are coming to understand that this power rests in their hands, rather than in the hands of any ruling clique, and provides the legal weapon for the preservation of the local security by their direction. They realize that the maintenance of internal order in the nation as a whole, subject to the safeguards provided by law, is dependent upon the manner in which each community administers the police power corresponding to its local responsibility. Here, too, difficulties are being experienced due to the present maladjustment of government finance, but this problem, as pointed out, is in process of solution. Apart from this, progressive strides have been made towards implementation of the new concepts embodied in the police law, and the police services are being administered with restraint, tolerance and commendable efficiency. The danger that a police state will re-emerge or that the police system as now constituted and manned will fail to maintain reasonable law and order is non-existent.

Progress of trade unionization during the past year, despite a degree of freedom unsurpassed in modern civilization, has been somewhat impeded by the machinations of an irresponsible union leadership, but its rank and file are showing an increasing awareness of this threat to labour's legitimate objectives and are moving to insist upon moderation and objectivity. Workers in the public service, through the functioning of a modernized and enlightened civil service system established by law, for the first time in Japan's history, find protection of their rights and interests adequately provided for, without continuous struggle on their part, with machinery established for the hearing and adjudication of individual or collective grievances. This has resulted in a marked uplift in individual morale and greater attendant efficiency in the conduct of the affairs of government.

The enfranchised women of Japan are exerting an increasingly beneficial influence upon Japan's political, economic and social life. They are responding magnificently to the challenge of the attending responsibility and give every promise of proving a powerful and effective force in the shaping of Japan's peaceful destiny.

Economically, Japan is still in transition from an economy of survival to one of health, but the past year has witnessed significant progress along a broad front. Foremost of the gains made lies in the development of a more positive leadership and an increasingly informed public opinion.

Both leaders and people are coming to understand that representative democracy draws its strength from the support of a broad majority of the people imbued with the belief that under it they may attain a standard of living commensurate with the capabilities of modern civilization—that a prerequisite to that condition is individual freedom of activity in the field of economic enterprise, for no individual bound in economic thraldom can be politically free. Thus, for the vast majority of those who earn their living in industrial and commercial pursuits there could be no political freedom so long as their economic destiny was determined by decisions made in the closed councils of the few families which formerly controlled the vast bulk of the productive and financial resources of Japan. Nor could there be any political freedom for those who work the soil so long as they were economic serfs under a feudalistic system of land tenure. The fruition during the past year of the plans laid down by the Occupation and carried out by the Japanese Government to remove, through the Economic Deconcentration Programme on the one hand and the Land Reform Programme on the other, these barriers to the existence of a free society has established in Japan the economic basis for the existence of a broad middle class which, having a stake in the economic well-being of the country, will support the ideal of democracy as their way of life and will reject with scorn any will-of-the-wisp economic utopias which require the surrender of the individual's freedom to the state.

With patience, fortitude and self-discipline the Japanese people withstood the privations of the immediate post-war period. With comparable energy, industry and hope they are now launched on the huge task of making Japan once again self-supporting among the family of nations. On the way to that goal great obstacles have been overcome, although some still remain. Since the summer of 1945, when productive activity in Japan was utterly paralysed, the production of commodities and goods for home consumption, for industrial use and for export has risen steadily until now it is rapidly approaching the average level for the years 1930-34 prescribed by the Far Eastern Commission as an interim standard. Coal, basic to so much of Japan's industry, is now being produced at a monthly rate of 3·2 million metric tons as contrasted with less than 1·7 million metric tons in 1946. Electric power, another basic ingredient of industrial activity, has attained a monthly volume of 3·2 billion kWh, as compared with 2·8 billion one year ago. Production of chemicals, necessary both for industrial uses and for the protection of the public health, has attained a volume of 105 per cent of the 1930-34 average, as compared with 76 per cent one year ago and 21 per cent in January 1946. Equally significant advances have been made in other fields of economic activity, such as in the construction of dwellings and business buildings to replace those destroyed by war, and in the production of an increasing variety of goods both for home consumption and sale overseas.

To acquire the raw materials needed to feed her industrial machine as well as to overcome the deficit in her indigenous food production, Japan must export a large volume of goods and services. Despite existing handicaps, chiefly the limited availability of raw materials from those sources which customarily supplied Japan in the pre-war years, progress in this direction has been heartening. In 1946, Japan's total exports were $103,000,000·00 ; in 1947, $173,000,000·00 ; in 1948, $258,000,000·00, and in the first six months of 1949, exports had already exceeded the total for the full year 1948 by a sizeable margin.

In the past 12 months two significant decisions to promote the economic rehabilitation of Japan were taken by the Government of the United States. One was that of May 1949, to cease the removal of industrial plants for reparations. This action dispelled the pall of uncertainty which had previously paralysed entrepreneurial initiative and restored the incentive to the investment of capital in the rehabilitation and construction of capital plant and equipment. The second was the authorization by the Congress of the United States of limited budgetary appropriations for financing the importation into Japan of materials needed for rehabilitation purposes in addition to the appropriations previously made for the importation of primary necessities such as food, fertilizer and medicines to protect the Japanese people against widespread suffering and disease.

The enactment by the Japanese National Diet in the spring of 1949 of a national budget which for the first time in many years achieved a true balance, and subsequent action to sharply curtail the cost of government by streamlining its structure and reducing its personnel, have struck at one of the contributing factors in the post-war inflation and are gradually effecting greater stability. To prevent the spectre of inflation from rising again, a firm and determined course based upon sound fiscal and financial policies is now being pursued by the Japanese Government. This, accompanied by maximum utilization of indigenous resources and efficient employment of the manpower of Japan in the useful pursuits of peace, will speed the day when the Japanese economy will be stabilized and its dependence on American subsidy eliminated.

To stimulate productive endeavour and to strengthen the foundations for the growth of free private competitive enterprises in Japan, the economic controls necessitated by the war-generated shortages of critical materials have been removed as fast as the availability of adequate supplies has obviated their necessity. The timing of progressive further relaxations will, of course, depend on the progress of the transition from an economy of scarcity to one of normalcy.

Since 1 October 1945, nine and one-half million people have been added to the population of Japan—five million by repatriation and the rest through natural increase. Yet there has been no mass unemployment, no social unrest and no large-scale dole. In June 1949, persons reported as totally unemployed were fewer than 400,000. Further, despite recent reductions in the number of government employees in the interest of governmental economy and efficiency and the current rationalization of industry necessitated by the adoption of a single foreign exchange rate for foreign trade and the transition from subsidized to competitive industry, total unemployment by the end of August 1949 is estimated not to exceed one-half million persons. During the 12 months ended 30 June 1949, the total number of persons at work in any given week averaged over 34·5 million, as compared with 32·9 million in the preceding 12 month period, or an average increase of 1·6 million in the total number of persons at work. In June 1949, the total number of persons at work stood at an all-time high of 37·4 million. These figures reflect an orderly absorption of the working energies of the increasing population in an expanding number of employment opportunities in industry, agriculture and small-scale family enterprises. Unemployment, therefore, presents no major problem at the present time, and the expanding areas of employment in the work of reconstruction will stand safeguard against any acute unemployment problem in the foreseeable future.

Since the full employment of Japan's industrial potential requires a vigorous revival of her foreign trade and since among her chief customers in the past were the countries bordering on the Pacific basin, the question as to whether Japan will regain her traditional trade with China, despite the stranglehold of Communism upon that tragic land, has been mooted with increasing frequency. This question is largely academic. Foreign trade requires production in excess of domestic needs. Human experience demonstrates with striking clarity that the further removed a people become from the economic philosophy of free enterprise in like ratio does its productive capacity deteriorate. This deterioration proceeds until, as under Communism, with incentive completely lost, the human energy and individual initiative which find their expression in production give way to indolence and despair. In such an unhealthy climate industry and commerce cannot thrive and realism warns that the potentialities of trade with any people under the structures of a collectivistic system must be discounted accordingly. For the time being, therefore, and for some time to come, Japan must look elsewhere for the sources of her needed imports and the markets for her manufactures. Against this need Japan has already initiated foreign trade with 113 other countries and territorial areas.

I dare say that no operation in history has been subject to such an extraordinary divergence of opinion carried in the media of public expression than has the Occupation of Japan. Some writers have been extravagant in their praise, other no less extravagant in their criticism. The truth, awaiting the judgement of history, will rest somewhere in between.

Nor has there been any operation subject to such a variety of influences and pressures—the ideological protagonists, the special pleaders, the vindictive and the lenient—many seeking to influence public opinion through prevarication of the truth. In the search for sensationalism, incidents in Japan, elsewhere scarcely worth the public notice, have been exaggerated out of all proportion to their true significance, with the serenity and order and sincerity of purpose normal to post-war Japan all but ignored. And time and again simultaneous attack has been levelled against Occupation policy, by the leftists as too reactionary and by the conservatives as too liberal. Such an atmosphere, while giving assurance that our moderate course is well charted, does not contribute to an objective public appraisal of the situation.

The great and noble effort by the American people, with the wholehearted support of other Allies, towards the reorientation and reconstruction of post-war Japan, beyond peradventure of doubt, will prove eminently successful. Long hence history will record of the Occupation that its greatest contribution to the progress of civilization was to introduce into Japan the great concepts of personal liberty and individual dignity and to give the Christian ideal the opportunity to advance into Asia.

Of the Japanese people, I can pay no higher tribute than to repeat that they have fully and faithfully fulfilled their surrender commitments and have well earned the freedom and dignity and opportunity which alone can come with the restoration of a formal peace.

Contemporary Japan, Vol. XVIII, Nos. 7-9, July-September 1949, pp. 398-404.

GENERAL MACARTHUR'S NEW YEAR
MESSAGE TO THE JAPANESE PEOPLE

To the people of Japan :

On this fifth New Year's Day following hostilities' end, one fact inescapably stands out—although Japan is still technically at war, there are few places on earth more completely at peace.

In keeping with my announced purpose to transfer the authority of government to your chosen representatives just as rapidly as they demonstrated the will and the capacity firmly to discharge the attending responsibility, the past year has witnessed progressive and far-reaching relaxation of Occupation controls. We have, indeed, gone a long way and internally have virtually arrived at a *de facto* peace. Your new leadership, strengthening under the stimulus of responsibility, is rapidly becoming safe guarantee against either the re-emergence of those institutions which brought your race to the brink of destruction or the substitution of alien concepts no less provocative of disaster. The ideal of human freedom, vigorously taking root in Japanese hearts, is progressively asserting itself through expression of the public mind whenever suppressive forces arise to challenge it. The myth of an unbridgeable gulf between the ways of the East and the ways of the West has been thoroughly exploded by the lesson of experience and no longer dominates man's thinking. For men now know that humanity, whatever the origin, race or cultural environment, is fundamentally the same in the impelling universal desire for higher personal dignity, broader individual liberty and a betterment of life. Given the opportunity, any segment of the human race thus will draw upon the best of the East and the best of the West, and from the resulting blend of tried and proved ideas will fashion a way of life best adapted to advance its own well-being. If, therefore, out of the bankruptcy, chaos and despair left in war's wake there emerges an ethical base for New Japan's embodying many sound ideas which in practice have raised the standard of Western life and provided the moral basis of Western thought, it will be but another triumph of common sense in its age-old struggle to apply enlightened knowledge as the guide to human decision.

During the past year Japan has scored impressive gains along almost every front and the confidence reflected in my message to you of a year ago has found complete support in ensuing events. Despite the convulsions in many lands where the concept of human freedom is suppressed or under assault, Japan's free institutions progressively have strengthened. The individual citizen is grasping with increasing understanding and firmness the political responsibility which attaches to the sovereign power. The public opinion is giving striking evidence of its insistence upon responsibility in government and public officials are showing a growing consciousness of their responsibility for the stewardship of public affairs. The police of Japan have made rapid strides in organization and training and proved that they can adequately cope with the problems of enforcing the law and preserving the public order as servants, rather than masters, of the citizenry.

With the continuation of the noble support of the American people tendered a prostrate Japan in her hour of most desperate need, a further broad advance has been made towards the self-supporting economy which is the goal of every Japanese citizen. The adoption of a truly balanced consolidated budget in the last fiscal year and the projection of one similarly balanced for the next has largely corrected the inflationary fiscal practice which persisted in the immediate post-war years, strengthened the Government's financial position and established the foundation for a sound system of public finance based on the capability of the people's support. The volume of currency outstanding has been stabilized, and for the second consecutive year provision has been made for debt retirement. Marked improvement in tax collections evidences an increasing consciousness of the individual's responsibility to support the operation of his public institutions. The implementation of the Government's plans to establish a more equitable tax structure and a fair and more efficient system of tax administration will equalize the burden and, it is my hope, will permit substantial future tax reductions over a broad base.

Production has continued the forward march initiated in 1946. Coal, utilities and other basic components of industrial activity are gradually approaching their pre-war levels, thus furnishing the sinews for overall industrial recovery. Consumer goods have become available in increasing quantities, and the production and collection of foods, benefited by good crops and a large catch of marine products, have reached new post-war highs. The farmers and fishermen thus are not only acquitting well their responsibilities towards securing the people's livelihood but are providing a striking demonstration of the fruits of free enterprise.

Labour, too, by its energy and patriotism is making a splendid contribution to the national recovery. Turning from an irresponsible leadership of the past, it is now becoming well oriented towards an objective and healthy future. And its demand for moderation evidences that labour is coming to understand that in a society which

726

is truly free the individual standard of life must bear a direct relationship to the constructive energies the individual contributes to life—
that every segment of society must earn its own way, as the
arbitrary advancement of one segment at the expense of another
inevitably weakens political and economic freedom.

Correction of the fiscal maladjustment and elimination of many
shortages have made it possible to approach a condition where stability of the price structure derives from the equilibrium of normal
economic forces rather than from artificial devices. Thus, the economic control exercised through rationing, price ceilings and subsidies
during the period of acute shortages and inflationary pressure has
been lifted as rapidly as conditions in the various fields have war-
ranted. With the latest relaxation of control, export trade was
returned to a private basis on 1 December, as is import trade being
returned today, retaining in the hands of the Government only
such control as is necessary to safeguard Japan's foreign exchange
position, the stability of her currency, and the equitable distribution
of essential commodities still in short supply. Japan thus rapidly is
approaching that economic ideal—free private competitive enterprise—which alone can provide hope for progressive advancement of
the living standard.

In foreign trade the gains initiated with the post-war resumption
of exports have continued. Reflecting the accelerated industrial
production and reopening of foreign trade outlets, exports this year
approximately doubled those of the last. Coincident with the expansion of international trade, definite gains are being made towards
attaining a balance between imports and exports. All this, indeed,
shows healthy progress in the building of New Japan and foretells
the day not long hence when political maturity, social justice, and
economic self-sufficiency will make of Japan a sturdy and highly
respected member of the society of free nations.

This synopsis of the present etches the pattern of the future. It
reflects the steady, unswerving progress of a people who, with backs
to a discredited past, see a lofty goal ahead and are determined to
achieve it. It gives unmistakable answer to those voices of men—
the uninformed or misinformed, the informed but pathological cynic:
the indoctrinated of Japan's old and discredited order, so blind
that he 'will not see'; and the subversive who would sabotage
the people's faith—raised during the four years and more of occupation in self-ordained omniscience to forecast from time to time with
insatiable persistence the imminence of economic disaster, the re-
emergence of political reaction, the widespread absorption of the
Communist hypocrisy, and the social convulsions inevitable from
any effort to integrate Western ideals with Eastern culture. It is

to the credit of both the American and Japanese peoples that these prophets of gloom have had their say without marring in the least the pattern of steady progress.

As we enter the new year, two basic and yet unresolved problems cause concern in every Japanese mind—the global ideological struggle brought close to Japan by the Communist hold over China, and the international procedural conflict delaying the call of a Japanese peace conference. Such concern is indeed most natural. But the solution of these problems does not lie within Japan's present capability, and should not directly be drawn within the orbit of Japan's internal politics. Pending such solution, however, Japan's road ahead is clearly delineated. She must continue steadfastly and invincibly forward along the course so well charted by the constitutional precepts. To do so is not only to strengthen Japan's own free institutions, but by example to strengthen the free institutions of others as well.

Some contemporary cynics deride as visionary Japan's constitutional renunciation of the concept of belligerency and armed security. Be not over concerned by such detractors. A product of Japanese thought, this provision is based upon the highest of moral ideals, and yet no constitutional provision was ever more fundamentally sound and practical. While by no sophistry of reasoning can it be interpreted as complete negation of the inalienable right of self-defence against unprovoked attack, it is a ringing affirmation by a people laid prostrate by the sword, of faith in the ultimate triumph of international morality and justice without resort to the sword. It must be understood, however, that so long as predatory international banditry is permitted to roam the earth to crush human freedom under its avarice and violence, the high concept to which you are pledged will be slow in finding universal acceptance. But it is axiomatic that there must always be a first in all things. In this historic decision, you are the first. The opportunity, therefore, is yours to exemplify before mankind the soundness of this concept and the inestimable benefit resulting from the dedication of all energy and all resource to peaceful progress. In due course other nations will join you in this dedication, but meanwhile you must not falter. Have faith in my countrymen and other peoples who share the same high ideals. Above all, have faith in yourselves.

Contemporary Japan, Vol. XIX, Nos. 1-3, January-March 1950, pp. 136-9.

LISTS OF REFERENCES

AND

INDEX

FOR

CHINA, KOREA, JAPAN

LISTS OF REFERENCES

CHINA

PART I

SECTION I

1 Text supplied by Chinese Embassy, New Delhi, 1948. Arts. 174-5 re-edited from Ch'ien Tuan-sheng, *The Government and Politics of China* (Harvard University Press, Cambridge, Mass., 1950), Appendix D.
2 *China Magazine*, May 1948, p. 23.
3 *United States Relations with China*, pp. 740-41.
4 *China Newsweek*, No. 235, 24 April 1947.

SECTION II

5 *United States Relations with China* (Department of State Publication 3575, August 1949), pp. 706-10.
6 ibid., pp. 697-9.
7 ibid., pp. 699-702.
8 ibid., pp. 703-4.
9 ibid., pp. 749-56.
10 ibid., pp. 826-8.
11 ibid., pp. 839-40.
12 ibid., pp. 834-6.

SECTION III

13-17 *China Information Bulletin*, Vol. I, No. 16, New York, 1 September 1948.

SECTION IV

18 *United States Relations with China*, pp. 756-8.
19 *Hsin Sheng Pao*, Taiwan, 23 December 1947.
20 *United States Relations with China*, pp. 847-9.
21 ibid., pp. 920-2.
22 *China Digest*, Vol. V, No. 8, 8 February 1949, pp. 9-11.
23 *Hsin Chiang Jih Pao*, Tihua, 28 January 1949.
24 *China Digest*, Vol. VI, No. 2, 3 May 1949, pp. 19-22.

731

25 *United States Relations with China*, pp. 710-19.
26 *China Digest*, Vol. III, No. 4, 13 January 1948, pp. 3-5, 14-18.
27 ibid., Vol. IV, No. 1, 18 May 1948, pp. 9-11.
28 ibid., Vol. IV, No. 1, 18 May 1948, p. 11.
29 ibid., Vol. IV, No. 5, 13 July 1948, pp. 6-7.
30 ibid., Vol. 5, No. 3, 30 November 1948, pp. 8-9.
31 ibid., Vol. VI, No. 2, 3 May 1949, pp. 9 and 18.

SECTION VI

32 ibid., Vol. VI, No. 6, 28 June 1949, pp. 3-4.
33 *The Common Programme and Other Documents*, reprinted from *Labour Monthly*, December 1949.
34 *Daily News Release*, New China News Agency, Nos. 153-82, 1 October 1949, p. 2.
35 ibid., pp. 62-4.
36 *The Common Programme and Other Documents*, pp. 29-40.
37 *Daily News Release*, New China News Agency, No. 154, Peking, 3 October 1949.

PART II — EXTERNAL RELATIONS

SECTION I

38 *United States Relations with China*, pp. 686-9.
39 ibid., pp. 763-4.
40 ibid., pp. 764-74.
41 ibid., pp. 815-16.
42 ibid., pp. 816-17.
43 ibid., pp. 817-22.
44 ibid., pp. 869-71.
45 ibid., pp. 981-3.
46 ibid., pp. 991-3.
47 ibid., pp. 994-1001.
48 ibid., pp. 1004-6.
49 ibid., pp. 888-9.
50 ibid., pp. 889-90.
51 ibid., pp. 922-3.
52 ibid., pp. 290-91.
53 ibid., pp. 1006-42.
54 ibid., pp. 1042-53.

SECTION II

55 *Daily News Release*, New China News Agency, No. 289, 8 October 1949.
56 *UN Document* A/1123, 21 November 1949.
57 *Daily News Release*, New China News Agency, No. 262, 20 January 1950.

KOREA

PART I

SECTION I

1 *Korea 1945 to 1948*, US Department of State Publication No. 3305, Washington D.C., October 1948, pp. 43-4.
2 *The Soviet Union and the Korean Question* (Documents), Ministry of Foreign Affairs of the USSR, Moscow, 1948, pp. 36-8.
3 ibid., pp. 42-6.
4 ibid., pp. 47-8.
5 *Korea 1945 to 1948*, pp. 50-51.

SECTION II

6 *Official Records of the Second Session of the General Assembly, Plenary Meetings, 16 September-13 November 1947*, Vol. I, Lake Success, New York, pp. 21-2.
7 *Korea 1945 to 1948*, pp. 51-61.
8 *Official Records of the Second Session of the General Assembly, Resolutions, 16 September-29 November 1947*, Document No. A/519, pp. 16-181.
9 *UN Document* A/AC. 18/23, 16 February 1948.
10-11 *UN Document* A/AC. 18/6, 6 February 1948.
    UN Document A/AC. 18/27, 17 February 1948.
12 *Reports of the Interim Committee of the General Assembly (5 January-5 August 1948)*, *General Assembly Official Records ; Third Session*, Supplement No. 10 (A/578, A/605, A/606), Paris 1948, p. 21.
13 UN Department of Information, *Press Release*, 18 April 1948, as quoted in *Korea 1945 to 1948*, p. 72.
14 UN Temporary Commission on Korea, *Press Release 70*, 30 June 1948, as quoted in *Korea 1945 to 1948*, pp. 72-3.

15 *Official Records of the Third Session of the General Assembly, Resolutions, Part I, 21 September-12 December 1948*, Document No. A/810, pp. 25-7.

16 *Report of the United Nations Commission on Korea*, Vol. I, Chapter IV, *General Assembly Official Records*, Fourth Session, Supplement No. 9 (A/936), pp. 30-34.

SECTION III

17 *The Soviet Union and the Korean Question*, pp. 66-7.
18 ibid., pp. 68-9.
19 *Documents on International Affairs, 1947-8*, Royal Institute of International Affairs, pp. 701-2.
20 *Korea 1945 to 1948*, pp. 113-14.

SECTION IV

21 ibid., pp. 73-7.
22 ibid., p. 78.
23 ibid., pp. 78-95.
24 ibid., pp. 95-8.

SECTION V

25 Tewksbury, Donald G. *Source Materials on Korean Politics and Ideologies* (Mimeographed), International Secretariat, Institute of Pacific Relations, New York, 1950, pp. 98-114.
26 ibid., pp. 119-20.

PART II

SECTION I

27 *Korea 1945 to 1948*, pp. 98-9.
28 ibid., pp. 99-100.
29 ibid., pp. 100-1.
30 ibid., pp. 103-4.
31 ibid., pp. 104-12.
32 ibid., p. 116.
33 *Department of State, Bulletin*, Washington D.C., 19 June 1949, pp. 781-3.

SECTION II

34 *The Soviet Union and the Korean Question*, pp. 72-5.
35 ibid., pp. 76-7.
36 ibid., pp. 78-9.
37 ibid., pp. 82-3.
38 ibid., p. 84.
39 Tewksbury, Donald G., *Source Materials in Korean Politics and Ideologies*, pp. 127-8.

FURTHER LIST OF BOOKS ON KOREA

Report of the United Nations Commission on Korea covering the period from 15 December 1949 to 4 September 1950. General Assembly Official Records, Fifth Session, Supplement No. 16 (A/1350).

Report of the United Nations Commission for the Unification and Rehabilitation of Korea. General Assembly Official Records, Eighth Session, Supplement No. 13 (A/2441).

The Korean Question : Reports of the Neutral Nations Repatriation Commission covering the period 9 September 1953 to 21 February 1954. General Assembly Official Records, Eighth Session, Supplement No. 18 (A/2641).

US Marine Operations in Korea 1950-53, Vol. I, The Pusan Perimeter, *A.D.I.* 1110.

The Korean Problem at the Geneva Conference, April 26–June 15, 1954, *A.D.I.* 11251.

JAPAN

SECTION I

1 *Political Reorientation of Japan, September 1945 to September 1948*, Report of Government Section Supreme Commander for the Allied Powers, US Government Printing Office, 1949, 819337, Appendix A : 13, pp. 428-39.
2 ibid., Appendix C : 21, pp. 671-7.

SECTION II

3 *Political Reorientation of Japan*, Appendix H : 19, pp. 968-76.
4 ibid., Appendix H : 21, pp. 1022-35.
5 ibid., Appendix D : 7, pp. 705-6.
6 ibid., Appendix H : 30, pp. 1062-71.
7 ibid., Appendix H : 34, p. 1089.
8 ibid., Appendix H : 40, pp. 1151-3.
9 *Contemporary Japan — A Review of East Asiatic Affairs*, Vol. XVII, Nos. 7-12, Tokyo, July–December 1948, pp. 404-9.

SECTION III

10 *Political Reorientation of Japan*, Appendix H : 9, pp. 872-84.
11 Text Supplied by the Japanese Government Overseas Agency, New Delhi, August 1948.
12 *Political Reorientation of Japan*, Appendix F : 42, pp. 780-82.
13 *Contemporary Japan*, Vol. XVII, Nos. 4-6, April–June 1948, pp. 211-14.
14 *USSR Information Bulletin*, Washington D.C., 6 October 1948.
15 *Documents on International Affairs, 1947-8*, Royal Institute of International Affairs, London, 1952, pp. 725-8.

SECTION IV

16 *Contemporary Japan*, Vol. XVI, Nos. 4-6, April–June 1947, pp. 227-8.
17 *Contemporary Japan*, Vol. XVII, Nos. 1-3, January–March 1948, pp. 98-100.
18 *Documents Concerning the Allied Occupation and Control of Japan*, Vol. II (Political, Military and Cultural), pp. 4-10, compiled by the Division of Special Records, Foreign Office, Japan, 1949.
19 Contemporary Japan, Vol. XVII, Nos. 1-3, January–March 1948, pp. 100-07.
20 ibid., Vol. XVII, Nos. 1-3, January–March 1948, pp. 107-8.
21 ibid., Vol. XVII, Nos. 1-3, January–March 1948, pp. 110-11.
22 ibid., Vol. XVII, Nos. 1-3, January–March 1948, pp. 111-17.
23 ibid., Vol. XVIII, Nos. 4-6, April–June 1949, pp. 256-9.
24 ibid., Vol. XVIII, Nos. 10-12, October–December 1949, pp. 567-72.

SECTION V

25 ibid., Vol. XVII, Nos. 4-6, April–June 1948, pp. 214-22.
26 Department of the US Army, *Press Release*, 18 December 1948.

27 *Contemporary Japan*, Vol. XVII, Nos. 7-12, July–December 1948, pp. 434-5.
28 ibid., Vol. XVIII, Nos. 1-3, January–March 1949, pp. 140-43.
29 ibid., Vol. XVIII, Nos. 1-3, January–March 1949, pp. 143-5.
30 ibid., Vol. XVIII, Nos. 4-6, April–June 1949, pp. 259-66.
31 *Documents Concerning the Allied Occupation and Control of Japan*, Vol. III (Financial, Economic and Reparations), pp. 294-300, compiled by Section of Special Records, Foreign Office, Japan, 1949.
32 *Contemporary Japan*, Vol. XVIII, Nos. 7-9, July–September 1949, pp. 386-98.

SECTION VI

33 *Political Reorientation of Japan*, Appendix F : 39, p. 776.
34 ibid., Appendix F : 148, pp. 788-9.
35 *Contemporary Japan*, Vol. XVIII, Nos. 1-3, January–March 1949, pp. 126-8.
36 ibid., Vol. XVIII, Nos. 7-9, July–September 1949, pp. 383-5.
37 ibid., Vol. XVIII, Nos. 7-9, July–September 1949, pp. 398-404.
38 ibid., Vol. XIX, Nos. 1-3, January–March 1950, pp. 136-9.

INDEX
CHINA, KOREA AND JAPAN

A

Agrarian Reforms, Mao's report to the Central Committee of the Communist Party of China, 131-4, provision in the Common Programme, 162-3

An Oa, 102

Ashida, Hitoshi, 460, 579, 612, Statement of policy, 647-8 Speech in the Diet, 648-54

Assam, 305

Attlee, Clement R., 120

Australia, 330, 331, 333, 362, 368, 455

B

Baker, John Earl, 290

Barr, David, 190

Bevin, Ernest, 120-1

Bowen, Howard R., 707

Bowman, Isaiah, 264

Bulgaria, 476, 489

Burma, 305, 455

C

Cairo Declaration, 327, 389, 427, 438, 470

Canada, 330, 331, 362, 455

Ceylon, 192

Chang Chih Chung, 181

Chang Chun, 6, 9, 187, 215-17

Chang Hsi Jo, 181

Chang Lan, 74, 181

Chang Man-yun, 102

Chang Nai-chi, 102

Chang Nan Hsien, 181

Chang Po Chun, 102, 144, 181

Chang Tung Sun, 181

Chang Wen Tien, 323-4

Chang Yun Yi, 181

Chen Cheng, 130, 209

Chen Chiyu, 102, 144

Chen Kuo-fu, 6n.

Chen Li-fu, 6n., 134

Chen Shu Tung, 181

Chen Yi, 181

Chen Yun, 181

Cheng Chien, 181

Cheng Ming Shu, 181

Chiang Kai-shek, 4-6,
  Radio broadcast, 7
  statement on State Council's reorganization, 42-4
  peace proposals, 54-5
  broadcast on Sino-Japanese war anniversary, 59-68
  speech to the Central Executive on the President's election, 92-5
  New Year message, 95-8
  letter to Truman for more aid, 246, 317, 327

Chiang Monlin, 290

Chien Po-tsan, 102

Chien Tuan-Sheng, 39

China, Nationalist Government,
  Civil war, 88-112
  Communists, 113-153
  constitutional developments, 19-43
  Kuomintang economic measures, 74-87
  political developments, 44-73
  relations with the United States, 197-315

People's Republic of,
  constitutional developments, 154-82
  relations with the Soviet Union, 316-21

742

Date Due

AUG 2 4 '60		
AUG 1 1 '61		
NOV 30 '62		
JAN 5 '66		
⒢Ⓑ PRINTED	IN U. S. A.	